1943 December, Chief of Staff to Commander Aircraft Pacific Fleet

1944 March, Assistant DCNO (Air), Washington, D.C.

1944 May, additional duty as member JCS special committee on reorganization of defense establishment

1944 October, to sea as COMCARDIV, Fast Carrier Task Force

1945 23 September, relieved as COMCARDIV and Commander TG 38 for duty with Commander-in-Chief, Washington, D.C.

1945 7 November, reported to Secretary of the Navy to head Navy effort on "unification"

1945 18 December, DCNO (AIR); also head of unification effort. Promoted to Vice Admiral

1947 February, Commander Second Fleet (Atlantic)

1948 January, VCNO

1948 December, cruise with Royal Navy; visits to Britain, Italy, Turkey, Saudi Arabia, Kuwait, Egypt, Morocco

1949 30 April, promoted to Admiral (four-star); duty as CINCPAC, CINCPACFLT, and HICOM, Trust Territory of the Pacific Islands

1949 28 May, visit to General Douglas MacArthur, Supreme Comm... Tok... Phili...

1949 26 Jun... ...aroline Islands

1949 9 August–21 October, B36 hearings

1950 15 April–11 June, visits to Canton Island, American Samoa, Australia, Trust Territory of the Pacific, Philippines, and Japan

1950 13 July, conference with JCS and General MacArthur in Tokyo

1950 15 October, at Wake Island meeting with President Truman and General MacArthur

1951 November, visits to French Indochina and Southeast Asia

1952 January, defense of Formosa and Philippines transferred from CINCFE to CINCPAC

1952 August, meeting with ANZUS Council

1952 November–December, accompanied President-elect Eisenhower to Japan and Korea

1953 12 May, nominated by President Eisenhower as Chairman JCS

1953 15 August, sworn in as Chairman JCS

1957 15 August, retired from USN and from two terms as Chairman JCS

1973 17 August, died at Bethesda Naval Hospital

From Pearl Harbor *to* Vietnam

Admiral Arthur W. Radford, USN, as Chairman, Joint Chiefs of Staff. *Courtesy of Mrs. Arthur W. Radford*

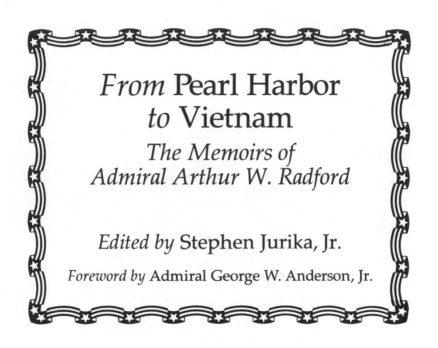

From Pearl Harbor *to* Vietnam

The Memoirs of
Admiral Arthur W. Radford

Edited by Stephen Jurika, Jr.

Foreword by Admiral George W. Anderson, Jr.

HOOVER INSTITUTION PRESS
Stanford University, Stanford, California

*The Hoover Institution on War, Revolution and Peace, founded at
Stanford University in 1919 by the late President Herbert Hoover,
is an interdisciplinary research center for advanced study on
domestic and international affairs in the twentieth century. The views
expressed in its publications are entirely those of the authors
and do not necessarily reflect the views of the staff, officers,
or Board of Overseers of the Hoover Institution.*

Hoover Institution Publication 221

Designed by Elizabeth Gehman

Contents

Foreword

The life of Admiral Arthur W. Radford (1896–1973) spanned the first seven decades of the twentieth century, a dynamic period in American history. During these decades the United States grew to be the strongest nation in the world politically, industrially, militarily, and, at times at least, morally. Its strength derived primarily from its human resources: people descended from immigrants of many races, religions, and social strata. Dedicated leadership, guided by the concepts of America's Revolutionary fathers, melded this nation's material resources with the best resources of its people to nurture growth, and to cope with external threats to the country as well as its inherent social and economic problems.

The objective of American leadership has been consistently "to provide for the common defense, promote the general welfare and to assure the blessings of liberty for ourselves and our posterity," as set forth in the preamble to the Constitution. Enlightened interpretation of this objective has been to keep the horrors and devastation of war beyond our homeland, to help our allies help themselves resist and overcome aggression, and to build the social, political, and economic conditions conducive to peace with justice for all. The phrase "and our posterity" requires the American government carefully to avoid expedient solutions for the short term, at risk of possible future catastrophic dangers.

Essential for American security is the training of officers of the armed services to prepare and implement military policies that are consistent with coordinated political and economic policies; to fight successfully on land, at sea, and in the air; to advise civilian officials of military requirements and the military implications of political and economic undertakings. In these seven decades the military did indeed produce officers and personnel capable of meeting and eventually defeating foreign aggressors. The United States, through mobilization of its human and industrial resources, especially scientific and technical talent, emerged from World War II as the bastion of power for the free world. Its military forces were at the peak of their strength; its factories, farms, laboratories, and transportation and communication systems were undamaged; and it had a temporary monopoly on atomic weaponry. But at that crucial point, the country rushed into a drastic demobilization that emasculated diplomatic efforts to establish conditions conducive to lasting peace.

Admiral Radford was one of those who could visualize future hazards to the United States and the free world and who could perceive the need for timely measures to thwart communist strategy. He thoroughly supported the North Atlantic Treaty Organization and its efforts to maintain the security of the Atlantic area. As a result of his experience as Commander-in-Chief Pacific, he had a thorough knowledge of the Far East; he and General MacArthur were the foremost authorities of the armed forces on affairs of the Orient and their impact on American interests. The long-term threat to the United States, that an alien power gain control over Japan with its technical and industrial capability, China with its manpower, and Southeast Asia with its markets and raw materials—which was the menace posed by Japan itself at the onset of World War II—has remained a potential threat from certain communist powers. Thus it was essential that communist aggression be defeated in Korea and Indochina.

Admiral Radford and General MacArthur were convinced that, when it was necessary to employ U.S. armed forces, there could be no substitute for victory; that the United States should fully exploit its air and naval power; and that capabilities of indigenous friendly ground forces should be maximized with U.S. assistance in equipment, training, and leadership. But national policy set in the United States and stimulated both by communist propaganda and pressure from European allies precluded a victory in Korea and set the base for a debilitating war and a capitulatory "peace" in Vietnam. It is therefore fitting that Admiral Radford's account of developments pertaining to Korea and Indochina up to the time of his retirement as Chairman of the U.S. Joint Chiefs of Staff be added to the historical record.

Over the many years of my association with Admiral Radford, my admiration for his superior capabilities was reciprocated by a confidence in me on his part that was genuine and very special. I found him quite different from the impetuous, swashbuckling, and arrogant figure sometimes conjured by his media. The Admiral was perceptive, patient with his staff, and prudent in his decisions while unafraid to accept their consequences. He was an attentive listener and avid questioner. Above all, Admiral Radford was an articulate examplar of the cool professional, dedicated to serving his navy and his nation at whatever personal cost—and that cost was often high.

Admiral Radford, General MacArthur, and General Eisenhower: the last of the great American military statesmen. Would that we had another, today.

GEORGE W. ANDERSON
Admiral, U.S. Navy (Retired)

Editor's Note

In 1965 I wrote to Admiral Radford, urging him to tape-record the highlights of his unique career. Perhaps my plea contributed to his decision to set down his memoirs. From 2,000 pages of typed manuscript, my associates and I have distilled the essence into this volume. The entire manuscript is in the archives of the Hoover Institution on War, Revolution and Peace at Stanford University.

Seldom has a confidential record of personal opinion, of conversations with men who shape the world scene, and of participation in international crises been made public so soon after its author's death.

I have thoroughly checked the accuracy of the manuscript, adding first names and other details here and there, and have provided the notes, bibliography, and other materials. Bracketed interpolations in the text are mine; those in parentheses are Admiral Radford's.

Special mention must be accorded to Marianna Radford (Mrs. Arthur Radford), who made the Radford papers available to the Hoover Institution and authorized the publication of this volume. Her unwavering support, high interest, and invaluable assistance made this project possible.

My thanks go to the staff of the Hoover Institution on War, Revolution and Peace, especially Associate Directors Richard Burress and Richard Staar; Mickey Hamilton of the Hoover Press; and Captain Paul B. Ryan, USN (Ret.). All were ever courteous, helpful, and encouraging.

STEPHEN JURIKA, JR.

Abbreviations

AA	Anti-aircraft
BUAERO	Bureau of Aeronautics
BUNAV	Bureau of Navigation
CAP	Combat air patrol
CINCFE	Commander-in-Chief Far East
CINCPAC	Commander-in-Chief Pacific
CINCPACFLT	Commander-in-Chief Pacific Fleet
CNO	Chief of Naval Operations
CO	Commanding Officer
COMAIRPAC	Commander Air Force Pacific
COMCARDIV	Commander carrier division
CV	Large carrier
CVL	Light carrier
DCNO (Air)	Deputy Chief of Naval Operations (for Air)
EDC	European Defense Community
HICOM	High Commissioner
JCS	Joint Chiefs of Staff
JSSC	Joint Strategic Survey Committee
MAAG	Military Assistance Advisory Group
MAP	Military Aid Program
MDAP	Mutual Defense Assistance Program
NSC	National Security Council
ROK	Republic of Korea
RAF	Royal Air Force (British)

R.N.	Royal Navy (British)
TF	Task force
TG	Task group
UMT	Universal military training
VCNO	Vice Chief of Naval Operations
VF(N)	Fighter aircraft (night)

Prologue

A dmiral Arthur William Radford, United States Navy, was the first naval officer to become Chairman of the Joint Chiefs of Staff—a post he held under President Dwight D. Eisenhower from 1953 to 1957.

A naval aviator with a distinguished World War II record as a carrier division commander, Radford was closely involved with nearly every important development of naval aviation in the fleet, particularly the concentration of carrier aircraft against fleet and shore targets. Following the war, he was the driving force behind naval participation in the major interservice issues of unification of the armed services, organization of the new Department of Defense, and formulation of the roles and missions of the services.

During the late 1940s, as Deputy Chief of Naval Operations for Air and later as Commander-in-Chief Pacific, Admiral Radford unremittingly prepared for a war that was not long in coming: Korea 1950. He lent strength and increasing naval support to our Korean War ground forces; initiated Allied planning and coordination with Australia and New Zealand (ANZUS); and later represented the United States in interpreting the touchy role we should play in French Indochina.

The Admiral was a close friend and adviser of the first Secretary of Defense, James Forrestal. He served Presidents Truman and Eisenhower; and he worked with Secretary of State Dean Acheson, with generals of the Army and Air Force, with senators and congressmen, and with many heads of state and their chief advisers. He habitually recorded in a diary, or in a memorandum for the file, the tenor of his meetings with the great and near-great. Articulate, perceptive, and witty, he was recognized as a preeminent leader by his colleagues.

When the Eisenhower New Look defense posture for the nation, which called for major reductions in Army and Navy personnel and equipment and support for the "long pull" over the years, came under attack from many factions, it was defended by Admiral Radford in eloquent articles and speeches. But he always insisted that no one arm or service could win a war, and that no single weapons system would be the "right" one or the adequate response to aggression.

Admiral Radford's incisive comments on certain political figures, coupled with his conclusion that political expediency sometimes plays a part in the shaping of our national security interests, strongly suggest that domestic political considerations can be key elements in security decision-making. As a military man Radford studiously avoided involvement in political matters, but he was never afraid to record his views when asked for an opinion. He did so in calm, measured, and closely reasoned phrases. His insatiable appetite for knowledge on a wide range of subjects and his warm personal concern for individuals were recognized and appreciated by all who knew him.

In the crisis years of the Eisenhower presidency, the President leaned heavily on Radford's temperate, even counsel. Adam Yarmolinsky, a veteran White House adviser, put it well:

> *In practice, Eisenhower depended on the Joint Chiefs less than had Truman . . . But at the same time, Eisenhower used one military man in the kind of top-level advisory role that Truman reserved for his civilian secretaries. From 1953 to 1957, Admiral Arthur W. Radford, the JCS Chairman, occupied a place in Eisenhower's foreign policy councils second only to that of Secretary of State John Foster Dulles. His period as Chairman and Marshall's as Army Chief of Staff probably mark the two points at which professional military men have had the biggest voice in presidential decisions.* (The Military Establishment, *p. 30*)

On 15 August 1957 Admiral Radford's distinguished career of service to the nation was climaxed when he received from President Eisenhower a fourth Distinguished Service Medal, stepped down as Chairman of the Joint Chiefs of Staff, and retired from the active list of the Navy after 45 years of service. It was at once a poignant moment, a proud occasion, and the happy beginning of a new personal life with his wife Mariana, to whom he had often confided, "we make a great team."

Many major corporations offered directorships or chairmanships of the board and inducements in the form of pay and perquisites for the privilege of using the Admiral's name and fame. He responded slowly and with care to avoid even a hint of conflict of interest, ultimately deciding to become a consultant on the development of foreign and domestic business for the Bankers Trust Company, a position he held from 1957 until his death in 1973. He also accepted several directorships. In all these business associations the Admiral's integrity, sound judgment, and knowledge of world affairs made his assistance invaluable.

☆ ☆ ☆ ☆

This volume is Admiral Radford's story. He wrote most of it in longhand during the late 1960s and early 1970s at the Washington Navy Yard, referring frequently to personal and official diaries, memoranda, and letters to flesh out dates, details, and dialectic. He drew heavily upon accounts of the Vietnam war compiled by the history branch of the Joint Chiefs of Staff, a branch he had worked hard to strengthen and monitored personally as JCS Chairman.

Admiral Radford did not write his memoirs with a view toward publication in book form. He wished merely to record memories of his life for the benefit—and the enjoyment—of those who would follow.

1

Pearl Harbor

I t was a peaceful Sunday morning on the golf course of the Pensacola Country Club, and we had reached the third or fourth hole.

Suddenly a Navy car appeared, charging up the fairway at top speed and sounding the horn, headed directly for us. It stopped near Albert Read, one of my companions. A young officer jumped out and handed him a dispatch. He glanced at it quickly and passed it to Artemus Gates, who read it aloud:

JAPANESE HAVE ATTACKED PEARL HARBOR—THIS IS NO DRILL. PLACE RAINBOW FIVE IN EFFECT AT ONCE.

We stood for a moment, looking at one another blankly. Mr. Gates broke the silence. "We'd better get back to Washington. But first I'd like to take a look at RAINBOW FIVE."

All of us crowded into the car and drove back to the clubhouse, where someone told us of a radio broadcast that the Japanese were attacking Pearl Harbor. We quickly changed clothes while Captain Read, Commanding Officer of the Pensacola Naval Air Station, went to ready our plane for the return trip and break out a copy of RAINBOW FIVE, the current major war plan.

We were in Captain Read's office in a few minutes. Chagrined, he announced that RAINBOW FIVE was in a safe with a time lock that could not be opened until 8:00 Monday morning. Mr. Gates, who was Assistant Secretary of the Navy, was horrified to discover that in a time of such crisis a large naval command could not get at its instructions.

Back in Washington, we found a mob milling around the office of Secretary of the Navy Frank Knox. Mr. Gates went inside for further details while our other companion of that morning, Capt. D. C. Ramsey (Assistant Chief of the Navy Bureau of Aeronautics), and I waited outside. He returned with word that neither the Secretary nor his assistants had definite information on what had happened at Pearl Harbor. But they all seemed very pessimistic and felt it had been a disaster for us.

We each called home, then talked in Mr. Gates's office before breaking up. There was nothing we could do that night so we went home. I found Mrs. Radford listening to the radio, which was still broadcasting speculative stories. She had been busy at home in the morning when a friend telephoned and told her to turn on the radio, that the Japanese were attacking Pearl Harbor. We went to bed that eventful evening knowing little about what was going on in Hawaii.

The Bureau of Aeronautics (BUAERO) was fully manned long before 8:00 A.M. the next day, 8 December 1941. Admiral John Towers, its chief, had called a meeting of all division heads for 9:00. Waiting for it, I discussed with my staff plans for enlarging our training establishment. I was on temporary duty under Admiral Towers then, and had been in Pensacola en route to visit our principal flight stations and aviation mechanics' schools.

At 9:00 Admiral Towers told his division chiefs what had happened in Pearl Harbor and read several dispatches giving details. We were stunned to realize what a complete success the Japanese attack had been. Japanese losses seemed negligible.

I could hardly believe what I heard. When I had left Pearl Harbor only six months before, we were having numerous anti-aircraft drills and were otherwise preparing to repel an attack. Navy patrol planes were flying extensive searches in the dangerous quadrants. Everyone, so far as I knew, considered a surprise Japanese attack on Pearl Harbor likely as early as April 1941. Now it had happened, yet we had been caught flatfooted.[1] I simply could not understand it.

I also remembered well Grand Joint Exercise Number Four, in 1932. This large-scale exercise had involved a surprise attack on Hawaii by the U.S. fleet, using its carrier aviation power, which had been defended by the U.S. Army, principally the Air Corps. The exercise had received wide publicity. It was common knowledge, for example, that the Air Corps felt that daylight attacks on Sunday morning, though permitted under the rules, were on the dirty side. The Japanese navy had apparently read all the publicity in detail. Their attack on Pearl Harbor was almost an exact duplicate.

Admiral Towers made a brief statement regarding the responsibilities facing BUAERO. He asked each division head how much money would be needed to execute plans made earlier to expand activities. My answer was $100 million, and my plan was to immediately begin building up the physical facilities of the training establishment. To turn out combat-ready pilots we had to establish an operational training command in which graduates of our naval aviators' course would move on to service [operational] aircraft and specialize. This new organization had been discussed the week before and was effected immediately. We were to have a primary, an intermediate, and an operational training command. Students would receive their wings after completing intermediate training.

That first day of the war, two former naval officers, graduates of the Naval Academy, called to tell me they were having difficulty getting back into the

Navy. On applying, they had both been referred to junior reserve officers, who demanded transcripts of their college careers. They replied that this information was already in Navy files, since they were graduates of the Academy; nevertheless, they were told they must get the transcripts themselves and present them with applications for commissions. I asked each man if he had been approached by the Navy regarding his willingness to serve in case of emergency. Each said no. One of them was a classmate of mine who had served in submarines after graduation and qualified for command. Some twenty years after leaving the service under honorable conditions, having been successful in business in the meantime, these two men in their early forties were volunteering for active duty and having difficulty getting back!

If there was anything we needed at that time it was capable, trained naval officers. I was appalled to think that in the preceding months, with war almost a certainty, graduates of the Naval Academy in civilian life had not been contacted and given tentative mobilization assignments. I helped these two men come back, stating that I wanted them in my training organization and they joined me in about a month.

In the first month or so of the war the training division, like all of BUAERO, worked literally from dawn to dark seven days a week. I walked between my apartment and work—my only exercise. Social life was almost nonexistent.

Several important accomplishments mark that early period. Almost immediately, in conjunction with the Army Air Corps, we reduced the minimum educational requirements for pilot training from two years of college to a high school diploma. This automatically generated additional ground school requirements to bring students up to the level required for flight training. We decided to set up preflight schools that would give this additional schooling plus complete physical and survival training. I looked for an officer to head the activity and found him close at hand. Commander (now R. Adm., ret.) Tom Hamilton, former Navy All-American football player, tells the story:

> You outlined your aim to train our naval aviators in the most thorough and comprehensive manner so that they would not only be vastly superior to our enemies and would win, but would also have maximum chances to survive . . . Having analyzed the qualities a successful pilot should have, you had come to the conclusion that many of these characteristics, in addition to the necessary flying skills and academic knowledge, would be developed by utilizing various sports training. This would not only breed the competitive spirit but such attributes as quick reactions . . . mental and bodily agility, strength and stamina, perseverance even though fatigued or injured—in general the will to win and survive. Your idea intrigued me greatly. I heartily concurred with your thoughts.
>
> You asked me how the Navy could obtain the required instructors for this training. I suggested that you send someone to the Detroit convention of the NCAA and the American Football Coaches Association to explain the proposal and ask

for volunteers from the top coaches and physical educators of the colleges and high schools . . . I received word that you wanted me to go to Detroit and make the presentations to the assembled coaches . . . The flood of applications caught everyone by surprise and how to handle them was a problem.

Initial plans called for four preflight schools, with a capacity of 1,800 cadets each, to induct a new class of 300 every two weeks for a twelve-week course. Facilities at four universities were selected and operations started. The schools eliminated young men who were not qualified and who might have failed or been killed later on. They turned out groups who were eager to fly and who were able to (and later did) take care of themselves and come home safely.

On one of these early days I went up to "the Hill" to call on Carl Vinson, Chairman of the House Naval Affairs Committee, to tell him about the preflight schools. I found it helpful to keep Mr. Vinson aware of my plans because he always found out about them quickly, somehow or other.

Outlining the scheme, I said we would have one preflight school each in the south, the mid-Atlantic states, the midwest, and the west coast. We were hoping to interest universities in taking on this responsibility, since their enrollments would be down.

Mr. Vinson listened carefully, then said in his soft Georgia drawl, "Captain, that sounds like a fine idea. You don't have to look further for the southern university; it will be the University of Georgia. You will get great cooperation there." And that's the way it turned out. In 1965, when I read of the turmoil in our universities—riots, anti-ROTC demonstrations, and so on—I thought of those great days in 1942 when almost everyone in the academic world was trying to help and many climbed into uniform. I wondered what had happened to our great country.

At the Naval Academy, each midshipman's space was halved so that we could conduct four month-long indoctrination classes for selected officers. With the cadres trained, four preflight schools were opened by the end of April 1942. Some 2,500 officers were selected from 25,000 applicants. The selection system worked well and provided top leadership in officer, instructor, and administration groups.

In mid-December, I wrote to the chief of the Bureau of Navigation (BUNAV) asking if the Bureau was planning to organize a women's reserve to serve during the war. In surveying requirements for officer and enlisted billets in the air training establishment, we felt we could use competent, trained women to great advantage—particularly in jobs that did not require physical exertion, such as running flight simulators. To my surprise, BUNAV had no such plans. I concluded that the best way to get action would be to discuss the matter with Carl Vinson, which I did. I never knew exactly what happened, but soon afterward I received a request from BUNAV asking for the number of women reserves who could be used in aviation training. The figures were bandied about, and many plans were made and unmade; but eventually the wonderful Wave organization came into being and grew much larger than originally planned. At the end of the war there were 23,110 Waves in the naval aeronautic organization, most of them in air training.

By this time, BUAERO had established a program for training administrative officers, which we had to enlarge. Training for air combat intelligence officers was under discussion. The Naval Intelligence Division had trained a few intelligence officers for the aeronautical organization, but their program and curricula did not meet our needs. It was decided that we would start our own school.

Quonset Point, Rhode Island, was chosen as the location of the new Aviation Indoctrination School and the Air Combat Intelligence School. Lieutenant Commander J. J. Schieffelin of the Naval Reserve Air Base Atlanta, a capable and energetic individual was selected—perhaps in typical manner these days— as Commanding Officer of the Aviation Indoctrination School. His name came to me as we were completing plans to start the school within a week. On a Thursday or Friday I called him and said: "Jay, this is Captain Radford. We are starting a new school for aviation administrative officers at Quonset Point, Rhode Island, hopefully next week. The first class will report in about two weeks. You have been selected as the Commanding Officer and I'd like to have you there by next Monday, although you could delay until Tuesday morning if necessary. I hope you will volunteer!" There was a pause at the Atlanta end of the line, then Jay's voice came back, "Aye, aye, Sir." Another pause, then, "Where did you say that new school was to be?"

Jay Schieffelin is now [1965] a Rear Admiral, USNR (retired). His record at Rhode Island was as outstanding as I had expected. The graduates of Quonset Point staffed the administrative billets of the naval aeronautical organization ashore and afloat with distinction. Some of the Aviation Indoctrination School graduates were selected for further training at the Air Combat Intelligence School, with Lt. Comdr. John Mitchell (soon relieved by Lt. Comdr. Harry Davison, Jr.) as Officer-in-Charge. They, too, were a splendid group.

Most of the special training units established under great pressure and urgency in 1942 performed amazingly well. But I think these two schools—in the development of which we received tremendous support from the academic world—were in a class by themselves insofar as their overall contribution to the war effort was concerned. In the squadrons the pilots and mechanics were, simply, superb. But the aviation ground and air combat intelligence officers, mostly well-educated and successful young business and professional men who had volunteered for this training, added a maturity of judgment and experience that made the total endeavor, in most cases, magnificent. The same things were true of carriers and staffs. Gratitude is forever due this splendid group, who gave up several years—and in some cases their lives—to serve their country so well.

Along with officer training programs, the training of enlisted men had to be greatly expanded. Our greatest problem was to find good instructors. In the aviation mechanics' schools we relied heavily upon civil service instructors, many of whom were recruited from vocational high schools and put through a teacher-training course at Great Lakes, Illinois. We endeavored to mechanize or audiovisualize as much of the instruction as possible so that we could standardize it, for our instructors were of varied backgrounds and ages.

Our peacetime aviation mechanics were generally men of considerable special schooling and experience. For the wartime training program, we broke down requirements of the various specialty ratings into three or four segments, each of which could be taught in a fraction of the usual time.

When war began, we had a sizable but widely scattered enlisted training program. We concentrated by retaining a large technical high school in South Chicago and establishing two big technical training centers, one at Memphis, Tennessee, and the other at Norman, Oklahoma.

By the end of 1942 the total naval aviation training effort was enormous. The specialty training schools alone required personnel, money and special equipment never imagined in prewar training plans.

In the specialty training schools of the enlisted training program, I was fortunate to have the assistance of one of the most remarkable men I have ever known, Mr. Jamison Handy. Mr. Handy's firm, the Jam Handy Company of Detroit, had been making moving pictures and slides and preparing manuals for training officers and men. At our request they also began training officers and men (including Waves) to operate the special training devices being installed in our schools and air stations.

Jam Handy volunteered as a dollar-a-year man to act as my eyes and ears in checking the performance of our many new schools—the way of handling classes, the adequacy of the curricula, and so on. An expert in all aspects of education, he could not have been a better assistant for such work, which he thoroughly enjoyed. When I asked who would take care of his company during his absence on trips for me, he said simply that they were organized to get along without him.

By the end of 1942 our training program was really rolling. But I was having trouble holding on to my wonderful assistants, and I too was getting restless as news of the war kept rolling in. Commander Artie Doyle came to me in about June 1942, saying he had just found out there was a chance for him to be Executive Officer of *Saratoga*. I knew how he had found out: the new skipper had simply asked him. To Artie's surprise, I told him I would not let him go to be just an executive officer; I would let him go when he was offered a command (and I did). He protested he could not get a command without experience as an executive officer, but he was wrong.

In April 1943 I was relieved of duties in Washington and ordered to report to

Commander Aircraft Squadrons, Pacific Fleet, for duty as a Carrier Division Commander. Assistant Secretary Gates, about to make an inspection trip to the Pacific theater including Australia and Guadalcanal, invited me to join him. I accepted with great pleasure, knowing I would have time before my new flagship, the *Independence,* was ready.

2

Air Strikes on the Gilberts

Believing that I was going to sea for the remainder of the war, Mrs. Radford and I decided that she should take up residence in Carmel, California, and that we would sell our Ford sedan. This was a mistake, as I was back in Washington less than a year later.

Meanwhile, I arrived in Pearl Harbor after our brief Pacific trip and reported on 8 June 1943 to Adm. Frederick Sherman, Commander Carrier Division (COMCARDIV) 2. The balance of the month was spent observing flight operations and carrier tactics, riding first one and then another of the carriers operating out of Pearl. Obviously, great improvements in carrier air operations and tactics had been made since I had left *Yorktown* in Bermuda just over two years before.

I was impressed with the routine operation of carrier task groups in circular formation and their maneuvering by simultaneous turns in order to land or launch planes. This new formation permitted groups to concentrate anti-aircraft (AA) fire in case of air attack. I consider its adoption one of the greatest advances in the art of carrier warfare and the most important reason for our overwhelming successes in the later stages of the war. I believe Admiral Sherman was responsible for its development. I do know that he had considerable difficulty in selling the idea to some carrier skippers and seniors. I have a copy of a letter to him dated 11 March 1943, signed by Adm. William Halsey, forbidding him to restrict individual maneuvers of carriers when under air attack. "As you well know," Admiral Halsey wrote, "it is a matter of great concern to the *Saratoga* when in company with the *Enterprise* to be able to have plenty of sea room for violent and radical maneuvers during air attacks." *Saratoga* and *Lexington*, not as maneuverable as later carriers, were hard to handle in company with ships of *Enterprise* class.

On 30 June I was ordered to Mare Island, California, where I joined *Independence*, one of the new cruisers converted to light carriers. Upon promotion to Rear Admiral in July, I would be COMCARDIV 2, with *Independence, Prince-*

ton, and *Lexington*. Admiral Towers thought it would be a good idea for me to get acquainted with my flagship, so I cruised to Hawaii in *Independence* in July. This carrier, one of ten conversions, was much smaller than the new *Essex* class. But the ten had the speed to maneuver with the larger carriers, and they carried 36 planes, usually 27 fighters and 9 torpedo planes. They were much more sensitive to rough seas, rolling and pitching a great deal. Flight operations on *Independence*-class carriers required great skill on the part of the pilots and the ship's company, particularly the landing signal officers.[1]

Summer 1943 marked the beginning of the U.S. naval offensive in the Pacific war. As new carriers arrived in Pearl Harbor, Admiral Towers and his staff put them through stiff training courses, topped off when possible with a combat exercise against a Japanese-occupied island. For the rest of July and August, I put light carriers (CVLs) through their paces off Pearl and assisted in working up plans to build an airfield on Baker Island in the central Pacific.

Rear Admiral W. A. Lee commanded the expedition to build the fighter-bomber strip on Baker where a fighter squadron of 19 P40s was to be stationed. I had the covering force of two light carriers and four destroyers.

Intelligence reported that Japanese naval aircraft from Tarawa and Makin Islands, coral atolls in the Gilberts, flew regular patrols to the vicinity of Baker. Our B24 and PBY [patrol plane] watches in that area were similar, operating from Canton Island. If we could surprise and destroy the first Japanese patrol plane near Baker without giving it an opportunity to radio a report, we could unload our ships and almost complete the landing strip before the next flight.

Initial landing was made on Baker on 1 September, and a combat air patrol (CAP) was established over the island at sunrise. Carriers operated about 50 miles to the east with three destroyers, while the fourth destroyer with a fighter director[2] aboard took station just west of Baker. About 1:00 P.M. the fighter director unit picked up a bogey [unidentified aircraft] to the west and vectored the CAP to intercept. Some 25 miles out, attacking out of the sun, they shot down in flames a Japanese four-engine flying boat of a new type.

Three days later a similar intercept took place a little further to the west at about the same time and altitude. This time the Emily [Japanese patrol plane] sighted the intercepting fighters and began evasive maneuvers, attempting to utilize cloud cover. The Emily radioed a report of the attack, but again the units of Task Force 11 were not sighted. But the Japanese knew that something was going on.

On 8 September a third Emily was intercepted considerably to the south of Baker Island, apparently attempting a sly new approach but still at about the same time of day. The Emily sighted its pursuers and tried without success to escape.

The destruction of three latest-model Japanese flying boats, without permitting them to sight our surface forces, was a feather in the caps of the air groups in *Princeton* and *Belleau Wood* and certainly pleased me.

By 10 September the landing field was ready for the P40s, and the following day they arrived from Canton Island. Our mission was accomplished.

Shortly after our arrival off Baker, and after intercepting the first Emily, I decided that once the landing field was completed it would be a good idea to hit Tarawa and Makin Islands before returning to Pearl. Because we did not have enough offensive air strength in the two CVLs, I sent a message to Admiral Towers suggesting he send an *Essex*-class carrier to join us so we could really work over the islands. My suggestion fell on fertile ground. Task Force 15 was organized, with R. Adm. Charles Pownall in *Lexington* joining our task group.

I transferred to *Lexington* the next morning to confer with Admiral Pownall and give him the intelligence we had collected. I felt we might consider withdrawing on the first afternoon of attack and returning at daylight the next day, probably catching the Japanese by surprise. Admiral Pownall would not commit himself to a second day's operation but said he would consider it when he saw how things went the first day.

The task force maneuvered as a unit during our eight attacks. The original launching time was advanced at the request of air group and squadron commanders, who felt there was sufficient moonlight for predawn bombing. This proved erroneous, and the attack group remained over the target for an excessive period until daylight; so the element of surprise was lost.

Nine twin-engine Japanese bombers and one dive-bomber were destroyed on the runways at Tarawa, and two twin-engine bombers were shot down by the CAP during our withdrawal. At Makin three or four four-engine flying boats were destroyed on the water by strafing. Neither planes nor military installations were observed at Abemama, a third target we had decided upon. Numerous fuel dumps, barracks, and warehouses on the islands were damaged or destroyed. A small freighter was sunk and another left sinking, and many small craft were heavily strafed and damaged or sunk.

Anti-aircraft fire from Tarawa was heavy; at Makin it was light; at Abemama there was none.

One U.S. fighter, two dive-bombers, and a torpedo plane failed to return, missing the ship and landing in the water. Searches failed to locate the crashes or rubber boats. One dive-bomber was hit by AA and landed in the water. The strike leader sighted the crew in their rubber raft and broadcast their position to our rescue submarine, but the crew was captured by the Japanese and spent the rest of the war in prison camps.

As an exercise, the Tarawa raid was valuable for both ships and air groups. Joining combat for the first time is an experience never forgotten. Units with combat behind them perform much more efficiently. I was sorry the task force Commander decided not to repeat the strike on the second day, for I sensed that one more day, even with the same number of sorties, would cause much greater damage. I never knew what factors caused Admiral Pownall to make this decision.

In Pearl Harbor the operation was carefully reviewed. It was by such analysis and discussion that our carrier operating techniques were improved. In this particular case, our most important deficiency was night fighters equipped with intercept radar, which could operate from the carriers: we had none. The Japanese were apparently aware of this, for their scouting planes moved into plain sight when our last CAPs were landed on the final day. Before I had left the training assignment in Washington a night fighter school had been established, so I knew that fighters with intercept radar were due in the fleet soon; but the urgency of the situation demanded an interim solution.

Another important deficiency was the air discipline of squadrons and air groups in predawn launch and rendezvous. Obviously more practice was required, and this was emphasized in my report of the operation.

For the next operation, an attack against Wake Island on 5–6 October 1943 (the largest U.S. carrier operation of the war until then), I shifted my flag to *Lexington*. Task Force 14, commanded by R. Adm. A. E. Montgomery, consisted of six carriers accompanied by three heavy and four light cruisers, with destroyers and oilers.

Wake was an important Japanese base, a stepping-stone for aircraft en route to or from the Marshalls and Marianas. Intelligence indicated it was defended by approximately 30 fighters and 15 twin-engine bombers, some dive-bombers, and perhaps a flying boat or two. Besides heavy air attacks, the island was to be bombarded by the cruisers.

The Wake enterprise was a great success—and it showed conclusively how much could be gained by a second day's operation—but the rough edges and deficiencies were still apparent. Communications between ships and aircraft were improving; those with the rescue submarine were even better, and the sub did a wonderful job rescuing downed pilots. Carrier training was still short of the desired level.

It was these small offensive operations, coupled with intensive training ashore and on carriers at sea in Hawaiian waters, that prepared carriers and air groups for the major offensive operations following the Wake Island attack.

Task Force 14 returned to Pearl Harbor where the force was dissolved and units reported to their administrative commanders. Flag officers of the carrier task groups reported to Admiral Towers, discussed the operation in detail, and were briefed by the Admiral on the next operation, the first big step on the road to Tokyo. It was code-named "Galvanic" and was to get under way in late October, commanded by Adm. Raymond Spruance—the victor of the battle of Midway and the gentlemanly former Commandant of the Tenth Naval District in San Juan, to whom I had reported when I took command at Trinidad.

Galvanic was the first time our carriers would face Japanese land-based air in strength. We would have to slug it out with them for command of the air while Marine and Army units fought Japanese troops for possession of the islands.

For this first amphibious assault Tarawa, Makin, and Abemama Islands were selected. They were some four hundred miles south of the Marshalls, which had been developed by the Japanese into a formidable air base and naval anchorage complex in violation of the terms of their League of Nations mandate.[3]

Twenty-five years after Galvanic it is difficult to understand the anguished concerns of the planners when they fleshed out details. To the amphibious commanders, their proximity to the strong enemy air forces in the Marshalls was of great concern. To the fleet Commander it was also an anxiety, but he had other worries. If the Japanese high command, expecting a major strike from forces they knew were gathering at Pearl, could forecast its time and place they could make our task more difficult by moving submarines into the area ahead of time. The Japanese fleet with its carriers was still a powerful force that could be thrown into action at a critical moment. These concerns were very real to us as we studied the operation orders.

The wisdom of our westward advance through Micronesia seems clear now, but in summer and fall 1943 many strategists regarded it as very chancy because it would take our ships beyond the range of Allied shore-based air power. As it turned out, the Japanese were surprised by our movement in force into the Gilberts, and their reactions were slower than expected. Attacks by our south Pacific forces against Bougainville and damage inflicted on enemy cruisers and destroyers in Rabaul by *Saratoga* and *Princeton* kept the Japanese high command uncertain and off balance regarding where our next blow would strike.

Galvanic had the largest naval force ever assembled under the American flag: some 200 ships carrying about 108,000 soldiers, sailors, marines, and aviators. The fast carrier force, Task Force (TF) 50, commanded by Rear Admiral Pownall, was the greatest carrier force ever concentrated, consisting of six large and five light carriers that operated more than 600 aircraft—fighter, dive-bomber, and torpedo. Two escort carrier groups, totalling six escort carriers, transported 200 more. Shore-based Army and Navy patrol and striking groups aggregated over 150 additional aircraft. Total air strength of the Fifth Fleet was over 1,000 planes, a truly powerful force.

Task Force 50 was organized into four carrier task groups and two air support groups. Northern Carrier Group 50.2 was under my command, with *Enterprise* (flagship), *Belleau Wood*, and *Monterey*.

The planners in Pearl placed great emphasis on protection of the two amphibious assault groups during the time they were taking Makin and Tarawa. Admiral Towers and his staff were not too happy with the protective role of the fast carriers, but having done their best accepted it. When Rear Admiral Montgomery and I returned from the Wake strikes early in October and were fully briefed on the projected air operations we were most unhappy. We pointed out that far more protection could be given to surface forces in the Gilberts if the fast carrier group took the offensive against Japanese air fields in the Marshalls prior to D-day, eliminating enemy air and damaging airfields until they ceased to be a factor. In partial agreement, Admiral Towers gave us permission to see Admiral Spruance in an effort to have the basic air plan changed. Admiral Spruance received us with his usual courtesy and listened carefully to our arguments. His decision was: no change. He felt that detailed preparations could not be changed in time, particularly in an operation over such an enormous area. We could not but agree with Admiral Spruance that our suggestions for change had come too late.

Looking back on Galvanic, and knowing the value of taking the offensive in carrier operations, I am certain that TF 50 could have done a much better job of protecting surface forces had we struck first, hard, and often enough to eliminate enemy air power in the Marshalls before D-day. On the other hand, I must admit that we did very well. Our fighters did a remarkable job of intercepting daytime strikes. Our success in repelling night torpedo attacks was due partly to skill, good luck, and some Japanese stupidity but mainly to excellent maneuvering at high speeds in close formation, presenting the attackers with a concentration of AA fire such as they had never seen.

Carrier groups 50.1 and 50.2 sortied from Pearl Harbor, using the fairly direct passage to the Gilberts for AA and air training exercises, to weld the squadrons and groups into effective combat units. The fast battleship division joined us at a refueling rendezvous, then both groups commenced the run-in for attacks on D-day, 19 November.

During the passage from Pearl to Makin, I worked with Lt. Comdr. "Butch" O'Hare, the air group commander in *Enterprise,* on developing a night fighter unit. I was convinced that our carriers must have night offensive capacity. The Japanese air commanders followed a set pattern when faced with a carrier attack. First they sent out search planes to locate us, then they launched bombing and/or torpedo plane attacks in force. As long as we had no night fighter capability, their scouting planes could report our carrier movements while the attacking force was on its way out. This did not hold in the daytime. While our CAPs were airborne, we usually shot down Japanese scouting planes whenever they approached. It was rare that a lone Betty (reconnaissance plane) could close at low level before being discovered.

The result of discussions in *Enterprise* was the organization of two units that we called the Black Panthers, consisting of one torpedo and two fighter aircraft each. Our torpedo planes (VTs) were equipped with radar that was to be used for night attacks but that could also be used to pick up other aircraft. The VT made a good night search plane, and since it carried two .50-caliber fixed machine guns it had offensive power also. Its only drawback was lack of speed. The Black Panthers included the VFs [F6 fighter aircraft] for that reason. With the VT to lead the VFs close enough to an enemy plane or formation for the latter to see them or pick up their exhaust flames, it was hoped that the fighters could surprise and shoot down single enemy planes and disperse formations.

Lieutenant Commander O'Hare and Lt. Comdr. John Phillips, the Torpedo Squadron Commander, evolved plans for the two night fighter units. On 18 November, the day before our first attack on Makin, I sent the following message to Task Group (TG) 50.2.

Upon the assumption that night air attacks by torpedo planes are difficult to make unless the target can be located and tracked, if snoopers appear after sunset *Enterprise* may launch planes which will endeavor to shoot them down. Failing in this, these planes will be used as radar pickets in an effort to locate the attacking group as far out as possible and possibly break up their formation. When it is apparent that attack is developing, our planes may be directed to attempt to confuse the attackers by dropping float lights and flares at some distance astern of the formation if and after the enemy has attempted to mark our position in this manner. Aircraft launched as outlined above will initially be VT with extra tanks which should enable them to fly until after sunrise. If the attack develops after midnight and visibility is good, two additional fighters may be launched. All these aircraft will be ordered to stay well clear of own formation unless engaging enemy aircraft. If they have a deferred forced landing for any reason the formation may be maneuvered to rescue them or they may be directed to land alongside a screening vessel, which will be ordered to drop astern for that purpose. In either case formation will be notified over the TBS [Tactical Voice Radio].

On 24 November by 3:00 A.M. the task group had returned to an area about 50 miles northeast of Makin and was in a good position to intercept enemy flights bound for Makin or Tarawa. Both Black Panther units were launched to intercept enemy fighters picked up by our radar. Unfortunately the bogeys picked up were over 100 miles to the west, apparently headed for Tarawa, so our Panthers had no practice except in operating together.

I was standing on the flag bridge hoping to see any action they might stir up when, shortly after 5:00, the darkness to the west was suddenly lit up by what appeared to be a terrific explosion. It looked almost like a sunrise but was in the wrong direction. It was 50–75 miles away and we heard no sound. What we had sighted was the explosion aboard *Liscombe Bay*, flagship of R. Adm. Henry Mullinnix. Both the admiral and his Commanding Officer were lost, as were over 600 others. The explosion apparently was in a bomb magazine touched off by a torpedo hit from a submarine.

The rest of D+4 day was routine, and by sunset the group was all buttoned up and cruising in an area of intermittent rain squalls. Shortly after 8:00 P.M., well after dark, several bogeys were picked up flying separately and rather aimlessly but closing slowly. My Japanese Intercept Officer, Lt. W. L. Kluss, was listening to the bogeys' chatter and said they had not sighted us; their main concern was the arrival of their reliefs. With poor surface visibility, I slowed the group to bare steerage way so that we left almost no wake. The task group was notified not to open fire on any aircraft coming close unless ordered to do so. A lone bogey gradually worked nearer us and finally flew directly over the formation at about 500 feet; we could see his exhaust flames clearly as he passed over *Enterprise*. Had we fired we undoubtedly would have brought him down but we would have disclosed our position to the others. Quite likely we would have been attacked in force about an hour later. The radio intercept group under Lieutenant Kluss paid big dividends on this occasion and many others. I knew my ship commanders thought I was crazy to let that Jap get away but I could not tell them the story at that time.

With the sinking of *Liscombe Bay* and other reported sound contacts, we knew that Japanese submarines had at last moved into the Galvanic operating area, and our patrols were doubly alert. After sunset on D + 5 day, 50 miles west of Makin, a number of bogeys appeared on the screen. They closed in, dropping flares apparently in preparation for torpedo attacks. Their attack developed so quickly that I decided against launching our Black Panthers. Screening vessels opened fire: *North Carolina* shot down one Betty certainly, another probably. Shortly afterward, for no apparent reason, all enemy planes withdrew.

At 11:15 P.M. the destroyer *Radford*, screening the group on circle 6,[4] made a depth charge attack on an excellent sound contact. Shortly thereafter several ships reported a surface contact almost due west, and *Radford* was detached to search. At 5.8 miles the surface target suddenly faded, indicating a submarine making a crash dive. *Radford* made three more attacks on excellent contacts, with a large explosion following the last one. A strong odor of oil and considerable cork and wood debris were noted and recovered. *Radford* was awarded only a probable kill, but Japanese submarine I-19 (in that vicinity at the time) never surfaced again.

The next day was again routine, with CAPs heavy at times over Makin and the task group. After sunset, just after all CAPs had been recovered, several bogeys appeared on the horizon, closing the group. Our intelligence indicated that a large group of enemy planes would follow them. On the bridge, as I decided what to do, Lieutenant Commander O'Hare approached me and requested that I send one of the Black Panther groups out. At 6:00 P.M. they were launched.

The bogeys escaped, but even before the Black Panthers had rendezvoused, 30 or 40 enemy planes appeared. They dropped float lights astern of us, evidently marking a base point. Then a section dropped a string of some 25 powerful flares to the west and rather close aboard. The task group was lighted up as if in daylight. By now we were in close AA formation, with carriers on the 1,000-yard circle and six destroyers and three battleships on the 2,500-yard circle, a tight and formidable target. We were steaming at 25 knots and maneuvering by simultaneous turns to keep the Japanese planes from gaining a position on our bows.

possibility before, so he was prepared for my recommendations and was sympathetic. We jointly drafted a dispatch, which he promised to get to Admiral Nimitz as soon as possible. This was either on 1 February or on the next day at the latest.

Later the same day, Admiral McMorris called to say that Admiral Nimitz had released the dispatch after making only one change: instead of "directing" the operation he "suggested" it be considered. I was sunk. I was almost certain that this would mean a fatal delay and that when it took place we would find Truk practically empty. That is exactly what happened.

On 2 February CINCPAC suggested a carrier strike on Truk "before enemy ships leave it," and the next day more detailed suggestions were made to Admiral Spruance regarding the attack. The dispatch also noted that Admiral Halsey was expected to photograph Truk the next day. Reading over these dispatches 26 years later I can see that I misunderstood what went out to Admiral Spruance on 2 February. The second message sent contained the gist of what I suggested, but the urgency I had endeavored to indicate was missing.

The photographic flight was made as directed, and some choice targets were spotted. Admiral Mineichi Koga's Combined Fleet was there, less some ships that had departed for Palau. At anchor in Truk Lagoon were a battleship, 2 carriers, 5–6 heavy and 4 light cruisers, 20 destroyers, and 12 submarines, as well as numerous merchant ships. Tipped off by our reconnaissance flight, Admiral Koga sent most of the combat ships to Palau while he returned to Japan in *Musashi.*

Admiral Mitscher with TF 58 assembled in Maloelap Lagoon after the D-day strikes. The task of destroying Japanese air power in the Marshalls had been well done. Other than a strike against Roi by six Japanese seaplanes from Saipan, there was no enemy air action in the Marshalls or in Eniwetok after 29 January.

Task Force 58 had a good rest in Maloelap and were raring to go against Truk, the fabled Japanese bastion of the Pacific, when they finally sortied on 12–13 February. Admiral Spruance shifted to *New Jersey,* one of the new fast battleships, to be in on the Truk raid (operation Hailstone) and to see as much action as he could. In Pearl, I had been biting my nails wondering when this operation would get under way, although I knew that the element of surprise would be missing and that our most important quarry had already gone. Writing this 26 years later, it seems strange that Admiral Spruance did not sense the urgency about this operation that I thought Admiral Nimitz' two messages had indicated. He may have explained his delay to Admiral Nimitz; if he did, I did not see the messages. Undoubtedly he wanted to see the major objectives, Kwajalein, Roi, and Namur, taken. By the time they were taken, he probably knew that major units of the Combined Fleet had left Truk, and perhaps he decided it would now be better to delay a little more. An operation that could have started on 3 or 4 February and caught major units of the Japanese fleet did not get under way until nine days later. A surprise strike that might have shortened the war by months became just another history-making carrier strike.

Operation Hailstone began just before sunrise on 17 February. Task Force 58 made a high-speed approach from the northeast and was undetected by Japanese air searches. Of some 365 aircraft on Truk, fewer than 100 remained after the first surprise attacks. A predawn fighter sweep the next morning was unopposed by enemy aircraft, whereas on the first morning some 75 Japanese fighters were airborne.[2]

With Japanese air opposition all but eliminated the first morning, Admiral Mitscher turned his attention to merchant shipping and those combatant ships still in the lagoon. Two auxiliary cruisers, a destroyer, an aircraft ferry, 6 tankers, and 17 marus [cargo ships that can carry passengers or troops], a total tonnage of about 200,000, were sunk.[3] It was a sad day for the Japanese merchant marine.

Shortly after sunset, still on 17 February, Admiral Mitscher's three carrier task groups were maneuvering within sight of one another about 100 miles northeast of Truk when they were attacked by six or seven Japanese Kates, torpedo planes launched from Truk. This was the first and only Japanese counterattack.

That night Admiral Mitscher launched the first carrier night bombing attack with planes of VT 10 from Enterprise. The squadron, commanded by Lt. William Martin, had trained for months. Martin, assisted and advised by Lt. Henry Loomis, had devised the equipment and tactics that made the TBF1C a good night attack plane.

Twelve torpedo planes, commanded that night by Lt. Van V. Easton because Martin had been incapacitated by an accident, took off at 1:00 A.M., rendezvoused, and successfully attacked Japanese shipping in the Dublon and Eten anchorages. They were detected crossing the outer reef; a Japanese hospital ship switched on her lights, and heavy AA fire opened at once. The planes remained for 20–30 minutes locating ships by radar in their assigned areas and making masthead-height runs at them. This single night attack caused about a third of the total damage to shipping by the entire carrier force.

This first night carrier attack won the great debate raging in Pearl Harbor concerning the future of night carrier operations. The impact of the Truk strike resulted in the designation of night carriers (Enterprise, Independence, and Bataan), fitted out primarily for night offensive operations, which joined the fast carrier task force early in 1945. By then the Essex-class carriers were successfully operating their own fighters (F6Fs with radar) on night CAPs.

Full-scale operations against Truk resumed at dawn on 18 February. Since there was no air opposition and the lagoon was clear of live targets, special attention was paid to airfield hangars, storage tanks, and fuel dumps. When orders to retire were given at noon a total of 1,250 combat sorties had been flown against Truk, 400 tons of bombs and torpedoes had been used against shipping, and some 94 tons had been dropped on airfields and shore installations.

This first carrier strike on Truk was in many respects one of the most successful carrier operations of the war. It destroyed not only immense amounts of supplies and large numbers of scarce merchant ships and aircraft but perhaps more important, five tankers. It seemed also to have had a depressing effect on Japanese morale, for it was the first real dent in their second defensive perimeter. In Japan and the United States at the time, Truk had been considered impregnable. Reports indicated that the defenders had been badly mauled.

Truk was still usable for planes, and many buildings were undamaged until after a second carrier raid in April 1944, but its usefulness as a fleet anchorage and advanced naval base was over. One can only imagine the magnitude and consequences of this victory had it included the sinking of the Japanese fleet flagship *Musashi* and all the other ships that had been at anchor there on 4 February.

The spectacular success of the Navy's operations in the Gilberts and Marshalls, together with the knockout punch delivered by the carriers at Truk, boosted morale in the Pacific Fleet and the country at large. The Navy had redeemed itself for the losses at Pearl Harbor and the setbacks in earlier Pacific operations.

Our losses in men and aircraft were light but would have been much heavier had it not been for the splendid work of rescue submarines and seaplanes. *Sea Raven* rescued the entire crew of a torpedo bomber from *Yorktown*. Seaplanes from *Baltimore* and *Massachusetts* made rescues in and near Truk Lagoon. The downed pilots were covered by fighter patrols that were relieved on station while the rescue operations were organized. In the rescue of Lt. George M. Blair, of *Essex,* shot down in the 18 February dawn fighter sweep, the CAP had to strafe and drive away the Japanese destroyer *Fumizuki*, which was trying to capture Blair.

Closer to me personally, Lt. George Bullard, who became my aide in 1948, was shot down on the second day and managed to make his way to an islet on the reef. Through a mixup his fighter patrol was not relieved on station and his location was lost. Japanese took him into custody and vented on him and the few other prisoners captured the bad feelings engendered by their decisive defeat. George was flown to Japan and spent the rest of the war there. Released in September 1945, he weighed only 120 pounds. When he served with me he was troubled by problems attributed in part to dietary deficiencies suffered while a prisoner. He did not harbor a grudge against the Japanese, and pointed out their treatment of one another was not much better than their treatment of prisoners. Promoted up the line to Rear Admiral, George made up for time lost as a prisoner but died of a heart attack in 1966. His experiences in Japan must have taken a lot more out of him than he realized.

By spring 1944 there were in service ten heavy and nine light carriers. The new air groups showed the results of the longer training syllabus put into effect after the war started. The young pilots arrived in the fleet ready to take their places in the squadrons. For me, these were great days as I read the dispatches of the successes of TF 58. One can therefore imagine my shock when I received orders to Washington early in March. I had left there not quite a year before and did not want to go back.

☆ ☆ ☆ ☆

I found many changes in the Navy Department that rather surprised me when I reported for duty in Washington as Assistant to the Deputy Chief of Naval Operations (DCNO) for Air, V. Adm. J. S. McCain, in April. From December 1941 to April 1943, the attitude of practically everyone with whom I did business in the Department had been one of complete cooperation. The desire to get on with the war had enabled me to get rapid approval of radical changes in plans, programs, and appropriations. The American people had been badly shaken. They were frightened enough to forget their differences in order to get on with the business of winning the war. It had been a wonderful experience to serve in the Navy Department during the first months of the war.

I found that the questioners had returned. Naval ideas and suggestions had to be well documented, and everyone in a high position had by then surrounded himself with a staff whose most obvious mission was to keep him from making mistakes. It took much more effort to get things done, and there was evidence that people in high places were thinking only about winding up the war.

Admiral McCain practically apologized for ordering me back to Washington so suddenly. He said there were some specific problems he wanted me to work on; but he indicated he would help me get back to the Pacific.

Mrs. Radford and I had a difficult time finding a place to live. Rents had skyrocketed in the year we had been gone. We tried to get our old apartment or one like it, but for the next six months, the length of my tour, we bounced from one temporary home to another.

Admiral McCain was not one to waste time. On 12 April I received the precept for an informal board of which I was senior member, to develop a policy for the retirement of aircraft that were overage or otherwise outmoded and to develop an integrated maintenance, material, and supply program based upon such policy. In our precept there was wide latitude for procedure. We were given to understand that the matters involved were urgent and that our report was desired as soon as possible.[4]

The board plunged into its work, holding hearings in Washington, Norfolk, and Alameda, California, at which representatives of interested offices and bureaus appeared. Fifteen meetings were held and the final report submitted to DCNO (Air) on 4 May. There was a remarkable unanimity of opinion among our witnesses on the problems involved, and our report—quite radical in some respects—represented the consensus of experts in many fields.

We found that the naval aeronautical organization had been swamped by the avalanche of material pouring into it once the manufacturing facilities involved were able to get rolling. Until our report was accepted and its recommendations placed in effect, the system of receiving and keeping track of aircraft, spares, engines and their spares, and the thousands of other items in aeronautical inventory remained much as it was in December 1941. The offices and organizations that managed these functions had been expanded as personnel became available, but the system had never been changed. By spring 1944 utter chaos was just around the corner. At the end of the pipeline, in the Pacific, I had been one of the most vociferous critics of this supply system, which made it so difficult to maintain our planes in combat readiness. It was likely that one or more of my caustic messages had led to my nomination to the board.

Looking back on this particular experience, accomplished under great pressure, I believe it was helpful to me in every way. I learned a great deal about the aviation supply system and the individuals who ran it. The solutions we recommended received wide publicity, and I became acquainted with many civilians in the higher echelons. Luck plays a great part in one's advancement. In this instance, my assignment as senior member of what became known as the Radford Board (authors of the Radford Report), helped my naval career a great deal.

Our recommendations were accepted almost in their entirety and put into effect immediately. Assistant Secretary Gates gave us his complete backing, so reluctant bureaucrats were overwhelmed and could not drag their feet.

My six months in Washington were more of the same after the Radford Report. I restudied the training program and found it going well. I then gave considerable thought to the postwar naval aviation reserve problem, and with Capt. Irving McQuiston, USNR, drafted a plan to keep most of our primary training stations as naval aviation reserve bases after the war.[5]

Shortly before the end of August, Admiral McCain called me into his office to say that he was leaving to take command of the fast carrier task force of the Third Fleet under Admiral Halsey. In a reorganization about to take effect, Admirals Spruance and Halsey were to alternate in command of the fleet under Admiral Nimitz. Under Spruance it would be the Fifth Fleet, under Halsey the Third. Admiral Mitscher was to command the fast carriers under Spruance and Admiral McCain would command them under Halsey. Whichever Fleet Commander and Fast Carrier Force Commander were not at sea would be in Pearl, working on plans for the next operation. It was a good arrangement, but—as the "working men" in the fleet began to see later on—changing drivers and not horses made it very tough on the individual ships and staffs who stayed on.[6]

Admiral McCain had promised to let me go after six months and in fact I got away on 4 October. My orders were to report to the Commander Fast Carrier Task Force, in such port as he might be. I was in Saipan until 26 October, living aboard the former Pan American yacht *Southern Seas*, while the momentous events of 23–25 October unfolded. Information was fragmentary at best; but we ten officers and men awaiting transportation to Ulithi to join the Third Fleet did our best to find out what was going on.

We knew that Gen. Douglas MacArthur's initial landings on Leyte were being given close cover by units of the Seventh Fleet under Adm. Thomas Kinkaid. We also knew that the Third Fleet under Admiral Halsey—especially Task Force 38, the fast carriers under Admiral Mitscher—were giving more distant cover, interdicting Japanese land-based air from many bases in the Philippines and Formosa and searching for units of the main Japanese fleet that could be expected to intervene.

It is difficult to recall just how much we actually knew then, but we had an idea of the broad picture. The senior officers saw copies of intercepted dispatches, for the communicators on *Southern Seas* were able to decode dispatches from CINCPAC to Commander Third Fleet. I remember reading an intercepted copy of the famous dispatch sent by Admiral Nimitz to Admiral Halsey that read, WHERE IS TASK FORCE 34. The padding (words added before and after a message to make it more difficult to break the cipher) supplied by CINCPAC communicators very suitably read: ALL THE WORLD WANTS TO KNOW. Indeed, all the world did want to know where Admiral Halsey's fast battleships were when the Japanese heavy ships began to engage Admiral Kincaid's escort carriers in the Gulf of Leyte early that morning.[7]

On 25 October resounding victory or smashing defeat was possible. On the *Southern Seas* we awaited the outcome with suspense. We read Admiral Kinkaid's frantic messages calling for help from Admiral Halsey and Halsey's reply, after what seemed an interminable delay, that TF 34 was with him engaging an enemy carrier force at a position so far north that he could not possibly intervene in the action off Leyte.

The air was filled with urgent messages, not necessarily decoded in the sequence in which they were sent, that fateful day. We were alternately fearful or exulted as the reports were laid before us. By evening we knew that, by some miracle, the Seventh Fleet had been saved—largely through the heroic action of R. Adm. Clifton Sprague's escort carriers and their destroyers.[8] The Japanese heavy ships that had come through the San Bernardino Strait and engaged our fleet off Leyte had unexpectedly broken off the battle and retreated through the same strait. We were uncertain just what Admiral Halsey had finally done. It was late that night before we turned in, as exhausted as if we had taken part in the various engagements that had cost so many lives and so many splendid ships in the expanse of the Philippine Sea.

I shall never forget my visit to *Missouri* when I was finally able to report to Admiral Halsey on 17 November. First I met with my classmate and friend "Mick" Carney, Chief of Staff. I was bubbling with curiosity on several important points and did not hold back. To my surprise, the usually garrulous Mick was rather noncommittal, and the same was true of Admiral Halsey and several other members of the staff. The impression that remained with me was definite: they did not want to talk about those days in October. I felt distinctly that all were displeased with their performance but had not yet agreed on the reasons for it. On later occasions, particularly after the war, I heard those who had been members of that staff defend every action taken with vehemence, much as Admiral Halsey did in his autobiography.[9]

Subsequently at Ulithi, and at various times since the war, I talked with all the other principal flag officers involved in the carrier actions of this second Battle of the Philippine Sea. Without exception they felt that Admiral Halsey's decision to leave the Strait of San Bernardino unguarded on the night of 24–25 October was a great, and nearly fatal, error.[10] Reading Halsey's own story of these events, I am not impressed that he did not consult with Mitscher or, in fact, with any of his task group commanders. Knowing the many variables that exist in intelligence estimates, that a fleet commander would not consult with experienced subordinates if he had time seems strange. Admiral Halsey had the time, and he had good communications with his task force and task group commanders on that evening.[11]

4

Ulithi to the Indochina Coast

In *Ticonderoga,* part of Task Group 38.3 under Admiral Sherman, I sortied with the group on 2 November 1944. They had expected more time in Ulithi for repairs, rest and recreation after the strenuous operations of the last two months, but urgent calls for assistance from General MacArthur and Admiral Kincaid at Leyte necessitated additional carrier strikes against Japanese shipping and airfields in the northern Philippines. We operated with Task Groups 38.1 and 38.2 against southern Luzon and the Visayan Islands, our targets enemy shipping, combat vessels, airfields, and aircraft.

The first taste of fast carrier action since the Gilberts operation a year before was revealing. Ship tactics and task group operations were much improved but air groups varied a great deal. Sheer numbers of aircraft furnished the power for victory, but I sensed that individual groups were not as well trained as before. On 7 December I wrote a letter to my relief as Assistant DCNO (Air), R. Adm. John Cassady, covering some of the particulars.[1]

Task Group 38.3 paused only briefly in Ulithi after the supporting strikes of early November. A conference at Tacloban between Gen. Douglas MacArthur, Gen. George Kenney, and Admiral Sherman resulted in agreement that the fast carrier forces continue to concentrate on rehabilitation and improvement of material condition for future amphibious operations. This canceled strikes against Japan that Admiral Halsey had been hoping to make before the end of the year.

It was obvious that the Japanese air force was making a tremendous effort to reinforce the Philippines and there were further U.S. actions against northern Luzon and Manila in late November. By then pilots, air crews, and ships' crews were exhausted from the almost continuous action since early September. *Princeton* had been lost, and *Cabot, Intrepid, Lexington, Franklin* and *Belleau Wood* needed extensive repairs. Kamikazes, the enemy's suicide planes, were a serious menace, and some time was needed to develop a counter to them as well as to rest the whole force.

We finally entered Ulithi on 2 December. The whole task force was there, so impressive a sight that a famous contemporary photograph showing seven fast carriers anchored in a row at Ulithi was captioned "Murderers Row." The fast carrier force had caused the Japanese to lose so much shipping and aircraft that they had great difficulty reinforcing and resupplying the troops left on Leyte.

At Ulithi, there was planning to counter the devastating kamikaze attacks. Study, analysis, and conferences finally resulted in a strategy. All information on damage resulting from kamikaze attacks was kept very quiet and officers and men returning to the United States and Australia were warned not to talk about them or the damage they had caused. We did not want the enemy to find out how successful he had been with this new weapon. Mail censors also carefully eliminated any mention of this new problem. Not until April 1945 was the kamikaze story broken to the American public and by that time the fleet was prepared to handle it.

Admiral McCain and his staff consulted with other experienced officers and pilots and worked out new tactics to meet the kamikaze problem. Radar picket destroyers equipped with the latest radar and aircraft homing devices were stationed about 60 miles from the task force on strike days, on each side of the target-bearing line, to give advance warning of enemy aircraft. Returning strike planes were required to make a full turn around the picket destroyers known as Tom Cats, within certain altitude limits. This permitted "delousing"—the weeding out of kamikazes trying to sneak in on the task force with our planes—by CAPs known as Sheep Dogs.

One thing was obvious. Task Force 38 must operate in strength to provide maximum defense and at the same time conduct offensive operations that would hurt the enemy. The 13 fast carriers available were reorganized into three instead of four task groups.

Changes were made in the complement of aircraft on the carriers. Where each *Essex*-class carrier had carried some 38 fighters, 36 dive-bombers and 18 torpedo planes, the new complement was 73, 14, and 15, respectively. Hellcats and Corsairs were modified to be all-purpose planes; they could carry up to 2,000 pounds of bombs and fly bombing missions unescorted, intercept enemy strikes, or fly combat air patrols. These important changes had great repercussions along the training and logistics line. The carriers' effectiveness was almost doubled.

Task Force 38 sortied from Ulithi on 11 December to make preliminary strikes on Luzon airfields in support of the Mindoro landing, General MacArthur's next step after Leyte en route to Manila. Admiral McCain tried out another tactic that had long been discussed but could not be attempted earlier for lack of fighters. It was called the Big Blue Blanket: keeping an umbrella of fighters over the Luzon airfields day and night so that enemy aircraft could not take off to attack the carriers or the Mindoro convoys. When fighter cover was being relieved, bombers would attack grounded planes. The blanket was maintained for three days and a good part of two nights.

Admiral McCain wrote, after trial of the new tactics:

> Before the innovation of suicide attacks by the enemy, destruction of 80 or 90 percent of his attackers was considered an eminent success. Now 100 percent destruction of the attackers is necessary to preserve the safety of the task force. New developments—the Jack Patrols, Moosetrap Exercises, all night combat air patrols, and Tom Cats—are designed for 100 percent destruction. These new offensive and defensive requirements inherently conflict and making the correct compromise is the continual task of the force comander.[2]

It was expected that after the operations in mid-December TF 38 would be released from support of General MacArthur. Admiral Halsey was anxious to enter the South China Sea, where he hoped to catch remnants of the Japanese fleet. The Navy high command did not feel the time was ripe for this operation, so the fast carriers headed instead for a rendezvous with their refueling group. In trying to make this rendezvous Admiral Halsey unwittingly made one with the worst storm of the year in the Philippine Sea.

There have been many stories written about this storm and the losses suffered by the Third Fleet as a result of it. My story may well differ from others. I was still riding *Ticonderoga* as an observer. Anxious to see everything I could, I spent practically all my time on the flag bridge in my favorite spot, a seat on the starboard wing. There I had a wonderful view, with my eyes about 75 feet above the sea.

We joined the tankers early on the morning of Saturday 17 December, and fueling commenced. Admiral Halsey was anxious to finish soon in order to strike Luzon two days later in accordance with a promise to General MacArthur. But the ships had difficulty refueling, so about noon Admiral Halsey delayed the process and put the task force on a northwesterly course for a new rendezvous. Many of the destroyers, very low on fuel, were rolling heavily in their deballasted condition.

I sat in my perch all that Sunday afternoon watching the turbulent sea and the ominous sky. *Ticonderoga*'s aerologist felt we were experiencing a tropical disturbance but not a cyclonic storm. Weather reports were decidedly sketchy but the fleet was in an area that spawned typhoons. As the ship's motion increased I was convinced that our tropical disturbance was likely to be a typhoon. I remember calling for a copy of Bowditch's *The American Practical Navigator*, a text used at the Naval Academy when I was a midshipman. I reread the chapter on cyclonic storms, particularly the section "Early Indications of Tropical Cyclones." Captain Dixie Kiefer, commanding *Ticonderoga*, felt as I did that we were in for it and issued orders to secure for a typhoon. We estimated the location of the center of the storm, which indicated that we were practically in its path, but we erred on the pessimistic side. With an opposite view a different conclusion could have been reached—and was, for by the next morning at daylight the Third Fleet was in the typhoon, nearly at its center. *Ticonderoga* was rolling heavily, probably 35–40 degrees. From my seat on the flag bridge this was exaggerated, of course. As we rolled to starboard it seemed as though the crest of the next wave was on my level and that I could put my hand out and touch it.

Monday morning was a wild one. The storm was evidently increasing in severity, but Admiral Halsey made one last effort at refueling that was cancelled soon afterward.

By 9:00 A.M. the winds were gusting at 50 knots. Rainfall was so heavy as to greatly restrict visibility and the formation was beginning to disintegrate. Destroyers and light carriers were forced to maneuver to reduce motion, in the interests of safety, and the fleet was becoming strung out over a wide expanse [2,500 square miles] of ocean.

The large carriers rode well, although the extent of their rolling can be judged from the fact that *Hancock*'s flight deck, 57 feet above the waterline, scooped up green water on one roll. The battleships and cruisers rode out the storm without great difficulty, and only the cruiser *Miami* sustained serious damage.

But light carriers were having difficulty. Rolling heavily, their planes began to go adrift as even the extra-heavy lashings began to snap and some of the steel padeyes [rings] in the flight decks pulled out. Two ships caught fire, and there was much damage to ships and their planes.

The escort carriers with the refueling and replenishment group did well under the circumstances, rolling heavily but suffering no great material damage. Total aircraft losses in the fleet, including those blown overboard or jettisoned, were 146.

Destroyers had the worst experiences. *Hull*, a 1,370-tonner, together with two destroyer escorts, was screening four fleet oilers. At about 11:00 A.M. the unit commander in *Monongahela* ordered a change of course. While this was being executed the wind increased to over 100 knots. While proceeding to her new station, incident to the change of course, *Hull*'s helm failed to respond to any combination of rudder and engines. She lay "in irons" [unable to move, pinned down by wind and sea] yawing in the trough of the sea. Her whaleboat, depth charges, and almost everything else on deck were swept off as she rolled 50 degrees to leeward. Just before noon the rolls increased to 70 degrees. She recovered from two or three, but finally a gust estimated at 110 miles per hour pinned her down on her beam ends. Seas flooded the pilot house and poured down her stacks. A few minutes after noon she went down. Of her complement of 18 officers and 246 men, only 7 officers and 55 men were rescued. It can be noted that, at the time of *Hull*'s loss, she had 70 percent of fuel on board. She had not reballasted with salt water, but it was not considered necessary then for a ship of this class to reballast with that much fuel on board.

The stories of two other destroyers, *Dewey* and *Alwin*, are also epic. They, too, survived rolls of 70–75 degrees and suffered tremendous damage close to the center of the storm. Individual acts of heroism by officers and men were legion, but one stands out in my mind. When the eye of the storm passed *Alwin* close aboard around 11:00 A.M., her steering control was lost and her engines were stopped: she rolled 70 degrees to port and then lay down on her side for 20 minutes. Steering control, regained intermittently, was employed to bring her stern to windward, using the bow's surface as a headsail to keep steerage way. This maneuver kept the wind at about 30 degrees abaft the starboard beam, but she frequently fell into the trough. From 1:00 P.M., when the lowest barometer reading, 28.55, was observed, the ship did not roll *more* than 60 degrees. Engine rooms were abandoned when temperatures reached 180 degrees because blowers had failed. Lieutenant E. R. Rendahl, USNR, and Machinist Mate First Class T. Sarenski remained on watch in the terrific heat to protect the electrical circuits. They stayed too long at their posts and when they could stand it no longer crawled out on deck through the only exit, a hatch so small that they had to remove their life jackets. They were immediately overcome by the change of temperature and collapsed, and before anyone could help them, they were washed overboard and lost. *Alwin* finally got underway at seven knots with water sloshing above her floor plates, but she managed to control the flooding that night and survived.

This typhoon was comparatively small, as they usually are in lower latitudes, but because the Third Fleet ran smack into it with a number of deballasted destroyers, more damage was inflicted on the Navy than by any other storm since the famous hurricane at Apia, Samoa, in March 1889. Three destroyers capsized, six or seven other ships were seriously damaged, and almost 800 officers and men were lost. As Admiral Nimitz later said: "this was the greatest uncompensated loss that the Navy had taken since the Battle of Savo Island."[3]

Sailors mourn shipmates lost through the dangers of the sea if possible even more than those killed by enemy violence. Certainly, all of us in the Third Fleet on 19 December, as we surveyed the damage under clear skies and searched for survivors in a massive hunt covering hundreds of square miles, were depressed by the loss of so many fine men but individually thankful to be spared.

The Third Fleet spent Christmas in Ulithi repairing typhoon damage. Admiral Nimitz spent the holiday with Admiral Halsey and heard about the typhoon firsthand from numerous officers. Later on, after a court of inquiry had rendered its report placing the responsibility for storm damage with Admiral Halsey, Admiral Nimitz issued a fleet letter entitled "Lessons of Damage in Typhoon." The letter is a lesson in sound seamanship. I am sure Admiral Halsey realized as he read it that Admiral Nimitz, too, placed responsibility for the loss of men and damage to ships of the Third Fleet squarely on his, Admiral Halsey's, shoulders.

A hundred years ago, a ship's survival depended almost solely on the competence of her master and on his constant alertness to every hint of change in the weather . . . While to be taken by surprise was . . . serious, the facilities for avoiding it were meager. Each master was dependent wholly on himself for detecting the first symptoms of bad weather, for predicting its seriousness and movement, and for taking the appropriate measures, to evade it if possible and to battle through it if it passed near to him . . .

Seamen of the present day should be better at forecasting weather at sea, independently of the radio, than were their predecessors. The general laws of storms and the weather expectancy for all months of the year in all parts of the world are now more understood . . . and more readily available in various publications. An intensive study of typhoons and western Pacific weather was made over a period of many years by Father Depperman at the Manila Observatory, and his conclusions have been embodied in the material available to all aerologists. What Knight and Bowditch have to say on the subject is exactly as true during this war as it was in time of peace or before the days of radio. Familiarity with these authorities is something no captain or navigator (or aerologist!) can do without. The monthly pilot charts, issued to all ships, give excellent information as to the probable incidence and movements of typhoons . . .

The safety of a ship against perils from storm, as well as from those of navigation and maneuvering is always the responsibility of her Commanding Officer, but this responsibility is also shared by his immediate superiors in operational command, since by the very fact of such command the individual commanding officer is not free to do any time what his own judgment might indicate . . .

It is most definitely part of the senior officer's responsibility to think in terms of the smallest ship and most inexperienced commanding officer under him. He cannot take them for granted . . .

In conclusion, both seniors and juniors must realize that in bad weather, as in most other situations, safety and fatal hazard are not separated by any sharp boundary line, but shade gradually from one into the other. There is no little red light which is going to flash on and inform commanding officers or higher commanders that from then on there is extreme danger from the weather and that measures for ships' safety must now take precedence over further efforts to keep up with the formation or to execute the assigned task—this time will be a matter of personal judgment. Naturally no commander is going to cut thin the margin between staying afloat and foundering, but he may nevertheless unwittingly pass the danger point even though no ship is yet "in extremis." Ships that keep on going as long as the severity of wind and sea has not yet come close to capsizing them or hacking them in two, may nevertheless become helpless to avoid these catastrophes later if things get worse . . . The time for taking all measures for a ship's safety is while still able to do so. Nothing is more dangerous than for a seaman to be grudging in taking precautions lest they turn out to have been unnecessary. Safety at sea for a thousand years has depended on exactly the opposite philosophy.

C. W. NIMITZ

☆ ☆ ☆ ☆

All of us who were in Ulithi for Christmas thoroughly enjoyed the relaxation from the tension of the past two months. But I was getting restless and anxious to take command of a fast carrier task group, and on 9 December I received the rather surprising orders to relieve Admiral Montgomery in command of TG 38.1. Since TF 38 had orders to sail the next day there was little time to effect the transfer. I immediately visited *Yorktown*, Admiral Montgomery's flagship, and found that he had been injured. He had slipped and fallen between boat and gangway while disembarking and was now in a hospital ship with undetermined injuries to his back. He was terribly disappointed to lose his command, particularly because he felt that on this next operation TF 38 might enter the South China Sea for long-expected strikes against the Asian mainland.

To sortie from Ulithi in command of one of three groups in the fast carrier task force of the Third Fleet, the most powerful naval striking force the world has ever known, was thrilling. Sitting on the flag bridge and looking over my part of that mighty armada, I felt very proud and fortunate. As I reviewed events of the past year, 1944, I was amazed at the success of our naval campaign. Last New Year's Day I had been in Pearl Harbor, working hard on arrangements for the Marshalls operation and trying to convince some of my senior commanders that the carrier forces could do better on the offensive. Now they were convinced. The record established by naval air power in 1944 had been beyond the expectation of even its most enthusiastic proponents. How the carriers and their squadrons had compressed the original timetables for our advance into the western Pacific! This had been the year of aggressive young carrier pilots led by one of the greatest air leaders of all time, Adm. Marc Mitscher.

On 2 January the task force refueled and commenced its high-speed run-in to the launching point for two days of strikes on Formosa. Every precaution had been taken to achieve complete surprise, including anti-snooper patrols out of Saipan and Leyte to intercept possible search planes, and complete surprise was achieved.

Bad weather hampered air operations and prevented accurate damage assessment for the two days. Admiral McCain, the Task Force Commander, estimated that a total of some 170 enemy planes were damaged or destroyed. Although the Task Force lost 22 planes in combat, the strikes paid off. They helped the Luzon attack force, because no planes from Formosa participated in the fierce attacks on our ships in Lingayen Gulf during the following week.

After refueling, TF 38 at daylight on 6 January launched strikes and sweeps against Luzon airfields; TG 38.1 took those to the north.

Searching for counter actions to stop the kamikaze, recommendations had been made to convert *Enterprise* to a night carrier. On 5 January, in time for these strikes, TG 38.5 was formed, a night-flying carrier group consisting of *Independence*, *Enterprise*, and six destroyers. During the day they operated as part of TG 38.2 but pulled out for independent operations when directed by the Task Force Commander. *Enterprise* trebled the offensive night capability of the task force and permitted the Commander to tighten blanket coverage around the clock. By the time these strikes ended on 7 January, the Japanese air forces on Luzon were almost wiped out.

Task Force 38 refueled and hit Formosa on 9 January, the day of the landings in Lingayen Gulf. On that day B29s based in Kunming, China, attacked Kirun Harbor in Formosa, while 72 of those from the Marianas dropped 122 tons of bombs over Japan, one-third of them on the Musashino aircraft plant in Tokyo. We were certainly closing in on the Japanese in January 1945.

The Third Fleet's direct support of the Lingayen operation ended with these strikes on Formosa. In one week, 3–9 January, TF 38 flew a total of 3,030 combat sorties, dropped 700 tons of bombs, and lost 86 planes, 40 operationally. These operations, combined with the all-out efforts of the escort carriers and the Army Air Corps, made the Lingayen landings possible.

Shortly after retiring from the launching area, TF 38 received a dispatch from Admiral McCain to the effect that TG 38.1 would have the honor that night of leading the Third Fleet through Bashi Channel into the South China Sea. I remember the excitement of reading that message, realizing that my task group would be the first unit of an Allied surface force to enter the China Sea since December 1941, when *Prince of Wales* and *Repulse* were sunk.[4]

The logistic group entered the South China Sea on the same night through Balintang Channel, to the south. Neither this group of some 30 oilers, plus escort carriers, destroyers, ammunition ships, and fleet tugs, nor TF 38 were discovered by the Japanese.

In the South China Sea at last, after planning this operation for months, Admiral Halsey took full advantage of his opportunity to harass and hurt the enemy. The immediate objective was Camranh Bay,[5] where it was hoped we would find some major units of the Japanese fleet. Important Japanese convoys from Singapore passed close to the Indochinese coast near Saigon, and we hoped to intercept one or more of them.

On 11 January the whole task force refueled and the following day Admiral Halsey's plans for the attack on Camranh Bay were effected.

The Admiral's report that TF 38's score that day was "one of the heaviest blows to Japanese shipping of any day of the war" was not exaggerated. The essential Japanese supply routes from Singapore, Malaya, Burma, and the Dutch East Indies were severed and were always thereafter in danger.

At sunset we headed over from the Annamese coast at 20 knots. Admiral Halsey was on a northeasterly course at high speed not only to confuse enemy searches but to escape an approaching typhoon. Fortunately, it hit the Indochina coast well to the south and hung there for several days. But the seas it kicked up bothered us, and made fueling difficult for some ships and impossible for others. Searches for enemy shipping made to the south on both days of refueling were negative. The Japanese had taken cover after their surprise.

Unless one has personally experienced heavy weather during the monsoon season in the South China Sea it is hard to describe the difficulties experienced by TF 38 and the logistic group under Capt. Jasper Acuff during these two days. By the greatest effort and expert ship handling, all destroyers were finally topped off [filled to the brim] and heavy ships refueled to about 60 percent capacity—all the fuel the tankers held.[6]

Admiral Halsey had received orders for the Third Fleet to intercept enemy forces approaching Lingayen Gulf from the north or south. The high command in Washington, Pearl Harbor, and the Philippines was still crediting the Japanese navy with an offensive capability which they hardly had left. Admiral Nimitz authorized Halsey to strike Hong Kong at his discretion.

Operating generally in the center of the South China Sea, TF 38 was in a position to strike Hainan Island, Hong Kong, China north of Hong Kong, and Formosa for the next five days, as well as to search for the old Japanese battleships *Ise* and *Hyuga*, which Admiral Halsey thought were hiding somewhere along the Indochina or China coast.

Task Force 38 headed north almost directly into strong northerly monsoon winds. Speed was limited to 16 knots because destroyers and other smaller ships could not make more without excessive damage. I remember watching our screening destroyers putting their bows out of water as far aft as their five-inch gun mounts as they crashed into the heavy seas every few minutes. It was a time when those of us on the big carriers and battleships were happy to be there.

At daylight on 15 January strikes and sweeps were launched against the China coast and Formosa. Task Force 38.1 was given objectives—airfields—in the Canton area and northern Formosa, a division of effort that I thought strange at the time and still do.

Late in the afternoon the force headed for a position east of Hong Kong to complete the devastation of shipping off the south China coast and in Hong Kong. It was the consensus among the flyers that AA fire over Hong Kong was the heaviest experienced in the war to date.

It was difficult to determine enemy losses, especially in Hong Kong, but postwar records show that it was heavy both in ships damaged or sunk and in facilities damaged ashore. Our planes unintentionally started quite a large fire on the Kowloon side.

Tokyo Rose informed the world that TF 38 was bottled up in the South China Sea. She threatened its annihilation saying, "We don't know how you got in, but how the hell are you going to get out?" This was, in view of the continuing strong monsoon winds and heavy weather, indeed a problem for Admiral Halsey, who originally had planned to leave the South China Sea via Balintang Channel but decided later on Mindoro Strait, Sulu Sea, Mindanao Sea, and Surigao Strait. I was surprised to receive a message telling me that TG 38.1 would lead TF 38 in a high-speed run through these waters. It was a questionable honor and a great responsibility. A study of the charts and available additional information indicated that it would be a very dangerous operation, particularly the first night. We could not rely on any navigational aids—they might not be in place or lighted. Navigation by radar would be difficult in the most dangerous areas, where reefs extended for miles off island shores. It was possible to make such an exit but I felt the risks to valuable ships were too great. We could still expect some harassment from the Japanese air force and kamikazes, too. There would certainly be many more gray-haired admirals and skippers after an exit through these waters!

Fortunately for TF 38, and for me in particular, Admiral Nimitz was quick to question the advisability of debouching through southern Philippine seas. He did not forbid Admiral Halsey to leave by that route, but he listed several disadvantages that he considered serious enough to warrant a delay in waiting for better weather in order to leave via the Balintang Channel. His main concern was that the Japanese might sight the force as it transited Surigao Strait, and their high command might then decide to venture naval strikes against the Mindoro-Lingayen logistic line, which could prove embarrassing to General MacArthur at such a time. Admiral Kurita's undetected sortie from the San Bernardino Strait at the time of the Leyte landings was still very much on CINCPAC's mind.

Admiral Halsey was evidently convinced, for on 19 January, he headed for Balintang Channel. The weather moderated to permit this northerly exit during the next night.

The operations in the South China Sea for these 11 days were eminently successful, even though no major units of the Japanese fleet were sighted or sunk. Our fleet wreaked havoc along the Indochina and South China coasts. The merchant shipping losses were a blow to the war effort in Japan.

One of the most striking features of this operation was the logistic support of the vast fleet while it was operating in what had been enemy-held waters for over four years. The oilers, ammunition ships, and fleet tugs under Captain Acuff, with their escorting carriers and destroyers, did a superb job under very difficult circumstances.[7]

☆ ☆ ☆ ☆

The operations against Formosa, which began with strikes launched against airfields and shipping at daylight on 21 January, soon brought TF 38 back to the hard facts of life. The China Sea cruise, with little or no enemy air action, had perhaps caused us to become a little lax in our defensive tactics. Two actions early in the morning were so near the force that it was evident the enemy knew our position.

Just before noon one of our Tom Cats reported a bogey, which no one else could confirm, about 40 miles away and closing TF 38. Shortly thereafter *Ticonderoga*, in TG 38.3, was hit by a kamikaze. The plane crashed her flight deck and a large bomb penetrated to the hangar deck where it exploded, causing an intense fire among closely spotted planes about to be launched for a strike. Spreading fires were still being fought when a second kamikaze struck the ship's island structure, sending flaming gasoline over it and parked planes on the flight deck. By 2:15 *Ticonderoga* had all fires under control, but her casualties were heavy and she had lost 36 planes.

Langley in TG 38.3 and destroyer *Maddox* on picket duty were also hit that day. But in spite of our heavy losses the enemy suffered more than we did. Flying weather was the best we had had over Formosa, and in that one day the force flew a total of 1,164 offensive sorties against aircraft and shipping. Over a hundred enemy aircraft were destroyed on the ground, and Takao, Tainan, and Kirun harbors were heavily hit. A postwar check showed ten *maru*s, including five tankers, sunk and, in the Pescadores, the destroyer *Harukage* damaged.

That evening a special task group was detached and ordered to escort *Ticonderoga* to Ulithi. I had left most of my clothes and other personal effects on *Ticonderoga* when I shifted to *Yorktown* in December. I wondered how much I had left.

The task force steamed north during the night en route for strikes against the Ryukyus. The principal objective was photographic coverage of Okinawa in preparation for the campaign to capture that island. After the operation we headed south, arriving in Ulithi on 26 January for a badly needed rest.

The task force had been under way for 28 days and had steamed 12,129 miles at an average speed of 18.5 knots. During January it had destroyed some 300,000 tons of enemy shipping. The total Japanese losses during that period were 248,000 tons of freighters and 182,000 tons of tankers. Enemy aircraft claimed destroyed totaled 615. The cost to us was 201 carrier aircraft, 167 pilots and air crewmen and 205 sailors killed in kamikaze crashes on 21 January. We had proved our ability to operate in almost continuous bad weather. As a result of our operations Admiral Halsey wrote, "The outer defenses of the Japanese Empire no longer include Burma and the Netherlands East Indies; these countries are now isolated outposts and their products are no longer available to the Japanese war machine except with staggering and prohibitive losses en route."

I felt that in our operations we still had room for great improvement. Fearless leader though he was, Admiral Halsey either suffered from poor advice in connection with carrier air operations or insisted on making his own decisions, which could be worse.

In my task group action report for the period 30 December 1944 to 26 January 1945 I made comments and recommendations designed to improve our operational efficiency.

Strikes by this task group were considerably reduced in effectiveness for the following reasons:

1) Distance from the launch point to assigned targets was, in general, excessive so that the greater part of the flight time was used in transit to and from the target.

2) At times the separation of targets assigned to this task group was so great that it was impossible to strike any of the targets in sufficient strength to be decisive and all mutual support was lost . . .

3) We had a very high percentage of fighters committed to defensive patrols . . .

4) Extensive searches on strike days were usually required while operating in the China Sea, with distances usually to four hundred miles. This caused further reduction in VF and VT planes available for offensive operations.

At midnight on 26 January 1945, in Ulithi, Admiral Spruance relieved Admiral Halsey in command of the fleet, which again became the Fifth Fleet. Concomitantly, Admiral Mitscher relieved Admiral McCain in command of the fast carrier force, now Task Force 58.

5

Air Strikes on Japan and Okinawa

I n summer and fall 1944 there had been great arguments in the high command about the course U.S. forces would take after having established themselves in the Philippines. Admiral Ernest King (Commander-in-Chief) favored taking Formosa and as usual expressed his opinions forcefully. Admirals King, Nimitz, and Spruance and Generals Millard Harmon and Simon Buckner conferred in San Francisco, where future plans were thrashed out. Admiral Nimitz presented a carefully drafted memorandum urging that there be a staggered two-pronged advance toward Japan. The first move should take Chichi Jima or Iwo Jima, the second a large island in the Ryukyus. The first objective would secure emergency landing facilities for the Saipan-based B29s and their fighter escorts bombing Japan. The second would secure and develop a large and complete air and naval base to support the invasion of Japan.[1] The Iwo Jima operation would follow Luzon because it was thought to be easier than that in the Ryukyus. The same fleet would have to cover and support both.

Admiral Spruance fully supported Admiral Nimitz' recommendations, so Admiral King had given in. He carried the word to the Joint Chiefs of Staff, who had issued a directive to General MacArthur and Admiral Nimitz:

1) General MacArthur was to seize and occupy Luzon, target date 20 December 1944, and to provide support for subsequent occupation of the Ryukyus by Admiral Nimitz' forces.

2) Admiral Nimitz, after providing covering and support forces for the liberation of Luzon, was to occupy one or more positions in the Bonins-Volcano group, target date 20 January 1945, and one or more positions in the Ryukyus, target date 1 March.

As it turned out, both operations had to be postponed about a month.

Task Force 58 had a good rest in Ulithi, but it was also busy getting ready for another long grind at sea. On 10 February 1945, under Admirals Spruance and Mitscher, the fleet sortied for the beginning of a long and arduous campaign, probably the supreme naval effort in the western Pacific.

Rumors were rife that we would strike Tokyo for the first time since the Doolittle raid of 1942, so one can imagine the excitement as the fast carriers, now organized into four task groups, moved to the open sea. There were nine large *Essex*-class carriers and five light *Independence*-class CVLs. Our aircraft strength totaled approximately 1,100. My group was TG 58.4, with carriers *Yorktown* (flag), *Randolph*, *Langley*, and *Cabot*, heavy screening battleships *Washington* and *North Carolina*, cruisers *Santa Fe*, *Biloxi*, and *San Diego*, and 17 destroyers.

En route to Tokyo, planes from CAP of TF 58.2 strafed a small Japanese fishing craft. *Hailey* from our screen was detached to investigate and to sink the vessel. One survivor was picked up, a Japanese in his late teens who came aboard willingly. He had minor wounds and was delivered to *Yorktown* for treatment.

Our first prisoner of war created a great deal of interest. He was a fisherman, whose craft had been blown out to sea after engine failure and had drifted south for 20 days. The crew of three had subsisted only on the raw fish they were able to catch. As a consequence our prisoner had a built-in fragrance even after a thorough washing. His companions had been lost in the strafing and sinking.

The young man remained with *Yorktown* until the end of this operation, when he was transferred to a prisoner-of-war camp on Guam. He became a favorite with the crew, although he was confined most of the time. His Marine guards taught him English of sorts, and his replies to greetings were usually quite startling. I saw him just once, as he was about to leave the ship, because he had pleaded to stay with *Yorktown* and to enlist in the U.S. Navy. When I called on him, through an interpreter, his fish smell had gone and he had gained weight on good Navy food. He said he had never been happier, that he now knew the U.S. would win the war, and that he wanted to stay with us. We could not keep him, of course, and he was taken ashore in Ulithi sobbing.

On our high-speed run-in extraordinary precautions were taken to prevent detection, for example, radio deception, scouting ahead by submarines to dispose of any picket vessels on our route, and scouting by B29s and Navy Liberators from Saipan and Tinian. Thanks to these measures and generally thick weather, the force arrived undetected. Launching position was approximately 125 miles southeast of Tokyo but only 60 miles off the coast of Honshu. This was a great change for the better in carrier tactics. Admiral Mitscher was fully aware of the offensive advantages in coming close to targets.

Despite cold, rain, and intermittent snow squalls, heavy fighter sweeps were launched on schedule to destroy aircraft at fields around Tokyo Bay. Planes from TG 58.3, whose targets were to the west, had the pleasure of finding clear weather and the distinction of being the first carrier planes to fly over Tokyo.

The next day there were fighter sweeps and bombing strikes against industrial plants near Tokyo. Close to noon, with the weather deteriorating, Admiral Mitscher suspended further strikes and the task force set course for Iwo Jima.

The results of these first strikes against Tokyo, while not spectacular, were substantial.

On the morning of 18 February patrols and fighter sweeps were launched against Chichi Jima and Haha Jima.

Three days later *Saratoga* was caught alone en route to her station as a night carrier north of Iwo Jima. In two vicious attacks by 12 kamikazes, she suffered heavy bomb and fire damage. Casualties were 123 killed and 192 wounded and she lost over 40 planes by fire and jettisoning. Under her own power, *Saratoga* steamed to the west coast of the United States, where repairs took almost three months.

The loss of *Saratoga* and the discouraging results of this battle, coupled with a reported distaste of night carrier pilots for their work, slowed the development of special dawn-to-dusk carriers and their aircraft. Admiral Mitscher was not favorably impressed with their performance. Later, in the Ryukyus operation, there was but one night flying carrier, *Enterprise*; but she did so well that Admiral Mitscher changed his mind about night carrier operations.

Saratoga was not the only ship to catch hell that night. The escort carrier *Bismark Sea* was attacked by kamikazes east of Iwo Jima and sunk after having been abandoned. At the same time the escort carrier *Lunga Point* was attacked by torpedo planes, but damage was slight and there were no fatalities.

Admiral Mitscher ordered *Enterprise* to assume *Saratoga*'s role in close night support. She had two main tasks, to fly dawn-and-dusk CAP over the escort carriers whose planes supported the troops by day, and to interdict the airfield at Chichi Jima. With the aid of five planes transferred from *Saratoga*, her night fighter squadron began hanging up a new record. Night and day for 174 consecutive hours ending at midnight on 2 March, this squadron kept planes airborne.

Further sweeps commenced against airfields north of Tokyo. This time we had been detected during our approach so were not surprised to encounter heavy airborne opposition over the airfields assigned. Bad weather cancelled further operations, so the force retired southwest.

During this 20-day cruise, TF 58 reported 393 enemy planes shot down and 250 destroyed on the ground. Our plane and pilot losses were heavy: 84 planes with 60 pilots and 21 crewmen in combat, 59 planes with 8 pilots and 6 crewmen operationally. But we had successfully attacked the heart of the Japanese homeland, just over three years after our disaster at Pearl Harbor. Rebounding from that defeat, the United States had accomplished miracles in building up its offensive might.

The task force arrived in Ulithi on 4 March, filling the lagoon almost to capacity. Activity was intense, for everyone was getting ready for the second and longest phase of the spring offensive, which began with the assault on Iwo Jima and ended with the capture of Okinawa.

One evening I was sitting in my cabin reading when I heard a plane pass low overhead. This surprised me, for our planes were forbidden to fly over the anchorage after dark. As I rang for my orderly, to ask the duty officer if night AA exercises were scheduled, I heard a muffled explosion to port.

Yorktown was loading ammunition that night, and my first thought was of an explosion in the ammunition lighter alongside. At that moment the general alarm sounded for general quarters and, grabbing my helmet, I started for the flag bridge.[2] The immediate vicinity was lit up by an intense fire in *Randolph*, anchored in the next berth.

There was great confusion at first. I learned that a Japanese plane had crashed on one of the islets in the lagoon that was used for outdoor movies. Evidently the pilot was attracted by the bright screen and thought it was on a ship.

Finally we learned that two Japanese twin-engine planes, apparently from Truk some 400 miles east, had crashed in kamikaze fashion, one on *Randolph*'s flight deck and the other ashore. *Randolph* suffered extensive damage to her flight and hangar decks, as well as many casualties.

☆ ☆ ☆ ☆

Action for us in the next operation, against airfields on Kyushu, the southernmost large Japanese island, started at 7:39 the morning of 18 March, when a Judy (bomber) suddenly emerged from the clouds at about 500 feet and dropped a 500-pound bomb on the flight deck of *Enterprise*. The bomb bounced, detaching the detonator, which exploded against the island structure. The bomb stopped on deck but did not explode. At 8:00 a twin-engine Frances attempted to bomb *Yorktown*. The ship opened fire and hit the plane, which started to burn and crossed the bow to crash 1,500 yards away. Another Frances seven minutes later dove on the formation and was shot down in flames close aboard *Intrepid*, killing 2 men and wounding 43. That afternoon there were more attacks on *Yorktown*. One bomb blew two large holes into her side, well above the waterline.

It was a busy day. Our Combat Information Center tracked a total of 54 raids, 6 of which materialized into attacks on the task group. In the meantime, our air strikes concentrated on fields in northeast Kyushu. Seventy-eight enemy planes were destroyed, 25 probably destroyed, and 134 damaged. Our losses were 9 aircraft and 3 pilots.

At day's end I walked into my emergency cabin, where I lived while the ship was under way, and found the whole room covered with shards of glass. Anyone in the room when that bomb had struck in the afternoon would have looked like a pincushion. I replaced the glass port with a steel one, as I should have done earlier.

The next day TF 58's strikes were directed primarily against Japanese naval vessels in the Inland Sea. But on this day R. Adm. Ralph Davison's TG 58.2 bore the brunt of enemy attacks. Shortly after sunrise, *Wasp* had just launched two-thirds of her aircraft when an enemy plane arrived overhead undetected and dropped a bomb that caused fierce fires on five decks simultaneously. So efficient was damage control that all fires were out in 15 minutes and the ship was recovering aircraft by 8:00. A few minutes later a kamikaze missed the carrier by a few feet, the bomb exploding alongside. Casualties from the first explosion were heavy, but *Wasp* continued to operate for several days before retiring for repairs.

At almost the same time, Admiral Davison's flagship *Franklin* was struck by two bombs from an undetected plane while launching her second strike of the morning. The first bomb exploded on the hangar deck, spreading destruction and lighting huge fires among parked and armed planes. The second bomb struck the flight deck aft, exploded above the hangar deck, and spread fires among planes that were turning up ready to be launched. Almost immediately the ship was enveloped in flames and a pall of heavy black smoke.

Some 15–18 miles away we could see these clouds of black smoke and subsequently mushroom clouds several thousand feet high caused by explosions of Tiny Tim Rockets. *Franklin* had a squadron of planes armed with these new heavy rockets, some on the hangar deck and some ready for launching. As the intense heat set them off they "whooshed" in all directions as they exploded. We could not believe that anyone remained alive on a ship undergoing such travail. I mentally said goodbye to my classmate Admiral Davison and to *Franklin's* skipper, my friend Capt. Leslie Gehres.

The successful fight to save the *Franklin* is one of the most fascinating stories in Navy annals. As Admiral Davison was shifting his flag to *Santa Fe,* a cruiser he had ordered alongside for that purpose, he authorized Captain Gehres to abandon ship. The Captain replied that he thought she could be saved, and save her they did.

Captain Gehres ordered all but key officers and men to leave the ship for *Santa Fe* and rescue destroyers. By 10:00 fire and engine rooms had been evacuated due to intense heat and *Franklin* lay dead in the water. By noon all fires were under control, the starboard list was stabilized, and all wounded had been evacuated. *Santa Fe* had taken on board 826 men in 30 minutes and stayed alongside for three hours.

Pittsburgh now took *Franklin* in tow and after some difficulty steadied on a southerly course at about six knots. The sea, fortunately, was calm. A heavy CAP kept enemy aircraft away from the cripple and her escort as they headed south. At 3:00 the next morning *Franklin* regained power. By 9:30 she had steering control but still no compass. At 11:00 she was ready to make 15 knots and by afternoon she was making 20 knots on her own, *Pittsburgh* having cast off the tow line.

Franklin was by far the most heavily damaged carrier in the war. She was saved by the ability, fortitude, and sheer guts of her officers and crew who survived fires and explosions to fight for her. Casualties were 724 men killed or missing and 265 wounded—almost 25 percent of her complement. Stories of individual courage read like a novel.

But it was know-how as well as courage that enabled our ships' crews in the last year of World War II to conquer fires such as those raging in *Franklin.* Improved fire-fighting schools were established soon after the war started, and the damage control party of every new ship was trained as one of them. The objective was to convince the sailor that, properly equipped with fire mask and helmet, handling an all-purpose nozzle and applicator, he could boldly advance to the source of a blaze and not get hurt.

Changes were also made in the carriers' fire mains. In addition to some 14 mains dependent on ship's power, two mains operated by individual gasoline or diesel engines. One of these in *Franklin* threw fog for eight hours continuously when all other mains were out because of power failure.

Franklin headed home under her own power. With only one stop at Pearl Harbor, she made a 12,000 mile voyage to New York City, where she was given a tremendous welcome.[3]

Following the Inland Sea strikes, TF 58 retired slowly. On the afternoon of 21 March, a large group of bogeys was picked up to the northwest. The raid numbered 48 aircraft, 18 of them twin-engine Bettys carrying a new device slung under their bellies: the "baka" bomb, we called it (which means "fool" in Japanese), a 4,700-pound bomb with stub wings, rocket propulsion, and a human pilot. Fortunately the Japanese did not have many of them, for they were small and fast when cast off from their carrier plane.

The big flight was intercepted some 60 miles out. The Bettys with their bomb cargo were sluggish and were easy prey for our fighters. Almost all the Japanese planes were shot down, only a few escaping to the north.

On Easter Sunday, 1 April 1945, the amphibious landings started on Okinawa. This tremendous operation, for which plans had been initiated a year before, was under way at last. Air strikes and air cover for the amphibious forces were furnished by TG 58.4, in company with groups 58.1 and 58.3. Just as in the Gilberts a year and a half before, the fast carriers were tied to a support job for troops ashore and thus limited in our freedom to move. We also had to supply CAP for amphibious forces and the radar picket ships. When we could we interdicted airfields in Kyushu and in the Ryukyus chain north and south of Okinawa. This assignment was tough for the carriers in many respects; in the Okinawa campaign it was tougher than ever before. Had any of us known how long we were to be tied down this way we would have been downhearted, to say the least.

Admiral Turner, who commanded all naval forces in the immediate area of

Okinawa, was responsible for planning support strikes that carriers were to furnish. Late each afternoon the Commander TF 58 would receive detailed requests for support missions of the next day: size of strikes, armament, and so on. Generally task group commanders received this information at the same time and could start on the air operations schedule for the following day. Of course, in addition to the support strikes, the groups had to supply their local CAPs, large CAPs for the amphibious forces and the 16 radar picket stations, and special anti-submarine and search flights. The air schedules for each carrier and the working out of deck spots was a difficult and time-consuming task. My Operations Officer, his assistants, and all ship's air personnel were often busy until late at night getting ready for the next day's operations, which always started before sunrise. Besides all the above complications, every other night the large carriers (CVs) in each group operated their own night fighters. The strain of this added chore was reduced by putting ready night fighters all on one CV before sunset, to be launched by catapults. The other CV would keep a "ready" deck, its planes spotted forward, so the planes could land. Air departments had personnel on duty almost all night.

After 1 April our schedules followed the above outline for three days out of four. The fourth day each group would retire for refueling and replenishment. By comparison those were days of rest, but they were still very busy, as the ships took on tremendous loads of provisions, ammunition, and fuel and conducted limited flight operations for local CAP and landing replacement aircraft.

We were naturally very interested in what was going on ashore, particularly on L-day, Easter Sunday. Most of us thought the landings would be contested on the beaches as they had been at Iwo Jima. We had been directed to stand by for a major air support effort if called upon. Intelligence reports estimated that the island was defended by at least 60,000 Japanese troops—although few had been sighted during the previous week of air and surface bombardment.

To everyone's surprise, the landings were practically unopposed. The weather was excellent and the landings commenced practically on schedule at 8:30 A.M. Amazingly, both Kadena and Yontan airfields were in our hands by 10:00 that morning instead of on L + 3 day as the operation plan anticipated. And the Japanese had failed to destroy them, which made it even better.

That afternoon Admiral Turner reported to Admiral Spruance that some 50,000 of our troops were ashore; that there had been only sporadic and light opposition on the beaches; and that he had ordered the landings continued with general unloading to commence at once.

In the carriers we were overjoyed at the good news. It looked as though our preliminary work had paid off handsomely and that we would soon be released from our close support activities. How wrong we were!

On the next night, the destroyer *Franks* collided with *Missouri* and suffered considerable topside damage. Her commanding officer (CO), on the bridge at the time, and one other officer were seriously injured. *Franks*, on plane guard station for flight operations, had been near the center of the formation. Ordered to her screening station, astern on the course we were making at the time, her CO misjudged distances and relative speeds in the darkness and almost cut across *Missouri*'s bow as he made a hard right turn. He managed to complete the turn but scraped the battleship's side almost from bow to stern, taking off the port side of his own bridge, from which he was conning the ship.

This incident shows how fast things can happen when a formation is steaming at 20 knots. *Franks* could have slowed to drop back, quickly clearing heavy ships astern. Instead, her CO elected to expedite the maneuver, with disastrous results to himself and to his ship. Naval officers pay a high price for an instant of bad judgment or carelessness.

The unloading of troops, equipment, and essential supplies continued at a rapid pace. Large and most small ships retired south at night but suffered continued harassment by kamikazes that must have come from Okinawa or others of the Ryukyus. In the carriers, we were vigilant toward the Japanese reaction that was bound to come.

Six April turned out to be the day we had all been waiting for.

Admiral Toyoda, commanding Japanese air forces in the East China Sea, managed during the first week of April a partial concentration of aircraft on Kyushu and Formosa to carry out operation Ten-Go, a massive air attack by both kamikazes and conventional bombers.[4] The operation had been planned by Imperial General Headquarters in March to defend the Ryukyus, where an attack was expected after the Iwo Jima operation. Task Force 58 strikes on 18–20 March and B29 strikes on 27 and 31 March had interrupted preparations in Kyushu for Ten-Go. The Japanese, with some 700 planes available, commenced their first strong attacks on Okinawa. These were the first of ten swarming kamikaze attacks that the Japanese named *kikusui*, floating chrysanthemums.[5]

The first massed air attacks of operation Ten-Go struck Okinawa and TF 58 on 6 April. Admiral Turner estimated that his ships were attacked by 182 planes in 22 groups, mostly in the late afternoon. Fifty-five planes were destroyed by CAP and 35 by ships' AA fire, and 24 kamikazes were destroyed in crashing our ships—a total of 108. On the same day TF 58 claimed to have shot down 246 planes, 65 by *Essex* airmen alone. That these claims were little exaggerated is indicated by the fact that the Japanese reported 355 kamikaze planes and 341 bombers committed to this operation, the first and greatest of their *kikusui* attacks.

Total casualties in the Fifth Fleet were heavy: 3 destroyers lost, 1 landing ship tank and 2 ammunition ships sunk, 10 ships with major damage and heavy casualties. But Japanese claims for the day amounted to 60 U.S. vessels (including 2 battleships and 3 cruisers) sunk and 61 badly damaged!

The kamikaze blitz continued into the next day when some 20 planes attacked near Okinawa. But meanwhile TF 58 had other excitement. Still on 6 April TG 58.4 had received orders to rendezvous with groups 58.1 and 58.2 the next morning, prepared to search for and destroy a Japanese naval task force of two large and six smaller ships that had been sighted by our submarine *Threadfin* on a southwesterly course through Bungo Suido, the strait between Shikoku and Kyushu. In accordance with orders, *Threadfin* passed up a chance to attack in order to flash her contact report. Later *Hackleback* also sighted this force and sent four contact reports.[6]

This final impetuous effort of the Japanese Combined Fleet boasted the super battleship *Yamato*, the light cruiser *Yahagi*, and eight destroyers. As an element of operation Ten-Go, their objective was U.S. survivors of the 9 April air blitz in Hagushi roadstead, off Okinawa. The sacrificial nature of this operation was clear: *Yamato* had been fueled for a one-way trip to Okinawa.[7]

The specially armed strikes of groups 58.1 and 58.3 totaled 280 planes, 98 of them torpedo bombers. With the weather misty and cloudy, the attack was a melee. It was impossible to dive-bomb from high altitudes and poor visibility required torpedo planes to come in close on the deck [just above the water]. The attacks could not be coordinated because of poor visibility and poor radio communication caused by Japanese jamming of the circuits.

Difficult as it was for our attacking forces, it was even tougher for the Japanese. For about two hours they were under almost continuous attacks. *Yamato* received two bomb hits near her mainmast and shortly afterward her first torpedo hit. The destroyer *Hamakaze*, hit by a bomb and a torpedo at about the same time, plunged to the bottom. *Yahagi* also suffered bomb and torpedo hits and lay dead in the water before sinking.

The first two groups badly damaged *Yamato*; even so, when the TG 58.4 attack group reached the scene, she was making good speed with two escorting destroyers nearby. *Yorktown* pilots were able to coordinate their maneuvers, and a series of dive-bombing and torpedo plane attacks finished her off. *Yamato* rolled over and exploded violently as she sank. A mushroom cloud like that from an atomic blast blotted out the actual sinking, and for a while there was an argument whether she had sunk. Admiral Mitscher was finally convinced when he received the *Yorktown* pilots' photographs.

By the time TG 58.4 pilots had left, short on gas, *Yamato* and *Yahagi* were sunk, two destroyers were afire and apparently heavily damaged, and three destroyers were apparently undamaged.

It was a great victory for the U.S. Navy and almost the coup de grace for the Imperial Japanese Navy. There was elation in TF 58 that night, but we had bogeys on the screen and much work to do.

Of the Japanese force, all four remaining destroyers were damaged in varying degrees but managed to reach Sasebo. *Yamato* lost all but 23 officers and 246 men of the total of 2,767 on board. I could hardly believe it. One would think that the suddenness of her sinking, accompanied by tremendous explosions, would have killed everyone on board. One of our patrol rescue seaplanes, seeing a group of Japanese survivors amid some wreckage, landed and took prisoners—as many as he could who would come with him.

Under orders from Admiral Spruance, Adm. Morton Deyo had taken command of the battleships and cruisers at Okinawa and headed north to intercept *Yamato*. When he heard of her sinking by TF 58 soon after he started out, he goodnaturedly broadcast his regrets to his force and to Admiral Mitscher.

☆ ☆ ☆ ☆

By now I was convinced of a pattern in the Japanese air operations against us. Each night they tried to keep us under surveillance. If our night fighters prevented this, as they increasingly did, the Japanese sent out searches early in the morning. If these searches were intercepted and destroyed at some distance from the task force, or before they sighted us, the chances were that we would have a quiet afternoon and evening. But if a searcher got close enough to sight us and had time to get off a report, all hell would usually break loose in the afternoon. Nightfall did not stop the attacks, it only changed the type.

In the afternoons, AA practice against drones was conducted by all ships which had finished replenishment. During the Okinawa operations no opportunity for AA practice was missed. The Task Force stayed in the same area each night, preparing for a repeat performance of the day's activities. We were still tied to Okinawa because of continuing requirements of CAP and special support sorties. All the group commanders and Admiral Mitscher were chafing under this restriction to our movements, which made it almost impossible for us to fully interdict the Kyushu airfields, from which most of the attacks were coming. Admiral Turner was adamant in his refusal to release TF 58 until he felt secure on Okinawa, for which we could not blame him. We knew that Air Corps and Marine aircraft were being ferried into Okinawa, yet requirements laid on us were not diminishing. A message I sent to Admiral Mitscher on 8 April is an example of my feelings:

From CTG 58.4 to CTF 58: *Yorktown* pilot who spent last night at Yontan reports Marines there with 94 F4Us and one squadron of VF(N) are ready and itching to go to work.

Shortly after 1:00 A.M. on Friday 13 April, as TF 58 was about to begin another active day, ALNAV [All Navy Message] 69 was received announcing the death of our Commander-in-Chief, President Franklin D. Roosevelt. The message, sent by Secretary of the Navy James Forrestal, was a great shock to the fleet and the troops ashore. We had had no idea that the President was seriously ill, and we knew that the services in general and the Navy in particular had lost a great friend and leader.

Hardly any of us in the fleet knew anything about our new President, Harry S. Truman, and there was much speculation about what changes, if any, could be expected.

All ships of the group received the following message:

All ships in TG 58.4 have been directed to follow movements of *Yorktown* in half-masting colors from 0800 14 April to sunset 13 May inclusive. During this period *Yorktown* will display colors at half-mast except when in condition I for enemy action or when enemy units of any type are sighted.

Operations on 12–14 April consisted of interdicting nearby Japanese airfields, which were heavily bombed and usually hit late each afternoon with a number of delayed-action bombs mixed with the others. In spite of our best efforts the Japanese, using the most primitive equipment (wheelbarrows, for example), would repair runways on most of these fields and begin to use them during the night. They had many wrecks and our delayed-action bombs must have run up their casualties, but they persisted. Our daily photographs showed the newly wrecked planes, though, so we knew we were wearing them down.

The Japanese were trying everything they could think of to annoy, harass, embarrass, and sink our ships and shoot down our aircraft.[8] In turn, we were doing all we could to anticipate their new tactics. We began to notice that quite often small groups of kamikazes were accompanied by a single plane at high altitudes. Interrogation of some captured kamikaze pilots revealed that new kamikazes were not completely trusted to crash themselves. The high-altitude escort observed the action of a particular group. He could, if he returned safely, report which kamikazes were on their way to heaven so that earthly rewards promised to their families could be made.

As the Japanese made new moves we tried to counter them. When they began coming in at high altitudes we boosted our CAPs and by the middle of April had one section of CAP in each task group at 30,000 feet or better. Interceptions were made at times at over 35,000 feet. These were difficult but rewarding operations for pilots, for we shot down search planes that had been reporting our positions and bringing out the kamikazes about three hours later. The high-altitude missions for CAP, and sometimes for communications relay, were dangerous in other ways. Off Japan in April, winds at that altitude could be very strong—100 and sometimes 150 miles an hour from the west. It required constant alertness on the part of pilots and ships' radar men to prevent planes on high-altitude missions, ususlly above a solid overcast, from being blown away. Four Marine fighter pilots who had been on high-altitude CAP over Okinawa and were blown out to sea were rescued by TF 58.4. Our alert fighter director picked them up and vectored them to *Yorktown*, about 80 miles east of Okinawa.

Just about daylight on 14 April as we were launching our CAPs, a Japanese Jake (single-engined seaplane) passed about five miles from our screen, flying very low. A section of our CAP shot him down. The crash was hard and no survivors were seen or expected.

Two more planes were splashed by our CAP in the afternoon about 50 miles north. This was only the first of many small three- or four-plane raids that began converging on us from a wide arc, west to northeast. Most of the attacks were against the TF 58 destroyer picket line. In the midst of this matinee, standing by our chart table, I noticed that our maneuvers had brought us almost to the spot where the Jake had been splashed that morning. As I turned to suggest a search in that vicinity, *Guam* reported sighting a man in the water. Destroyer *Melvin* investigated and found three men, the crew splashed that morning: one young officer pilot and two enlisted men, a bomber and a tail-gunner. The pilot and one of the enlisted men were glad to be rescued; the second at first resisted, then thought better of it. They were transferred to *Yorktown*.

The pilot confessed he had been en route from Formosa to Kagoshima, on Kyushu, that morning and had become lost. He ran into our formation just at daylight and not knowing which way to turn kept on going until splashed. Apparently well educated, he admitted inexperience but said he was sure the Japanese government would be willing to exchange several American prisoners of importance for him. This proved to be just talk on his part. He had only recently been stationed on Formosa and had little knowledge of what was going on. He seemed glad to be rescued and out of the war. His greatest concern after coming aboard *Yorktown* was that the ship would be sunk. He apparently had great confidence in the ability of the kamikaze pilots.

TF 58 had now been under way for over a month and under extreme pressure for nearly all that time. Individuals were tired. Admiral Mitscher was concerned about the situation but nothing, it appeared, could be done except to stick it out. Apparently the Army Engineers had not been able to build the necessary additional airfields on Okinawa in the time originally estimated. Air Corps support units, to be based ashore, could not therefore be brought forward. The fast carrier force could not be relieved of its support of the forces on Okinawa until that happened. But to us, progress seemed excruciatingly slow.

On 17 April, having lost *Enterprise*, *Intrepid* and several destroyers in *kikusui* attacks the day before, Commander TF 58 decided to temporarily disband TG 58.2. Units of that group were directed to join other groups. We received *Independence*, *Flint*, and Destroyer Division 105.

That afternoon was routine, interrupted only when a lone Frances was detected near the force and shot down after quite a chase. The observer survived and was picked up by a destroyer and delivered to *Yorktown*.

A message I sent to Admiral Mitscher indicates how important it was for us to recover and interrogate prisoners of war:

Preliminary interrogation cooperative 19 year old observer member of crew of *Frances* . . . Prisoner had heard of Viper bomb and called it Tokontai which may

also refer to special attack corps which flies bomb. Believed many Vipers man-
ufactured but disappointing lack of applicants for opportunity to fly same. Believed Betty only plane equipped to carry. Viper attacks take off from Kanoya.
Mentioned Izumi, Miyazaki, Kanoya as bases where planes from all over Empire
collecting for attack on Blue [U.S. forces]. Kanoya most important. Only old
planes and trainers used as suiciders and pilots ordered to fly these missions. No
shortage of fuel but critical shortage planes and pilots. Prisoner witnessed carrier
fighter attack which took Izumi by complete surprise on 16 April. Five planes
destroyed, others damaged, operations disrupted. Believed Japan had lost war
and said men in barracks and civilians of acquaintance felt likewise. Further details by mailgram.

In an effort to keep up morale during this long and strenuous campaign,
bulletins were sent to the task group when information that could be passed on
came to hand. This was especially appreciated by the screening ships large and
small, which did not have contact with flying activities.

I quote a sample bulletin of 18 April:

POW Bulletin—Second Issue. Two more Japs riding with us. One is pilot who
parachuted from Zeke shot down near picket DD at 1310 on April 14th. His
combat experience in this war began and ended with CAP encounter when
splashed. He took off from Kanoya, Kyushu at 1100 on 14th with orders to report
position of remnants of this force (note: Japanese press was reporting heavy losses
of our ships). Other POW was observer in Frances shot down seven miles southwest of this group at 1415 yesterday. He says high percentage of one way pilots
most demoralizing in Empire where aviators are not a dime a dozen. Reports that
in his opinion Japan has lost the war and that this feeling is shared by others both
military and civilian. Both POW doing nicely in sick bay but are still apprehensive as to our intentions.

On 19 April the all-out attack against the heavily defended and well dug-in
Japanese positions on Okinawa commenced. H-hour for the jump-off was 6:40
A.M. Naval gunfire support was provided at near maximum weight. After a
night devoid of star shell illumination, an intense bombardment of enemy positions was laid at 5:40 by six battleships, six cruisers, and eight destroyers.[9] In
addition, the south and southwest coasts were bombarded. Ashore, 27 battalions
of artillery rained some 19,000 rounds of shell fire on enemy lines for 40 minutes
before the jump-off. Some 650 Navy and Marine planes added bombs, rockets,
napalm, and strafing to the general din. The assault platoons then advanced,
hopeful that the great weight of explosive metal had destroyed the enemy or left
him so stunned that he would be helpless. They were quickly disillusioned,
stopped cold when the relatively untouched Japanese came out of their deep
holes and manned their well-designed defense positions.

For the next five days bitter fighting continued and progress was measured in yards. Although naval gunfire and air support were generous it was essentially an infantry battle.

By evening on 23 April, General Ushijima's outer line had been penetrated at several points and he decided to withdraw to his next line. This retirement was effected at night under cover of fog and artillery barrages. Such was the pattern at the southern end of Okinawa, where the majority of Japanese forces were dug in. Each line of defense was held until the sheer weight of attack penetrated and forced abandonment. The battle for Okinawa was the toughest and most prolonged of any in the Pacific since Guadalcanal. It was similar to Iwo Jima but there were more Japanese to eliminate and more terrain to capture.

From 20 April to the end of the month carriers in TF 58 were not molested by the enemy. They continued to furnish air support and CAP over Okinawa and to make daily fighter sweeps over the northern Ryukyus.

Admiral Mitscher announced a rotation plan for the three task groups still supporting Okinawa; this was welcome news, though for TG 58.4 it was still a long way off, another month. But by this time we had settled into a pattern of operations against the enemy that made life a little easier. Our high-altitude CAPs frustrated their snoopers and kamikaze "mother ships," which apparently were important to them. Our night fighters were doing superb work, with the result that few Japanese reconnaissance planes could locate our carrier forces. Night fighter interceptions were often made at great distances from the force, giving no definite information to the Japanese even if they received reports of the interceptions.

On 4 May Commander TF 58 sent the following message to the force:

> Today, we in this force have reached and well passed one thousand enemy aircraft shot out of the air by aircraft and ships gunfire since 1 April. The enemy cannot take it at such a murderous rate much longer. Be alert and keep them splashing.

On 9 May TG 58.4 received very welcome orders to continue operations on 10–11 May, returning to Ulithi at their conclusion. I sensed that we would see more action on the eleventh, for the Japanese tried hard to pinpoint our location the day before with their high-flying aircraft. Even the splashing of these high flyers could be pinpointed pretty well by Japanese radar.

Early on the eleventh, a bogey was chased by one of our VF(N) but was not intercepted and left the area. We had been successfully snooped. By 7:00 Japanese planes were attacking Okinawa and at 8:30 bogeys started closing our formation. They came in intermittently, using cloud cover to avoid our CAPs; four were splashed.

Shortly after 10:00 all enemy planes seemed to be gone from the task group and from Okinawa. But *Yorktown*'s fighter director was concerned that bogeys were concealing themselves in the vicinity of flights returning from Okinawa. I passed the word to Commander TG 58.3, who did not appear concerned and was about to top off destroyers. Within a minute or so TG 58.3 was under attack. Two kamikazes crashed *Bunker Hill*, Admiral Mitscher's flagship. Bombs from them exploded, and huge fires started.

With the carrier's flight and hangar decks aflame, *Wilkes Barre* and several destroyers moved in to fight the fires and rescue crew members who had been blown overboard or had jumped to avoid the flames.

About 11:00, by visual signal, Admiral Mitscher passed command of TF 58 to Admiral Sherman, Commander TG 58.3, and prepared to move his staff and flag to *Enterprise*. By 3:30 P.M. fires were under control and assisting ships cast off.

With the exception of *Franklin*, *Bunker Hill* was the most heavily damaged carrier to survive the Pacific War. She suffered heavy casualties, many from smoke suffocation: 343 dead, 43 missing, 264 wounded. Almost all pilots of the ship's fighter squadron, waiting in their ready room, were asphyxiated. Material damage was so extensive that the ship had to return to the Bremerton Navy Yard for repairs.

Just before TG 58.4 steamed south to Ulithi, news of the German surrender reached the fleet. It had a stimulating effect on all of us in the Pacific, for we knew that now the full effort in Washington would be directed to backing us up.

6

The Last Air Raids and the Surrender

Just before leaving Ulithi I learned that two guests of the Secretary of the Navy, Mr. Henry Luce and Mr. Roy Alexander, both of Time, Incorporated would join *Yorktown* there. I had met Mr. Luce but did not know him well, but Roy Alexander, the managing editor of *Time,* was a close friend. I looked forward with pleasure to having them aboard. This class of visitor was something new. I had known that Mr. Forrestal was anxious to have distinguished newsmen and publishers visit our naval forces, but President Roosevelt would not authorize such guests. As I heard it, the president particularly had not wanted Colonel McCormick of the Chicago *Tribune* to visit the front lines, and accordingly, no one could be allowed to go. Secretary Forrestal had wasted no time in getting the rules changed following President Roosevelt's death.

As we greeted one another, Roy asked how long they would be aboard. I said, "Roy, I have no idea—how long do you want to stay?" "Well," he replied, "Mr. Luce never stays anywhere more than 24 hours." I answered, "Mr. Luce is going to have an entirely new experience. You'll be with us a week or more, at least." [The guests remained aboard from 24 May until 1 June.]

Mr. Luce amused himself by roaming all over *Yorktown* in the days that followed, having coffee with gun crews, hangar deck crews, air crews, engine room crews, and everyone else. He was very gregarious and enjoyed meals in all the messes. The only fixed engagement he had was at my request: unless action interfered, he would dine with me in my flag cabin. Our conversations were interesting to me, for he was a fascinating man and I could understand why he had been so successful. Born in China, the son of an American missionary, he had a great interest in and feeling for the Far East. We talked at length about China and I accepted an invitation to have dinner with him in Peking after the war. But we could not agree on a date until it was too late and the communists had taken over what Henry Luce said was the most interesting and one of the most beautiful cities in the world.

Roy Alexander also found much to do. For one thing—good Catholic that he was—when he found that Father Moody, the *Yorktown*'s daily newscaster (by loudspeaker), held mass each morning, he attended faithfully. I accused him of doing this to get ahead in his church-going so he could relax when he got back to New York.

On 24 May 1945 the task group, larger and more powerful than ever, sortied toward a rendezvous with the rest of the task force. We now had three CVs in the group, *Yorktown*, *Shangri La* and *Ticonderoga*; one CVL, *Independence*; battleships *Iowa* and *Wisconsin* and battle cruisers *Alaska* and *Guam*; and eighteen destroyers as our screen. Personnel totaled almost 28,000. Days and nights en route were busy with all sorts of exercises. The group had to be honed again to a fine point of readiness for action so our guests had quite a show. There was daily AA firing; the air groups simulated attacks against the ships; and there were night surface tracking exercises for radar personnel and destroyers, as well as practice for night interceptions and torpedo attacks.

Admiral Halsey relieved Admiral Spruance and the fleet again became the Third Fleet, the task force was 38, commanded now by Admiral McCain, and my group 38.4.

On 29 May TF 38 launched a series of supporting strikes for the ground forces on Okinawa. We were back in the old routine, still tied to the ground operations against Japanese forces on the island. The fighting there was still almost hand-to-hand combat for each foot of advance.

Operations were routine until 2 June, when Commander TF 38 directed long-range fighter sweeps against southern Kyushu airfields. Planes were launched from 100 miles east of southern Okinawa—a round trip of 600 miles with scant leeway for errors in navigation and little allowance for time over the target or extra fuel in combat. This was our first indication of a rather radical change in tactics by the new commanders. I felt strongly that fighter sweeps from this distance were unproductive and unnecessarily hazardous. I urged that the task groups proceed at least 100 miles north before launching such sweeps.

On one of these sweeps two *Shangri La* planes ran out of fuel and did not return. An unsuccessful search was launched for them. On another one, two planes from *Independence* lost their way while returning and were not found.

A typhoon was reported to the south on 4 June. My information about it was not specific, but because I had been operating in the area for over two months, dodging fronts and other bad weather, I had definite opinions. My estimate of the situation was that in heading east as ordered we were making a mistake and very likely heading into the path of the typhoon rather than away from it. I prepared a message to Commander TF 38, saying I estimated we would intercept the typhoon if we continued at our present course and speed. I received only an acknowledgement from Admiral McCain. This was the second suggestion I had made in as many days, and I had the distinct feeling of a chip-on-the-shoulder attitude from the flagship toward the "old-timer" group commanders, who perhaps thought they knew too much about the operations.[1] I made no more comments at the time.

That afternoon, again on orders from Commander Third Fleet, we changed course to intercept groups 30.8 and 38.1. This seemed an even worse decision to me.

About 1:30 A.M. Commander TF 38 was in tactical command; he apparently decided to maneuver to the west of the storm, in the safe semicircle, based on his information regarding the typhoon path. But the storm center continued to close our formation, its speed estimated at 22 knots. Now task group commanders were authorized to maneuver independently. I increased speed and made course changes to the left until the storm center passed us. At 7:00 the barometer read 29.06 and the center was approximately 15 miles south of TG 38.4. By that time TG 38.1 was caught in the typhoon center and having a very bad time. My group, by great good fortune, was riding easily and suffered negligible damage. By 10:50 the weather had cleared and the seas moderated to such an extent that we could launch CAPs—partly, on orders from Admiral Halsey, to search for groups 38.1 and 30.8. The former had suffered severe damage to several ships.

With the benefit of hindsight, and having studied the explanations of the various participants in this disastrous encounter with the elements, I came to the unequivocal conclusion that Admiral Halsey was completely responsible and in this instance culpably negligent.[2] Vice Admiral McCain bears a lesser degree of responsibility; I have never been able to determine just how he judged the situation as it developed.

The Commander-in-Chief Pacific (CINCPAC) weather service was not what it is today. We did not have continuous air tracking of a storm center, but in my opinion that is not a good excuse. Seamen of all generations have been taught to watch the weather, and a "peek is better than a finesse." In times like that afternoon, among other things one should break out the old Bowditch, reading in particular the part on earliest indications of tropical storms. I had just done that before I sent my message to Admiral McCain and after I had read all the weather messages and looked over the situation from the bridge. Too many naval officers, it seemed, made their weather judgments in their cabins (at night) without looking outside.

The responsibility of a fleet commander in such a situation is awe-inspiring. It is hard for me to believe that Admiral Halsey and his staff gave the problem the study it deserved. Why he tried so hard to get all three task groups together remains a mystery to me; the individual groups could have done much better on their own. My group would have escaped the storm by remaining where we were. I certainly had no feeling of being dangerously close to a lee shore—the East China Sea was just on the other side of the Ryukyus. The Navy should make a careful and objective analysis of this and the earlier typhoon situation and publish them for the benefit of sailors everywhere.[3] Finally, neither Admiral Halsey, Admiral McCain, nor their staffs were exhausted. They had just rejoined the fleet, and they could have asked the judgment of some of us who had been operating continuously in those waters for almost five months.

At sunset on 10 June, to the surprise of everyone, TF 38 was released from its Okinawa duties and set course for Leyte Gulf in the Philippines, our new base in the western Pacific. We arrived there closing out almost three months of continuous operations in support of Okinawa.

We felt the Okinawa job had been well done and in Leyte all hands could read the congratulatory messages from Washington, Pearl Harbor, and Guam to prove it. This stay was for rest and recreation as well as for upkeep, and everyone took advantage of it.

I was so exhausted that I slept almost 24 hours straight after our arrival. Then there was the interminable paperwork to catch up with, and letters to write.

Five or six days later I received a message from a close friend, V. Adm. J. L. Kauffman, Commander Naval Forces Philippines. "Reggie" invited me to visit him in Manila and made it sound interesting. I thought it over but decided the comfortable life aboard *Yorktown* would be better. I was really too tired and lazy to go ashore. I declined, and Reggie's reply was characteristic:

> I WILL NOT TAKE NO FOR AN ANSWER. AM ARRANGING PLANE FOR TOMORROW MORNING. YOUR ROOM IS READY.

I spent a memorable week with Admiral Kauffman, who confessed he had caught a glimpse of me at a conference in Leyte and saw that I was tired and needed a change of scene.

I saw all the sights and met all the famous Americans in Manila at the time, from General MacArthur on down. Reggie's quarters were on Dewey [now Roxas] Boulevard, in a house that had been only partially destroyed by Japanese troops as they evacuated. Almost all the fine homes on Dewey—the Michigan Avenue of Manila—were in various states of destruction, and I learned that many of the families who owned them had been massacred when the houses were destroyed. Downtown Manila was a shambles, including the famous Army-Navy Club and the Manila Hotel. As this was my first visit, I could not quite appreciate how beautiful it must have been before.

I wanted to tour the harbor to see the many wrecks of Japanese naval and merchant vessels. Our attacks had concentrated on the port facilities, not the city, and they were in ruins. Commodore W. A. Sullivan, the Navy's salvage expert engaged in raising sunken hulks that interferred with port operations, showed me around, complaining that in too many cases our aviators had damaged the vessels more than they had to. From the Commodore's standpoint one nice, clean hole, just enough to sink a vessel, was quite enough. When the damage included a broken keel and near destruction his work was much harder. He told me that sometimes, alongside a dock, he would find two or three small ships sunk one on top of the other. Commodore Sullivan did such a good job of clearing Manila Harbor that it could be used by our military forces almost as soon as the city was retaken.

Driving around Manila at that time, the happiness of the Filipino people released from the rigors and cruelties of Japanese occupation, was heartwarming. I found friends of Washington days. Commander Charles Parsons and his family were back in Manila, building a home to take the place of one they had owned on Dewey Boulevard that had been destroyed. "Chick" Parsons' contributions to the victory over Japan are too numerous to mention. On many visits to the Philippines during the Japanese occupation (he was landed and taken off by submarine), he encouraged and organized Philippine guerrilla resistance forces so successfully that the Japanese put a price of $50,000 gold on his head, dead or alive. During the war years his wife's mother continued to live in Manila, her home for many years. At first she was unmolested, but toward the end, as their defeat became more certain, the Japanese military became convinced that in some way Mrs. Jurika must have assisted her famous son-in-law. She was arrested and not long before the fall of Manila executed by beheading along with some 29 other Americans and Filipinos suspected of collaboration with the Americans.[4] All are buried in the Heroes Monument in the North Cemetery, Manila.

One feature of the Manila landscape in June 1945 was the squatters. As the Japanese withdrew, destroying or damaging much of the beautiful historic part of the city, Filipinos from the countryside who had lost their homes and others who wanted a change of scene moved into damaged homes or onto the property around them. All over the city shacks sprang up, built mostly of material salvaged from damaged buildings. The house in which Admiral Kauffman was now living had been completely stripped of plumbing, hardware, and light fixtures. The squatters had certain rights under Philippine law, and they remained a problem in downtown Manila even on my last visit 25 years later.

The highlight of my 1945 Manila visit was a call on General MacArthur. Admiral Kauffman kept asking if I wanted to call, but I was reluctant to do so, knowing the General was extremely busy. One morning, driving past government buildings in the center of the city, Reggie pointed out a large one with few signs of damage. He suddenly told the driver to stop and said we would look inside. He walked up a corridor to a door with a sentry, and told him that Rear Admiral Radford, U.S. Navy, wanted to pay his respects to General MacArthur and was accompanied by Vice Admiral Kauffman. I could hardly back out then.

We chatted for certainly half an hour. If the General had worries or pressing appointments he gave no evidence of concern. Even then I felt that he was a great soldier and leader. I was to get to know him well later, in Japan, and this first meeting set the stage for our friendly cooperation.

☆ ☆ ☆ ☆

The next basic operation order called for attacks against airfields, aircraft, shipping, and industrial targets on or near Hokkaido, Honshu, and Shikoku. We knew there were still important units of the Japanese fleet in existence but did not expect trouble from them. Submarines were still a threat, which we were prepared to meet. Japanese shore-based aircraft were known to exist in considerable numbers but trained pilots were scarce. We knew the kamikaze menace was still great, but we were organized to make it tough for them to get to us.

We sortied on 1 July, and again I commanded TG 38.4, one of three groups of the fast carrier TF 38 under Admiral McCain. All groups consisted of 3 CVs and 2 CVLs but TG 38.4 had an extra CV—a powerful group. Looking over the six carriers formed up outside, I reflected on the immense advances made by U.S. naval aviation in the almost four years since Pearl Harbor. We had built a force to strike repeatedly against the heart of Japan, which all of us felt would contribute greatly to victory by the end of 1945.

En route north we had several submarine scares, one of which turned out to be almost amusing—afterwards—because it had probably been caused by a porpoise. Before that had been concluded it gave all hands a pretty bad night.

Beginning early on 14 July our sweeps and strikes against Hokkaido and northern Honshu were launched.

Aerial opposition was practically nil and few planes were destroyed on the ground. The greatest damage was against shipping, particularly the great fleet of 12 railroad-car ferries that traveled between the two islands.

Simultaneously with the air operations, TF 34 under R. Adm. John Shafroth bombarded three major industrial tragets. There was no enemy opposition and damage to plants was extensive. These shellings were the first of a number of such operations that continued until the end of the war. They indicated to the Japanese as nothing else had how impotent their remaining naval and air forces were. After all, ships cannot retreat, as do aircraft—and the Japanese, a seafaring people, understood such things.

Task Force 38 retired on 15 July and headed south for strikes against the Tokyo area. Following these attacks rendezvous was made with 30.8. In a replenishment operation that took three full days, in what was probably the greatest logistic feat ever performed on the high seas, the task force received 379,157 barrels of fuel oil, 6,369 tons of ammunition, 1,635 tons of stores and provisions, 99 replacement aircraft, and 421 replacement officers and men.

Targets were struck next in the Inland Sea, Osaka, and Miho areas. On one day alone 1,747 sorties were made. There was little aerial opposition, and much shipping was destroyed. Major vessels of the Japanese fleet hidden in the Kure area were ferreted out and many were sunk or heavily damaged. Four days later, Japanese naval vessels in Kure were again hit heavily. At last there was little left of the once formidable Japanese fleet. Only their remaining submarines could threaten our operations if we were not alert.

After operations ended on 28 July the task force steamed south, preparing for further strikes and sweeps against Tokyo. In the course of these attacks a *Yorktown* VF, hit by AA fire, was forced to land in Maizuru Bay not far from the Japanese base. His shipmates maintained a fighter cover over the downed pilot, Lt. (j.g.) D. R. Penn, and radioed for a rescue seaplane. *Yorktown* launched four VF(N) to escort the rescue plane, piloted by Lt. John Rairich, Army Air Corps. From the time he started, Lieutenant Rairich knew that he would have to return after dark and that he would probably have to make a night landing in the vicinity of the task force, since he did not have sufficient fuel to reach his base at Iwo Jima, where he was part of the Fourth Emergency Rescue Squadron of the Twentieth Air Force.

Shortly before dark, Lieutenant Rairich landed alongside Lieutenant Penn and made his first rescue. But a Japanese destroyer escort had entered the harbor, sighted our pilot in his life raft, and headed for him. The fighter escort overhead immediately attacked the ship, strafed it heavily, and drove it off temporarily. Lieutenant Rairich got into the air with enemy shots falling around him just as a fighter from the escort was forced to land in almost the same spot. Again the courageous pilot made a landing and picked up the second pilot, with shots continuing to fall all around.

Lieutenant Rairich displayed not only flying skill of the highest order but a courageous determination to do the job that probably equaled any act of heroism in the war to date. With his VF(N) escorts, Rairich in his lumbering plane made his way back across Japan to TF 38, 150 miles south of Tokyo. Two of our destroyers proceeded to a point about five miles from the formation, one to turn on a searchlight into the wind and the other to take station about half a mile upwind. Lieutenant Rairich landed about 9:30, and the crew and rescued pilots were taken off and the plane sunk. Thus ended one of the outstanding rescue efforts of the war. Incidents like this, which showed our organization for and ability to make rescues under the most difficult circumstances, kept up the morale of our carrier pilots. I recommended Lieutenant Rairich for the Navy Cross and hope he received it.

At the beginning of August, TF 38 remained in a southerly position to avoid a typhoon. We then steamed north for strikes against Kyushu, but they were canceled. Something more than a typhoon seemed to be delaying our operations, but in *Yorktown* we did not know what it could be. On 7 August I was ordered to report to Admiral McCain in *Wasp*. I learned that on the day before an atomic bomb had been dropped on Hiroshima by B29s of the Twentieth Air

Force. Even the word "atomic" was new to me and had to be explained. I was impressed with the tremendous power released by an atomic explosion and assumed, as did my informers, that Hiroshima had been wiped off the map. I also learned of plans for amphibious landings in Japan later in the fall; and I was informed that I would not be relieved as I had expected—about the first of September—but would stay on as a task group commander for two or three months more. This was all right for me, but I pointed out that some of my staff were too exhausted to keep going. I would have to have reliefs for them, which was agreed.

I was told that Admiral Nimitz had intelligence to the effect that the Japanese navy planned a suicide operation against our B29 bases. They were reported to be assembling about 200 bombers on airfields in northern Honshu and planning to carry some 2,000 suicide troops for crash landings on the bases in the Marianas and Okinawa. General MacArthur was very disturbed by the possibility of such an attack.

Targets for all missions on 9 August were airfields on Honshu. Careful briefing of pilots and attacks by them at treetop level were successful in rooting out camouflaged aircraft widely dispersed in revetments and concealed in wooded areas. No fewer than 392 planes were destroyed or damaged on that day. It was evident that General MacArthur's fears were well grounded, and a major Japanese air effort of some sort was spoiled by TF 38.

That evening we learned that a second atomic bomb had been dropped on Nagasaki. Pressure was mounting on the Japanese government and people.

On 10 August strikes were again directed primarily against airfields on Honshu. Two previously undetected fields were hit, destroying planes that were being assembled for strikes on the Marianas. Task Group 38.4 alone destroyed or damaged 43 planes on the ground.

About 9:00 that night a dispatch was received that Japan had sued for peace. Five minutes later, the *Yorktown* CO announced over the ship's public address system that Japan had made overtures for peace. Loud cheers rose from the blackness on the flight deck where crews were respotting planes.

Admiral Halsey decided that it was more important than ever to keep up the pressure. It was planned to again hit the Tokyo area; if the Japanese were vacillating maybe we could help them make up their minds.

About dawn on 12 August we launched the first of four sweeps and two strikes directed at airfields near Tokyo. The Japanese were in the air early that morning also, and during the day a total of 22 planes were shot down by our CAP. All afternoon we were busy with small raids that continued into the evening, when our dusk CAP shot down 6 planes and the rest turned back. It did not look as if the Japanese air force were suing for peace. The task force score for the day's operation was 254 planes destroyed on the ground and 149 damaged, not counting those destroyed by the CAP.

After refueling, we headed for the launching point off Tokyo. At 4:11 A.M. on 15 August we started launching the day's first fighter sweep.

I hated to see our planes take off that morning, feeling that the war would be over within hours. I recommended to Admiral McCain that we delay our offensive operations. He felt we had to keep the pressure on, so off went the planes. At 6:35 Admiral Halsey directed Admiral McCain to recall all strikes then airborne and to cancel remaining strikes but to continue CAPs. The Japanese had accepted the surrender terms and CINCPAC had ordered all offensive air operations suspended.

Our second strike was approaching the coast when they got the word. They jettisoned their bombs and returned. Some of the first strike were not so fortunate. Six VF from *Yorktown*'s VF88 got the word over Tokorozawa airfield. The strike leader had barely acknowledged when the formation was attacked by 15–20 Japanese planes. A wild fight ensued, the last important air battle of the war. Although badly outnumbered, the Hellcats shot down nine of the enemy but lost four of their own, our last combat casualties. Their loss was a personal tragedy to me on that day of victory. I felt I should have been able to convince Admiral McCain to delay offensive operations.

About 10:00 that morning Admiral Halsey received orders from CINCPAC ordering the Navy to "cease all offensive operations against Japan." An hour later, Commander Third Fleet broke [unfurled] his four-starred Admiral's flag, and *Missouri* blew her whistle and sounded her siren for a full minute to celebrate the end of the fighting. Other flag officers and ships followed suit. I still have the two-star flag that *Yorktown* broke for me.

In the next two hours several Japanese planes approached the force and were intercepted and shot down by patrols. Task Force 38 commenced retirement with CAPs still overhead; we were taking no chances on being surprised by Japanese pilots who either had not received the cease fire order or did not want to obey it.[5]

My emotions for the rest of the day are hard to describe. The end of the fighting came as a great surprise to me in spite of the advance information. It was difficult to believe, after months and months of such grim action.

I sat down at my desk that morning and wrote a letter to Mrs. Radford in Carmel. I told her I thanked God that the war was over and that my life had been spared. I realized how fortunate I had been in so many ways, able to play an important part in this great conflict, and I had seen and done things I had never dreamed of being able to do. I would be coming back to the States in a month or so, when we would end this long separation, and I wanted to make it our last. Having been so fortunate in my naval career, I was thinking of retiring so we could be together and I could do some of the many things I had always wanted to do; after all, I had over 30 years of service, so I could retire. I wanted to get this letter off so she could be thinking it over before my return.

The shooting was over, but we had only a cease fire, pending arrangements for a formal surrender. The task force had much to do; we continued to operate, practically on the same war basis, off the east coast of Honshu. In fact, our tasks seemed to increase. Task Group 38.4 was ordered to furnish CAPs and air support for the Tokyo area. Other air missions included airfield prisoner-of-war (POW) camp reconnaissance, with food and supply drops to the latter. We provided air cover for airborne troop movements, and air support for Third Amphibious Force landings. Extensive preparations were made for the American occupation of Tokyo, and Marine and Bluejacket landing force units were organized. These operations proceeded without incident and culminated in the formal signing of the surrender documents on *Missouri* on 2 September in Tokyo Bay. I was able to let all flag officers in the task group attend the ceremony except myself. I had the responsibility for air cover during the ceremony and could not leave. There was still the outside chance that some wild-eyed kamikazes might try to interrupt the proceedings on *Missouri*'s quarterdeck.

The interval between 15 August and the ceremony on 2 September was busy, but we also had time for historically interesting operations. On Admiral Halsey's orders all task groups, including the British TG 38.5, massed for aerial photographs. Then our planes had their turn. Both shows were tremendous. Never before nor since has so much naval power been concentrated in one force. *Yorktown* launched 96 planes for the aerial parade, which totaled about 1,300 planes.

The British TG 38.5 was broken up on 20 August, most ships returning to Leyte for rest and rehabilitation; but their two battleships, two cruisers, and four destroyers joined TG 38.4 temporarily. I now had a powerhouse manned by approximately 47,000 officers and men.

Planning for the actual surrender and the occupation of Japan began with the cease fire. Much of the detail was unknown to me at the time, but I saw many of General MacArthur's dispatches to the Japanese directing them to make certain preliminary arrangements. The General's appointment as Supreme Commander of the Allied Powers for the surrender and occupation of Japan had been announced by President Truman on 15 August immediately following his announcement that Japan had accepted Allied surrender terms.

There were many details to be resolved before actual occupation took place; one was the Japanese government's problem with members of its own armed forces who would not accept the surrender.[6] General MacArthur directed the Japanese government to send a "competent representative" by air to Manila to receive instructions for the formal surrender and the reception of occupation forces. The delegation was delayed two days, partly because of problems in forming a new cabinet and partly because hotheads in the Japanese air force threatened to shoot down any surrender mission that took off. Japan's Vice Chief of the Army General Staff, Lieutenant General Kawabe, headed the delegation that finally took off in darkness and secrecy in two planes, painted white with green crosses, from Kisarazu airfield for Ie Shima, where they transferred to a U.S. aircraft for the flight to Manila.

Delays such as the above kept us all on our toes. Our CAPs and airfield reconnaissance flights remained vigilant.

In Manila, the Kawabe delegation met with General MacArthur's staff and with Admiral Sherman, Admiral Nimitz' representative. They were presented with a copy of the "instrument of surrender" and instructions for reception of the occupying forces. When told that the first troops would arrive in Japan on 23 August the Japanese asked for more time, noting the problems of controlling their armed forces and pleading that delay would enable them to prevent regrettable incidents. The date for the first airborne soldiers to arrive was set for 26 August, the first major landings for two days later.

The Japanese delegation was impressed by the firmness but fairness of the American officers. As one Japanese expressed it, their attitude was stern, but they were neither arrogant nor mocking.

Meanwhile, many outlying Japanese garrisons obeyed the Emperor's orders even before the formal surrender. At Mili in the Marshall Islands, 2,395 ragged and half-starved soldiers, sailors, and construction workers surrendered to Capt. H. B. Grow, in U.S.S. *Levy*. Tiny garrisons near Okinawa began to surrender to the Tenth Army on 29 August, and on the same day Maj. Gen. H. H. Johnson on Morotai took the surrender of all Japanese in the Halmahera group: 36,700 servicemen and 5,000 civilians. About 2,500 emaciated troops on Marcus Island surrendered to R. Adm. F. E. M. Whiting in *Bagley* two days later.

Admiral Halsey was getting anxious to anchor in sheltered waters, and permission was received to enter Sagami Bay on 27 August.

The Japanese Navy had been ordered to send us an escort through the mine fields, and to deliver officers empowered to arrange the surrender of the Yokosuka Base. When the escort came into view, we identified her as the destroyer *Hatsuzakura*. As stipulated, her guns were depressed, their breeches open, her torpedo tubes empty, and no crew was topside except enough men to handle a small boat. Mick Carney and I watched her from the *Missouri*'s flag bridge. She was so frail, so woebegone, so dirty, that I felt ashamed of our having needed four years to win the war.[7]

The organization for recovering POWs had been set up, but General MacArthur had directed that no action be taken until the Army was ready, so nothing had been done. On the night of 27 August a picket boat from the Third Fleet, patrolling close inshore, heard a yell from the beach. The boat picked up two British prisoners whom they delivered to Commodore Rodger Simpson, commanding the rescue operation. Commodore Simpson heard such a tale of inhumanity that it was hard to believe until corroborated the next day by a

Swiss doctor of the International Red Cross. Listening to the story, Admiral Halsey told Simpson to take his task group, which included the hospital ship *Benevolence,* to Tokyo and stand by for a signal. Admiral Nimitz arrived from Guam two days later and was told about the POWs and urged to permit recovery operation to commence.

"Go ahead," Admiral Nimitz said. "MacArthur will understand."

Carrier planes had located a number of POW camps and had been dropping food, clothing, toilet articles, and cigarettes. Planes from the fleet were able to guide Commodore Simpson and Commander Harold Stassen's small boats up estuaries in the Tokyo area leading to the nearest camps.

By 7:10 that evening the first POWs were aboard *Benevolence*. By midnight 794 had been brought out, and within two weeks every one of 19,000 Allied prisoners in the Navy's area, the eastern two-thirds of Honshu, had been liberated and hospitalized or sent off for a quiet convalescence.

General MacArthur gracefully yielded to Admiral Nimitz on the selection of a place for the formal surrender ceremony: the *Missouri,* named for President Truman's native state and christened by his daughter, Margaret. *Missouri* was Admiral Halsey's flagship for the last two months of the war and a part of my task group.

Missouri was anchored in Tokyo Bay not far from Commodore Perry's second anchorage on his visit to Japan 92 years before. On a bulkhead overlooking the spot selected for the surrender ceremony was featured the 31-starred flag that Perry wore into Tokyo Bay in 1853. In contrast to Perry's tiny fleet there were now anchored in Tokyo Bay some 258 warships, from battleships to the smallest amphibious types, representing all the Allied nations that had been at war with Japan. Most of the aircraft carriers were at sea preparing to launch planes for a big flyover after the surrender had been signed.

The setting was severe, the atmosphere frigid, as was proper. The Japanese preserved their dignity, impassive but tearful.[8]

After all required signatures had been affixed, General MacArthur spoke a final word. "Let us pray that peace be now restored to the world and that God will preserve it always. These proceedings are now closed."

General MacArthur and Admiral Nimitz felt compassion for the defeated foe; Nimitz had earlier revoked an order from Halsey to the CO of *Landsdowne* not to offer coffee, cigarettes, or other courtesies to the Japanese delegation. The Japanese delegates received side honors [accorded to all visiting dignitaries] as they boarded and left *Missouri,* to symbolize that they were no longer enemies.

As the formalities ended the sun shone through, and a flight of some 600 carrier aircraft and several hundred from the Army Air Corps roared over *Missouri* and the rest of the fleet. At higher altitudes, not taking part in the review, was a heavy CAP from TG 38.4. We were still taking no chances.

What remained of TG 38.4, the carriers and their screening destroyers, was still at sea that day. I missed the ceremony aboard *Missouri* but heard the running comment broadcast to all ships and stations. In some ways this was even more moving, and it gave me time to think. I was impressed by the valedictories of Admiral Nimitz and General MacArthur, and I wanted to be a part of the world movement for peace. Although my small family had been hit by the tragedy of war in June,[9] I approved of the compassion shown by our two great war leaders for our recent enemies. I felt that the armed forces of the United States had done a superb job for four long years. Now it was up to the statesmen to take advantage of the complete victory we handed them. Certainly on that one day, Sunday, 2 September 1945, practically all the people in the Far East except the Japanese seemed our friends. It is difficult to determine just why we have made so many mistakes after such a glorious start.

☆ ☆ ☆ ☆

Task Group 38.4 was kept very busy until after the surrender. After that our responsibilities gradually diminished and we became rather lonesome, for everyone else was being ordered into Tokyo Bay.

On the first of September, Vice Admiral Towers relieved Admiral McCain as Commander Fast Carrier Task Force. After the surrender ceremony, Admiral McCain left for home. Ten days later he was dead of a heart attack, as truly a war casualty as it was possible to be. I had lost a great friend.

On 5 September my task group designation was changed to 38.1. I still had three CVs, one CVL, three cruisers, and nine destroyers. Our daily flight operations were still heavy; over 400 flights a day, mainly in connection with locating, photographing, and supplying POW camps in the Tokyo area. We were astounded at the number of camps found and photographed.

Meanwhile, of course, the Great Demobilization had commenced.[10] The great fleet that had won the victory from Japan was being swiftly put out of action by orders from Washington. Our sister service, the Army, was no better off. Our government was in a great hurry to "bring the boys home."

My own orders had arrived. At the discretion of Commander Third Fleet, I was to be detached and ordered to Seattle for duty as Commander Fleet Air Seattle, which I had listed as my first preference. A generous Navy Department also allowed me 15 days' delay in reporting, to count as leave—after nearly 11 continuous months of the most strenuous war duty one could possibly have.

The details of demobilization came thick and fast. A sample message received from the Chief of Naval Operations (CNO) gives some idea of the urgency of the situation—as seen from Washington, that is—before the ink was dry on the signatures written on the *Missouri*.

Commanding Officers shall immediately reconsider the cases of all personnel who meet the required point scores and are being retained on the basis of quote military necessity unquote. Continued retention of such personnel shall be based only upon a literal and realistic interpretation of the term quote military necessity unquote.

Commanding officers in my task group, which was still under way and still on war footing, were given no particular consideration. What hurt was that the most experienced and competent officers and men were the ones with the highest point scores, who deserved to go home.

We did our best and our operations continued. At sunset on 8 September navigational lights were turned on. *Yorktown's* war diary contains the entry, "this is the first night in the life of the ship that she has not been blacked out while under way at night." Washington evidently considered that all Japanese submarines had been accounted for.

Commanding officers in TG 38.1 kept me continuously advised of their personnel situations regarding their ability to continue operations. I passed news on to Commander TF 38 and Commander Third Fleet, warning them that my group—the last one still at sea—was rapidly approaching the point where we would have to anchor somewhere. We were detaching our skilled petty officers in droves. Finally, with our airfield reconnaissance and POW camp missions tapering off, we were ordered into Tokyo Bay on Sunday morning 16 September. We had been under way since 2 July, 75 days. It felt strangely quiet on the ship in the silence of the great power plant that had served us so well since leaving Leyte Gulf.

Many of the *Yorktown* company had not been off the ship since it had sailed from Pearl Harbor on 24 October 1944. The attractions ashore in wartime fleet bases in the western Pacific were seldom an inducement to overcome the difficult boating situations. But now everyone was anxious to see Japan, the country that had put up such a fight. For a month all hands had been getting ready for this liberty.

The time had finally come, and our liberty parties were ready to leave the ship. But there were no boats! Despite assurances received while still at sea that boat service for the group would commence upon anchoring, we sat on board fuming that lovely Sunday morning, waiting for service that never came. Immediately upon anchoring I sent personal messages to friends on ships already in port, but for the most part they had gone ashore. To say I was disappointed was putting it mildly. I was mad as hell, to think that the thousands of men in my ships were being stood up because of the failure of some individual to do his job.

It was nearly noon before our boat service commenced. We were permitted to send only small parties ashore at a time, and none overnight. Trips to Tokyo were by special arrangement only, since transportation was by electric train. Buses and cars were at a premium in Japan and most were driven by gas generators mounted on the rear in clumsy, box-like contraptions.

Somehow we survived that first day in port. Our liberty parties got ashore and back safely to begin stories of adventure in Yokosuka, Japan's largest naval base. A few officers visited the naval base itself and the officers' club. I covered a good deal of Yokosuka in a walk late that afternoon. I was amazed at the poor layouts in the shops, the mostly dirt floors and the nondescript mixture of machine tools. The Japanese workmen were obviously underfed but seemed busy with their jobs.

The Japanese naval officers' club had been taken over, of course, and by that evening it was in pretty fair shape. My dinner there was not Japanese food, but rather poorly prepared American food. It *was* different from my ship's fare, as I had anticipated—but it was not better.

I learned that I would be detached as soon as I could close out my paper work and see that my staff were started home. I made one trip to Tokyo. Because of my rank I was given special transportation: an ancient Packard V12 probably commandeered by the Japanese military from some wealthy Japanese at the outbreak of war. It had seen hard service. I had doubts about it as I set off for Tokyo, but most of our trouble was with tires. We had three or four flats on the way, each of which had to be repaired on the spot. I would have done better by train but would not have seen as much of the people and the countryside.

From Yokosuka to Tokyo via Yokohama was about 30 miles by road, mostly through urban areas. From Yokohama on, most of the buildings had been destroyed by fire from incendiary bombs. The remains, as far as the eye could see, were a stark forest of brick chimneys. Occasionally there were patches or groups of buildings still standing in good shape, and I was informed by the Japanese guide that these were red light districts. I could not figure out whether our Air Corps had been smart enough to spare them or the Japanese had moved the girls into the only available housing after the bombings. At any rate they were open for business and already causing U.S. commanders ashore plenty of trouble.

Downtown Tokyo was not destroyed and was open for business under General MacArthur's rather strict rules. Our servicemen were swarming everywhere and buying everything offered, probably at outrageous prices. The exchange rate was 360 yen to a dollar. I wanted a few souvenirs to take back to the States, but the crowds in the department stores and the scarcity of goods were too much for me. The Japanese people with whom I came in contact that day could not have been more friendly or polite. There was not the slightest evidence of hostility anywhere; and our Army seemed to be doing a remarkable job of getting things running again.

I had just a week in Japan before I was relieved by my friend R. Adm. Donald Duncan. I saw my flag come down with mixed emotions, glad that the war was over but hating to leave this wonderful ship, my staff, and her crew, with whom I had been through so much in the last ten months. This, I thought, was the end of my experience with warfare. By our great and complete victory we had, in all probability, made future wars impossible. How wrong I was!

My route back to the States was via Pearl Harbor. As I came down the steps from the plane at Hickam Field, Oahu, I noticed a young officer waiting at the foot, looking at me. He saluted and handed me a dispatch directing me to proceed to Washington and report to Admiral King for temporary duty. I read it, thanked him, and walked to a waiting car. He seemed surprised, as if he expected me to climb back into the plane and continue to San Francisco. I had other ideas. In spite of the implied urgency, I felt I had to pick up the clothes I had stowed at Ford Island and get another good night's sleep. I did, and arrived in San Francisco on the afternoon of Friday 28 September for a glorious reunion with my lovely wife, who had been waiting in Carmel all these long months. That was the end of the war for me and I was so glad to be back in the most wonderful country in the world.

7

Back to Washington: The Unification Uproar

After a year's absence I was finally at home in Carmel, enjoying the California bungalow that my wife had arranged to keep in the hope that we could spend our leave there. Instead, because of Admiral King's insistence, I had only a little more than a weekend with my family. After Saturday and Sunday in Carmel, Mrs. Radford and I drove to Santa Monica to visit my parents overnight, and on Tuesday I left for Washington. Mrs. Radford returned to Carmel for another period of waiting; had she traveled to Washington with me we would have had to pay her expenses, so we thought it best that I find out how long my stay would be before we changed our plans.

I reported to Admiral King (Commander-in-Chief, a Fleet Admiral) in Washington on 3 October 1945 and found that I was one of three officers selected to comment on the Navy's Basic Post War Plan Number 1. The others were V. Adm. H. W. Hill and R. Adm. W. H. P. Blandy. Admiral King was definite in his brief instructions to me. He wanted *personal* comments on the plan. I could, of course, discuss problems with other officers and civilians in the Navy Department, but what I wrote was to be my own comment, as nearly as possible uninfluenced by others. He remarked that in selecting Hill, Blandy, and me he had picked individuals with a reputation for independent thinking.

We went to work immediately, impressed with the importance of our task. The month in Washington was strenuous and, in many respects, very disturbing. Talking to numerous friends in the Navy, in the other services, in the Congress, and in civilian life made me realize what a turmoil our government faced in the years ahead. The end of the fighting did not mean, automatically, a settlement of the many problems that had much to do with starting it. This did not seem to bother a great many of our citizens, and it bothered their representatives in Congress even less. The political demands for speedy demobilization were increasing in spite of Herculean efforts on the part of the services to retain some semblance of order in the process. Washington was really a wild place, not what it was in December 1941, when everyone was working together to get things done. In November 1945 there was little evident cooperation; and there was a rather ruthless drive for a unified military organization, being pushed by the Army and the Army Air Corps with the full backing of the President. The Navy seemed to be without a plan but did not like the Army plan.

I read Basic Post War Plan Number 1 carefully. In a letter dated 5 November 1945 transmitting the plan to the Secretary of the Navy and enclosing our comments, Admiral King was careful to point out that the plan was flexible and that it was to be reviewed and revised as often as necessary to meet changing conditions. He made it clear also that the active fleet in the recommended postwar Navy would be ready for instant action at the end of demobilization in fall 1946. While this was undoubtedly true there were many other facts to consider, which the Admiral also knew well. A tentative force plan that is already in effect is difficult to change with time.[1]

In his letter of transmittal Admiral King listed the assumptions on which the plan was based:

a) There is no prospective enemy in possession of a large fleet.

b) There is no prospective enemy that is largely dependent upon imports as was the case with Japan. Consequently, the field for submarine action will be more limited than it was in the last war.

c) Enemy action on the sea (if war came before the end of 1947) will consist largely of operations by submarines, land based aviation, and cruiser raids.

d) Possible action (by the U.S.) which would be necessary would consist of air attacks on enemy production centers and lines of communication, conduct and support of amphibious operations.

The plan also provided vessels that would be used to train the Navy's allocation of men under a plan for Universal Military Training (UMT), which was being considered by Congress; and, finally, Admiral King was assuming that the personnel ceiling for the plan was to be 500,000 men. He believed we could and should provide an adequate Navy without going above that number. Admiral King promised the Secretary of the Navy another review of the plan, based on data then available, in January 1946.

As might be suspected, the three consultants differed, primarily in their recommendations regarding the offensive forces, the so-called fast carrier task force. In the basic plan, these comprised:

    5 BB (battleships)
    3 CB (battle cruisers)
    8 CA (heavy cruisers)
   16 CL (light cruisers)
    4 CL(AA) (anti-aircraft cruisers)
   36 subtotal

    3 CVB (heavy carriers *Roosevelt* type)
    7 CV (medium carriers *Essex* type)
    4 CV (medium carriers with 20–30 percent complement)

Admirals Hill and Blandy recommended that carriers (CV) in active commission be increased to a total of 12. I recommended an increase to a total of 20. My reasoning is quoted from my letter to Admiral King:

The Striking Force. Viewing the proposed fleet composition in the light of war experience, I am immediately struck by the lack of carrier air power. There are ten active CV-CVBs. Their total embarked aircraft will number 1,150. In one carrier task force, their offensive striking force would never total more than 800 aircraft and would probably be less—yet this is the force that is to "strike hard and promptly to forestall at its beginning any attempt to disrupt the peace of the world."

To me it appears fundamental that our naval striking power must be built around a mobile naval air force superior to any shore-based air power that a potential enemy can bring to bear on it. If we are entitled to any extravagance in our estimates, it would be in the composition of this force, whose defeat would be disastrous in any sudden war of the immediate future.

Therefore, until the world settles down—until we know where we stand—the Navy cannot afford to be conservative in estimating its needs for air power. I strongly recommend that we maintain as the backbone of our striking force an embarked aircraft complement of 2,000 planes. This will require 20 CVB-CVs in active commission. For each embarked air group there should be one reserve group in training, making the total combatant air force approximately 4,000 planes. This should be organized into task groups with four carriers in each—one (group) of which may be employed at all times for training. At least four of these five groups should operate in the Pacific, ready to concentrate on short notice.

A general rundown of my views on issues of the plan follows.

The Submarine Force. Given the number of submarines in the plan, I felt that a division of submarines could directly support the fast carrier task force in any theater of operations.

The Amphibious Force. I felt the composition of this force was satisfactory except for the lack of fire support ships. I assumed that they were to be furnished for training purposes from the heavy support ships assigned to the fast carrier force, and that in case of war there would be time to activate the bombardment groups shown in the reserve fleet. I favored retaining Marine air groups in the CVEs (escort carriers) directly assigned to the amphibious groups.

The Service Force. The Service Force should be adequate to furnish support to the active peace-time fleet and to supply on-the-spot service to the striking force in case of sudden hostilities. I felt that within the service force there should be representation of all types so that we could continue to improve the actual transfer of fuel, ammunition, and food at sea. I noted (rather gratuitously, it appears, 24 years later) that I was not at all enthusiastic about the record of the service force in the Pacific war; that the ability of the fast carrier force to operate at sea for extended periods was more a tribute to the ingenuity of their personnel "to get along without." The magnitude of the task and the lack of trained personnel accounted for much of the difficulty, but I also felt that there was some lack of imagination, a decided tendency to be satisfied with the job. I felt that the service force deserved the most intensive study and every possible assistance.

The service forces outlined in the plan could be reduced considerably, although reduction would depend largely on the number of fleet bases retained. I recommended reduction in the number of transport CVEs.

Mine Force. I recommended that the peacetime active mine force be reduced to a nucleus of types sufficient to keep alive the art of minelaying and minesweeping.

Fleet Air Wings. A sizeable reduction in the number of patrol squadrons had been made in the plan, but I recommended a further cut in the total number of either aircraft or squadrons. For psychological reasons in dealing with the Army I felt that reducing squadrons was preferable, but from an organizational point of view fewer planes per squadron would be better. I recommended that patrol wings be reduced from 12 to 8 and patrol squadrons from 48 to 32, with 3 wings assigned to the Atlantic and 5 to the Pacific. In spite of their impressive record, Navy patrol squadrons would be under constant fire from the Army Air Corps. Retention of land-based planes of this type would be difficult, but we must have them and must continue their development as a type with high priority.

Fleet Air Ships. I felt these should be eliminated as an operating force, retaining one experimental and developmental unit.

Training Unit (UMT). Within the UMT period of one year, the Navy now planned to give each naval trainee three months' training at sea. The difficulties and expense of such a plan outweighed its advantages. We had learned to train ashore, where synthetic training devices freed us from the vagaries of weather and other restrictions aboard ship. I recommended a restudy of the UMT plan as applied to the Navy, and that this training force be eliminated from the estimates. Personnel not needed for the shore training establishment would be available for other assignment. The ships allocated to UMT could be reassigned or placed in the inactive reserve.

Operational Training. I recommended elimination of vessels assigned solely to this force, for necessary training afloat can be accomplished by temporary assignment of ships from the operating forces or in district craft.

Experimental and Development Force. I felt this should have the highest priority in every respect and that it should include at least one battleship.

Advance Bases-Sea Frontiers-Naval Transportation Service-Naval Districts.
The forces in this category, particularly patrol craft and minesweepers, were
ripe for a second approximation.

I summarized my recommendations to Admiral King generally as follows:

a) The number of active carriers should be increased by ten.

b) If reductions in personnel recommended by elimination of UMT force plus
such reductions as can be made in Service Force, Mine Force, etc., cannot
provide the personnel required for the additional CVs recommended above,
then I would obtain them by reducing the support ships in each carrier task
group to six, decommissioning the excess in the following priority: CV, BB.

c) Except as noted in (*b*) above, I have made no recommendations for the decommissioning of battleships or battlecruisers, as types. If the UMT plan is
not adopted or if shore training is substituted, I assume that all *Washington*
class would enter the reserve fleet, leaving five *Iowa*s and three *Alaska*s in the
striking force. Approximately double the number of cruisers could be substituted in the active fleet for the same cost in money and manpower required
to maintain these eight BBs and CBs. I recommend that all but one BB
(*Iowa*) and all three CBs be placed out of commission, and that the one BB in
active commission be assigned to the experimental and development force.
Cruisers in excess of those required in the striking force could then be assigned directly to the Amphibious Force or to training duty.

d) I do not believe it practicable or desirable to attempt to operate ships, particularly the larger types, with 20–30 percent of complement.

☆ ☆ ☆ ☆

I have limited myself to direct comments on the composition of the postwar fleet
and have made recommendations that I believe are justified in the light of war
experience. The most important recommendation has to do with a large increase
in the air power of the striking force. Perhaps this recommendation will be approved. Whether it is or not, the fact that it has to be made is to my mind the
most important issue that faces the Navy today. It is an issue that must be discussed with frankness and settled once and for all. Are we to have an air-sea
Navy in the future, or is it to be in the immediate future the sea-air Navy of pre-
Pearl Harbor days and ultimately no Navy at all?

In World War II the Navy demonstrated to the world what air power, backed by
sea power, could do—air power really teamed with the surface ship. When the
detailed history of the war is written and prewar claims compared with actual
performance, no air force will have a better record in that respect than that of the
Navy. Naval aviators exceeded their claims in every respect and proved beyond a
reasonable doubt that the airplane is, for today at least, the Navy's primary offensive weapon.

To me, any recommendations for a postwar fleet that lacks carrier air power is a stunning surprise. It is an indication that even the war has not brought unanimity of opinion within the naval service.

The issue becomes that old controversy: the battleship versus the airplane. A striking force which includes eight battleships and cruisers and ten carriers in full commission is backed up by a training force of six battleships and four carriers in reduced commission. Under conditions which dictate maximum economy the Navy proposes to retain in commission what amounts to a battleship-carrier ratio of 14:14. Assuming that the composition of combatant forces in the fleet should reflect naval consensus as to the relative offensive values of the various types (as they are available), I look to past performance and the best estimate of the future that can be made to justify the retention of battleships in the postwar fleet.

In World War II, the battleship:

a) proved invaluable as a unit of the amphibious force

b) engaged in two successful night actions against Japanese heavy ships

c) bombarded shore targets at various times, particularly in the last two months of the war

d) furnished AA support to the fast carriers.

Today, only amphibious support can best be performed by battleships. Lack of air power set the stage for the surface actions mentioned above; sufficient air power will prevent them in the future. Ordinary shore targets such as those bombarded in Japan can be more effectively destroyed by air attack. Lighter, more maneuverable vessels can furnish more effective AA support to the carriers.

In World War III, the battleship:

a) in its present form will still be of great value to the amphibious forces—provided World War III reaches that stage

b) perhaps modified with a heavily armored hull might be an efficient launching platform for long-range rockets or guided missiles.

I conclude that the battleship is obsolescent. Its usefulness, aside from amphibious support, does not justify its retention in numbers in the active postwar fleet where economy in men and money is a consideration. That other navies have battleships is no argument in their favor. But that we have them should be the greatest incentive to salvage some of our huge investment.

On the other hand, I am making no long-range claims for the aircraft carrier as we now know it. The World War II record will support the statement that the aircraft carrier is the most valuable offensive ship we have. We should retain as many carriers in the postwar fleet as are necessary to give us a mobile air force that cannot be defeated by any probable enemy. When I mention "air" in connection with long-range plans I mean whatever offensive weapons of the air can be adapted for naval use, including long-range rockets and guided missiles. The aircraft carrier of the present may be as obsolete in ten years as the battleship is now.

I am optimistic regarding the *possibilities* of the future insofar as the Navy is concerned. No armed service in the world has a better technical background with which to face the atomic age than the U.S. Navy. I am pessimistic about the *actualities* of the future unless there is an immediate renaissance within the service—a change in the naval "attitude," for want of a better expression. Now or never is the time for a critical and ruthless self-examination. Now is the time to eliminate self-interest or sentiment from acts of the present or plans for the future. *We must realize that the time is past when Navy recommendations on naval matters will be accepted without question!* Requirements of national security demand that the armed services integrate their plans. Our own plan will receive scrutiny by the other services.

Stubborn insistence that the battleship is still the "backbone" of the fleet will not win public confidence, for the public is historically too well informed to believe it.

I believe that an *air-sea* Navy has a future, that a *sea-air* Navy is but a step removed from the transportation service that extreme proponents of air power envisage.

I believe that an early marriage with "Air" is essential to win the public confidence that is so necessary if the Navy is to continue as an important arm of the national defense. No more candy, flowers, and promises, but a church wedding to which the public is invited. We must obtain unanimity of opinion within the service, alive to the implications of the present and preparing for those of the future.

I signed this letter to Admiral King on 29 October. By the time he had forwarded it and those from Admirals Hill and Blandy to the Secretary of the Navy, I was back in Carmel, resuming with much pleasure the two weeks' leave that had been interrupted before it began.

The letter had been difficult to write. I was in every sense a loyal naval officer, but I felt that I had to be critical and outspoken if I were to do any good. I do not know what good, if any, my comments accomplished. I never discussed the letter with Admiral King or anyone else; but on 6 November, as I was relaxing in the California sunshine, I had a call from my friend and classmate, R. Adm. Bill Fechteler, in Naval Personnel, to let me know that he was issuing orders for me to proceed to Washington, reporting to the Secretary of the Navy.

I was flabbergasted. Bill said he would send a plane to Monterey for me immediately. He expected me in Washington late that night.

Our plans were again in a mess. As I threw my clothes into suitcases, Mrs. Radford and I decided that we should give up the house in Carmel and that she would follow me to Washington as soon as she could. It looked as if our plans for a peaceful postwar stay in the northwest had gone out the window and they had.

On arrival in Washington, I wasted no time in reporting to the Secretary [James Forrestal]. He said something like this:

"Radford, I have become increasingly concerned with the situation in regard to the merger fight or unification of the services. The Navy has no adequate organization to handle this important problem—it has not even had a plan of its own until recently—and has done practically nothing to educate its own people, the public, and particularly Congress on the grave problems it would face if some of the hasty and poorly thought-out solutions now being talked about on the Hill were included in permanent legislation.[2]

"I have, therefore, had you ordered back to take charge of the Navy's efforts to insure, if at all possible, that legislation on this subject, which is sure to be passed in the not-too-distant future, is satisfactory from our standpoint. My personal position is that an improved and unified defense organization is needed. The President wants one quickly, and the Army is pushing for speedy action with his complete backing. You are to set up an office, under me, and go to work as soon as you can. My staff will do everything to help you get the people you want and the space you need."

To say that I was surprised is putting it mildly: I was stunned. I said, "My God, Mr. Forrestal—I don't know *anything* about merger or unification—I may even be for it. I think you have made a great mistake to pick me for this job."

The Secretary smiled. "I don't think so, Raddy. I know you will do your best and that is all I ask. Take a couple of weeks to acquaint yourself with the details and come to me whenever you get stuck."

I left the Secretary's office in a daze, feeling stumped. I hardly knew where to begin. Looking over the record now, I am surprised at what the little organization I gathered around me so quickly was able to do, but I am still puzzled over how they were able to do it.

It is easy for the Secretary of a service to issue orders, as Secretary Forrestal did as he gave me this assignment. I was to have "the people and the space needed," but there was much wailing and gnashing of teeth before my new organization was under way. One incident illustrates this pretty well.

Captain Arleigh Burke was attached to the Bureau of Ordnance, following his distinguished wartime service as Admiral Mitscher's Chief of Staff. He was one of the first individuals I thought of as I put down my requirements for personnel, for I was a great admirer of his abilities. His chief, R. Adm. George Hussey, was a classmate and friend of mine. I called him and told him of my new duties and problems. I mentioned the blank check I had from Mr. Forrestal in regard to staffing the organization, concluding the conversation by telling him that I wanted Arleigh Burke to work for me—right away.

There was silence at the other end. George cleared his throat and said, "Raddy, I would just as soon lose my right arm as to lose Arleigh Burke. I'm sorry. You can have anyone else in the Bureau but Arleigh." I said, "George, I'm sorry too, but I have to have Arleigh so you might as well prepare to amputate your right arm."

He remained firm, so the conversation ended; but Arleigh reported for duty soon afterward. I was not making myself the most popular man in the Navy Department. Multiply the above incident numerous times for an idea of the problems that faced me. Getting space to house our activities was almost as difficult. Since we had to be reasonably close to the Secretary's office, we had to displace some VIPs congregated in that vicinity. Secretary Forrestal received appeals from some of them but they did not come back to me. In a surprisingly short time the new organization was in business, without a name. When I heard it was being called the Radford Committee, I asked for suggestions. It was decided we would be SCOROR, the Secretary's Committee of Research on Reorganization, which sounded stuffy to me, but we had to move fast and had no better idea.

Secretary Forrestal's concern regarding the unification problem was fully justified, I rapidly discovered as I plunged into my new job. Things were really in a mess. The Department as a whole and, worse, the Navy at large had no guidance. Along with the President, the Army and several influential members of the military committees of both houses of Congress were pushing for rapid action. It appeared we might be defeated before we could get started.

The situation was reversed by the Herculean efforts of this small SCOROR, assisted in every way, of course, by the Secretary and by an increasingly united Navy effort. Members of Congress, the public, and finally the President became convinced that the Navy's plan for unification had merit. We were given, reluctantly at first, the time we needed to present our ideas, which differed radically from the much simpler Army plans that had been presented up until November 1945. The several Army plans were much easier for Congress and the public to understand. As the risk of great oversimplification, I feel that, in general, the Army said, "Put us in charge of everything—including a new and separate air force—and things will be all right."[3]

Over the years, particularly after service in Washington during the 1920s, I had learned a good deal about the Army and the Army Air Corps. I found that the Army, at least in peacetime, was not very unified. The Cavalry, Infantry, Field Artillery, Coast Artillery, Engineers—all went their separate ways, pretty much. The occasions on which they came together for large-scale maneuvers were few and far between; but this was not their fault, for there simply was not money nor were there many areas large enough for large-scale joint exercises. Army officers attended many schools together, which helped but did not meet the basic problem.

In the Navy we lived close together aboard ship. We had to get along and we did by understanding the other fellow's problems; for the modern Navy too had many specialties.

By 1946 I had a broad knowledge of the problems of the services. In my new job I tried to establish and define my own position. I concluded that:

> There was no doubt that the services could not return to the earlier status quo, two separate and independent Departments of War and Navy.

Any new organization must attempt to coordinate military with national planning in political and economic fields.

A "joint chiefs of staff" organization, similar to the one that had worked so well under President Roosevelt in World War II, must become a statutory body.

Other major questions presented themselves, of course, the most important being the control of air power in the new military organization. On that subject Army plans were quite general. They asked for an autonomous air service, equal in status to the Army and Navy. In nearly every case there were some provisions for "naval air" of some kind, principally on carriers. Actually, the Army planners (including those of the Army Air Corps) envisioned an Air Force similar to the Royal Air Force of Great Britain, which had absorbed all air units of the Army and Navy. This was confirmed not long after I had returned to Washington. General Carl ("Tooey") Spaatz of the Air Corps asked me to lunch with him. Our acquaintance went back over a number of years. Although we had never served closely together I admired him as an excellent pilot and courageous leader.

Tooey was frank. He wanted our naval aviation organization in the new Air Force, which he felt would be set up in the near future. He intimated that we would be included whether we liked it or not, so he was really giving me a chance to voluntarily get on the right side. He felt that if I would join forces with him in this effort he could promise that I could soon succeed him as Chief of Staff of the Air Force.

It was an alluring prospect and I felt highly complimented. I told Tooey that. I also told him that I simply could not accept his offer, for I felt too strongly that such a reorganization would not be in the best interests of the United States and the armed services. I also regretted the situation I sensed was developing, a bitter fight between the Army and Navy over this matter of Air. I remarked that the Air Corps had already embittered the majority of naval aviators by its tremendous propaganda campaign to prove it had won the war almost singlehandledly, and that neither I nor any other aviator could change the majority thinking.[4]

We went our separate ways during the remainder of the unification battle but always remained friends. Tooey was a square shooter. He was a tough antagonist, but this was one fight he did not win.

By early December 1945 my personal position on unification had solidified as follows:

I was for a secretary of defense, joint chiefs of staff, a national security council, and a national security resources board—all of the unified top suggested by the Eberstadt Report prepared at Mr. Forrestal's request, which became the Navy's plan.

I was for two departments, quite independent and each with its own air, as before, but I had become convinced that this was no longer possible. The Army and Air Force wanted to be separate and there was nothing that could be done to stop this feature of the new organization.

I had had a conversation with Ferdinand Eberstadt shortly after I set up SCOROR. The Eberstadt Report had been distributed and I had studied it carefully. It provided inter alia for a separate and independent air force, presumably the former Army Air Corps. But nowhere in the report was there justification for this recommendation. I concluded that Mr. Eberstadt felt that a separate air force was inevitable and had therefore put it in his plan. I asked him if this were the case and he admitted it was.

By mid-December, the Navy Department had an official position on unification that was generally accepted and for which we were prepared to argue before Congress. Since early November, the Senate Military Affairs Committee had been holding hearings on a new military organization, and one of the major problems I had faced from the first day of my new job was finding and briefing witnesses to appear before these hearings. The Navy was really stalling for time while we solidified our own ideas.

The Senate Committee hearings were pretty dull and were getting nowhere fast. President Truman was getting madder by the minute. He had long ago made up his mind what he wanted in the way of a new military organization and he was tired of what he felt was unnecessary delay. On 19 December, he acted, sending a message to Congress recommending a reorganization of the armed services into a single department along broad lines.[5]

In the Navy Department, we were stunned by the President's action. Although he had ostensibly included in his unification plan some of the Navy's concepts contained in the Eberstadt Report, we felt that actually his thinking had changed very little. He was a hard-line Army man and he had put us in a very difficult position. When a president has spoken as definitely as President Truman did in this matter he has established the government's position. The Army and Navy Departments could no longer oppose the organization proposed by the President. The Navy's opposition, if it was to continue, had to be a matter of individuals expressing their personal ideas. Mr. Forrestal took this matter up with the President at a cabinet luncheon on 18 December, the day before the message on unification was sent to Congress.[6]

On the same day he sent a memorandum to Judge Samuel Rosenman [the President's principal speech-writer] in the White House:

As you know, and as the President knows, I am so opposed to the fundamental concept expressed in the (President's) message that I do not believe there is any very helpful observation that I could make on the draft you referred to me.

You asked for a check to make sure there are no misstatements of fact. I challenge many statements that are made because they seem to be conclusions rather than facts. Examples are the comments on the Joint Chiefs of Staff, the statement that the services did not get along with each other, and the statement that the Army and Navy each normally constructs its own airport, even though the total operation does not exceed the capacity of one of the fields.

I cannot refrain from comment on the next to the last paragraph. The only hearings held thus far on the legislation now pending for merging the War and Navy Departments have been held by the Senate Military Affairs Committee. That committee does not have adequate background with respect to Naval Affairs. Moreover, the attendance of its members during testimony by Naval Officers has been extremely limited. Only the chairman heard the testimony of Admiral Hewitt, our most distinguished Naval Commander in the war against Germany, who visited the United States for the express purpose of testifying. The presentation of Navy testimony has not yet been completed.

In addition, there are many civilians who have been intimately connected with both the War and Navy Departments during World War II . . . I believe that the views of these men and others who occupied positions of importance in the government during the war, would be extremely helpful to the President and the Congress.

I would urge that the President send no message and take no stand on this matter until the hearings are completed.

[signed] FORRESTAL

Secretary Forrestal's efforts were in vain, as the President's message went to Congress the next day. Mr. Forrestal then released a message to the Naval establishment:

In view of the President's message to Congress urging the passage of legislation for a Department of National Defense, officers of the Navy and Marine Corps are expected to refrain from opposition thereto in their public utterances in connection therewith, except when called as witnesses before committees of Congress [where] they will of course give frankly and freely their views and will respond to any questions asked.

Naval Officers may continue to advocate at all times the importance of the Navy as one of the major components of the National Defense and the great importance of seapower to the National Security and welfare . . .

These were bleak days in the Navy Department and in ships and stations worldwide. The President's message seemed so final that pessimism was the order of the day. But, under the leadership of Mr. Forrestal, those of us engaged in selling the Navy's plan for a new unified defense organization rallied and decided that perhaps the President's action would prove to be an aid to us.

Amid the gloom on the unification front, I had a pleasant surprise. On 18 December my temporary duty orders under Secretary Forrestal were canceled and I was ordered to relieve Vice Admiral Mitscher as the Deputy Chief of

Naval Operations for Air—a great promotion, carrying with it the rank of Vice Admiral. I could hardly believe that at age 49 I was to obtain this rank and all the responsibility that went with it. By agreement with Mr. Forrestal I would continue as head of SCOROR. I had misgivings about handling both of these jobs but decided that with the excellent help I would have in both offices I could give it a try.

As 1945 ended, unification was by no means the most important problem faced by the United States. Unification had been catapulted into prominent public position by the precipitate action of the President in his message to Congress. Advised by cabinet members other than Mr. Forrestal that such action would undoubtedly generate a bitter fight that he (the President) might lose, Mr. Truman persisted in his effort to reach a quick solution. He was backed in this effort by the Secretary of War and by the Army hierarchy, including General Eisenhower. Army and Air Force both thought this was the time to push for what they wanted, that the Navy was on the ropes and needed only the final knockout to end the battle.

I believe that ranking unification high in the list of problems that our leaders had to study and attempt to solve in those immediate postwar days was one of the gravest mistakes ever made by a president.

From September through December 1945 our leaders were faced with increasingly difficult problems connected with (1) the rapid demobilization of our armed forces, (2) the atomic bomb and its future, (3) how to get along with the Russians, who were obviously not demobilizing and who were showing unmistakable signs of taking advantage of our weakened military posture, (4) how to placate the great majority of American citizens by a rapid return to what they considered a "normal" peacetime existence with much lower taxes, (5) what to do about Europe, (6) what to do about China and the Far East, and (7) what to do about the Middle East. Reading the headlines in fall 1969 it is easy to recall the international situation at the end of 1945, with perhaps one great exception: in 1945 we did not have the wave of disloyalty of 1969. At both times the country suffered from the unconscionable actions of members of the Congress, both Senate and House, who placed their political future before the good of the country although, in almost every case, they knew better.

In 1945–1947 the country made many mistakes—errors of omission more than commission, perhaps—but was saved by the efforts of great leaders in Congress, by the courage and forthrightness of the President in times of real crisis, and by the understanding support rendered by that majority of intelligent American citizens.

A precise forecast of what was in store for the nation was made by Assistant Secretary of War John McCloy, who returned to Washington on 5 November 1945 from a round-the-world trip. According to Mr. McCloy, these were impressions one received throughout the world:

The postwar problems are global; that is, the conditions of anarchy, unrest, mal-
nutrition, unemployment, etc., which exist in Europe and the Middle East are
duplicated throughout Asia and Southeast Asia—the economic dislocations are
profound and far reaching.

The tremendous position and prestige enjoyed by the United States is the one
beacon of hope everywhere, but the dependence upon us to be the salvation for all
the ills of the world may not be an unmixed blessing; the disappointment, frustration and bitterness of the end of next winter may be in exact proportion to the
confidence expressed in us now.

[There is a] universal fear of the Russian Colossus, both in terms of the size of
that country and the locust-like effects of their occupation wherever they may be
. . .[7]

As I recollect those three years and my many contacts with Mr. Forrestal, I
realize now how much more he could have contributed to the resolution of overall problems had he not been so enmeshed in the unification issue. As it was, he
saw more clearly than most the dangers our country faced in the postwar period.
He was particularly concerned with the aims and ambitions of the USSR with
respect to the free world. His fears were well grounded; had his advice been
heeded, the late forties and the fifties would have been much more peaceful. The
Korean War might not have taken place.

8

The Hardliners on Unification

I t is difficult for me to place a priority on my efforts after becoming DCNO (Air) in January 1946. I was still head of SCOROR and responsible for the Navy's efforts to convince the Congress that there were better ways to restructure the postwar military establishment than those proposed in the so-called Army plan and by President Truman.

As DCNO (Air) I was plunged into demobilization problems that were numerous and serious in the aviation branch of the Navy. I was responsible for planning postwar naval aviation and working into those plans the technical advances that were bringing about such great improvements in performance of our combat aircraft. We had many combat aircraft that were almost new and perfectly flyable, but they were already relegated to the reserve by gas turbines and pure jets. The computer was also to have a great effect on our new material. We could perform our engineering computations much faster and more accurately and we could look forward to tremendous advances in the automation of controls for both aircraft and their weapons systems. In the field of aircraft performance we could forecast major changes for the near future that automatically outmoded nearly everything we had developed for World War II. These new, faster, and heavier aircraft must operate from our carriers, which had to be correspondingly modernized at considerable expense. The new horizons in military effectiveness must be "sold" to a Congress and a public who were tired of war and had been told that our enemies were soundly defeated and that the new United Nations organization would prevent future wars. It was no easy task.

Fortunately for the Navy we had Mr. Forrestal, who had no illusions about the international situation and realized that only a strong United States would guarantee postwar peace for any length of time. President Truman had articulated a simplistic formula for the size of the total peacetime military budget, to which he frequently referred. Annual service on the national debt required $6 billion. The armed services could have one-third of what was left of the national income after that charge had been made. He was for a balanced budget.

In dividing my time among my several duties I simply did the best I could, though unification took the larger share of my time for at least the first six months of 1946. Shortly after the President had delivered his unification message to Congress in December 1945, the Senate Military Affairs Committee assigned a subcommittee to draft a new bill that would take into account the President's recommendations. Senator Elbert Thomas, the committee chairman, asked Secretary of the Army Robert Patterson and Secretary Forrestal to furnish him with liaison officers to sit with the subcommittee and advise them on the details of military matters. The Army nominated Lt. Gen. Lauris Norstad of the Air Corps; Mr. Forrestal nominated me. He helped me by informing Senator Thomas that I was being placed in a rather difficult position, and by approving a statement that I read to the committee when I reported on 10 January.

> ... I cannot say I am glad to have this assignment. My personal feelings on the matter of reorganization of the armed services are approximately those of the Navy Department as expressed in Secretary Forrestal's press release of November 28, 1945, but I feel further that this whole matter has become unnecessarily complicated in the eyes of the public. The Army and Navy can and should get together on this matter of national security. The details can and should be worked out on a basis of give and take. The public is entitled to a thorough and exhaustive study of this matter with partisan feelings submerged for the common good.
>
> Real unification, as the President so aptly said, will take years. My interest and that of the naval services is to see such unification started with joint education now.
>
> The pressing need of the moment is not for detailed legislation. What both services need is a breathing spell to put their own houses in order and at the same time permit their two great leaders, General Eisenhower and Admiral Nimitz, to get together and with assistance of a legislative committee prepare legislation for strengthening the national defense.

My association with the subcommittee was just about what I expected. I sat through hours of deliberation with little or no opportunity to make constructive suggestions because the committee's collective mind was made up. They were endeavoring to draft a bill that would include the President's recommendations as well as much of the so-called Army plan, which they had adopted in previous drafts. Senator Thomas could not have been more thoughtful and polite, but it was obvious that I was present only so it could be said that a naval officer had taken part in drafting the new bill.

Senator Thomas was optimistic in his initial estimates of the date on which the redrafted bill would be presented to the full committee and to the President, mentioning the end of January. Actually, the hearings dragged on, there was much speculation in the press, and the delay heated up the controversy between the services, whose propaganda battle was carried on through their friends in Congress. It was plain to me that the Navy's public image was being hurt. The majority of our citizens had a simplistic view of the problem, believing that the President and the Army wanted a new and unified organization for the armed services that would save money and manpower and above all would insure that air power attained its rightful place. The new Air Force would be an independent service. Pretty heady stuff, to be sure, and the Navy's real position became obscured in the public clamor for action.

The Thomas subcommittee finally produced a draft bill, which they presented to the full committee and the President early in April. I had kept Mr. Forrestal advised of the committee's progress. He did not like their new draft much better than the one they had submitted in December, before the President's message, and neither did I.

Through some parliamentary maneuvering, which surprised me at the time, Sen. David Walsh, chairman of the Senate Naval Affairs Committee, secured permission to hold hearings on the Thomas Unification Bill. Secretary Forrestal testified on 1 May, giving a dignified and carefully reasoned outline of his personal position, similar to that expressed many times before.[1]

The Walsh hearings fanned the flames of controversy to such an extent that President Truman stepped in again. At a news conference the day after Mr. Forrestal's testimony, with all present expecting him to be critical of the Secretary's testimony, the President—a little testily according to reporters—said that Mr. Forrestal had had a perfect right to say what he did and that he, the President, had authorized him to say it.

Obviously the President was concerned by this latest outburst, which showed plainly that feelings in the services were running high and had to be controlled. On 13 May he called a conference of Secretaries Patterson and Forrestal and their top military assistants for Army, Navy, and Air Corps. The President was frank. He said he wanted the services to get together in a serious attempt to settle their differences on details of a new unified organization. He realized he could not order them to agree but he wanted them to try, to list their points of agreement and disagreement and submit the list to him. He indicated that after reviewing the matter he would make his own decision on the points of disagreement, embodying it in a directive that he would expect all services to observe.[2]

To the Navy the President's remarks indicated a great change in his ideas, in contrast to those expressed in his December message to Congress, but we had to remember that these were only remarks and that written answers to specific questions remained to be thrashed out.

Secretaries Patterson and Forrestal lost no time in getting to work on their report. In contrast to their previous attempts to resolve the problems of unification, they now found a large measure of agreement. The Navy's efforts to sell the Eberstadt plan had borne fruit. The Army would now buy a "council of common defense," a national security resources board, a central intelligence agency, a military munitions board. They had definite reservations on a central research and development agency but accepted continuance of the present joint chiefs of staff arrangement. They also agreed to three autonomous departments, army, navy, and air. One major point of disagreement remained: the powers to be given to the single overall secretary of defense. The Army favored full powers, while Mr. Forrestal and Admiral Nimitz favored limitations, particularly in the field of administration.[3]

As is often the case in such discussions the first flush of agreement proved somewhat elusive as the deadline approached. In their report to President Truman on 31 May the Secretaries, while noting a considerable measure of agreement, were forced to identify basic disagreements on organizational form. The Army insisted on a strongly centralized department of defense under a powerful secretary, with army, navy, and air reduced to three coordinate "branches" of subordinate status.

The Navy, on the other hand, favored unification in less drastic form. While it would have preferred to see the Army integrate its air component with its ground forces as the Navy had done, it realized that was the Army's problem and it would assent to a separate department of air provided the status of the naval air forces was assured. The Navy also wanted department status for its organization, with cabinet rank for its secretary.

The Army's statement of responsibilities for the new air force indicated basic disagreement with the Navy. They proposed to concentrate in the air force total responsibility for the military air resources of the nation, excepting only ship- and water-borne aircraft and certain minor service aircraft that would be left to the Navy.[4] Finally, the Army would limit severely the functions of the Marine Corps in amphibious warfare.[5]

At a meeting with the President the two Secretaries, accompanied by General Eisenhower and Admiral Nimitz, presented their reports. Mr. Forrestal wrote that after the Army presentation both Patterson and Eisenhower "went to great pains" to emphasize that no matter what decision the President made they would loyally support it. He felt that Patterson's remarks emphasized the feeling that the President was still pretty much on their side;[6] and he felt, and all of us close to him on this subject agreed, that Patterson's statements had been designed to put him, Forrestal, on the spot with the President. For Secretary Forrestal's own part, he stated simply that whatever the President's decision, the Navy would abide by it.

Mr. Forrestal's diary of this meeting contains a later, additional entry explaining his position in greater detail. His aim, he said, was

(1) to try to keep the Navy intact as a Service as distinct from a merely subordinate branch of a vast Department; (2) to obtain the improvements in our national defense organization that the war indicated should be made *but without sacrificing the autonomy of the Navy*; (3) to discharge my responsibilities to the President as a member of his Cabinet, which means that I must go as far as I can in accepting and promulgating his views, always having the alternative, when I can no longer do so honestly, of resigning . . .[7]

There was an official hiatus in the unification argument while the services waited for President Truman to complete his study of the Secretaries' report and prepare his directive. Again, in my opinion, President Truman had placed himself in an anomalous position, just as he had in December. As Commander-in-Chief he could issue orders to the services, orders which they would have to obey; but in the case of service reorganization the president was not the court of last resort. President Truman could come to firm conclusions on details of the new military organization, but Congress alone had the power to draft the legislation for presentation to him. In the course of renewed congressional hearings that were bound to follow the presidential decisions of June 1946, Secretary Forrestal and high civilian officials would undoubtedly testify as they had before, and so would prominent naval officers. The many friends of the Navy in Congress certainly had the power to block or at least delay final action on a bill that was unacceptable to them.

It seemed to me that President Truman was actually playing into the Navy's hands. I saw him quite frequently, usually in company with Mr. Forrestal. He knew the assignment I had been given by the Secretary and he had at times in my presence jokingly referred to me as the chief culprit in blocking his plans for unification. I was somewhat surprised, therefore, by a story told me by a newspaper man who called on me one day. He introduced himself as a reporter for one of the Kansas City papers who was friendly with the President and who was frequently invited to join a select White House group for a bourbon and branch water at the end of a hard day. He said that on several occasions recently President Truman had expressed himself forcibly on my activities in connection with unification. The newsman said that these outbursts at first did not strike him as serious, but having heard them several times he decided he should at least tell me about them. He said they might mean nothing, or they might be serious as far as my future was concerned. I thanked the young man for his concern, saying there was little I could do under the circumstances but that I did feel that President Truman, inclined as he was to "pop off," was basically fair in his final judgments.

President Truman announced that he would make public on 15 June his decisions on the points of disagreement in the Secretaries' reports. I remember that day, a Saturday, as if it were yesterday. I kept in touch with Mr. Forrestal's office, ready to report there immediately when the President's letter arrived. About noon, with no word from the White House, Mr. Forrestal decided to relax on the golf links at Chevy Chase, leaving word that he was to be notified immediately the President's letter was received. After lunch I joined a group in Mr. Forrestal's office, waiting there for the blow to fall, for we were quite sure that the President's decisions would go largely against the Navy. It was almost 5:00 when we received word from the White House that the President's letter was on its way.

Almost simultaneously the White House released all the correspondence: the two Secretaries' reports, the President's long reply, and letters to the chairmen of the military and naval affairs committees of the Senate and House laying down a 12-point design on which he believed unification should be established. As Mr. Forrestal had anticipated, the President's decision on the points of difference represented a substantial defeat for the Navy's position.

In his memoirs President Truman says,

> In this decision I supported the War Department view that a single Department of National Defense was necessary to effective unification. I also supported the War Department's opinion that a separate Air Force should be established, and that the Air Force should take over all land based aviation, including naval reconnaissance, anti-submarine patrol and protection of shipping. It seemed to me that no one could give a valid reason for continuing the expensive duplication of land based air services then existing.

> I took the Navy's view that the function of the Marine Corps should continue undisturbed. I felt that if a Marine Corps were necessary, efforts to draw a hard and fast line as to the extent of land fighting would be futile. I saw much justification in the Navy's position that the Marine Corps should be permitted to do those things essential to the success of a particular naval campaign.[8]

The President also approved the establishment of a council of common defense, a national security resources board, a central intelligence agency, a procurement and supply agency, a research agency, a military and training agency, and the statutory establishment of joint chiefs of staff. He urged passage of legislation toward unification of the services at the earliest practicable date.

Our little group in Mr. Forrestal's office was gloomy indeed. The only consolation I had as I read the President's letter was to recall Mr. Vinson's repeated statements to the effect that Congress would not accept the President's decisions in these matters.

Word had been sent to Mr. Forrestal that the President's letter had been received, but it took some time for him to get back to his office, or at least it seemed so to me. Before he returned we heard that Secretary Patterson had already released a copy of his brief reply to the President's letter saying that he heartily supported his decisions and would be glad to do everything he could to expedite action in regard to legislation. This information came to us from newsmen calling to find out what Mr. Forrestal had done, so we knew that the Secretary was already on the spot.

It was nearly 6:00 when Mr. Forrestal returned, full of vim and vigor. Golf always seemed to buck him up. He sat down and read all of the correspondence very deliberately. Then he looked at me and said, "Raddy, I want you to draft a reply to the President's letter, for my signature." I said, "Mr. Secretary, the only reply I can think of would be your resignation." He thought a moment, then said, "I don't think I can let the Navy down that way." Still in a gloomy mood, I said, "Mr. Secretary, in my opinion you would let the Navy down if you did not submit your resignation." He made no direct reply then, switching the conversation. Later he asked V. Adm. "Duke" (De Witt C.) Ramsey (Vice Chief of Naval Operations—VCNO) to draft a reply.

In the next few days I recovered from the depression into which the President's letter had plunged me. There was certainly much good as well as bad in it, and those of us working on the unification issue could plainly see that we had changed the President's mind on several important points.

Newsmen continued to hound the Navy Department for a copy of Mr. Forrestal's reply to the President. Not until his diaries were published did I read his account of what must have been his first meeting or conversation with President Truman after 15 June.[9]

As he presented his case to the President, Mr. Forrestal outlined clearly his personal position. In his book I do not believe he represents President Truman's real feelings on some of the controversial issues, although the President quite likely replied as Mr. Forrestal reports. In my opinion, President Truman had high regard for Mr. Forrestal. Speaking on a subject he felt was important, the Secretary usually spoke rapidly and forcefully. I have been with him when he has made such a presentation to Mr. Truman and have heard the President indicate approval of a course of action that was obviously a change of position— but which we later have found was not as explicit a change as we had thought. The President could really be fascinated as he listened to Mr. Forrestal, so fascinated that he said things he did not mean.

Admiral Ramsey drafted a letter to the President for Mr. Forrestal's signature; it was shown to me and I was astounded. I of course had not read the record of Mr. Forrestal's talk with the President, and without that understanding the draft hardly made sense. I talked with Admiral Sherman by phone. He had seen the draft and felt as I did, that it was completely unsatisfactory.

I had lunch with Mr. Forrestal and we discussed the draft. I urged him not to send it. He said he would do nothing until he talked with Admiral Nimitz, who was away until 23 June.

There was much pulling and hauling in Secretary Forrestal's office. The draft letter was modified several times. He received conflicting advice from his staff, but most agreed that a written answer to the President was necessary.

On 24 June Mr. Forrestal signed the final draft of the letter and sent it to the White House. I did not see it but was told about the changes by the Secretary's office. I said that if the letter had to go I approved it very reluctantly.

The White House released Mr. Forrestal's letter two days later. Immediately I was deluged with calls from the press. Jack Steele of the *New York Herald Tribune*, for example, wanted to know what the Secretary meant by the statement that "he was glad to note that the Navy had a part in the development, research and procurement of land planes." He felt that might have been part of Mr. Forrestal's conversation with the President on 19 June. He asked if I understood that the Navy would handle design, procurement, and so on. I told him, "No—unless that was an understanding made between the President and Mr. Forrestal in their conversation." We agreed that the President might intentionally or otherwise misinterpret or forget that conversation, as he had so many others in the past.

Lloyd Norman of the *Chicago Tribune* phoned with similar requests for clarification on the reference to the statement that the Navy was to have a "continuing part in the future development of land planes for reconnaissance, anti-submarine warfare and protection of shipping." He said he did not want to quote me but wanted to find out where the Secretary got the basis for that interpretation. I told him I did not know but guessed it came from the President.

There was quite a flap over Secretary Forrestal's letter, but he had left Washington for the Bikini atom bomb tests and a trip around the world that kept him away for about a month.

The Senate Naval Affairs Committee held some hearings on the Thomas bill early in July, but with adjournment coming on unification, in spite of the President's wishes, was put aside for that session.

☆ ☆ ☆ ☆

Though the first nine months of 1946 were devoted mainly to demobilization problems, postwar planning, particularly in the area of new aircraft and helicopters, had an important place also. In April 1946 I had my first flight in a Sikorsky helicopter, at Washington National Airport. I was impressed with its performance and felt that for naval and marine use it would become important.

On 1 July there were still 30,033 aviation officers in the Navy, of whom 25,195 were reserves and 76,854 enlisted aviation ratings. A year later these numbers had been reduced to 12,679 officers, of whom 2,435 were regular navy enlisted men and warrant officers with temporary commissions, 3,029 were reserve officers tentatively retained for the fiscal year or on contract, and 87 were Waves. The number of enlisted aviation ratings declined to 37,862.

The organization under DCNO (Air) was placed on a more efficient peace-time basis in September. Although many details of demobilization remained, this change ended the period in which principal emphasis was on reducing the wartime aviation establishment. Thereafter, the greater effort was placed on the development of a permanent aeronautic organization and on the preparation of plans for future emergencies.

Among the rapid technical developments of the time, none was more important than the guided missile, offensive and defensive. When the post of DCNO (Special Weapons) was disestablished in November, the guided missile section of that division was transferred to DCNO (Air).

Guided missiles could not be classified solely as aircraft or ordnance but embodied features of both. Of interest to both the Army and the Navy, they called for close collaboration between the services. A review of existing development programs indicated that neither service could support all that had originally been planned and that there were similar programs in the plans of both. The requirements of the service with lesser experience or interest were included in the program of the other, thus reducing the total number of projects and effecting savings in personnel and money. Interservice cooperation in this field was very good.

My office diary for 2 July shows that even then the Navy had an interest in "space." DCNO (Air) was also very interested in the so-called CVBX, a new carrier design started by Admiral Mitscher about the end of the war. The new ship would be much larger than any carrier in service. It was to have a completely flush flight deck (no island structure for smoke stacks or navigating bridge). The Navy was anticipating difficulty in the operation of large land planes for anti-submarine work and reconnaissance. The flush deck would permit large planes of these types to operate from carriers. The Army Air Corps had become aware of the Navy's CVBX studies and were concerned about them. They realized that if we could in fact successfully build a large flush deck carrier it could operate heavy land planes of at least B29 size. This capability would permit the Navy to challenge the Strategic Air Force and, as can be imagined, they were not about to help us with our new carrier plans.

The atomic bomb tests were held in July. They went well and furnished the Army and Navy with much important information. My personal conclusion, after studying reports of the tests regarding damage to naval vessels, was that naval aviation must redouble its efforts to insure interception of atomic weapons carriers far from the fleets or task groups. This problem, incidentally, might well be less difficult than similar protection for shore bases. In the years that followed, the Navy was very successful in efforts along both lines.

Secretary Forrestal returned from Bikini having covered an incredible itinerary in a short time, and those traveling with him were exhausted. The Secretary had remarkable recuperative powers: an evening at home and he was "back to battery." His diary entries covering the trip reveal his intense concern with communist expansionist policies everywhere he visited, the Far East, the Middle East, and Europe.[10] After his return he referred constantly to American failure to coordinate military policies with foreign policy objectives. The latter, he felt, were nebulous in many instances due to the reluctance of the State Department to make hard decisions. He also expressed great concern about the caliber of our Foreign Service representation abroad and the necessity of encouraging our best young men to enter that field.

Mr. Forrestal was certainly a realist. With his keen and perceptive mind he could cut through to the heart of a matter. I thought then, and still think, that as Secretary of State he could and would have persuaded the President to adopt policies that would have changed the course of postwar history. Instead of our fumbling efforts in 1945–1947, which gave the Russians a tremendous head start, as a nation we could have led the way to postwar stability instead of to the frustrations encouraged by our lack of policies. Mr. Forrestal again began to press for more use of the Navy in the Far East and Mediterranean areas. Displays of naval strength, he felt, would help prevent further deterioration of our national image in those important regions. He was pressing for increased strength in the Seventh (Far East) Fleet and trying to get authority to establish a permanent naval force in the Mediterranean (ultimately the Sixth Fleet).

In spite of a troubled world situation, which required firm positions on the part of the United States, our military posture in the summer of 1946 continued to deteriorate. The Navy, already struggling with reduced budget estimates for fiscal 1948, was suddenly called upon to reduce current expenditures by some $700 million. The Army faced similar reductions. At almost the same time the Joint Chiefs of Staff (JCS) were meeting with the British to examine the availability of military forces in case of trouble with the Russians regarding their demands on the Turks concerning use of the Dardanelles!

During summer 1946 the unification problem was on the back burner. That autumn, in several meetings with the President and at least one or two with Secretary Patterson, Secretary Forrestal went on the offensive. It seemed to all of us on the Navy side that the Army was happy to let unification matters simmer until the next session of Congress in January. We felt this did not entirely satisfy the Army Air Corps, though we could not be certain. Mr. Forrestal felt that action on his part might stimulate things to the point where the Navy and the Air Corps could force the Army to negotiate instead of waiting for the President to force his ideas upon Congress.

I believe Secretary Forrestal accomplished a great deal toward unification in late 1946. He made the President feel that he was taking the lead in trying to reach an agreement on those points in dispute. At some of the larger meetings in the White House he made Secretary Patterson appear to be delaying the whole business. Throughout these conversations the Navy's desire for an overall "secretary of common defense" with limited powers was emphasized.

President Truman told a group including both Secretaries, General Eisenhower, Admirals Nimitz and William Leahy, and Clark Clifford that he proposed to have Leahy and Clifford draft a bill "that would become the doctrine of the administration," and that after it had been mulled over by all interested parties he would expect support for it in Congress. Mr. Forrestal replied that he could not support a bill before Congress violating principles that he honestly believed were essential. Rather than agree to that he would ask the President to accept his resignation. The President said in response to this statement that "he expected no such necessity need arise."[11]

Mr. Forrestal's clear exposition of his position and the President's reply took the wind out of the Army's sails. Both Patterson and Eisenhower joined in recommending their previous position: merge now and let the details be worked out later. Why, they said, should the Navy fear that any such subsequent actions would impair their ability to perform their missions? Secretary Forrestal's reply was blunt: the Navy *did* have deep apprehensions, with good reason he thought, in regard to the Marines and certain aspects of naval aviation.

This September meeting was a milestone in the unification talks, which had been going on for over a year. It set the stage for formal and informal negotiations that fall, mostly between Mr. Forrestal and Mr. Symington and involving the differences between naval aviation and the Air Corps.

At a meeting in Admiral Nimitz' office on 15 October with all DCNOs present, my chief assistant in SCOROR presented the latest developments. He recorded several conversations, including one of mine with Mr. Forrestal about an attempt by the Air Corps to have the Bureau of the Budget remove funds for operation and procurement of naval land planes to be used in anti-submarine work. BUAERO and many of my own subordinates were quite exercised about this rather backhanded move. Navy Budget Officer Bill McNeil, an old friend, felt strongly that the Secretary would have to personally get into the picture. When I spoke to the Secretary he admitted he was stalling on the matter but intimated that he had some other irons in the fire. I did not push further, feeling that things would turn out all right. And they did. Secretary Forrestal always had several ways to skin a cat—or the Air Corps.

On Thursday 7 November I was told that Mr. Forrestal was having Norstad and Secretary of the Air Force Stuart Symington for luncheon at his home and that he wanted Sherman and me to join them later for coffee and discussion. The idea of the luncheon had sprung from a conversation he had had with Symington during golf the previous Saturday. It appeared to him that Symington and the Army Air Corps were somewhat unhappy with Patterson and his unwillingness to negotiate. Mr. Forrestal wanted to exploit that unrest. At the afternoon meeting he wanted to discuss the Navy's use of land-based aircraft. I told him it was not my idea, or the Navy's, to exclude the Army Air Corps from anti-submarine operations. We wanted to be the experts, developing tactics and equipment. We wanted to be able to train them to assist us, when they could. We pointed out to them that when they assisted us we must control their squadrons. The Navy felt it was completely impracticable to use a plane on one day for anti-submarine warfare and on the next for strategic bombing.

The meeting turned out to be friendly. I think the discussion, carefully guided by Mr. Forrestal, brought out facets of the land-plane problems of the Navy that had never been fully appreciated by the Army Air Corps. Sherman and I thoroughly expanded on the subject. The meeting adjourned about 4:00, after a suggestion by Secretary Forrestal that Norstad and I draft a paper on the land-based plane problem of the Navy, trying if we could to reach agreement. I suggested that Admiral Sherman work with Norstad. It was agreed and worked out well. From then until a basic document was submitted to the President by Patterson and Forrestal, Sherman and Norstad worked together and deserve the major credit for removing the impasse between the services.[12]

I give prominence to this meeting because in my opinion it was the most important one of that fall. As a result of it a statement was drafted of the agreed principles that could be used as a basis for legislation about to be drafted by Clark Clifford. In the matters of Marine and naval aviation missions, which it was assumed would not have to be included in legislation, the agreement would be submitted for presidential approval.

From the meeting Mr. Forrestal seemed to grasp the significance of the Navy's position on the Marines and the problems of naval aviation. Before then in discussions with him I had often felt that he could not quite understand our insistence on these points. Seemingly he wanted us to "give a little" to help him out. But from that time on he was firm in his negotiations in these areas.

Again on 4 December Mr. Forrestal had a luncheon for Symington, Norstad, Sherman, and myself. As is often the case in important negotiations this meeting seemed a great setback. Norstad and I had some sharp exchanges, and it became apparent that he was not getting his Air Corps conferees to reduce their opposition to the Navy's use of land planes. Symington, too, had had his back stiffened. The meeting broke up, almost on a discordant note, and I was sure that Mr. Forrestal was deeply disappointed.

Admiral Mitscher had been in Washington on a flag officers selection board (of which I was also a member) for several weeks prior to this time and of course was kept au courant on our meetings. On the day following the setback, Secretary Forrestal had Admiral Mitscher to his office for a farewell luncheon. Admirals Denfeld and Sherman were present. Questioning Mitscher about the difficulties of naval aviation vis-à-vis the Army Air Corps the Secretary heard, more forcibly, the views I had expressed the day before. Mitscher also brought up the fact that the Air Corps was trying to persuade some of our best young officers to join them. One of our lieutenant commanders with a fine war record was trying to arrange a transfer to the Air Force, where he had been promised a promotion to lieutenant colonel.

The same day, Mr. Forrestal spoke to R. Adm. C. R. Brown, Navy representative at the Air University, Maxwell Field, Alabama. I heard Admiral Brown tell the Secretary that, at the University, officers openly proclaimed their ultimate objective (for the new air force) to be complete domination of all military air activities in the United States. It was important to me to have the Secretary hear this corroborative testimony from other senior naval air officers at frequent intervals. Without it he was inclined, very naturally, to feel that I was an obstructionist.

December was a critical time in the unification struggle. I am sure that the chief negotiators, Admiral Sherman and General Norstad, received a great deal of advice. Senior officers on both sides who had taken undeviating positions on the question began to be disturbed at the growing evidence of bitterness between the services. About this time Admiral Towers, CINCPAC, visited Washington and told me that we should stick to the two-department setup and have *nothing* to do with a separate Air Force. Admiral Mitscher recommended no equivocation whatever. I tried to remain flexible but found it difficult at times, being so close to the realities of the political situation in Washington.

Reading the Forrestal *Diaries*, I was impressed with the entry for 3 January 1947 in which Mr. Forrestal recounts that Secretary Patterson rode with him from a cabinet meeting to the Navy Department. Mr. Patterson said "he was much disturbed in the growing evidence of bitterness between the Services," and that if "Army and Navy officers went down to testify in a mood of bitterness and hatred, they would do serious damage to the Services and the national defense." Mr. Forrestal replied that he was simply stating what he had stated all along, that unless the two services were honestly and thoroughly behind a plan for integration and coordination it would not be successful.[13]

This reversal of Patterson's earlier "take it or leave it" attitude was revealing. It is positive proof of the success of Mr. Forrestal's tremendous efforts during fall 1945 and all of 1946 to clarify the unification matter. There is no doubt in my mind that had the War Department been successful in its earliest efforts, with President Truman's wholehearted backing, to sell the Collins Plan or something similar to the Congress, our country would have been in real trouble.[14]

The progress that Sherman and Norstad seemed to be making in settling some of the most important differences, Patterson's shift to a more flexible position, and, most important, the convening of the new Congress all tended to make Mr. Forrestal push harder for a unification agreement. On 16 January he announced at a conference in his office that Symington, Sherman, and Norstad had agreed on the draft of a letter (to be signed by Patterson and himself) reconciling Army and Navy views on unification. The letter was addressed to the President and was in effect a sequel to the joint letter to him of 3 May reporting disagreement on four important points. They were now agreed on all aspects of the proposed legislation and were recommending (1) a single secretary of defense with coordinating powers, (2) a national security council, (3) a smaller war council, (4) a national security resources board, (5) a central intelligence agency, and (6) a command structure headed by the JCS. This was practically the organization that Mr. Forrestal had been recommending. It was agreed that roles and missions assigned to the three proposed services should not be included in the basic law but should be covered by an executive order, and a second letter to the President contained an agreed draft of such an order. The wording of the second letter was less exact, although in general it represented an acceptance of the Navy's position in the disputed areas. The Navy was given primary responsibility for anti-submarine patrols and overwater reconnaissance by patrol planes, with the further understanding that it could determine what types of aircraft should be used. The Marines were accorded primary responsibility for the development of the tactics and equipment for amphibious warfare.

Senior naval officers on the whole accepted the Secretary's efforts, as did I. I felt that the three-department organization would be difficult to administer and probably more expensive in the long run, but I had been so closely associated with the unification negotiations for over a year that I realized full well that the Navy had no alternative.

There was another fact to face. Agreement by the two Secretaries and the President did not end the matter; Congress still had to initiate and pass the legislation, and opposition from the services could be generated through friends in Congress. Mr. Forrestal realized all this and said as much in his remarks to the audience in his office on that important occasion.

President Truman was gratified to hear of the agreement between the Secretaries and to receive their letters. The next day he issued a public statement and an executive order setting forth in full the responsibilities of each branch of the service (roles and missions). He informed Congress that a unification bill was being drafted for its consideration.

The President transmitted his draft of the bill to Congress, and it was passed on 25 July 1947 in substantially the recommended form. It was not as strong as the original proposal, since it included concessions on both sides for the sake of better understanding. I doubt that it or any similar legislation could have been passed that year had it not been for Mr. Forrestal. His unceasing efforts were almost entirely responsible for the agreements that made the new unified military organization possible.

9

Forrestal and the Fight for Naval Air

Admiral Mitscher died of a heart attack on 3 February 1947, leaving vacant the post of Commander-in-Chief Atlantic. Since it was important that such a vacancy be filled, the changes in commands were announced quickly. Admiral Blandy, Commander Second Fleet became Commander-in-Chief Atlantic. I relieved him, and Admiral Duncan, Chief of Staff for Admiral Towers, relieved me.

I was surprised but delighted to get these orders. They meant leaving Washington just as the battle over unification moved into Congress, but I could not help but feel that both personally and officially this was for the best. I suspected that Secretary Forrestal had acquiesced in my detachment because he felt I had been too much of a "hard-liner" on unification details.

For over five years, since 1 December 1941, I had been working at top speed with practically no letup, and this would be a wonderful change. The postwar year and a half in Washington had been far more strenuous in many ways than my wartime service there, when everyone was trying to get things done and cooperation was the order of the day. Postwar duty was almost the exact opposite. Delay or direct opposition was common and made for great frustrations. Add to those the problems of the unification fight, and I believed I was entitled to the rest I envisaged in my seagoing assignment.

As it turned out, my command of the Second Task Fleet at Norfolk, Virginia was not a long one but it was a most welcome and interesting interlude. I had time to think, read, relax and wonder of wonders, play a little golf for the first time in years.

I divide my interests in the ten months of this job into three categories. First, and still very important, was my concern for the final details of the unification legislation. Second, almost immediately after relieving Admiral Blandy I became painfully aware that the postwar Navy afloat had deteriorated a great deal from its wartime peak of efficiency. My principal effort from then on was to determine the extent of that deterioration and what could be done to remedy it.

Last, and in some ways most important, was the opportunity this assignment gave me to become personally acquainted with the helicopter. As DCNO (Air), I had not been too successful in selling helicopters to the high command, particularly Admiral Nimitz and Gen. Alexander A. Vandegrift. The former had refused to approve a suggestion I made to him that seaplanes be removed from battleships and cruisers and replaced by helicopters. I sensed that he felt I was really trying to get aviation out of these ships. In General Vandegrift's case, he was too busy worrying about keeping a Marine Corps to be interested, and I could not blame him.

Since my first helicopter flight I had been pushing for their further development. How much we would have appreciated helicopters in the carriers during the war! I persuaded the Sikorsky Company to assign one, with pilot, to cruise to Trinidad in spring 1947 on a carrier as a demonstration. Now, as the new fleet commander, I had the privilege of pushing such demonstrations, which soon sold the helicopter to the fleet—first as a rapid pilot recovery vehicle after plane crashes, and second as a convenience for personnel and mail transfers between ships at sea. Its usefulness in anti-submarine work was demonstrated later.

The fleet remained anchored for a few days off Trinidad. The new Assistant Secretary of the Navy for Air, John Brown, traveled there for an indoctrination cruise on *Franklin D. Roosevelt*, one of the new *Midway*-class carriers that had joined the fleet after the war. This class was considerably different from the wartime *Essex* class. They were much heavier, with armored flight decks and as a consequence less freeboard. I was much interested in observing the performance of *FDR* and comparing her with the two *Essex*-class carriers in the task unit. With the Secretary was Charles McCarthy, of the United Aircraft Corporation. Mr. McCarthy, a longtime friend and a former naval officer, was responsible for assignment of the Sikorsky helicopter to *FDR* and was very interested in the demonstrations it was to make.

The Second Task Fleet, as made up for these tactical exercises, was a sizable organization consisting of an amphibious force, carrier force, surface action and support force, submarine force, land-based air force, and logistic force. In much reduced form it was analogous to an offensive fleet of the late years of World War II in the Pacific. The exercises, the first on such a scale to be held in the postwar Atlantic, had been planned in detail by Admiral Blandy before I relieved him just prior to the last phase, a full-scale amphibious landing on Culebra Island, off Puerto Rico. During late 1945 and most of 1946 the personnel situation in the fleets had precluded such exercises: all ships suffered severe personnel shortages, and many were unable to get under way. It is a matter of historical record, and not one to be proud of, that never before had such a mighty army, navy and air force been so quickly destroyed as were those of the United States in the period August 1945–July 1946.

Our days at sea were busy, with the carriers conducting every imaginable air exercise and the ships shooting at drones and simulating anti-submarine attacks. The amphibious exercises were completed in March, with all the thrills of a wartime operation including actual bombardment by the heavy guns of *Missouri* and the cruisers, and submarine attacks on the surface ships. To those of us fresh from the real thing there were many evident rough spots. To our visitors, who on the last day included Under Secretary of the Navy John Sullivan and several members of the House Naval Affairs Committee, it was a spectacular success.

Saturday morning, 15 March was a busy one. The carrier group with *Missouri*, headed for Norfolk, was subjected to air attacks by shore-based aircraft of the Army Air Corps and the Navy, most from bases in Puerto Rico. The Air Corps units entered into this exercise against carriers with gusto and carried out many attacks almost to the point of disaster. Watching from the bridge of *Missouri*, it all brought back memories of kamikazes that I had watched in real attacks less than two short years before.

Back in Norfolk, I found time to take Mrs. Radford on a ten-minute flight in the Sikorsky helicopter that had made the cruise aboard *FDR*. Mr. McCarthy generously dedicated the helicopter's last afternoon in Norfolk to indoctrinating as many wives as were willing to try a flight. He was smart to do this, and I appreciated his thoughtfulness. Having the wives' approval of anything can be very helpful in the Navy or anywhere else.

As soon as I had an opportunity I called Admiral Duncan, the new DCNO (Air), to find out what was going on in Washington. It was no surprise to hear that (1) unification hearings were going full blast on the Hill and, (2) flight pay boards were meeting. The latter, joint Air Force-Navy boards attempting to establish new regulations concerning flight pay status, represented the one field in which the two services always worked well together. Flight pay, often under attack from various sources, was now the subject of a new bill tossed into the pot by Chairman Vinson of the House Naval Affairs Committee. Mr. Vinson's latest effort would abolish flight pay altogether, but I felt that the old gentleman really had something else in mind. He probably enjoyed hearing the Air Force and the Navy testifying on the same side of the fence.

Also, according to Admiral Duncan, the Appropriations Committee was very active and its chairman had several of his bright young men combing the Navy Department looking for new places to cut back Navy appropriations! Everything was just as I had left it. The more things change, the more they remain the same.

As the unification hearings progressed it became evident that I should testify at some time. Strangely enough, I had never testified in any of the numerous committee sessions from fall 1945 on; my responsibility was to keep Navy witnesses ready to testify as long as the proceedings continued, and I kept myself in reserve.

On 18 June a Captain Waller in DCNO (Air) called to tell me that he had just read a copy of a letter addressed to me by Congressman Clare Hoffman (Michigan), mailed in Washington on 17 April. Mr. Hoffman was now asking why he had not received an answer. I told Waller that I had never received the letter and could not understand why because it was properly addressed. Waller said it referred to hearings that Mr. Hoffman's Committee on Expenditures in Executive Departments was preparing to hold and wanted to know if I would be available to testify.

It would have been relatively easy for me to avoid testifying before the committee, first, because it had no lack of prospective witnesses and second because I was not stationed in Washington and could plead that because of my duties it might be difficult to predict my availability on a particular day. I knew, the more I thought about it, that my testimony would not please Mr. Forrestal, and I sincerely regretted that for I considered him a great friend. On the other hand few officers in the services had been so close to all details of the unification argument as I, thus I felt I owed the Congress my comments and recommendations.

The bill under consideration was House bill number 2319, its short title "The National Security Act of 1947." It was the bill drafted as a result of Mr. Forrestal's efforts in fall 1946 to iron out differences between the two services. It provided for a national defense establishment presided over by a Secretary of National Defense and consisting of three separate departments, Army, Navy and Air Force, as well as all other agencies created within the defense establishment.

The Secretary of Defense was empowered, under the direction of the President, to establish policies and programs for the national defense establishment and the departments and agencies therein. He exercised direction, authority, and control over such departments and agencies. He was directed to *formulate* and *finally determine* the budget estimates of the defense establishment for submittal to the Bureau of the Budget (these estimates were to be submitted to him at such time and in such manner as he might direct); he was to *supervise* and *control* the budget programs of the national defense establishment under the applicable appropriation acts provided; and here were the big kickers—(1) the Departments of the Army, Navy, and Air Force were to be administered as *individual units* under their respective secretaries, and (2) "nothing herein contained shall prevent the Secretary of any such Department from presenting to the President, after first so informing the Secretary of National Defense, any report or recommendation relating to his department which he might deem necessary."

There were, of course, a good many other provisions of importance but those that I have noted were the critical ones. I directed my remarks for the most part to them.

On 26 June I appeared before the committee, speaking from notes. I was on the stand most of the morning and was subjected to detailed questioning by practically every member. Reading these proceedings nearly 23 years later there are certain statements I would change, but on the whole I believe the gist of what I said is my position today. Since then I have served as Chairman of the Joint Chiefs of Staff and have worked closely with a Secretary of Defense.

The duties, responsibilities, and authority of the secretary of national defense outlined above give tremendous power to the secretary. Under the parliamentary system of government as it exists, say, in England, it can work well. In H.R. 2319 these provisions came originally from the Eberstadt Plan and represented Eberstadt's adoption later approved and recommended by Mr. Forrestal, of the British solution. I had originally accepted these ideas as a good answer to our problems; but the more I learned about the ways of Washington and service relationships with congressional committees and individual members of Congress, the less I thought they would do for us. In effect, the bill would still give free rein to the three independent departments in their relations with Congress after the secretary of national defense had made his budgetary decisions. These are still, and certainly were then, the guts of the whole problem of interservice relationships.

The main thrust of my testimony on that day was to convince the committee that we should have not three departments but two. I pointed out that mathematically it was four times harder to coordinate three departments than two.

On the other hand, I was emphatic in my statements regarding the importance of air in our military organization. I said, "I consider that at this time in this period, and this period will extend for some years, the most important part of our whole national security organization is the air organization. All indications of the future point to air as the most important [factor] offensively and defensively, for both services." As to the bill, I said I felt it complicated and proliferated our military organization at a time when there was every reason to simplify it. What I tried to make plain in my testimony was that the Air Force, if not given independent status as a separate service, should have much more power within the Army, just as naval aviation had reached the point in the Navy where naval aviators occupied billets in the command structure that gave them a voice in all policy decisions.

I felt strongly on the subject of a three-department organization and I had this exchange with Congressman John McCormack of Massachusetts following my statement that I thought the bill before them would further separate the services:

MR. MCCORMACK: Admiral . . . on that theory why would it not be better to have one service, following your reasoning?

ADMIRAL RADFORD: Mr. McCormack, I feel that if the immediate alternative was three departments or one, I would prefer one. On the other hand, I feel that we are not ready for one department. I think we have to carry on for another generation and I would be hopeful that we could have, eventually, when this new generation grows up, one service.

Hearings before the committee continued until July, but the chairman was pressured to report his bill to the House. The Senate had already passed its version of the Unification Bill when the House passed H.R. 2319 on 19 July. The conference report was not delayed; Congress approved it, and on 26 July the Unification Bill became law. Concurrently the President signed the nomination of James Forrestal as Secretary of Defense, and the Senate promptly confirmed the nomination. Approval by the President of an executive order, "Functions of the Armed Services," completed the merger package. The new unified military organization was a fact after nearly two years of argument.

☆ ☆ ☆ ☆

I had been planning a trip to Bridgeport, Connecticut, where the Sikorsky plant was located. I wanted to become better acquainted with Mr. Sikorsky and I was anxious to hear his ideas about the future of helicopters. I also hoped to work in some flight instruction. Mrs. Radford and I spent three days in Bridgeport. Mr. Sikorsky, and everyone in the plant, could not have been more hospitable. He assigned his son-in-law and chief pilot, George Von York, as my flight instructor and I flew in the morning each day.

I soon found out what I wanted to know, that it did not take a qualified heavier-than-air pilot long to learn to fly a helicopter. I was more than ever convinced that for the Navy and Marine Corps helicopters would be extremely valuable.

Mr. Sikorsky and I had several long talks. He told me that now in 1947, he considered the helicopter in a stage of evolution comparable to conventional aircraft in 1914. Its future size depended on the development of metal rotor blades and lighter, probably gas turbine, power plants. He said that, given adequate financing, he could undertake then to build a helicopter that could lift a 50,000 pound useful load, but he preferred a more gradual development.

His predictions have all come true. The helicopter can do everything he thought it would do. For the military it is a most valuable adjunct. Many young men are alive today who were seriously wounded on mountaintops in Korea and Vietnam from which they were evacuated to hospitals by helicopter in a few minutes, who would otherwise have died while being carried in stretchers down the mountain paths. Mr. Sikorsky lived to see, and contributed much to great advances in aeronautical science. I do not believe I know a man whom I admire more. With all the honors that have been heaped upon him he is still a quiet, modest man.

A visit to the Navy's submarine base at New London followed. I saw our latest submarines and heard of prospective developments that would make them even more efficient. Aviation and submarines had worked together closely during World War II and that liaison was continuing. I could never forget the splendid, courageous work of our lifeguard submarines in many carrier actions in the western Pacific.

Fall 1947 passed quickly. The unified defense organization was slowly getting started in Washington and I was keeping in close touch with developments. It became apparent early that the newly independent Air Force would aggressively challenge even the maintenance of the Navy's present carrier strength, let alone any plan to build larger, flush deck types.[1] The Army, too, still seemed determined to shrink the Marine Corps down to boy's size—a naval police or guard force—if it remained at all. The future looked grim indeed for the Navy.

Shortly after Mr. Forrestal was sworn in as Secretary of Defense and three new service secretaries (Kenneth Royall, Sullivan, and Symington) were installed, Admiral Nimitz let it be known that he wished to retire when his term as CNO expired in December. President Truman selected Adm. Louis Denfeld to relieve him, which pleased me because I admired Louie Denfeld and had worked closely with him during and after the war.

Shortly thereafter I heard rumors that I was being considered for duty as VCNO, the relief for Admiral Ramsey who, it was rumored, was to become CINCPAC replacing Denfeld. I also heard that great opposition, headed by Air Force Secretary Symington, was being generated to prevent my selection. Mr. Forrestal later stated flatly that Secretary Symington had done just about everything he could to prevent my orders being issued. But in a call I made on Mr. Symington he told me that rumors that he had opposed my return to Washington were wrong.[2]

With Washington in a turmoil for numerous reasons, international, domestic, political, and organizational, I stayed away except on rare occasions during November and December.

Admiral Denfeld assumed office on 15 December and let me know shortly thereafter that he was asking that I be assigned as his Vice Chief. This was a great compliment and I was naturally very pleased but not sure I would get the job. I looked forward to such an assignment with no illusions. We would be taking over at a critical time and would certainly bear the brunt of the interservice squabbles that were clearly in the offing.

My telephone rang repeatedly during the next week or so with calls from friends with advice and counsel. On Friday, 19 December Admiral Denfeld telephoned to say that Secretary of the Navy Sullivan wanted to see me in his office on Monday morning.

Mr. Sullivan came to the point immediately. "Raddy," he said, "Admiral Denfeld has nominated you as his Vice Chief and in spite of considerable opposition has insisted upon you for the job. I've conferred with the President about the matter and have left with him a recommendation that your orders be issued. The President was quite frank. He said that since you had been extremely active in opposing unification he wanted to know how you felt in regard to the new defense organization. Would you try to make it work if you were to be ordered as VCNO?"

I said, "Mr. Sullivan, as you well know I did oppose the bill which was finally passed. I felt it had some extremely bad features and that it could and should be improved. My arguments failed to sway the majority of the committee, which reported the bill favorably, and it was passed. It is now the law of the land. If I am ordered to duty as VCNO I will do the best I can to make it work."

Mr. Sullivan then said, "That's what I told the President I thought you would say. He informed me that if you did he would approve your orders, so that's settled and they will be issued immediately."

I thanked him, walked down the hall, and thanked Louie Denfeld, telling him I was leaving for California that night but would return right after New Year to relieve Admiral Ramsey.

Mrs. Radford met me on the west coast. We spent the holidays with my parents in Santa Monica, California—the first Christmas I had had with them for some years.

On our return to Washington, a large group of friends including Admiral Denfeld met us and escorted us to Quarters "A," now designated as the home of the VCNO in the old Naval Hospital Grounds. This was our first experience in government quarters. We found everything ready including food in the icebox from our thoughtful well-wishers. My most important recollection of this arrival was the knowledge that this time the Radford family would not have to go through the usual throes of house hunting while I was trying to learn the ropes and carry out the duties of a difficult new job.

I found little change in the Navy Department after ten months' absence. In rapid succession I confronted many of the problems that had haunted me as DCNO (Air), plus a few new ones, so time did not hang heavy on my hands. I came to the firm conclusion, after only a week or so, that unification was not working. The services seemed to be separating rather than unifying, and this in the face of a deteriorating world situation which was perfectly obvious to everyone in the Defense and State Departments.

President Truman had to deal with a Republican Congress and at the same time lay the groundwork for his presidential campaign in the fall. The country was fed up with war, having just successfully (so it was thought) finished the largest one in history. Both Congress and the President were in an economy mood. Now three instead of two services were fighting for every available dollar.

From a total defense expenditure in fiscal year 1946 of about $45 billion, 1947 saw a reduction to $14.2 billion. On my return to Washington we were in fiscal year 1948, with expenditures estimated at $10.7 billion—a reduction from the estimates in the President's message of January 1947 due largely to congressional pressures and President Truman's own idea of economy. In his budget message of January 1948 President Truman held out little prospect of an increase in military expenditures for 1949; his estimates were only slightly higher than those for 1948.

In fall 1947 the Air Force in particular was protesting the current division of the military appropriations funds. Mr. Forrestal was told by Gen. Alfred Gruenther that "there was a general impression throughout the Army and the Air Force, but particularly in the latter, that the amount of money provided for the Navy was disproportionate to the tasks of the Navy and its use in a future war.[3] In my opinion, this was a fair statement of the situation in which the Navy found itself that fall and winter as the three services endeavored to put together the first "unified" budget.

I was destined to be VCNO for a little over 15 months, or until April 1949. As I look back, these months were the most difficult and frustrating of my 45 years of service. Only the fact that with Admiral Denfeld (a calm, cool, tremendously energetic man) as its military head the Navy was fully united made it possible to keep going.

Two important committees that had been investigating the national air policy (the President's Air Policy Committee headed by Mr. Thomas Finletter and the Congressional Air Policy Board headed by Sen. Owen Brewster and Congressman Carl Hinshaw) were about to make their final reports and demanded the attention of the Defense Department. But Admirals Duncan, my relief in Norfolk, and John Price, who was to become DCNO (Air), were taken ill and delayed in being relieved. When I should have been free to work on the larger problems of the Navy I suddenly found myself again in the position of DCNO (Air), making presentations.

Mr. Forrestal was at that time pushing hard on the subject of "duplication," still a dirty word in the new unified defense organization. With a very limited staff of his own, the Secretary would tell one of his assistants that he wanted to hear presentations on such-and-such a subject by two services in order to ferret out "duplications" that he had been told existed. Some of my notes in January 1948 in regard to conferences of this kind seem humorous more than 20 years later, but they were dead serious at the time. The details of one in particular seem worth recording because of an important aftermath.

On the afternoon of Wednesday 28 January, Army Brig. Gen. Leroy Lutes phoned to say that Secretary Forrestal had directed him to set up a presentation to be made sometime later that week, probably Saturday, on the capabilities of naval aircraft. The Air Force was to prepare a similar presentation for the same time. The idea was to give Mr. Forrestal information on the types of planes each service would buy if given additional funds. General Lutes mentioned amounts of $300 million in fiscal year 1949 and $500 million in 1950.

The General also said that later, probably the following week, Mr. Forrestal wanted a presentation similar to one that I had recently made to the Brewster-Hinshaw Committee. I pointed out to the General that in that presentation I had included the information Mr. Forrestal wanted in the first presentation but in much greater detail. I had projected our plane purchases to five years, if we could finance such a program. Lutes thought the Secretary might like that. He suggested I talk about a two-year program now with a view to extending it to five years later on. I asked him for a written memo on these presentations, which I could pass around, and he promised it quickly. I immediately gave Admiral Price, who had just reported, the information concerning the presentation to Mr. Forrestal just three days later. It involved a great deal of work for a number of people in the next two days.

The following day I received a telephone call from Mr. Larkin, also in Mr. Forrestal's office, giving me a little more detail on what the Secretary wanted. The gist of his call was that Mr. Forrestal had for some time been questioning the performance and capabilities of different types of aircraft, particularly big bombers. It seemed that the Air Force had engineers coming in to make a presentation, probably Saturday afternoon. There would be another presentation a couple of days later, and Mr. Larkin had told Secretary Forrestal that at this second presentation he thought I should give the presentation I had recently made to the Brewster-Hinshaw Committee. He complimented me by saying that he had heard it and thought it was impressive.

From the two phone calls and the memoranda that followed I prepared to do two things: first, if called upon Saturday afternoon, I would be ready to tell Mr. Forrestal what planes the Navy would buy if given additional funds for fiscal 1949 and 1950. I would be prepared to give performance characteristics for these planes and estimates extending such a program to a total of five years. Second, I directed that the presentation given to the Finletter and Brewster-Hinshaw Committees be reworked and given to Mr. Forrestal during the following week. I was hoping that Admiral Price would feel able to make this talk, although I realized it was asking a lot for him to get ready on such short notice, and that to be prepared to answer the kind of questions he would get from Mr. Forrestal would be difficult. This presentation was rather an elaborate one and involved at least four or five assistants as well as the presenter.

The above done, I waited for details. For the Saturday appearance, I thought I would take Admiral Price with me so he could listen and get acquainted with Mr. Forrestal's method of handling such affairs.

On Saturday morning my office received word that Secretary Forrestal's first presentation would be given on Sunday afternoon. On that day Mr. Forrestal's office seemed quite busy, but I finally found an aide and introduced myself and Admiral Price, who was to sit in the presentation with me. The aide disappeared but soon returned to tell me the conference was about to start, but only I could go in. Admiral Price would have to wait in the outer office until later, when he would be called in.

I was surprised to find a number of people in Mr. Forrestal's office, mostly Air Force but also including Generals Gruenther and Lutes, Mr. Larkin and several others whom I did not know. Mr. Forrestal greeted me warmly, and I told him I had brought Admiral Price but had not been permitted to bring him in. The Secretary, seemingly a little harassed, said that Price could be brought in later but for now he wanted to get on with the presentations.

I sensed that presentations had been going on, that the conference had started some time before, and certainly that the ground rules for attendance favored the Air Force. It did not seem to be the cozy little informal affair that Mr. Larkin had described.

Air Force engineers seemed to be presenting performance figures on new aircraft, with great emphasis on a new bomber, the B50C, which they expected to have in quantity in 1952. So far so good. I listened intently, as did Mr. Forrestal, and took copious notes, for to me most of this was quite new even though I was supposed to have such information as a matter of course.

The Air Force finished and Mr. Forrestal called on me for the similar Navy information, which I gave. That over, Lieutenant General Norstad gave a strategic presentation based largely on the performance figures of the new aircraft that had just been described, which certainly left the naval air forces out in the cold. We were not counted in and very evidently were not needed.

I was astounded. This was no small, informal presentation but a show staged with great skill and preparation.

By that time it was nearly 5:30. Mr. Forrestal turned to me and asked if I had a strategic presentation to make. I said, "Mr. Secretary, I have given you the only presentation I was asked to prepare for you today. I will have a strategic presentation ready to give you next week but it will not fit very well with General Norstad's ideas, which you have just heard and which are in many respects new to me."

The room was very quiet after my statement. Mr. Forrestal hesitated a moment, then adjourned the meeting and left the room. I lost no time in getting out myself. I was so mad I decided it was best to leave as quickly as possible and to find out later just what had gone wrong. Of one thing I was certain: the Navy's contacts with the office of the Secretary of Defense were not good and must be improved—soon!

The next morning I went to Admiral Denfeld's office and told him what had happened. He knew in detail what we had prepared so could well understand my surprise and great concern at the way things had turned out. I concluded by saying, "Louie, we have to get closer to Mr. Forrestal. The Secretary [Sullivan], you, I—all of the Navy's top administrative offices have to move to the Pentagon [from the old Main Navy Building on Constitution Avenue]. At one time we were asked to move, you remember, and promised about a third of the space. I realize what a job it will be to move, but after this experience yesterday I can tell you we are rapidly losing out. I still don't understand exactly what happened, but in Mr. Forrestal's office yesterday the Navy was the country cousin, just asked to the party for the sake of appearances."

Admiral Denfeld understood the situation. My experience fitted with recent indications that he had observed, so he discussed the matter with Secretary Sullivan, who agreed that the move should be made. We lost no time in presenting the matter to Mr. Forrestal, who was pleased to hear of our change of heart.

This is the story of the Navy's move to the Pentagon; I must say that we never had reason to regret it.

☆ ☆ ☆ ☆

Mr. Forrestal realized, I believe, what confusion there had been at this conference, particularly when Sullivan and Denfeld called him to ask that the Navy be permitted to move to the Pentagon. My description of the confusion could have been applied to many other similar meetings around that time. The Secretary's habit of telling the first man he could get hold of in his office what he wanted done was really the basic cause of the trouble. In his days as Under Secretary and later Secretary of the Navy, he had always had a capable naval officer to handle his orders, a military man well acquainted with the naval organization and its people. As Secretary of Defense he lacked such an aide primarily because none was available. Some of the more brilliant young flag officers might have filled the bill but the Secretary was reluctant to take them from important jobs—he was always a very thoughtful man, not inclined to hurt people or to ask for too much for himself.

Mr. Forrestal also had often said and still felt that his new office should be staffed primarily by civilians. But with civilians there was the problem of seniority, for how could one determine who was most important? Mr. Forrestal had several top civilians, excellent men all, on his staff, but he used them as equals and often gave more than one of them orders to do things that were part of the same assignment. Problems were generated down the line before the individuals in question realized they were working on the same project. The difficulty was partly his way of working and partly that he was trying so hard to do too many things too fast. By January 1948 he was beginning to realize that the problems of making the new unified military organization work were far greater than he had anticipated. He was driving himself with that relentless energy which was his great ability but his troubles were mounting in spite of his efforts.

Mr. Forrestal had opted early in the game for legislation that would give the new Secretary of Defense policy-making powers plus control of the three independent departments. In addition, the Secretary had to put together and present to the Bureau of the Budget a single budget for the Defense Department.

In January–March 1948: (1) Mr. Forrestal was discovering that his authority was *not* clearly spelled out, that the three departments were still quite independent and could delay and drag out his efforts to get things done. (2) He was also, in my opinion, discovering that Army and Air Force agreement to go along with the unification bill he had supported was more a tactical move than a change of heart. (3) The Army, as a whole, resented the Marine Corps and the Air Force was still determined to become the *only* air force. (4) Mr. Forrestal had believed that, if service roles and missions were spelled out, as they were in President Truman's executive order, it would be fairly easy to work up the three departmental budgets. One would simply divide the available funds to take care of the primary service missions.

By the time the Navy moved to the Pentagon, Mr. Forrestal was in real trouble. The defense budget for fiscal year 1948–49, presented to Congress by President Truman in January 1948, had been put together in fall 1947 after the merger had become effective; but it was in reality the old two-department budget worked out in spring 1947 only slightly warmed over. The Air Force was dissatisfied with its share. As 1948 began and work started on the 1950 budget—the first budget to be worked up completely by the new Department of the Air Force—the fun began and Mr. Forrestal's troubles mounted daily.

Mr. Forrestal had acquiesced in the defense budget for fiscal 1948 primarily because he realized that Congress was unwilling to go any higher and that the President was in an economy mood also, for political if no other reasons (the election loomed in the fall). The Secretary realized that the services were being squeezed too hard. He particularly wanted to get contract authority for new aircraft, which he realized would be badly needed in the next few years. In President Truman's cabinet, which included Gen. George Marshall, Mr. Forrestal alone appreciated the seriousness of the Soviet threat worldwide.[4]

In response to the critical global situation, which obviously called for a bolstering of the country's military strength, President Truman again proposed a UMT program. Secretary of State Marshall backed him, saying that money spent on such a program would convince the world that we were ready to follow through on our military policy and would save large sums. Both the President and the Secretary of State felt that UMT would add greatly to our national military strength, a feeling that was not shared by senior military men in the new Defense Department nor by Mr. Forrestal.

As I write this in 1970, with daily headlines crises in Europe, the Middle East, and China, it would seem that little has changed in the 22 years that have passed. Our country has fought two wars since then and is not yet finished with the second. The world is not much improved.

On 24 February 1948 the communist coup in Czechoslovakia shocked Washington profoundly, but the main reaction in a military sense was the administration's efforts to push further for UMT.

Congress had just received the reports of the Finletter and Brewster-Hinshaw Committees advocating increased air strength, primarily for the new 70-group Air Force. The effect on the Hill was the conclusion that increased air strength could be substituted for UMT, which was politically unpopular.

Secretary Forrestal of course was in the middle of this controversy. At the same time he was concerned with the failure of the JCS to agree on a revision of the roles and missions of the armed services. The need was urgent for better strategic planning and better service integration, but progress could not be made while the chiefs disagreed. He told the President that if the chiefs did not produce decisions in the near future he would make them himself.

On Wednesday 10 March, Mr. Forrestal informed a press conference that he was convening a prolonged meeting of the JCS outside of Washington, to thrash out "who will do what with what. If they fail, I shall have to make my own decisions."[5] He added that the services now agreed that some form of compulsory military service was necessary. If there were no UMT the draft would have to be revived.

To add to the seriousness of the world situation, on the same day Jan Masaryk, Foreign Minister of Czechoslovakia and son of the country's first President, a figure well known and liked in all Western capitals, fell to his death from a window in his official residence. An official announcement said he had committed suicide, and the event only added to the concern over the communist takeover.

Admiral Denfeld and I represented the Navy at the JCS meeting called by Mr. Forrestal in Key West the next day.[6] On the first evening there was a cheerful and interesting dinner in the comfortable old Commandant's House (recently renovated for use as a winter White House by President Truman), as well as an opportunity for all of us to size up the seriousness of the situation. Mr. Forrestal's welcoming remarks left no doubt as to what he expected. The meeting was a milestone in the long road toward unification, and an important one. Admiral Denfeld and I knew that the Navy was on the spot. But we felt we had a good case to present, and that with Mr. Forrestal present we would have the opportunity to present it. Admiral Leahy, we believed, would try not to inject himself into the discussions, and that proved to be the case.

By Sunday morning the chiefs were finally agreed on "certain broad, basic decisions."

1) For planning purposes the Marine Corps is to be limited to four divisions. [A sentence in the final document states that the "marines are not to create a second land army."]

2) The Air Force recognizes the right of the Navy to proceed with the development of weapons the Navy considers essential to its function but with the proviso that the Navy will not develop a separate strategic air force, this function being reserved to the Air Force. However, the Navy in the carrying out of its function is to have the right to attack inland targets, for example, to reduce and neutralize airfields from which enemy aircraft may sortie to attack the fleet.

3) The Air Force recognizes the right and need for the Navy to participate in an all-out air campaign.

4) The Navy is not to be denied use of the atomic bomb.

5) Navy is to proceed with the development of an 80,000 ton carrier and development of high altitude aircraft to carry heavy missiles therefrom.

It was further agreed that, since existing forces had shrunk below those authorized, voluntary enlistment was a failure; UMT could not furnish additional men fast enough, so the JCS would recommend immediate reenactment of the draft law. A restudy of the custody of atomic weapons was also requested, with the intent of authorizing such bombs to be turned over to the armed services [from the Atomic Energy Commission].

To U.S. military men today these decisions and conclusions undoubtedly seem reasonable and not particularly startling, but to Admiral Denfeld and me they were very important. For the first time, mainly because we had the time we needed to explain our reasons, and the understanding help of Mr. Forrestal, the Army and Air Force agreed that the Navy had collateral ability and missions that could under certain circumstances aid them. Even these measures of agreement and indications of the beginning of interservice understanding would not have been possible without the presence of Tooey Spaatz, who broke the logjam. A no-nonsense debater and a tough opponent, Tooey is willing to listen and can be convinced, as he was at Key West.

Before leaving Key West, we discussed the world situation in considerable detail and decided that our armed forces were inadequate for possible actions we might have to face. Discussion of amounts was general, and I believe it was Mr. Forrestal who suggested asking for a supplemental appropriation of approximately $4 billion, which would have brought the total defense appropriation for that year to a little over $15 billion. There was no particular magic to the $4 billion figure, though it did approximate the generally estimated cost of UMT. Mr. Forrestal may have thought he could persuade the President to forego UMT in order to build up our forces in light of the unfavorable world situation.

Mr. Forrestal returned to Washington on Monday afternoon, saw the President, and reported on what had happened at Key West. The Secretary was surprised to learn that Mr. Truman, previously advised that revival of the draft was recommended by the JCS, had two hours earlier announced that he would deliver a message to Congress the following Wednesday, going all out for selective service and UMT.

Admiral Denfeld and I briefed Mr. Sullivan and the assistant secretaries on the Key West meeting; a meeting followed with the senior officers of the Navy Department to acquaint them with actions to be taken in carrying out the new JCS agreements. Without question the top echelons of the Navy were pleased with the situation reported to them by Admiral Denfeld. As VCNO, I initiated the detailed planning for the enlarged programs that all of us thought would follow soon.

10

★

1948: Truman, Marshall,
and the Cutback in Military Power

O ur euphoria was short-lived. Rumors reached the Navy Department that
Air Force Secretary Symington was furious at the agreements reached at
Key West and supposedly at his representatives who agreed to them. To me this
was no great surprise. I figured that for our three steps forward we might, temporarily, have to take one backward. That Key West paper still looked good to
me.

On 17 March 1948 President Truman, accompanied by his cabinet, proceeded to the Capitol, where he addressed a joint session of Congress. His
speech was forceful. For the first time he identified the USSR as the one nation
that was blocking all efforts toward peace and that was, furthermore, aggressively threatening the free world. "The United States," he said, "must meet
this growing menace . . . there are times in world history when it is far wiser to
act than to hesitate."

Listening to these words over the radio, I was elated. The President had at
last recognized the danger and would certainly approve the buildup that the
military felt was so necessary. Then came the recommendations. The President
asked for three things: (1) prompt enactment of the Marshall Plan program
of economic aid to Europe, (2) the adoption of UMT as "the only feasible
means by which the *civilian* components of our armed forces can be built up to
the strength required" (italics mine), and (3) the "temporary" reenactment of
selective service "in order to maintain our armed forces at their authorized
strength."[1]

I am sure that most senior officers in the armed services felt much as I did
when the President concluded this address, which had started out so well. I was
astonished. I knew perfectly well that there was no plan in being to implement
the buildup agreed upon at Key West, but that the JCS and the services were
working on it. Had he wanted to the President, without committing himself in

detail, could at least have let Congress and the public know that our military strength must be increased. I think Congress was expecting some such recommendation and that the public felt it was coming. Certainly the Pentagon felt let down.

A week later Secretary Forrestal presented the administration program for strengthening our armed services before the Senate Armed Services Committee. The Secretary's opening statement was powerful and left no doubt of his own feelings regarding the world situation: "The record shows that despotism, whatever its form, has a remorseless compulsion to aggression ... Today another power, wearing the false mask of freedom for the people, seeks to spin its web over all Western Europe."[2]

The program presented was a balanced one to increase strength on ground and sea and in the air. It made plain, as the President's message to the Congress had not, that what was wanted was an immediate increase in the regular military establishment, as well as the cumulative effect of UMT, which would provide adequate reserves.

The Air Force had presumably agreed to the program, but when questioned by sympathetic members of the committee at this hearing they did not try to conceal their conviction that increases for the Air Force should be much greater and should include a 70-group program. Symington went further, estimating that the 70-group program could be provided for an additional $800 million.

Mr. Forrestal was recalled for questioning. He told the Senators that an establishment based on a 70-group air force, with the other services in proper proportion, would cost not $800 million but more like $15 billion. He pointed out that he was asking for a minimum balanced-force increase, with emphasis on those unglamorous elements the weakness of which was the source of our helplessness and current embarrassment in dealing with world affairs.

The hearing ended in confusion. It was evident that this was the beginning of a new and bitter controversy.

The Russians chose the end of March to notify General Clay in Germany that on 1 April they would institute a new system of inspection and validation of personnel and materiel entering or leaving the Russian zone. In effect, this meant the right to inspect personnel and materiel entering or leaving the Allied zones in Berlin.

The struggle over division of the supplemental military appropriations went on for nearly a month. In the House of Representatives, meanwhile, air power enthusiasts prevailed, passing an amended aircraft procurement bill with $822 million added for a 70-group Air Force.

Mr. Forrestal would not give up. He struggled with the JCS in private, and on 21 April presented a revised supplemental program to the President that totalled $3.481 billion, with a division of funds agreed to by the JCS. The President authorized its presentation to Congress. That afternoon Forrestal appeared before the Senate Armed Services Committee to deliver a long and detailed statement on its behalf.

The JCS, he said, had agreed that from purely military considerations what was required was a balanced establishment based on 70 air groups and a total of two million men at an estimated cost of $9 billion in additional funds. He then described the 3.481 billion supplementary program agreed upon unanimously by the JCS, with its total of 1,795,000 men. The Air Force expansion was to 66 groups (from 55) but would be accomplished by reactivating mothballed B29s rather than by purchasing new aircraft.

The interservice battles were far from over, but in those four weeks of controversy Mr. Forrestal, through his patience, tolerance, and gradualism, carried his main points. The Air Force, while seemingly the main gainer, had not by any means won the complete victory its Secretary had anticipated due to the apparent willingness of Congress to appropriate for air power as the easy way out politically. Mr. Forrestal had, almost singlehandedly, averted the danger that the whole rearmament effort would be swept by the public enthusiasm for air power into an expansion of the Air Force alone. I say singlehandedly because Mr. Truman, for reasons best known to himself, did not openly intervene to help his Secretary of Defense.[3]

In the country at large, however, Mr. Forrestal's efforts did not appear to be generally appreciated, and there was a feeling that he was not tough enough on the military. But had he failed in his efforts to obtain this balanced buildup of the armed forces, with enough money for new naval carrier aircraft included, our situation in June 1950 when the Korean War was forced upon us would have been far worse than it was. Our first Secretary of Defense merits the country's thanks for these pioneering efforts to bring the services together. I admit frankly that at that time I could not have written so objectively. I thought Secretary Symington should have been fired for insubordination.

On Capitol Hill that spring and summer confusion reigned. Powerful members of Congress opposed the President's programs in many ways. It was an election year, with all the accompanying political maneuvering.

When the President authorized Secretary Forrestal to present the program to Congress, he also ordered it submitted to him again via the Bureau of the Budget.[4] James Webb, Director of the Budget, was there to hear that order. I took the results of the 21 April meeting as an approval by the President of the budgetary increase, expecting no serious problems to be developed by the Director's review. This was the general viewpoint of interested military men at that time. We were, perhaps, too optimistic after several months of terrific interservice infighting; but another factor intervened that most of us had not considered.

In March and April, exploratory conversations between the United States, Britain, and other allied Western European nations had developed as a result of Ernest Bevin's proposal to Secretary Marshall of a plan for Atlantic security to be built around the five-power Brussels Pact. The reinstitution was being discussed of some form of lend-lease of military equipment which would assist the European nations to reoutfit their military forces. An off-the-cuff estimate late in April by Under Secretary of State Robert Lovett gave a figure of $3 billion for such lend-lease, greatly disturbing Mr. Forrestal. His diaries for 24 and 30 April note his concern about this new drain on U. S. resources and record a conversation with the President and the Secretary of State in regard to the matter.[5]

On 6 May his fears were realized when he met with Budget Director Webb in connection with the latter's review of the supplementary military program already before Congress. Mr. Webb presented an analysis of the program, which Budget review had reduced from $3.481 to 3.1 billion. His analysis showed that if the 3.1-billion program were approved it would result in an appropriation buildup in later fiscal years from 15.5 billion in fiscal 1949 to 18.2 billion in fiscal 1952. Mr. Webb commented further that, if prices continued to rise, the 18.2 figure could easily become 20 billion. This would mean a 50-billion national budget, an unheard-of amount.

Mr. Webb proposed that the supplemental program be reduced to a total of 2.5 billion by reducing personnel and collateral procurement programs so that total cash and appropriation authority could be held to 15.3 billion in fiscal 1950 and would level off at about 15 billion thereafter. The reduction would require reverting to 55 air groups in 1949, deferral of vital Navy programs, particularly in naval aviation and anti-submarine warfare, and considerable reduction in Army material support.

Mr. Forrestal then posed a question: "Is the world situation such as to warrant appropriations on this order at the present time?" Answering his own question, he told Mr. Webb that he would have to support the larger, 3.1-billion program because of his belief that *the next eighteen months to two years were a critical period in our relations with Russia* (italics mine).

Mr. Webb then asked, "Can we carry out such a military program, support the European Recovery Program (Marshall Plan), provide a merchant marine program and implement the atomic energy plans without having available the controls and sanctions [over the civilian economy] which it seems very doubtful that we will get in this election year?"

Mr. Forrestal replied that authorization of the larger program was essential and probably could be accomplished with certain preemptive authority but not necessarily with across-the-board controls. While he did not like the reduction to 3.1 billion, Mr. Forrestal would have tried to live with its suggestions. He knew he would have great difficulty in getting agreement by the JCS. But the second Webb proposal was a totally different matter. Aside from its specific military effects, the program would have reopened the whole span of our military programs and thrown overboard the results of weeks of painstaking work by the Secretary and the JCS.

As the basis for his second and revised proposal, Webb had brought out in the open the question of future additions to the military budget. Were they to grow? Mr. Webb proposed that the military "structure" be reduced to a point where its annual costs would level off at about 15 billion. This was the first suggestion of a hard-and-fast ceiling on military spending and therefore on military strength. "Suddenly, it appeared that it was Mr. Webb who was in control of American military policy rather than the Secretary of Defense," Forrestal comments in his diary.

Mr. Forrestal felt he had to know at once whether Mr. Webb was speaking for the President. A meeting was arranged at the White House for the next day so the Secretary could have a full discussion with the President about his objectives in lifting the financial sights on the 1948–49 budget. The President, instead of answering directly, asked Secretary Marshall to comment. Marshall said, Forrestal reports, that "the policy of this country was based upon the assumption that there would not be war and that we should not plunge into war preparations which would bring about the very thing we were taking these steps to prevent." He added that he had "always regarded UMT as the best manifestation to Europe—both as to the Western friendly countries and the Iron Curtain countries—of the continuity of our policy and of our determination to continue our position in European matters."

The President approved the statement of the Secretary of State. He said he wished to make it clear that the increases he had approved through augmentations in the budget should not be construed as preparation for war. "We are preparing for peace and not for war."

President Truman added that "the very people in Congress who would now vote for heavy Air appropriations are those who a year from now would deny anything to the Armed Forces, and . . . if we permit the military budget to rise to proportions that cut too deeply into the civilian economy, the ones that will suffer in the long run will be the Armed Services."

Mr. Forrestal made no comment in his diary on this meeting, but it is not difficult to imagine what a shock it was for him to hear both the Secretary of State and the President deliver such a rebuff to the Defense Department.

I recall that it did not take long for those of us in the top echelons to get the word on the President's position in regard to a buildup in the military budget. Again, to most of us, it was confusion compounded. What we could not understand then, and what I still find difficult to understand, is how the President and Secretary of State could reach such obviously different conclusions in regard to the world situation from the Secretary of Defense and the JCS, from the same set of facts available to all. Thinking over the contretemps in the light of subsequent information and 22 years of hindsight, I have come to the following conclusions bearing on these very important differences of opinion.

First, I must restate the very close personal relationship between President Truman and Secretary Marshall. Their admiration was mutual, and Marshall was serving because the President had, for the second time since the General's retirement in fall 1945, requested that he come back to help in a critical situation.[6] Second, one would presume that a man with General Marshall's background would have had somewhat the same concerns in regard to our lack of military strength as did Mr. Forrestal and the JCS. Quite obviously he did not. I believe he did not share the feeling of urgency that existed in the Defense Department because: he felt the services as presently constituted were adequate (he looked back to pre-World War II figures, which were much smaller); he was not yet convinced that the Russian threat was a serious one; and as a close friend of the President he wanted to help control the budget and the economy, which he knew was most important in the President's program. Although not a politician, General Marshall was aware of the implications that could help or hurt in the fall campaign. The positions he took were helpful to the President but certainly not to Mr. Forrestal or the armed services. Further, Marshall was Secretary of State during a critical period. He was in and out of Washington attending various conferences of great importance and was undoubtedly feeling the aggregate effects of the ailments that forced his retirement in January 1949.

I have concluded that General Marshall sided with the President because his views, in general, coincided with the President's and not with those of the Defense Department. He actually did, I believe, feel that UMT was the best way to impress upon the rest of the world that the United States was serious in its determination to resist the spread of communism, particularly in Europe.

Here also I must inject another aspect of the complex situation at the "top." On my return to Washington in fall 1945 I had become well acquainted with Mr. Forrestal and had worked closely with him. I admired him but I also began to worry about him. Often I was with him in conferences with the President at the White House. I knew how loyal he was to Mr. Truman and I knew, too, that the President had initially had great respect for him. As time went on, particularly after I returned to the Navy Department in January 1948, I sensed on occasion that Mr. Forrestal had begun to lose his standing with the President. The President still admired his Secretary of Defense, but as Mr. Forrestal continued to press for increased military appropriations and to warn of the world situation in more alarming terms than those presented by any other cabinet member or close associate, his relative status in Mr. Truman's eyes gradually decreased.

On 13 May President Truman outlined his military budget policy to Mr. Forrestal, the three service Secretaries, the JCS, and Budget Director Webb.

The President went into some detail on the supplemental request, noting that it had been reduced by Budget from $3.481 to 3.1 billion. He said that although this was more than should be asked of Congress at this time he was willing, in view of the uncertainty of the world situation, to submit this supplemental on one condition: *that the armed forces not spend it.* Specifically, the armed forces were not to create a military structure in the next eight months that would require more than approximately 15 billion in the following fiscal year (1950). "I do not want immediate action taken toward the activation of all the units contemplated—and by that I mean such things as Army training camps, naval air stations, and air groups."

The President ended the meeting by saying that he expected these orders to be carried out wholeheartedly, in good spirit, and without mental reservation. He invited comments, for "once this program goes forward officially, it will be the administration program and I expect every member of the administration to support it fully, both in public and in private."

So the tremendous efforts in spring 1948 to rebuild U.S. military strength to a "safe" level were almost completely negated. True, out of this did come in June the passage of the Selective Service Act, a great help in maintaining at least authorized personnel levels. Also, in the heated discussions preceding JCS agreement on a total increase, Mr. Forrestal had maintained the principle of balanced forces and the services had begun to learn how to get along with one another.

I have devoted considerable space to the efforts of Mr. Forrestal and the JCS in that spring to improve the military posture of the United States; for the services were below authorized strength and suffered from rapid turnover of personnel recruited for short-term enlistments. The Army had large commitments for occupation forces in Germany and Japan; the Navy and Air Force were not only undermanned but had ships and aircraft squadrons that could not function. Facing these facts and viewing the deteriorating world situation it is no wonder that the armed services were concerned. It was their duty to be ready for emergency calls that might be made upon them by their Commander-in-Chief, and it was their duty as well to make clear their reduced capabilities to both the President and Congress.

In 1947, as the armed services had worried about meeting their commitments, various crises had caused them even more concern, particularly when President Truman took positive actions that in effect created national policy that they had to integrate in their planning. A good example is the Greek-Turkish crisis, which the President took to Congress on 12 March 1947 in an address broadcast to the nation. His announcement of policy on this occasion became known as the Truman Doctrine.

As a result of this stirring speech and subsequent legislation requested by the President, Congress had appropriated $400 million for economic, technical, and military aid: 250 million for Greece and 150 million for Turkey. The President was informed by Mr. Forrestal and the JCS at this time that any sizeable commitments of troops to Greece or Turkey would require partial mobilization, as there were insufficient uncommitted reserves in the United States.

A similar crisis arose in spring 1948 when, following the coup d'état in

Czechoslovakia and recurring difficulties in the Far East, which led directly to the JCS meeting in Key West, the President had agreed to ask Congress for UMT and renewal of the Selective Service Act.

These two public announcements by President Truman sparked the services to urgent efforts in March and April 1948 to work with Mr. Forrestal on the minimum supplementary budget that could purchase adequate military strength. The letdown following the meeting with the President on 13 May was tremendous.

Senior officers today who think they have problems might feel better if they reviewed in some detail the situation faced by their predecessors in this critical 1948 period. In the first place, we had occupation forces in Germany and Japan. Our difficulties with the USSR were increasing, particularly in connection with Berlin, where problems regarding interference with Allied transportation had been mounting since March. On 24 June 1949, the day Mr. Dewey was nominated by the Republican party, the Russians really clamped down. They halted what little traffic was moving into Berlin and started a blockade that lasted nearly a year and was overcome only by an unprecedented massive airlift maintained by U.S. and British forces.

Another indication of turmoil to come, although few Americans appreciated it then, was the recognition of the new state of Israel by the United States on 14 May 1948. President Truman had taken the matter out of the hands of the State Department several days before. They were notified as the announcement was made. In foreign policy the President made decisions in much the same way as he did in connection with the military budget.

The failure to sell the rather small supplementary budget to President Truman set the stage for more and longer lasting interservice controversies in summer and fall 1948. The first of these concerned service roles and missions, supposedly settled at the Key West conference in March. At Key West no accurate record of the proceedings was kept, and when General Gruenther tried to obtain agreement on a draft that he constructed after returning to Washington, difficulties arose. Another problem concerned use of atomic weapons. The Air Force felt that they should be carried only by the heavy bombers of the strategic force, while the Navy felt that there would be occasions when naval operations could benefit by their use and that, consequently, no restrictions should be placed on naval use.

Mr. Forrestal concluded after listening to both sides that another out-of-town meeting of the JCS was in order. This time Newport, Rhode Island, was selected and the chiefs and their assistants gathered there on Friday 20 August. We were billeted in the vacant quarters usually assigned to the president of the Naval War College. Room assignments were designed to get the services better acquainted. My roommate was Army Gen. Albert Wedemeyer.

That evening Mr. Forrestal hosted a very pleasant dinner. No one could be more genial and attractive than he when he wanted to be, and I am sure the others felt as I did about the evening as we retired.

Albert Wedemeyer and I shared a rather large room and turned in immediately. I was awakened some time later by someone talking, apparently in the room. I sat up to see what was going on, and in the bright moonlight I could see that my roommate the General was carrying on a one-sided conversation while sound asleep. The fact that I might get some valuable information struck me immediately so I tried to decipher what he was saying. It was no use, and as the talk gradually subsided I went back to sleep. Next morning, Al asked almost immediately, "Did I talk in my sleep last night?" I said, "Al, you certainly did and I'm so glad I was here to get all that confidential information!"

In the years that followed Al tried again and again to find out what he had said. Finally he shifted his story and now tells mutual friends that I awakened him by telling the story of my life. The best defense is a good offense, as Al well knows.

The Newport Conference was well organized. Mr. Forrestal had an assistant keep a verbatim record, found to be so necessary after the Key West meeting. The fact that such a record was being kept, I felt, made the conferees more careful in expressing themselves and contributed greatly to the important agreements reached.

A memorandum of the decisions taken at Newport began with: "Control and direction of atomic operations: It was agreed that, as an interim measure, the Chief, Armed Forces Special Weapons Project would report to the Chief of Staff Air Force." This gave operational control for the time being to the Air Force. But the memorandum went on: "It was agreed to postpone any decision concerning the permanent future organization for the control and direction of atomic operations until the current study of the Military Liaison Committee could be completed."

The second decision clarified the term "primary mission" in the Key West agreement. In the fields of its primary missions, each service "must have exclusive responsibility for planning and programming," but "in the execution of any mission all available resources must be used ... For this reason the exclusive responsibility and authority in a given field do not imply preclusive participation." In other words, the Air Force was obligated to use any strategic bombing capabilities the Navy might have or develop. The Joint Chiefs noted that this was not "in any wise a victory or defeat for any service" and they agreed "to so explain it to their respective services and to the public."[7]

The last item on the agenda was significant. Forrestal and the chiefs developed two systems of unified international command for Western Europe, one for "immediate" use, the other for "use in event of war." The second plan, for "U.S. information only," provided for a Supreme Allied Commander-in-Chief (West) "who should be an American," and outlined other provisions, all of which became effective on the appointment of General Eisenhower as Supreme Commander.

The handling of the Newport conference, both at the meeting itself and subsequently, up to and including the Pentagon conference that followed, was masterful and almost completely Mr. Forrestal's idea. With its finale, the informative conference that passed the word to the planning groups of the three services, the Secretary of Defense had accomplished all he could to bring the services together. From then on it was up to them.

The JCS continued their budgetary efforts without mutual agreement in spite of the understandings reached at Key West and Newport. It is not difficult to see why they had such difficulties. The new military budget for 1949–50 was not to exceed $15 billion, including the appropriations for stockpiling and funding of atomic projects. This left about $14.4 billion to be divided between the three services.

More important was the declared determination of the Army and Air Force to reduce the Navy's share of the budget. In November 1947, General Gruenther had informed Mr. Forrestal that the Army and Air Force were convinced that the Navy was getting more money than it was entitled to considering its tasks in emergency war planning. Both services pointed to the large inventory of vessels the Navy had, as compared with their own shortages. The fact that the Army had abandoned tremendous amounts of equipment overseas at the end of World War II and that the Air Force had simply declared most of their fighters and bombers obsolete did not seem to make any difference. The argument existed.

The McNarney board, three high-ranking "budget deputies" appointed by the JCS, had been laboring to scale down the separate and competing demands of the three services. Their progress was not encouraging. Sometimes their debates bordered on the ridiculous, as when Gen. Joseph McNarney announced that he saw little value in the carrier force and would have recommended its elimination except that we had a national commitment to keep one carrier in the Mediterranean. He also realized that a deployed carrier had to return to the United States from time to time for overhaul and repairs. For that reason he was willing to agree that the Navy should be permitted to have two carriers in active commission!

Other arguments centered on funding for the new flush deck carrier that had been authorized in the Navy shipbuilding program of the 1949 budget. On 23 July 1948 President Truman authorized the construction of several ships including CVA58, the *United States*. The Army and Air Force would have eliminated or slowed down the construction of this ship by cutting out the second-stage funding in the 1950 budget.

I was not continuously engaged in the budget discussions. That burden was carried by Admirals Denfeld and Carney. My job was to see that they were furnished the information and assistance they needed. I did take part in some of the meetings at which aviation matters were discussed. After one such meeting Mr. Forrestal, who was also present for a while, asked me to stop by his office when I was through. In a very serious mood, he said, "Raddy, as one of my old Navy friends why can't you help me more by agreeing to some of the Navy cuts proposed by the Army or the Air Force? You know how difficult it is for me to have so many decisions thrown in my lap, many or most of which I really know little or nothing about." Taken completely by surprise, I said, "Mr. Forrestal, this is exactly what you had to do when you were Secretary of the Navy. You had to make the final decisions on matters that could not be agreed upon down below." Mr. Forrestal could not remember any such situations in the Navy Department so I reminded him of a few, which he dismissed as not in the same category of importance.

Our conversation went on for a time and I finally told him that representatives of the services *expected* him to make the decisions. They could not go back to their offices and admit giving in unless some evidence had been brought up. A decision by the Secretary of Defense, whom we all admired, was something else. We could accept that and blame ourselves for not making better presentations.

I certainly failed Mr. Forrestal on this occasion and returned to my office feeling unhappy about it. I was again aware of the terrific strain under which he was laboring.

Mr. Truman, campaigning hard during fall 1948, took little part in the military budget discussions. Mr. Forrestal, feeling that "there is no question that foreign policy is a function of defense and vice versa," did inform the President in October that with a $14.4-billion ceiling we would probably have only the capability of reprisal by air attack, using Great Britain as a base, against any possible enemy. The Mediterranean would be ruled out. He told the President that he planned to submit a budget based on the 14.4-billion limitation but would also prepare another budget, probably on the order of 18.5 billion, predicated on a capability of exploiting the Mediterranean.

The President said he wished this latter budget to be held in reserve, that its presentation would be interpreted as a step toward preparation for war. He added that the additional amounts would be kept as supplemental estimates to be presented if and when the situation became more dangerous. Even a president who had courage to announce the Truman Doctrine of 1947, and who must at that time have been keenly aware of the importance of the Mediterranean line of communication, seems to have flinched from translating national policy into military and budgetary terms during the political campaign of 1948.[8]

Shortly after this meeting Mr. Forrestal told the JCS that he expected a recommendation on the division of funds between the services under the 14.4-billion ceiling. The JCS refused, saying that they could agree on no program within that limit.

Mr. Forrestal did not give up. He persuaded General Eisenhower to come to Washington to help in the budget discussions and he tried again to get General Marshall to assist him in relating military posture to foreign policy problems. Eisenhower was a great help to the Secretary, but Marshall was again unresponsive.

President Truman was reelected and, with a Democratic Congress to back him up, was more positive than ever in his decisions on military budgetary matters.

In a meeting with the President on 9 December Mr. Forrestal had with him the service Secretaries, the Joint Chiefs, and General Gruenther; Budget Director Webb and R. Adm. Sidney Souers were also present. The Defense Department had an elaborate map and chart presentation of an intermediate budget, finally agreed to by the JCS, that totaled 16.9 billion and provided a military establishment of 1,980,000 men and 59 air groups as of 30 June 1950. The President listened politely, said it was all very interesting, and made no other comments. The meeting lasted less than an hour.

When the President sent his budget to Congress on 10 January 1949 it provided 14.2 billion for the armed forces, exclusive of stockpiling: there would be 1,617,830 men and 48 air groups as of 30 June 1950. Actually, when war came in Korea as fiscal 1950 was ending, our military strength was much less, having been eroded by further economies introduced by Mr. Forrestal's successor, Louis Johnson. Military manpower on 24 June 1950, the day the North Koreans attacked, totaled only 1,465,000.

From fall 1945 through 24 June 1950, all our services were mere shells of their former tremendous wartime strengths. Their military heads, and the civilian Secretaries who were holdovers from the war, were perfectly aware of these weaknesses and did their level best to convince President Truman that the U.S. military establishment was inadequate to back up the foreign policy he so courageously espoused. General Marshall, experienced military man that he was, elected to back the President in economizing on the military budget in order to carry out other heavy burdens: the Marshall Plan, Aid to Greece and Turkey, and so on. Both President Truman and General Marshall were gambling on Russian intentions and they knew it—Mr. Forrestal and the Chiefs certainly made it plain to them on numerous occasions in those five years.

Looking back on that period I conclude that President Truman and General Marshall placed much more importance on our atomic power than was justified at the time. They correctly assessed it as a deterrent that would prevent another major war with the USSR. They fully realized that in the several hot spots of those times—Greece and Turkey, the Middle East, Korea—conflict was a possibility, *but* such possibilities were always looked upon as involving the USSR versus the United States.

☆ ☆ ☆ ☆

Those of us old enough to remember what happened in June 1950 will recall that the Russians were careful to keep out of the actual fighting in Korea.[9] The advisers they had with the North Korean forces kept well back.[10] Only one Russian pilot was shot down for certain. Papers found with the body identified the man as a major in the Soviet air forces. The Russian government was officially notified and told that we were prepared to return the remains. No reply was ever received. Later, perhaps in 1951, a combat air patrol in the Sea of Japan shot down two Migs headed toward them. The two planes crashed in the sea but their pilots were not recovered. Again we heard no comment or protest from the Russians.

I mention these facts to indicate how careful the Russians were to *officially* keep out of the Korean War although they had quite openly trained, equipped, and provided material support to the North Koreans.

Russian strategy in this war was new to us. We were actually fighting the Russians and the North Koreans, but our atomic bombs were not useful as a deterrent under the new circumstances. President Truman had made a great mistake in dismantling our military establishment. The Russians watched its erosion in 1945–1946, as well as the internal arguments about rebuilding it during 1947–1949. They watched, with tremendous satisfaction I am sure, the further reductions made by Secretary of Defense Louis Johnson, who relieved Mr. Forrestal in April 1949.

President Truman, with General Marshall's help, probably saved $8–10 billion during the three years before the Korean War broke out by restricting the size of the military establishment. Because these savings were made, the USSR elected to have us fight the Korean War. Perhaps this is a strange way to put it but it is true. It cost the Russians something, of course, for they had to train, outfit, and support the North Koreans and later the Chinese who had to be brought in. Perhaps the Russians spent $6 billion on the Korean War; but they did not lose 47,000 young men as we did.

During the Korean War we spent some $17–18 billion.[11] Since the armistice of July 1953 we have probably spent [up to 1970] another 15 billion or more in South Korea and have kept two divisions of our troops there during the 17 years that have passed.[12] Some 30 billion spent as against some 10 billion saved. Not a good exchange.

The history of our mistakes leading to the Korean War is clear. The mistakes, some of them ours, that led to the war in Vietnam are not so plain, and our leadership in the latter had been neither as courageous nor as astute. The temper of vocal America is more hysterical as I write in 1970, and I can imagine with what gratification the debates in Congress and the statements of some of our leading Senators are read aloud in the councils of Moscow, Peking, and Hanoi.

11

The Middle East Visit / Forrestal's Last Days

In September 1948 Admiral Sir Roderick McGrigor, R.N., Commander-in-Chief of the British Home Fleet, visited Washington for a few days. At a stag dinner in his honor at the British Embassy I had the pleasure of sitting next to him and having a good chat. I flooded him with so many questions about what had happened to the Royal Navy since the war, particularly to their air arm and carriers, that he suggested I join him in his flagship, H.M.S. *Duke of York*, in Bermuda in November for a cruise back to Britain.

I conceived the idea of flying on from London to Greece, Turkey, and the Middle East, returning to Washington by 29 December, and Admiral Denfeld concurred. My greatest difficulty was selling the additional trip to Mrs. Radford, who would be alone over most of the holidays; but she approved, and I was in business.

I gathered a group to join me on the trip, and on Sunday 28 November *Duke of York* and other units of the Home Fleet got under way for exercises en route to Portsmouth, England.

My host kept me busy during this passage. Nearly every morning I inspected part of the flagship. Knowing that the First Lieutenant would have everything slicked up if he had time to arrange things in advance, I was not cooperative. When my guide and a ship's master-at-arms came for me I told them which part of the ship I wanted to see that very morning. As a consequence I saw what *Duke of York* looked like on an average day. Although she was not brand new, she was one of the latest British battleships, but she certainly was not being kept up, to our standards at least.

The majority of the younger seamen seemed physically below par compared to our own young sailors. Talking it over with the Senior Medical Officer, he told me that they were, on the whole, poor physical specimens. They were of the wartime generation who had suffered from lack of vitamins during the critical growing age due to strict rationing in England.

Always an admirer of the Royal Navy, I began to realize what Britain had been through during her six-year struggle for existence in World War II. Evidences of strict economy were plain everywhere, from the wardroom on down.

Duke of York had a large quarterdeck. In choppy weather an occasional sea would break over the deck but the water did not drain off quickly. I was surprised to find that scuppers were set in the teak deck along the deck edges but that there were no waterways along the edges as in our ships. Water simply sloshed back and forth until it managed to find a scupper. I was told that line officers in the Royal Navy had little to say about details such as this. Naval constructors in the Admiralty made these decisions and many others affecting the comfort and appearance of ships. This I could not believe. It meant that senior line officers in the Royal Navy simply did not pay enough attention to details during or after construction. In many instances, they assumed that their constructors were the best in the world and let it go at that.[1]

Operation Chicken started 4 December. It first involved the Bermuda detachment joining the carrier *Illustrious*, then with *Illustrious* on our side, intercepting a force coming up from the south consisting of two more carriers, *Theseus* and *Vengeance*, and eight destroyers. The weather was squally with occasional strong winds, the sea not rough but choppy. *Illustrious* operated aircraft but *Theseus* and *Vengeance*, which were smaller and somewhat like our CVLs, did not. I was not impressed with the handling of the ships and air groups.

Three days later came Operation Sunrise, in which the Royal Air Force was to play an important part. Admiral McGrigor and his staff assumed that RAF bombers using atomic bombs would attack at night in coordination with attacks by R.N. submarines.

With my aviation background I was brought into the staff discussions as a "consultant." Since the carriers were not prepared to operate night fighters (they did not have any), only defensive arrangements could be made by the Fleet Commander. After listening to all the details I suggested that the best protection would be a large circular formation that could maneuver by simultaneous turns and that did not have the heavy ships in the center. I explained that the RAF bomber pilots, at altitudes of 15-20 thousand feet to avoid heavy AA fire, would be on instruments and using radar. At that altitude they could not positively identify heavy from light ships but would probably assume that ships in or near the center of the formation were the larger combatant ships and probably the carriers they would want to knock out. My advice was taken. Although the formation did expose some of the larger ships on outer circles to submarine attacks, it certainly misled the RAF pilots, who bombed the center of the formation where there were a few destroyer types, able to maneuver radically after the bombs were dropped. Since the submarines were not active at the same time, the Home Fleet came through practically unscathed.

I was informed later that my hosts and the RAF had arguments about the formation used at that time. The RAF thought it was not entirely cricket!

When preparing for the cruise I had inquired from knowledgeable friends about a present I might give my host, Admiral McGrigor, and my friend Fleet Adm. Sir Michael Hodges. The consensus was that a large American ham would be a most welcome gift in ration-starved England. I mention these hams because of the great excitement they caused when presented. I felt almost ashamed to realize what a gift of a whole ham meant to an English family at that time. Certainly in the United States we did not appreciate the fact that our British allies were still being strictly rationed as late as December 1948.

My four days in London were busy, with briefings at U.S. Headquarters, Royal Navy calls, and a call on Minister of Defense V. A. Alexander and the Commandant of the Imperial Defense College, Air Marshall Sir John Slessor. I also had an opportunity to visit the Royal Naval Museum and the Royal Naval College at Greenwich. The museum in particular fascinated me; one comes away with a real appreciation of the important role of the Royal Navy in the building of the British Empire.

My party departed London for Naples on 17 December, and two days later we arrived at Yeşilköy airfield.

This was my first visit to Turkey. I had been told that the Turks, particularly the armed services, were great for details and energetic in carrying them out, but I was not prepared for the whirlwind that followed our arrival and that, with rather short breaks for sleeping on our two nights there, continued until we took off. The mere recollection tires me 20-odd years later!

As we circled to land at Yeşilköy we had a good view of the Sea of Marmara, the Bosporus, and the city of Istanbul with its beautiful mosques; we could see patches of snow on the field and evidence that a strong wind was blowing.

A large naval honor guard and many naval officers awaited our debarkation. Not a single detail was missed in our reception. In spite of the chilling wind I inspected the whole guard and was introduced to the Turkish custom of greeting the men in ranks and receiving their greetings in return. As I came to each unit of the guard I would say "Good morning, men" (in Turkish, which I had just learned) whereupon the men in ranks would shout out, "Good morning to you, sir," also in Turkish. It was a unique touch that I have never seen duplicated elsewhere.

Honors over, our party, accompanied by the senior officers of the Turkish Navy and a few representatives of the Army and Air Force, embarked on the Turkish destroyer *Demir Hissár* for the naval base at Gölcuk on the Asiatic side of the Sea of Marmara. Although *Demir Hissár* was by no means a new ship she was well kept up and our ride was very comfortable. I was told, for the first time, that the whole Turkish fleet was assembled at Gölcuk and standing by for my inspection. Since we were to arrive about 3:00 and it would be dark by 5:30 I could not possibly conduct the whole inspection myself. Five inspection parties were quickly organized, headed by the line officers in the party. This solved the problem but still required a strenuous workout on arrival at Gölcuk.

Our Turkish visit continued at this rapid pace. That night there was a large buffet dinner. At 8:00 we boarded the train from Istanbul to Ankara as it passed through a nearby town. This train, with its old but comfortable sleeping cars, was the famous Berlin-to-Baghdad Orient Express of pre-World War I days, about which so many mystery stories have been written.

We were given a detailed briefing on the military situation in Turkey and the part that our military aid program was playing in stabilizing the political situation, domestically as well as vis-à-vis the pressures being steadily applied by the USSR. Some of my notes made at the time read now almost like current news dispatches from that part of the world.

Following visits with Chief of the Turkish General Staff Omurtok and Minister of National Defense Cakir, we were able to meet with President İnönü, which pleased me very much.

The President greeted us warmly. A very nice-looking man of medium height and build, probably in his middle or late seventies, he spoke excellent French and a little English, so we were able to carry on an interesting conversation.

Quite naturally, the question of U.S.-Turkish cooperation came up. The President said he realized that Turkey must always look out for its own interests first, and that the U.S. must of course do the same. But he felt that in view of our mutual interests we should be able to discuss with some degree of frankness our plans in certain eventualities. I replied in effect that I agreed with him, adding that I thought a forthcoming visit by Adm. Richard Connolly would lay the groundwork for just such discussions since he was the JCS Commander for the Middle East at that time; I mentioned that he could speak for the JCS. This seemed to please the President, as I had hoped it would, but later I found that our Ambassador, James Wadsworth was somewhat concerned, feeling that I had made too definite a commitment. Writing to Connolly after I returned to Washington I mentioned the incident and told him that the Ambassador had made a resume of the conversation and would probably discuss it with him on his next visit to Ankara. I said I felt I had committed him to nothing, but that I did feel strongly that the time had come when, in our conversations with the Turks, we must be prepared to discuss details.

Into Istanbul again, the whole party was given a hasty but very interesting tour of the downtown area before the long flight to Dhahran, Saudi Arabia. We had received special clearance to overfly Egypt upon failing to get clearance to overfly Syria and Iran.

After cool weather in Britain, Italy, and Turkey we were looking forward to the heralded warmth of Saudi Arabia. To our amazement, it was raining and quite cool in Dhahran. Our Aramco hosts assured us that the weather was most unusual—that the rain was general throughout Saudi Arabia and would probably average two to three inches! The comforts of the Aramco Executive House were welcome that night.

Our first visit was on Bahrein Island, an independent sheikdom under a British protectorate, not far off the coast. There we called on Sir Rupert Hage, the British Resident, and then on His Highness Sheik Sir Suliman bin Hamad al Khalifa, a most interesting man who was of course very wealthy from oil revenues but who lived simply. The Sheik seemed conscious of his responsibilities to his people and reportedly was trying to improve their education and health. At the same time, there was no question of his authority: he was an absolute monarch, benign in many respects but tough when the situation called for toughness.

That evening, in Dhahran, Sen. E. V. Robertson of Wyoming and I had a conference with Aramco's J. MacPherson, Vice President and Resident Administrative Officer, and J. Terry Duce, Vice President and Chief Geologist. Mr. MacPherson wanted to brief us on Aramco's problems with the Saudi government prior to our audience the next afternoon with King Ibn Saud. Mr. Duce spoke of the development of the oil fields in Saudi Arabia and noted their size and worldwide importance. I was impressed with his description of the reserves. He said the total Saudi proven reserves were estimated in 1948 at some 30 billion barrels, a figure comparable to the total proven reserves in the continental United States. The great difference, he explained, was that the Saudi reserves had been proven by drilling about 100 wells whereas the United States reserves had been gradually proven over a much longer period and by drilling approximately 1,000 wells per year!

Mr. MacPherson and Mr. Duce also emphasized the outside pressures being placed on the Saudi government not only by other Arab governments but by the Russians. Middle Eastern oil was already a prize coveted by many and destined to cause trouble for the world. It was to get just such information firsthand that I was visiting there.

Flying over Saudi Arabia, one is most impressed by its rugged desolation and utter barrenness. It is almost inconceivable that some four to six million people can exist in such a wasteland, somehow finding food for their horses, camels and sheep. But beneath these deserts lies one of the greatest oil pools ever discovered, a sort of Aladdin's lamp that can bring to these nomads almost every worldly benefit if they can learn how to exploit its power and value.

In a report to me after the trip one of my companions, R. Adm. Luis deFlorez, who had been closely associated with the U.S. oil industry, wrote, "I feel that Russia must be casting its eyes on this part of the world and that it is not beyond the realm of possibility that the growing national ambitions of Israel may include the oil lands of Arabia."

We were met in Jidda by American Minister J. Rivers Childs and his staff.

Not all of our party made the trip because of limitations on the number to be present at the audience with the King.

The meeting with the King, His Majesty King Abdul Aziz Ibn Abdurrahman al Faisal al Saud, had first been suggested by Admiral Connolly, our Naval Commander in London. I had said I would be glad to meet the King but doubted that the audience would be worthwhile from his standpoint. Initial efforts to arrange the meeting had been opposed by Minister Childs. Unknown to me, my good friend Bob Lovett (Under Secretary of State) had put pressure on the Minister and the meeting was finally set. Since King Saud was then resident in Mecca, the Moslem holy city barred to all other faiths, I could not meet him there. It had been arranged that the King would motor to Hadda, the country residence of his Minister of Foreign Affairs, some 23 miles from Mecca on the road to Jidda.

Without much delay the audience commenced in a rather large room. The King, an imposing man some six feet four or five inches tall and weighing over two hundred pounds, sat in a large and higher chair at one end of the room in front of large doors that opened into a courtyard garden. His retinue, including the Deputy Foreign Minister, sat on his left. All furniture had been removed from the room except chairs for the King and his audience. The floor was covered with an enormous Persian rug, one of the most beautiful I have ever seen.

The King greeted Minister Childs, who replied for all of us. While this exchange was going on (it took time for translations) several enormous and very black men in elaborate uniforms, including short swords, moved into the room with small coffee cups and black Arabian coffee. These huge men were almost identical in appearance, well over six feet tall and with a series of tribal scars on each cheek; with colorful turbans, they were a fierce-looking group. I learned later that they were Nubian slaves supplied to the King from a particular tribe in Africa.

We all sipped our coffee in an exchange with the King, as though it were a toast. The cups were collected by the Nubians immediately afterward. I noticed that if there was still coffee in a cup, the tough-looking collectors emptied it on the beautiful rug in a sweeping, disdainful sort of motion. I decided that I would drink all of mine if I were served again.

Coffee break over, the serious business of the audience got underway. After remarking on recent business with our Minister, the King began a long statement which was translated for us, in essence as follows:

> I welcome my visitors from the United States, a great country which is friendly to Saudi Arabia.
>
> In Saudi Arabia when a man says to another man, I am your friend, he follows up that statement with actions designed to prove his friendship. The friend in

turn does likewise. There is a mutual exchange which continues between the friends as the years go on.

Your President visited me here in Saudi Arabia several years ago and we made our vows of friendship, which to me continue today. Recently, however, I am puzzled. I send a message to your President, asking a question and months go by, no answer come back. (At this point I whispered to Minister Childs asking if this were true. He replied that, unfortunately, it was.)

This is very disturbing. Now I am not naive; I know there are problems coming between us, the problems of Palestine and its partition. I would like to see them settled but there are complications. We Arabs feel that the Jews are anxious to expand their holdings. We feel that they will not be satisfied with what they now have. We believe that they want to get the oil of the East, the oil we have here in Saudi Arabia, in Bahrein, in Kuwait.

Some kind of settlement must be reached if a long and mutually disastrous war is to be avoided. I have thought long and hard on this matter and have reached a conclusion which I would like to have the Admiral take back to his President.

If the United States and the United Nations, but principally the United States, will guarantee the present boundaries of Israel I believe I can get my Arab brothers to agree.

The King's remarks included more, of course, particularly intimations that the British were proving to be better friends to the Arabs than the United States. The British were furnishing arms while we were taking the opposite course.

The audience lasted for an hour, interrupted briefly when the King stepped out on the balcony for a short devotional service. Curtains were pulled as he stepped through the doors, but we could hear his booming voice making replies to the calls of a priest somewhere in the distance.

The audience over, we bade farewell to King Saud, who returned to Mecca. Our party was ushered into an adjoining room, where an enormous and elaborate buffet was set out. We were not hungry but did our best to be polite, although we could not make a dent in the meal set before us. The Minister and I had a brief conversation about the King's unusual message. He promised to get the word to Washington at once and expressed the hope that our government would take action on it immediately.

We returned to Dhahran via Kuwait, by then independent but with a British Political Agent still resident. Kuwait was important from my standpoint not only as an oil-producing country, and one in which the original concession was held by an American Oil Company, Gulf Oil of Pittsburgh, but because it was located at the head of the Persian Gulf not far from Abadan, Iran, where the Anglo-Iranian Oil Company had one of the largest refineries in the world.

I have not visited Kuwait since that short stop in December 1948, but I occasionally read of the amazing developments that have transformed the sleepy little town we visited on Christmas Eve. Kuwait was then just emerging from the poverty of centuries. The people were poor. There was little or no industry except boat-building, fishing, and trading in commodities brought in by the Kuwait dhows, which sailed as far as the African coast for their cargoes. The port also served the Iranian hinterland to the north.

We first called on British Political Agent Jordan to pay our respects. His establishment was a modest one and he seemed a very nice, quiet young man. Mr. Jordan drove us around the city and to the oil fields to the south and southeast. At his home for lunch, we heard his estimates of oil reserves in this small country. The figures did not approach those given us by Aramco for Saudi Arabia but they were huge. Mr. Jordan felt that Kuwait sat on top of one of the largest single oil fields ever discovered. The years have proved him right.

Unable to get a clearance for either Iraq or Iran, we flew from Kuwait over the head of the Persian Gulf at an altitude high enough to see something of the country to the north—the valleys of the Tigris and Euphrates rivers, irrigating the fertile fields of what is now Iraq and Syria, and that of the Karun River, headed toward the high mountains of central Iran. While not as large as the Tigris or the Euphrates the Karun was strategically important. Its valley was the pass to the north, to Teheran, the Caspian Sea, and the oil fields in northern Iran. It would probably be the preferred route for a Russian strike toward a warm, saltwater port and the oil fields of the Persian Gulf region. Abadan, its refinery, and its tanker docks were just below us, teeming with activity. The valley of the Karun headed north and we could see the roads and railroads that furnished transportation northward from Abadan.

Our observations to the north complete, we headed back, south to Dhahran. The view in this direction was equally spectacular. The southern coastline of Iran stretched out ahead for hundreds of miles on our port hand, while to starboard were Kuwait, the neutral zone, Saudi Arabia, Bahrein, the Qatar Peninsula and the Trucial Coast dimly visible to the south. On Christmas Eve 1948 in Dhahran there was strict compliance with rules imposed by the Saudi government. It was like prohibition days in the States: only private stocks of liquor were available and what drinking took place was done in privacy. Those of us who wanted to attend church services that evening found there was only one choice, a midnight mass to be held in the new Aramco cafeteria building by a Catholic priest who was permitted to hold three or four services over the holiday period. No Christian or other non-Muslim churches were allowed in Dhahran or other Aramco settlements at that time.

On Christmas Day, touring the town, we were impressed by the care taken to make things livable for all who had to work there for Aramco, native and European. The town was built in the desert; though there was practically no vegetation and fresh water was too scarce and expensive to use for flower gardens, it was well laid out. European housing was built in clusters, each served by a central air conditioning unit. There were schools for the young and vocational schools for adult Arabs who were needed to man the increasing activities of Aramco over an ever-widening area in Saudi Arabia. The dispensary-hospital installation was unusually complete.

We visited a native Arab camp on the open desert near Dhahran. Apparently it was typical of nomadic family groups, which still comprised most of the native population. We were told that this particular group numbered about a hundred adults and children, plus their horses, camels, and sheep. Their tents appeared to be made of hides. There we saw a demonstration of falconry preceded by a ritual tea served by our Arab hosts that took considerable time. We drank sparingly in spite of the fact that we had seen the water boiling actively before the tea was brewed.

Formal farewells were exchanged and we drove back into Dhahran. We were impressed with the desolation of the desert, which literally lapped at the boundaries of civilization.

Headed west toward home, we spent the following night as guests of General Sir John Crocker, the British Middle East commander at Fayid in the Suez Canal Zone. I had assumed we could fly directly there from Dhahran, but the Egyptians allowed only British planes to use the Fayid airfield, so we had to leave our plane at Cairo and change to an RAF transport.

The British Army occupied the Suez Canal Zone. They had originally set up this defensive position in World War II when North Africa became a German objective. There were still large British forces there, and the occupied territory was fenced off from the rest of Egypt with barbed wire. Emotions were running high between Egyptians and British, the former feeling that with the war over there was no need for British troops to remain on Egyptian soil. At our briefing on the problems faced there by the British, I heard the word "Fedayeen" used for the first time, meaning an Egyptian terrorist trained to infiltrate into the Canal Zone to destroy military equipment, buildings, or personnel. General Crocker made no effort to belittle the seriousness of the situation and, while he did not say so directly, he seemed to feel that Britain would soon have to withdraw from the Canal Zone entirely.

The next day's flight was one of the most interesting I have ever made. We flew generally along the North African coast, the areas fought over so bitterly between the British and Americans and the German Afrika Corps under General Rommel. Since this was almost all desert we could still see many signs of the fighting. Tank tracks were visible, as well as the wreckage of tanks, trucks, and aircraft. The positions of major engagements were marked on our charts and we could easily confirm the locations from our altitude of some 15,000 feet. Places such as El Alamein, Sidi Barrani, Quattara, Tobruk, Benghazi, and many others were thrilling to see as we passed above them.

Senator Robertson made a remark as we flew over Libya that I shall never forget: "You know, I am an amateur geologist with a particular interest in petroleum. I would say that some day great quantities of oil will be found under these deserts below us." He was right.

Coming in over the mighty Atlas range that extends from the Mediterranean coast of Algeria almost to the Atlantic coast in the Spanish Sahara, the forests and valleys of northeastern Morocco stood out in the fading light of a beautiful sunset. There was a good deal of snow on the high peaks, a surprise to those of us not familiar with the North African climate.

During World War II, the U.S. Navy built Port Lyautey, in Morocco, into a tremendous airbase for both land and seaplanes. It was an important terminus for trans-Atlantic planes and a staging point for flights to Britain, Europe, and the Middle East. It was also of strategic importance as a base for anti-submarine patrols. After the war it was one of the key bases in the redeployment program. At the time of our visit it had been reduced to an "air activity," the station having been returned to French Navy control almost exactly a year before. My official call there was on Rear Admiral Jozan, Commander of the French Naval Forces in Morocco.

On 29 December we were back in Washington. It had been a strenuous but eventful and very useful trip to me, and it had certainly given all of us a feel for our national, military, and particularly our naval problems in Europe and the Middle East. As I read the headlines today, it is plain that our problems in both places are still important and critical. But at the time of my return, I felt that the message I carried for our President from King Saud might be very helpful and I was optimistic.

I was back in my office in the Pentagon on the morning of 30 December, facing a mountain of correspondence and being brought up to date on budgetary and other interservice matters. By noon it seemed as if I had never been away. I had already reported the highlights of my trip to Admiral Denfeld, mentioning particularly the message I had received from King Ibn Saud. I told the Admiral that Senator Robertson had promised to see President Truman without delay. Since I had to go through Secretary of the Navy Sullivan and then Secretary of Defense Forrestal before seeing the President, I had not wanted the message to be delayed.

Senator Robertson saw the President that afternoon or the next morning. He told me that the President was very much interested in details of the whole trip but particularly of the message from King Saud, which the Senator told him was to come to him from me.

I was unable to see Secretary Sullivan until early the next week but gave him a complete rundown on the trip when I did. He too was impressed with the importance of the message from King Saud and urged me to get to Secretary Forrestal with it as soon as I could.

It was Saturday 8 January before I was able to meet with Mr. Forrestal at luncheon at his office. He listened carefully to the details of the trip, asking me not to skip anything. When I came to the message for the President he was impressed. He expressed the opinion that with circumstances as they were in Palestine and the Middle East generally, this offer might prove to be a key to the situation. It was my understanding when I left Mr. Forrestal's office that afternoon that he would make a date to see President Truman as soon as possible and would take me with him.

This is where the story ends, so far as I know. Mr. Forrestal saw the President and undoubtedly discussed the King's offer with him. The President could not have been surprised by it, for he had heard the outline from Senator Robertson.

What I did not realize, having been away from Washington for over a month, was that the relationship between Mr. Forrestal and the President was probably somewhat strained, not only because of the Secretary's great efforts to enlarge the Defense Department's budget during the previous three or four months but also because Mr. Forrestal was very concerned about the situation in Palestine. The president was reported to feel that the JCS and the Secretary of Defense were not backing his policy in the Middle East.

It seems to me quite likely that in bringing King Saud's offer to the attention of the President and perhaps urging its acceptance in strong terms, Mr. Forrestal's efforts had the opposite effect. The President did nothing about it.

There is another possibility: that President Truman consulted with his staff after hearing of Saud's offer from Senator Robertson. Prominent on that staff at the time was Judge Rosenman, who was in touch with Zionist leaders who, if consulted as they must have been, probably recommended against acceptance of a binding commitment on the boundaries of Palestine.

I never discussed the matter with Mr. Forrestal again, and he had opportunities to bring it up had he wished to. I never heard directly or indirectly from the White House. Senator Robertson left Washington and the Senate within a week after seeing the President. He had no further communication with the President on this subject but seemed surprised to learn from me several months later that the White House had not been in touch with me.

There is the final possibility that the matter had reached the President through the State Department and had been decided one way or the other before my return. I think this is quite unlikely, since it had been only a week since our visit to Jidda. Minister Childs' message probably did not reach the State Department before Christmas Eve. I doubt that any action was taken on it even at lower levels until Monday 27 December. There is little likelihood, in my opinion, that it reached higher levels and the White House before Senator Robertson's call on the President.

Over the years I have given considerable thought to this matter. Did I push hard enough, individually? In retrospect, I do not think I did. However, for many reasons I was not in a position to do much pushing. I was extremely busy with all sorts of problems and catching up with my own work, and, having talked at some length with Mr. Forrestal, I felt certain that he would carry the ball. He seemed in agreement with me that this offer was a most important one. Certainly he must have urged careful consideration on President Truman. I must conclude from evidence that came to me later that Mr. Forrestal was no longer one of President Truman's trusted advisers.

One other incident comes to mind which may throw a little light on Mr. Forrestal's state of mind in January 1949.

President Truman's inauguration took place on 20 January. Secretary of State George Marshall was relieved by Dean Acheson and Robert Lovett, the Under Secretary of State, was succeeded by James Webb, Director of the Budget.

Two days later I received an invitation to a stag dinner at Mr. Forrestal's home. The other two guests would be Bob Lovett and Artemus (Di) Gates, both close friends of Jim Forrestal. Di Gates was a close friend of mine from war days, with whom I had kept in touch since. I also knew Bob Lovett well officially and socially. I looked forward to an interesting and pleasant evening.

The others were assembled when I arrived. Bob Lovett was in high spirits, saying that he had just that afternoon completed and been relieved of his duties in the State Department. He had been on the wagon during his tour as Under Secretary, he said, and was now getting off. Martinis were ordered. Bob is a top storyteller at any time, but that evening he was superb, covering one tale after another in perfect dialect: first he was an Irishman, then a Portuguese, a French Canadian, a Southern planter, a cowboy. The rest of us were in stitches as he reeled them off. I had never seen Jim Forrestal laugh so hard or seem so relaxed as early that evening with his two old friends.

At dinner the jolly conversation turned serious. Di and Bob brought up the fact that Drew Pearson and Walter Winchell had been crucifying Mr. Forrestal in their columns and their radio broadcasts within the past ten days or so. Winchell had started it on 9 January with a prediction that President Truman would accept Mr. Forrestal's resignation within the next week. He also alleged that the Secretary of Defense had formed a Canadian corporation in 1929 in an effort to reduce income taxes. Winchell had been a hostile critic of the Secretary since the start of the Palestine controversy. A week later Drew Pearson joined the attack on Mr. Forrestal, first writing that Winchell's prediction that President Truman was about to accept his resignation was correct. Only the fact that Winchell predicted it kept the President from taking that action.

Both Lovett and Gates were familiar with what background there was to these stories. They discussed details and urged Forrestal to sue both commentators for libel. At first the Secretary took an active part in the exchange, bringing up details himself, but as the dinner went on he became more and more silent.

Dinner over, we moved back to the living room for coffee. Bob made an attempt to liven things up again, with no great success. The Secretary quickly excused himself about that time and we thought nothing of it, expecting him to rejoin us in a moment. With the exchanges between Di and Bob still very active and with me thoroughly enjoying every word of their conversation, time passed quickly. We suddenly realized that our host had been gone for over half an hour, that he had left us. We filed out quietly after the butler said he "supposed" the Secretary had gone to bed.

There were other instances in the next three months that tended to confirm a feeling that had been growing, as far as I was concerned, that Secretary Forrestal was nearing a nervous breakdown.

☆ ☆ ☆ ☆

In January 1949, important underlying differences of opinion between the services still existed and caused increasing tension. The Secretary of Defense had lost the battle of the budget but there were still pressures from Congress and other departments of the government to reduce the money spent for national defense. The international situation, in Europe, the Far East, and the Middle East, was one of increasing tensions due almost entirely to the aggressive actions of the USSR. There was evidence that Stalin and his cohorts were taking full advantage of the postwar turmoil to extend their power. While President Truman had become aware of this at the time of the Greek and Turkish difficulties and had taken, publicly, a strong position in defending free societies, he had never been willing to go full out for increases in the military establishment, increases which his Secretary of Defense and his JCS felt were necessary to give credibility to the tough positions he took from time to time vis-à-vis the USSR.[2]

There are many similarities in the situation faced by our government today, in 1970, and those faced by President Truman. In both 1949 and 1970 congressional concern was chiefly with domestic problems. Both President Truman in 1949 and President Nixon in 1970 had access to intelligence that they were not always able to use in arguing for more military strength, even if they had desired to do so. Both were aware of risks they would run if our military forces were too small to oppose Russian aggression in any one of several exposed areas. Russian leaders in 1949 were fully aware of the situation in the United States, militarily as well as politically.[3] They had watched our declining military strength and had had plenty of time to decide what they would do about it. Eventually they decided to unleash the Koreans in June 1950. I have often wondered why the Koreans decided to strike when they did across the thirty-eighth parallel. They had access to our military debates in 1949 and spring 1950. Had they paid attention to details they would have known that the further cuts in our military strength planned for fiscal 1951 would have left us with practically nothing in the western Pacific by June 1951. Had the Korean War started just one year later than it did South Korea would have been overrun before we could have mustered sufficient military strength to intervene.

I often wonder if—and where—we will have another Korea. Perhaps the Communists will just heat up the war in Vietnam after we have withdrawn most of our troops.

But to go back to 1949. Our Navy budget for 1950 had gone through pretty much as it was when I left for England. The flush deck carrier had survived, largely due to Mr. Forrestal's help. Within our Navy family differences were fairly well under control, but interservice difficulties were still simmering and ready to erupt at any time.

Many felt that Mr. Forrestal was about to leave and there was much speculation about his relief. I do not recall that Louis Johnson was mentioned to me as a possibility, but by mid-February that was the consensus.

Just then occurred one of those unexpected personal decisions with far-reaching effects on others. Admiral Denfeld received a letter from his friend Admiral Ramsey, whom I had relieved as VCNO and who was by then CINCPAC and Commander-in-Chief Pacific Fleet (CINCPACFLT). Duke told Admiral Denfeld that he had decided to retire. He had received an offer from the Aircraft Industries Association that he found difficult to turn down. He was letting only Louie Denfeld know in advance to give him a free hand in arranging for relief.

Admiral Denfeld called me in to read Duke Ramsey's surprising letter as soon as he had read it. An unexpected change in one of the few four-star billets could have a domino effect throughout the high command of the Navy and required careful consideration. Louie asked me to keep the information confidential but to realize that I myself might be involved and to be thinking it over.

At first I dismissed the possibility of relieving Duke Ramsey as out of the question. I was relatively junior and also younger than most of my contemporaries. I would be 53 on 27 February. I had been handpicked as VCNO by Louie Denfeld and I was certainly a key man in handling the Navy's problems with the Air Force. I did not think Louie would want to let me go.

Considering the matter further, I thought perhaps it might be a good idea for reasons I had not previously considered. I had been intimately connected with the unification struggle almost from its beginning and had naturally become identified as public enemy number one by some leaders of the Air Force, particularly Secretary Symington. If I were to leave, and particularly if I found a relief who had good contacts with the Air Force, it might smooth things over at what was bound to be a critical time when Mr. Forrestal left. It suddenly occurred to me that just the man for my job would be my close friend Admiral Price, the DCNO (Air). John was already my alter ego in handling interservice air matters and thus was thoroughly familiar with current problems in that field. Extremely competent, he was also well liked by everyone.

Another reason for its being a good idea was that at that time, in both the

Army and the Air Force, the vice chiefs of staff (number two military men) were four-star officers. When appointed I had hoped the Navy would follow that policy, and as I became better acquainted with the job I was convinced that as Vice Admiral VCNO I could not do as well on the Hill and in public as I might have done as a four-star admiral. It is difficult to argue for one's own promotion, however, and I realized that there were many good reasons for the present situation. With the idea of a move to CINCPAC, I conceived a solution. I would be willing to shift to CINCPAC as a Vice Admiral and thus make a four-star billet available for my relief as VCNO.

Louis Denfeld did not bring up the subject of CINCPAC for perhaps a week or ten days. He had to discuss the matter with Secretary Sullivan, and that usually took a little time. When he did mention the subject again I gave him my thoughts on the matter, particularly the reasoning outlined above. Maybe Louie had been thinking along the same lines, or maybe Secretary Sullivan suggested my going, I never knew. At any rate, about the first week of March Admiral Denfeld told me he would recommend that I relieve Duke Ramsey. He did not go along with downgrading CINCPAC to three stars, but thought he could get the VCNO promoted. From then on the matter was in the hands of the Secretary of the Navy and President Truman, with Mr. Forrestal and Mr. Johnson being consulted, I presumed. At this time Mr. Forrestal's own future was under discussion at the White House. Apparently, on 1 March President Truman asked the Secretary of Defense for his resignation, which was received on 2 March.[4] The following day the White House released the exchange of letters between the President and Jim Forrestal and announced the appointment of Louis Johnson as the new Secretary of Defense.[5]

March 1949 was not a particularly happy month for me or for most military men in the Pentagon. Louis Johnson, the new Secretary of Defense, was more and more in evidence as the days passed. He made it quite obvious that he was planning great changes in the Defense Department as soon as he took over. General Eisenhower was in Washington most of this month, working with the JCS on the budget for fiscal 1951 at Mr. Forrestal's request. With pressure for even deeper budget cuts, interservice tensions were growing and the groundwork was certainly being laid for the explosion that took place later on that spring and summer, the B36 inquiry.

Mr. Johnson relieved Mr. Forrestal on 28 March in a brief and to me very sad ceremony at the Pentagon. Mr. Forrestal seemed in a sort of daze on that occasion.

Toward the end of the month the three service secretaries, Royall, Sullivan, and Symington, gave a farewell dinner for Mr. Forrestal—a black tie affair with the principal civilian and military men from the three departments as guests. It was plain from the time Mr. Forrestal sat down that he was under a great emotional strain. All of us understood that President Truman was to join us later in the evening for a few remarks, but we were surprised that Louis Johnson was not present. Toward the end of dinner, Louis Johnson strolled in, dressed in a brown suit, and took an extra seat placed for him at the head table. If it had seemed strange that he was not included in the guest list in the first place it was even more unusual to have him join the party as he did.

The President joined us soon afterward, in black tie and apparently in very good spirits. His remarks followed soon and, under other circumstances, would have pleased everybody. He eulogized the outgoing Secretary for his outstanding service to the country over a long period of years, then went on to say that he had wanted very much to have Mr. Forrestal stay on but that the latter had pleaded important personal reasons for leaving, which he had been forced to accept. I am quite sure most of the guests that night knew or suspected that President Truman had asked for Mr. Forrestal's resignation, and there was a noticeable lack of applause when the President sat down. During the President's remarks Mr. Forrestal sat very quietly, a stony expression on his face.

The dining room was quiet as the Secretary of Defense rose to reply. He had completely regained his composure and his brief talk was very much to the point. He stressed the seriousness of the times and the importance of the military to the security of the country and the free world. He regretted his personal inability always to convince the Congress and the people of military needs but felt certain that his relief could do better. It was a simple and direct talk, the kind Mr. Forrestal at his best would make. I am sure all the guests left the dinner that night with heavy hearts, as I did.

I saw Mr. Forrestal at the relieving ceremony and that was my last brief glimpse of him. On the day after he flew to Hobe Sound, Florida, to visit Bob Lovett, who had a home there. Even after his departure, Admiral Denfeld and I had good reasons to be concerned about Jim Forrestal's welfare. In our personal contacts during the last few months of his service, we had noticed a marked deterioration, especially in the week before his relief. A few days before, he had called Louie Denfeld to tell him of his great concern for security in his own home. He felt, he said, that it was bugged and that "people" were getting ready to steal his "papers." Louie assured him we would have the Office of Naval Intelligence check his home for security but could only assure protection of his papers by removal to a safer place. Mr. Forrestal asked that they be put in the White House for safekeeping, at least for the time being.

In Florida, Jim Forrestal evidenced all the symptoms of a complete nervous breakdown. He was unable to get any rest and was almost constantly in fear for his own safety. These reports came to Admiral Denfeld and me on 30 March. I recommended sending Capt. John Gingrich, Mr. Forrestal's naval aide during the war years, who was very close to him, and a Navy psychiatrist, Capt. George Raines, to Hobe Sound immediately. They were no sooner on their way than I received a message from Ferdinand Eberstadt in New York asking that the

Navy not send anyone to Hobe Sound. He was getting Dr. William Menninger of the Menninger Clinic to go there the next day, and he was fearful of exciting Jim too much with the arrival of several people. I assured Mr. Eberstadt that we could rely on John Gingrich to see that nothing of that kind happened but that it was too late to recall him. In fact, the Secretary seemed to trust Johnny and to be more relaxed with him present, and Dr. Raines stayed in the background. Johnny kept Admiral Denfeld and me informed of the situation.

Eberstadt and Dr. Menninger arrived on 1 April. Apparently the doctor at once realized the seriousness of the situation and recommended immediate hospitalization. Jim Forrestal flew back to Washington with Johnny Gingrich and Dr. Raines; Johnny seemed to be able to exercise more control over him than anyone else. The Secretary was admitted to the Naval Hospital at Bethesda, Maryland. During April he responded very well to treatment. To his many friends who were allowed to call on him he seemed his old self most of the time. Even President Truman, who visited him, thought he was well on the road to complete recovery. By mid-May his physicians anticipated his discharge in another month or so. As part of the treatment they risked a relaxation of the restraints that had been imposed on him. This was a tragic error; for on the night of 21 May at about 3:00 A.M., the Secretary fell to his death from the window of a small diet kitchen near his room on the sixteenth floor, which was unguarded. Thus the country lost one of its greatest and most selfless public servants. I have often thought how much James Forrestal could have contributed toward solving the problems our country has faced in the years that followed his death.

☆ ☆ ☆ ☆

My own status was being discussed in high places, and it was not until 3 April that President Truman sent my nomination as a four-star admiral to the Senate for confirmation, announcing that I was to be CINCPACFLT. I was scheduled to fly from Los Angeles to Honolulu on 28 April after a week in Santa Monica visiting my parents.

I was just getting accustomed to a relaxing vacation routine in Santa Monica when I received a telephone call very early one morning from Secretary Sullivan, directing me to return to Washington at once. Secretary of Defense Johnson had, the day before, ordered that the construction of the new flush deck carrier *United States* be stopped.[6] Secretary Sullivan planned to protest this action and wanted me to assist him.

The keel of the *United States* had been laid in 1949, marking the culmination of four years of effort on the part of the Navy to build a prototype carrier that could operate heavy and comparatively long-range aircraft. During those years the flush deck carrier had been discussed in great detail in the JCS and in the press. Through the latter, certain Air Force elements accused the Navy of planning to get into the atomic bomb-carrying business by means of the new carrier and its heavy planes.

But Mr. Forrestal had backed the carrier proposal from the start, always with the condition that his approval extended only to the first ship. He would wait, he said, to see how she worked out before recommending others. His influence was responsible for a tentative approval to this carrier design given by General Spaatz at the first Key West Conference in March 1949.

As VCNO until 16 April 1949, I had been intimately connected with the halting progress of CVA58 and realized, as did all the Navy high command, that our success was in large part due to the constant backing given us by Mr. Forrestal after he became Secretary of Defense in 1947.

As I left the Navy Department on that day, happily en route to my new assignment in the Pacific some 4,000 miles away from the turmoil of Washington, I did not know that the new Secretary of Defense had, the day before, sent a letter to General Eisenhower, the temporary presiding officer of the JCS, stating that he would like the current views of the chiefs on the proposed aircraft carrier *United States*. In this letter, Mr. Johnson stated that he had "no preconceived notions with respect to this carrier" and that he had "not as yet formed any opinion as to whether or not its construction should go forward." Copies of the letter were sent to each of the Joint Chiefs for their information but I am quite sure that Admiral Denfeld had not received his copy before I left.

On 23 April the unilateral views of each of the chiefs on the proposed carrier were submitted to the Secretary of Defense. On the same morning Secretary Johnson ordered work on construction of the carrier stopped.[7]

In Santa Monica I had some difficulty getting a plane, and I finally called Admiral Price, who had just relieved me. Through his efforts I finally located a cargo-type DC4. John asked me if I would bring his daughter and her two children to Washington with me. I was glad to do so. In addition to John's daughter, her little girl about six, and her son about three, we picked up a few other stray passengers.

The trip was not too comfortable but was enlivened by the antics of John's grandson, who was an air travel enthusiast and was all over the plane. When he wasn't taking off all his clothes he was trying to dismantle things. He seemed so expert at unscrewing nuts and bolts that for a while I was afraid he would loosen some important part.

Late in the afternoon, over Columbus, Ohio, I received a message from Secretary Sullivan that President Truman had approved Secretary Johnson's action, that he was submitting his resignation as Secretary of the Navy, and that I did not have to return to Washington.

There was nothing for me to do but to continue with my passengers, which I did. I spent the night with Admiral and Mrs. Price and flew back to the coast the next day.

The story of the CVA-58 was, in fact, the "straw that broke the camel's back." Many naval officers had bitterly opposed the final unification legislation and were still unhappy about it. The trend of events since the first of the year, particularly the appearance of Louis Johnson on the scene (a former Army man and Under Secretary of the Army) and Mr. Forrestal's almost abrupt departure, indicated to these officers that the Navy was in for difficult times. President Truman's acceptance of Louis Johnson's action in canceling construction of a ship that represented the future of the Navy to most knowledgeable Navy men without even consulting the Secretary of the Navy, was probably the worst blow we had received and it ultimately convinced some of this group that the time had come for drastic and public reaction. Then too, we were losing our scrappy Secretary of the Navy and would most certainly get a new one who would agree to go along with the Secretary of Defense.

Time had printed a story on 11 April 1949 about Louis Johnson's first press conference, the day after he relieved Mr. Forrestal. The new Secretary proclaimed his plans for an enforced peace "right now, in one bite, as far as the law will permit." He also admitted that he had a "pretty fair conviction" of how the competition between the Air Force and the Navy's air arm should be decided. Anyone who objected, he said, "would have a chance to argue me out of that conclusion in the next couple of days." After that anyone who still disagreed would get out; "there will just not be room for them around the Pentagon and I told the three Secretaries that."

The *Time* story added:

> Four days later Johnson followed up that threat with a major personnel change which looked like a first crackdown. Vice Admiral Arthur W. Radford, wartime task-group commander, was relieved of his post as Vice Chief of Naval Operations and made Commander-in-Chief of the stripped down Pacific Fleet. Able, popular "Raddy" Radford would get the four stars of a full Admiral, but officers of the Navy and the other services got the point: Radford had been the most articulate, determined foe of what the Navy regards as an Air Force threat to the functions and size of the Navy's air arm.

Strangely enough, on a Sunday morning just before I was detached I had occasion to go to the MATS [Military Air Transport Service] Terminal at Washington National Airport to meet a group of VIP civilians who had just visited an operating carrier off Norfolk. They were guests of the Secretary of Defense under a program started by Mr. Forrestal to acquaint prominent civilians with the armed services. Shortly after I arrived to wait for the group Mr. Johnson also arrived, accompanied by several newsmen. He greeted me cordially and as we walked up and down said casually, "I noticed a story in the press the other day to the effect that I was sending you to the Pacific to get you out of Washington. I want you to know that there is nothing to it." I thanked the

Secretary and added that I had seen the story but had not worried about it because I knew it was not true. Later on one of the *Time* reporters, a good friend of mine, who had overheard this conversation said that at a press conference Secretary Johnson had also made such a remark!

In my long Navy career I met many civilians who served in high places in our government. I became quite well acquainted with many who served as Secretary of the Navy. All were gentlemen, and most were outstanding men who had made a success of their civilian careers but who, when it came to purely professional naval matters, took the advice of their military assistants. Louis Johnson was certainly an exception to this rule. At that time, I am sure, he had not the slightest doubt of his ability to fairly settle any question, military or otherwise. In the second report of the Secretary of Defense for fiscal 1949 he included a paragraph entitled "Aircraft Carrier Decision," which reads in part as follows:

> At the request of the Secretary of Defense, the Joint Chiefs of Staff considered the advisability of continuing work on the super-carrier *United States*, construction of which had previously been authorized and begun. The question was, to what extent such a carrier was required as a matter of progress in carrier aviation in order to fulfill the Navy's mission under present or projected strategic plans. The Joint Chiefs were unable to reach agreement. They conveyed their views individually to the Secretary of Defense, who made the decision to abandon the project.

Mrs. Radford and I flew from Los Angeles to Honolulu on 28 April. I will never forget getting up early on the morning of our arrival and watching the beautiful Hawaiian Islands as they loomed on the western horizon. We were on our way at last to a new assignment to which we both looked forward with great anticipation.

12

CINCPAC

On 30 April 1949 I relieved Admiral Ramsey as both CINCPAC and CINCPACFLT, the latter the naval component of the Pacific Command. The ceremonies were brief but to me impressive. I watched my new four-star flag as it was broken at the masthead with a feeling of great pride, mixed with regret that my mother and father could not be there to see it also.

Mrs. Radford and I, alone that evening in our comfortable quarters—where Admiral Nimitz had lived during World War II—wondered how long we would be in this lovely place. We hoped it would be a full two years because we had been moving pretty rapidly during and since World War II.

My new office was a short walk from our quarters, in the headquarters built for Admiral Nimitz. From my office I looked directly down the hill toward Pearl Harbor and the sunken hulk of *Arizona*. The oil storage tanks, which the Japanese could and should have destroyed during their attack, were strung out at the foot of the hill below the headquarters.

To anyone who has never lived in Hawaii it is difficult to describe the excitement of rising to greet each day. From my bedroom windows I would look out toward the lovely sunrise in the east, then drink in the beauty of the mountains, the pink clouds and the whole of Pearl Harbor to the west. Even our few rainy days had their own wet sort of beauty. In the four years I lived at 37 Makalapa Drive, I never ceased to reflect as I started each day how fortunate I was to be where I was!

Headquarters was manned on a 24-hour basis. I issued orders to the duty officers that when in the slightest doubt about whether to call me at any hour of day or night they were to err on the safe side. I had not forgotten the delays in reaching important people in Washington on the morning of 7 December 1941.

The day after the relieving ceremonies I was informed that the longshoremen's union in Hawaii had walked out on strike at midnight. A strike of this kind in Hawaii is particularly serious because so many important items of food and material arrive by sea. This strike was not unexpected, and Admiral

Ramsey had discussed it with me. I knew that the armed services would soon be called upon to help the civilian economy, for military shipping would continue to operate and the striking unions would continue to furnish stevedoring services to the military.

Once I had gotten acquainted with my two staffs, with prominent local officials, and with immediate problems in the Hawaiian area, I made plans to visit fleet activities in the whole Pacific area. A call on General MacArthur, the Commander-in-Chief Far East Command (CINCFE), my neighboring Unified Commander, was given high priority. At that time CINCFE had responsibility for Japan, Korea, the Ryukyus, the Marianas (except Guam), Formosa, and the Philippines, so far as U.S. military activities and planning were concerned. In the Pacific command I had Guam, the Trust Territory of the Pacific Islands (the Caroline and Marshall groups), Midway, Wake, Johnson, Palmyra, Canton, and American Samoa.

Under my CINCPACFLT hat came all naval ships and activities in the Pacific area, which were in the Pacific Fleet: I was responsible for their personnel, training, and support. In one of those strange organizational quirks that sometimes exist after large wars, CINCPACFLT was still Naval Governor of the formerly Japanese Bonin and Volcano Islands, including the inhabited islands of Chichi-Jima and Iwo Jima, where we had an Air Force detachment and an operational airfield. Our military activities in Korea at this time were controlled from Washington, through the Army. Later, when General MacArthur assumed the added direct responsibility of the Korean War, my Pacific command was enlarged to include the Ryukyus, the Marianas, Formosa, and the Philippines.

As High Commissioner (HICOM) of the Trust Territory, I had an important obligation to visit as many of the inhabited island clusters as I could, soon. This visit was pressing because the U.N. was taking an active interest in the Territory, and in Washington there was chatter that it should be transferred to the control of a civilian department, probably the Department of the Interior. I felt strongly that I would have to see for myself how well the naval government had been doing and find out how the majority of the islanders felt about the proposals for change.

In that initial week I had my first formal press conference, beginning a pleasant relationship with the local newsmen that continued during my tour in Hawaii. Questions at the conference concerned the size of the Pacific Fleet and the many rumors that there were to be further reductions in ships and shore activities. I had to agree that I would like to see more than two large carriers in the Pacific. I added that, having helped as VCNO to make the Pacific cutback decisions, I understood the necessity for reduction of forces there because of strategic emphasis elsewhere. I pointed out that a shift of emphasis back to the Pacific could be made any time.

In addition to the longshoremen's strike, another urgent problem was put in my lap that first week. Pressures from Washington were mounting to force relocation of the field headquarters of the Trust Territory staff from Guam, which was not part of the Territory. The Navy had been in control of practically all this vast island area when fighting ceased in August 1945, and its administration was passed to CINCPAC. President Truman emphasized the interim nature of the arrangement by appointing in October 1945 the Secretaries of State, War, Navy, and Interior as a committee to draft recommendations on problems of administration of the islands. Their deliberations involved whether the area should be made a trusteeship or annexed outright, and which governmental agency would have permanent responsibility for its administration.

The security aspect was uppermost in postwar discussions concerning control of the islands. Although the JCS considered in June 1945 that the military and strategic implications of the draft United Nations Charter were, as a whole, in accord with the military interests of the nation, many Army and Navy officers did not agree with this estimate of security within the framework of the U.N. Arguments continued throughout the next year and a half between the State, War, and Navy Departments. Army and Navy could not agree on which should run the island governments, although both agreed the military should control them. Many prominent persons and organizations thought the U.S. should annex them. This outcry grew when news of the decisions at Yalta, concerning the award of Southern Sakhalin and the Kurile Islands to the Soviet Union, was first revealed in February 1946.

Former President Herbert Hoover urged American control of the islands in a speech at graduation ceremonies of the School of Naval Administration (of civil government) at Stanford:

> We require a very large extension of these island holdings over what we had prior to 1941 if we are to maintain the defense of the United States. With the development of air power we have to extend the periphery of our defense materially and it is my hope that we are going to hold to the Pacific Islands as primary to the safety of the American people. The holding of these islands is not an extension of imperialism because we have no designs of economic exploitation . . . What we are doing is looking after not only our own defense but . . . the defense of the world.

Arguments over the future of the islands continued throughout summer and fall 1946. In November President Truman issued a statement that the United States was prepared to place the islands under a strategic trusteeship. A draft agreement to this effect would be submitted to the Security Council for approval.

Naval military government of the former Mandated Islands was ended on 18 July 1947, and on the same day the Trust Territory of the Pacific Islands, with the United States as administering authority, came into being. The U.S. Navy was given interim authority to administer the Territory. That did not allay the efforts of organizations and individuals who wanted civilian control. Much criticism continued as opportunity offered, to the time I inherited the responsibilities of HICOM of the Territory. I realized that my every action would be subject to close scrutiny by those anxious for a change. Consequently, I appreciated the import of what might otherwise have seemed an unimportant question of a shift in location of the staff of the Territory government.

Early in May I had to make some hard decisions in regard to my responsibilities as HICOM. The steps I took were not regarded with favor by the Territory staff in Guam or by the majority of the naval government group in the field. As I became better acquainted with many of them I was to find that my actions were construed as an attempt to militarize the rather easygoing naval government.

The Navy Department's directives on the shift of administrative headquarters were specific: it could not stay in Guam, but was to be moved into the Trust Territory soon. In the CNO's opinion, and apparently in that of the U.N. Trusteeship Council, the preferred location was on Truk Atoll. But I was informed by my Deputy HICOM that there was only one place he could move his staff: to Saipan, which had been a center of U.S. military activities during and just after the war. In Washington that suggestion was not well received because Saipan was north of the large mass of islands in the Territory, and its inhabitants were much more sophisticated.

I asked for more time, telling the CNO I wanted an opportunity to see for myself before I made a recommendation. I favored a move to Saipan but recognized the important disadvantages, particularly in U.N. circles.

My first trip to the western Pacific began on 24 May. In all my travels as CINCPAC/CINCPACFLT, I was interested in meeting people and inspecting facilities. Knowing that the "big boss" always sees things at their best, insofar as local commanders can arrange it, I organized my accompanying staff and the plane crew into an inspection party. The younger officers and the senior crew chiefs were adept at discovering incipient troubles and problems of all kinds. They were instructed to pass news they considered serious to me or my senior staff officer at once so I could discuss it with the local CO before departing. This procedure, which I followed during my four years in the job, worked well. I surprised many of my hosts with questions on matters that were new to them.

The period of my tenure, 1949–1953, was one in which all the services suffered from lack of experienced personnel as well as rapid changes of plans. On this first trip to the western Pacific, every command I visited was reducing its activities and in some cases preparing to decommission entirely. Just over one year later, we were all engaged in a rapid buildup and in reopening bases that had been closed only a few months.

One of the highlights of this trip was a reception in Tokyo given by V. Adm. Russell Berkey, Commander Naval Forces Far East, who had invited members of the local American and British colonies. He felt I would be interested in talking to these people and probably would not meet them otherwise in a schedule heavy with entertainment by the U.S. armed forces. Berkey was right: the people I met that afternoon were most interesting to me, particularly a group of American and British businessmen who had just come out of Shanghai as the communists were about to take over the city. Old China hands for the most part, they had differing views of what was going on in China but thought their forced visit to Japan was only a pleasant interlude. "We will be back soon doing business as usual," I heard from many of them. Their conviction was that the Chinese communists were first of all Chinese, and therefore interested in business and their personal economic welfare. The American businessmen were mostly representatives of the larger American oil companies and were the principal suppliers of "oil for the lamps of China." I found the oilmen not so optimistic as their British counterparts about their future opportunities in China under the communists. As I write it is almost 22 years later; few if any of this group ever saw Shanghai again. A curtain settled over China in 1949 that has become considerably more opaque in the years that have followed.[1]

That evening, Admiral Berkey and I were guests at dinner of Lt. Gen. W. H. Walker, Commander Eighth Army. General Walker, who led our troops in the early part of the Korean War, was killed there in an accident. Major General William Dean, a division commander, also a guest that evening, was captured and tortured in Korea. But a war in Korea was farthest from anyone's thought that evening, I'm sure, as we talked about problems of the occupation.

The next day I called on General MacArthur. The protocol was impressive, for the General, as Supreme Commander Allied Powers in Japan was a "head of state" and was treated thus by his staff.

General MacArthur remarked early in the conversation how much he loved the Navy and I'm sure he saw my slight smile, for he quickly added, "I admit I didn't always feel that way—but the extremely loyal and expert support I received from my naval confreres during the late war changed my mind." Our general exchange of wartime recollection was most interesting to me.

In answer to questions, the General expanded on his problems as Supreme Commander. He was concerned with the economic situation in Japan: the destruction of heavy industry had had a very adverse effect, and he was worried about the future. Touching on the situation in the Far East, the General indicated that he was quite unhappy with the overall situation, particularly the failure of the United States to support General Chiang Kai-shek against the Chinese communists. I shared his opinions, and it was no satisfaction to me to realize later how fully our joint fears were justified.

On one day in Japan my party were driven to Miyanoshita, a mountain resort in the vicinity of Mount Fuji. The countryside was simply beautiful, and in the clear air Mount Fuji and other peaks looked like storybook pictures.

From Japan we flew to Okinawa, where I had arranged a meeting with V. Adm. Oscar Badger, Commander Naval Forces Western Pacific, who had just pulled his ships out of China. En route we cruised at eight or nine thousand feet, often below the scattered clouds, because I wanted to see all I could of the islands and the sea in their vicinity. We were flying over many of the areas where, in Task Forces 38 and 58, I had taken part in actions during the last year of the war. As we neared Okinawa I could visualize the bloody battles with hordes of Japanese kamikazes in spring 1945. It was hard to match my recollections with the calm and beautiful ocean beneath us.

Admiral Badger was an experienced and energetic naval officer who had been in this command for some 15 months, generally the period when the fortunes of our allies, the Chinese Nationalists under Chiang Kai-shek, had deteriorated. He had been responsible not only for U.S. military participation in the many and diversified activities in China, but he was also charged with the protection of American citizens. His period in command included resumption of U.S. military aid to the Nationalists following the embargo on such aid that had been successfully recommended and enforced by General Marshall in his efforts to force a coalition government (with the Chinese communists) on Chiang Kai-shek.

I made no claim to being an expert on Far Eastern affairs, although I had always been interested in that part of the world and had read much of its history. I felt, when World War II ended, that the United States had, militarily, done an excellent job in the Pacific; I realized it was now up to our political leaders and diplomats to secure a lasting peace, but it seemed to me that that would not be too difficult. During my tour as VCNO my misgivings had begun. When we suddenly pulled our Marine division out of northern China, where they had been guarding the railroad from Tsingtao to Peking, I could not understand the reason for such a decision. I was told that General Marshall [then Secretary of State] had recommended it. I remembered talking to General Wedemeyer in 1948, just after he had reported to General Marshall on his China mission. He told me that it was the "end of a beautiful friendship," so I knew that General Marshall had not been pleased with the Wedemeyer report. In fact it was suppressed at that time.[2]

Clearly, I was anxious to talk to Admiral Badger. He was depressed. The Chinese communists were rapidly consolidating their victory on the mainland, and his remarks showed that he blamed our government for their success. He said, for instance, "You will hear it said that the Nationalists never lost a battle for want of ammunition. I want to assure you that while this may be technically true, it is also true that there were many battles that they could not fight because they had no ammunition." Many Chinese Nationalist divisions had been armed with U.S. weapons, and when our embargo shut off spare parts and ammunition they were in trouble.[3]

It was Admiral Badger who first told me that the Russians were rearming Chinese communist armies with the equipment they had obtained from surrendering Japanese divisions in Manchuria; also, that they had used for the same purpose military equipment and supplies shipped to them in Vladivostok by the United States before the end of the war. This was the first time I had heard that the United States had shipped military supplies across the Pacific to the Russians in order to get them to come into the war against Japan. I later read in General MacArthur's *Reminiscences* that "The great mass of military supplies we had sent them [the Russians] at Vladivostok during the latter stages of the war was largely transferred to the Chinese [communist] Forces."[4]

Admiral Badger gave me chapter and verse on our "mistakes," for so many of them seemed designed deliberately to destroy the government of our allies, the Nationalists. He mentioned, for instance, military aid shipments to the Nationalists that the United States had resumed late in 1948 after an embargo from August 1946 to July 1947. These he said, were often shipments of weapons such as machine guns. When the boxes were opened they frequently contained mixtures of parts—bolts for a different type of gun, for instance. He had been shown evidence that many of these shipments had been deliberately sabotaged by packers in the United States.

My afternoon and evening with Admiral Badger convinced me that most of our postwar troubles in China were of our own doing. For some reason the U.S. government switched its policy of support for the government of China in the latter part of 1945 and, for most of the next four years, or until the communists took over the mainland, largely withheld that support.[5] The success of the Chinese communist armies was made possible by the support and supplies given them by the Russians at the same time that we were refusing all military aid while trying to force the Nationalists to accept a coalition government with the communists. It is a performance in history of which this nation cannot be proud. Our actions, or lack of them at times, in these same years led *directly* to our later involvement in two more wars, the Korean War and the war in Vietnam.[6]

I left Okinawa feeling depressed. Certainly a communist victory in China would make my job as CINCPAC much more complicated. I was also disturbed at how badly our political leaders and diplomats had handled the postwar Far Eastern situation.

It was in Manila that I first heard of a promise apparently made by U.S. authorities when the Philippine government was established, to remove all American military or naval activities from Manila Bay. For the Navy this meant that Sangley Point would be turned over, probably to the Philippine navy. I mention this because during my tenure as CINCPACFLT I was planning for such a move. The Navy Yard at Olongapo, Subic Bay, also had orders that in the next year would greatly reduce its scope.

My visit to Guam was devoted to inspection of military activities on the island and familiarization with problems of the government, as well as with those of the Deputy HICOM, my number one assistant. After two strenuous days there I went to Saipan, to assess its possibilities as the proposed interim capital of the Trust Territories.

In conversations with the Deputy HICOM on Guam I had found that he much preferred to stay there; considering the difficulties of a move, this was understandable. If they were forced to move, Saipan offered the only alternative. The Island Governor of Saipan was pleased with the prospect of having the Trust Territory staff located there and was certain they could be adequately housed within the financial limitations imposed. But in conversations with some of the more prominent native Saipanese, I sensed that they were not anxious to become the so-called capital of the Territory. There was a feeling that they were not really part of the ethnic groupings in the vast area of the central Pacific. There was no question in my mind that this was true. The Saipanese—Chamorros—were neither Polynesians, Micronesians, or Melanesians. They were part Malay, probably related to the Filipinos, and part Spanish, and they were certainly more sophisticated and much better educated than the Marshallese or Carolinians. To me it was evident that the Saipanese considered themselves socially better than these other groups and wanted to become part of the United States like Guam, where the natives were also Chamorros. [In 1978 Saipan and Tinian were granted commonwealth status.]

As I toured Saipan I was given a detailed account of the battle for its capture. Fighting had been heavy and most Japanese soldiers had refused to surrender and fought to the death. A last surviving group of military and civilians were reported to have committed suicide by jumping off high cliffs into the sea at the northern end of the island. By now little evidence remained of the heavy wartime damage.

On my return to Pearl Harbor I learned that the situation in the Pacific command was generally normal, except for the continuing longshoremen's strike. The first intimation had arrived, no surprise to me, that serious trouble was brewing in Washington from interservice difficulties. I had expected something of the sort ever since Secretary of Defense Johnson had canceled construction of the *United States*. Personal correspondence and news clippings indicated that some naval officers and Navy civilian employees were determined to bring about a congressional investigation of the relationship between the Navy and the Air Force. Apparently Chairman Vinson of the House Armed Services Committee had decided to go ahead with such proceedings.

The next day, I received a personal message from Admiral Denfeld saying that Mr. Vinson had requested him to notify me that he would want my assistance during the proposed B36 investigation, probably in July or August. I organized a small group on my staff to track what was going on in Washington and draft a comprehensive statement for me to make when called upon to testify. Throughout the summer and into October I devoted a great deal of time to the matters under investigation in Washington and toward finding out what I could regarding other complaints of naval officers or civilian personnel.

But a problem that had to be settled soon was relocation of the administrative staff on Guam. I had enough information to assess the problems in that area. Regarding the pressures, mostly from the U.N., to move everyone on Guam to Truk and to make that the new capital, I was not so sure. The matter was important enough to go see for myself, so I flew to Truk for 24 hours—enough to get a good look at what everyone in the United States had once believed was the strongest and most important Japanese base in the Pacific.

My main concern, the suitability of Truk as the proposed capital of the Trust Territory, was soon satisfied. It would require extensive and expensive installations. Obviously, with a limitation of $50,000 laid down by the Navy Department, Truk could not become the capital.

Back at headquarters I decided on recommendations: that my Deputy and his staff, except for a small field headquarters at Truk and and a small staff on Guam, return to Pearl Harbor, where office space was available and the civilian community could absorb those without furnished government quarters. After all, CINCPAC/CINCPACFLT headquarters, and the educational and scientific resources of Honolulu, were the real backup for the Trust Territories and the hub of their communications with the outside world. A new civil government, expected within the next two years, could function best initially if its headquarters were in Hawaii.

In October the move was accomplished. My problems in that area of responsibility became at least controllable. I am certain that the whole staff, once settled in Hawaii, were glad the move had been made. The Saipanese, I am equally sure, were glad their island had not been selected as the capital.

13

The B36 Battle: Round One

M y involvement with what became known as the "B36 hearings" started
with the receipt of a message from Admiral Denfeld that Carl Vinson,
Chairman of the House Armed Services Committee, would want my assistance
during the hearings and that I could expect to testify at some stage. Louie's
message was not very detailed and I was more or less in the dark. I soon found
out that the same situation existed in the Navy Department. So I relaxed as
much as I could and tried to assemble the basic information needed.

It was not too difficult to trace the problem, almost from its beginning. In
addition, I soon found that I could count on help from the Air Force, as individual officers in that organization began to write to me and it became evident
that enthusiasm for the B36 was not shared by all Air Force pilots. But what
seemed in June–August 1949 to be a rather complicated affair with uncertain
beginnings is quite different when reviewed almost 22 years later.

The story of the B36 hearings starts with the postwar pressures for unification put on the Navy by the Truman administration, many influential members
of Congress, and the Army (including of course the Army Air Corps). At the
time I took office as VCNO in 1948 I first heard of Air Force plans to reduce
B36 procurement—apparently because they already considered the B50 and
B54 better aircraft. During the traumatic budget experience of my tour as
VCNO, Air Force representatives made clear their efforts to curtail naval aviation. Then, with years of tremendous effort on the part of the Navy to develop a
flush deck carrier pushed down the drain by the sudden and arbitrary orders of
Secretary Johnson, developments spawned in rapid succession. Secretary of the
Navy Sullivan resigned feeling that he had been undercut by the new Secretary
of Defense and therefore his usefulness was at an end. Principal leaders of the
Air Force, including Secretary Symington, feeling that their efforts to reduce
the size and scope of naval aviation were now on the road to complete success,
shifted into high gear.

The new Secretary of the Navy, Francis Matthews, a lawyer from the midwest, was handpicked by Secretary Johnson. Knowing absolutely nothing about the Navy, its history or its present problems, he was in no position to lead the fight for what many naval officers felt was its very existence. Furthermore, he felt he had to give Mr. Johnson his complete loyalty and was inclined to suspect the loyalty of his immediate subordinates in the Navy. Senior civilian and naval leaders under Mr. Matthews realized the seriousness of their new situation and were prepared to slug it out as opportunities appeared in an effort to educate the new Secretary of Defense, but a group of younger naval aviators, all with outstanding war records, and a few dedicated Navy civilian employees who had been feeling that normal channels of communication and education would not suffice decided to kick over the traces. They were convinced that only a congressional investigation would bring out facts that were being suppressed. These "facts" were mostly rumors, first spread in conversation but then picked up by a few columnists. These Young Turks were convinced that the Air Force so controlled public opinion through the normal communications media that the Navy could not get a fair hearing in the court of public opinion.

Most of these young men were good friends of mine, and some had asked for my blessing in their efforts. In every case I tried to stop them, feeling that theirs was a hazardous and insubordinate course and one not likely to succeed. The great majority of naval officers including myself were just as worried as this younger group, but we who had been on the Washington scene felt that the Navy *did* have friends in high places and that ultimately our positions would be justified. We felt too that there were some wild men in the Air Force who would eventually be repudiated.

George Sokolsky, a great newspaper man and a good friend, summed up the situation from the public point of view in a column in the *Washington Times Herald* on 23 September 1949.

> No one can absolutely guarantee that a Navy will not be vulnerable in the next war any more than anyone can guarantee that there will not be a next war. Louis Johnson, Secretary of Defense, is pledged to achieve amalgamation of the Armed Services and he is personally pledged to economy, to the elimination of duplication and waste.
>
> It is now the general impression that this is to be achieved by reducing the Navy to a subordinate arm of the defense—by its reduction from the pride of our country to an auxiliary ferry service.
>
> If this is what needs be, then sink the Navy. After all, bows and arrows were not retained through sentimentality after their usefulness as a weapon of offense and defense had disappeared. But who, in the year 1949, is prepared absolutely to guarantee that there will be no naval warfare in the next war? The man who does make such an assertion now assumes a very great responsibility indeed.
>
> It, of course, is being asserted that all warfare will be in the air, with a ground force to take over and hold areas captured by air power. The atom bomb is to

devastate entire nations, wipe out the civilian population and the national industry.

Then along comes somebody else who says . . . that chemical warfare and biological warfare will really do the job . . .

Of course, there is no experience with all this. The atom bomb was hurled at Japan, but the Japanese had been brought to their knees before that . . .

That does not mean that the atom bomb and the germ will not do infinite damage in the next war. It does mean that we do not know, from actual experience, what it will do . . .

Everyone denies that he wants to sink the Navy, but that precisely is happening. The morale among naval men is the lowest that it has ever been in our history.

Pretty nearly every naval officer I personally know—and I know a good many— is looking around to see what he will do next—and none of them expect to go into the Army or Air Force. They are an embittered group and they will not keep quiet.

They are today particularly embittered because the Navy is not permitted to present its cause to the American people.

This is bad public relations by the department of defense . . .

If the Navy has no case, an open hearing would establish the fact. If the Navy has a case, then the country is entitled to know what it is. Few of us are expert in these matters and many who pretend to be, merely repeat the prejudices of the side they favor.

. . . Unification does not mean suppression of the truth, nor will it mean anything but tragedy if it is done without regard to the significance of all weapons in the next war.

There is a further error in not permitting the Navy to state its case. It gives to laymen like myself the impression that there must be a motive for silencing the Navy, while giving the other arms ample opportunity to defend their judgment. That is not a good impression to get about.

Louis Johnson is doing an admirable job that calls for the support of the entire country. Unification is a sound doctrine. Waste is inexcusable. Duplication of costs is outrageous. But is it necessary to sink the Navy?

A chronological precis of the B36 hearings can best begin with a speech made in the House by Congressman James Van Zandt, a member of the House Armed Services Committee, on 26 May 1949.

Mr. Van Zandt first reminded the House that one of their most solemn obligations was to maintain at all times an adequate national defense. Because of this and other equally serious obligations as a House member, he was introducing a resolution providing for an investigation of military aircraft procurement. He wanted to assure, he said, that American taxpayers were getting a dollar's worth of defense for every dollar of taxes paid, and he wanted to determine the truth of ugly rumors circulating in Washington to the effect that the B36 program was being controlled by politics. Having been declared obsolete, the plane was now being touted as the best heavy bomber in existence. Contracts for its procurement, once about to be canceled, were now being increased, while other contracts were being reduced to furnish the money needed for the additional B36s.

According to Mr. Van Zandt, there were rumors to the effect that Mr. Symington's former company, Emerson Electric of St. Louis, was being favored to the extent of some $20 million in contract renegotiations. Throughout the aircraft industry there were rumors of disturbing circumstances surrounding these transactions, culminating in well-founded reports that Floyd Odlum, Chairman of the Board of Consolidated Vultee Aircraft Corporation, had actively assisted Louis Johnson in raising campaign funds in September–October 1948. Mr. Odlum's success in this regard coincided both with the improvement in the status of Consolidated Vultee Corporation and with the reputation of the product on which its financial future was staked: the B36.

Mr. Van Zandt was careful to say that none of the rumors were more than that. But he maintained that there was sufficient evidence to warrant the congressional investigation proposed by his resolution.

As a result of Congressman Van Zandt's speech, Mr. Vinson submitted a resolution of his own to the committee and then to the House on 1 June. House Resolution 234 of the Eighty-first Congress authorized and directed the Committee on Armed Services to thoroughly investigate matters involving the B36 bomber and other issues.

From the wording of the resolution and the agenda, the investigation, if carefully pursued, was bound to result in thoroughgoing testimony from both sides (Air Force and Navy), each critical of the other, and bearing directly on weapons. Many naval officers felt strongly that placing ourselves in such a situation was a great mistake—that while matters of "strategy" could be debated behind closed doors they should not be discussed in the detail of a public debate; furthermore, it was traditional that individual services be allowed to select the weapons they felt were best to carry out their assigned missions. In the Navy Department, during the first weeks of the effort to work out Navy position papers on all agenda items, this "family" argument had first to be settled, and it was not easy.

But the fact was that Mr. Vinson, acting for Congress and the people, had decided that the time had come to investigate in a public hearing the rumors and charges concerning the B36 and related matters. It would be undignified in many respects, a real cat and dog fight in the arena of Mr. Vinson's choosing, the hearing room of the House Committee on the Armed Services. I took a prominent part in this fight because I was ordered to do so and because I concluded it had to be done. I had many misgivings but I was certain of one thing, there was no alternative. Mr. Vinson was a determined and thorough man. It seemed to me that a satisfactory presentation of the Navy's position in these hearings offered probably the first and last chance to recapture a position in public opinion that would give the Navy a fair shake in the give-and-take of future military budgets.

For reasons I did not then understand, and which do not entirely make sense to me now, the leaders of the Air Force had elected in 1949 to try to do away with the Navy's attack carriers and particularly with the threat they felt from the new and larger prototype design, *United States*. To accomplish this feat they had resuscitated a dying bomber model, *one which they had previously and publicly announced was obsolete*. Because this plane could carry an atomic bomb to a point 4,000 miles away, drop it, and then return to its takeoff point, the Air Force said the initial problems of a war with the USSR within the next four or five years would be solved. They added, or intimated, that their solution did not require large new carriers.

This Air Force position, not entirely new but considerably refurbished and slicked up about the time Mr. Forrestal left the Defense Department, was carried by the press in great detail in February–April. The Air Force press campaign was alarmingly thorough. With cancellation of the building of *United States* it seemed to many of us in the Navy that at least Secretary of Defense Johnson, and probably President Truman, had bought the Air Force story.

The B36 hearings opened formally on 9 August. The first witness was Robert Lovett, who had been Assistant Secretary of the Army for Air during World War II. He described in detail his connection with aircraft procurement and particularly the circumstances surrounding the decision to undertake design studies for a long-range high-altitude heavy bomber in April 1941, a bomber with a range of 10,000 miles and capable of carrying a load of 10,000 pounds for half that distance. This design study resulted in orders for the procurement of two experimental planes, the XB36 and the YB36, in 1941. Circumstances in summer 1943 made it advisable to speed up procurement of production models of the B36 without waiting for tests of the two experimental models, so a letter of intent was signed and given to Consolidated Vultee Corporation for the purchase of 100 B36s. After VE Day but before VJ Day, the air staff recommended to Mr. Lovett that, along with other contracts, the B36 contract should be continued. When Mr. Lovett returned to civilian life in December 1946 the contract for 100 B36s was still in effect but none, including the two models, had been delivered.

Major General Frederick Smith, Jr., USAF, Assistant for Programming under the Deputy Chief of Staff (Operations), gave a detailed account of the history of the B36 in the Air Force. He stressed that the genesis of an aircraft and its place in the Air Force is in the Air Force mission assigned by the JCS. The Air Force must try to meet the requirements of that mission with the weapon (or aircraft) best suited to its accomplishment.

From the background of the strategic bombing mission assigned to the Air Force by the JCS, requiring long-range high-altitude bombing planes, General Smith traced the development of the B36 from a conference in August 1941 that had determined range and bombload. Requests for preliminary designs were submitted, the Consolidated design was selected, and that company was asked to build the two prototypes. By summer 1943 the War Department was concerned about losing all bases on the Continent, and a gamble on a production contract of the B36 was considered desirable; so the contract was signed for production of the 100 B36s. At the end of the war the air staff had recommended that this contract be continued.

In December 1946 Gen. George Kenney, USAF, Commander of the Strategic Air Force, recommended that the B36 contract be reduced to a few experimental test models. He did not like the plane: its range was not sufficiently greater than that of the B50 to make it acceptable. By that time the first experimental model, the XB36, had flown, so General Kenney had this additional background for his estimate of the plane.

The USAF Chief of Staff referred General Kenney's letter to the Air Material Command for comment. General Nathan Twining did not agree with Kenney and strongly urged completion of the contract for 100 B36s, citing several new and favorable developments: Pratt-Whitney had developed an improved engine giving 3,500 horsepower instead of 3,000, which gave the plane much greater performance. There was also a newer and even more promising power plant, the Pratt-Whitney VDT engine, which the command wanted to try. The B36 contract was continued.

In August 1947, General Smith continued, at the first meeting of the new Air Force Aircraft and Weapons Board, there was considerable argument over the B36. Some members wanted to cancel the contract, thinking the plane outmoded; others wanted to order more. This board also canceled the proposed VDT engine installation. On the whole, the board showed little enthusiasm for the B36.

Funding the B36 contract after July 1948 was a problem due to the expiration of wartime funding, requiring the Air Force to juggle available longer-term funds to cover the contracts they wanted to keep going. Consolidated was very concerned, pointing out that the huge Fort Worth aircraft plant would have to be closed if the B36 contract was terminated. Possible closure of that plant was of great concern to the Air Force also, for it would immediately scatter a large, skilled working force. The Air Force directed Consolidated to get in touch with the Northrop Company to study the possibility of building the production contract for B49s (the flying wing) at the Fort Worth plant.

In fall 1947, Consolidated tried again to interest the Air Force in the VDT engine installation, particularly in the last 34 B36s. After study by the Air Material Command the matter was again referred to the Aircraft and Weapons Board. This time all members except General Kenney voted for the idea.

During spring 1948 the general worsening of the world political situation, particularly with the USSR, gave impetus to Air Force studies of long-range bombing, with particular emphasis on aerial refueling as opposed to large, heavy aircraft. In April, studies were concluded which showed that the VDT engine installation was not suitable for the B36 and that it actually resulted in a slower airplane. General McNarney, then head of the Air Material Command, notified the USAF chiefs of this failure and made alternate recommendations in regard to B36 production. Concurrently, flights of B36 test models established new records that changed the whole picture. An Air Force conference received information on these tests and was extremely pleased. They felt the B36 picture was looking up. The conference recessed until late June in order to get the Air Material Command's review of the new data. When it was confirmed, all members agreed that the B36 contract (by then it was for 95 airplanes) should continue. At this time the Berlin blockade was just starting.

In fall 1948 the B36 was recommended as a long-range reconnaissance plane for the Strategic Air Force and 36 more were requested. Meanwhile as a result of President Truman's budgetary plans for succeeding fiscal years, the Air Force was required to cut back from 59 to 48 groups, necessitating reexamination of all aircraft procurement. The Board of Senior Officers (successor to the Aircraft and Weapons Board) convened in late December to do this. General Curtis LeMay, commanding the Strategic Air Force, recommended using B36s in two additional groups of heavy bombers and one additional group of reconnaissance planes; the board approved this and further recommended that the additional aircraft be funded by canceling other contracts for B49s, B45s, and F93s. In all, a total of 170 B36s were ordered.

General Smith finished testifying on 10 August and returned for questioning the next day. That morning I reported to Mr. Vinson and was asked to sit at counsel's table during the remainder of the hearings. Mr. Keenan, the committee counsel, had apparently asked for a senior naval representative to be present during the rest of the hearings, to be available as necessary to answer questions. At my request, Mr. Vinson was asked by Under Secretary of the Navy Dan Kimball to publicly clarify my status in the hearing room, which he did.

A total of 31 witnesses were heard in these first hearings before the committee and a subcommittee, including practically all active-duty senior officers of the Air Force, several heads of aircraft companies, Secretaries Johnson and Symington, Under Secretary Kimball, and several civilians.

At the outset of the hearings Mr. Vinson made it clear that priority was to be given to the first two items on the committee's agenda: (1) Establish the truth or falsity of all charges made by Mr. Van Zandt and by all others the committee may find or develop in the investigation; (2) locate and identify the sources from which the charges, rumors, and innuendoes have come.

A great deal of testimony from the senior Air Force officers was repetitive. All were convinced that in the event of war with the USSR an early strategic bombing offensive, carried out from bases on the North American continent and by striking at important targets in the USSR, was very important. I did not disagree. They were unanimous, but with varying degrees of enthusiasm, in declaring the B36 the best long-range heavy bomber in the world and an aircraft that could accomplish the job. Most seemed to think there was some magic in an altitude of 40,000 feet. Only George Kenney and Curtis LeMay differed definitely and sharply on an essential point.

Kenney testified that when he took command of the Strategic Air Force in October 1946 he did not like what he heard about the B36 from friends in Dayton. He recommended to General Spaatz that the B36 be reconsidered, giving as his main reasons its lack of performance. The Air Material Command answered his criticisms and generally said that things "were better than he thought," but did not entirely satisfy him. By June 1948, many troubles had been corrected, a new engine installed, and envelope curves developed. "The airplane astounded me," he said, "and I bought it."[1]

He said he wrote a letter to Secretary Symington in June 1949 in which he explained his feelings on the B36. It culminated in an opinion that the B36 would do very well as a *night* bomber at 40,000 feet, *where no fighter could then touch it.*

In the question period after his statement, General Kenney stuck to his opinion of the B36 as a *night bomber* only, readily agreeing that it could be shot down in daylight. He had not heard anything about high-altitude tests with the Navy's new Banshee fighter. In amplification he said, "if they (any enemy) get a night fighter with a good search radar that can operate at 40,000 feet the B36 will become *just another tanker*" (my italics).

Asked if he thought the large carrier *United States* should have been disapproved, Kenney replied that he thought "it was a wise decision." Questioned about Russian aircraft in general and fighter planes in particular, he said, "I am not worried about Russian aeronautical development being so good (that) we are outdistanced."

In an exchange regarding Navy night fighters and their ability, Kenney maintained "it would be five years before a night fighter could be developed which would take the B36 at night at 40,000 feet."

General LeMay, present Commander of the Strategic Air Force, said his first knowledge of the B36 was in December 1945 when he assumed the job as Deputy Chief of Staff in charge of Research and Development. It was he who suggested the formation of the Aircraft and Weapons Board, consisting of all major Air Force commanders, to pass on future aircraft and weapons for the Air Force. Too large and unwieldy, the board had been succeeded by the Senior Officers Board of four officers. Asked if he had attended any meeting of either board when the B36 was discussed, he said yes, on 3 January 1949, when he was commanding the Strategic Air Command. He had requested the board to increase the B36 groups in his command from two to four. (At that time, he said, a group was 18 aircraft; it was later increased to 30). He also said that 18–20 B36As were in existence but none had been delivered to his command. The board had seemed to have other ideas about the B36 and called LeMay back to ask what he would want if he could not get all the B36s he had asked for. He told them he would want the B47 (new Boeing all-jet bomber).

At another meeting of the board, LeMay had recommended cancellation of the B54 program in order to buy more B36s. After considerable discussion this recommendation was approved. He also had recommended that all 95 B36s have jet pods installed. He asserted in answer to questions that there had been no outside influence on his recommendations, that the B36 was the best airplane, and that if called upon to use it in action he would be in the first one out.

Asked if the B36 could be shot down by fighters, LeMay said, "Yes." Answering a question about day fighters shooting down a B36 at 40,000 feet, he thought "it would be very difficult." He testified that he expected to train his command to bomb day or night, in good weather or bad weather, singly or in formation. When the time came, he would decide what use to make of his forces. Asked if he now felt, with all advances and improvements in the B36, that it was possible to use them in attacking any potential target from any base in the continental United States, LeMay replied, "Yes I do."

Congressman Dewey Short then said, "If that is true, I am wondering why this government and we, as elected representatives of the people, should be spending billions of dollars in arming the countries of Western Europe. Should we not, perhaps, put more emphasis on building and improving the B36s here, because we can get them out and get them back without relying on anyone else?"

General LeMay's answer was, "Sir, I said we could take off from here and go and bomb any target any place that you asked us to. I did not say that in so doing we would win the war. I think that the proper balance of forces of land, sea, and air forces should be determined by the JCS. I think they are working on that problem." The General persisted in arguing for balanced forces in a unified, balanced team during a continuation of this exchange with Mr. Short.

Mr. Van Zandt then asked LeMay, "Do you concur in the statement of General Kenney that the B36 is purely a night bomber?"

LeMay said, "No I do not." Asked if he thought it was an around-the-clock bomber, the General replied, "I think I would employ it in the daytime under certain circumstances. I believe we could run the B36 in over a target at the present time, and not only get it over, I doubt if they would even know it was there until the bombs hit. But I do not know whether I would do it that way or not, and I won't until the time comes."

Questions continued. The General was asked if there were planes in existence that could go high enough to avoid being detected by radar. He said, yes he thought the "B36 is one such plane." Regarding the B36 versus fighters, he agreed that ultimately certain fighters would be able to shoot it down. But he said, "By that time the Air Force would have better bombers which would be relatively invulnerable."

General LeMay was followed by Gen. Hoyt Vandenberg, USAF Chief of Staff, who read a prepared statement that was very good. He outlined the threat from the USSR and the agreed requirement for instant retaliation "in order to *prevent* war." He quoted a statement by General Bradley: "We (JCS) confirm the premise of most airmen that the fear of *instant retaliation* at the hands of our strategic air offensive is the most substantial deterrent to war today . . . first things must come first—and the first is readiness in air strength." The General also quoted from a statement which he said the JCS had written to Chairman Vinson. "The JCS separately and jointly are of the firm opinion that the concepts of strategic bombing, and the extent of its employment as now planned, are sound."

General Vandenberg then reviewed circumstances in 1941 which had caused initiation of B36 contracts: "danger of Germans overrunning all of Europe and England, leaving the United States without overseas bases and facing a European enemy." To meet this possibility, "we required a bomber that could take off from the Western Hemisphere, deliver its bomb load, and return again to North America, an intercontinental bomber."

Strangely, the General and other high Air Force civilians and officers did not seem to recall that this was the exact situation faced by the United States in the Pacific in early 1942 after the Japanese had driven the allies out of their Far Eastern bases, which we had finally overcome by a naval offensive spearheaded by carrier air; and that now, in 1949, we had the capability to initiate an offensive across the Atlantic, if necessary.

In answer to a question, General Vandenberg said it was "public knowledge" that he thought the building of the carrier *United States* should have been canceled.

Secretary of the Air Force Symington followed reading a prepared statement. He emphasized the fact that "the only war you really win is the war that never starts."

The Secretary made a detailed rebuttal of the charges in the famous anonymous letter[2] and covered in Congressman Van Zandt's statement on the floor of the House.

Mr. Vinson thanked Mr. Symington on conclusion of his statement, saying it was frank and candid and answered every allegation made against the Air Force or himself personally. An argument ensued among committee members: some felt that if the Chairman felt Mr. Symington had completely answered the charges, there was no need to go on with the hearings. Mr. Vinson overruled the argument and the proceedings continued.

The Secretary said he first saw a B36 mockup in San Diego in 1942. Questioned about its range, Symington said it "had flown a good deal farther than 10,000 miles after carrying a 10,000-bomb load well beyond the halfway point."

Congressman Melvin Price asked the Secretary if he knew who had written the anonymous document. Symington astounded the committee and everyone else in the room by calmly answering "Yes." This brought on a series of exchanges, not always friendly, between Symington, Vinson, and Van Zandt. Mr. Keenan, the committee counsel, also seemed upset by Symington's assertion, since he had been trying to find the author of the anonymous document. I am sure I felt like every other spectator in the room, expecting the Secretary to be asked for a name. For some reason this was not done.

The Chairman announced that the committee would adjourn until 22 August in order to give a subcommittee, headed by Mr. Price, time to hold hearings on the west coast.

☆ ☆ ☆ ☆

The first witnesses before the subcommittee were the heads of the Northrop and Boeing Aircraft Companies.[3] Then the committee heard Donald Douglas, Robert Gross, and J. H. (Dutch) Kindelberger—real aviation pioneers, who headed the Douglas Aircraft, Lockheed Aircraft, and North American Companies, respectively.

All expressed great confidence in Air Force procurement methods and understood the necessity of occasional cancellation of contracts. Each, asked about mergers, had been involved in discussions but nothing had come of them; nor had they been pressured to go through with such mergers. Bob Gross and Dutch Kindelberger, when questioned about the integrity of Air Force leaders, expressed nothing but praise.

The committee then met in San Francisco with Gen. H. H. Arnold, USAF (retired), the wartime leader of the Army Air Forces and the man generally credited with building those forces to the peak of efficiency.

General Arnold gave a most interesting account of bomber developments from the Barling Bomber of the 1920s through the B15, B19, B17, and B29 to the B36. He stressed that, while he was intimately connected with these developments, he was largely the prodder. The developments came quite naturally as technological and engineering advances were made. The General stressed that there were no politics in selecting individual aircraft for production. He did say, however, that during World War II because of pressure for quantity he had overruled his engineers in some instances, mentioning particularly the P51.

The General then explained how the JCS decided certain questions, such as numbers of aircraft to be built, who would do strategic bombing, and the use of atomic bombs. He expounded on the qualifications of his principal wartime assistants, mentioning Kenney, LeMay, Norstad, Spaatz, and others, and gave them high marks. He felt strongly that in this postwar period we could maintain world peace only by maintaining our military strength. He was concerned that we might not do this. Under questioning, General Arnold said that in his opinion it was the Air Force plus the atomic bomb that was maintaining world peace.

Mr. Price observed near the end of the session that he thought that "all Americans who are of the opinion that *no* other nation will some day have the atomic bomb—are living in a fools' paradise."[4]

☆ ☆ ☆ ☆

General Carl Spaatz was the first witness when the full committee resumed its hearings in Washington, D.C., on 22 August.

The General read a statement on the B36 insofar as he was connected with it. He mentioned particularly having received critical comments from General Kenney in 1946 and the reply by General Twining, which he had had to adjudicate. He presented an eloquent dissertation on the value of strategic bombing in a war against a power such as the USSR.

General Spaatz expounded on the problem of shooting down bombers in formation but seemed to forget some of the serious losses suffered in World War II by USAF formations. He agreed that top officers in the Air Force would not be subject to political influence. He stated that he thought these hearings were a great disservice to the country by forcing the Air Force to disclose performance figures on the B36. I wondered what figures he was referring to, since the Air Force had disclosed practically all important performance figures in their own public releases or in leaks to the press in the previous four or five months.

The General did *not* recommend that military foreign aid funds be used to bring the Air Force from 48 to 70 groups but he did, by inference, say that he thought the Air Force should have priority over the Army and Navy. In other words, the division of funds between Army and Navy should be only after the Air Force 70-group program had been funded—General Spaatz was a direct and forthright witness!

The remaining witnesses that day were Generals Muir Fairchild, Howard Craig, and McNarny, all USAF. Generals Fairchild and Craig testified mainly on their connections with the Senior Officers Board meetings regarding B36 procurement. Both agreed that there were no outside pressures on board members.

General McNarney described his career, ending with his present assignment as Chairman of the National Defense Management Committee in the office of the Secretary of Defense. The committee job, he said, was "to institute a continuing program to reduce expenditures of the national military establishment—*without reducing our combat capabilities* and also in accordance with statutory authority."

Witnesses in the next days were Generals Twining, Norstad, and Edwin

Rawlings. General Twining, after having outlined his career, covered his connection with the development of the B36, commencing with his review of General Kenney's comments in 1946 when he was in command at Wright Field.

General Norstad sketched his career in the Air Force, ending with his present assignment as Deputy Chief of Staff, Air Force Operations. Questioned on his connection with the B36, he recalled joining in recommendations to General Arnold for the B36 in 1945. He was questioned about the ability of senior Air Force officers, whom he considered a fine group of men. Asked if he had read the anonymous letter, he said not all of it. He remarked that it had undoubtedly damaged morale in the Air Force.

General Rawlings, Comptroller of the Air Force, was asked if his books reflected the cost of the B36 program from the beginning to date. He said they did. Total dollars allotted to the B36 program to date were $988,506,574. Paid to contractors was about half the total cost. There were changes that probably would make the total dollar cost of the program $1,022,000,000.

Total unit flyaway costs of the first 95 B36s, including spares, the General gave as $4,693,392 prior to modifications, $6,248,686 after modification. The total termination cost of all aircraft contracts terminated by the Air Force from fiscal 1947 through fiscal 1949 was $56,013,700.

That afternoon, Secretary of Defense Johnson specifically and in detail denied any activities covered in the anonymous document which related to him.

On the following day there was quite an argument, started by Mr. Van Zandt, who demanded that the Chairman subpoena the author of the anonymous document and get him before the committee. Mr. Keenan, the counsel, objected, saying he felt that to bring out a name in this way would be most unjust; the man would be pilloried by the press before it was known for certain that he was the author. Mr. Vinson, who at one stage of the proceedings had said he knew the name of the author, now said he knew only the name of the man who had given the document to Congressman Charles Deane. The Chairman sent for Mr. Deane. Mr. Keenan said he would bow out if the proceedings were changed. The matter was temporarily recessed, and the committee decided to proceed with General Omar Bradley, USA, the new chairman of the JCS, as witness.

General Bradley, under questioning, said that the JCS decided who should conduct strategic bombing—the Air Force—and that the Air Force should be helped by the Navy, if possible. The JCS also passed judgment on the equipment used for strategic bombing and the proportionate relation of that equipment to the equipment required for other uses, such as tactical air.

He said the JCS were twice asked in early 1949 to approve additional B36 procurements and the modification of some B36s already built. The JCS had no objection to the switching of Air Force funds that was necessary in order to buy more and modernize other B36s. The JCS felt that the B36 was the best intercontinental bomber available at this time and probably the best that would be available within the next few years.

Asked if he knew certain senior officers of the Air Force, mentioned by name, General Bradley said he did and felt that all were outstanding men.

Discussing the evaluation of the B36 by the new Weapons Systems Evaluation Group, he said it would have to be a thorough one and was certainly of high priority.

The General agreed with a recent statement by Army Secretary Gordon Gray to the effect that we could not win a war with intercontinental bombers alone but must have bases in Europe.

The next witness was L. L. Tyler, a lawyer and former FBI man retained by the committee counsel to find the author of the anonymous document. Mr. Tyler said he had been running down leads, so far without success.

Chairman Vinson then called Cedric Worth to the stand. Questioned by Mr. Vinson, Mr. Worth identified a document handed to him as one relating to the B36 and said it looked like the one he had given to Congressman Deane. When asked his position in the Navy Department, Mr. Worth said he was a special assistant to Under Secretary Kimball.

Asked where he got the document he had given to Congressman Deane, Worth told a hushed audience that he wrote it. He said no one had known he was writing it, no one helped him with it, and that the information it contained came from many sources.

Mr. Worth was questioned in great detail by Mr. Vinson and insisted that the information contained in the document came from many sources, including the press, but that no one else had known he was writing it. He said he gave four copies to members of Congress: Deane, James Van Zandt, Styles Bridges, and Millard Tydings. No high-ranking officer ever saw it. He said Mr. Kimball did not know he had written it until four or five days before, when Worth had told him. He said that Mr. Glenn Martin [President of Martin Aircraft] had given him much of the information in the document and probably knew he was writing it. The Chairman then introduced the anonymous document into the record of the proceedings.

Asked by Mr. Vinson what prompted him to prepare this document, Mr. Worth replied, "I was greatly concerned. As the document indicates, it appears to me that the defenses of the country are going in the wrong direction and are being materially weakened by propaganda which is not true."

Mr. Van Zandt questioned Mr. Worth in some detail. Then Mr. Keenan took over the witness, telling him first that anything he said could be used against him in possible criminal proceedings. A little later, Mr. Worth claimed unfamiliarity with some details of the document, and the committee adjourned to let him reread it.

Mr. Keenan, resuming his questioning of Mr. Worth, covered his career in detail. Mr. Worth was then subjected to general questioning about whom he had spoken to in the last six months in regard to the B36, roles and missions of the Air Force and Navy, and so on. Counsel and Mr. Vinson were evidently trying to establish a tenuous connection between him and various articles that appeared in the press. This merged into questioning concerning when and how he had come to write the anonymous document, and when and under what circumstances he had come to meet Congressman Van Zandt.

Having testified that he had informed Mr. Kimball that he was the author of the document, there was now a complex of questions and answers indicating that this was not true. Worth admitted it was not. As a result, Mr. Kimball was called for questioning. It appeared from his testimony that he had never known or suspected who had written the document until he had heard of Worth's testimony late the previous day. He had then suspended Worth from his job. Mr. Kimball testified at length about the efforts he had made to find out who had written the document, never suspecting that it could have come out of his own office.

Floyd Odlum, chairman of Consolidated, was the next witness. Questioning developed on how Mr. Odlum had become interested in buying into Consolidated; how he had first met Mr. Symington; and how they had met again, in July 1948, when Mr. Odlum was told of the plan to put the B49 (flying wing) into production at the Fort Worth plant in order to keep that plant busy after the B36 contract was finished.

Further questioning developed information on contributions to the Democratic party during the presidential campaign of 1948. Odlum said he had contributed about $5,000 himself and had forwarded an additional $25,000 from some of his directors and officers.

Odlum discussed the financial status of Consolidated soon after his takeover and during 1948, when a serious loss took place due to faulty estimates on the cost of building the Convair liner. He then read a prepared statement categorically denying all charges made in the anonymous document and excoriating Mr. Worth.

Colonel John Sessums, USAF, testified that he had no knowledge of a paper recommending cancellation of B36 contracts having reached his desk in January 1948 as alleged in the anonymous document; he also had no recollection of having discussed such a document with Harvey Tafe, Washington representative of Consolidated. Mr. Tafe also denied allegations in the document which mentioned his name. A Mr. Welsh of the New York law firm Simpson, Thatcher and Bartlett, denied statements in the anonymous document which said an industry rumor had it that his law firm had been retained by the Air Force to negotiate the cutbacks necessary to buy additional B36s.

Mr. Worth was then recalled and questioned by Mr. Keenan in regard to statements and charges in the document. In every case Mr. Worth agreed he had been wrong in making such statements or charges and regretted having done so.

Finally, the Chairman said he thought that agenda item number one had been disproved and that the committee would adjourn until 5 October, when counsel could present further evidence, if any. The committee could then decide what to do.

The delay was quite a surprise to me and to the officers working with me on the statement I expected to make when called before the committee. It gave us more time to get ready for our presentation, but kept the whole business hanging over our heads.

14

B36: Round Two

S o it was that I spent Friday 26 August 1949 cleaning up odds and ends in the Navy Department and left for Pearl Harbor that evening.

My desk at headquarters there was naturally piled high, and I spent a day trying to catch up. Admiral Badger, who had been relieved as Commander Naval Forces Western Pacific, was about to arrive so I planned a conference and luncheon for him.

Admiral Badger briefed a conference of flag officers on the Western Pacific situation. He was just as pessimistic on the outlook in the Far East as he had been when I visited him in Okinawa the previous June. The Communists, Russians, Chinese, and North Koreans, he said, were elated with the success they had had in China. They were bound to take advantage of the reduction in our forces that was then taking place in accordance with the latest directives from Secretary of Defense Johnson. He could not, of course, pinpoint where new crises would break out but had a feeling that Formosa and/or South Korea were likely spots. It was rather a sober group at the luncheon following the conference, not helped by the situation I described in Washington in which the unified budget for 1951, which provided for further large cuts in naval and other forces, was being put together by General McNarney's committee.

Secretary of the Navy Matthews and his wife visited us from 2 to 7 September, having come to dedicate the new national cemetery in the Punchbowl, where hundreds of military dead of World War II had been reburied. The dedication ceremony was impressive and I could not help but think, as I stood there with the Secretary facing acres of graves, how quickly we, as a nation, are apt to forget. Here we were, the Secretary of the Navy and the Commander-in-Chief of the Pacific area, taking part in a solemn ceremony honoring the dead of a huge war ended barely four years before, but also engaged in reducing our naval and other armed forces to the point where we were almost certain to invite tension and further conflict from our dedicated adversary, international communism.

Mrs. Radford and I found the Matthews a charming couple and enjoyed showing them what we could of the beautiful island of Oahu. I must confess, however, that the better I got to know Mr. Matthews the more certain I became that his appointment as Secretary of the Navy verged on a national catastrophe. The Secretary knew that I was to be leadoff witness for the Navy when the House Armed Services Committee resumed its hearings, but he did not want to discuss the matter. I offered to let him read my prepared statement, practically in its final form. He declined, saying that he wanted to avoid the slightest pretext for accusations that he was trying to influence my testimony.

The Secretary's visit over, I devoted most of my time to getting ready for resumption of the B36 hearings. Mr. Vinson's decision to have me present during the hearings in August, which I had originally not liked at all, had proven to be a great help. Listening to questions and answers, hearing the prepared statements read by the civilians and high-ranking officers of the Air Force, left me with no illusions about the seriousness of the situation faced by the Navy. The Air Force had presented a united front and an impressive array of witnesses, who had *almost* unanimously praised the B36. There was a tiny chink in the armor left by General Kenney's blunt statement, "If they get a night fighter with a search radar that can operate at 40,000 feet—the B36 will become just another tanker."

During Kenney's testimony Mr. Vinson had referred to the 12 August 1949 issue of *U.S. News and World Report* as conveying the impression that the Navy was "all washed up." Actually there had been two such articles on the topic, that one and one in the next issue. The first article was entitled "Shift Ordered in U.S. Defense: A Plan to Concentrate Power in Air Force." It stated:

[Reprinted from "U.S. News & World Report."]

Secret orders [by the Secretary of Defense] show the coming shakeup in U.S. fighting forces. A basic overhaul of defense strategy is planned.

Navy, as blueprinted, is to lose importance as Air Force gains. Navy, Marine Air Arms are down for 50 percent cuts. Shift stresses big bombers as first line defense. It leaves Navy to protect convoys, move troops, fight submarines. This basic shift in the nation's vast military structure is to occur, if the secret orders are followed through, in the year starting next July 1 [1950].

To bring about this shift in the pattern of U.S. defenses, Louis Johnson, Defense Secretary, is moving a long step beyond that taken when he canceled construction of a super carrier for the Navy. Under powers given by the unification act as just amended, he now is acting to alter the weapons and roles of the services, to reduce the Navy's mission to that of sea patrol, and to give the Air Force a virtual monopoly of U.S. military air strength.

Shift in defense plans of U.S., based in large part on this change in the relative strength of Navy weapons, is to be along these lines.

Navy role, after such changes are made in the proportion of air and sea weapons, is certain to be limited almost solely to anti-submarine warfare. Strength of the

Navy, if the secret orders are carried out, will be concentrated in weapons for convoying U.S. cargoes abroad. Offensive weapons, and the plans for using carriers as floating bases for strategic bombing missions would be out. Major job of the Navy then will be to operate and protect a newly organized Military Sea Transport Service.

Air Force role, in turn, is to take over much of the offensive missions now held by the Navy. Air striking power of the United States will be almost wholly Air Force power, not half Air Force and half Navy.

Net result of the secret orders, thus, is to be an increase in the importance of Air Force bombers as the only remaining quick means of retaliation, and increase in the striking power of the Army and a sharp reduction in the striking power of the Navy in U.S. defense planning.

Behind this shift in the basic strategy for U.S. defense is a new set of powers given to Mr. Johnson by Congress to centralize control of the armed forces and cut competition between the services. Under new amendments to the Unification Act, for example:

> *Top policy* decisions are to be made, in the end, by the Defense Secretary rather than by the Joint Chiefs of Staff. In the past nearly all such decisions have been compromises worked out by the three Chiefs of Staff. Now any disagreement among these officials is to be reported by a new military chairman to Mr. Johnson, who has the power to decide such policy matters himself. Moreover, he is to be the *only* cabinet member from the military services, so that the President will tend to accept his decisions, even though contested by civilian heads of the military departments.

The second article of 19 August, was headed, "The New Defense Set Up: The Lines of Command." Its first two paragraphs are a precis:

> Louis Johnson, Secretary of Defense, now is taking on the job of streamlining the big and growing U.S. defense structure.

> Mr. Johnson has just been given more power by Congress. He becomes undisputed boss of the Army, Air Force and Navy, subject only to the superior power of Mr. Truman . . . He is given power, within broad limits, to shape the form and character of U.S. defenses.

> [Copyright 1949 U.S. News & World Report, Inc.]

The two articles also forecast that the 1950–51 budget for the Navy would reduce large carriers from eight to four, small carriers from ten to eight. Carrier air groups, Marine air groups, and patrol squadrons were to be reduced proportionately. Only the Navy's anti-submarine air squadrons would remain at nearly the same strength, cut from eight to seven.

As far as the Navy could ascertain, these two articles were an accurate forecast of Secretary Johnson's plan for the immediate future: preparation of the 1950–51 budget. From the testimony of Generals Bradley and Vandenberg, members of the JCS, in the first part of the B36 hearings, and from what was known of General McNarney's ideas (as Chairman of the Secretary's Budget

Committee), it was quite plain that the Navy had to make a tremendous impression—not only on the House Armed Services Committee in the second part of the hearings but on the public as well—if it were to retain any control whatever over its future status.

The rest of September passed quickly as I tried to get ready for the hearings and handle many military and semi-diplomatic problems as numerous visitors came and went. One incident that month has continued to stand out over the years. On Wednesday 14 September Miss May Craig and Mrs. Doris Fleeson, two of Washington's top newspaper women, paid a call.

I had known the ladies well in Washington and was very glad to see them. I think I had more questions to ask them than they did me. We had an interesting exchange about almost everything going on in Washington, including the B36 hearings. Toward the end of the interview, in answer to a question, I voiced great concern over what Louis Johnson was going to do to the armed services in general, and the Navy in particular, the way he was headed. To my surprise, Doris Fleeson said, as I recall her words, "You will not have to worry about Louie Johnson too much longer—he has had his throat cut but does not yet know it, and will be leaving." I could hardly believe my ears. Doris amplified her statement by saying that Mr. Johnson had tangled with Secretary of State Dean Acheson, who had taken the matter to the President. Mr. Acheson, she said, had won out and Mr. Johnson was to go at the first opportunity. May Craig did not contribute to this particular discussion but agreed with Doris Fleeson's estimate of the situation.

I often thought of this incident later, particularly, of course, when Mr. Johnson was summarily relieved by President Truman a few months after the Korean War started. While reading Dean Acheson's biography, I found out why Doris Fleeson had said what she did.[1]

Mr. Vinson's committee reconvened briefly in October as a special committee and completed its investigation into agenda items one and two. They reconvened the next day as a regular standing committee of the House, to investigate the remaining items on the agenda. For this part of the hearings the committee had no special counsel.

Mr. Vinson, opening the hearings, made an interesting statement.

Under the Constitution, the Congress is given the responsibility for raising and supporting an Army. This responsibility cannot be delegated by the Congress . . .

The House rules go on to say . . . each standing committee of the Senate and House of Representatives shall exercise continuous watchfulness of the execution by the administrative agency concerned of any laws, the subject matter of which is within the jurisdiction of such committee . . .

. . . this committee determined four months ago to conduct the inquiry commencing this morning. The committee felt last June, and recent events have confirmed that view, that there have been sufficient concern and so much obvious disagreement within the Department of Defense and that these disagreements involve such basic subjects involving the national defense, that this committee could not properly ignore the situation.

So this hearing this morning is pursuant to the committee's decision of four months ago, not—as the morning press might indicate—the results of events occurring within the last day or so or the last few weeks.

... it is the intent of the committee that all testimony given shall be frankly and freely given and be given without reprisals in the Department of Defense against any individual presenting testimony during the course of these hearings.

... we want these witnesses to speak what is in their minds, to put their cards on the table and to do so without hesitation or personal concern. We are going to the bottom of this unrest and concern in the Navy.

The Chairman then asked Secretary of the Navy Matthews to take the stand.

The Secretary stated:

... I am conscious of the responsibility involved in my mission here this morning.

In the light of that fact, I want to suggest ... that in the proceedings which I anticipate will transpire here, there will be offered matters which, in my opinion, are and should be classified matters. For this morning's consideration I refer particularly to the statement that is to be made by Admiral Radford, which I have had the opportunity to read. I think personally that the presentation of that statement and the publicizing that will result by reason of its presentation in an open meeting of this committee will have a definite effect upon the national security of our country. And I feel that I would be derelict in my duties as Secretary of the Navy if I failed to suggest to this committee that I think Admiral Radford's statement—and I speak only of that statement now because it is the only one of the statements that I have seen—should be heard by this committee in Executive session ...

To say that I was astounded by Secretary Matthews' statement is putting it mildly. Mr. Matthews had declined in Pearl Harbor to read my statement. The evening before the hearings resumed, I received a request from his office for a copy of the statement. I heard nothing further from the Secretary until this statement before the committee.

In working up the Navy's presentation, those of us most involved were worried that we would not get publicity, that our story would be considered dull and uninteresting when compared to the Air Force presentation, and that it would be carried on the back pages rather than on page one. Our presentation did seem dull to me—perhaps because I had heard it so often—but also because we were forced to discuss highly technical subjects in a manner that would not interest many people. With these thoughts ever on my mind, imagine my surprise on this morning when the Secretary, unwittingly I am sure, provided the missing ingredient to our presentation: intense human interest.

The committee's decision was ideal from the point of view of publicity. I was to present my statement to the committee in executive session that afternoon, with representatives of the Army and Air Force and Mr. Matthews present. The committee would then decide whether the statement would be given the next morning in open session, and if so would notify the press and radio. One can imagine the nationwide interest generated in the Navy's story overnight.

After the exchange about my statement, Secretary Matthews was asked to proceed. The statement he read was skillfully prepared. He gave much real support to the Navy's overall case but also plainly indicated that he favored the Secretary of Defense solution in particular (important) instances.

He sketched the problems of the Navy's lowered morale, as charged by some senior officers, generally ascribing it to the major cutbacks in naval appropriations. He pointed out that, in particular cases, officers who were greatly concerned about low morale were the same officers who had opposed unification legislation and, presumably, were still opposing it although it was the law of the land. He concluded that, generally speaking, Navy morale was good.

Finishing his polished statement, the Secretary was questioned closely and on a wide range of subjects. I was amazed at his ability to handle even the hottest questions. It showed that he had worked hard to prepare himself for this ordeal.

Before adjournment, Mr. Vinson had the committee clerk read the list of Navy witnesses who would appear. There were 23, with some very prominent names including Admirals King, Nimitz, Halsey, and Spruance; there were also some young officers, specialists in their lines.

That afternoon I read my statement before the full committee. Since the members did not feel it contained matter that could be called classified, it was decided that the press and public would be notified that the committee would convene the next morning and that I would read my statement and be questioned in open session.

The committee's hearing room was packed the next morning. There was standing room only, and the crowd overflowed into the corridors. Press and radio were there in force, thanks to Secretary Matthews' statement of the day before.

Mr. Vinson got things off to a good start with a few pithy remarks: "Before we start there must be order in the committee room. There is a large number in the audience this morning. I suggest you keep the doors open. It gets hot in here. Let a little fresh air flow through. We have to keep things on an even keel. Everyone be quiet now. Guests must take seats or stand up against the wall and stay still. All right, Admiral."

The Navy's story was to be told in an entirely different manner than that of the Air Force. The latter had a succession of senior civilians and high-ranking officers who, in general, covered the same subjects in written statements. Questioning was by counsel, and that, too, followed a pattern and was repetitive. Their story was that the B36 was an intercontinental bomber, the only one in existence, and that it was an excellent aircraft in all respects after a somewhat difficult development period. It was *almost* invulnerable because it could fly at 40,000 feet. There was some danger if it flew its missions in daylight, but practically none if they were flown in darkness because there were no night fighters in existence that could reach 40,000 feet and had search radar to help find a target in darkness at that altitude.

One strange element about the aggregate Air Force presentation, to my mind, was that they had no young pilots testify, none of the B36 squadron pilots. I noticed their absence because I had heard directly from several who told me that the B36 was not a good plane and that they did not like it. One or two even offered to testify to that effect before the committee. Several of these young men attended some of the hearings and commented in writing on the Air Force testimony. I met only one of them and did not want them to get into trouble. With this shortcoming in the Air Force presentation, the Navy wanted to put on its specialists: the young men who tested new aircraft, those who flew night fighters at high altitude, the radar experts, and so on.

My statement was general. I covered the Navy's whole story as a background for the detailed presentations to come. Reading it over 22 years later, I would change some details in light of further experience; but on the whole it filled the bill, and it certainly expressed my feelings at the time.

I concluded by summarizing my views. I said the B36, under any theory of war, was a bad gamble with national security. Should an enemy force an atomic war upon us, the B36 would be useless defensively and inadequate offensively. The plane itself was not so important as the acceptance or rejection of the theory of atomic blitz warfare that it symbolized. It was fortunate that honest doubts about the adequacy of the B36 had served to bring this more vital issue before the country.

I did not believe that the threat of atomic blitz would be an effective deterrent to a war or that it would win a war. I did not believe that the atomic blitz theory was generally accepted by military men. But if, after careful study of all sides of the question, the retaliatory atomic blitz were to become the determined and studied policy of the United States, then we must have a much more efficient weapon than the B36 to deliver it. We were now capable of procuring more effective and more efficient planes than the B36 for the task.

Development in the Air Force of planes suitable for tactical and fighter missions had suffered from overemphasis on the heavy bomber. This was apparent from inspecting the proportions for each category, not in terms of numbers of groups and planes, but in terms of money—research and development funds earmarked for tactical and fighter types. The lack of adequate fighters might have grave consequences for future security of our bases and our homeland. It was not only wasteful but might be disastrous to an unsound theory of warfare.

The unusual procedures used to push the B36 program to its present status were not justified. They undermined all unification; they prevented progress toward mutual trust, understanding, and unified planning; they shortcut the vital and proven procedures developed through experience for safeguarding the security of our country.

Any service must be permitted to bring an experimental weapon through development into test and evaluation stages. On the other hand, any service must be prevented from procuring any weapon in quantity until it has passed these stages.

We should develop weapons capable of maximum effectiveness from all land and sea areas that we control. We should push research and development of weapons to this end. We should not, however, base our war plans on such weapons until they are proven. Our defense budget should not be used for unproven weapons. American taxpayers cannot afford billion-dollar blunders. Nor can they afford expensive military procurement on a stop-and-go basis, involving costly cancellations for which our country receives nothing.

Strategic bombing should be a primary role of the Air Force, I said. But it would not be sound for the United States to rely on the so-called strategic bombing concept symbolized by the B36 delivering the atomic blitz to its present extent. In the minds of our citizens this fallacious concept promised a shortcut to victory. Our citizens must understand that its military leaders cannot make this promise, that there is no shortcut, no cheap, no easy way to win a war. We must realize that the threat of instant atomic retaliation would not prevent it, might even invite it. We must grasp that we cannot gamble that the atom blitz of annihilation could even *win* a war. We must remember that if war is forced upon us we must win it, and win it in such a way that it can be followed by a stable, livable peace.

I spent the rest of the day on the stand, after reading my statement. My emphasis on the fact that in some instances I did not think the Navy, particularly naval aviation, was getting a square deal in the Secretary of Defense's office led Mr. Vinson to bring in two financial witnesses the next morning: Adm. Herbert Hopwood, the Navy Budget Officer, and Mr. Wilfred McNeil, comptroller of the Defense Department.

Chairman Vinson made an introductory statement:

I think it is highly important to call to your attention and put in the record what the Congress has authorized in the 1950 budget. Here is what [it] . . . will do to naval air:

It provided 2,922 fewer operating aircraft in the 1950 fiscal year than was planned for as of June 30, 1949. It authorized the procurement of 480 fewer aircraft than were authorized in 1949 fiscal year—843 in 1950 compared to 1,123 in 1949. It deactivated 9 naval air stations. It failed to provide for the modernization of aircraft carriers by strengthening the flight deck and increasing fuel capacity—although the Secretary of Defense more recently has seen fit to make such an authorization on his own initiative rather than on the initiative of the Congress. It provided $30,000,000 less for aviation research and development—knocking out aircraft and engine prototypes in 1950 on projects under way. It reduced attack carrier air groups from 15 to 14, these being major units of the Navy's striking force. It decreased patrol plane squadrons from 34 to 30. It reduced naval aviation personnel by 550 officers and 11,903 enlisted. It forced the discontinuance of the use of fleet carriers to train reserve air groups. And by its providing less than half the number of new aircraft required to maintain even the reduced active aircraft authorized, it planned for reduction of the fleet air arm to not more than 3,000 aircraft within the next two or three years.

All of this without regard to the action of the Secretary of Defense on the carrier cancellation.

So I may say it seems to me easy to understand why the naval aviation leaders and the personnel of the Navy are considerably concerned.

It would appear that the Congress intended to let naval aviation wither on the vine by failing to give enough aircraft to maintain the required number of operating aircraft. *And it would also appear that the leaders in the Pentagon in the other services and in the office of the Secretary of Defense are themselves out of sympathy with naval air power, for it was their recommendation that persuaded the Congress to take the action as stated* [editor's italics].

Now let us see what is proposed to be done with the 1950 budget *after it has been enacted.* (The budget to which Mr. Vinson was referring was still in Congress.)

I have seen a reputable document, stating it as a fact, that decisions have been reached in the Department of Defense to cut naval and marine aviation strength about in half, and that the Air Force is to be given an expanded role, with big bombers becoming to even a greater extent the first line of defense, leaving the Navy only the role of protecting convoys, moving troops, fighting submarines. It is my understanding that secret orders have already been issued to that effect in the Pentagon.

Now I understand further that the Navy as a whole is to be cut under the 1950 budget, which is now pending in conference and will be voted on by the House of Representatives Monday or Tuesday—by $353,000,000 ... naval aviation is to sustain $203,000,000 or 57.5 percent of the total cut, far out of proportion to the total cut, far out of proportion to the rest of the Navy. And on top of this, flight hours per pilot are being sharply reduced.

I also have it on good authority that the Air Force is taking the position in Pentagon deliberations that no large aircraft carriers or their air groups should be kept in active commission in the Navy.

I am also advised that early last month, General McNarney, Chairman of the National Defense Management Committee, and a top ranking Air Force officer reduced the allocations for naval aircraft procurement in the 1951 budget, which of course is in a tentative state, from the $700,000,000 approved by the Joint

Chiefs of Staff under the direction of General Eisenhower to $600,000,000, and simultaneously increased by $100,000,000 the $1,100,000,000 approved for the Air Force by the Joint Chiefs of Staff.

In the making up of the 1951 budget it is reliably stated that this is what is going to happen:

Large classes of carriers will be reduced from 8 to 6, just after the 1950 budget, still in Congress, has proposed a reduction from 11 to 8.

Small carriers will be cut from 10 to 8. Carrier air groups will be cut from 14 to 6. Marine air squadrons will be reduced from 23 to 12.

Patrol squadrons will be cut from 30 to 20. Anti-submarine squadrons will be cut from 8 to 7.

Now . . . it looks to me as though it is not difficult to comprehend the concern of the air arm of the Navy and the Navy in general . . .

Admiral Hopwood confirmed that the Navy Department had been asked to reduce its 1950 spending by $353,000,000, the amount Mr. Vinson had mentioned.

The Chairman brought out the fact that in order to meet such a reduction the Navy would have to take most of it from aircraft procurement funds. Secretary Matthews admitted that a reduction of this magnitude in naval appropriations was a "reduction" in the combat capability of the Navy, not a "saving" in the sense that with reduced funding the Navy could keep the same forces but operate them more efficiently.

Mr. Vinson commented on Mr. Matthews' remarks:

I am glad to hear you say that. I want the country to know it. It is not a saving at all. It is a reduction. Now, if Mr. Johnson adheres to what has been proposed by the Management Committee, what effect will that have upon the Navy's ability to perform its roles and missions?

SECRETARY MATTHEWS: Well, it will very definitely curtail its ability to perform its roles and missions.

VINSON: Does it necessarily impair the security of the country? It would to a certain extent, would it not?

MATTHEWS: That is our opinion of it.

VINSON: And you feel when you and your associates and your predecessors went before the Appropriations Committee and told them you needed these various items which are identified, you were justified from a national security standpoint?

MATTHEWS: We were convinced that we were; yes, Sir.

VINSON: And you know of nothing now that has happened in the country or in the world that causes you to reach the conclusion that you can afford to have a reduction of $353,000,000?

MATTHEWS: I have so stated in my letter to the Secretary of Defense.

VINSON: Now, what disturbs me, members of the committee, is this: The basic question is whether or not Congress has a voice in this matter or whether it is to be entirely set by the Secretary of Defense. That is the basic thing. That is fundamental. Here it is, after months of hearings by one of the most distinguished groups of men in the Congress, who reach a decision. And I will tell you that when an appropriation committee composed of a Mr. Mahon, Mr. Engel, Mr. Sheppard, Mr. Plumley, and Mr. Sikes gives you an appropriation it is certainly justified. Now they reach a decision. Then Mr. Johnson, without the slightest information as to what effect it is going to have, sets lower figures and tells these departments to disprove them. The country must know what is going on in the Pentagon. *It is time Congress knows what is going on.*

This delving into the budgetary machinations of the Secretary of Defense brought out much information that was new to me and reinforced my feeling that Secretary Johnson was determined to reduce the combat roles of the Navy while increasing the combat responsibilities of the Air Force and the Army.

Mr. Vinson was a determined and thorough man. On this morning he brought before his committee incontrovertible proof of the Navy's main case, that it was being destroyed as a combat force by the combined efforts of the Secretary of Defense, the Army, and the Air Force. Unification had not yet provided the integrated service *team effort* that had been desired by the country and predicted by the Secretary of Defense.

The statement of Capt. Frederick Trapnell (CO of the U.S. Naval Air Test Center in Patuxent, Maryland), the first of the Navy's technical witnesses, was thoughtful and carefully prepared.

The Navy has for several years . . . taken for granted that it must be prepared to defend itself against bombers which would fly at very high altitudes and at very high speeds, altitudes and speeds way above any which have been discussed in these hearings so far. All of our new interceptor fighter designs provide the ability to do this, but production of such airplanes is very costly . . .

If, at this late date, a potential enemy should announce to the world that he would attack us with a very large, slow, unescorted bomber, we would immediately be released from a considerable burden of very costly research and development in fighter design. Yet, this is precisely the relief which we would confer on our potential enemies if we confirm our extraordinary investment in the B36.

During the past three years, the Navy has acquired considerable experience in the operation of a series of jet fighters culminating in the Banshee. This airplane gives us altitude performance superior to any other U.S. airplane presently in service. But it is not an interceptor fighter. It is a general purpose fighter carrying a large fuel load and having comparatively great range. Nevertheless, the Banshee flies at speeds and altitudes far greater than those of which the B36 is capable. But we expect to be confronted with more modern bombers and feel that we must have the still higher perfomance provided by the interceptors now under construction.

There is every reason to believe that the enemy will have fighters as good as ours. The British do. And the Russians have publicly demonstrated numbers of very advanced designs . . .

The development of jet bombers has not been comparable to that of jet fighters, for the simple reason that their very high fuel consumption has made it very difficult to provide the range required for land-based operations. That is a severe handicap for us—but it is not so for our potential enemies . . . One-way bombing missions, requiring one-half the bomber performance in range, are a thoroughly practical undertaking for them and may very soon be within their jet bomber capabilities.

With our experience, backed by the lessons of World War II, we find ourselves in sharp disagreement with the proponents of the B36. This controversy has, in effect, been submitted to the press and to the public. The technical decision which a nontechnical public is in the process of making is based on information which is incorrect in specific particulars. The importance of interpreting all such information correctly will be apparent.

Arguments in support of the B36 have led to erroneous impressions as to combat conditions at 40,000 feet.

These are specific examples:

The *false premise* that radar is ineffective against the B36.

The *false premise* that the fighter pilot has trouble in seeing or finding his target.

The *false premise* that the interception can be completed only with great difficulty.

The *false premise* that the intercepting fighters lack the performance and the maneuverability to attack effectively at high altitudes.

The *false premise* that the B36 can defend itself successfully if it is attacked.

And the *false premise* that no night fighter in existence can make an interception . . .

As for the radar problem, at the Naval Air Test Center we get good results in detecting, tracking, and controlling jet fighters—at altitudes well above 40,000 feet—with radar equipment that is four years old and without any special electronic aids in the planes. Because the B36 is a vastly more favorable target than these jet fighters, we expect even better results against it. From our experiences we see no grounds for the statement that the B36 can go undetected in enemy territory, simply because it is flying at 40,000 feet.

In fact, there is nothing significant about the figure 40,000 when considered without regard to the fighter's performance capabilities. As we increase altitude from 30,000 to 40,000 or 50,000 there are no surprises, no sudden changes, no discontinuities . . .

The top altitude of any satisfactory jet fighter is far above that of the B36. At all such altitudes, high speed and maneuverability are limited by those phenomena which appear as we approach the speed of sound. This approach is expressed in percentage of the speed of sound. The fighter can fly at a figure which is greater by at least one-quarter than the maximum figure for the B36. The fighter's speed is greater by a margin of 100 mph. And I might mention that with our new interceptors these margins will be greatly increased.

The widespread impression that, at 40,000 feet, the fighter pilot has difficulty in seeing the target in daylight is a false one. There is no loss of visual acuity, the air is generally clearer and in many cases the target produces vapor trails, which it may not do at lower altitudes, and which make it extraordinarily prominent. The B36 is the most easily located of all air targets because it is the largest. The widespread impression that interceptions at 40,000 feet can be completed only with great difficulty is a false one. It becomes solely a matter of rate of climb of the fighter.

Rate of climb figures may not be released in open session, but the time required by present Navy fighters to climb to 40,000 feet has been quoted in the press as less than 12 minutes. This is fast enough to insure interception of any propeller-driven bomber if the radar warning net is effective.

As regards the doctrine that fighters cannot attack effectively at 40,000 feet: if you were to ride as an observer in a B36 at 40,000 feet during joint exercises you would see Banshees diving and zooming all around you and apparently making repeated gunnery attacks with a speed advantage of over 100 mph.

You might notice that the maneuvers of these fighters were more deliberate than at lower altitudes, that their turns were not so sharp, and that they do not attack from broadside or directly overhead ... But they do have the ability to make coordinated attacks from all other bearings, including those most favorable to the fighter. They have, in effect, the same superiority over the B36 that the fighters had over the bombers of World War II. When these bombers were unescorted, this superiority was decisive.

In regard to the doctrine that the B36 can defend itself successfully against interceptor attack: except for the limitations I have just mentioned, the effect of altitude on the gunnery problem is negligible. At the moment both planes will mount guns of the same caliber. Gun for gun the interceptor is comparatively vulnerable but is a very small maneuvering target. Interceptor superiority is favored by the factors of surprise, initiation, and deception, and is assured by numbers. A Japanese pilot, for instance, in a single Banshee would undoubtedly press his attack all the way home and both planes would be destroyed in a collision—which would be a most economical way of dealing with very heavy bombers ... American pilots, however, are entitled to a sporting chance and, were they attacking an enemy B36, would consider that two Banshees provide a fair fight.

Three Banshees would positively insure the destruction of the B36. In larger numbers the Banshees will work progressively through a bomber formation, concentrating on parts of it with even more favorable ratios ...

You have already received testimony that we may not expect for five years to encounter any night fighter capable of intercepting the B36. This evidence has to be reconsidered in the light of the following facts.

The Corsair night fighter now in service has a performance adequate to intercept the B36 at 40,000 feet. It has a radar which is effective for ground control. The Douglas Skyknight, a two-seat jet night fighter which will soon go into service, has the performance and has radar adequate under all conditions to intercept the B36 at 40,000 feet. It completed five successful night interceptions above 40,000 on its first test.

It should be noted particularly that the target plane in this case was another small jet fighter—a poor radar target. The night fighter version of the Banshee, with overwhelmingly superior performance, will also go into service very soon. It *must* be concluded that the B36 is not, even now, safe from interception at night.

To summarize these points: we have convincing evidence that the radar will detect and track the B36; that the fighters will find and intercept the B36; that the unescorted B36s will be attacked and shot down in numbers which will be prohibitive; and that the night fighters are today a threat which cannot be ignored.

If we disregard completely the question of economy, I concur with the testimony that the B36 has some virtues as a night bomber because of the complications involved in interception and attack during complete darkness. But our knowledge of radar definitely contradicts the unqualified statements made before this committee that any ground target can be bombed at night, just the same as it might by daylight.

In addition to the very questionable accuracy of any kind of bombing from 40,000 feet, it is certain that a large percentage of strategic targets are in areas devoid of the physical characteristics which are essential if they are to be located and identified by radar. On this point alone, and without regard to the vulnerability of the B36, the chances of success of any strategic night bombing mission are extremely uncertain.

The great size of the B36 is particularly favorable to all aspects of the interception problem under all conditions. It also suggests that other methods of attack, such as bombing with proximity fuses against highly developed surface targets, might be very effective against the B36—particularly in view of the fact that it is incapable of maneuvering to any significant extent . . .

We are nearing the time when interceptor fighters will be equipped with rockets or missiles in lieu of 20-mm cannon . . . it is generally agreed that a great increase in effectiveness will result. Equivalent improvement in defensive armament of the bomber is not now feasible, and the bomber will suffer another severe setback in its contest with the interceptor fighter.

In this contest with the interceptor the B36 has raised the potential bombing altitudes by not much more than 5,000 feet over that of the B29. It has greatly extended the range, with the net result that the possibility of escort is completely eliminated.

The experience of the Navy in the operation of the fighters at high altitude may perhaps be unique in certain respects; but if so, it is impossible to avoid criticism of the Air Force's design policy with respect to fighters. There is a tendency in Air Force design to concentrate on high speed at considerable sacrifice of high-altitude performance. This tendency is most inconsistent with the bomber policy exemplified in the B36 program.

Many of the foregoing statements will be challenged by proponents of the heavy bomber. Such controversy is not easily resolved because of the complexity of the factors involved. At this point, comparative tests, carefully run and carefully evaluated, must be made. In light of the Navy's experience with existing equipment at high altitude, equipment which has not heretofore been considered, the B36 program seems unquestionably ill-advised.

It is impossible to reconcile the publicity in favor of the B36 with the reluctance to engage in joint comparative tests with the Navy. This employment of the equipment would be the most valuable possible training for both services.

I believe, however, that it would result in cancellation of any further B36 production. Even though this raises a specter of utter confusion, the issue is one which must be faced. It appears that the eagerness to be free of dependence on foreign bases, and to establish a simple method of fighting a war, has led us into error on a very large scale.

Mr. Vinson led off the questioning following Captain Trapnell's statement, which evidently impressed the members of the committee, by asking whether the information in the statement was available to the Air Force. The Captain replied that it *was* available. Although no formal presentations had been made to the Air Force, he felt certain that his conclusions should be as obvious to Air Force test pilots as they were to him.

Congressman Lansdale Sasscer remarked, "Whether your suggestions were available to the Air Force . . . they have made no effort to avail themselves of the research that you have made, have they?"

Captain Trapnell replied, "No, Sir, I feel that there has been a *distinct tendency to avoid coming to us for information or acknowledging our progress in any field*" (my italics).

Further questioning brought out again that Navy requests for a B36 to act as target for our fighters in test exercises had been refused by the Air Force.

The committee recessed. I felt certain that Captain Trapnell's testimony had made a great impression on them. Here was the Navy's chief test pilot, giving them facts that he stood ready to back up with tests controverting a good deal of the Air Force testimony on why they were purchasing the B36.

A careful and technically competent reader of Captain Trapnell's statement who was also acquainted with the Captain's record as a test pilot might still wonder why the Navy was devoting so much effort to developing fighters. Was the Navy going as far overboard in accenting fighters as they claimed the Air Force was going in the case of the high-altitude bomber?

In the development of naval aviation in general and carrier warfare in particular, the fighter had always been of primary importance to the Navy. Earlier, I pointed out that one of the greatest handicaps of our carriers at the outbreak of World War II was lack of fighters, and that this lack had been caused by erroneous conclusions drawn from fleet exercises where the *rules of engagement*, drawn up largely by nonaviators, placed too much emphasis on scouting and patrol planes. Flag officers in command of opposing forces wanted information, and long-range scouts (which could double as bombers or torpedo planes) gave them this capability. They insisted that carrier groups have a preponderance of such aircraft. Fighter types, on the other hand, did not produce much in the way of peacetime dividends. The war game rules at one time required that a single patrol plane had to be attacked by at least four fighters to be put out of action (and the four fighters were lost, too). Fighter pilots were certain that one good fighter pilot could knock down several patrol planes flying singly. The rapidly maneuvering fighter was not a good target for the gunners of a patrol plane. Read "heavy bomber" for "patrol plane" and you can see that naval aviation had been through this fighter-versus-bomber controversy long before the B36 inquiry. As soon as carrier fighter production could be stepped up after World War II started, our carrier groups had fighters in the ratio of four or five to one instead of one to four. When we improved the all-round capability of the fighter type with dive bombing, we had a valuable and versatile offensive-defensive weapon.

Another reason for Navy accent on the fighter and the night fighter during the war was the Japanese torpedo-bomber and its proficiency in night attacks. A carrier force had to protect itself around the clock, and that took good fighters, day and night, and good radar. My task group had night fighters in the air some 50 of the 90 nights when we fought off Okinawa. These fighters were usually stationed 75–100 miles from the task group at 20,000–25,000 feet altitude. We were very successful at intercepting and shooting down Japanese scout-bombers attempting to locate us at night. During daylight, and again during the days off Okinawa, we routinely stationed combat air patrols at 30,000–35,000 feet above our task forces. We had learned from experience that Japanese kamikaze groups were usually accompanied by a high-altitude observer. If we were able to intercept and shoot him down the kamikazes became confused and lost their aggressiveness.

So naval aviation entered the postwar era with a full-fledged fighter development program that was already paying great dividends when the B36 hearings took place, as Captain Trapnell pointed out to Mr. Vinson's committee. But the Air Force had shown a *"distinct tendency"* to avoid coming to the Navy for information or acknowledging in any way *our progress in any field*. By 1949 the Navy had at Patuxent one of the finest engineering test pilot schools in existence, already recognized in military aviation circles around the world. It was more than strange, it was sad, that Air Force generals such as Kenney and LeMay were not acquainted with our fighter development programs, as well as those in the rest of the world.

This is not the case today, nor has it been since soon after this famous confrontation in 1949. Air Force test pilots attend the Navy school at Patuxent and vice versa in Dayton and at Edwards Air Force Base.

Following Captain Trapnell were seven Navy technical witnesses who covered in great detail the reasons why the Navy differed with the Air Force in the important issues at stake in the B36 problem.

Lieutenant Commander Edward Harrison, radar expert attached to BUAERO, gave a broad picture of the worldwide development of radar, pointing out that the first known article on the multicavity magnetron (the heart of the radar) had been published in Russia. He said: "I believe, in view of Russia's demonstrated capabilities in other fields, having information on the performance of large high-altitude bombers and using information in radar design already made available to her, she will be ready with an adequate air defense system for use against this type of bomber." He noted that "radar is now available for fighter aircraft operating above 40,000 feet, and thus is added the final link to form an effective air defense system for use against large bombers."

Harrison ended his presentation stating that "we have, and can expect any potential enemy to have, radar equipment capable of intercepting and bringing about the destruction of large, very heavy bombers regardless of how high they fly."

Commander William Leonard, commanding Fighter Squadron 171, was the next witness; he was a Naval Academy graduate and had been a naval aviator for nine years, six with the fleet and three at the Naval Air Test Center. His appearance before the committee had been arranged in order to dispel some of the mystery that seems to becloud high-altitude fighter capabilities.

Commander Leonard stated:

I am acquainted in general with performance of jet fighter aircraft at home and abroad . . . [which] forces me to conclude that the performance of the fighters of my squadron is not unique. The airplanes of my squadron are representative of a continuing advance in fighter design . . . which is not the monopoly of any particular country. *Right now* the performance under discussion exists in jet fighters of the United States, is paralleled in Great Britain, and is boasted of in other parts of the world.

Leonard said his squadron consisted of sixteen F2H general-purpose carrier fighters, known popularly as Banshees. In the squadron training program, high-altitude operations received major emphasis.

The reason for this is technical but simple. In common with most jet aircraft, the Banshee uses its fuel most economically at high altitude. The altitude for most economical operation of the Banshee happens to be above 40,000 feet; therefore the airplane climbs to and operates at this level routinely, as a matter of choice and as a practical matter of economy. It can be truly said that the region above 40,000 feet is the domain and natural element of the F2H Banshee. It is a lonely domain. In all the hundreds of hours the squadron has operated in this region none of its pilots has ever encountered or even seen any other type airplane . . .

[The Commander covered all the points at issue in high-altitude operations, then concluded his statement.] In summary, gentlemen, Navy jet fighters currently operate freely and effectively in the regions above 40,000 feet. They have proved their ability to intercept, overtake, and shoot down targets that are much faster and more difficult than the B36 class of bomber could be at its best. In the face of current worldwide jet fighter capabilities, a bomber with performance no better than the ultimate attainable in the B36 has a negligible chance of survival.

Commander William Martin, who had specialized in instrument flying and the application of radar to combat air operations since 1940, was the next witness. He had been a Commander in the first night group operations in the Pacific war. At the time of his appearance he was assigned to the All Weather Training Unit, Pacific Fleet.

Commander Martin opened his statement by informing the committee that

should war come to America, we [the Navy] will have a small but capable defense force against raids by the so-called intercontinental bomber of the B36 type at its best combat altitude and speed, day or night.

The B36 type can be effectively attacked by fighter aircraft above 40,000 feet at night.

Single aircraft at 40,000 feet have been reliably detected by radar at ranges which permit fighter interception far from the controlling surface radar. This has been accomplished repeatedly by U.S. fighters.

Furthermore, British reports of successful interceptions have been *available to both the Navy and the Air Force for some time.*

Commander Martin sketched the night fighter situation in the Navy. The transitional night fighter, the Corsair, was operational in the fleet; the Douglas Skyknight, with many recent improvements, was under test. It carried a radar operator in addition to the pilot, making it possible to solve the most complicated interception problems with minimum aid from the ground. Its new intercept radar was many times more powerful than those used in our wartime night fighters. The Skyknight had passed many of its tests and successfully accomplished interceptions at night *above* 40,000 feet.

A night fighter version of the proven McDonnell Banshee was soon to be delivered. Plans for a night version of the high-performance Chance Vought Cutlass were under consideration. All of these jet fighters had wide speed margins over the B36 type. Recently developed air-to-air rockets also increased the armament advantage of the fighter.

Commander Martin concluded:

The Navy today is capable of intercepting and shooting down very heavy bombers of the B36 type at any altitude and speed it can attain under combat conditions, day or night.

Worthwhile target systems in the land of our most probable enemy are located at high altitudes where periods of darkness are short during the summer months. There are less than six hours of darkness during May, June, and July over Edinburgh, Helsinki and Moscow at 40,000 feet.

It is generally not so dark at 40,000 feet. Ordinarily heavy clouds do not extend much above 33,000 feet. The moon shines half of each month.

Commander Alfred Metsger, who had been head of the Fighter Design Branch of BUAERO, from 1945 to April 1949, stated:

> In repeated studies of the fighter-versus-bomber-development contest we always find that the fighter retains its decisive advantage over the bombers . . .
>
> To do its job, the fighter has advantages in speed, altitude, and concentrated fire power. This applies to both day and night fighters. The primary difference between these types is that the day fighter omits the radar in order to have an added increment in performance . . .
>
> We know that fighters armed with self-propelled missiles—rockets—have a large added advantage. Messerschmitt jet interceptors armed with rockets inflicted shocking losses to our bombers late in the last war. These rockets cannot be used by the bombers shooting back at the fighter, for on being shot they weathercock into the wind.
>
> . . . the fighter airman knows that a major step toward success in penetration of enemy territory is the performance of the modern jet bomber . . . But bombers, even . . . superb modern jet bombers, remain utterly dependent on their fighter escort. Lacking such support, large bombers operating at long range over enemy territory cannot expect to get by without disastrous losses, night or day. It could not be done here or over Europe.

Abraham Hyatt, head of the Aviation Design Research Branch, BUAERO, was the next witness. Saying that he felt "a serious error may be committed if we place reliance on the B36 as an unescorted intercontinental bomber," Mr. Hyatt explained the background leading to his finding that

> to fly a deep penetration mission of about 4,000 miles the B36 must fly a major portion of the distance over enemy territory at about 235 miles per hour and at about 23,000 feet altitude. From my calculations that would approach suicide.
>
> . . . unless some revolutionary development in engine or bomber design occurs, which cannot be applied equally well to fighter aircraft, the losses that will be sustained in unescorted intercontinental bombing raids could well prove catastrophic.

Commander Eugene Tatom, head of the Aviation Ordnance Branch of the Navy's Bureau of Ordnance, followed Mr. Hyatt.

> . . . you have heard testimony before this committee to the effect that our proposed bomber force can strike any probable major target in the world, day or night, in good weather or foul weather. It is the purpose of this statement to point out some of the difficulties of bombing and to show that radar bombing from great heights cannot be classified as precision bombing . . .
>
> In the last war, for night bombing of relatively nearby targets in familiar areas, which were fully and accurately charted, it was found necessary to employ spe-

cially trained pathfinder groups to precede the main force and lay down marker flares, and even these trained crews with radar and radio assistance frequently misplaced their flares and voided the effort of the main attack. They even bombed neutral Denmark and Switzerland by mistake.

... If we are forced to use the "A" bomb we cannot afford to miss.

Contrary to popular opinion, the effect of the atom bomb, while completely devastating in the immediate vicinity of its burst, is rather limited in its area of destruction. You could stand in the open at one end of the north-south runway at the Washington National Airport with no more protection than the clothes you now have on, and have an atom bomb explode at the other end of the runway without serious injury to you ...

To have a reasonable assurance of destroying a particular installation from 40,000 feet at night or in daylight, we must send enough planes to saturate the area with bombs, after allowing for expected operational losses and combat losses of aircraft before the target is reached, even when using atom bombs.

The great majority of the bombs will fall wide of the target and wreak havoc in the surrounding areas. These areas will most often be thickly populated.

... Just let me assure you, gentlemen, that *precision* bombing of military targets deep in enemy territory from 40,000 feet at night or in daylight is a myth.

I realized as soon as I heard the statement about standing safely in the open at Washington National Airport that it would cause great controversy and possibly vitiate the value of Commander Tatom's excellent testimony. I was sorry he had included such a statement, whether or not it was true. I doubted it, myself.

The net effect of the lengthy committee questioning and the newspaper publicity that resulted, which laid great stress on this startling statement, was in fact to negate the important points the Commander was trying to make: that even with atomic bombs it was necessary to drop them on target, because near misses were likely to result in reduced damage to important targets.

The last Navy technical witness was Capt. John Sides, a guided missile expert.

... Before some of the big bombers now on order are delivered, we expect to make a decided improvement in the effectiveness of our air defenses by means of target-seeking guided missiles which will readily intercept and knock down big bombers, even above 40,000 feet ...

The Army, Navy, and Air Force all have missiles approaching operational test which will be fired either from the ground or from other planes, and which will seek out and destroy the really fast jet bombers now on the drawing boards, day or night, and in any kind of weather in which bombers on instruments can operate.

A missile just good enough to knock down a B36 would not be good enough for a place on our development program, because we would not expect any potential enemy to use a plane so slow and vulnerable as the B36.

From the lack of questions by committee members I concluded that Captain Sides's presentation had made a great impression on all of them, particularly those who tended to favor the Air Force side and who were usually quite aggressive in follow-up questioning. It also occurred to me that a similar presentation could have been made by an Air Force Ordnance specialist in January 1949, when the Air Force Senior Officers Board was considering the purchase of additional B36s. I could think of no good reason why it had not been made.

The Navy technical presentation was completed. We had proved—to our satisfaction at least—that we already had day and night fighters that could operate above 40,000 feet at speeds well above that of the B36. And we had newer and better night fighters coming into service very soon.

Admiral Radford transfers by highline to assume command of Admiral
Montgomery's carrier division: World War II. *U.S. Navy Photo*

Carrier Division Commander Admiral Radford on the flag bridge: World War II.
Courtesy of Mrs. Arthur W. Radford

At Key West, 1948: from left, Admirals Radford and Denfeld, General Gruenther, Fleet Admiral Leahy, Assistant Secretary of Defense McNeil, Secreatary of Defense Forrestal, Generals Spaatz, Norstadt, Bradley, and Wedemeyer. *Courtesy of Mrs. Arthur W. Radford*

President Truman being welcomed to Hawaii by Admiral Radford (then CINCPAC) and other naval officers: October 1950. *U.S. Navy Photo*

Generalissimo Chiang Kai-shek, in plain tunic, smiles as Mrs. Radford admires the calligraphy and scrolls in his austere office: 1951. *Courtesy of Mrs. Arthur W. Radford*

Admiral Radford. *Courtesy of the U.S. Naval Historical Center*

General MacArthur, Supreme Commander Allied Powers, meets Admiral
Radford at Haneda Airport, Tokyo: April 1951. *U.S. Army Photo*

Fleet Admiral and Mrs. Nimitz chat with Admiral Radford at
Moffett Field, California: July 1951. *U.S. Navy Photo*

President Eisenhower presents a fourth Distinguished Service Medal to Admiral Radford on his retirement, as Vice President Nixon looks on: the White House, August 1957. *Courtesy of Mrs. Arthur W. Radford*

Former President Eisenhower and Admiral Radford at Gettysburg: July 1966. *Courtesy of Mrs. Arthur W. Radford*

Admiral and Mrs. Radford at the White House, August 1957. *Courtesy of Mrs. Arthur W. Radford*

15

B36: Revolt of the Admirals

The Navy presentation continued with some 13 witnesses, truly a parade of "stars," with statements by or for Fleet Admirals King, Nimitz, and Halsey, Admirals Denfeld, Spruance, Kinkaid, and so on.

The hearing room was crowded for the testimony of Admiral Denfeld (CNO) because of interest generated by stories in the press about what he was going to say. His statement was a remarkable document, a clear and objective analysis of the Navy's predicament and its problems, which had been brought about by unification.

> We [the Navy] endorse the spirit of unification as Congress conceived it and the public demands it. We maintain that those principles and objectives are not being realized and will not be achieved unless the Navy is admitted to full partnership.

> Gentlemen, the Navy is not seeking to destroy unification, as has been publicly charged. The Navy, whose inherent functions are as old as sea power, knows from experience the valuable results which follow the spirit of real unification, real coordination of effort. Our functions have long required operations on the sea, under the sea, on the land, and in the air, utilizing the basic principles of unity of effort. The success the Navy has achieved can be directly attributed to avoiding arbitrary separation of functions on the basis of the elements, the land, the sea, the air.

> The fact that the Navy is not accepted in full partnership in the national defense structure is the fundamental reason for the apprehension you have heard expressed here. The entire issue is the Navy's deep apprehension for the security of the United States. This apprehension arises from the trend to arrest and diminish the Navy's ability to meet its responsibilities . . .

> On April 15, 1949, the Joint Chiefs of Staff were asked for their individual opinions on the flush deck carrier project which was well under way . . . It is no secret that General Bradley reversed his earlier approval of this project. I again strongly recommended its construction, pointing out in detail its importance to the evolution of carrier aviation and naval warfare. General Vandenberg again opposed its construction.

As senior member of the JCS, it fell to me to sign the forwarding letter to the Secretary of Defense enclosing the three opinions. It was delivered to the Secretary . . .

Forty minutes later I was handed the already mimeographed press release of the cancellation order.

. . . Unification should not mean that two services can control a third. Up to now, there have been many instances in which that has happened . . .

. . . The Army and the Air Force have disapproved proposals advanced by the Navy pertaining to naval aviation and the Marine Corps. There is no intention to impugn the motives of any person in this respect; rather, [the problem] arises from lack of study or lack of experience in naval matters, or both. Nevertheless, these disapprovals constitute a pattern which I cannot ignore.

. . . I can understand the view that it is regrettable the basic differences revealed in these hearings have been aired in public. I believe, however, that it would have been immeasurably more regrettable had these issues remained hidden and a false sense of security been permitted to prevail . . .

What does the Navy propose should now be done?

First, expedite the report of the Weapons Evaluation Group in order to determine the military worth of the B36.

Second, literally support the National Security Act and the Key West agreement on roles and missions of the armed forces.

Third, support the principles that each service within budgetary limitations be permitted to design and develop its own weapons.

Fourth, provide the Navy adequate and appropriate representation in key positions within the Department of Defense.

Fifth, limit the scope of the activities of the JCS to those specifically mentioned in the National Security Act.

Sixth, [note that] in the present stage of unification, it must be recognized that the views of a particular service are entitled to predominant weight in the determination of the forces needed by that service to fulfill its missions.

The accomplishment of these points will not in itself solve all our national security problems. It will, however, go far toward providing a framework which will permit a unified approach to the grave problems of national security. We must get on with these problems, for in their solution lies the whole hope of life, liberty, and the pursuit of happiness—not only for this great country but for the entire world. The time is now!

I express the wish of the entire Navy when I say that we not only hope, but sincerely believe, that the opportunity afforded the Navy to make this presentation can but lead in the final analysis to a clearer understanding of unification and hence to a more expeditious realization of its sound objectives.

Mr. Vinson said, "Admiral Denfeld, in my judgment you have rendered a great service to the nation by making this statement . . . putting the chips on the table and letting the country know the facts." Minority leader Dewey Short also complimented the Admiral: " 'Amen' . . . to your magnificent statement . . . this committee is sympathetic to your problems, and I personally appreciate the frankness and courage that you have exhibited here. It is something that needed to be said and it was forcefully and beautifully said."

The committee's final report of the Navy's stance in the B36 hearings stated:

The Navy position was in sharp opposition to high-altitude bombing of urban areas, using either atomic bombs or TNT bombs, and in criticism of the giant B36 bomber which, for the immediate future, must be the carrier of the bombs to those targets from bases in this country.

The Navy view was a case against the present-approved theory of "strategic bombing" and against the B36 both as a weapon and as a symbol of this type of warfare against specific military targets.

The committee wishes . . . to emphasize that the testimony presented on these subjects by all witnesses was at the request of the committee and directed in answer to the committee's own agenda. There were no unsolicited "charges" and "attacks" as many have alleged, in and out of the service. There was extended honest and frank testimony, and this was as the committee intended and expected.

The Marine Corps was represented by Gen. Clifton Cates, Commandant of the Corps; the former Commandant, Gen. Alexander Vandegrift; and Brig. Gen. Vernon Megee. General Vandegrift made a short statement that was so different from most others and to me so important that I quote from it here.

The first matter [I shall discuss] is a disquieting one. It poses the question whether the problems of warfare have not grown so technical in character as to lie beyond the capacity of modern warriors to assess. It asks whether such matters should not better, in this year of 1949, be left to the trained appraisal of the military mind. Such [questions], and the trend in public thought which they portray, are disturbing.

There have been periodic crises in or among our armed services since the founding of the Republic. In nearly every case, the Congress, acting in accordance with the responsibility entrusted to it by the Constitution, has first inquired and then reached its own decision . . .

. . . The real and enduring success of the American military system rests on the fundamentals of civil control of the military function. The great weakness of any military system is that it cannot reform itself. Reform must come from without, and only in a democracy is found a civil authority of sufficient force to regularly impose its will on the military people to reform it, and to reorganize it and to retain it as the servant of the people.

The Congress has countless times performed this role and it has seldom, if ever, been in error. On the contrary, the American Congress can point with pride to the times when its judgment was vindicated even when in opposition to an important segment of professional opinion. In fairly recent years, for example, Congress acted against the strongest opposition of those in high military positions in forcing our Army to substitute the motor vehicle for the horse, to equip its troops with modern high-speed tanks and to lay the foundation for a modern air force . . .

On all these occasions, as it is doing in this inquiry today, Congress was judging not technology but men and the soundness of their ideas. It was providing that ultimate forum which our military system required, since Americans, whether in or out of uniform, cannot accept the complete suppression of an authoritarian rule.

It is, therefore, my earnest hope that the Congress of the United States will never entertain a doubt as to its competency to discharge for itself those military responsibilities entrusted to it by our Constitution and that it will never succumb to the logic of those who would see it divested of one of its greatest powers.

With respect to the unification of the armed services, I note about the national capital the same signs and portents that were present here in 1946 and 1947 when the National Security Act was being enacted. It seems as though we . . . stand no closer today to deciding these vital matters than we stood in 1946.

Then, as now, these matters were the subject of negotiations behind the scenes under the sanctuary afforded by rubber stamps marked "Confidential" or "Top Secret." Then, as now, matters which should have been presented openly to Congress for solution were withheld from the light of public inspection.

It was the Congress, acting with characteristic thoroughness and decision, that brought the matter to a solution in the National Security Act . . . [which] stated in detail the roles and missions of the Marine Corps . . . [and] guaranteed the Marine Corps its long-established status as the nation's force in readiness and its primacy in the field of amphibious warfare . . .

Hearty applause followed General Vandegrift's statement, with which the Navy-Marine Corps case was completed.

☆ ☆ ☆ ☆

The Army and Air Force began their testimony on items of the committee's agenda regarding the Navy's strategic case the next day, 18 October. Secretary Symington, Generals Vandenberg, Bradley, Marshall, J. Lawton Collins, Dwight Eisenhower, and Mark Clark were witnesses.

Secretary Symington read a statement criticizing and refuting, directly or indirectly, practically all the naval testimony. He flatly stated that the B36 could do everything the Air Force claimed it could, but he refused to answer questions relating to its vulnerability. He said that the Air Force was in favor of carriers; and that as a service they did not want a single Air Force. He blamed Admiral Nimitz for starting the whole interservice controversy through a speech made in January 1948 in which the Admiral, according to Mr. Symington, spoke of the desirability of the Navy bombing Russia's heartland. This showed that the Navy wanted to get into strategic bombing and caused the present trouble!

I listened intently to the Secretary's statement and to his answers to the many searching questions put to him by members of the committee. It seemed to me that he had either not paid much attention to the testimony of Navy witnesses or that he had decided to completely disregard, or deliberately misinterpret, what they had said. He was on the stand all day, adroitly answering questions; but he did not impress the majority with the soundness of his arguments.

General Vandenberg's statement the next morning was also intended as a complete rebuttal of charges against the B36 by Navy experts, and as a refutation of more general charges on the subject of strategic air warfare.

It was evident that both General Vandenberg and Secretary Symington thought it perfectly all right to stop construction of the carrier *United States* and thus *prevent* the Navy from "developing" this most necessary naval weapon of a new class.

At the same time both felt that it was *not* all right to require the Air Force to put *some* of their first 100 B36s through careful evaluation tests before buying 75 more.

Secretary Symington and General Vandenberg had, it seemed to me, made their statements too strong. Consequently, during the question periods committee members cornered both of them, to their embarrassment, in several instances.

To keep the record straight, the Navy had no objection to the purchase of the first hundred B36s; that was water over the dam. But it did feel that the hurried procurement of 75 additional ones, before any of the first had undergone a thorough evaluation test, was a great mistake. [As a member of the JCS] Admiral Denfeld had not voted against this procurement because he thought it was Air Force business. Further, the Navy did not think the B36 would pass a strict evaluation test as an intercontinental bomber and was prepared to prove its point.

Regarding the carrier *United States,* the Navy felt it had been approved by the President, the Secretary of Defense, and Congress as a *new development.* Under the Key West agreement each service was permitted to carry a new weapon through the development stage. Air Force representatives had heard Secretary Forrestal say on several occasions that he approved the building of one such carrier. Additional carriers would be built only if the first one proved a great success. The Navy thus felt that Generals Bradley and Vandenberg had violated the Key West agreement in voting to stop construction of the carrier when asked for their opinions by Secretary Johnson. The Navy felt too that Secretary Johnson had handled the matter in an arbitrary and unfair way.

General Bradley, chairman of the JCS, was the next witness. He read a long, involved statement which he said was entirely his own and which he had not shown to anyone, from the Secretary of Defense to the JCS. He must have been fuming when he wrote it. There was evidence throughout of an almost uncontrollable temper. His military arguments suffered, either for this reason or because his overall knowledge of some subjects was insufficient.[1]

General Collins' rather general and nonaggressive statement did no harm and may have soothed some feelings, ruffled after hearing Generals Bradley and Vandenberg.

General Eisenhower followed, with an impressive statement in the nature of a review, trying to determine from previous experience just what was wrong in the Pentagon—what had brought about the violent differences of opinion that in turn had brought about the investigation.

He told how difficulties in the JCS had resulted in Mr. Forrestal's calling him back about a year before, and how he had failed to find a formula to bring the chiefs together. He told of bringing questions to Mr. Forrestal, and of how the Secretary, when he made decisions, always requested that those he had decided against come to see him if they wished.

General Eisenhower said that the trouble in the JCS had been over money: the allocations of dollars (which the JCS had to make) in the military budget. He suggested that the committee might move closer to that problem (which also came to them) if they went to the Pentagon or had the chiefs come before them at an earlier stage in the budget proceedings.

He would not take sides or suggest solutions, General Eisenhower said. He believed in unification and thought that, ultimately, it would work. He inferred that the services *had* to learn how to work together.

General Clark did not have a prepared speech but reported on a "unification program" that Secretary Forrestal had directed him to carry out in July 1948 in nine western states. He had been told, he said, to "establish a pilot program." In general, he had received most opposition from the Navy. He thought there were still people (officers) who opposed unification, and he recommended "ruthless elimination" of them. His testimony seemed to impress the committee favorably.

General Marshall, with no prepared statement, said he could bring to the committee only his point of view as formed by his experience before and during the war and later as Secretary of State. He had concluded that the military budget would always total what the president and politicians said the country could afford; the JCS would have to divide that pie between the services. He felt the unification law should have required the chiefs to annually estimate what they thought was required for national defense. I found his remarks, which were of a philosophical nature, most interesting.

Secretary of Defense Johnson gave a long, detailed defense of all his actions as Secretary, in such a way as to make them all sound very plausible except for the story on cancellation of the *United States*. That was certainly not convincing to all members of the committee, nor to Secretary Sullivan, Admiral Denfeld, or me.

Part of the testimony was in regard to the "savings," as opposed to "reductions," that Mr. Johnson expected to make in the military budgets for fiscal 1950 and 1951. Here the Secretary managed to completely confuse his audience, even Chairman Vinson. I simply shuddered to think what was going to happen to our armed services in the next two years. We would certainly be cutting bone *and* muscle, not "fat" as Secretary Johnson maintained.

There was little questioning. Chairman Vinson appeared to be pleased with the Secretary's testimony in general; but it was not always easy to tell just how Mr. Vinson felt.

The "Unification and Strategy" part of the hearings was over. Mr. Vinson told the committee to "take all this testimony ... evaluate it ... take a little vacation, get in touch with your constituency, come back here in January and try to reach a decision as to what course of action is important."

☆ ☆ ☆ ☆

On 10 January 1950 Mr. Vinson signed and forwarded to Speaker of the House Sam Rayburn a report of the House Armed Services Committee's investigation of the B36 bomber program. The committee found Mr. Cedric Worth to be the author of an anonymous document that leveled unsubstantiated charges at many public officials, and recommended that he be discharged by the Navy Department.

The committee's Report of Investigation on Unification and Strategy, on the second part of the hearings, was larger and more involved. It was dated 1 March 1950—more than five months after the hearings had ended. The report is a masterpiece of its kind and certainly one of the more important congressional investigative reports.[2] On the so-called "rebel admirals" it is explicit:

> The committee wishes ... to emphasize that it solicited from each witness his own personal viewpoint and urged that his testimony be presented without restraint or hesitation ... therefore, the fact that the presentation of Navy views revealed fundamental disagreements within the Pentagon Building should not, in the view of the committee, be distorted into a charge against the witnesses that they were performing in any manner unbecoming their positions in the government.

This portion of the report closes with a statement that in my opinion should be reviewed and reaffirmed by the House Armed Services Committee at the commencement of each session of Congress:

> Should the time ever come when personnel of the Army, Navy, Air Force, or Marine Corps, or other officers or employees of the Executive branch, are fearful

of, unwilling to, or restrained from voicing their frank opinions and convictions before Congressional Committees, then will be the time when effective representative government in this country is gravely imperiled.

The next 38 pages of the report are grouped under the heading "Testimony by subject matter and committee conclusions," with subdivisions (1) Strategy, (2) Air Power, (3) Strategic Bombing, (4) Tactical Aviation, and (5) Unification. The reports under each heading are exceptional in their restrained detail, giving the view of each service with frankness and sympathy and, in general, approving of the current responsible service views because the unified organization was still too new to expect more sophisticated cross-education.

Section V of the report is a summary of the 33 committee views:

1) All testimony presented was based on the committee's agenda and rendered at the committee's request. Personal views of the witnesses were solicited. Criticism of the witnesses for presenting their frank views under these circumstances is unworthy and a disservice to the Nation's defense.

2) The witnesses would have been subject to censure had they failed to present their convictions to the committee on the subjects covered in the committee agenda.

3) The national objectives proposed by General Bradley appear to the committee to be sound, but should not be assumed by the military leaders. The Secretary of Defense should initiate a study in the National Security Council to provide a firm statement of principles upon which the Joint Chiefs of Staff may rely as an official expression of their civilian leaders.

4) The Secretary of Defense should initiate a study in the National Security Council on the relationship to the national objectives of atomic warfare and present strategic planning for the use of atomic weapons . . .

5) In view of the terrible destructiveness of modern weapons, the Nation can no longer afford lackadaisical planning or complacency as to its defenses. For an indefinite time, the Nation must maintain sound, modern, alert defensive forces capable of anticipating and dealing with a sudden enemy attack.

6) Intercontinental strategic bombing is not synonymous with air power. The Air Force is not synonymous with the Nation's military air power. Military air power consists of Air Force, Navy, and Marine Corps air power, and of this strategic bombing is but one phase. The national air power consists of the military air power of the various services plus commercial aviation plus the national industrial and manpower resources pertaining to aviation.

7) Navy leaders are not opposed to "strategic air warfare" but do oppose "strategic bombing" if, by the term "strategic bombing," is meant mass aerial bombardment of urban areas.

8) There is possibility of serious damage to the Nation's defense if too much joint planning is concentrated on individual service questions of a highly technical nature during the formative period of unification. The committee has strong doubts that it is a service to the Nation's defense for the military

leaders of the respective services to pass judgment jointly on the technical fitness of either new or old weapons each service wishes to develop to carry out its assigned missions.

9) Difficulties between the Air Force and the naval air arm will continue because of fundamental professional disagreements on the art of warfare . . .

10) The committee expects the services to resolve their professional differences fairly and without rancor . . .

11) A political body cannot of itself reach, through deliberative processes, final answers on professional military questions but must depend upon and encourage a continuation of the process of exploration, study, and coordination among our officers of the several services to preserve a satisfactory doctrine of defense, to have ready applicable plans, and to devise units, suitably equipped, to meet the most probable circumstances of any emergency. The significant thing is to insure that the national defense structure insures adequate consideration of all professional views, especially during those early days of unification.

12) The Committee on Appropriations should make a thorough analysis of present and projected aircraft procurement to verify whether or not the present and planned level of procurement will support the required air power for the Nation.

13) A closer relationship should be established between Marine Corps aviators, the Army Field Forces, and the Air Force for the development of sound close air support tactics and techniques . . .

14) There should be joint training activities between tactical aircraft of the Air Force and Navy to resolve questions of relative performance of these aircraft.

15) All services have been at fault at one time or another in the unification effort . . .

16) Prudent administration of unification, sensitive to the many imponderables of spirit and emotion and service loyalties, can greatly ease service tensions and difficulties over the years that must pass before cross education of the services will truly produce the "one-armed-force" concept . . .

17) Cross education of the services holds the ultimate key to the perplexing problems of interservice relations . . .

18) There is no justification whatsoever for barring naval aviation personnel from Strategic Air Command activities of the Air Force . . .

19) Joint training centers should be established in all areas of greatest interservice controversy to remove lack of understanding which breeds suspicion, rivalry, and questioning of motives . . .

20) There should be an augmentation of interservice war games to resolve such questions as the Banshee versus the B36 in order to eliminate or at least reduce the tensions between the services, as well as contributing to their combat-readiness.

21) The committee firmly supports unification, but emphasizes that it is a con-

cept requiring definition . . . its meaning should always be examined to determine whether the particular concept being applied or proposed is the
proper one.

22) Civilian control of the Nation's armed forces is integrally a part of the Nation's democratic process and tradition; it is strongly supported by the committee. But in supporting civilian control of the armed forces, the committee
does not mean

   1) preventing free testimony before congressional committees by members
   of the armed forces, or

   2) the relegation of the United States Congress to a bystander role in issues
   pertaining to the national defense.

23) The Joint Chiefs of Staff structure, as now constituted, does not insure at all
times adequate consideration for the views of all services. The committee
will sponsor legislation to require rotation of the position of chairman of the
Joint Chiefs of Staff among the services after a two-year term, and to add
the Commandant of the Marine Corps to the Joint Chiefs of Staff as a member thereof.

24) The committee will ultimately reexamine the entire Joint Chiefs of Staff
structure to determine whether the structure, as amended as proposed in this
report, insures adequate consideration of all service views.

25) The evaluation of the B36 is properly within the province of the Joint Weapons Systems Evaluation Board; future mass procurement of weapons should
not be undertaken until the recommendations of this Board, except in time
of emergency, are available to the Joint Chiefs of Staff.

26) The Air Force holds the primary responsibility for conducting strategic
bombing. It has maintained that the B36 bomber is its foremost weapon to
carry out that mission and that the B36 can do its job. The committee holds
that the Nation must rely upon the judgment of its professional leaders in
their respective fields in matters of this nature . . .

27) The committee deplores the manner of cancellation of the construction of
the aircraft carrier *United States,* but, because of the pressure of other shipbuilding programs at the present time and the existing budgetary limitations
on the Navy Department, will withhold further action—for the present—as
regards the construction of this vessel. The committee considers it sound
policy, however, for the Nation to follow the advice of its professional leaders
in regard to this subject in the same manner as has been heretofore done in
respect to the B36 bomber. In the committee's view, the Nation's leaders in
respect to naval weapons are the leaders of the United States Navy.

28) The appropriate role of the Joint Weapons Systems Evaluation Board is to
evaluate weapons after they have been developed, not to instruct the services
what types of new weapons they will or will not develop.

29) The committee will sponsor legislation to require, within reasonable limits,
consultation by the Secretary of Defense with the Appropriations Committees of the Senate and House of Representatives before appropriated funds
are withheld by administrative act.

30) The Appropriations Committee should augment its staff in order to keep in intimate touch with the development of national defense budgets ...

31) The Management Committee of the Department of Defense should be placed under the direction of the Comptroller of the Department of Defense on all fiscal and budgetary matters.

32) The appointment of a career military officer as chairman of a committee composed of civilians on the Assistant Secretary or Under Secretary level is an unfortunate and undesirable precedent which inverts the civilian-control concept so closely identified with unification.

33) The removal of Admiral Denfeld was a reprisal against him for giving testimony to the House Armed Services Committee.[3] This act is a blow against effective representative government in that it tends to intimidate witnesses and hence discourages the rendering of free and honest testimony to the Congress; it violated promises made to the witnesses by the committee, the Secretary of the Navy, and the Secretary of Defense; and it violated the Unification Act, into which a provision was written specifically to prevent actions of this nature against the Nation's highest military and naval officers.

The committee voted unanimously to approve items 1–32 of this summary. The vote was 23–8 in favor of item 33. The view of the eight dissenters follows:

... there is nothing whatsoever in the record of the committee hearings to support the finding the committee has reached.

The letter, contained in the report, from the Secretary of the Navy to the President, giving his reasons for removing the Chief of Naval Operations, is the only official evidence available to the committee pertaining to this action. That letter specifically states that the Secretary of the Navy informed the President, in the presence of the Secretary of Defense, before the committee's October hearings began, that Admiral Denfeld's usefulness as Chief of Naval Operations had terminated in the opinion of the Secretary of the Navy.

There is absolutely nothing before the committee, privately or publicly, to controvert this statement of the Secretary of the Navy.

Purely on supposition—exclusively on the basis of a priori reasoning—the committee has cast aside the carefully weighed words of the Secretary of the Navy and, in effect, stated that the Secretary has misrepresented the facts to the President.

The undersigned members of the committee cannot support either the finding of "reprisal" under these circumstances, or the method by which the finding was reached ...

Ten members of the committee signed a supplemental statement urging that the entire record of proceedings be turned over to the Department of Justice so that a determination could be made of whether the statutes of the United States relating to the protection of witnesses had been violated:

The committee . . . has found that there has been a reprisal—a punishment inflicted upon a witness for having testified before a committee of the House of Representatives. To allow such a precedent to be established, that is, to acquiesce in the punishment of a witness before Congress, is to circumscribe for all time the power of Congress to perform its functions . . . Fortunately, the statutes [of the United States] provide a means whereby those who commit acts of reprisals against witnesses, or in any other way tend to injure them, may be brought to the bars of justice . . .

This concludes my story of the B36 hearings, which occupied so much of my time for more than five months of 1949 and which undoubtedly had a great deal to do with my subsequent career.

In many ways these hearings were a traumatic experience for the loyal professional career officers who took part and also for the many capable and equally loyal reserve officers who rounded out the teams for all services.

From the standpoint of my subsequent service career plus the experience of the years that followed my retirement, I look back on the B36 hearings as the most important congressional activity during my naval career. With Mr. Vinson at the helm giving sage guidance, the House Armed Services Committee gave its time, energy, and competence to the job of straightening out a morass of conflicting service views that, had they been left to grow, would have ultimately hurt all the armed services but might have destroyed the Navy. The nation owes Mr. Vinson and his committee a great debt of gratitude.

16

Spring 1950

By the time the B36 hearings were over in October 1949 I had been CINCPAC for almost six months. When I took over from Admiral Ramsey I decided to "see" the whole command for myself. In July I had visited American Samoa and some of the Marshall Islands on my way south. Now, back in Pearl Harbor, I worked on my travel schedule for the rest of the fiscal year, hoping to visit the remaining islands of the Trust Territory.

There were other pressing concerns. First, I had no idea what kind of report Mr. Vinson's committee would make. From day-to-day communications with the Defense Department, and from my end of the line, I could see no change in the apparent determination of the Secretary of Defense to continue his great reductions in defense expenditures. And the punitive and cynical removal of Admiral Denfeld by the Secretary of the Navy just five days after the hearings were over seemed an action in contempt of the committee.

The Pacific Fleet shore establishment was particularly hard hit by budget cuts, and forces afloat were to be greatly reduced during the remaining months of fiscal 1950. Rear Admiral C. C. Hartman, passing through Pearl on his way to the Seventh Fleet in the Far East, expressed great concern at the lack of naval air power available for defense of that fleet. I could only agree with him and tell him I was doing all I could to persuade the powers in Washington that our situation in the Pacific was becoming critical.

International problems were pressing also. Negotiations were in progress with the Philippine government, which wanted all U.S. military bases out of the Manila Bay area. This particularly affected the Navy.

The Chinese Communists were making every effort to get all American diplomatic and consular representatives out of China. Our government seemed paralyzed and unable to make up its mind just what course to pursue in Asia. Britain had recognized Red China almost as soon as President Chiang Kai-shek had moved his government to Formosa, and there were frequent rumors in the press that the Truman administration was about to follow suit. It seemed to me incredible that the United States would cold-bloodedly turn its back on a faithful ally of many years' standing; but I knew that powerful political forces were at work to persuade President Truman to do just that.

I soon found out why Honolulu was known as the "crossroads of the Pacific." It seemed that every famous person in the United States and the world was on the move, and that most if not all wanted to spend a day or so in Honolulu.

My official guestbook of that time shows such names as Al Jolson, Clark Gable and his wife, and Sidney G. Holland, Prime Minister of New Zealand. Naturally, Pearl Harbor was a great visitors' attraction; and I soon realized that the Navy would have to find ways to take care of the flood of visitors. I incurred the dislike of the District Commandant when I finally ordered him to build a suitable platform on the above-water part of the wreck of *Arizona,* erect a flagpole, and see that the colors were flown from it daily. He told me my orders were illegal, contravened Navy regulations, and so on. I replied that I knew all that, and that I was trying to get *Arizona* replaced on the list of naval vessels in commission (which could be done by the Secretary of the Navy), so far without success. Feeling that I could wait no longer, I gave him orders to do the next best thing I could think of. On 7 March 1950 I had a ceremony on *Arizona* and for all intents and purposes made her USS *Arizona* again. There she remains, although a suitable memorial has since been added [and she has been recommissioned] to make her even more impressive to the thousands of visitors who come each year to pay their respects to the heroes of that fateful Sunday in 1941.

Mrs. Radford had been after me for a long time to take a real vacation, and I realized I was tired, particularly after the events of the summer. We went to the Army Rest Camp at Kilauea for two weeks. In the brisk, cool air I rapidly recovered and returned to Pearl to tackle the daily problems with renewed vigor and somewhat less pessimism.

It is difficult to write objectively of the remaining months of 1949 and the first half of 1950, but I will try.

President Truman had not had an easy time, from that day in spring 1945 when he took over on President Roosevelt's death. In the immediate postwar years, after completely dismantling our great military organization he had come to the realization that the Soviet Union was not a friend and ally. He had courageously countered communist expansion in Europe, particularly Greece and Turkey. He had met the Berlin blockade with the airlift and he had pushed the formation of NATO. During all this time he had kept a tight rein on appropriations for our armed forces. By fall 1949 the Army, Navy, and Air Force were in a truly sorry state and headed for worse trouble under a Secretary of Defense who seemed impervious to advice of any kind.

I admired President Truman, as a man and as president, in many ways, but I have never been able to figure out why, with General Marshall so close, he let our national security posture decline to the dangerous point it finally reached in

June 1950. I have reluctantly come to the conclusion that it was really General Marshall's fault, in that he did not pay particular attention to the status of our forces. The General was very busy with other things, his missions to China and his duties as Secretary of State and head of the Red Cross. As far as the armed services were concerned, he wanted in those years only one thing, universal military training. With that great asset he felt, it seemed to me, that we would be safe. The three services knew full well that the cost of UMT would be enormous—that we could have little else to go with it, and no real security. In the years when General Marshall might have tried to convince the President that our military strength was so dangerously low that it might invite attack, he elected not to do so.[1]

During these years, while President Truman held the Russians at Bay in Europe, he let the situation deteriorate badly in the Far East. In early 1950 there was great pressure on the President to recognize Red China—and in effect turn over the Far East to the Chinese—and I believe his advisers who wanted recognition of Communist China came very near succeeding.[2]

While I of course was intensely interested in the global picture and was kept pretty well informed on it, my particular responsibility was the Pacific Command and its usefulness in furthering U.S. policy in the Pacific and Far East. I kept in close touch with General MacArthur's Far East command through his naval headquarters which, for naval support purposes, was part of my command. From my visit to Tokyo in May I knew MacArthur was having plenty of difficulty. American policy objectives were not clear in the Pacific area; so in protesting cutbacks in military forces, commanders could in many cases only assume what the U.S. position would be if certain circumstances arose.

Admiral Sherman, Commander of the Sixth Fleet in the Mediterranean, had been ordered to Washington as the prospective CNO at almost the same time as Admiral Denfeld was detached. His selection as Denfeld's relief was a surprise to many naval officers but not to me. Of the whole naval high command he had been practically the only one not directly involved in the B36 or the unification and strategy hearings. In command of the Sixth Fleet, he had been well clear of the unusually bitter interservice arguments that began early in 1949. I am not certain Secretary Matthews had even met Sherman before he arrived to take Denfeld's place, but I am sure that Sherman came well recommended by President Truman and Secretary Johnson.

Admiral Sherman's assumption of his new office was greeted by many of his top subordinates, including myself, with mixed emotions. Since Admiral Denfeld had been fired because he had disagreed with policies of the Secretary of the Navy, undoubtedly approved by the Secretary of Defense, it seemed likely, to me at least, that Forrest Sherman must have been closely questioned about his own views prior to acceptance. I assumed his views were sufficiently close to those of his civilian superior to assure his selection as CNO.[3]

Sherman had been my shipmate and was a longtime friend. He was two years behind me at the Naval Academy, but we had both chosen naval aviation as a career specialty and had thus more or less grown up together. After World War II we had teamed in presenting the Navy's case for unification. Sherman had been selected by Secretary Forrestal to work with Norstad to reach agreement on a unification bill. His work directly set the stage for passage of the first unification legislation in summer 1947.

I knew that Generals Bradley, Collins, and Vandenberg, his colleagues on the JCS, would lean over backward to get along with Admiral Sherman. Professionally, the Navy could not have a better representative on the JCS—if he were free to be his own man. I made up my mind to delay congratulations until I had had a chance to talk to him, to ask him if he had been required to make any precommitments before being nominated for the new job. I knew he would notice this and would not delay in arranging a meeting. I was perfectly willing to request retirement if he wanted someone else in my job as a result of my feelings.

Our meeting, in January 1950, was very pleasant and interesting. In reply to my question about precommitments Forrest said, "I was not asked and did not make any such commitments, Raddy." I thanked him, congratulated him, and said that I for one was sure he was about the only man who could handle the job at that difficult time. In my opinion, Forrest Sherman made an outstanding CNO during the relatively short time he had the job. He was recognized in Washington as the outstanding member of the JCS.

By the end of March the reductions in Pacific Fleet forces for fiscal 1950–1951 were established. The situation in the Far East was quiet, at least as far as the Chinese were concerned. I felt I could schedule several important trips. These instructive journeys took me away from Pearl during most of the next two and a half months. But mid-June I was back again to greet Secretary of Defense and Mrs. Johnson, traveling with General and Mrs. Omar Bradley on the latter's first inspection trip to the Pacific area. In my conversations with Mr. Johnson then I could say that I had covered my entire Pacific and Trust Territory responsibilities.

My first trip was an indoctrination visit to Los Alamos and Sandia Base in New Mexico. Under Admiral Sherman's influence the Navy's future atomic program was being greatly enlarged, and all senior flag officers were required to become familiar with details which had until then been classified and limited to a few officer specialists.

I next visited American Samoa for its Golden Jubilee, celebrating fifty years under the American flag, first hoisted on 17 April 1900 in Pago Pago. I felt proud of Navy achievements in administering the government of the island for all this time, keeping Samoan customs and traditions alive and thriving among this intelligent and cultured people.

Following three exciting days of colorful celebration, there was a business conference in the office of Capt. Thomas Darden, the Naval Governor. The subject was the logistic problems of American Samoa and how they could best be handled by the new civilian government to be established early in 1951. Without the Navy to come to their rescue when orders for food and other necessities were forgotten or not anticipated in time for a scheduled shipment, the Samoans were going to suffer at times.

The third trip came about through the invitation of the Australian government for Mrs. Radford and me to be their guests during the celebration of Coral Sea Week, starting on 1 May. The celebration was to commemorate the raging two-day battle of the Coral Sea, in which a combined American-Australian naval carrier task force defeated two similar Japanese task forces in an engagement.

This was the first decisive naval battle in history in which the opposing forces did not sight each other and did not exchange naval gunfire.[4] The battle dealt the Japanese their first really severe blow and scattered the greatest concentration of Japanese warships, planes, and transports gathered since the Battle of the Java Sea. Admiral Weneker, the German naval attaché in Tokyo during the war, felt that the defeat was the greatest single shock of the war to the Japanese, for they had thought they would conquer Australia by late 1942. What a catastrophe for the Allies, particularly the United States, that would have been.

The margin between victory and defeat in this naval engagement was small, very much smaller than was realized in Australia at the time or for a number of years afterwards. But the important thing was that the victorious Japanese advance southward was stopped, the effect on morale in Australia and throughout the Allied Pacific forces was electrical, and the Japanese were shocked.

A memorable part of this trip was Mrs. Radford's first press conference. I wondered just how it would turn out. I was not to find out until the day after, though, for her conference was held simultaneously with one of mine. She had a fine time at hers but would not tell me what she said. To my surprise, I read in the papers the next morning that she had expressed a great desire to see a Koala bear. I stopped worrying about her press conferences.

The Royal Australian Navy had been charged by the government with coordinating a schedule for my visit that would both satisfy me and give the Australians a chance to see me on occasions and hear what I had to say. After several months of correspondence the schedule had been finalized, and it kept me busy almost from dawn to midnight every day. There were four principal addresses, the most important at a Coral Sea luncheon in Melbourne given by the Australian-American Association.

Australia in 1950 was far different from Australia today, as Mrs. Radford and I know from subsequent visits. Then the country had not yet modernized and was just awakening. A Labor government, in power for some eight years, had been defeated. The new Conservative government, under Prime Minister Robert Menzies, was just getting started.

One of our first impressions then was of the lack of service. For instance, to meet my schedule I had to be ready for breakfast at 8:00 every morning. But at that hour I could get no breakfast in the Menzies Hotel and there was no room service. After much discussion the management finally came up with the idea that I could be served tea and toast with the maids who came on duty at 8:00. This and the lack of heat in a cold Melbourne May did not detract from our wonderful stay.

The Australians had been left shaken in World War II when, with practically all their troops serving in the Middle East, the British defeat at Singapore left them exposed to attack by the Japanese. They were interested in discussing the whole Far Eastern situation and in hearing my assessment of what the Russians and Chinese were up to. At the Coral Sea luncheon, the Army Chief of Staff asked, "Do you conceive of Russian aggression over and above the submarine threat?" I answered that in my opinion there was no possibility of a large-scale aggressive movement by the communists for some time to come. Their cold war activities were working out so satisfactorily that it would be foolish for them to precipitate a hot war. This exchange took place a little less than two months before the North Koreans attacked across the thirty-eighth parallel.

Our Australia trip—climaxed by the beautiful Coral Sea Ball, with a guest list that read like an Australian *Who's Who*—was a full and memorable one. The Australians went full out to show us how sincerely they appreciated the help the United States had given them in the critical stages of World War II; and they succeeded.

After only a few days at Pearl Harbor, I left on one of my longest and most strenuous trips. For a month in May and June I visited 21 of the most important islands of the Trust Territories, as well as naval installations in the Philippines and Japan, besides making my second call on General MacArthur in Tokyo.

Travel arrangements for a trip of this magnitude were complicated. The timing was largely dictated by the availability of the heavy cruiser *Rochester,* deploying to the western Pacific for duty as the flagship of the Commander Seventh Fleet. I could use her to good advantage for the most difficult part of the Trust Territory trip because she carried a helicopter. Visiting many of the Pacific islands by more conventional means—ships, boats, native craft—was often difficult and in bad weather sometimes very dangerous.

The Trust Territory tour was arranged to cover several of the Marshall Islands, islands in the Ponape and Truk districts of the eastern Carolines, and those in the Palau district of the western Carolines. The Trusteeship was spread over an enormous ocean area, some three million square miles; the total population was approximately 54,000, located on 97 lush atolls and islands. I wanted to see and know the larger and more important islands of the Territory, as well as representative smaller ones. I expected to be succeeded as High Commissioner by a civilian early in 1951 and wanted to know all I could about the organization before he arrived.[5]

At each of the islands or atolls I met with the high chiefs and the village councils. I listened carefully to the recital of their economic and social woes, then wove into the fabric of my reply the intent of the United States to assist the islanders. It was usually possible to suggest some concrete move or new direction under vigorous leadership of a local chief.

The health and general well-being of the people was important to me, as was the preservation of those elements of traditional culture that flavor the unique ethnicity of Micronesia. The islanders—out of sight and out of mind, half a world away from Washington—needed a link to their past.

Before my journey was over I had learned that, given almost identical resources, some of these native communities would adopt one and some the other of two quite contrary courses of action. Some were noticeably concerned with the future, others merely reveled in abundance; some attacked each new problem with vigor and common sense, others lacked the confidence to surmount the problems of everyday life. It was an object lesson of importance. What a difference a few competent and energetic leaders can make in the development of self-sustaining communities!

One of the interesting stories in the Trust Territory is of the "street of stone money" in Yap, part of the western Carolines. Along both sides of this narrow, tree-bordered thoroughfare there are round, flat stones three to ten feet in diameter and about six inches thick. The area is called the "bank of Yap," for it comprises all the wealth of the community in Yapese tradition. Many years ago these large disks were transported via outrigger canoe from the Palau Islands, about 225 miles southwest of Yap. A square hole was cut in the center of each, in which was inserted a pole that was lashed to two or more outrigger canoes for the perilous journey north. The value of each piece was established after it had been determined what amount of energy and time was expended and how many lives were lost in moving it to Yap.

Some years ago, an enterprising trader named O'Keefe with a good-sized schooner called at Yap and learned the value of the islanders' stone money. He made a direct run to the Palaus, where he had turned out, on a near assembly line basis, a number of these round disks, which he took to Yap. To his dismay the Yapese placed no value on his pieces of stone, since there was no perilous journey involved or lives lost in the making of the money or in its transportation.

From the western Carolines I flew to the Philippines for an annual visit to inspect U.S. naval activities there in my capacity as CINCPACFLT. The Philippines were at that time in General MacArthur's area of responsibility so far as military planning was concerned.

When the United States gave the Philippines their independence in 1946, we agreed to remove all military activities from the Manila area. By 1950 this had been largely accomplished except for the Navy's activities at Sangley Point, south of the city. Although the Filipinos were not pushing us, I felt we should move out and I wanted to find a place for another naval air station, preferably one with deep water near which a carrier pier could be built. The Navy had no place west of Pearl Harbor where carrier planes could be unloaded from a ship and taxied to an adjacent air strip or vice versa.

Besides Sangley Point, our principal naval activities were located at Olongapo in Subic Bay, northwest of Manila on the South China Sea. Because Subic Bay was a large natural harbor surrounded by a U.S. naval reservation, I had hoped to find a location for the new air station close to activities on Olongapo but had had no luck. Finally, with the help of the U.S. Army Engineers, who were mapping the Philippines and had more information on them than anyone else, a site was located on Subic Bay that was almost adjacent to the Navy Yard at Olongapo; it was called Cubi Point. I had visited Olongapo only once and could not visualize the new site from maps. I intended to look at Cubi Point on this trip but was not optimistic that it could fill the bill.

Our first stop was at Baguio. This was the first time we had flown to the mountain summer capital of the Philippines, and it was quite a thrill to land there in our DC3. The Baguio airstrip was just adequate for a DC3 if one approached it over a deep canyon, put the wheels on the ground as soon as possible, and rolled on, uphill, to almost the end of the strip. Taking off was even worse: you revved up the engines from a standing start at the upper end of the runway and charged downhill, hoping for enough speed to stay airborne by the time the strip dropped off to the canyon.

In Baguio, with its pine forests and pleasant climate, I met with President Quirino, and with the American Ambassador and practically the whole Manila diplomatic corps.

On the next day I had a good look at the site proposed for our naval air station and was pleased to find that it had great possibilities. It would require leveling a rather high hill, but otherwise the problems were quite straightforward. The Seabees were looking for good-sized training jobs, and I hoped they would be interested in looking this one over.[6]

Rear Admiral F. P. Old, Commander U.S. Naval Forces Philippines, had been insisting that I find time to call on Gen. Emilio Aguinaldo at his residence in Kawit, near Sangley Point on the road to Manila. As a youngster I had read about General Aguinaldo and his rebellion against the United States after the Philippines had been captured from Spain. I had great admiration for his courage and determination, and went willingly with Admiral Old to call on him.

I suppose General Aguinaldo was in his mid-eighties when I met him and his charming wife that afternoon. Both seemed in excellent health, the General particularly spry and interested in everything. They lived in a large, lovely old home, and his "office" was in a room at the top of a tower, three or four flights up rather steep stairs. He said he kept busy reading, to stay up to date on world affairs, and writing, mostly his memoirs.

As one listened to General Aguinaldo relate some of his experiences, one could imagine what a wonderful leader he must have been as a young man. By the time of my visit he was, of course, a great friend of the United States and grateful for our help to his country during and after World War II. He was intensely interested in the details of the naval war in the Pacific against Japan and deluged me with questions indicating the depth of his studies of that conflict. Admiral Old and I said goodbye to this most interesting man with great reluctance.

I was committed to arrive in Tokyo promptly at 5:00 on the afternoon of Friday 2 June, having received word that General MacArthur intended to meet me at Haneda Airport. Our pilot pulled up to the ramp at exactly 5:00 and there was the General, accompanied by Admiral and Mrs. Joy and members of the staff. This was something the General did not have time to do very often, I knew, and we very much appreciated his courtesy.

We were in Japan for a week and had an active social calendar, but I had plenty of time for my inspections and conferences with General MacArthur and V. Adm. Turner Joy, Commander Naval Forces Far East. When the Korean War surprised us all about three weeks later, I was certainly glad of this opportunity to bring myself up to date on their naval problems and their views on Japan and the Far Eastern situation in general.

I have always remembered that in my conversations with General MacArthur on this visit he again stressed his great concern about the economic situation in Japan. Unemployment was high, partly because of restrictions placed on heavy industries by the Allies. The General was trying to solve the problem, with little or no success then. Within the next month or two, demands upon Japanese industry because of the Korean War turned things around in a hurry.

On arrival in Manila the week before, I had received a dispatch from Secretary of Defense Johnson saying that he was traveling to the Pacific in June with General Bradley and a party of about eight others. General MacArthur had also received this notice. We speculated on the reasons for the visit and all that we hoped the Secretary might get out of it. Both of us were greatly concerned with reductions in our forces scheduled for fiscal 1951, which would begin on 1 July 1950.

I had one formal and one informal off-the-record press conference for the American press while in Tokyo. Reviewing the records now, I am impressed with the great concern of all these men and women regarding our relations with the Russians. With nothing specific to go on, their noses for news must have been telling them things that I, for one, did not foresee. For instance, on one day I had a complete briefing by General MacArthur's Intelligence Officer that took well over an hour and included much interesting information—but no premonition that the North Koreans were about to attack the South. I heard in some detail of the heavy equipment, tanks, and artillery being supplied to the North Korean army, in comparison with the very lightly-armed division we had organized, equipped, and trained in South Korea, but there was no prediction that this would cause trouble in the near future.

I conferred with Prime Minister Yoshida twice, and my admiration for his abilities increased each time. Japan was fortunate to find such an able leader in these immediate postwar years.

Mrs. Radford and I spent two days in Kyoto—a great treat for both of us, as we had seen little of Japan outside of Tokyo. Mrs. Radford was almost overcome by the many opportunities to buy beautiful things of all kinds. She was careful in making up her mind before she purchased anything, and in later years I have appreciated how wisely she selected the oriental objects d'art in our home.

The dispatch waiting at Pearl from Secretary Johnson, outlining the itinerary for his forthcoming trip, was brief. He indicated there would be eight in his party, and stated "no honors at landing desired or expected" [a most unusual procedure]. The message ended, "We expect to confer with senior commanders at each command. Official receptions and engagements will be held to absolute minimum." I thought it an unnecessarily brusque message when I received it but was even more annoyed when I received a personal letter from the Secretary's aide, Capt. Kenneth Craig, U.S.N.

Captain Craig informed me that for the first evening "an official reception is in order. [The Secretary] is sending regrets to all social events except for this one reception." He added that the Secretary wanted me to set up a meeting the following morning for the top military officers in Pearl; "up to two hours may be devoted to this conference." On Wednesday a trip to Hilo and lunch at the Volcano House was to be arranged. "A suitable plane *is required*." Departure would be at 11:00 P.M. that evening. But the end of Captain Craig's letter really threw me: "Stopover is primarily for recreation." This was a surprising comment, when the Pacific command was one of only five commands under the JCS and presumably the Secretary of Defense would be interested in becoming acquainted with some of his principal military subordinates and their problems.

I can hardly say it was a pleasant visit. I felt that the Secretary was almost bored with our efforts to entertain him and was barely polite to our friends who met him. I believe he was beginning to feel the effects of the brain tumor that took him out of public life not long afterward.

Once the Secretary and General Bradley had left Honolulu for their visit to the western Pacific, I settled down to catch up with the many problems and the mounds of paperwork that had accumulated during my absence on the Trust Territory-Far East trip. The orders I had received regarding further reductions of naval and other strength in the months to come appalled me. It seemed to me that Washington was out of touch with reality, but there was nothing further I could do except carry out my new orders. I had made protests several months before, to no effect.

By Saturday 24 June I had been working steadily for ten long days and I was getting quite depressed. Mrs. Radford suggested that we invite our good friends Sandy and Ana Walker to have dinner with us, with a little canasta before.

It was a lovely June afternoon. As we sat down at the card table on our big verandah, Sandy remarked that on the way to Pearl he had heard on the car radio that the North Koreans had attacked South Korea. He wanted to know if I had word of such an attack. I said I did not but that I would call my office.

The CINCPAC duty officer had heard the same radio news announcement, but he had nothing directly from Washington. But he added that a rather long coded message was just coming in that he would send me as soon as it was decoded. I told Mrs. Radford and the Walkers what I had heard and asked them to excuse me. I believe they had a nice dinner together, but I was busy until nearly midnight with most of my staff.

17

The Korean Eruption

The message from Washington on that Saturday night told of an unprovoked attack across the thirty-eighth parallel, the temporary boundary between North and South Korea, at approximately 4:00 A.M. on Sunday morning, 25 June, Korean time.[1] It seemed incredible to me that the North Koreans would have the audacity to attack South Korea, running the risk of having the United States come to the South's rescue.[2] On the other hand, I could not help but recall my recent briefings in Tokyo, to the effect that the North Korean army was well trained and very well equipped. A cold-blooded assessment of the situation could not be optimistic about the outcome unless the United States was prepared to move fast.

At least, we had more U.S. forces in the Far East than anywhere else. In Japan there was the Eighth Army of four infantry divisions on occupation duty, plus 18 fighter squadrons, a light-bomber wing, and a troop-carrier wing. Then U.S. Naval Forces Far East, under General MacArthur, consisted of one cruiser, four destroyers, and several amphibious and small cargo vessels. Also operating in the western Pacific was the newly formed Seventh Fleet under V. Adm. Arthur Struble, consisting of *Rochester,* the aircraft carrier *Valley Forge,* and destroyers, submarines, and auxiliary vessels. All these forces except the Seventh Fleet were under General MacArthur's command, and the Seventh Fleet command could easily be passed to him.

Another consideration which puzzled me then, and to which I have never found an entirely satisfactory answer, was the apparent failure of the communists to read American newspapers of June 1950. There they would have found that, in another year or less, all U.S. forces would have been greatly reduced— to the point, I am certain, where they could not possibly have intervened successfully in Korea. This would have been true, of course, if Secretary Johnson had been allowed to have his way, but there was always a chance that the increasing opposition to his ruthless cuts might have caused a change.[3] Perhaps the Russians were smarter than we then thought, for they took a gamble that was almost successful, and that caused us the loss of tens of thousands of young

Americans in a vicious war and the expenditure of countless billions of dollars in the years that followed. They lost very few Russians and a lot of military equipment, but they kept North Korea and are now, in 1971, to all intents and purposes pretty well prepared for another attempt to take over South Korea.

As CINCPAC and CINCPACFLT I had no direct responsibility in the Korean War. I knew that the Seventh Fleet would be turned over to General MacArthur's command immediately. I expected to play a supporting role under whatever action President Truman chose to take, and I spent that first evening going over all the possibilities that my staff and I could think of. I ordered certain ships that were ready to the western Pacific immediately. They could always be recalled if not needed, while the advantage of even 12 hours in their time of arrival might be crucial. Knowing that Admiral Joy's staff was inadequate for the increased load it was bound to get, I canvassed our Pacific Fleet resources for qualified officers and ordered them to be ready to leave within 24 hours. It was a busy Saturday evening.

I was informed that there were two Korean navy submarine chasers in Honolulu Harbor, en route to Korea. They had been turned over recently to the Korean navy in a demilitarized condition—with no armament. I ordered them to Pearl Harbor so we could reinstall the weapons that had been removed and send them on their way. The young Korean commander in charge of the two craft, Sohn Won Il was very attractive and seemingly very competent. He appreciated our thoughtfulness and was on his way to Korea as soon as the Navy Yard had installed his new weapons and given him ammunition and fuel. Later I met him often in Korea and watched him advance in rank, to Chief of Naval Operations and ultimately to Secretary of Defense.

On the next two days we were not deluged with news or orders from Washington. From the press we had a general idea of what was going on. President Truman had taken the invasion of South Korea to the U.N. Security Council, which first called upon the invading North Korean troops to cease hostilities and withdraw to the thirty-eighth parallel and then, when no attention was paid to this directive, called upon all U.N. members to render every assistance in execution of the first resolution.

On Monday morning my Intelligence Officer reported that two columns of North Korean troops were advancing almost unchecked toward Seoul.

On Tuesday morning the nation received a message from the President entitled "President Truman's Statement on Korea Issued Today at the White House after a Conference with Military, State Department, and Congressional Leaders." This remarkable document, in which the President stated that he had ordered U.S. air and sea forces to give the Korean government troops cover and support, was the first important step in establishing a coherent, up-to-date U.S. policy for the Far East—something we had badly needed, something to which the armed forces could tie their planning.[4]

The first week of the Korean War was confusing to me. I had several teletype conferences with various branches in the Navy Department that added little specific information to what I knew or could assume. Evidently the Defense Department was also in a state of confusion.

I complained that I was not receiving copies of directives to General Mac-Arthur which, I was certain, contained information on which I would have to take action. What I suspected turned out to be true: the General was receiving many of his orders via teletype, and in the confusion even the Navy Department was not being informed.

The complications of these early days is hard to describe. Most of us were frustrated, wanting to hurry up and do something. For the Army units rushed into Korea it was almost catastrophic.

The gallant but relatively futile first action of Task Force Smith, the first American Army unit in combat in the Korean War, is related in *War in Peacetime,* by Gen. J. Lawton Collins. They found that they were up against a strong, competent enemy that was well trained and well led.

In Pearl Harbor planning went forward at high speed. We were doing our best to recommission combat vessels, particularly carriers. The Navy Department received permission to call back reserve officers and men in July.

On 10 July I received a message from Admiral Sherman asking me to represent him at a conference with General MacArthur, General Collins, and General Vandenburg in Tokyo. On arrival I went directly to General MacArthur's office, where the conference was already in session, entering just in time to hear conversations on the number of troops required for Korea. As I walked toward my seat I thought I heard General Collins say that General MacArthur would have to get along with the troops he had. As I sat down I volunteered to Joe that the Fifth Regimental Combat Team in Honolulu was ready to load out, fully manned and brought up to full equipment by borrowing from the Hawaiian National Guard. Further, I was holding some ships there, just in case, so they could get going fast. To my surprise Joe said, "We have other plans for that unit."

The conference went on, with no great decisions made but with a complete account of events in Korea from General MacArthur. He was now fully aware of the problems there because he understood what little reliance he could place on the South Korean forces and what a well-trained and well-equipped enemy he faced.

In his book General Collins gives a clear report of this conference, mentioning General MacArthur's insistence on high priorities for his theater, and his urging immediate and maximum effort in support of his command from the start, rather than a gradual buildup. MacArthur, according to Collins (pp. 82–83), wanted "to grab every ship in the Pacific and pour support into the Far East" stating, "To Hell with the concept of business as usual."

I realized the problems facing Collins and Vandenburg, but I also knew there were no definite answers to the questions they posed to MacArthur: "We needed to know when General MacArthur expected to be able to launch his major counter offensive, what his requirements would be to reestablish the thirty-eighth parallel position and what strength he would need thereafter."

General MacArthur replied that it was impossible to say when he would be able to pass to the counter-offensive. He hoped to stop the North Korean advance when three American divisions were in action and then launch an amphibious operation to cut enemy lines of communication and routes of withdrawal, following that with an overland pursuit of the withdrawing North Koreans. He meant to destroy their forces, he said, not merely drive them back across the thirty-eighth parallel. He thought a total of eight infantry divisions and an additional Army headquarters would be required. He added that he hoped to block off support for North Korea from Manchuria or China. He was sure the communists would try to reinforce the Koreans but was equally sure this could be prevented by medium bomber attacks. He was convinced the Soviets would not go to war at this time but would make a maximum underground effort.

General Collins wrote that General MacArthur concluded the conference with the statement that the situation in the Far East should not be clouded with questions of priorities. "We win here or lose everywhere; if we win here, we improve the chances of winning everywhere." Joe also noted, "Admiral Radford expressed agreement with the remarks of General MacArthur," which is an understatement if anything. I fully agreed with a major effort to win this war and I thought at the time that there was a good possibility the JCS would see the light and convince the President to that effect. Certainly General MacArthur's outline of the situation was almost prophetic. I did not believe then, nor have I ever been convinced since, that the JCS should have divided their efforts between the Far East and Europe in trying so desperately to build up our armed forces from the low point they had reached in June 1950.

I next met with Adm. Turner Joy, serving under General MacArthur with a small staff that I had started to build up. Joy was given a rough schedule of ships that we hoped to get to him as fast as we could have them manned.

That evening I met with General MacArthur, who asked my support in planning an amphibious landing to cut the supply lines of the North Korean army; *even at that time* he mentioned Inchon as the preferred place. As our conversation ended he thanked me for the Navy's full support to date, saying, "if I had the same support from my own service I would have no worries."

My lasting impressions of this first visit to Tokyo after the outbreak of the Korean War were: first, General MacArthur's masterful summation of the situation as he saw it then and his plans for the immediate future; second, his ideas of how the war should be fought and why; third, his immediate military plans, which included the Inchon landing; and fourth, his estimate of where the present enemy offensive would be stopped. On the latter point he showed me Taegu on the map in his office and said, "I think this will be about their high point." It was.

I have voluminous records of what went on in the Navy in the summer and fall 1950. I do not believe people ever worked harder than did the Navy staffs in an effort to bring order out of chaos and to see that our naval units on the front lines had proper support.

The general public, and even many intelligent and otherwise knowledgeable high government officials, have little appreciation of the important followup actions that must be taken to insure that important orders *can* be carried out. For example: combat ships recommissioned in the United States came through Pearl Harbor on their way west. Here the Pacific Fleet staff gave them a final inspection, clearing them for western Pacific and combat or holding them for further training or repairs. If there was a disagreement of serious importance I decided it, particularly in the case of carriers, which I personally inspected if I possibly could.

Further, a great effort was made to increase the trans-Pacific airlift. Planes were diverted from other runs, taken out of mothballs, chartered, and loaded with high-priority personnel and air freight for the Far East. But before we could fly them we had to have facilities and fuel along the route. We had just decommissioned the air station at Midway in spring 1950. Now we had to recommission it immediately, and its deterioration in less than six months was surprising. Facilities at all the island stops had to be augmented. As a result of Herculean efforts on the part of all services the combined Pacific airlift was a tremendous success, *but* 98 of every 100 pounds that was transported to Korea went by surface shipping!

Recommissioning of merchant cargo vessels was another high-priority activity in June. It too was successfully accomplished on time, but lack of adequate shipping control later caused much difficulty.

Early in July I decided to keep a record of our naval problems and how we solved them. I obtained permission from Admiral Sherman to set up what was called a "continuing evaluation of the Korean War effort." I had discussed the matter with General MacArthur, explaining what I wanted to do and also the fact that members of my evaluation group would have to contact Army and Air Force units in many cases to obtain their appraisal of certain Navy efforts that affected their operations.

Three courses were to be followed in the evaluation:

(a) Recording in detail what happened within the various naval operational and administrative commands in the Pacific. *(b)* Establishing the difficulties, deficiencies, and problems, as well as the successes of naval commands in the Pacific. *(c)* Undertaking detailed staff studies of functional components of the Navy with the view of submitting constructive recommendations for improvements.

In undertaking these tasks, the basic concept was held that it was the Navy's responsibility to have its own house in order, and that it was neither the responsibility nor the right of the Navy to extend beyond those parameters into other services except where naval operations were adversely affected. Neither was it considered within the purview of the basic directive to inquire into national policy or major strategy.

The complete evaluation report, *Naval Operations in the Korean War,* is in 18 volumes. The chronological narratives of the Pacific Fleet commands and the Naval Forces Far East contain a wealth of information on what happened, when it happened, and the problems and difficulties experienced.

These volumes were a gold mine ready for use when the war in Vietnam was thrust upon the services. (I am told that the Navy used the report to full advantage, but I am not certain that the Navy passed on useful information to the Army and Air Force. For example, the first paragraphs in the report under "Major Features of the War in Korea" are entitled "Pattern of War." I include this section here because it is so true and so important. It was undoubtedly read by many young officers, but probably not by the JCS, in 1963 and 1964.

A. Pattern of War

The Russian Nation from the time of Napoleon has evidenced a high degree of aptitude for irregular and guerrilla warfare on land and later, defensive mining of seaports. These methods on land were developed during periods of military adversity, and generally have resulted in ultimate military victory over what were considered relatively superior forces. The soviets trained the North Korean Army, which demonstrated high capability in irregular and guerrilla warfare as well as a high degree of effectiveness in more orthodox types of military action. The soviets are presumed to have given training to Chinese Red Communist armies who have utilized the same type of tactics with considerable effectiveness. *Chinese Communists engaging the French in Indochina have been using similar tactics successfully.*

It appears reasonable to assume that soviet trained satellite nations as well as the soviets themselves will again use such tactics when forced to do so (italics mine).

U.S. Naval Forces, particularly Navy and Marine Air, should make every effort to develop ways and means of countering such actions—particularly with interdiction weapons and techniques that will tend to reduce the necessity for major engagements between ground forces.

Certainly the type of war fought in Vietnam indicated little recollection of the same problems only a few years before in Korea. One of the difficulties faced by military leaders was how to get their *civilian superiors* to read and understand such important military history.

In July and August 1950 the Eighth Army forces in Korea, together with those units of the South Korean army still in existence, were pushed back into the "Pusan perimeter." The fighting along the perimeter then and in early September was vicious. The North Koreans threw their attacking forces against our understrength divisions and the South Korean units without regard for losses. Time and again they broke through our lines, only to be checked by the rapid use made of his few valiant reserve units by Gen. W. H. ("Johnny") Walker, Commander Eighth Army.

I would add laurels for the men of the First Provisional Marine Brigade, who arrived in Pusan in August after organization and deployment to Korea by ship all within a month. In the next six weeks this brigade of some 5,000 officers and men participated in three major actions, twice prevented a breakthrough that threatened the complete collapse of the Pusan perimeter, and destroyed two entire North Korean divisions as effective military units, causing casualties estimated at twice the Marines' original strength. After this amazing series of actions, the brigade reembarked in Navy amphibious ships and participated in the Inchon landings as part of the First Marine Division Assault Force.

I also want to highlight for posterity the gallant Navy and Marine airmen and their support shipmates who spent most of this time interdicting North Korean forces and in close air support of the Pusan perimeter. It is impossible to recreate the tension of those early days and the dogged courage of the first lonesome forces on the scene of this bitter conflict in Korea.

I have often wondered how President Truman and Secretary Johnson must have felt as they read of these terrific battles, basically brought about, as I have noted, by the steady and well-publicized reductions in our armed forces. Called by these gentlemen a "police action," nothing could have been less descriptive. There was full-scale war in Korea that summer.

In Tokyo, under General MacArthur's guidance, planning for an amphibious landing on South Korea's west coast moved steadily forward. The General wanted to make the landing on 15 September, and there was much to do to get ready.

By mid-August the JCS had to make up their minds, and quickly. The Marine Corps had promised to have their division ready for the 15 September date, and the Army felt that their Seventh Division could also take part in the landing, if not the assault. General Collins and Admiral Sherman were delegated by the JCS to go to Tokyo to confer with General MacArthur and his planners and to return with firm recommendations. I joined them to hear the presentations.

I knew full well that most of the Army, Navy, and Marine Corps planners did not like Inchon as the site. With its tremendous rise and fall of tide—up to 36 feet at times—and its narrow, twisting approach channels and vast mudflats at low tide, it was an ugly, dangerous place for an amphibious landing. Its principal advantage was that the many obvious disadvantages would also be apparent to the enemy and they might be inclined to cross it off as an unlikely target for the same reasons, thus increasing the chances of surprise. Discussions of the pros and cons had been many and sometimes disagreeable, as tempers flared.

But by the time of the Tokyo conference I had become convinced that Inchon was the place to land.

Two days before the meeting, I had my only visit inside the Pusan perimeter during the fighting. General Walker's briefing was interesting and complete. He did not avoid describing the precariousness of his position—constantly emphasized by enemy shells falling within a mile or so of us. General Walker told us that he was prepared to move back, abandoning this advanced headquarters, on an hour's notice if he had to. It was not a cheerful presentation, but the General's cool courage was admirable.

The conference with General MacArthur and the JCS representatives on 23 August was a full-scale presentation of all details—many pessimistic—by the planning groups and some of the prospective task group commanders.[5]

General MacArthur listened intently to the briefing and all the comments. General Collins writes (p. 125):

> He continued sitting in silence for a few moments as we waited for his reaction. He then spoke quietly, in a matter-of-fact tone at first, gradually building up emphasis with consummate skill. Even discounting the obvious dramatics, this was a masterly exposition of the argument for the daring risk he was determined to take by a landing at Inchon.
>
> MacArthur said that he recognized all of the hazards that the Navy and Marine Corps had so clearly pointed out but that he had confidence in their ability to overcome them. He said that the Navy and Marines had never let him down throughout his campaigns in the Pacific and that he was sure they would not now.

The General's brilliant exposition left his audience spellbound. I felt that everyone but General Collins was convinced. Collins felt that Sherman and many of the Navy and Marine officers were still dubious. But this was late August, not quite four weeks to D-day, and actions to insure readiness by that date had to go forward rapidly.

I favored the plan and so did Joy. Sherman had doubts but I felt sure he would vote for it. General Lemuel Shepherd, my Fleet Marine Force Officer, who had practically single-handedly convinced the Marines that they could ready the First Division by 15 September, was certain it would be a tough operation but thought it could be done.

Actions in the next month still leave me puzzled, and they certainly must have been disappointingly confusing to General MacArthur. A fair appraisal of the situation in Washington was that the Army members of the JCS did not want to approve the Inchon landing but did not know how they could turn it down. They knew that the alternative, of reinforcing General Walker to the point where he could break out of the Pusan perimeter, would take additional troops, considerable time, and terrific losses of men. I concluded that they approved General MacArthur's plan, reluctantly, because they had no good alternative. Their action in this case probably had a great deal to do with later actions of great importance when the going got tough.

It is difficult to believe that a final decision on such an important operation could be delayed until one week before D-day, but it was in this case. After several interim exchanges and further reassurances from General MacArthur, the JCS wired on 8 September that the plan had been approved and the President so informed. Daily air bombardments of the fortified island in Inchon Harbor commenced two days later. This was just one of many instances that led General MacArthur to believe that authorities in Washington were not supporting him wholeheartedly and which, in my opinion, led to the final showdown that resulted in his abrupt relief.

Inchon is one of the classic amphibious operations of all times and certainly one of the most crucial. Without it the Korean War might have burgeoned into World War III, been a great defeat for the United States and its allies, or degenerated into a stalemate favorable to the communists. I am sure no one was more pleased than I to get the details of this highly successful operation, nor more sincere in the congratulations I sent to General MacArthur. It was truly his personal show.

As I mentioned, at the conference in Tokyo on 13 July General MacArthur had said he would follow up the amphibious maneuver with an overland pursuit of the withdrawing North Koreans, as he meant to destroy their forces, not merely drive them back across the thirty-eighth parallel. This was the crux of the next holdup in his operations.

I was not privy to all the orders and instructions given General MacArthur, but through many conversations with him and his principal assistants I was well aware of his intentions in this and other important objectives. His plans were, on the whole, sound militarily. General Collins raised no questions to this early outline of MacArthur's plan for winning the war, and he must have included these positive thoughts in his report on returning to Washington.

General Collins explains in his book (p. 143) what he calls the

dilemma at the 38th parallel. The capture of Inchon and Seoul ended the first phase of the Korean War but created new dilemmas as difficult as those that followed the North Korean invasion of South Korea.

Should the victorious United Nations Command stop at the 38th parallel? Should it simply drive the North Koreans back to where they came from, or should the North Korean Army be destroyed completely? Should all of Korea be occupied by United Nations forces and a United Korean government be established under the protection of the United Nations? What would be the reaction of the Soviets and Communist China under any of these conditions?

Former Secretary of State Dean Acheson, in his interesting and revealing *Present at the Creation,* had a great deal to say about the Korean War from its start almost to the signing of the armistice. His book contributes much to a better understanding of why, within our government, we had so much difficulty transmitting to our Commander-in-Chief in the field clear and definite orders.

Mr. Acheson wrote (p. 416):

> From the very start of hostilities in Korea, President Truman intended to fight a limited engagement there. In this determination he had the staunch and unwavering support of the State and defense departments and the Joint Chiefs of Staff. Such a war policy requires quite as much determination as any other kind. It also calls for restraint and fine judgment, a sure sense of how far is far enough; it may involve, as it did in Korea, a great deal of frustration.

I could add that, most important, it requires starting from a position of military strength, not from the nadir of national military weakness to which President Truman had brought the United States in the almost five years since the end of World War II.

Experienced military men know that the decision to keep a war or a "police action" *limited* is not, and cannot be, the decision of one side. The enemy has a great deal to say about that. So it was in the Korean War. I am quite certain that the JCS originally felt strongly that they had to hold out enough resources to take care of possible trouble in Europe, which they were afraid might come. But I do not feel that as military advisers they could have given the President their unwavering support for a policy of limited war. When our Eighth Army was backed into the Pusan perimeter, desperately fighting for its very existence, I am sure the JCS were doing everything they could to save it, and so were all the rest of us.

General MacArthur saved the day at Inchon and gave everyone, from the President down, a breathing spell. Unfortunately, the administration was not ready to take advantage of it. In particular: although two and a half months had elapsed since the start of hostilities, and General MacArthur had carefully informed Washington of follow-up plans that he considered an integral part of the Inchon operation—that is, pursuit of the remnants of the North Korean Army beyond the thirty-eighth parallel in order to destroy them—the administration had not yet made up its mind.

True, there were complications with our allies, with the U.N., and with criticism from the opposition party in Congress. What had seemed like such a good idea in June, to fight under the banner of the U.N., was causing trouble, and it was difficult to keep the war limited. In addition, the dispatch of two U.S. divisions to Korea in early July put matters of defense planning in a different perspective and made it an immediate budget issue. The midyear (July) report of the Council of Economic Advisers took a "relaxed view of affairs" that not only assumed the fighting would be kept localized but concluded that no standby economic control powers were necessary.

The State Department was unanimous in agreeing that not only what the country did but what it was obviously preparing itself to do, if necessary, would greatly affect what it might be called upon to do. In other words: not only the immediate enemy, North Korea, but its communist backers were watching us carefully. They could follow in detail the rate at which we were able to build up our depleted military strength and could distinguish a bluff from the real thing without much difficulty.

Mr. Acheson had brought these feelings to the attention of President Truman at a cabinet meeting on 14 July and convinced him that action should be taken to speed up increases in military strength. Five days later the President sent a message to Congress that did just this; stating that the United States would have to increase its military strength and preparedness to deal with the aggression in Korea and also to increase our common defense with other free nations.

It is one thing to ask for and receive additional appropriations for increased military strength and another thing to achieve that increased strength. Without unusual economic powers, such as are conferred in a state of national emergency, the armed services cannot always get the necessary high priorities for persuading manufacturers to give them the necessary facilities priorities. The Korean War was the first large international war in which we did not have time to build up our strength but started from a minimum base. The armed services had not developed the close liaison between industry and defense that existed later. Even this advanced planning cannot be effected without wartime powers granted to the President by Congress. (This most important liaison between industry and defense is now under almost constant attack by left-wing organizations. The Russians, who understand the problems of keeping industry ready to serve their military forces, are fully behind this destructive effort and are willing to go to almost any lengths to eliminate the liaison. They, if no one else, realize how important it is to our security.)

The delays in approving Inchon and giving General MacArthur permission to pursue the North Korean army were due not only to domestic political difficulties and to misunderstandings with the U.N., and some less than helpful allies, particularly Britain and India, but also to the fact that the Secretaries of State and Defense, and General Bradley and the JCS, had to devote much of their time to negotiating difficult NATO organizational problems and a proposed peace treaty with Japan. In the higher echelons of the U.S. government, summer and fall 1950 was truly a three-ring circus that might have been humorous had it not been so serious.

Probably because of a hiatus when Secretary of Defense Johnson was replaced by General Marshall, the JCS directive to General MacArthur concerning his crossing the thirty-eighth parallel was not transmitted until 27 September. It read as follows, quoted from Mr. Acheson's book (pp. 452–453):

Your military objective is the destruction of the North Korean Armed Forces . . . you are authorized to conduct military operations . . . north of the 38th parallel in Korea, provided that at the time of such operations there has been no entry into North Korea by major Soviet or Chinese Communist Forces, no announcement of intended entry, nor a threat to counter our operations militarily in North Korea. Under no circumstances, however, will your forces cross the Manchurian or USSR borders of Korea and, as a matter of policy, no non-Korean Ground Forces will be used in the northeast provinces bordering the Soviet Union or in the area along the Manchurian border. Furthermore support of your operations north or south of the 38th parallel will not include Air or Naval action against Manchuria or against USSR territory.

In the event of the open or covert employment of major Soviet units south of the 38th parallel, you will assume the defense, make no move to aggravate the situation and report to Washington. You should take the same action in the event your forces are operating north of the 38th parallel, and major Soviet units are openly employed. You will not discontinue Air and Naval operations north of the 38th parallel merely because the presence of Soviet or Chinese Communist troops is detected in a target area, but if the Soviet Union or Chinese Communists should announce in advance their intention to reoccupy North Korea and give warning, either explicitly or implicitly, that their forces should not be attacked you should refer the matter to Washington.

Soon after the JCS had forwarded their instructions to General MacArthur, Secretary of Defense Marshall sent him a dispatch for his eyes only, saying (Acheson, p. 453): "We want you to feel unhampered tactically and strategically to proceed north of the 38th parallel." General MacArthur replied, "Unless and until the enemy capitulates, I regard all Korea as open for our military operations."

In the light of all subsequent happenings, I submit the following. (1) The JCS directive to General MacArthur was somewhat equivocal and certainly on the timid side.[6] If this directive had reached the Russians and/or the Chinese it would have encouraged just what happened: the Chinese "sneaked" into North Korea and remained hidden until they could surprise the U.N. forces. Even after they were discovered the fiction was maintained that all the Chinese were "volunteers," not regular People's Liberation Army units ordered into North Korea. (The Chinese commander in Manchuria must have been surprised when half or three quarters of his army turned up missing!) (2) The directive was sent during the time that Burgess and MacLean were operating in London and Washington and the Russians had returned to the U.N. It is not unlikely that both Russians and Chinese learned of the American orders to the U.N. Commander, General MacArthur. (3) General Marshall's message to General MacArthur complicated matters. General Marshall was a man who usually said exactly what he meant. Perhaps he did in this case, though Secretary Acheson and General Collins thought otherwise.[7] (4) If the exchanges showed anything, they indicated that it was time for the President, the Secretary of State, the Secretary of Defense, and the JCS to call General MacArthur back to Washington for a conference.

In a way, that is what President Truman seemed to think. On 11 October he announced publicly a meeting with the General in the Pacific, to discuss "the final phase of United Nations actions in Korea ... We should like to get our armed forces out and back to their other duties at the earliest moment ... Naturally I shall take advantage of this opportunity to discuss with General MacArthur other matters within his responsibility."

☆ ☆ ☆ ☆

The meeting was to be held on Wake Island, on 15 October. This was my first experience with the problems and responsibilities of hosting the President of the United States. Next to my quarters at Pearl was a standard set of officers quarters used for official guests, which would be the President's for the three nights that he would spend in Hawaii. Secret Service men in the advance party swarmed over these quarters, particularly the downstairs bedroom, the President's. They insisted upon having a single bed against an inside wall, which made the arrangement of other furniture in the room very difficult but at least kept the bed away from the windows. Then they demanded a large overstuffed chair for the bedroom, a type not used much in that tropical climate. We located a rather shabby old chair and had it recovered that very day.

On the day of his arrival, following full honors and inspection of the honor guard, I presented to the President local flag and general officers, as well as the Governor of Hawaii, the Mayor of Honolulu, and other local dignitaries.

Mrs. Radford was to greet the President at his quarters and present him and his party with leis. She was on the entrance porch as the President walked up the steps, and she stepped forward with a gorgeous red carnation lei and attempted to put it around his neck. He looked rather surprised and recoiled, but Mrs. Radford was too quick for him and managed to get it on. As *Time* said, "The President acted as though the lei was made of poison ivy and took it right off." The lei incident received worldwide publicity and much comment pro and con. Mrs. Radford says that she said to the President as he tried to back away, "Mr. President, it is a custom of the Islands."

That afternoon, the presidential party toured the military bases in the Honolulu area, including as the final stop Tripler General Hospital, where there were many wounded soldiers and Marines from the Korean conflict.

The President walked quickly through the wards, occasionally stopping to greet a particular patient with a few words. As we came through one large ward I noticed a rather small young man sitting straight up in his bed, very evidently waiting to greet the President. He had a patch over one eye but the other, a piercing black one, was riveted on the President as he approached. Mr. Truman noticed him and stepped toward him with his hand outstretched just as the youngster, a Marine, said, "Mr. President, you called this a 'police action'—it's a big war!"

The President seemed really taken aback, shook the boy's hand, and said something about being "sorry"; but we hardly slowed down.

It was on that day that President Truman asked whether I would like to go to the Wake Island conference with him. I was of course delighted and accepted with pleasure.

General Collins writes of this meeting (p. 151): "The President and the General greeted one another cordially at the airstrip . . . After the usual picture-taking the two drove in an old Chevrolet to the quonset-hut office of the local airline manager. There they talked alone for some while before joining the official party for the main conference in another building."

In the conference room, places were arranged for the President, General MacArthur, Sec. Frank Pace, General Bradley, Amb. Averell Harriman, Amb. Philip Jessup, Dean Rusk, Amb. (to Korea) John Muccio, Col. A. L. Hamblen, and myself. This is the list at the head of the famous transcript at the conference prepared—without my knowledge, at least—by Miss Vernice Anderson. Miss Anderson was nowhere in sight as everyone was arriving; she must have come earlier and taken up her post in a little side room. She kept out of sight for the whole time as far as I can remember.

My copy of Miss Anderson's notes was handed to me soon after we returned to Pearl. I read the so-called transcript with considerable amazement, thinking it a poor and misleading record.[8] General Collins says of it (pp. 151–152):

> Unknown to either the President or General MacArthur, and reportedly without instructions from anyone, Miss Vernice Anderson, Secretary to Ambassador Jessup, was in the next room, the door of which was open, taking shorthand notes throughout this conference. Bradley and others in the President's party openly took notes, which were combined later into a top secret memorandum. A total of fifty-nine copies of this memorandum were distributed to officials of the White House and of the State and Army Departments, to the JCS, and to General MacArthur's Headquarters. As always seems to happen in Washington in the case of such controversial memoranda, especially when so widely disseminated, a copy was "leaked" to the press . . . During the congressional hearings on the relief of General MacArthur the General took umbrage at the fact that any "record" of the conference had been kept. He said that he had not read the copy of the memorandum when it was received at his headquarters but simply had it filed.

During these hearings Senator Russell asked the General: "So you are not in a position to state whether or not there are inaccuracies in that report or whether it is a reasonably accurate statement of what transpired on Wake Island?"

General MacArthur replied: "No, Sir; I have no way of telling you that. I have no doubt that in general they are an accurate report of what took place."

Had I been questioned six months later on the same subject, perhaps, I would have made a somewhat similar answer; but my immediate reaction on reading Miss Anderson's transcript was quite different. I don't see how she possibly could have been accurate. The half-door to her hideaway was *not* open, I would testify to that, and it would have been remarkable if she had heard all the individual conversations. How she could identify voices she had hardly heard before, such as mine, I did not know.

I took no part in preconference discussions; I came into the meeting cold, expecting to hear a detailed discussion of how General MacArthur would handle the military situation in North Korea. On the date of the conference U.S. forces were advancing into North Korea but had not proceeded far, although the South Koreans had captured Wonsan five days earlier.

The President seemed in a jovial mood and opened the conference by saying, "Now, General, suppose you start things off by telling us how things are going in Korea."

General MacArthur did just that, giving a very lucid and certainly optimistic description of the situation. He mentioned resistance in North Korea by about 100,000 North Koreans, whom he identified as replacements, mostly poorly trained and poorly organized. In South Korea he said there was little resistance from only about 15,000 (I presumed he meant the remnants of the North Korean army) and that the winter "will whip those that we don't." He thought military operations would end throughout Korea "by Thanksgiving" and said he was planning to withdraw the Eighth Army to Japan by Christmas, leaving the X Corps in Korea. He hoped the U.N. would hold elections in Korea by the first of the year. When these elections are held, "I expect to pull out all occupying troops. Korea should have about ten Divisions with our equipment and supplemented by a small but competent Air Force."

He ended his remarks thus: "I emphasize the fact that the military should get out the minute the guns stop shooting and the civilians take over. Korea is a poor country. It has been knocked down a long time and a little money goes a long way. It has been estimated that it will take $900 million to $1.5 billion for Korean rehabilitation. I believe these estimates are far too high. One hundred fifty million dollars per year is enough and three years of that should make us self-sustaining."

The conversation continued on details of the rehabilitation program. Then the President asked, "How will Syngman Rhee like the idea of elections?" MacArthur answered unhesitatingly, "He won't like it."

Assistant Secretary Rusk interjected, "We must not undermine the present

Korean government. We must have local elections all over Korea. Local officials in North Korea should get in touch with those in South Korea and in 1952 [we] should have general elections."

Mr. Harriman asked, "How about the interim period?" General MacArthur replied, "North Korea will be under military control. The U.N. calls for the maintenance of local government, but this is not possible. Local government will be maintained by appointing Republic of Korea [ROK] officials."

Mr. Harriman: "What about war criminals?"

General MacArthur: "Don't touch war criminals. It doesn't work. The Nuremberg trials and the Tokyo trials were no deterrent. In my own right I can handle those who have committed atrocities and if we catch them I intend to try [them] immediately by military commission."

The President then asked, "General what is your idea about a Japanese peace treaty without including Russia and Communist China?"

MacArthur answered, "I would call a conference and invite them. If they don't come in, go ahead. After the treaty is drawn up, submit them a draft of the treaty and if they don't sign, go ahead with the treaty. The Japanese deserve a treaty."

President Truman asked, "What would the effect on Japanese security be when our troops leave?"

General MacArthur: "We are organizing four divisions of Japanese troops (police reserves) to secure Japan. [The] present draft of the treaty by the State Department, which is very good, will call for the security of Japan . . . by the U.N. with the United States acting as the agency of the U.N. until the U.N. is in a position to do it itself."

The President: "Would we have to maintain three or four divisions in Japan until the Japanese can secure themselves?"

MacArthur: "Yes, the Japanese would not object, if they did not have to pay the bill for the support of these divisions."

Then General Bradley inquired: "Will the Japanese expect to receive this treatment from the troops when they return from Korea?"

General MacArthur: "Omar, there is complete camaraderie between troops and the Japanese. The Japanese like our troops; they spend lots of money."

General Bradley: "The Eighth Army is returning to Japan soon. We have the problem of getting troops to Europe. As it now stands, it will be April before we can get troops into Europe at the earliest. Could the Second or Third Divisions be made available to be sent over to Europe by January?"

My recollection of this last exchange is that General MacArthur promised to release one division about the first of January and a second possibly about the first of February.

The conference continued on the subjects of the Japanese peace treaty and problems in connection with the cost of occupation, then shifted to general

Asian problems when President Truman said he would like to discuss Pacific security. Indochina, and the difficulties of working with the French there, was discussed.

President Truman then remarked that he had talked at some length with General MacArthur about the [economic] situation in the Philippines, saying that the General suggested that Joseph Dodge (an American financial expert in Japan) would be able to help out.

The President said, "General MacArthur and I have talked fully about Formosa. There is no need to cover that subject again. The General and I are in complete agreement."

A conversation between MacArthur and Bradley about foreign contributions to the fighting in Korea, and the difficulties of their use, was followed by an exchange between MacArthur and Rusk about a reported Indian suggestion that the frontiers of North Korea be guarded with Indian and/or Pakistani troops instead of South Koreans. General MacArthur was dead against this.

It was obvious that the conferees were running out of steam, and at this point the President suddenly changed the subject: "General MacArthur, I am told that there are some three or four hundred thousand Chinese troops in Manchuria, just across the border from North Korea. Are you concerned about them? Do you think they might try to intervene to help the North Koreans?"

General MacArthur replied, "Mr. President, those Chinese troops have been there in Manchuria practically all the time since the Korean trouble started. There is always the possibility that they might decide to try to intervene but I believe that if they did I could take care of them."

To me General MacArthur's reply was very plain. He meant that if the Chinese crossed the border he would use his air force to bomb them—not just the troops, but their logistic bases in Manchuria. On 13 July in Tokyo I had heard him tell General Collins that he was sure the "communists" would try to reinforce the (North) Koreans but was equally sure that this could be prevented by medium bomber attacks. In other discussions with me he had elaborated on the vulnerability of the Chinese logistical bases in Manchuria to attacks by B29s. I thoroughly agreed with this line of reasoning and so did the leaders of the Far Eastern air forces, so far as I know.

This last exchange ended here. The President apparently accepted General MacArthur's statement, and he certainly did not say, "But General, remember you cannot attack the Chinese bases in Manchuria." Neither was there comment from Secretary Pace or General Bradley to this effect.

Secretary Acheson [who did not attend the conference] mentions this subject briefly (pp. 456–457), noting that General MacArthur told the President "that the Chinese would not intervene. If, however, they should do so, not more than fifty to sixty thousand could cross the Yalu, and they would be slaughtered if they attempted to go south." I do not believe this is a fair report of the exchange.[9]

The conference was over. President Truman said that a communiqué would be submitted as soon as possible, that General MacArthur could return immediately, and that it had been a most satisfactory conference.

Secretary Acheson reported (p. 457):

> The party returned full of optimism and confidence in the General. The President's speech two days later in the San Francisco Opera House exuded both. In explaining his journey to Wake, he concluded: "I also felt that there was pressing need to make it perfectly clear—by my talk with General MacArthur—that there is complete unity in the aims and conduct of our foreign policy."

Mr. Acheson added, "that perfect clarity did not outlast the month."

I felt as the President did. I thought it had been a very good conference, although I was surprised that more details of the proposed operations in North Korea had not been discussed. I incorrectly assumed that these had been discussed by the President and the General in their private conversation.

What went wrong at Wake Island? I still do not know, but I suspect that the whole conference had been informally thought up and was too informally conducted. Perhaps the State Department representative thought that the details State wanted discussed (and they must have had some important ideas) had been covered by the President when alone with the General.

General Bradley, the JCS representative, did not bring up the differences that we later learned still existed between the chiefs and their Unified Commander. A great opportunity to clear things up was lost; and I, who sat there and listened to it all, thought it had gone very well. I do not think the President was well served by his staff, but, again, they did not know what the President and the General had discussed in private.

The repercussions of the failure to reach a complete understanding at Wake Island were serious and continue to this day. At the end of the conference, if President Truman or General Bradley had said, "But General, you cannot attack across the Yalu," and the matter had been thoroughly discussed, the Korean War would have ended much differently. I feel that General MacArthur could have convinced the President that he had to attack Chinese bases in Manchuria if Chinese troops attacked his forces in North Korea. If the discussion had ended thus, we would have had a victory in Korea and many young men who died in combat in the next two years would have lived out their lives. What a shame! What a catastrophe!

18

Truman, MacArthur, and Limited War

T he next two and a half months are not pleasant to write about, and I can add little to the detail in which they have already been covered by historians. Instead of contributing to a better understanding between General MacArthur and the authorities in Washington, the Wake Island meeting seems, in retrospect, to have exacerbated them. One thing remains clear: General MacArthur either thought he had complete authority to decide all military matters in Korea or else decided on his own to do so. Secretary Acheson describes the situation at the Washington end in considerable detail (pp. 456–468, quoted below). One incident was particularly interesting to me. It relates to an order—certainly a sweeping one—issued in early November 1950 by General MacArthur to Gen. George Stratemeyer, his Air Force commander,

> to use his full air power to knock the North Koreans and their allies out of the war. [General MacArthur said] "Combat crews are to be flown to exhaustion if necessary," the Korean ends of all Yalu river bridges were to be taken out, and . . . every means of communication, installation, factory, city and village in North Korea, destroyed.
>
> General Stratemeyer informed the Pentagon of his orders three hours before his planes were due to take off on their mission against the bridges from Sinuiju to Antung . . . Mr. Lovett [Deputy Secretary of Defense] brought the order to me in the State Department, saying that he doubted whether the bombing would importantly interrupt traffic across the river and that the danger of bombing the Manchurian city of Antung was great.

Assistant Secretary Rusk, who was with them, said (in Acheson's words) that "we were committed not to attack Manchurian points without consultation with the British."

The JCS were asked to postpone MacArthur's action until the President's instructions could be obtained. The President was reached by telephone in Kansas City and the situation explained to him. He said he "would authorize anything necessary for the safety of the troops." MacArthur was finally authorized to hit the Korean end of the bridges.

But both Washington and Tokyo were confused after these exchanges and the bridges were not taken out. Horizontal bombing plus the order not to fly over Manchurian territory made the task almost impossible.

Mr. Acheson describes other difficulties with MacArthur and says,

> All the President's advisers in this matter, civilian and military, knew that something was badly wrong, though what it was, how to find out, and what to do about it they muffed. I have an unhappy conviction that none of us, myself prominently included, served him as he was entitled to be served.

What was going on, of course, was that Washington was trying to limit the war and General MacArthur was trying to win it and later save his Army from destruction.

During this time I knew that our Air Force, as well as Navy and Marine Forces, were trying desperately to stem the tide of defeat. I knew we were not allowed to attack targets in Manchuria. I felt this was the crux of the situation and the reason our Army was being pushed back. I still think so, believing to this day that the Air Force with the help of carrier air could have destroyed the Chinese air forces in Manchuria and the Chinese army's logistic bases as well, if the President really had wanted to do "anything necessary for the security of the troops." I do not know why these restrictions were retained, British consultation or not.

During November and December the Eighth Army was engaged in almost continuous heavy fighting while it withdrew close to the thirty-eighth parallel by Christmas. The X Corps, in a remarkable amphibious operation in reverse, withdrew from Hungnam and was transported to Pusan. The ROK I Corps, also evacuated from Hungnam, was disembarked at Sanchok on the East Coast of South Korea, ready to anchor that end of a defensive line.

On 23 December General Walker was, as usual, traveling by jeep along his front lines to "see things for himself." On a narrow road he started to pass two trucks parked on one side just as a Korean truck pulled out from behind the parked vehicles. The General's jeep was hit and overturned, all its occupants thrown out. General Walker was killed almost instantly. It was a sad ending for this wonderful man who had fought so hard from the perilous days of the Pusan perimeter through the pursuit to the Yalu and the surprise Chinese attack there that had again put his army on the defensive.

General Matthew Ridgway, Deputy Chief of Staff for Operations and Administration under General Collins, who had been selected as General Walker's successor when and if needed, arrived in Tokyo late Christmas Day. After a brief discussion, which MacArthur ended by telling Ridgway he was prepared to turn over full control of military operations in Korea to him, Ridgway asked whether MacArthur would object to a decision to attack. MacArthur replied, "Do what you think best, Matt, the Eighth Army is yours" (Ridgway, *Soldier,* p. 201).

General Shepherd, Commander Fleet Marine Forces, had made several trips to Japan after the Inchon landing. A visit late in December brought him back to Pearl in a very pessimistic mood. He said General MacArthur was even concerned about the ability of the Eighth Army to stay in Korea. This attitude—which Shepherd sensed but could not positively confirm—had been occasioned by another misunderstanding between Washington and Tokyo in regard to a new directive to MacArthur, about which Shepherd and I could not know at that time. It was straightened out once President Truman had sent MacArthur a clarifying letter, but it resulted in further serious confusion and contributed ultimately to the final break in April.

On 20 January 1951, at Admiral Sherman's urging, I made a trip to Tokyo and Korea, followed by stops at Okinawa, the Philippines, and Hong Kong. I wanted principally to assess the morale of our naval units, as well as to make my own judgments about Korea.

After a meeting in Tokyo with General MacArthur, Admiral Joy and his staff provided me with a good cross-section of opinion on all phases of our naval operations. There seemed to be no pessimism in the Navy's high command.

This trip was the occasion of my first meeting with General Ridgway, in Pusan, and I was impressed. He had that élan that all good field commanders have; and as he spoke of his plans to drive the Chinese back north, his quiet confidence convinced me that here was a man who knew what he was talking about. He was well acquainted with his new command although he had been there less than a month. From everyone I heard that he had spent practically all his waking hours getting acquainted with his troops and their leaders, and that Eighth Army morale was noticeably high in the U.S. units. The South Korean units were in much better shape too. Still apt to cave in when attacked in force by Chinese troops, they could more than hold their own against the North Koreans. My meeting with General Ridgway was very satisfactory from my standpoint—particularly as he added high praise for the performance of all Navy and Marine units and for their cooperative spirit.

Off the North Korean coast I helicoptered to our carriers *Princeton* and *Philippine Sea* to witness flight operations, hear the pilots briefed before their missions, and listen to their reports on returning. Their principal mission was the interdiction of communist supply lines from the north, with particular attention to railroads, bridges, highways, and almost anything that moved north of the thirty-eighth parallel.

After visiting several other ships based in Japan, I went to Yokosuka, to the large naval hospital crowded with wounded Marines from Korea. It was depressing to walk through ward after ward of fine young men wounded in the hard fighting in North Korea as the First Marine Division had fought its way in, and then out, against terrific opposition by hordes of Chinese and in vicious weather, often much below zero. The division had a total of almost 10,000 casualties, over 6,000 of them frostbitten, and many were still in this hospital. I was heartened, however, by not only the spirit of the wounded men but by the dedication of the obviously overworked hospital staff.

On 27 January I lunched with General MacArthur and the Honorable John Foster Dulles, whose principal responsibility at the time was preparation of a Japanese peace treaty. This was largely the subject of our conversation. I believe that, in criticizing General MacArthur, bureaucrats in Washington were apt to forget that in addition to his Korean responsibilities he still had very important and time-consuming duties in Japan as Supreme Commander Allied Powers. While he was permitting General Ridgway full freedom of action in handling the Eighth Army, General MacArthur had to work many long and extra hours to keep up with both jobs.

I had been trying to arrange for the use of Hong Kong as a liberty port for some of our larger ships, with little success so far. I had decided that a face-to-face meeting was in order, which proved correct. Other than Yokosuka and Sasebo our ships had no good ports to visit in the entire Far East. Only Manila was available, and that was not suitable for large liberty parties.

Governor Alexander Grantham, a splendid diplomat, helped us work out an agreement that continues satisfactorily to this day. He was frank in outlining his concerns: large liberty parties might cause trouble with Chinese communists, who lived in Hong Kong although they did not control it. We compromised by agreeing to allow no more than 1,000 men ashore at any one time and promising thorough indoctrination of all who were allowed to go on, for example, the perils of communist trickery in starting riots. For those kept aboard ship, we permitted selected Chinese merchants to sell their wares on the ships. The plans worked well for many years, and thousands of our men have enjoyed their visits to this fascinating city.

In my two conversations with General MacArthur on this trip I had no indication of his gradually worsening relations with Washington, which are so evident in the histories of misunderstandings that existed between the President-State-Defense-JCS on the one hand and General MacArthur on the other, during December 1950–March 1951.

Nevertheless some incidents that increased the bad feelings received wide publicity, and I along with many others was well aware of the increasing tensions between the President and his Commander in the field. Looking back upon my feelings at the time, and adding to them later knowledge of differences as they developed, I confess to being torn between my sympathy for a Commander who saw his men being killed and wounded in the field *when he thought they did not have to be* and a courageous President doing what he thought was right as Commander-in-Chief of the armed forces and the elected civilian leader of the country.

The problems between President Truman and his advisers and General MacArthur had their genesis, not only in the problems of fighting the Korean War once the President had decided to take that step in June 1950, but in the cumulative acts of his administration for the several years he had been in office.

Truman, an astute midwestern politician with limited formal education, became President in April 1945 as a result of a series of near accidents. He was catapulted into the enormous responsibilities of his new office with little chance to prepare himself. A man of great native intelligence, he handled himself extremely well under the circumstances and learned fast.

I attended conferences between Mr. Forrestal and President Truman. I came to the conclusion that the President admired the Secretary for being everything that he himself wanted to be but was not—that is, a poor boy who had educated himself at Princeton and who later became a successful businessman—but that he did not like him and perhaps was jealous of him. President Truman took strong likes and dislikes to people without very good reasons in many cases. He told me once that he just could not stand President Chiang Kai-shek. Surprised, I asked if they had ever met. He said they had not but that he read and heard a great deal about the Generalissimo. I remarked that I thought of the Generalissimo as one of the great men of our times and let it go at that.

In my contacts with President Truman I came to realize that he was inclined to lean heavily on a few intimate advisers, and that once he had made up his mind he did not change it readily. The advisers to whom he listened, whoever they were, must have insisted that the communist threat was overrated, for he was still demanding that military expenditures be reduced when the Korean War started.

Every now and then some of our obviously sincere but extremist antiwar advocates make the point that by our large expenditure for military forces and hardware we force the Russians to follow our course: the U.S. fuels the fires of militarism by its own actions. These people have short memories, or perhaps they had not yet been born in 1945–1950. If ever an example of what they want was set, President Truman set it in those years. The country was rewarded not with peace but with the Korean War.

During those fateful few days at the end of June 1950, when decisions were made to go to the rescue of South Korea, the JCS, principal military advisers to the President, made clear what a low ebb our military posture had reached and what risks the President would be taking if he decided to fight. I believe that the JCS were well aware of the risks the President was taking and *that they assumed that he was, too,* since they had made this clear to him in many conversations on the military budget before the Korean crisis. They knew and voiced concern regarding U.S. ability to keep the Korean action limited. It takes either two to cooperate in that regard, or else well-known and overpowering strength on one side. In June 1950 we had neither of these requisites. We knew, or should have known, that the leaders of the USSR were behind the Korean aggression and that they were not going to cooperate with us in our efforts to defeat it. These leaders, and the rest of the world, knew that our military strength was at its nadir and that it would take considerable time to rebuild it. The USSR counted on a quick victory in Korea.

President Truman had successfully countered earlier communist threats in Iran, Greece, and Berlin because he had acted quickly and positively. He must have thought he could do this again in Korea. The fact that the Secretaries of State and Defense agreed with him is not important. What did the JCS advise? I believe it all happened so fast, and over a weekend, that the chiefs did not make their position entirely clear until it was too late—or that they counted too much on the ability of four U.S. divisions in Japan plus a South Korean army (which really did not exist). Certainly the United States was well committed by the time Generals Collins and Vandenburg met with General MacArthur in Tokyo on 13 July 1950; yet, in this conference General Collins wanted to know what U.S. army forces General MacArthur needed to stop the North Koreans and drive them back to the thirty-eighth parallel.

My point is that the earliest and, to my mind, very proper decisions made so courageously by President Truman were not backed up by sound military advice or planning but were the beginning of a great gamble.

For reasons that must have been at least partly political, our military buildup in the first six months of the war was not as rapid as it should and could have been. True, Congress appropriated quickly a great deal of money for the armed services, but that unfortunately is only the first step. President Truman did not proclaim a state of emergency until 15 December 1950. Under that proclamation the services can really speed their buildup; but by that time we were in great trouble not only in Korea but in the U.N. and also with our allies in the fighting.

At the Washington end, by the middle or end of December General MacArthur was taking the blame for serious military reverses the U.S. had suffered after the heavy Chinese attacks at the end of November. General MacArthur, I think, felt that the blame rested in Washington because he had not been permitted to attack Chinese bases in Manchuria to slow down their attacks on the Eighth Army and the X Corps in Korea. On this particular point of difference I have no firm evidence to support either side.

General MacArthur had this to say, in *Reminiscences* (p. 374):

> I will always believe that if the United States had issued a warning to the effect that any entry of the Chinese Communists in force into Korea would be considered an act of war against the United States, that the Korean War would have terminated with our advance north. I feel that the Reds would have stayed on

their side of the Yalu. Instead, *information must have been relayed to them* (my italics), assuring that the Yalu bridges would continue to enjoy sanctuary and that their bases would be left intact.

He quotes an official leaflet by Gen. Lin Piao, which he says was published in China:

> I would never have made the attack and risked my men and military reputation if I had not been assured that Washington would restrain General MacArthur from taking adequate retaliatory measures against my lines of supply and communication.

I am inclined to agree with General MacArthur in this argument and to feel that at the end of November 1950 his Far Eastern Air Force, with considerable assistance from our carrier air (four large carriers), could have destroyed the Chinese air forces in Manchuria and their armies' logistic bases. There is the possibility that Russia might have joined the Chinese in air and other attacks against our forces in Korea, but I have never believed that this would have happened. All such possibilities should have been considered in June 1950, when we decided to go into Korea. Quite evidently they were not, probably for lack of time.

Differences between Washington and Tokyo continued during early 1951. General MacArthur several times used interviews with newspapermen (later published) to publicize certain of his views. One incident led to another until, on 20 March, the General replied to a personal letter he had received from Joseph Martin, Republican minority leader in the House of Representatives, in a manner that evidenced his difference with national policy as laid down by his superiors in Washington (no surprise to them). Dean Acheson makes it plain that publication of MacArthur's letter to Martin convinced President Truman that his insubordinate Commander-in-Chief was violating orders, and the President decided to relieve him of his command. The letter said in part:

> My views and recommendations . . . have been submitted to Washington in most complete detail . . . they follow the conventional pattern of meeting force with maximum counter-force as we have never failed to do in the past . . . It seems strangely difficult for some to realize that here in Asia is where the communist conspirators have elected to make their play for global conquest, and that we have joined the issue thus raised on the battlefield; that here we fight Europe's war with arms while the diplomats there still fight it with words; that if we lose the war to communism in Asia the fall of Europe is inevitable; win it and Europe most probably would avoid war and yet preserve freedom. As you point out, we must win. There is no substitute for victory.

General MacArthur says in *Reminiscences* (p. 386):

> I have always felt duty-bound to reply frankly to every Congressional inquiry into matters connected with my official responsibility. This has been a prescribed

practice since the very beginning of our nation, and is now the law. Only in this way, and by personal appearance, can the country's law-makers cope intelligently with national problems.

I know of no law that would require General MacArthur or any other military man to answer a communication like Congressman Martin's in detail and in a way that would make plain his differences with the administration. On the other hand, any officer testifying before a congressional committee is required to give his personal opinion, if asked for it, even if it discloses a disagreement with higher authority. In General MacArthur's case, he could have replied through the War Department, asking them to forward his letter to the Congressman.

There were other exchanges between General MacArthur and the JCS around this time that I am sure enraged the General. He felt—and with good reason—that the diplomats, not the soldiers, were running the war in Korea.

For instance, in the new directive given to General MacArthur by the JCS on 30 December 1950 he had, as Collins describes it in his book (p. 248), "two interdependent and, from MacArthur's viewpoint, conflicting possible courses of action. On the one hand he was told to defend Korea, subject to the proviso that he must save his command from destruction and still be prepared to defend Japan from invasion. On the other hand he was to withdraw without further ado."

General Collins explains the JCS thinking (p. 248), but then says

> I must admit that I personally, and, I believe, the JCS as a group, had considerable sympathy for MacArthur in the dilemma presented to him by this directive. In our regular periodic meetings with representatives of the State Department the Chiefs constantly tried to pin down at any particular time after the Chinese intervention, just what our remaining political objectives were in Korea, but our diplomatic colleagues would always counter with the query "What are your military capabilities?" . . . The Chiefs could only deduce that our State Department co-workers, torn as they were by often conflicting domestic and international political considerations, wanted us to attain the maximal military results within our military capabilities. But the military would have to assume all the responsibility if things went wrong.

This is a fair assessment of the situation, I believe, but even so the JCS did pass the buck to MacArthur. Why they laid so much stress on the defense of Japan all this time is beyond me. Certainly if the Navy had the capability to move the Eighth Army from Korea to Japan in the face of a Russian threat to invade that country, then the Navy had the strength to keep the Russians from coming over. I think the chiefs could well have left the defense of Japan out of this complicated picture and trusted the Navy to stop it if attempted.

Apparently President Truman spent almost a week considering General MacArthur's relief, consulting with the Secretaries of State and Defense and receiving through the latter the unanimous recommendation of the JCS [who decided on 8 April] that he be relieved. On 10 April Acheson, Marshall, Harriman, and Bradley met the President with draft orders to put their decision into effect. The President approved and ordered the decision sent by State Department code to Ambassador Muccio in Pusan. The Ambassador was to deliver the orders to Secretary of the Army Pace in Korea, who was to fly at once to Tokyo and present them to General MacArthur.

This complicated procedure was designed to prevent "leaks" and save General MacArthur from embarrassment. It did not work. After waiting some time for notice from Ambassador Muccio, who had been told to acknowledge receipt at once in the clear [not in code], it was finally decided to send the orders through regular War Department channels to Tokyo.

General MacArthur says of it all in his book (pp. 389, 395):

> At one o'clock in the morning of April 11th, President Truman summoned the press to the White House and announced my relief from command in the Far East. His action was fraught with politics as he was apparently of the belief that I was conspiring in some underhanded way with the Republican leaders . . . I was first apprised of the action through a press dispatch over the public radio . . . The order for my relief reached Tokyo on the afternoon of the 11th as the radios broke through their normal programs to announce a special bulletin from Washington: "President Truman has just removed General MacArthur from his Far Eastern and Korean Commands and from the direction of the occupation of Japan."

In Honolulu we received the news late in the evening of 10 April, by news broadcast relayed to me by my headquarters. It was not unexpected as far as I was concerned. Mrs. Radford and I had discussed the possibility and concluded that if it happened we would invite the MacArthurs to be our guests at Pearl Harbor when they came through Honolulu, as they surely would, on their way to the mainland. I immediately sent a dispatch through Navy channels to Admiral Joy, thinking this the quickest and surest way to reach General MacArthur, asking him to call on the General and personally extend not only our regrets at the news but our warmest invitation to Pearl. In accepting our invitation General MacArthur commented, "Whenever I get in trouble the Navy comes to my rescue."

General MacArthur's welcome in Honolulu was as tumultuous as it was everywhere else. He agreed to drive through the city for a ceremony at the university and a visit to the National Cemetery at the Punch Bowl. But most of the time he was busy writing the speech he had been invited to give to a joint session of Congress on 19 April.

I had little opportunity to talk to General MacArthur privately while he was my guest, but what contact I had showed me that he was his normal, gracious self. I heard not one word of regret, not one word of criticism of the President.

The speech to Congress was a masterpiece. Congressman Dewey Short, one of the great orators in the House, told me that MacArthur had made one of the two great speeches he had heard in his lifetime.

The entire speech is recommended reading so far as I am concerned. But I quote here, from *Reminiscences* (p. 404) what I consider the most important part:

> Men since the beginning of time have sought peace. Various methods through the ages have been attempted to devise an international process to prevent or settle disputes between nations. From the very start, workable methods were found insofar as individual citizens were concerned; but the mechanics of an instrumentality of larger international scope have never been successful. Military alliances, balances of power, leagues of nations, all in turn failed, leaving the only path to be by way of the crucible of war. The utter destructiveness of war now blocks out this alternative. We have had our last chance. If we will not devise some greater and more equitable system, Armageddon will be at the door. The problem is basically theological and involves a spiritual recrudescence and improvement of human character that will synchronize with our almost matchless advance in science, art, literature, and all material and cultural developments of the past 2,000 years. It must be of the spirit if we are to save the flesh.

The General was not, as charged by some, a man who would risk a larger war, a world war, for a small victory in Korea. He was a man who understood other men, a student of warfare, who realized that appeasement does not pay, that it only prolongs conflict.

The lack of understanding between the President and his advisers in Washington and their field commander in Korea brought about a stalemate instead of the victory General MacArthur had envisaged. No one will ever be able to *prove* who was right, but the long-term results are plain. A war that might have ended in victory by Thanksgiving Day 1950 goes on today, for we still have only an armistice in Korea. Expenditures in the billions, and the lives of tens of thousands of our young men, in Korea and later in Vietnam, can be charged to our failure to win the Korean War.

General Ridgway relieved General MacArthur, and Gen. James Van Fleet succeeded to command of the Eighth Army in Korea when Ridgway moved to Tokyo.

As Ridgway prepared to turn over the Eighth Army command he was aware that the Chinese and North Korean armies were preparing to resume the offensive, counting particularly on rainy spring weather to hamper movements of the heavy equipment of U.N. forces. He says in *Korean War* (p. 161):

> Eight days after I settled myself . . . the Chinese Communist Forces opened their two-punch fifth-phase offensive, destined to be their final all-out effort to cast us into the sea. It was an advance in great strength, and had the Chinese earlier

been able to trap any considerable number of our forces by luring them into unphased pursuit, they might have done us great damage.

The enemy offensive ran out of steam at the end of April, and General Van Fleet put the Eighth Army on the offensive immediately, hoping to catch them off balance. Advances were made but could not be sustained, so again we prepared to counter the new Chinese offensive that was sure to come.

According to Ridgway (pp. 174–175), "The Chinese resumed their efforts just after dark on May 15th, using an estimated 21 divisions with 9 North Korean divisions on the flanks." Chinese losses in this second phase of their offensive were heavy and they soon sputtered to a stop. By 20 May the U.N. forces had started forward again, melting resistance until at the end of the month the opposing armies were facing each other almost where they had started in April.

The end of the first year's fighting, in June 1951, found South Korea again free of the enemy and the two armies face to face in the general area in which they would remain for the next two years.

Toward the end of May 1951 I made another Tokyo and Korea trip. General Shepherd accompanied me because I was to tell General Ridgway that Admiral Sherman and Gen. Clifton Cates, Commandant of the Marine Corps, were concerned about the lack of close air support for the First Marine Division. All other efforts having failed to improve their situation, the First Marines now asked that one of four squadrons be positioned close to their rear and directed to support them. Theoretically, they would have much less support than before; but this way they would *get* what was available when they asked for it.

I found Ridgway familiar with General Shepherd's proposals yet politely but firmly against any change. He stated frankly that he could not approve any proposal that would in effect give the First Marines more air support than that given to the other U.S. (Army) divisions, even though I pointed out that the Marines were organized and able to use more close air support than were Army divisions.

I later told Sherman that though I could get no commitment for a change from Ridgway, I hoped he would pass the word to the Far East Air Force to do better for the Marines. I was sure that Ridgway was (1) generally satisfied with the close air support given to the Eighth Army (even though many younger Army officers passing through Pearl told me it was often inadequate) and (2) inclined to favor artillery for many missions for which Marines would use close air support. I also heard Van Fleet express much the same idea at a briefing at Tenth Corps headquarters after Gen. Edward Almond [Commander X Corps, Korea] had been outspoken in regard to the advantages of the Marine system.

During this trip General Shepherd and I visited the First Marine Division, which was on the move north after the last Chinese offensive. We flew up together in a helicopter with another helicopter escort, and spent a busy day visiting front-line positions and watching offensive operations in progress with and without air support. I suppose I was too interested to realize that we were overstaying our time, so when we did start the return trip I agreed that the young Marine pilot could head straight across the mountains to get to his field before dark.

We were just over the higher ridges when I began to notice that our engine was rough. Shepherd finally asked me if I thought anything was wrong with it and I told him I was afraid so. Just about then it stopped completely and we headed into a valley for our forced landing. It was desolate mountain country, with no sign of human habitation, but our pilot made a nice landing in what appeared to be an abandoned rice paddy. Pilot, copilot, and mechanic immediately jumped out of the helicopter, pistols and a rifle at the ready. The other helicopter landed close by.

I had felt that we were in uninhabited country and perfectly safe, so was amazed to find several dozen youngsters eyeing us from about 50 feet away within five minutes.

The Marine pilot suggested that General Shepherd and I leave immediately in the escort helicopter; we were glad to do so, realizing that we would indeed be prizes if taken by guerrillas, sometimes numerous in these mountain areas.

Both helicopters managed to beat nightfall, but I was not too proud of this venture. By my carelessness I might have caused a lot of people—including myself—a lot of trouble.

The end of the Chinese offensive of April and May, and the counteroffensive of the Eighth Army, evidently impressed the higher-ups in communist circles. The first call for an armistice was delivered by Jacob Malik, Deputy Foreign Minister of the USSR and Soviet delegate to the U.N., on 23 June.[1]

The next day, carrying out a directive from Washington, General Ridgway broadcast to the Chinese high command a message that if, as reported, they were ready for a cease fire, the U.N. command would be willing to send representatives to discuss an armistice. It took several days to make contact and agree upon a meeting place: the town of Kaesong, on the west coast of Korea just south of the thirty-eighth parallel.

The armistice negotiations opened on 10 July 1951. No one could have realized that they would drag on for over two years, and that grim fighting would continue for most of that time. General MacArthur noted in his book that three-fifths of American casualties were suffered during this time. When the negotiations started, there were high hopes in the United States and Korea that fighting would stop in a few weeks. We did not know the communists as well then as we do now.

19

The Far East: Political Problems

W ith a "stationary" war in Korea, and with U.S. naval forces having pretty well reached their projected peak, my problems as CINCPAC changed. For several months the JCS had been considering, for a number of reasons, relieving CINCFE of his additional responsibilities outside Japan. First, MacArthur had irritated certain members of the U.N. when he recommended, after a surprise visit to Formosa, the use of Chinese Nationalist troops in Korea. These members thought the U.N. Commander should not have such outside responsibilities. Second, the Japanese peace treaty was moving forward, and the JCS realized that, despite their objections to it, it would go through. This would do away with Supreme Commander Allied Powers and leave only a U.N. command that would also probably disappear upon settlement of the Korean War.

For several months I had been corresponding with Admiral Sherman about the additional planning responsibilities which, as CINCPAC, I would have: the defense of the Marianas and the Bonins, as well as the Ryukyus, Formosa, and the Philippines. I was also being brought into planning for possible emergency evacuation of U.S. nationals from Hong Kong and other areas in Southeast Asia.

Enlargement of CINCPAC's responsibilities required rather major changes in my activities, which almost coincided with the changed action in Korea. For the rest of 1951—and in fact for the rest of my tour as CINCPAC—I was busy acquainting myself with the people and problems of the western Pacific.

☆ ☆ ☆ ☆

Although Japanese fortification of the Bonin Islands, especially Chichi Jima, the largest and most important, had begun some 20 years before World War II, work was still in progress when war was declared. By 1941, all important gun emplacements and tunnels were nearing completion; repair shops, machine shops, oil storage, and magazines had been placed underground in concrete-lined, ventilated caves. The approximately 20,000 Japanese who garrisoned the island boasted that Chichi Jima was the Gibraltar of the Pacific. Credit for masterminding this fantastic network of underground tunnels and caves goes to the same Major Matoba who developed the fortifications on Iwo Jima.

Chichi Jima was fortified to ward off an invading fleet. Little emphasis had been laid on air defense. Once again Japanese strategy was in error. As U.S. air strikes began to hit the islands, attention was directed toward meeting this threat, without much success, but with an interesting development for the original Bonin Islanders. Their settlement, a little American-English-Hawaiian colony named Yankeetown, was at the head of the harbor and almost at the foot of a rather steep mountain. Most raids by American forces came over this mountain from the east, and because they were trying to destroy the naval base their bombs did not hit Yankeetown. The Japanese felt that the American group in the town must have had means of communicating with American forces! Partly as a result of this, and partly because civilians were in the way, all civilians were evacuated to Japan in July 1944, where they worked for the next year in ammunition factories near Tokyo.

After the armistice, U.S. authorities decided to return the descendants of the original Bonin group to Chichi Jima. Since then responsibility for them had been charged to CINCPACFLT.

Although Chichi Jima could claim one of the finest natural harbors in the Pacific, it had not been recharted. Japanese wrecks were not marked, and entry of even a destroyer would have been hazardous. On my first visit there, in May 1951, our party used a gasoline-powered boat from Chichi Jima manned by members of the Savory clan. Jerry Savory, one of the official greeters and president of the village council, told us that the boat had once been the property of Lieutenant General Tachibana, commander of all Japanese forces in the islands, who after the war had been tried, convicted, and hanged for atrocities he had permitted on Chichi Jima against captured American flyers. Fred Savory, Jerry's younger brother, had acted as the official interpreter during the trial.

I shall never forget the beauty of that two-mile ride into the harbor. The shores of the almost landlocked bay rose gradually and gracefully to the rather steep mountains that hem the harbor. The splendor of the island was magnified in the early morning sunlight. I could imagine the feelings of early explorers and the original Savory group as they entered the bay for the first time.

Hundreds of caves, many of which once held coastal guns, dot the mountainsides. To starboard as we entered the harbor was the former Japanese air strip, a short, steep cut through the mountains from the harbor to the sea, and plagued by fog and crosswinds. It could be used only by small light planes. According to Mr. Gilley, one of the Islanders, the Japanese labored nearly twenty years to build the field but it never was very successful.

The Islanders had been informed that my visit would be short, and that I wanted to see all I could of the administrative and residential sections of Chichi

Jima, particularly of Yankeetown. I wanted to meet with the men of the community to talk about plans for their future. Members of my staff would remain behind to estimate the amount of scrap metal on the islands. If there was enough to make its salvage worthwhile I wanted to let a contract for its removal, setting up the proceeds in a trust fund for future use of the community. (Eventually the trust fund was set up, with about $100,000 from this source.)

My inspection, mostly by jeep, did not take too long except for a difficult half-hour climb to the top of the first rise back of the settlement, where a century-old cemetery lay. As I stood there looking at headstones of the Savorys, the Gilleys, and others of the original little band, I could not help but think how the world had changed since they first came to Chichi Jima in 1830.

That morning the 38 adult male members of the community assembled in the schoolhouse, formerly the administration building of the naval station. I was impressed by their appearance. It was evident that they were descendants of a hardy group and were now living as they wished to live, as free men, for the first time in many years.

Six or seven months before I had received a petition signed by the individuals I was now meeting, asking that they be permitted to again become U.S. citizens. I say "again" because several of the original group were American citizens, and from the time of Commodore Perry's visit in 1853 all had felt that the United States had taken them under its wing. I was anxious to help them not only because of historical ties but because I felt that there were many good reasons for the United States to retain possession of this island group. Even before 1950 our State Department had successfully pressured the Defense Department into returning the Ryukyus north of Okinawa to the Japanese, and I knew this pressure would continue. In the Bonin Islands there was no local Japanese population to return to Japanese sovereignty and there were no natural resources that made the islands particularly valuable. There was local fishing, which furnished a good livelihood and which would suffice for many years to come. In the fine harbor of Chichi Jima and the airfields on Iwo Jima the United States could have an excellent advanced naval base to complement our bases in Guam and the Philippines. There could come a day when we might have to project our strength into the western Pacific again, without bases in Japan or on the mainland.

As the Military Governor, and as CINCPAC, I had already heard from the Japanese civilian group who had once lived in the Bonin group. They had organized and were attempting through the Japanese government to return to their former homes in the Bonins. Fortunately for me, our occupation authorities in Tokyo had obtained all the land records of the islands at the end of the war. Title to most of the land was retained by the Japanese government. Soundings in Washington indicated that buying up former Japanese civilian land might be practicable, and it would solve the most pressing and immediate problem. It might ultimately result in bringing the Bonins under the U.S. flag. This was the situation when I met with the men of the original Bonin group in May 1950.

I have never addressed a more attentive group than I did that bright morning on Chichi Jima. I told them of my intense interest in their history and well-being, of my knowledge of their hardships and my desire to help them. I had not visited the islands before but had been able to keep in close touch with the Islanders and thought I had a pretty good idea of their problems. I would not only be glad to receive but would appreciate any suggestions which they cared to make pertaining to the administrative, economic, and social matters of their community. I was able to tell them that their request had been granted that young men and young women of their group be permitted to marry Japanese.

Then I came to the highlight of the meeting as far as the Bonin men were concerned: their petition for citizenship. I read them a letter that I had written and signed as Military Governor: I had been directed to inform them that their petition had been received with deep appreciation and great interest and would receive careful consideration. I assured them that I would continue to urge its approval.

I wish I could report that my plans for this little community and the islands were finally and successfully negotiated, but I cannot. At the time of my retirement from active duty in August 1957 the Bonins were still under the American flag. The original group had grown to over 200 and was prospering. From 1951 to 1957 I had been able to fend off several attempts by the State Department to return the islands to Japanese sovereignty. Congress had appropriated the funds to buy all former Japanese civilian-owned land.

The Japanese Peace Treaty was signed in September 1951, and our first post-war ambassador to Japan was appointed: Robert Murphy, a career diplomat who had been closely associated with General Eisenhower in Europe and a good friend of mine. I believe we talked over the future of the Bonin and Volcano Islands several times but am not certain. At any rate, in 1952 I was very surprised to receive a copy of his dispatch to the State Department recommending that the islands be returned to Japan. I took immediate steps to delay any such action and urged him to meet me in Chichi Jima so that I could acquaint him personally with the Islanders, their problems, and the reasons why I felt we should not give them up. Bob was convinced that I was right after our visit, and he cooperated with me thereafter in my efforts to hold on to the islands.

Later, at the request of the Islanders, I financed a trip for four of their men to the U.N. in New York, where they petitioned for approval of their request for U.S. citizenship. I did not feel that their efforts at the U.N. would be helpful but I did feel they should be given a chance to try.

After my retirement I was able to help the Islanders and kept in touch with their progress, particularly in connection with their school. While I was still on active duty we had managed to hire two young Japanese men in Honolulu as teachers for the Chichi Jima school. This was a successful move, socially and educationally. But as the years passed, official Washington, including the Defense and Navy Departments, lost interest; and in June 1958 without my knowledge the islands were returned to Japanese sovereignty.

☆ ☆ ☆ ☆

On 9 July Mrs. Radford and I left Pearl Harbor for Washington, where we were guests of Admiral and Mrs. Sherman for a delightful week at his quarters at the Naval Observatory. Admiral Sherman and I had an excellent opportunity to exchange ideas on the many naval problems in the Pacific and the Far East, and I was thoroughly briefed on my changing status as CINCPAC, including the prospective added responsibilities of the Marianas, Formosa, and the Philippines and new responsibilities in connection with Southeast Asia in general and Hong Kong and Indochina in particular.

I had barely settled again at Pearl Harbor when I received news of Admiral Sherman's sudden death in Naples. I could hardly believe that this attractive, active, and seemingly healthy man with whom I had worked so closely during the previous week had passed away. His funeral date was set and I was to be a pallbearer. With a heavy heart I again flew to Washington, stopping at San Francisco to pick up Admiral Nimitz, for whom Admiral Sherman had worked so closely during and after World War II.

Forrest Sherman's death was a great loss to the country, and to the Navy in particular, coming as it did at a critical time for both. In the relatively short time he had been CNO, he had made a great place for himself. His advice and counsel would be sorely missed in Washington.

There was some speculation in the press to the effect that I might succeed him as CNO but I did not think so, nor did I think it was a good idea. I was very happy when Admiral Fechteler, a classmate, was nominated for this assignment. Bill Fechteler was a splendid selection, and I knew that we could work well together.

Summer 1951 was a busy one for American diplomats and military planners. In the Pacific the Korean armistice negotiations, begun in July, were moving at a snail's pace, with little promise. The negotiations for a peace treaty with Japan, on the other hand, were moving splendidly. John Foster Dulles, selected by President Truman and Secretary of State Acheson to draft and negotiate the treaty, had been busy with it since September 1950, passing through Pearl Harbor often and usually stopping in our guest house to break the long flights. I knew he was shooting for September 1951 for the formal signing.

I also knew that Prime Minister Shigeru Yoshida would head the Japanese delegation to the meeting, to begin in San Francisco on 4 September. If he followed the usual practice, he and his party would break their flight by an overnight stop in Honolulu. It was my responsibility to make security arrangements for such a stopover.

It was just six years since the end of a war that had begun with the Japanese attack on Honolulu and Oahu. Feeling had run high in Hawaii against the Japanese at the time of the attack and had subsided very gradually during the war. Many people in Hawaii had suffered as a result of the war, many had lost loved ones in the fighting. It was hard to determine just what the reactions might be to the first visit in U.S. territory of the head of the Japanese government. Asking the question of numerous friends, I received conflicting answers. Intelligence officers on my staff could do little better. Representatives of the FBI recommended that extreme precautions be taken to guard the Prime Minister and his party.

Secretary Acheson notes in his book (p. 541) "Never was so good a peace treaty so little loved by so many of its participants in the weeks preceding its signing as was this one." My only contribution was to make sure the Japanese delegation survived its stopover in Honolulu.

With the Governor and others, I met Prime Minister Yoshida and his delegation at the International Airport in Honolulu on the afternoon of 31 August. After brief ceremonies of welcome, the party was escorted to the Royal Hawaiian Hotel, where the top floor of the main wing had been reserved for them. Every contingency we could think of had been provided for except one: what to do if the Prime Minister tried to leave his floor for a walk outside. We did not want him to leave his floor until his departure the next morning and hoped the matter would not come up. If it did, the security officer was to ask the Prime Minister to wait until he could get me on the telephone. I then would have to tell Mr. Yoshida as best I could that we preferred he not go out, and why. Fortunately, the Prime Minister stayed in his suite until the next morning, and there were no untoward incidents in connection with the visit.

On the way back, Mr. Yoshida and his party again stopped overnight in Honolulu. Now he was the head of a friendly government, and we who were responsible for his safety were satisfied with the usual security measures.

The Prime Minister said he would like to call on me at my headquarters, in the large concrete office building built during the war for Admiral Nimitz and his staff. My office was at one end of the building, on the ground floor. Visitors arrived at a parking area in front of the building, which overlooked Pearl Harbor and particularly Ford Island, around which were the battleship berths that had been occupied on 7 December 1941. From my office I could almost see the wreck of *Arizona*.

The Prime Minister with one or two aides arrived promptly and we had a very pleasant visit. I had a feeling that he was a little uncomfortable when he arrived but decided later that I was mistaken.

I had a fine little Scottie—named after a Royal Navy friend, Adm. Sir Rhoderick McGrigor—who spent every morning with me. "Mackie" was stretched out in front of my desk as Mr. Yoshida entered. As Scotties will, he rose, walked slowly over to the Prime Minister, and allowed himself to be patted while carefully sniffing around his shoes and ankles. This started a dog conversation that took up most of the visit. I found that my guest was a great dog fancier and had raised Scotties of his own.

Years later, in a conversation with Mrs. Radford, the Prime Minister told how embarrassed he had felt on arriving at my headquarters that morning to find himself overlooking Pearl Harbor. The civilian driver who had brought him also seemed determined to give him a detailed description of what had happened on that fateful December day. Mr. Yoshida said that he was very much upset as he walked into my office and was so glad that my dog enabled him to start a conversation which took his mind off Pearl Harbor.

☆ ☆ ☆ ☆

I made a rather fast trip to Japan and Korea in October that was memorable for two reasons: Mrs. Radford and I spent a weekend sightseeing outside of Tokyo for the first time, and I had an overnight stay with Adm. Turner Joy at his Armistice Headquarters Camp near Panmunjom.

I had always heard of the spectacular fall colorings in the mountain areas of Japan, and I was prepared with at least two cameras and much color film. Lake Chuzenji, inland from Nikko and almost 2,000 feet higher, lies in a picturesque valley with a few lovely homes and one small village. The coloring of the maple and other deciduous trees was at its height. I have never seen anything more beautiful and I was able to capture much of it on film.

Our armistice delegation in Korea was housed in tents, and I well remember how cold my living quarters were when I was called the first morning. With no running water I had shaving problems, which Turner Joy solved by loaning me his electric razor, my first experience with this relatively new method of shaving. I bought one right away.

The negotiations had started approximately three months before. Admiral Joy gave me a detailed account of his frustrations and difficulties, covering many of the problems that he later discussed in his book *How Communists Negotiate*.

I particularly recollect his story (p. 102) of how communists deal with the "truth."

> Communists have two techniques with which to deal with the truth. One: they deny it. Two: they distort it. The flat denial of truth is the less frequent tactic of communists, because they have learned that truth is buoyant: submerged, it will pop to the surface at embarrassing moments . . .

The distortion of truth as practiced by the communists is a science. The basic procedure is to select out of the whole truth certain parts, which if put together in a particular way, produce a conclusion exactly contradictory of the whole truth. An example might be the story of the witness of a street fight. A man was accused of mayhem, it being alleged that during a street fight he had bitten off the ear of his opponent. There was only one witness . . . [who] was put on the stand by the lawyer for the accused. The lawyer asked, "Did you see my client bite off the ear of this man during the fight?"

The witness replied, "I did not."

The lawyer . . . pursued the point further.

"I want this to be very clear. You witnessed the entire fight, but you did not see my client bite off his opponent's ear?"

The witness replied, "No, but I saw him spit it out!"

Now the communist would never have allowed that last statement to appear. He would have halted the record at the witness' first reply, leaving an utterly false conclusion with the hearer.

The simple fact is that with all respect to the military power of the free world, truth is communism's most dangerous enemy.

Vice Admiral Ruthven Libby, another great friend of mine, served with Admiral Joy during the negotiations and wrote the foreword to a recent republication of Joy's book. Libby says in that foreword (pp. i–v):

The mistakes our side made during the Korean truce talks were many and varied, but were perhaps excusable on the ground of our inexperience in dealing with communists and our natural reluctance to believe it possible for human beings to be so inhumanly perfidious. Those of us who took part in these encounters, and every meeting was a battle, learned a great lesson. We saw at firsthand how a man's mind can be distorted by accepting a philosophy that denies everything which we were taught constitutes the eternal verities. We learned this lesson the hard way—by experience.

In my opinion—there was some excuse for the mistakes we made during the beginning of the Korean Armistice Talks—but there was no excuse for our making many of these same mistakes all over again when we started our talks over fifteen years later with the North Vietnamese.

One last point was made by Admiral Joy during our talk: "I have the distinct feeling that the communist side gets advance information in regard to new instructions which are sent to me. I can often tell as they listen to a new statement that they have expected it. We must have some serious leaks in Washington." This was before the two Britishers Guy Burgess and Donald MacLean were exposed. I am sure that Admiral Joy was right.

Back in Pearl Harbor, I began preparing for my first trip to Southeast Asia. Our two principal allies, Britain and France, were having difficulties there, the

French in Indochina and the British in Hong Kong and Malaya. In both countries the difficulties were communist inspired and supported.

Many people like to compartmentalize the world's troubles, and I have often been asked why the United States had to get involved in Asia in 1950 and 1951 when it was so obvious that we had our hands full trying to build a sound NATO alliance in Europe. The answer in the case of our Korean involvement is fairly straightforward. There the Korean communists, backed by the Russians, attacked a little country which they thought we would not protect, and our courageous President did the only thing he could do—come to their rescue. Only later did his advisers let President Truman down; they did not see clearly that Korea was only part of a worldwide communist offensive, an essential part that they could disregard only at great peril. Complaints that Korea was the "wrong war in the wrong place" were indicative of the fuzzy thinking in Washington. It was perhaps the wrong war in the wrong place so far as U.S. planners of the time were concerned but it was the right war in the right place to the Russians and Chinese.

By fall 1951, our diplomats and military leaders had realized that the problems of Asia were intimately related to the problems of NATO. In trying to build up NATO's European Defense Command (EDC) to include a German contribution, Secretary Acheson found both Britain and France very concerned with problems in the Far East that were draining them financially and militarily. They wanted assurances of American help in solving their Asian problems in return for help in again building up their former enemy, Germany, militarily. To build NATO into the strong alliance needed to counter Russian strength in Europe, the United States had to try to help Britain and France solve their Asian problems. My trip to Southeast Asia in November–December 1951 was in the nature of a survey to see what we might do. By far the most involved problem was Indochina.

Many factors contributed to the situation there. Almost without exception they could be traced to three fundamental causes: the abuses of the French colonial regime over many years prior to the outbreak of World War II; inflamed Indochinese nationalism; and France's ill-conceived attempt after World War II to reassert, practically without change, the government power structure and economic domination she had exercised since the 1860s.

France's original domination had been won by force and the threat of force. What is now Vietnam was once a single, sovereign Annamese state under its own emperor. France gradually extended its sway over this country and Cambodia, and by the end of the nineteenth century Laos too had been forced into what became the Indochinese Union. By 1938, less than 40,000 Frenchmen dominated 24 million subjects in a land one-third larger than France itself.

Indochina was a rich prize. In the 1930s it was the world's third largest exporter of rice. It also produced rubber, timber, fish, corn, pepper, cattle, coal, iron, tin, zinc, chrome, phosphates, manganese, tungsten, and bauxite. Industrial development was deliberately kept at a low level to avoid competition with French manufacturers. Indochina served French purposes as a source of raw materials and a market for French goods.

French investors and French capital enjoyed an especially favored position in the economic life of the country. Land could be purchased only by Frenchmen or by companies with a majority of French stockholders. France supplied 53 percent of Indochina's imports and took half its exports. The French policy was to carry on free trade with Indochina while levying on foreign imports into the colony virtually the same tariffs as on imports into France. French economic and political control of the country was reinforced by the breakdown of old Vietnamese social and legal structures.

The alliance of opportunistic Mandarins and French bureaucrats produced a state of affairs strikingly similar to conditions that led to the French Revolution. The number and size of large French estates increased and peasant ownership of the land became more and more precarious.

Among other misfortunes of the Indochinese was the government's monopoly of salt and alcohol, as well as opium, which constituted one of the main sources of revenue. French companies and Chinese agents, who paid dearly for licenses to sell these items, realized enormous profits. Opium was not widely used in Indochina before the arrival of the French. Thereafter, consumption increased rapidly. In France opium-smoking was a criminal offense; in Indochina, it was a financial prop of the government.

Nevertheless, French rule brought some genuine benefits to Indochina. The Pasteur Institute made important advances in the study and treatment of tropical diseases and greatly improved sanitation and hygiene. Hospitals and dispensaries were built. The French strengthened and extended the dike system, which for centuries had been incapable of holding back the waters of delta areas. Thousands of acres of farmland were reclaimed by drainage and irrigation and French agricultural experts helped increase Indochinese crop yields. Modern road systems were constructed in and around the cities and a main highway was built from Saigon to the Chinese border. The French also built the Trans-Indochinese and Yunan railroads; the latter linked the port of Haiphong with the interior of South China.

In pressing their own language upon the natives, the French unwittingly opened the way for the discovery by Annamese intellectuals of the historic French revolutionary tradition. Once acquainted with the political liberties of the French people, and impressed by the theories upon which those liberties were based, the Indochinese sought similar rights for themselves.

Many Vietnamese withdrew from public life in passive resistance to French rule. Others turned to violence and revolution, attempting to expel the French and reestablish imperial Vietnam. Each revolt, lacking organization or real popular support, was harshly put down by the French.

There was an upsurge of nationalistic feeling once the Russo-Japanese War of 1905 had destroyed the myth of white invincibility. World War I also played its part. Over 100,000 Annamites were sent to France as soldiers, farm laborers, and factory workers. Resentment over forced participation in the French war effort, coupled with new ideas such as that of the political party, was transformed into political action upon return home.

The most important political development in Indochina, particularly in Vietnam, in the twenties and thirties was the development of the communist party. This in turn is inseparably connected with the life and activity of Nguyen A' Quoc, later known as Ho Chi Minh, and the determination from the earliest days of their rule in Russia of the Bolshevik party to subvert the masses of Asia, particularly those in the colonies of European nations.

What impresses me about those days in Moscow was that the leaders of the Russian Communist party, with many problems of their own still to deal with, had time to select and to train young Asians like Ho who were destined to help them communize the Asian world when opportunity offered. Deliberately and thoroughly they expended their scarce funds to prepare for an uncertain future.

During World War II and especially during the Japanese occupation, Vietnamese political parties created coalitions in order to more effectively work for independence. Of these coalitions, Ho Chi Minh and his Communist party emerged as the most potent political party after the war. The sudden collapse of Japanese resistance in August 1945 caused a delay in the return of French governmental and military forces to Indochina, and Ho's Vietminh forces attempted to fill the gap. The returning French were not welcomed with open arms by the majority of Vietnamese but they seemed oblivious to the signs of discontent. They attempted to reinstall their prewar government structure, using in many important offices the very same Frenchmen who had occupied them in 1940.

The French occupation of Indochina was, of course, well known in U.S. government circles. American efforts to convince the French of the necessity for granting self-government were consistent in the postwar years. French foreign ministers seemingly agreed and made promises, but the word did not seem to reach the individuals in Vietnam who were running things. There was one exception, early in 1950. Marshall Jean de Lattre de Tassigny was appointed French High Commissioner and Commander-in-Chief of the armed forces in Indochina—head of the civil government as well as the military commander. An outstanding soldier, he was an excellent civilian leader as well. It was he who had extended to me an invitation to visit Indochina as his guest. When I finally did arrive in Saigon, on 6 December for a three-day stay, I was told that Marshall de Lattre had been delayed in Paris; his Chief of Staff, Maj. Gen. René Cogny, acted as my host. In truth, the Marshall was suffering from cancer and died in Paris in January. What I saw of his efforts in 1951 led me to believe that he might have saved Indochina for France had he lived. He had tremendous energy and great influence in Paris, and he could get things there that his predecessor and successors could not. He was aware of Vietnamese feelings about freedom, and I believe he could have convinced French leaders to grant the autonomy to which they gave only lip service. His death was a great loss to France, to the Vietnamese, and to the United States.

En route to Saigon, I stopped in Guam and then in the Philippines for five days. On the morning of 30 November I attended a breakfast at Malacañang Palace in Manila as a guest of President Elpidio Quirino. Among others present were Gen. Carlos Romulo and Secretary of Defense Ramon Magsaysay. Senator John Sparkman, on a swing around the Far East, was interested in the Huk [Hukbalahap] situation and in our aid program. President Quirino and Secretary Magsaysay both emphatically reported that foreign submarines (presumably Russian or Chinese communist) were invading Philippine waters and landing guns and ammunition to assist the Huks. The President wanted protection by the U.S. Navy; but his "facts" seemed quite nebulous.[1]

Secretary Magsaysay was beginning to make a name for himself handling Huk problems and I sensed rather strained relations between Quirino and him. A briefing for Senator Sparkman at the U.S. Embassy brought out another reason for Quirino's unhappiness at breakfast. Local interim elections a month before had resulted in a resounding defeat for the President's party in Congress. The President blamed Magsaysay's growing personal popularity for the rather abrupt decline of his own.

The next day I visited Subic Bay and our naval activities there, including the new air station being built at Cubi Point. I was very pleased with the Seabees' progress in expediting this important project, which involved an enormous earth-moving job.

My notes from Hong Kong, where I met with Sir Alexander Grantham, the Governor, and U.S. Consul General Walter Patrick McConaughy, read:

1) General impression, situation in Hong Kong much improved since visit last January. By that, I mean largely the morale or attitude of British and Europeans generally. They now feel fairly secure. Return of U.S. dependents and continued presence of U.S. Navy has had a lot to do with this feeling. The fact that Chinese Communists are so fully occupied in Korea also leads to the belief in Hong Kong that they will not undertake any additional action in the south.

2) Governor Grantham outlined Hong Kong's problems as unemployment due to

refugee population and due to shortages of certain raw materials (black plate and cotton principally). The colony is furnishing no direct relief but is making every effort to increase opportunities for work.

The governor defends the British policy vis-à-vis Communist China (recognition, etc.) as the only practicable realistic policy possible for them. It is based on their feeling that no Chinese opposition party can possibly be organized. Chiang Kai-shek is finished. At best, the long-range outlook is not optimistic according to Sir Alex. *It seems to me their policy stems largely from a feeling that they cannot muster the necessary strength for a stronger policy.* Their Far Eastern policy seems to rest on their desire to stay in Malaya and Hong Kong as long as they can by avoiding a direct clash with Communist China, or at least putting it off.

The British say, in essence, that they know what they want to do and are willing to take their time whereas the Americans don't know exactly what they want to do but are in a hurry to do it.

3) Consul General McConaughy feels that his position is better than it was last January and that, in general, he receives excellent cooperation from the British.

I left Hong Kong feeling admiration for Governor Grantham and his administration of this beautiful but overcrowded city. How the British manage to keep the place so clean and orderly with their rather small, and largely native, police force is a mystery to me.

From our altitude, flying across-country to Saigon, Vietnam looked peaceful, beautiful, and well cultivated.

Our arrival at Tan Son Nhut airport was the occasion for an impressive welcoming ceremony that only the French military can stage when they want to. I was to become very familiar with these Saigon welcomes, many in extremely hot weather with everyone dripping, others that went on without a hitch in spite of a heavy tropical downpour. But this was my first, protocol was demanding on the guest of honor, and I was glad when it was over.

The ride into the city kept Mrs. Radford and me hanging on for dear life and scared to death most of the way. The road, fortunately, was wide and generally straight. Our driver put the throttle to the floorboard and kept it there. Marshall de Lattre's special motorcycle escort, eight of them in fancy uniform, guarded us so closely all the way that a sudden swerve on the part of our driver would have knocked over one or two. On each side of the road French troops were stationed about every ten yards, facing away from the road and toward the crowds, who were probably on the way home from work and seemed only mildly interested.

I was never sure why we made this mad dash with so much protection. I had been led to believe that visitors were in no real danger, and later conversations with Amb. Donald Heath more or less confirmed this feeling, although he did admit that occasionally the Vietminh threw a bomb or hand grenade to liven things up at a parade or welcoming ceremony.

The Governor General's palace, the impressive building in which we were to stay, was located in the center of the city in a large park. The palace was built in tropical style with long covered balconies running the entire length of the upper floors and all rooms opening onto them. Our room was enormous. The ceiling was twenty feet or more high, and several large fans hung from it. The rooms apparently extended the width of the building. The windows had only shutters and the doors were also slatted.

The dinner hosted by General Cogny the night of our arrival, in the beautiful dining room of the palace on a warm, clear tropical evening, was as perfect as one could imagine. The group was small enough to give us a good chance to get acquainted with the other guests but large enough to meet the most important government officials, French and Vietnamese.

The most interesting of the next morning's visits was to Emperor Bao Dai. I found him a very pleasant and interesting young man, a little on the portly side. He did not impress me as a great leader, but he evidently suited the French. His palace was much smaller and less pretentious than that of the French HICOM.

On a short trip to Hanoi without Mrs. Radford, I was greeted by an honor guard: foreign legion troops, all German I thought, and over six feet tall. I do not believe I have ever seen a finer looking, more soldierly group of men.

General Raoul Salan, military commander in the north, gave me a detailed outline of the situation in the Tonkin Delta area and French plans for the immediate future. Marshall de Lattre was planning to make the delta secure behind a semicircle of fortifications whose radius of fire support overlapped.[2] These defenses were pretty well finished and I was to see them from the air on a flight the next morning. With the delta base secure, Marshall de Lattre could free his best troops for inland operations against the Vietminh. He hoped to destroy their logistics bases and force them to keep on the move.

That evening General Salan entertained at a large and very interesting stag dinner. The food was superb and the champagne the best I have ever tasted; my hosts insisted it was regular French army champagne. I was impressed with the French army officers present that evening—most, if not all, members of General Salan's staff. I think it can be said that the cream of the French army officers and men were in Indochina.

A disturbing note was the marked tendency of French officers to denigrate the capabilities of their Vietminh enemies. I thought it was very noticeable and too explicit. The few Vietnamese civilians and military men present did not seem to like it, although the Vietminh were their enemies also.

On the next morning there was a familiarization flight over the Tonkin Delta, which is beautiful from the air, particularly in the south where strikingly rugged limestone chimneys [deep fissures in cliffs, by which they can be climbed] rise near the coast and in some of the bays. Strong points were pointed out to me, and I could see something of both the Red River and Black River valleys to the west with the rugged Thai country—so called after the native tribes who originally predominated there—in between. On the northern limit of our flight we could see the border of China's Kwangsi province.

On our last evening in Vietnam, we met Ambassador Heath's staff at dinner at the Embassy in Saigon. The Heaths were genial hosts and everyone always had a good time at their parties. We particularly enjoyed that evening with only English spoken!

Ambassador Heath opined that the French position was greatly improved and that the educated Vietnamese were beginning to realize that they needed the French. He was inclined also to feel that the vast numbers of Vietnamese who had remained neutral during the struggle for independence would probably support France if the United States took a positive stand against possible Chinese intervention.

My notes on the visit mention that Vietnamese troops looked good, French troops excellent (but these were certainly selected troops, in the honor guards). I was also favorably impressed with the French senior officers whom I met, particularly army. I did not meet many naval officers, for they were deliberately kept in the background during this quick visit. Rear Admiral Paul Ortoli, the senior naval officer and a rather quiet little man, expressed his personal opinion that France must stay in Indochina to protect it, and should say so. It was unclear to me what he meant, or why he had brought it up, but I gathered that he was expressing opposition to any ultimate settlement that included complete withdrawal of France from Indochina.[3]

I now know that my visit took place at what was probably the high point of France's postwar position. Marshall de Lattre had greatly improved French military and civilian morale. This, in turn, had stabilized the overall situation.

I visited Thailand, then a prosperous country run by military cliques, because of its importance as the only independent country in Southeast Asia. As friends the Thais could be a great help in the U.N., and their value as an ally could not be overestimated. We had only a small military assistance program in Thailand at the time.

The senior military officers seemed primarily interested in politics. Certainly the navy seemed to lack competent direction; and many of its ships, anchored in the large river (Chao Phraya) that divided the city and was also its port, were relics and should have been scrapped.

Our Ambassador and our naval attachés were cooperative. I met all the Thai senior military men and the Prime Minister, and still had time to see many of the beautiful temples and palaces that make Bangkok one of the most striking cities in the world. A cruise on the river one afternoon was fascinating because so much of the city's activity and life is on the river or its backwater channels, called klongs. Uncounted thousands of Thais live their whole lives on the water. They drink it, bathe in it, catch their food from it, and appear happy and healthy. One glass of the river water would lay one of us low for sure and for some time, but the Thais thrive on it.

Singapore, still Britain's big naval base and Far Eastern Military Headquarters, was also their diplomatic headquarters. Malcolm MacDonald, son of former Premier Ramsey MacDonald, was British HICOM for Southeast Asia. My new planning responsibilities made it advisable for me to get acquainted not only with him but also with V. Adm. Sir Guy Russell, R.N., British Commander-in-Chief, and Gen. Sir Charles Keithley, CINC British Land Forces, who was in charge of the antibandit campaign in Malaya. I found all these gentlemen very interesting and friendly.

What impressed me in Singapore was that the British were tying their missions together in a way that we in the United States did not. As I traveled from embassy to embassy in Asia I found a great lack of contact between our ambassadors. It seemed to me that our State Department wanted it that way. They preferred to be the center and source of all information and control. I found myself explaining to each ambassador how his neighbor was handling such and such a problem, in which they both were interested. I later tried without success to convince both Mr. Acheson and Mr. Dulles that we could use a HICOM in the Far East. I even offered a site for his headquarters on our Subic Bay naval reservation. Apparently this was too much of a change for State, although it was discussed in Washington.

Mr. MacDonald made the interesting point that the governments of countries in Southeast Asia were friendly to democracies and against communism but could not openly take that position at that time. On the other hand, the people of Southeast Asia, while generally anticommunist, usually let their nationalistic feelings predominate. He felt that Japan was the key to the Far East and could become communist.

A briefing at Gen. Sir Charles Keithley's headquarters covered the details of the antibandit campaign in Malaysia, where some 8,000 bandits or guerrillas were fighting about 75,000 British and Malaysian troops. I made two suggestions that, I was later informed, were helpful in making this operation successful. I was told that it was necessary to clear away the jungle growth for about a quarter of a mile on each side of principal highways in order to prevent, or at least lessen, the chances of successful ambush. The growth of heavy jungle grasses required tremendous manpower to keep them out. I suggested solving the problem with a chemical weed killer used by Hawaiian sugar planters to kill grasses beside their plantation roadways. This proved to be a great success and saved thousands of man hours. The second point was in connection with hunting down small guerrilla bands in jungle areas where concealment was easy. I told of a recent conversation with Secretary Magsaysay of the Philippines in which he mentioned the use of police dogs to track down and locate guerrillas. The Philippine Army had a large dog-training program, and I knew that Magsaysay would be glad to have British army representatives visit the training schools. General Keithley took immediate action on the suggestion.

I was able to tour the great British naval base in Singapore, the city, and its busy harbor and was shown in detail the way the Japanese had made their successful attack in 1941. Britain had always assumed that any attack would come from the sea, but the Japanese came overland from Malaya.

Once again in Pearl Harbor, I felt it had been a busy and in some ways a successful year. Our government was at last aware that the Asian problems were basically caused by the same communists who were causing difficulties in Europe. They were beginning to take steps that I hoped would at least check international communism in Asia and that might conceivably stabilize the situation there.

Secretary of State Acheson and Secretary of Defense Marshall, and later Secretary [of State, then Defense] Lovett, aided by General Bradley and the other members of the JCS, were forced by the end of 1951 to take a much greater interest in the military and political problems of the Far East as they affected the United States, Britain, and France. Our Far Eastern problems could not be confined to Korea and Formosa. In our own national interest we were forced to give large-scale help to the French in Indochina, to assist the British when they called upon us, and to sit down with them and Australia and New Zealand to plan for military contingencies should the communists, Chinese or Russian, elect to again take the offensive.

My trip established the basis for contingency naval planning with the British and French as had the Radford/Collins [the first step toward ANZUS] agreement with the Australians. The possibility of a Russian submarine offensive against allied shipping in the Far East was the most serious naval threat we faced, so the Allied naval command had to plan for a shipping control and convoy organization. That work was under way at the end of 1951.

20

A Defense Strategy for the Far East

As 1952 began I was in Pearl Harbor. I had not visited Washington since Admiral Sherman's funeral the previous July, but had had extensive correspondence with my classmate and friend Bill Fechteler since he had become CNO. Knowing that he needed time to get acquainted with his new responsibilities and problems I did not push too hard on my own problems, but I sensed that I should get back to Washington. I was to become responsible for the defense of Formosa and the Philippines, but since Admiral Sherman's death decisions on that had been delayed. I knew that both the Air Force and General Ridgway were dragging their feet, but I also felt that time was of the essence. CINCPAC could best represent the United States in the Allied planning that had to be done and fit that planning into the defense strategy for the Philippines and Formosa. A great deal of this contingency planning was naval.

In Washington in January, I had good talks with Generals Omar Bradley and Walter Bedell Smith, as well as long sessions with DCNO (Air) trying to find out why it seemed impossible to speed the delivery of combat aircraft. It was over 18 months since the Korean War had started, and aircraft were dribbling off production lines at a rate much slower than that promised a year before. In fall 1951 I had written to a friend in the aircraft industry asking what was causing the delays in production. His reply was a blast at the procurement system in Washington, both Navy and Air Force. With names left blank, I gave it to the BUAERO procurement people. It may have done a little good but not much. We have to get really frightened in this country to eliminate red tape in the procurement field. Korea was still not considered a real war in Washington!

In an attempt to settle some problems I had been having with the Governor of Guam and the Trust Territory, I attended a conference set up by Assistant Secretary of Defense Frank Nash with representatives of the Department of the Interior. My presentation explained in detail the provisions of the U.N. Trusteeship Agreement with regard to foreign nationals in the Trust Territory. We, the United States, were required to either (1) open the Territory to the nationals of all members of the U.N. or (2) keep it closed. We could not show favoritism. Guam was different. It was a closed port in a defensive sea area, and aliens could be admitted only after clearance by military authorities. The rules were simple and explicit, but Interior Department representatives seemed unable to understand why they could not violate them "just a little bit." It was an afternoon completely wasted.

On the other hand, a meeting I had with General Bedell Smith was most valuable. We discussed one item that had recently caused us both some trouble with the White House. For some time the Navy had been covering the Sea of Japan, the China Sea, the Strait of Formosa, and the South China Sea with long-range aircraft patrols to check on merchant shipping entering or leaving major Chinese ports. Most large ships were photographed, showing their names, nationality, and degree of loading or draft. With these photographs Pacific Fleet intelligence officers were able to estimate within narrow limits the gross tonnages going into and out of Communist China by sea. Since the capacity of the trans-Siberian railroad was fixed, as were the requirements of the Russian maritime provinces by rail, my intelligence officers could figure out what Communist China had to live on in total tonnage. What we did not know but wanted badly to know was what these ships carried into and out of China.

We had been urging the Central Intelligence Agency to get us this information. Since most of the ships photographed flew the British flag, we thought the CIA could get what we wanted directly from the British. As time went on I grew impatient. The CIA reported that British authorities maintained that their ships took practically nothing into Red China and brought out the usual export items: tea, tung oil, silks, rugs, and china. We did not believe them. Our photographs indicated generally near maximum loading both ways. Requests for copies of ships' manifests, again made through our CIA friends, were refused.

In late 1951 my staff had a bright idea. Prime Minister Churchill was to visit Washington in January. We would give the White House Naval Aide a brief memorandum of the shipping problem. If he could get the President to bring the matter up with Sir Winston, the latter might put pressure on the right people in Hong Kong and Singapore to clear out the roadblocks. The idea was passed to CNO at the intelligence level and apparently approved there. I did not learn what had happened at the White House until I talked to Bedell Smith. He told me that President Truman had broached the subject after a pleasant dinner on the presidential yacht *Williamsburg*. General Smith did not know, of course, how the President had approached the problem, but he did know that Sir Winston's reaction had been rather violent. The two men were alone when this exchange took place and immediately called for their principal assistants, Secretary Acheson and Foreign Minister Anthony Eden. Apparently Acheson was able to calm things down by asking that he be allowed to investigate. According to Bedell, Acheson had later dressed him down for having participated in this "plot," about which he had in fact known nothing. Bedell thought Acheson had also jumped on the Secretary of the Navy but was not certain. I was able to verify later that the Navy Department had been told to keep out of diplomatic exchanges of this type, and apparently my original guilt was not discovered. I escaped censure in Washington and, although I was very disappointed not to get the information (to which I thought we were entitled) from our British allies, I let the matter drop.[1]

My good friend Dean Acheson died only a few months before I read his memoirs, otherwise I would have taken great pleasure in giving him the full story on how this particular naval intelligence had been gathered, analyzed, and appraised. It was certainly *not* raw intelligence as the Secretary so quickly assumed. The incident was, and may still be, a good example of how difficult it sometimes is to communicate at high levels between departments in Washington. I knew in 1952 that the State Department, generally speaking, was not pleased with the Navy's efforts to ascertain with accuracy the amount of British maritime trade with Communist China. What I did not appreciate was the distorted view of those efforts that finally reached the Secretary. I felt then that our British allies were not playing fair with us concerning their trade with our mutual enemy and that our State Department was, to a great extent, aiding and abetting them. I still do not believe I was far wrong.

While I was in Washington the JCS finally resolved the problem of transferring responsibility for the defense of Formosa and the Philippines from CINCFE to CINCPAC. Their order, of course, covered only the broad outline and left details to be settled between the two commands.

I was en route to Pearl Harbor when I received a message from General Ridgway suggesting a conference in Tokyo to effect the mutual agreements desired by the JCS. Having had the benefit of discussions with the JCS, I felt this would not be difficult. My reply suggesting an early transfer of the new responsibilities, with the understanding that CINCFE's existing orders would remain in effect until we could meet, was based on assumptions I knew were satisfactory to the JCS. What I was really saying was that I would undertake to do just what CINCFE was prepared to do if Formosa or the Philippines came under attack *while the situation remained essentially the same in Korea.* I had earlier discussed the matter of these changing responsibilities with Ridgway in these terms and he had seemed to agree with them.

To my great surprise, Ridgway replied immediately that he was unable to concur in my proposal prior to reaching mutual agreement on principles involved and on plans for the orderly transfer of responsibilities. What he was saying, so far as I was concerned, was: "I cannot let the Seventh Fleet carriers go because without them I cannot defend Japan."

While it was true that we had not had formal discussions on the transfer to me of what were then his responsibilities, we had talked about it several times.

He knew that only the carriers of the Seventh Fleet and their supporting forces were available to defend Formosa or the Philippines, and I knew he could not let them go unless the situation in Korea was more or less stabilized. Obviously he was afraid that if I once got hold of the fleet I would not let it go.

On the other hand, I had to admit that the JCS in their message directing the transfer of authority had, in a way, left the gate open for Ridgway to take this position. The chiefs had directed me to tell them what additional forces I needed to accomplish my new mission, knowing that I would ask for Seventh Fleet carrier forces. They had, at the same time, asked Ridgway what forces he could let me have "in the event of a conflict in requirements of CINCFE and CINCPAC." They had added this statement: "Support of United States Forces in Korea and Japan—including Ryukyus—has overriding priority over defense of Formosa, Pescadores, and Philippines."

This was a prime example of confusion caused by the JCS habit of trying to cover every eventuality—a habit that has caused untold trouble many times before and since, and that I tried to break when I became Chairman. When JCS orders are hedged about with so many qualifications it is almost better for them to keep the responsibilities in their own hands. In this particular case they might better have told each of us to make such new plans as necessary to carry out our changed missions, listing force requirements, and then added that they would direct, when needed, a transfer of such forces.

This was more or less the arrangement on which we finally settled. Ridgway kept the Seventh Fleet command and the carriers with their supporting forces most of the time. Occasionally, I would arrange for a display of force in the Formosa Strait by a special task force of three carriers, just to let the Chinese know that we were prepared to defend Formosa. In the meantime, Commander Seventh Fleet prepared contingency plans for defense of Formosa and was prepared to carry out other missions that CINCPAC might order.

The studies by both CINCFE and CINCPAC, undertaken to buttress their arguments for additional forces to support their new missions in early 1952, had some beneficial fallout. The JCS were impressed by the increased threat posed by the Chinese communists and their Russian supporters. Both of us were authorized to plan for further contingencies, coordinating our plans as necessary. Submission of these plans had the added advantage of impressing the JCS planners with the Far Eastern situation as their two commanders saw it. About a year after General MacArthur was relieved, with the Truman administration still in office, military plans were made to cover actions that MacArthur foresaw as desirable military possibilities.

Twelve years before our participation in the war in Vietnam, our political and military leaders were concerned with the growing communist menace in the Far East. It was not a secret at that time and was openly discussed in the press.

Vietnam was not the surprise that many of its detractors would now like to have us believe.

Early in February, following the death of Marshall de Lattre, I received a long, interesting letter from General Salan in Indochina. The General outlined the overall military situation, concluding that he was so busy he could not accept my invitation to visit Pearl Harbor. He asked if I would be willing to receive Vice Admiral Ortoli in his place—soon, as he thought our personal contacts should continue.

The size of the party, as well as rumors passed to me by our Naval Attaché, indicated detailed discussions on a number of subjects. Deciding that frankness was the best policy, I sent a message to General Salan and Admiral Ortoli saying that Mrs. Radford and I were looking forward to the visit with pleasure and that I would be prepared to discuss shipping control and related naval problems in detail, but that in regard to broader policy matters that might be brought up at General Salan's direction such discussions would be limited as necessary by my policy directives from higher authority.

I believe the Ortolis enjoyed themselves, although both were rather quiet people and it was hard to tell. On the official side of the visit, I was puzzled. A letter written to Admiral Fechteler shortly after they left indicates my feelings.

> . . . Reflecting on Ortoli's visit, I have come to the conclusion that General Salan sent him here with the idea that he might be able to convince me that the French were generally meeting with more success in their operations than press reports might indicate and, what is probably more important, Salan wanted to impress me, and through me impress you and other members of the JCS, that the French have no intentions of withdrawing from the Tonkin Delta or from Indochina. As far as Salan and Ortoli are concerned, they are there to see the whole business through to the bitter end, whatever that may be.
>
> I would like to specifically draw your attention to the fact that V. Adm. Ortoli says that the French forces could not evacuate the Tonkin Delta even if they desired to do so. He discussed the subject with me in considerable detail on two occasions. He stressed the point that should the French make a move which would indicate an intention to withdraw from Tonkin, the populace would generally turn on them and the net result would be . . . "a massacre." Certainly the evacuation plans which we now have would require a major naval effort and under circumstances which might be very difficult.
>
> Plainly the Gulf of Tonkin is not a good place in which to concentrate major naval forces. It is very shallow, and of course with an unfriendly Hainan, the problem becomes even more complicated.
>
> Ortoli and his party arrived without any advance arrangements in regard to an agenda . . . I asked him to 1) make a general presentation to the Secretary of the Navy on the next day (which he did), and 2) to arrange a presentation by his individual staff officers of the detailed papers which they had brought with them

... I feel sure that Ortoli understood and I know the various French staff officers prepared their presentations. About ten minutes before the presentations were scheduled to start, Ortoli came into my office and ... told me that he was not ready to make such a detailed presentation. I said that was perfectly all right with me, that I was only trying to help him. The meeting turned out to be a solo affair with only Ortoli making a general statement.

Very likely there is no significance in this action. There is a possibility that Ortoli did not understand my original proposal, but I heard through individuals on my staff that the French staff officers were taken completely by surprise inasmuch as they had prepared their individual presentations.

Ortoli is a very sincere, serious-minded, and I believe very capable naval officer. I will see him again in Manila during our conference there, of course. He is to be detached in May and ordered to duty as General Inspector of the French Navy ... in Paris.

This seems rather long and involved but I thought some of the information might be helpful to you.

It may seem peculiar that I would write such a long personal letter about a meeting that turned out to be of little importance. My only explanation is that, in our overall dealings with the French military, we had to take many insignificant moves or facts into account in estimating what they wanted, or what they were trying to do or convey to us. Part of the problem undoubtedly was the language barrier: few of the Frenchmen could speak English well and our officers spoke French badly. But a great deal of it was a reticence or reluctance of the French to discuss, or even admit, unfavorable points regarding their situation or future estimates. Only on a few occasions over a long period of frequent meetings and negotiations did I feel that my French counterparts were really frank with me on matters of serious import.

In the late forties and the fifties, representatives of the French regular services suffered from a massive inferiority complex. They were proud members of a distinguished military line that had suffered complete defeat early in World War II. I think they felt this most keenly when dealing with us or the British. The obvious result was that very often they entered into conversations or negotiations with chips on their shoulders.

☆ ☆ ☆ ☆

United States naval forces operating in Korean waters were busier than ever in January 1952. Early that month, responsibility for the overall defense, local ground defense included, of designated islands on both east and west coasts was assigned to the Navy. This was followed by a great increase in enemy activity directed against the islands. All islands north of the thirty-eighth parallel had been conceded to the North Koreans by U.N. negotiators, but failing a total armistice agreement they remained in our hands. The communists saw an opportunity to improve their prearmistice positions by capturing them. There were a number of sharp engagements in spring 1952, but we were successful in holding fast except in the Yalu Gulf.

In April I left Pearl Harbor on a quick swing around Japan, Korea, Taiwan, Hong Kong, and the Philippines. In Korea I conferred with the new Commander Seventh Fleet about the final report of the outgoing commander, Adm. Harold Martin (by this time detached), because its general tenor disturbed me.[2] It was a further indication that in Washington the tendency to maintain the strength of all units (Army, Navy, Air Force) at the *minimum* safe level was becoming policy. This was evidenced most in personnel policies and aircraft procurement for the Navy, where there had been a marked deterioration in the last six months of 1951.

The shortage of petty officers was seriously affecting readiness of the Seventh Fleet. This shortage was due to the Naval Reserve release program; losses through expiration of enlistment; and lack of petty officers remaining in the Reserve. The only trained petty officers left were veterans of the last war, and the only way they could be recalled was by a change in draft laws. The overall personnel situation in the Seventh Fleet was satisfactory, but the lack of trained petty officers was causing increasing hazards.

In regard to aircraft (naval aircraft and carrier types), we were paying the price for our failure to fully develop and begin enough production-line procurement of modern types in the post-World War II period. The Air Force and Navy were caught in the transition from propeller types to jet aircraft. In spring 1952, almost two years after the Korean War had started, both services suffered shortages of new jet aircraft and spare parts.

The Korean War, of course, was the first major war we had fought in five years; we did not have ample time to prepare for it, and it exposed serious weaknesses in our systems of procurement and handling of personnel.

In World Wars I and II all enlistments had been for duration of the war; but the Korean emergency was handled, in a personnel sense, almost like business as usual. The authorization to recall reserves at its outbreak saved us from disaster, or perhaps I should say enabled us to commission additional ships to carry on. But the release of naval reserves by 1952 and our inability to hold our trained career men brought on a real crisis. Only the skilled workmen in nearby Japan permitted us to keep many of our older ships operating during the last two years of the Korean emergency.

On 26 April I was in Manila for a tripartite conference with Adm. Sir Guy Russell and Admiral Ortoli. Much preparatory work had been done and everything went off smoothly. As a result we then had, in conjunction with the Radford/Collins agreement, workable plans for a shipping control system to cover the whole western Pacific area that could be placed in effect on very short notice.

On 6 May I made my first visit to Taiwan, landing in Taipei early in the afternoon. The Chinese were curious to know why there had been a change in responsibility for the defense of Taiwan and I could expect many questions from their press. I was anxious to meet Generalissimo Chiang Kai-shek and other senior officials and to inspect their military bases.

The Chinese forces were in good shape, lacking principally tanks, heavy artillery, and anti-aircraft weapons. Naval personnel were effective but they lacked modern ships. The air force lacked modern aircraft, having no jet types at all.

I was pleased at what I saw and impressed by the top civilians in the government and the senior officers in the services. I left Taipei feeling proud of our Chinese allies. Twenty years later I feel the same way.

☆ ☆ ☆ ☆

About the middle of June 1952 I first heard that the JCS might consider favorably a request made by Gen. Mark Clark to attack the electric power complex in North Korea, which included some four or five large plants. Suiho, the largest, had a capacity of some 300,000 kilowatts and was supposed to be the fourth largest in the world.

I urged Adm. Robert Briscoe (who had relieved Admiral Joy as Commander Naval Forces Far East) to offer assistance from the carriers. I felt that our ADs (attack bombers), the newest attack planes, which could carry up to 5,000-pound bombs, could do a great job in such an operation. I was delighted to hear that final plans included 36 ADs and other contributions.

James Field, in *United States Naval Operations in Korea* (pp. 437–439), tells the story of this operation very well.

> . . . since damage to Suiho offered a method of making trouble in Manchuria without crossing the border, approval from Washington was forthcoming.

> . . . not since the strikes on the Sinuiju bridges in November [1950] had the carrier attack planes crossed Korea to hit targets in MIG Alley. The Suiho Strike was to be a joint operation in which the carrier pilots had the place of honor . . . the other attacks were timed to follow it by a few minutes.

> [On 23 June] the carrier force began launching 35 ADs with 4,000 and 5,000 pound bomb loads for the Suiho attack. Forming up at 5,000 feet, the Skyraiders crossed the coastline at Mayang Do and then, keeping low to the mountains to avoid radar detection, headed straight for the target. Fifty miles from Suiho they were overhauled by 35 F9Fs (jet fighters) which had taken off 50 minutes later. Eighteen miles from the target the group commenced a climb to 10,000 feet, with one jet squadron going up to 16,000 feet as combat air patrol. Two miles from the target a high-speed approach was begun.

> The first squadron of F9Fs dove on the anti-aircraft gun positions on the Korean bank of the Yalu River, closely followed by the ADs and the other flak suppression jets . . . within a space of two and one-half minutes the attacking aircraft delivered 81 tons of bombs. At the power house, which was the main target, red

flames filled the windows, secondary explosions were reported, and photographs taken by the last ADs to drop showed smoke pouring from the roof. The anti-aircraft batteries had opened up as the attack began; heavy weapons and automatic fire was moderate and machine gun fire was intense but the defenses were overwhelmed. No plane was lost, and the only Skyraider to suffer serious damage made a successful wheels-up landing at Kimpo Airfield (near Seoul). Everyone else was back aboard ship by dinner time.

... the attack continued with interservice cooperation of a high order ... But— while the Antung field is only 35 miles from Suiho ... [no enemy MIGs] put in an appearance, and of 250 reported on the ground by Air Force pilots, two-thirds disappeared into interior Manchuria during the attack, a tactic for which, on the U.N. side at least, no firm explanation was ever devised.

While the attacks on Suiho were in progress, the Chosin plants ... [and those in Fusen and Kyosen] were attacked. These efforts were followed up the next day by carrier, Air Force and Marine attacks on all three complexes, and [later] the Air Force returned to Chosin and Fusen. Then the picture taking and the photo interpretation began, but in North Korea and Manchuria the lights had already gone out.

The results appear to have been first class. Something in the neighborhood of 90 percent of North Korean power production had been disabled; for two weeks there was an almost complete black-out in enemy country; even at year's end a power deficit remained. But if liaison between the Air Force, Navy and Marines was well nigh perfect, on the upper levels someone had forgotten to pass the word. The British had not been advised of the contemplated attacks, and in Parliament some ructions developed among the opposition.

Secretary Acheson covers the matter of British criticism in his book (pp. 656–657), writing of a visit to England in June 1952:

The attack ... asked for by General Clark had been widely cleared, including with me, and no objections had been interposed. A storm broke at once, and nowhere more violently than in London and in the Commons ... Mr. Churchill and Mr. Eden, conceding that Britain had not been consulted, manfully defended the operation: power plants were legitimate military targets; there was good reason to attack them; they regretted that Her Majesty's Government had not been consulted but there was no obligation to do so. No one could ask more but the House of Commons did.

... through the kindness of Mr. Eden I had been invited to address a group of members of all parties and both Houses of Parliament on June 26th ... in Westminster Hall. Need I add that I had not planned it this way? At any rate there was no need to worry about attendance, especially as I had agreed to respond to questions. The meeting was off the record, which gave me more latitude than would otherwise have been proper in a matter about which the government and the opposition differed. Reports of what I said leaked out in garbled form and began to arouse some of my easily agitated critics in the Senate. To calm them, the [State] Department released the transcript on this subject.

... You would ask me, I am sure ... two questions, and I should like to reply very frankly to both of them. One question you would ask is: Shouldn't the British Government have been informed or consulted about this? To that, my answer would be "yes." It should have been; indeed it was our intention to do it. It is only as the result of what in the United States is known as a "snafu" that you were not consulted about it.

I am sure that you are wholly inexperienced in England with government errors. We, unfortunately, have more familiarity with them, and, due to the fact that one person was supposed to do something and thought another person was supposed to do it, you were not consulted—you should have been. We have no question about that.

If you ask me whether you had an absolute right to be consulted, I should say "No," but I don't want to argue about absolute right.

What I want to say is that you are a partner of ours in this operation, and we wanted to consult you; we should have, and we recognize an error.

Now you ask me whether this was a proper action. To that I say: Yes a very proper action, an essential action. It was taken on military grounds. It was to bomb five plants, four of which were far removed from the frontier. We had not bombed these plants before because they had been dismantled and we wished to preserve them in the event of unification of Korea. They had been put into operation once more; they were supplying most of the energy which was used not only by airfields which were operating against us but by radar which was directing fighters against our planes.

My hearers seemed to approve. They applauded heartily when in reply to a question I said that the attack had been highly successful. Nevertheless, when I met privately with Eden, he pleaded for "no more surprises."

I mention this in the detail above because at the time it was my feeling that our failure to consult with the British had been deliberate. In too many instances about that time I had a strong feeling that somehow or other the communists were being given information that we had supplied to our allies or to the U.N. Only when we sharply restricted such consultations—did we avoid leaks. This was before I had ever heard of Burgess or MacLean!

In summer 1952, three more large interservice air operations took place. Air Force, Marine, and Navy planes struck Pyongyang gun positions, supply and billeting areas, and factories on 11 July. On 20 August a sizeable effort was conducted against a large west-coast supply area; and nine days later the enemy capital, Pyongyang, was subjected to a second attack, the largest air attack of the war.

The seven weeks since the first joint strike on Pyongyang had seen renewed movement of troops and guns into the North Korean capital. To get these targets—as well as to provide food for thought in Moscow, where Chou En Lai was conferring with the Soviets—another attack was laid on. On 28 August warning leaflets were scattered over the city and on the next day 1,080 aircraft, including planes from a British carrier and the ROK air force, attacked en masse.

In addition to these cooperative ventures, the fast carrier efforts were largely directed at maximum-effort strikes against industrial targets in eastern North Korea. In conjunction with the increasing boldness of enemy fighter pilots, this northward movement of carrier operations raised the prospect of collision, and several did in fact occur. We found that although the MIGs were faster and could avoid combat if they desired, once engaged they could be shot down by our slower but more maneuverable jets. On 10 September 1952 a Marine flyer in an F4U Corsair made history by becoming the first pilot of a piston-engined aircraft to shoot down an enemy jet fighter.

☆ ☆ ☆ ☆

I had known of a prospective ANZUS (Australia, New Zealand, United States) conference for some time and had urged that it be held in Pearl Harbor or nearby. The prime ministers of Australia and New Zealand, and my many military friends in both countries, had all mentioned that they felt rather left out of things. They did not belong to NATO and yet had a keen interest in all that went on there. They had been happy to join with CINCPAC in planning for shipping control and other wartime emergencies in the Radford/Collins agreement. But they wanted another connection, and if they could not belong to NATO they wanted to be on their own with the United States, not as partners in a pact including the British.

Mr. Dulles, in his travels through Pearl while negotiating the separate treaties preceding the Japanese Peace Treaty, told me he had offered help in getting an ANZUS treaty negotiated as part of the exchange for the Japanese treaties. Australia and New Zealand insisted they needed closer ties with the United States if they were to agree to our generous terms to Japan. They wanted assurance that never again would they be left so alone as they were in December 1941 after the attack on Pearl Harbor. They remembered that Britain had been unable to come to their aid in 1942 and that it had been the U.S. Navy and its carriers that had staved off a Japanese invasion of Australia at the time of the Battle of the Coral Sea in May 1942.

In mid-July I received a message from Secretary of State Acheson telling me that he was planning a conference with representatives of Australia and New Zealand in Honolulu, starting on Monday 4 August.

Here is Mr. Acheson's amusing description (*Present at the Creation,* p. 687) of a typical reception at the Honolulu airport:

> An official reception at Honolulu Airport is an ordeal difficult to surmount with an appearance of pleasure, to say nothing of dignity. The leis that are hung around one's neck, as once around sacrificial bulls, invariably conceal small crawling creatures that find their way down a shirt collar and induce an urgent desire to tear off one's shirt. Instead one stands in the hot sun and watches hula dancers shuffle about on a lauhala mat designed to preserve them from incineration on the cement. The thought occurs that such might be too kind a fate.

I think the Secretary had some such feelings on that Monday morning. He was a day late, he was a long way from familiar haunts, and he had not wanted to come to Hawaii in the first place. I was not overjoyed myself. I had not looked forward to the meetings because I had never met Mr. Acheson. His reputation, as I knew it, came mostly from his vociferous critics on the Republican side of the Senate, and I was inclined to blame him for most of our current difficulties in the postwar Far East.

Once in his quarters at Kaneohe Bay, the sheer beauty of the place and the opportunity to "delouse" himself, as he described it, made Mr. Acheson feel better. At luncheon, he briskly ordered a very dry martini. This cleared the air somewhat; nevertheless, as we downed the drinks John Allison, whom I knew quite well, tried to break what seemed an unusual silence by asking me a question. I knew at once that my answer would most likely not please Mr. Acheson. I answered John and watched his face turn red. Trying to anticipate a possible cutting remark from his boss, Allison said, "I am afraid, Admiral, that the Secretary won't like your answer." Smiling broadly as he took another sip of his martini, Acheson was the perfect host: "Don't worry about me, John, I'm very comfortable and happy. I am glad to get to know the Admiral." That relaxed the whole atmosphere and marked the start of a warm friendship that lasted nearly twenty years.

The Secretary of State faced an unusual and difficult situation. At this first meeting of the ANZUS Council, comprised of the foreign ministers of Australia and New Zealand and their counterparts in our government, the problem was how to make these small but very valuable allies feel that they were close to our political and military planning and that they would be given timely information that would provide them an opportunity to contribute constructive suggestions. Lurking in the background was another serious problem. The dynamic Mr. Churchill had informed both Australia and New Zealand of Britain's desire to be included in whatever new procedural or organizational arrangements evolved from this meeting. The Australians, most of the U.S. delegation knew, did not cherish such chaperonage, as they were an independent country in the Commonwealth and wanted to stand on their own. Smaller New Zealand felt the same way but was willing to give in to Britain if the issue was forced. But neither country relished facing up to an open rejection of Mr. Churchill's expressed desire. It was Mr. Acheson's job to find a diplomatic way out of this booby-trapped impasse. He describes these meetings in his book (p. 688) in a way that typifies his astuteness.

Mr. Acheson opened the first private working session with the most complete review of world affairs, from a U.S. point of view, that I had ever heard, before or since. I was fascinated and so were our visitors. From their feelings that they were remote and uninformed, and from their worries about the unknown, Mr. Acheson made them see that in these meetings the United States was holding nothing back. I followed suit on the military side as I covered the Pacific situation in detail. Reporting to the President, Acheson writes of this part of the conference (p. 689 of his book): "Admiral Radford and I decided that instead of starving the Australians and New Zealanders we would give them indigestion."

For the next two days the U.S. delegation went over every situation in the world, political and military, with utmost frankness. At the end of the meetings our guests were pleased with their political liaison through the Council and military planning through their military representatives working with CINCPAC. It was a most satisfactory conference that could have gone off the track with unfortunate results. I attribute its success almost entirely to Secretary Acheson's remarkable diplomatic and personal ability.

I reserved the evening of the final day, after our work was finished, for a trip to the Island of Hawaii, where the volcano Halemaumau obligingly put on a wonderful display of fireworks. I knew the Australians and New Zealanders were anticipating the jaunt, but Mr. Acheson told me ahead of time that he and Mrs. Acheson would drop out; they were just too tired. I was terribly disappointed. I told him I was afraid if he dropped out that our guests Foreign Ministers Casey and Webb might too, and perhaps the whole party would fold. I told him what an impressive sight a volcano in action is and urged him so strongly to reconsider that he did.

Dinner was on a veranda of Volcano House overlooking the active crater several miles away. The proprietor of Volcano House was a rather famous character, a Greek named George Lycurgus, then in his eighties and a great storyteller. According to him, about 1910 he had gone down to the waterfront in San Francisco to see some friends off for Honolulu by ship. The farewells on board were so prolonged and enthusiastic that George found himself at sea en route to the Islands with no chance to change his mind. Being young and a bachelor, he arrived in Honolulu, took an instant liking to it, and never went back. He established himself in the hotel business and eventually bought Volcano House. George realized, of course, that business was much better when the Volcano erupted, so he was not above trying to do something about it. Convinced that Pele, the Hawaiian goddess of volcanoes, had been introduced to gin by whaling seamen of an earlier generation and that she liked it, George undertook to bring a long period of volcanic quiet to an end by throwing bottles of gin into the crater. When a single bottle didn't bring action George threw in a whole case, whereupon the crater put on a great show. At the time of our visit he said he was giving Pele a case a week!

After dinner the park rangers escorted our party to the edge of the crater and permitted us to stand just inside a little fence where we could look down into the pit of molten lava, about a mile across. The lava bubbled and occasionally spouted up several hundred feet above our heads. As the evening ended, the most reluctant to leave was Dean Acheson. In his book he says the years have not dimmed the image of that evening, and he often mentioned to me how glad he was that I had insisted on his visit to Halemaumau.

It was in the aftermath of this visit that I realized how fortunate this country is to have been served by so great and human a man as Secretary Acheson. For one thing, I received an official thank you letter that pleased me especially because he named the officers on my staff who had done so much to make the meetings a success. He also wrote to Secretary of Defense Lovett, again mentioning the officers' names, and telling the Secretary that cooperation between the State and Defense Department members of the U.S. delegation had reached an unusually high level—a major factor in the success of the conference. I distributed copies of the letters to those concerned, who were as pleased as I. In addition, this tremendously busy man wrote me a note in longhand that I treasure.

The ANZUS Council meetings over, the next important task was to host a meeting of ANZUS military representatives in Pearl as soon as possible; this was a requirement of the Council. It posed some complications from my standpoint, since I sensed that State and Defense had not made up their minds on U.S. positions in joint planning to counter further aggression by the Chinese communists.

My first visit to Southeast Asia in 1951 had given me a good idea of what the British and French expected of the United States in the way of further military help should the Chinese decide to enlarge their area of aggressive military operations. Simply stated, they hoped for adequate military aid [equipment and training] and direct military help [participation] as needed, in Malaysia and Indochina.

In passing this information to the JCS I had recommended that Britain, France, Australia, New Zealand, and the United States jointly study the military problems posed by the Chinese threat in Southeast Asia. It was impossible for me as CINCPAC to make intelligent plans for defense of U.S. interests in that area without better policy guidance from Washington. I also felt that the JCS needed a better basis for their own decisions.

These exchanges, and State Department problems in negotiating with Britain and France on NATO matters, helped initiate a series of five-power military studies, the first of which took place in January 1952 in Washington. At the preliminary Five-Power Ad Hoc Committee meeting in Hawaii, V. Adm. Arthur C. Davis felt there could be no further reconciliation by further negotiation or discussion on the ad hoc committee level. [Davis was the USN representative.] The British and French views, according to Davis, could be simplified by saying: (1) The French want all the help and commitments they can get in connection with their immediate Indochina problem, and (2) The British position remains that of holding Hong Kong and Indochina if possible *while avoiding any action of consequence against Communist China itself.*

Davis sensed, further, that an underlying difficulty was refusal of the Five-Power Ad Hoc Committee to recognize that their task was simply an initial step in determining what to do about Southeast Asian problems, and was clearly hypothetical. When the Ad Hoc Committee meeting ended we (the United States and our allies) were about where we hád started, except for clarification of basic differences. Davis felt certain that the JCS would not agree to recommend warning the Chinese concerning "further acts of aggression" without prior firm agreement that, if such a warning were disregarded, actual retaliatory action would have the concurrence and participation of the other interested nations. On the other hand, it seemed likely that British and French views expressed in the Ad Hoc Committee were their national views. Davis doubted, therefore, if U.S. views would be supported on the British and French political levels even had they been supported by the British and French members of the Ad Hoc Committee.

I cannot state definitely, but I felt certain, that the report of the Ad Hoc Committee was also a great surprise to our State Department, which probably recognized at once that the British and French government positions *were* those put forward by their representatives on this committee and that, in this respect, Allied governments were further advanced than our own.

I think it safe to say that in Washington in 1945, most of 1946, and well into 1947 most effort was concentrated on European problems. Our Secretaries of State spent much time in European conferences and our most serious postwar problems seemed to be concentrated in that area.

The problems between the Chinese Nationalists and the Chinese Communists finally claimed the President's attention. He sent General Marshall to China to try and persuade them to form a coalition government. The outcome of that intervention almost certainly caused the defeat of Chiang Kai-shek and is one of the saddest stories of our times. The public did not appreciate the influence that a few communist sympathizers in high places in our government could have in government circles. The result was ultimately the Korean War, Chinese participation therein, and the predicament I was now concerned with in 1952: as CINCPAC, how to get our Allies to join us in preventing further Chinese aggression.

I am not trying to accuse our government of deliberately failing to do the right things in these busy postwar times. I am trying to tell what the consequences were. I write, too, with the benefit of nearly thirty years of hindsight, which is helpful.

In 1950–51 and into 1952, Secretary Acheson was devoting a great deal, if not most of his time to strengthening NATO. In this he had generally the whole-hearted backing of the Defense Department, although from time to time the Navy and General MacArthur jointly pointed out serious deficiencies in our Far Eastern policies.

By fall 1951 Acheson had found that in order to get British and French acquiescence in NATO matters—a move he felt was essential to a strong military posture in that organization—he would have to agree to help both countries with their Far Eastern problems. Both were trying to reestablish themselves in Asia: the British in Hong Kong, Malaya and Singapore, the French in Indochina. This reestablishment was economically important to them at a time when they were suffering from the inevitable postwar depression. Also, Britain in Malaya and France in Indochina were spending a great deal of military effort and money on fighting insurgency.

The North Atlantic Treaty had been signed on 4 April 1949 and French troops were expected to play a vital role in the European army that the United States proposed to equip. Yet French Union forces approximating 156,000 ground troops, three fighter squadrons, three transport squadrons, and a small navy were tied down in Indochina. By the end of 1949, the French Expeditionary Corps there had suffered 16,270 casualties. The consequences to France's prestige of an Indochinese defeat would likewise hamper her contribution to the European coalition. It was increasingly apparent to the United States that France's ability to become an effective partner in NATO would be indefinitely jeopardized by this continued drain on her limited resources. To a lesser but important degree, the same problems pertained to Britain.

For what they considered sound and obvious reasons, the British and French believed they were entitled to direct and generous U.S. military help in their Far Eastern outposts if the Chinese were to attack them. But neither country wished to stir up trouble with the Chinese by threatening them.

The French were wholly convinced that the United States had not done all it could to help them reestablish in Indochina after Japan's defeat, and to a certain extent this was true. Many Frenchmen were convinced that we wanted Indochina for ourselves. This was not true, but we did want the Indochinese to be given a more autonomous government in the postwar period. In all high-level diplomatic contacts between the United States and France this was made abundantly clear.

By September 1952 I had been informed of JCS reactions to the report of the ANZUS Council meeting with its recommendation that a military representatives committee be set up to advise the council. The official report did not make plain to Washington the feelings of Australians and New Zealanders that they had become part of an important joint consultive and planning body. Certainly Mr. Acheson and I were well aware of this fact. The ANZUS Council could not have been set up on a less impressive basis; nevertheless the JCS were not pleased. They seemed to feel that, in getting ready for the military representatives meeting, I was preparing to set up a combined ANZUS staff that would develop detailed war plans for Southeast Asia and commit the United States to military action that the JCS wanted to avoid. I knew that I had to thrash out the details in a face-to-face meeting, so went to Washington to do so.

I was not entirely satisfied with the outcome of my meetings with the JCS, but felt that at least they had a better understanding of my immediate problems in dealing with our allies. The meetings confirmed that the JCS did not fully face up to the importance of the Far East as a whole and Southeast Asia in particular. They were still too preoccupied with NATO problems and seemed to hope that if they disregarded those in the Far East they might go away.

The first meeting of ANZUS military representatives was held in Pearl Harbor in September. Australia was represented by Lt. Gen. Sydney B. Rowell, Chairman of their Chiefs of Staff Committee, and New Zealand by Maj. Gen. W. B. Gentry, who held the same position in his country. I represented the United States and was elected Chairman of the meeting. I was pleased with the results and am sure my counterparts felt the same way.

21

1952: A Visit to Turbulent Southeast Asia

I was convinced that American problems in the Far East were growing in magnitude and importance. Since President Truman was not a candidate for re-election we would have a new President in November, who was certain to become immediately interested in the problems of Asia as they affected the United States. As CINCPAC I wanted to give him the latest information, which I could obtain firsthand only by traveling and meeting people.

The itinerary for my longest trip as CINCPAC (over 24,000 miles) was toward that objective, and it was strenuous, with visits to Japan, Korea, Okinawa, Taiwan, Hong Kong, Philippines, Indochina, Thailand, Burma, India, Pakistan, Ceylon, and Singapore. There were two side trips, one to Iwo Jima and the Bonin Islands in order to meet with our Ambassador to Japan, Robert Murphy, to try to convince him that the United States should not return previous Japanese residents to those islands. The other was to fulfill a purely personal desire to visit the ruins of Angkor Wat in Cambodia. Because this trip was my most important as CINCPAC, I shall touch briefly upon events at many of the stops.

The pleasant weekend cruise from Chichi Jima to Tokyo in the cruiser *Toledo* provided an excellent opportunity to become better acquainted with Ambassador Murphy and his problems in Japan, where he was breaking new ground as the first U.S. diplomatic representative after the signing of the peace treaty. I also had time to brief him in detail on my ideas about our security posture in the western Pacific, including, of course, my feelings on the importance of the Bonins and Iwo Jima.

My first real opportunity to know Gen. Mark Clark came in Tokyo. I had much to discuss with him in regard to mutual problems, particularly those imposed on us by the JCS decision to transfer responsibility to me for the defense of Formosa and the Philippines. I felt that for the first time there was a sound and satisfactory meeting of minds between us.

One pleasant part of the Tokyo visit was the opportunity to renew my friendship with Adm. Sir Rhoderick McGrigor, R.N., now First Sea Lord.

Our visit after a luncheon given in his honor was of value to us both and gave us a chance to exchange ideas and experiences covering the four years since we had last met. This doughty Scotsman, a great sailor, impressed me more than any naval man I have met. He was small but very tough, and one felt certain that he was never holding anything back. I miss seeing him now and then; he has long since gone to the Old Sailors' Valhalla.

Mrs. Radford and I also had an opportunity to make a social call on Prime Minister Yoshida and his charming daughter, Mrs. Kazuko Aso, who acted as her father's hostess. This was the beginning of a friendship that lasted until the Prime Minister's death in 1964; we still keep in touch with his daughter.

In Korea, I found morale especially high in all services. The previous five months had seen many successful operations, particularly joint air operations, against the North Koreans and Chinese. Vice Admiral J. J. Clark, Commander Seventh Fleet since May, had established excellent relations with the Army and Air Force.

I had not visited Okinawa since my detachment as a Carrier Division Commander. I wanted to take a quick look at it and to discuss the Navy's construction program with the Commanding General, Maj. Gen. R. S. Beightler.

The scars of war on Okinawa, so evident in 1945, had almost disappeared. Naha was a busy city, and our air bases were tremendous activities. Even the climate seemed to have improved. General Beightler was so enthusiastic about his command that he reminded me of a California real estate salesman. I finally told him I had no desire to buy a lot and settle there, for I knew too much about the island and its climate.

We stayed five days in Formosa. Since I was responsible for defending the island I wanted to know all about it—its peoples and its military resources, its economic and natural resources—and I was prepared for a strenuous schedule. My schedule was pretty stiff but Mrs. Radford's was worse. It appeared the ladies were going to give her a real workout.

I don't know how we made it, but we were twenty years younger then. We actually enjoyed the visit and remember it with pleasure. When I left I knew enough about Formosa to plan intelligently for its defense. I was particularly impressed with the talent available there: the mainland Chinese who had escaped to Formosa included specialists in every imaginable category.

One evening in Taipei, Mrs. Radford and I and members of our party were dinner guests of President and Mrs. Chiang Kai-shek, who introduced us to a cross-section of government, diplomatic, and military officials. It was our first experience at a large official Chinese dinner, and it was a most interesting and pleasant one. I was impressed by the fact that there was no lingering; after dinner everyone departed. This seemed a splendid idea, which the rest of the world could well adopt.

In a beautiful valley in Formosa, inland from Taichung, is the Sun-Moon Lake resort and power complex, built by the Japanese. We spent the night there at the comfortable Han-bin Hotel. After a long, strenuous day, including driving many miles over dusty country roads, we looked forward to hot showers. There were no showers but there were two bathrooms with big tubs that were scrubbed and refilled for each occupant. I had just settled into my tub when the door opened and in walked a determined-looking young Chinese lady who, I learned, was to scrub my back. I could not talk her out of it and finally let her finish the job. We all had the same experience and decided it was a good idea.

Across the lake from the hotel was a village of Formosan aborigines, one of the few left. Their origins are lost in antiquity, but from their appearance I would judge that they are related to the same people who came up the island chain from Indonesia through the Philippines.[1]

The power complex at Sun-Moon Lake consisted of three plants, at different levels. I visited the largest, which had been badly damaged by our air forces during attacks on Formosa in 1945, and found it expertly rebuilt.

In Hong Kong, one of my problems was the consideration of plans to assist the British, if necessary, in defending that island. The urgency of this problem was diminished by Chinese participation in the fighting in Korea; but it could become critical if the Allies decided to act against the Chinese outside of Korea, in an effort to break the stalemate there or to relieve pressure on the French in Indochina.

I spent the next two days conferring with Lt. Gen. Sir Terence Airey, commanding British forces in Hong Kong, and Commodore Dickinson, Commander R.N. in Hong Kong, and in making a complete tour of the New Territories, the mainland extension of British holdings. I saw the important improvements in the colony's defense that had been made since 1945 and that were based, of course, on the experiences of the Japanese invasion. If Hong Kong was not completely defensible against a Chinese attack the British had at least made it a costly target. I thought their estimates of ground troops necessary for the colony's defense were accurate, but it was obvious that the few airfields were so vulnerable that they would have to be supported by carrier aircraft in strength. Only the United States could supply these.

We were impressed with the growth of Hong Kong and its great building boom. A visit to this island—and to Kowloon, alive day and night—is always a great experience. Hong Kong, with one of the most beautiful harbors in the world, is an endlessly fascinating city.

Visits to Manila were always busy, officially and socially, but this weekend was particularly so. Not only was the local political situation heating up, with Secretary of Defense Magsaysay being touted prominently as a presidential candidate, but we were about to have a Philippine/U.S. defense conference in Manila. The main problems were American bases, the status of our military personnel stationed in the Philippines, military and economic aid for the country, and, a perennial, the claims of Filipino guerrilla forces for pay from the United States for their wartime services. The conference promised to be prickly.

An extensive briefing shortly after arrival brought me up to date on the local situation. I then flew to Subic Bay for an inspection of the Olongapo base and our new airfield under construction at Cubi Point. Progress on the latter was amazing. Our Seabees had literally moved a mountain in the year since they started work. Governor Grantham in Hong Kong was facing a difficult problem locating a new airport there, and I dictated a letter to him suggesting that he send some engineers to Cubi Point to see what could be done with modern earth-moving machinery.

At this time, I was very anxious to assess the military progress made in 1952 in Vietnam, not only in respect to predictions in the briefings given me by General Salan a year before, but also regarding how much had been achieved in building up the Vietnamese army because of our substantial military aid program.

In Saigon, Ambassador Heath and I embarked on the series of official calls that were a necessary prelude to further business. Once these were over I could get on with my real business. With a French naval aide and my staff I took off for Hanoi the following morning. There I conferred briefly with General Salan, who outlined the rest of my schedule.

I shall never forget my flight over the Northwest Operational Zone that afternoon, with the Commander French forces in Vietnam, Maj. Gen. François de Linnares. In connection with the detailed briefing that followed my return to Hanoi, the trip gave me an insight into French military thinking that was disturbing.[2]

General de Linnares put me in the copilot's seat and sat slightly behind me. We flew toward Hoa Binh on the Black River, the scene of what was assumed to have been a very successful French operation against the Vietminh almost a year before.[3] From Hoa Binh, which had been evacuated by the French, General de Linnares directed the pilot to fly over a series of what General Salan later described as "strong points," on the western side of the Black River.

These strong points were 15–20 miles apart, all built on hilltops with airfields in the valleys below. As far as I could make out from questioning General de Linnares, each was held by a French force of some 200 officers and men, with supporting Vietnamese troops. All or most of the strong points depended for water on cisterns filled with rainwater, or on water brought in during a drought. All other supplies came by truck or air, usually the latter because of Vietminh interference. These so-called strong points were a relic of prewar Vietnam, when French forces controlled the country by their mere presence. They reminded me of the Foreign Legion outposts in North Africa in the movie *Beau Geste*.

I photographed the strong points as we passed over them and wondered how they could possibly resist a determined attack by an aggressive force.

I often think of the rides I took in that DC3, cruising at three or four thousand feet and circling lower when the General had something particular to show me. I am certain the Vietminh saw us but made no effort to shoot us down.

At Yen Bai we turned southeast and headed back to Hanoi. General Salan had told me that an armored force was to depart that afternoon for a raid up the Red River, to destroy the logistic bases in the Yen Bai vicinity. Sure enough, as we approached Hanoi we could see columns of dust over the road leading up the Red River valley.

My briefing, which started as soon as I returned, was complete. General Salan, I am sure, wanted to impress me with what the French forces had done in 1952 since my last visit and what they proposed to do the rest of the year, giving full credit to their new capabilities brought about by the sizeable U.S. military aid program.

Among other things, I questioned the General about his total reliance on the strong points I had seen. My feeling was that the enemy could easily bypass them or destroy them one by one. I mentioned our naval campaign in the Pacific against the Japanese. We had bypassed such strong points as Truk or Wake and had captured others like Kwajalein and Saipan, which we could use. His answers did not satisfy me. He simply argued that the Vietminh would respect the strong points. Subsequent operations proved him wrong.

My flight over the North Delta Operations Zone was also rewarding. General de Linnares pointed out that the system of fortifications started by Marshall de Lattre to protect the delta was almost complete. He believed that French operations the previous summer had well-nigh destroyed Vietminh forces inside the area.[4]

At Haiphong, I joined the French navy for a tour of the harbor and the installations at Cat Bi airfield.

Back in Saigon I had one day with Adm. Philippe Auboyneau and the French navy. First we went over the (U.S.) Naval Military Aid Program, which the Admiral thought should be enlarged, then I toured Saigon's naval installations and harbor. That day I also visited our Military Assistance Advisory Group (MAAG), under Brig. Gen. Thomas Trapnell, who were doing a great job under very difficult circumstances.

On 1 November we landed at Siem Reap, Cambodia, to visit Angkor Them and the Bayon, then Angkor Wat.

I had visited many famous places and was impressed by ancient and modern architecture, some of it beautiful, some not beautiful but impressive, and some neither beautiful nor impressive. But one usually stands before such examples with a feeling of awe, a feeling of wonder. How were these builders able to handle such heavy stones? How could they lift them so high? There are few definite answers and, in the jungles of Cambodia more than elsewhere, the visitor is left subdued and puzzled.

Mrs. Radford and I were the guests in Pnompenh that night of French Civil Governor Jean Risterucci and his wife. Ambassador Heath had cheered me by saying that recently a high French official had been murdered while visiting the Risteruccis. The Ambassador assumed that we would be occupying the same room and suggested I keep the windows closed and locked, as the assassin had climbed up and entered through one of them. I took his advice but had to explain why to Mrs. Radford because it was a warm night. Neither of us slept very well.

The following evening we were guests of young King Sihanouk for dinner on the royal barge. Each year in autumn Cambodians celebrate a harvest festival, similar to our Thanksgiving Day, giving thanks for the bountiful gifts of food which the Supreme Being has furnished. The King, who plays an important part in the celebration, must leave his palace and live on the royal barge on the Mekong River during the festival. Our visit coincided with the last night of the celebration, which included a parade on the river by beautifully decorated and lighted floats.

Dinner was accompanied by several beautiful dancing acts, for which the Cambodians are justly famous. Young Sihanouk, then a bachelor and probably in his early twenties, was an attentive host who spoke English quite well and gave us a detailed explanation of every dance.

Ambassador Heath predicted that Sihanouk would tell us of his training as a French cavalry officer and show us movies of his prowess as a horseman. This proved correct, and we enjoyed them. Then he played for us, both piano and saxophone; he had considerable talent as a musician. It was probably well after midnight when we returned to the Risteruccis.

We met the young King on another visit to Pnompenh several years later but by then he was no longer king. He had abdicated in favor of his father, who had agreed to resume the burdens of ruling the country which he had turned over to his son.

Following a short stay in Bangkok we flew to Rangoon, where we were met by Amb. W. J. Sebald, an old friend and a Naval Academy graduate. The Ambassador had resigned from the Navy in 1930, taken up law, and spent some years in Japan before World War II. There he had met and married a beautiful young lady whose father was English and mother Japanese. Mrs. Sebald is one of the most charming and attractive ladies we have ever known. We looked forward to staying with them on our first visit to Rangoon.

Ambassador Sebald and I immediately made three most interesting calls, on Minister of Defense U Ba Swe, Foreign Minister Sao Hkun Hkio, and Prime Minister U Nu. The three men were completely different but each seemed very capable and well suited to his specialty. U Ba Swe was obviously energetic and rather dictatorial; Sao Hkun Hkio suave; and U Nu pleasant, rather quiet, and seemingly interested in everything. All three were then prominent in Burmese politics.

I had assumed that we would have some news of our presidential election—at least the trend in the United States—in Rangoon, but difficulties with radio reception prevented this.

In a thorough briefing at the Embassy on our second day it was made plain that Burma, now independent, was suffering the pangs of independence. The usual shortage of competent leaders, particularly civil, was causing much difficulty. The country did not have an entirely homogeneous population; this resulted in numerous dissident groups causing political trouble. A mixed population along the northern border with China kept that area in a state of semi-revolution much of the time.

Burma had suffered a good deal of damage in World War II. The Burmese people, traditionally rather gentle and religious, had been upset by the war and the country was experiencing a crime wave that for them was very unusual.

There were still British advisers in the country, mostly with the Burmese armed forces. As in most countries of Southeast Asia, the government was anxious to build up its forces to levels that had not previously existed. They were anxious for military assistance and other aid from the United States. I must say, however, that their British advisers were conservative in their recommendations. They realized that the Burmese people would not willingly support a large military organization over any extended period. To attempt to counter China by military means would be hopeless anyway.

After listening to the Embassy staff I concluded that this little country was probably headed for deeper trouble and perhaps a dictatorship. That did happen but I do not recall having met the gentleman who took over, General Ne Win. I carefully searched the guest list at the functions given for us and his name does not appear. He was biding his time, I suppose.

I repeatedly inquired at the Embassy about election news from home. By this time it was well into 5 November in the United States and results were undoubtedly available, but not in Rangoon. The Ambassador, apparently accustomed to poor service, was not as distressed as I.

In New Delhi, Mrs. Radford and I dined with Ambassador and Mrs. Chester Bowles at their residence, which I did not feel was really suitable for the U.S. ambassador. I found out later that the Bowles could have taken a much nicer home but preferred the one we saw.

The Ambassador confirmed that General Eisenhower had been elected President. At last, two days after the election, I knew who my next Commander-in-Chief would be.

Ambassador Bowles had replied enthusiastically when I notified him before the trip that my chief interest in visiting New Delhi was to meet prominent civilian and military personnel. He had promised "a reasonable schedule with a minimum of social affairs which will give you the best possible opportunity to judge the forces at work here in India and likely developments" and had forwarded some interesting background material on individuals. I was delighted with the Ambassador's efforts. His schedule, while strenuous, was enlightening and helpful.

One afternoon Mrs. Radford and I joined the Bowles for luncheon with Prime Minister Jawaharlal Nehru and his daughter, Mrs. Indira Gandhi. This was certainly an unusual opportunity to become acquainted with a famous man who had done so much to obtain independence for his country. But after it was over, and I had had a chance to think things through, I was sorry it had taken place. My feelings for the Prime Minister had changed with this brief contact. He was an opinionated egotist, in my estimation, and his attitude toward our Ambassador verged on rudeness at times—why I cannot say, because it was evident that Mr. Bowles admired him. Mr. Nehru was correctly polite to me, probably because he did not know me.

Since that luncheon I have read some of Mr. Nehru's writings and concluded that his problem was a basic inferiority complex coupled with incredible ambition. While his contributions to his country were many and great in the aggregate, his personality and egotism prevented him from being the world figure that he might have been. His daughter is much like her father.

In the afternoon I called on Defense Secretary Patel, Deputy Minister Majithia, and finally Gen. K. M. Carippa, Chief of the Indian army. All three men were interesting and impressive, but I was particularly taken with General Carippa, with whom we later had luncheon on one occasion. Here was a career military man of whom India could be very proud.

Later that day I held a press conference, the first one on the Southeast Asia leg of my trip. Suggested by Ambassador Bowles, it turned out to be interesting and helpful to me. There were a dozen or more Indian newsmen present, as well as Mr. Trumbull of the *New York Times*, Mr. Pope of the *Chicago Tribune*, and Mr. Mullen of the Associated Press. They later filled me in on news from the United States, particularly details of the election.

One pleasant evening, at dinner in the Imperial Hotel with Capt. H. K. Awtrey, our Naval Attaché, we were well into the main course when Mrs. Radford remarked how tender the steak was. Captain Awtrey agreed, noting that it was camel steak. Mrs. Radford could not eat another bite.

On our ride into Karachi from the airport we passed makeshift refugee camps of Moslems who had fled India for Pakistan. I was assured that the government was doing all they could to improve the housing situation but could not cope with the flood of newcomers that was still averaging some 100,000 a week.

In Karachi and in other cities we visited, the sidewalks were full of sleeping refugees at night. The sidewalks were apparently a little warmer than damp ground. Although the daytime temperatures in Karachi in November were quite high the nights were cool.

A formal and beautiful dinner party was given for us in Karachi by the Governor General, His Excellency Ghulam Mohammed, one of the most interesting and likeable men I have ever met. In his late fifties, he seemed older, for he was partially paralyzed, and he had difficulty talking. He was much concerned about the future of his country and of India. He had been closely associated with Nehru in the Indian Career Civil Service for many years, and both men had worked for Indian independence. Ghulam Mohammed said that while Nehru was in jail he had called on him as often as he was allowed to, brought him reading material and mail, and took his letters out. They were close friends for many years. Now, he said, when it would seem possible for them to work together and by their example to bring their people closer, Nehru would not answer his letters. The Governor General remarked that this was undoubtedly because he had first written to Nehru on the subject of Kashmir and Hyderabad, states he felt had been illegally taken over by Nehru in clear violation of the basic act of separation. He felt that Nehru, knowing he had been wrong in these two cases and unable to justify them to a friend, would not answer him.

We traveled next to Peshawar, located at the northwest gateway to India, the Khyber Pass—a name that had always fascinated me, associated as it was with so much British and Indian history. We flew 600 miles up the cultivated valley of the Indus River, with the beautiful mountains of Baluchistan on our left. Khyber Pass, with the snowclad peaks of the Himalayas in the distance, is a break in these mountains. We landed at Peshawar, a jewel in a lovely valley setting with an altitude that gave it a temperate climate and gorgeous flowers, particularly roses; from there we drove to the Khyber Pass.

At Jamerud, ten miles from Peshawar, I inspected a guard of honor and was presented with four sheep, which I politely returned. At the Afghanistan border, Murad Khan, representing the Shinwari tribe, presented me with two sheep, which I also returned.

After luncheon I inspected a platoon of the Kyber Rifles, a very tough-looking group, then visited their officer's mess. Signing their guest book, I noticed many famous names, among them Gen. Arthur MacArthur, USA, and his son Capt. Douglas MacArthur, USA, who signed the book together around 1903. I photographed the page and sent a copy to General MacArthur, who told me that his visit there with his father was still a vivid memory.

Among the presents I received from the tribesmen was a beautiful locally-made copy of a .38-caliber British Webley revolver. I was told later of its only drawback: it was made from the steel of old railroad tracks which the tribesmen tear up and would probably explode in my hands after firing a few rounds. I never fired it but am sure it would make a great impression on a burglar if I got the drop on him.

We actually put one foot into Afghanistan at the border. An Afghani guard watched us closely to see that we didn't get into his country with both feet!

At Rawalpindi we were met by the Commander-in-Chief of the Pakistani army, General Ayub Khan [later president], and several other military men and civilians. I inspected local army units and had luncheon with General Ayub.

Mrs. Radford had been met by a group of English and Americans, Seventh Day Adventist doctors and their wives. They invited her to visit their hospital, which specialized in the treatment of glaucoma, prevalent in Pakistan at that time. Mrs. Radford demurred when she found it was twenty miles away, but gave in when told that hers was the usual reply Americans gave. The trip was rewarding, for she saw something of the remarkable work that this group of medical missionaries was doing in northwest Pakistan.

At the request of the Governor General, I spent half an hour alone with him in Karachi, hearing more of his problems and hopes for the future. This great gentleman lived only four more years. Granted good health and more time, he might have been able to get Pakistan and India to work together for their common good.

A beautiful reception under tents out of doors was given that evening in our honor by Prime Minister Kwaja Nazimuddin. With a myriad of lights and beautiful Oriental rugs and costumes, it was like some splendid scene from the *Arabian Nights.*

Ceylon [Sri Lanka] was important to me because of its strategic position along the trade route between Europe and Asia. It had been threatened by the Japanese during the early days of World War II but had been well garrisoned. The Royal Navy had a good naval base at Trincomalee on the east coast.

Prime Minister Dudley Senanayake, an intelligent and interesting man, seemed well aware of the tremendous political and economic problems his country was facing.

On a tour of Ceylon harbor one morning I noticed several merchant ships flying the Chinese communist flag, unloading rice and loading rubber from Ceylon. China was at that time suffering a serious and well-publicized rice famine. I photographed these ships to substantiate my story that China's leaders were probably more concerned about rubber tires for their military vehicles than rice for their hungry peasants.

Governor General H. R. Soulsbury's predictions of the probable course of events in Ceylonese politics, offered at luncheon at Queens House, were not only interesting but were almost an exact forecast of events. I sensed that he felt helpless to reverse the trend he saw coming.

In the years after my visit to this beautiful island I followed its trials and tribulations, political and economic. I have regretfully concluded that Ceylon can be regarded as a microcosm of the Far East. Its difficulties have always seemed to foreshadow similar difficulties ultimately faced by the larger countries in South Asia. It has been a fertile breeding ground for communism, both Russian and Chinese, but still seems to hold a near majority of freedom-loving citizens, undoubtedly due to their conservative British heritage.

☆ ☆ ☆ ☆

On this strenuous trip I had been able to get a feel for Southeast Asia, India, and Pakistan. That sprawling, brawling area, struggling to recover from the effects of World War II and the abdication of British and French political power, was economically and politically upset. Only Thailand could be considered reasonably stable, and it had many difficult problems. The communists, Russian and Chinese, were trying to take advantage of the turmoil in every country. Conditions were almost ideal for spreading the tenets of Marxism. The Russians, at least, had planned for this situation years before, when they began to train selected young men—Ho Chi Minh, for example—from these countries.

In the years that have elapsed since I made this survey, it has been mainly the power and determination of the United States that has denied the communists a victory in Southeast Asia. It is fashionable among American intellectuals to decry the so-called domino theory, on which our support of the French and later the South Vietnamese was based. Americans in positions of great responsibility in every administration since World War II, including that of President Truman, have believed that if the communists could take over Indochina, particularly Vietnam, the rest of Southeast Asia would become communist in a relatively short time. Time has not changed my own judgment to this effect. It is appalling to me that so many otherwise intelligent American citizens have forgotten the history of Southeast Asia since World War II.

22

Eisenhower Visits the Pacific

A lmost the moment I landed from my trip, I received a long message from Admiral Fechteler saying that the President-elect, General Eisenhower, would depart nine days later, 29 November 1952, on a trip to inspect Korea. Utmost security was to be maintained. The news media, to be represented by three members of the party, would be required to withhold news until the party was an hour out of Seoul on the return trip. Any military source or control of sources that might be used to divulge information relative to the trip was to be similarly restricted.

The dispatch outlined the itinerary and concluded with many details regarding security and the special measures I was to take in guarding the long overwater flights.

I answered that I anticipated no difficulty making satisfactory arrangements except in connection with news restrictions during the outbound stop in Guam. I suggested that consideration be given to stopping at Iwo Jima instead. The facilities there were satisfactory, weather is generally cooler and more pleasant, and the party might enjoy visiting the island. Security, I added, would of course be excellent; the only personnel on the island were USAF men.

For the next eight days I was busy with details and instructions. But now, writing about this famous trip that I generally remembered so well I could find practically nothing in my files. Even the log of my personal aircraft, which I knew I had used to fly to Iwo Jima to meet General Eisenhower, did not list the flight. I finally called my former Flag Secretary, Means Johnston (now, in 1972, a Vice Admiral on duty in Washington, D.C.), who had traveled with me, and asked him what had happened to the trip file, a record we made of any trip away from Pearl Harbor. He said, "Don't you remember, Admiral, you would not permit us to record anything in connection with that trip—you swore us all to secrecy?" I could not remember giving any such instructions but realized that I must have done so and that they had been literally carried out.[1]

During the evening we spent on Iwo Jima, General Eisenhower invited me to go to Korea with him.

Nearing Seoul, our pilot reported very cold weather: the temperature would be about $-14°$ F when we landed, he said. My billet in Seoul was a Japanese-style house with sliding paper doors, lightly built, and with only open charcoal braziers for heat. My room was not much warmer than the outside, and I was still cold after piling my overcoat on top of all the blankets I could find.

Next morning while it was still dark I was awakened by a Korean who informed me that it was my turn for the shower, there being only one. I thanked him and said I did not intend to take a bath until I left Korea; someone else could take my place.

Traveling with General Eisenhower, I got to know him well and to appreciate the many facets of his makeup. He would listen to advice from his staff and then, very decisively, announce his decisions. He had great curiosity, wanting details on everything. His mind retained what he was told. I began at once to appreciate what a great leader he was.

I also was glad to become acquainted with the prospective members of his cabinet and the close advisers who made all or part of the trip with him, particularly C. E. Wilson, George Humphrey, Herbert Brownell, Douglas McKay, and Gen. Lucius Clay. I had known Mr. Dulles well before.

The close association in the heavy cruiser *Helena*, on the return trip from Guam to Wake Island, gave me a chance to see cabinet conferences in action, which was very helpful to me later on.

On the long flight from Wake to Pearl Harbor I had a good opportunity to get acquainted with Mr. Wilson. In our discussions, he told me that he intended to run the Defense Department in much the same way he had run the General Motors organization as Chairman of the Board. I suggested he might have some difficulty in that regard. "For instance," I said, "would you not have trouble in General Motors if at the end of your fiscal year you did not know how much money you would have to run the company for the next year?" "Of course," said Mr. Wilson. "You can't run any organization that way." "Well," I said, "you will find out how to do it in the Pentagon. The Secretary of Defense often faces that problem. Congress," I added, "quite often does not pass annual appropriations bills until several months after the new fiscal year starts. The departments keep going on the basis of temporary resolutions that continue funding at the rate of the previous year. If this continues as long as four or five months, as it has done, the three services are in great difficulty, for the new appropriations bill does not cover each item in the same way as in the previous year. The shortages in various particular items can be serious." Mr. Wilson thought this system would have to be changed but later found he had to live with it.

Charlie Wilson stayed a few days in Honolulu, where I had the pleasure of showing him the military activities on Oahu, all of which were busy because of the Korean War. On his last day, as we were riding back to my headquarters, he quite suddenly asked if I thought I were qualified to become Chairman of the Joint Chiefs of Staff. I thought a moment and then said, "Mr. Wilson, I feel that my duties here as Commander-in-Chief of the Pacific area and my experience in previous important assignments have prepared me for such a job. But, assuming as I do that a naval officer is to be the next Chairman, I would hope that Admiral Fechteler would be promoted and that I could relieve him as CNO." Mr. Wilson replied, "We have other plans for Admiral Fechteler"; and nothing further was mentioned.

This exchange puzzled me, and I decided I should tell Bill Fechteler about it. But by the time I next saw him, after the inauguration and about the end of January, he still did not know what Mr. Wilson had meant.

After President-elect Eisenhower's departure in December, the Pacific Command and Fleet Headquarters tried to get back to normal. Admiral Fechteler wanted to schedule a conference in Washington with me and some of my important component commanders to discuss deployments to the western Pacific in case of a Korean armistice. I wanted to talk to him about these matters and about the report of the Five-Power Ad Hoc Committee conference, which had been held in Washington in October. This report had to be the basis for plans that the JCS had directed me to prepare in August, that I had first discussed with them in our brief meeting in September.

The report of the five-power committee was distinctly disappointing to the United States. The British and French made it abundantly plain that they were unwilling even to meet the terms of reference, which in essence required recommendations on what might be done *if* retaliatory action were taken. They insisted that such action should *not* be undertaken and that any military measures should be defensive. Except for clarification of basic differences, the U.S. member felt that we ended about where we had started. He also felt that the British and French would persist in a desire to set up a combined command in the Southeast Asia area. The British had made it clear, he said, that they thought any direct support operations by U.S. forces should come under the French in Indochina and under the British in Hong Kong.

I was not surprised at the reaction of our allies, since we had made it evident that the only forces we could make available were those engaged in Korea. Except for providing some direct air support and establishing a naval blockade of China, we could do little. They, on the other hand, felt that these actions would not really hurt China but would aggravate their own situations. They wanted desperately to keep their possessions in the Far East and thought they could do better by not stirring things up, if we would not promise them direct help including ground troops.

But the committee was unanimous in assessing Indochina as the most likely area of further Chinese aggression, and they considered it the front line of the cold war in Asia. If that front gave way, they said, Thailand and Burma would probably fall under communist influence and British difficulties in Malaya would be compounded. Communism would also have more favorable conditions under which to spread further into India, Pakistan, and ultimately the Middle East.

The Five-Power Ad Hoc Committee report was a shock to both State and Defense. Efforts continued during 1952 to find answers to the problems left unresolved by this first try. Included were directives to me as CINCPAC to prepare plans providing for these same contingencies in the event of retaliation. Given the same limitations as to available U.S. forces, I had consulted with the JCS in September and told them I could not plan realistically on that basis. I suggested, and they approved, that I plan on a requirement basis: that is, my various plans would stipulate what forces were required to carry them out.

In reviewing the Far Eastern situation at the time the Truman administration turned over its responsibility to Mr. Eisenhower, I do not want to give the impression that, at the time, I was fully aware of the mistakes we were making as a nation or what caused our principal allies to be so reluctant to cooperate with us; I certainly was not. I did feel that my seniors in the JCS, at the start of the Korean War, did not fully appreciate the seriousness of the situation in Asia. I concluded that because of their feelings the State Department and the President gave the initial fighting in Korea secondary importance to the security of NATO. But the most serious mistake made by Mr. Truman was to fight this new war on a "guns *and* butter" basis. He declared neither war nor a national emergency until after the Chinese had given us a bad beating in North Korea and driven us back practically to the thirty-eighth parallel. We were so slow to mobilize our industrial resources that we were still suffering serious shortages of new aircraft and other important military equipment and supplies well into 1953. These facts were as well known to the communists as they were to our allies. They indicated to both that we lacked the national will and the military strength to back up our threats. This was part of our difficulty in the five-power conferences.

Probably the most basic problem with our principal allies, Britain and France, derived from the fact that both nations had suffered severe personnel losses in both world wars. And, too, France had been soundly defeated in the early stages of the latter war. In both countries people were fed up with fighting, and their governments had to realize that. Demands for additional postwar military resources were extremely unpopular, particularly those from the Far East.

Their governments could have been—and were—turned out of office if they went too far.

I did not sense the seriousness of this political background until later. I do not feel that many persons in the Truman administration did, either. In his efforts with the British and French foreign ministers to strengthen the military capabilities of NATO, I believe that Mr. Acheson was probably the first to properly assess this feeling. On the military side, in the JCS and in my own case, I think we felt that our allies were reluctant to spend their own money when they thought they should be given our aid. I am inclined now to believe that Britain and France were so tired of war that our efforts to spur them on fell on near-deaf ears. If we wanted to do things on our own they would not object; if we wanted to help them in Malaya, Hong Kong, or Indochina, fine; but if we wanted them to assist in efforts that might bring on World War III or widen the war in the Far East, they wanted none of it. When I say "they," I mean their governments, who were in touch with their people and felt that they would not be supported in such situations.

The French and the British in 1952–1953 felt just about as Americans felt in 1972 about the war in Vietnam. They joined us in the Korean effort because it was the first great test of the new United Nations peace-keeping efforts, but by 1953 they felt that the United States had badly botched that effort. Militarily, we had bogged down in Korea. We had tied down in that "little" war almost half of our army, navy, and air forces. We did not look too good as a military ally.

I did not fully appreciate this at the time. I thought the British and French did not appreciate what we had done in World War II and were unwilling to put forth their best efforts to stem what many of us could see by then was a worldwide, concerted effort by international communism to subvert the free world.

In May 1950, President Truman had first approved economic support and military supplies for Indochina. Our aim and hope had been to enable the French to cope with the revolution that faced them, and to give them time to work out the political problems incident to the gradual but ultimate independence of the three Associated States of the French Union.

Discussions on courses of action in Indochina had continued off and on at the government level. The JCS tried to solve the problem at the military level by hosting the Five-Power Ad Hoc Conference in Washington in October, again with little success. The French continued to press for further military aid, but their military operations were not succeeding as they had predicted and promised, for reasons that American military men could not completely understand.

For example, during my visit to Hanoi I had seen an armored column leaving on an offensive mission to destroy the Vietminh logistic base at Yen Bai.

This action, according to General Salan, was to force the Vietminh to return to defend their base and to bring about an encounter that would enable the superior French forces to completely destroy, or at least seriously cripple, the enemy.

In November at the end of my long Southeast Asia trip, I found that the French column had advanced to the vicinity of Yen Bai but, for reasons unkown to us, had not destroyed that base. The French force had then headed back for Hanoi and been ambushed by the Vietminh, whose forces had crossed the Thai country to set up the ambush and had badly mauled the rear of the French column.

General Salan's operation seemed more like a disaster than a success. My intelligence officers could not account for it. I could not write to Salan on the subject so I sent Col. M. L. Curry of my staff, who spoke perfect French, to interview him and if possible to find out why this operation had not been carried out as he had said it would be.

I received a voluminous letter from General Salan and of course talked to my Marine aide, who had discussed the whole matter with the General. I concluded that Salan had either lost his nerve and ordered the sudden withdrawal or had received orders to do so from his political superior, Jean Letourneau. I have since realized, however, that there was far more political pressure on French military commanders to hold down losses than we understood then.

☆ ☆ ☆ ☆

When President Eisenhower and his cabinet took over, the government, including Congress, had become increasingly and somewhat painfully aware that the major burden of opposing both Russia and Communist China had fallen on us. We had started to build a NATO military alliance of free nations to combat the advance of communism, but we were also learning the hard way that our allies expected us to put up most of the money and much of the military strength.

Fortunately, President Eisenhower and Secretary of State Dulles were well acquainted with our problems in Europe. Mr. Dulles, from his work on the Japanese Peace Treaty, was also familiar with the situation in the Far East. As a result of the President's trip to Korea in December 1952, he (Mr. Dulles) and Secretary of Defense Wilson had decided to apply pressure on the Chinese to get the armistice talks going again.

I spent the first week of February in Washington, accompanied by some of my principal subordinate commanders. We concentrated on plans for Navy deployments in the Pacific when and if a Korean armistice were negotiated. My efforts were to assure that CINCPAC received sufficient naval forces to carry out offensive operations in Southeast Asia if they became necessary. I met with the JCS on one occasion and sensed that they were receiving new directives from the President and Secretary of Defense.

During this week I made a courtesy call on the President. As far as I was concerned it was to be just that, but a surprising incident occurred. I have never been sure whether it was planned by Jim Haggerty, the President's assistant for public relations, or whether it just happened. The President was very cordial, and our conversation was mostly small talk about his trip to Korea and his stop in Hawaii until I was about to leave. Then he remarked that, since my name appeared on his appointment calendar for that day, I could expect to be questioned by White House reporters when I left his office. He added something to the effect that, if the reporters questioned me about new actions in the Pacific, I could of course say that I knew nothing about them. With that I left his office and ran into the entire White House press group, who wanted my comments on the orders that had just been issued canceling President Truman's June 1950 restrictions on Chinese Nationalist forces. Most of them assumed that I had recommended the change, which I had not. I tried to be calm about the whole matter and said I did not know that a new order had been issued. I wanted to add that I would have recommended against it had I been asked but thought better of it. The press corps gave me quite a working over and I am sure most of them thought I was not telling the truth.

In the Pentagon I verified that such an order had been issued and found that, for some strange reason, it had not been referred to me for comment before release. I was also told that the order was not to be taken literally; it was to be part of a larger psychological warfare effort. Unfortunately, no one outside of Washington had been told that. Feeling that Maj. Gen. William Chase, USA, our MAAG chief in Taiwan, would jump at the chance to push the Chinese Nationalists into action as a result of this change in policy, I immediately released a message telling him to delay any action until he had further word from me. As I suspected, he had already passed the word to the Chinese military and they, in turn, were preparing with considerable enthusiasm to carry out his suggestion. I had some difficulty in undoing what Washington had so innocently, it appeared, started. My friends also credited me with selling the idea to President Eisenhower!

☆ ☆ ☆ ☆

I continued to be in touch with General Salan during the early months of 1953, and made another trip to Hanoi in April in an effort to find out why our best efforts to aid the French had resulted in so little military success.

I did not realize how serious I would find the situation in Indochina. It seemed impossible that in three months the French military position could have deteriorated so markedly. Somebody was at fault, but it was difficult to pin down the responsibility.

My message to Admiral Fechteler stressed that the situation in Indochina was serious, and that the Vietminh invasion of Laos had caused the French to deploy their forces defensively so that they were entirely dependent upon air transportation. With the rainy season coming on, they would have to supply their widespread forces by air and must have enough airlift capacity to take advantage of good weather breaks. I felt that the best they could expect was to hold the strong points they had selected. The worst could be a serious military defeat, the complete loss of Laos, and damage to the politico-military situation in Indochina and Southeast Asia.

I pointed out that the Vietminh were gambling heavily on their boldness and risking a great deal in giving the French a chance to cut the long and tenuous Vietminh lines of communication. With more good troops and *aggressive* leadership the French should, I felt, be able to inflict a serious and perhaps decisive blow against the regular Vietminh forces committed to the new Laotian offensive.

In his briefing I sensed complete frankness on General Salan's part, which in the past had not always been the case. Obviously the French high command was very concerned.

I felt that the military situation in Indochina was so fraught with adverse possibilities, as far as the United States was concerned, that we had to take whatever immediate actions we could to improve it.

I recommended, first, that a minimum of six C119 transport aircraft be delivered to the French as soon as possible. Salan had assured me that if civilian pilots, crews, and maintenance personnel could be recruited he could pay them. These aircraft were important because they could transport tanks, armored cars, and heavy construction equipment to outlying bases. The tanks and armored cars would help to make up for troop shortages and might have a decisive effect.

Second, I said I felt that Salan urgently needed more French troops but doubted that he would ask for them. If France would or could send out ten thousand troops from their African colonies, they might wind up the war in six months. I suggested that we urge this course, on a governmental level or through NATO.

I ended by telling Admiral Fechteler that in my opinion there was no time to lose in helping the French out of their present difficulties. I had criticized their leadership and lack of aggressiveness in the past and was not too happy about it at the time. But I felt we had no choice if we wanted to save any part of the heavy investment in military and economic aid we had already made in Indochina.

My requests were carefully and quickly studied in Washington. The C119s were delivered with crews and maintenance personnel after some delay due to recruiting problems. The French were asked for more troops, and for awhile it seemed that they might be flown to Indochina; but as in so many other instances, the "cons" overcame the "pros" in Paris.

I pushed with my staff for much more detailed information from the French and soon concluded that we would have to set up a whole new organization in

Indochina to get it. But if we had to supply most of the help, I felt we had a right to be in on the planning.

My trip, to Manila, Saigon, Hong Kong, Saipan, and Guam, had been designed to take care of the press of business at each stop; but the Saigon situation overwhelmed everything else. Nevertheless, on 23 April I made the first landing on the new airfield at Cubi Point in Subic Bay. The Seabees had made such phenomenal progress in construction of that new field and carrier pier, which I felt was so important to the future, that I was able to fly in and out almost a year earlier than originally expected. It was a great occasion for me and a thrill for the Seabees. I found that great precautions had been taken for several weeks to keep "unwelcome visitors" off the strip. Apparently the underground had reported that some Air Force pilots at Clark Field planned to make the first landing, sneaking in sometime when grading machinery was off the field. The Seabees took the rumors seriously and kept the runway blocked from one end to the other 24 hours a day until I arrived to make the "first" and relieve them of their worries.

Known then and for sometime afterward as "Radford's Folly," the base at Subic Bay has taken its rightful place as one of the most important naval activities we have. Our naval operations in Vietnam could not have been supported as they were without these facilities in the Philippines.

The last five-power conference in 1952, in October, had been thorough and had made some progress. Its report suggested that studies be made of present arrangements for intelligence exchange, of established communication systems, of the machinery for coordination of national plans that might be approved in the future, and of the most appropriate means to ensure continuity of the contacts and permanence of the above studies.

Our JCS, pushing for action in Southeast Asia, directed me in February 1953 to initiate arrangements with the principal military commanders concerned for an early meeting of our representatives to explore implementation of the coordinating measures mentioned in the October report. But they included in the agenda an item asking again for a planning study to determine possible courses of action or capabilities to counter further Chinese communist aggression in Southeast Asia.

This latter conference was held in Pearl Harbor in April and was quite successful. I had to report that the British representatives forced a less positive approach to the agenda item on planning studies for possible future courses of action, but I also said that definite progress was made toward general planning for such action. I felt that the recommendations of the April report formed a satisfactory framework around which effective and coordinated planning could be accomplished, and I urged its early approval in order to capitalize on an auspicious beginning that was characterized by a sincere, straightforward approach and a full consciousness of the situation by all participants. The JCS agreed, and I was authorized to initiate meetings of representatives to proceed with planning studies.

The staff planners to the military representatives of the five powers convened in Pearl Harbor on 15 June in a meeting that lasted until 1 July. The report resulting from these meetings was thorough. It furnished basic information for commanders on which detailed plans could be made. For governmental organizations, such as our JCS, it described the pros and cons of each suggested operation in a manner that permitted decisions to be made. I was pleased with it in 1953 and as I read it again now I still feel it is an excellent report.

The report showed plainly what it was possible for all of us to do militarily in case of future Chinese aggression. It was not overly optimistic but neither was it pessimistic. While the combination of Allied forces available would not be enough to do everything that should be done, the actions we could initiate could be maintained to a point where the communists would be hurting.

When I forwarded this report to the JCS in July 1953 I knew that I would be on the receiving end also. By then I had been nominated by President Eisenhower to relieve General Bradley as Chairman of the JCS, and the Senate had confirmed my nomination.

From the time Mr. Wilson had spoken to me in Honolulu about the possibility of my becoming the next Chairman, I knew my name would be considered when the selection was made. But, looking at the matter cold-bloodedly, I had decided that my chances were slim. I knew there would be strong opposition from Air Force sources and that it was possible that President Eisenhower himself might be reluctant to nominate me [due to Admiral Radford's earlier stance on unification]. I talked it over with Mrs. Radford. She agreed that my chances were minimal. We decided that if the nomination came to pass it would be a great compliment, but that in the meantime it was best that I not try to get it. I had put it out of my mind entirely for the next few months and was busy with CINCPAC responsibilities. In spring 1952, nearing the end of my third year at Pearl Harbor, I had written to Bill Fechteler and told him that if he felt it desirable for any reason to make a change in the CINCPAC assignment to just let me know. I had thoroughly enjoyed the assignment but realized it had to be rotated, and I would gladly ask for retirement whenever he felt it best that I should. I was similarly relaxed about the Chairman's job. If it came my way, I'd do my best. If it did not, I would be glad to step aside.

In May 1953 a joint State-Defense-Interior conference was held in Pearl Harbor to study the problem of security of the Trust Territories. With a new regime in Washington and a new Secretary of the Interior, I had again urged that the matter be studied on a high level, and the meeting was the result of my latest effort.

On Sunday 10 May the Ambassador-designate to Japan, John Allison, and Frank Nash, Assistant Secretary of Defense for International Security Affairs, arrived and I escorted them to my guest house at Pearl Harbor.

Frank Nash spent the afternoon with me going over details for the meeting. Later we had a swim and dinner at my quarters. As he left that evening he said, "On Tuesday morning your telephone will start ringing a little after seven. It will be the press in Honolulu asking for comments on your nomination as Chairman of the Joint Chiefs of Staff by President Eisenhower, which will have just been announced by the White House at twelve noon, Washington time." When I suggested that he was trying to kid me he swore he was not and said he had been authorized to tell me in advance.

I could hardly believe the news and said nothing to anyone, not even Mrs. Radford. But on Tuesday morning the telephone rang just as Frank had predicted, and it was the Associated Press office in Honolulu telling me of my nomination and asking for my comment. I said in response to a question: "I sincerely and deeply appreciate the honor of being nominated by the President as Chairman of the Joint Chiefs of Staff. My first reaction is an awareness of the tremendous responsibilities involved, and I can only promise to do my best." I was completely overwhelmed, even though I had had nearly 48 hours to think it over.

The next few days were pretty much of a blur. I was deluged with telegrams and letters of congratulation, and I also read a few stories that were anything but complimentary. Certainly the country was not unanimous on the subject, which kept me from getting a swelled head and made me realize even more seriously what I was to face in Washington.

I was notified that the Senate Armed Services Committee would begin hearings on my nomination on 25 May. I accepted an invitation from the Pentagon press corps to attend a stag dinner in my honor at the Carleton Hotel the evening of 27 May. I knew this would be quite an occasion and that I could expect almost anything. I was not disappointed. One gentleman who had been imbibing freely offered to bet me $50 that my nomination would not be confirmed. He said he knew that Senator Symington, former Secretary of the Air Force, would oppose it and that he, Symington, could undoubtedly convince a majority of the committee to agree with him. I tried to stall the man off politely, but finally had to be blunt. I told him that I would not take his bet and that I myself was not at all certain I would be confirmed, as I knew there would be a good deal of opposition in the committee. If Senator Symington could convince a majority of the committee that I should not be confirmed it was perfectly all right with me. Aside from this incident the party was very enjoyable, and I realized that most of the Pentagon press corps were my warm friends. For four subsequent years they proved that to me in many ways. Many are still in Washington and are still close friends. This evening was a good start for me, and I appreciated it. I have never forgotten it.

The next morning I appeared before the Senate Armed Services Committee for the confirmation hearings. I was expecting and was prepared for a thorough questioning and I was given one. The Senators explored in considerable detail my views on strategic bombing, the strategic air force, unification, and many variations on these subjects. A few brief examples will suffice to show how it all went.

QUESTION: Admiral Radford, anyone who reads the daily papers is aware that in 1949 you expressed certain views with respect to strategic bombing by long-range bombers and the so-called atomic blitz. Prior to these 1949 House hearings, testimony you had given regarding the 1947 Unification Act was regarded by some as being in opposition to the bill then under consideration. Do you still hold the same views on those subjects?

ANSWER: It is almost four years since the hearings you refer to. There have been developments, improvements in material, and other changes that would naturally cause me to modify some of my positions. We are going ahead too fast for fixed ideas. I did not say anything I did not honestly believe. Under conditions as they exist today I probably would modify some of my statements.

There have been references in the newspapers that I was against unification. It has never been clear to me exactly what people meant when they said you were for or against unification. If they mean as the object uniformity in all aspects of the Defense Department, then I am against it. I think you have to have three very strong independent services and can expect differences of opinion.

I do not think that you want men in the Defense Department who are going to agree for agreement's sake. Military men who have years of experience and training behind them have very strong feelings about certain aspects of their work, and I think that is proper.

I think that in time, with the joint schools we have, each service will have a body of officers who understand the problems of the other services much better than some of us, who did not have that opportunity when we were young, do now.

My ideas in 1947 were certainly that the status quo was not satisfactory. We had to have an improved defense organization. I felt that the bill before Congress was not the best bill that could be drawn. I stated my objections to it frankly. Congress passed the bill, and I have tried to make it work ever since.

QUESTION: In the event the Chiefs of Staff were of the opinion that a certain minimum military strength was necessary to defend the country and they were overridden by the Secretary of Defense, do you think there is any obligation on the chiefs to take that to the President?

ANSWER: I do.

QUESTION: Regarding your appointment: were you asked to make any advance commitments?

ANSWER: No one asked me for any, and I made none.

QUESTION: I think we all would be interested in your concept today of the role of strategic air and the emphasis you think should be placed upon it.

ANSWER: I feel that the strategic air force is one of the most important arms of our national defense and that we must have an efficient and powerful strategic air arm in the Air Force.

In due course Senator Symington questioned me. He said, "Admiral, when you were with the Navy, you worked hard for the Navy. What I would like to know is this: in this new job, will you consider it your duty to work as hard for the Army and Air Force as for the Navy?"

I said: "Senator Symington, in this new job I will work primarily for the United States and I will do my best not to favor any particular service. I will try to call my shots as impartially as I can."

Senator Symington then told the committee Chairman that he had no further questions. I was over that particular hurdle, in spite of what my friend of the night before had predicted.

For the next four years, and since, Senator Symington has been a close friend. While I was Chairman of the JCS he helped me with various problems. My only differences with him concerned the Secretary of Defense Wilson: for some reason, never clear to me, the Senator did not like Mr. Wilson, while I continued to admire him.

On 2 June 1953 the Senate unanimously approved my nomination as Chairman of the JCS. By that time I had returned to Pearl and was waiting for my relief and trying to say goodbye to my friends in the Far East.

On Sunday 31 May Mrs. Radford and I left for a brief farewell trip to the Far East. I felt an obligation to visit, among other places, Korea, to say goodbye to our principal units there. I did this in company with the Eighth Army Commander, Gen. Maxwell Taylor. For the first time, I was made aware of the Korean objections to certain provisions of the armistice to which the United States had agreed. I had heard, of course, that President Syngman Rhee violently opposed some of the provisions for handling prisoners of war and the use of the Indian Army as inspectors, but I had not realized that these feelings were being expressed by street demonstrations.

General Taylor met me at the airport and surprised me by suggesting that we helicopter to a light plane field in the city not far from his headquarters, casually mentioning that there were some disturbances in the city that he wanted to avoid.

Leaving the helicopter, I was put in a jeep with General Taylor. I noticed with some surprise that our column of some six vehicles was surrounded with an escort of more than twice that number of jeeps filled with armed Military Police. As we drove out of the gate at the airfield I saw why. Directly in front of us, barring the road we intended to take, was a riotous crowd of young Koreans. They were a motley group, apparently all civilians, although they seemed to be of military age. Our convoy slowed to a stop while the demonstrators gradually crossed the road. It was evident that whoever the leaders were, they did not want a direct confrontation with General Taylor and his

MPs; so we finally could proceed. What impressed me about this group was the strange look on their faces. I had a feeling that most of them were under the influence of some drug, for they had a sort of glassy stare.

General Taylor later said we had witnessed one of a number of such demonstrations, which he felt certain were being carried out under direct orders from President Rhee.

I saw President Rhee on several occasions during this stay. He did not complain to me directly, but he let it be known that he was inexorably opposed to any armistice agreement permitting the communists to hold any part of Korea. At this time he was also threatening to withdraw the South Korean army from the U.N. command and go it alone in a fight to the finish with the Chinese and North Koreans. I could sympathize with the old gentleman but could not really believe he intended to carry out these drastic threats. Later on, as Chairman, I had direct contacts with him and found out for myself just how stubborn he could be.

23

Chairman of the JCS

I n the month following my arrival in Washington in July 1953, I attended two National Security Council (NSC) meetings and was impressed by the depth and thoroughness of the planning that had been undertaken by the new administration in trying to improve the efficiency of government departments. In two long conferences with the President and in a number of discussions with Secretary of Defense Wilson, I was thoroughly briefed on President Eisenhower's ideas on national security. They made a great deal of sense to me, and I felt sure that my new colleagues would also be pleased. All of us had suffered in Washington during the lean postwar years under President Truman and I was certain that, as a group, we attributed the Korean War largely to the fact that our armed forces had been cut to the point of real weakness, a weakness that had invited the attack of June 1950.

As President Eisenhower took office, the world situation he faced included two active wars: one in Korea and one in Indochina. The United States was hoping for an armistice in Korea, but all concerned realized that this would mean not the end of a war but simply a cessation of fighting. During an armistice our forces would have to remain ready to resume fighting if the enemy elected to break it. History had recorded instances of armistices being broken unilaterally.

In addition to two wars in Asia, there was a very sensitive situation in Europe. In spite of our best efforts, the European Defense Command, originally proposed by the French, remained in limbo. French representatives at NATO conferences would report that EDC was just about to be approved; but French politics seemed always to block it at the last minute, although so far they had not been ready to kill it. From the U.S. point of view, EDC was a necessary part of the NATO military setup.

In the United States itself, the temperament of the American people, reflected in the attitude of the new Republican-controlled Congress, indicated that they were fed up with war in general and the Korean War in particular. There was every indication that "economy" would be the watchword on Capitol Hill when it came to military expenditures.

While many members of Congress viewed with alarm large military expenditures, there were also those who were concerned with unique inadequacies in our defense posture. President Eisenhower in a speech in April set guidelines for his military policies when he said that henceforth the United States would plan for the "long-term pull" in lieu of a "year of crisis" basis. Such thinking coincided with my own, and I felt happy at the prospect of working for a president who had such ideas on military planning.

President Eisenhower wasted no time in acquainting the new JCS with his ideas, including his views on how we should approach our new assignments. He had already clarified my responsibilities and given me more control over the Joint Staff. For one thing, he had directed that selection of every officer of the Joint Staff be approved by the Chairman of the JCS. He hoped thus to help divorce the outlook of the Joint Staff from that of each parent service and to focus their efforts on national planning for the overall common defense. This change in procedure made a great change in the Joint Staff. With few exceptions I found them a group dedicated to finding the best answers for the nation as a whole.

President Eisenhower asked the service chiefs to concentrate on the larger aspects of the job: their roles as members of the JCS. He said at one meeting that he was certain they could organize their offices so their vice chiefs could take care of the service details, freeing them for "national planning." It was after such a meeting that I had my first misgivings. The service chiefs did not want to give up their service responsibilities. They enjoyed them. It was the broader planning and national aspects of their jobs that they appeared more willing to delegate. Among ourselves they would agree that the President had to say such things, but they felt he knew how they actually had to operate.

In *The White House Years* (vol. I: *Mandate for Change*, p. 446), President Eisenhower outlined his thinking on the military establishment:

> I [was] convinced that the composition and structure of our military establishment should be based on the assumption that the United States on its own initiative would never start a major war. This meant that the nation had to maintain forces of greater strength and effectiveness than would be necessary if our purpose had been aggressive. So long as we were to allow an enemy the initiative, we would have to be capable of defeating him even after having sustained the first blow—a blow that would almost certainly be a surprise attack and one that would make Pearl Harbor, by comparison, look like a skirmish . . .
>
> The second guideline was that since modern global war would be catastrophic beyond belief, America's military forces must be designed primarily to deter a conflict, even though they might be compelled later to fight . . .
>
> A third was that national security could not be measured in terms of military

strength alone. The relationship, for example, between military and economic strength is intimate and indivisible.

A fourth consideration was that our armed forces must be modern, designed to deter or wage the type of war to be expected in the mid-twentieth century. No longer could we afford the folly, so often indulged in, in the past, of beginning each war with the weapons of the last ...

The fifth important guideline was that United States security policy should take into account the need for membership in a system of alliances. Since our resources were and are finite, we could not supply all the land, sea and air forces for the entire Free World. The logical role of our allies along the periphery of the Iron Curtain therefore, would to be to provide (with our help) for their own local security ... while the United States, centrally located and strong in productive power, provided mobile reserve forces of all arms ...

President Eisenhower has been criticized by many, in and out of the services, for some of his military policies. It has been my experience that most of his service critics were simply not familiar with the details of the reorganization he demanded and the rationales on which his decisions were based. The others, many senior officers, were familiar with the President's orders and the background for them, but each felt his particular service had not been given what it needed.

It seemed obvious to me in July 1953, when I first studied the President's ideas for what was called the New Look, that the organization that would evolve would have to be heavy in air power (both Air Force and Navy), and that the other services, Army, Navy, and Marines, would have to adjust to organizations that could be fleshed out rapidly in case of emergency. The Air Force, strong in strategic and air defense forces, could not have all it felt it needed in tactical air wings and air logistical activities. In short, after the deterrent forces were decided upon, almost every other activity had to give to a certain extent.

The other important point made by the President to the new chiefs was that national security could not be measured in terms of military strength alone. He says in his book (vol. I, p. 446) that America needs a

fully adequate military establishment headed by men of sufficient breadth of view to recognize and sustain appropriate relationships among the moral, intellectual, economic, and military facets of our strength ... they should have the capacity to dispose our forces intelligently ... to serve peacetime objectives and yet to be of maximum effectiveness in case of attack. They would, of course, have to realize that the diabolical threat of international communism—and our problems in meeting it—would be *with us for decades to come*. (My italics here and below.)

Finally, the President demanded "a realistic appraisal of what the maintenance of an adequate but *not extravagant* defense establishment over an extended period of time (say half a century) could mean to the nation" and urged *"that we do our best to create a national climate favorable to dynamic industrial effort"* (p. 452). He realized that an important part of our national security effort was the readiness of industry as a whole to help in emergencies, that is, cooperation in the essential *military-industrial relationships.*

Eisenhower wrote frankly about the problems faced by Adm. Robert Carney and General Ridgway in the reorganization of their forces under his directive. He understood their problems perfectly and sympathized with them in their concerns, which he knew were real. He also knew that the new organization would work only if he himself were ready to do his part. "But I was not pessimistic. *My intention was firm: to launch the Strategic Air Command immediately upon trustworthy evidence of a general attack against the West"* (p. 453). This statement was the key to the New Look and to the safety of the United States under President Eisenhower. Unfortunately, in eight of the years between his presidency and 1972 we have had presidents who (1) did not understand the national defense policies bequeathed to them and/or (2) had military and civilian advisers who did not approve of President Eisenhower's policies and were able to persuade them that the policies were wrong. Not until President Nixon won the White House have we had a president who listened primarily to his military advisers on military matters and had the courage to follow that advice when he approved it.

When I reported to Secretary Wilson he gave me a copy of a memorandum from President Eisenhower dated 1 July 1953. It is so important that I quote it here, for it shows plainly the President's ideas about revamping our military planning.

Memorandum for the Secretary of Defense

I wish the newly appointed Chiefs of Staff, before assuming their official duties, to examine the following matters:

a) Our strategic concepts and implementing plans,

b) The roles and missions of the services,

c) The composition and readiness of our present forces,

d) The development of new weapons and weapons systems and resulting new advances in military tactics, and

e) Our military assistance programs.

I do not desire any elaborate staff exercise. As a result of this a examination, I should like a summarized statement of these officers' *own* views on these matters, having in mind the elimination of overlapping in operations and administration, and the urgent need for a really austere basis in military preparations and operations. . . .

Such an examination should provide a fresh view as to the best balance and most effective use and deployment of our armed forces, under existing circumstances.

What I am seeking is interim guidance to aid the Council [NSC] in developing policies for the most effective employment of available national resources to insure the defense of our country for the long pull which may lie ahead.

For the purpose of carrying on this examination together, wherever it may take them, I want you to arrange the duties of these officers so that, beginning as early as possible in July and prior to undertaking the responsibilities of their new offices, they can give to the examination full time, uninterrupted attention, freed of all other duties.

[signed] DWIGHT D. EISENHOWER

With such definite orders I made every effort to get started on the project as soon as possible, but I encountered many practical difficulties. The other chiefs, Ridgway, Carney, and Twining, had already reported to their service secretaries and were part of the organizations they headed. Twining, in fact, had been Chief of the Air Staff since May. I quickly found that their idea of how to carry out the President's directive was to have studies made by their service staffs, then meet to piece them together. Since the President had been specific in his talks with me regarding how we should work I did not want to accept this course; besides, I had no staff to work for me!

After three meetings in my temporary office, with numerous interruptions, I decided we were getting nowhere. I asked Secretary of the Navy Robert Anderson if I could borrow his yacht *Sequoia* and take my colleagues to sea, keeping them there until we could agree upon an answer to the President's memorandum. He agreed and a date was set, not without grumbling from the others. Some thought that at least we should come back to Washington every night. But I was adamant. Thursday morning 6 August was set for departure. Only the chiefs were to be aboard, with two enlisted secretaries. *Sequoia* was provisioned for an indefinite stay in the lower Potomac.

The sessions were long and difficult, all day on Thursday and Friday. On both evenings we continued our discussions informally. On Saturday morning things began to fall into place, and by late that afternoon we had a paper that all were willing to sign. I have never been sure why agreement was reached on Saturday when Friday had been so difficult, but I suspect that Matt Ridgway, wanting to get home to his young bride for the weekend, began to see traces of merit in certain things he had opposed the day before. Our paper was typed before we docked. I felt we had done a good job. I called Mr. Wilson, told him about our cruise, and said I would bring the paper to him first thing Monday morning.

Mr. Wilson read our paper, discussed it with me, and then called the President in Denver where he was vacationing and suggested I fly there to show it to him. I found myself under way for Denver about noon. President Eisenhower read the paper carefully several times; he asked me a few questions, then handed it back. He expressed his pleasure with it and said he wanted it brought up at a meeting of the NSC as soon as he returned to Washington. I tried to give the paper back to the President but he would not take it. He said it was too hot to handle.

On my return to Washington I tried to give the paper to Mr. Wilson, but he too told me to keep it. As a result I still have the original copy, with all four signatures.

This paper became known as the New Look paper. It has never been published, but I consider it such an important part of the record of my term as Chairman of the JCS that I have had it declassified.[1]

The chiefs' New Look was the product of a careful survey of the U.S. military situation in July 1953. We all knew that the Korean War had resulted in a rapid and largely uncoordinated buildup of the armed forces. Each service, more or less on its own, had produced remarkable results in enlarging its forces from the skimpy base that had existed in June 1950. Congress, as usual, had responded generously to President Truman's requests for additional funds, and I am certain that most congressmen were pleased with themselves. Their contribution to the war effort was "on time" and all that was asked for! But the final and most essential ingredient of rapid mobilization in our free democracy, declaration by the president of a national emergency, had been put off until December 1950, almost six months after the fighting had started. All the services had had great difficulty in making contracts for essential military supplies and equipment. Industry *could* not, in many instances, cancel private contracts on which it was working to put its plants at the disposal of the military. Under these circumstances the services had to rely on their wartime reserve stocks, which in many cases were inadequate and in others, such as new aircraft, did not exist. Even as the new chiefs met to discuss the problems of readiness put to them by President Eisenhower we had serious shortages. We certainly knew what the President was talking about when he mentioned developing means for the military to cooperate with industry.

Another fact we all knew: the U.S. effort in Korea had just *barely* averted an early and serious defeat. The first Army contingent to land in South Korea fought its first action on 5 July 1953 and was almost annihilated. From then until the Inchon landing on 15 September, U.S. and South Korean forces in the Pusan perimeter had just managed to hold the line. There were times in August and September when we were on the verge of total disaster, avoided only by the uncommon valor of our forces. The men who served in those Army and Marine units were wonderful. The country owed them a lot, and many of them never came home to collect the debt.

☆ ☆ ☆ ☆

On Saturday 15 August 1953 I was sworn in as Chairman of the Joint Chiefs of Staff. The oath was administered by my predecessor, General Bradley. Although I had been preparing for this ceremony ever since the Senate's confirmation, I was overwhelmed by the actual event. The full realization of my enormous responsibilities suddenly dawned on me and never left me for four years, until I turned them over to my successor, General Twining.

President Eisenhower made it plain to me that he expected me, as Chairman, to call him directly whenever *I* felt it necessary, day or night and wherever he was. What a splendid and thoughtful man he was to work for. Secretary Wilson gave me the same orders, saying, "Whenever you feel you have to see me, come into my office. If I have someone else there and you tell me you must see me I will see you alone at once." During my four years' tenure I had quite the same relationship with Secretary of State Dulles, who also expected me to consult him whenever I felt it necessary.

What a difference the Chairman and other senior military men faced in these same situations during the regimes of Presidents Kennedy and Johnson, particularly in regard to contacts or conversations with Secretary of Defense Robert McNamara.

The fact that the President had ordered me to consult with him whenever I thought it necessary or advisable was known by members of his cabinet; consequently, I had no difficulty communicating with key men in the whole administration. From my point of view this was a great safety factor for the country, and it made my responsibilities much easier to carry out.

At one of my first meetings with the President in July he asked if I would like to have a weekly meeting with him. Surprised, I answered that I had not realized I would have to see him that often. He said, "Well, Raddy, if you don't mind, I'd like to continue the arrangement I've had with Brad, a meeting with you at 9:30 every Monday morning when we're both in the city." For one thing, it would seldom then be necessary for him to call me for a special meeting, which would always cause speculation by the press. Finally, he said, if I did not have anything in particular to take up with him he could just talk with me; it would be relaxing for him in the midst of a heavy schedule of appointments with individuals who generally wanted something!

My regular appointment on Mondays continued until his first heart attack, after which I saw him at more irregular intervals. But he was always available, and on short notice.

☆ ☆ ☆ ☆

In August the New Look paper was submitted to the NSC. I explained the thinking behind the paper and answered questions about it. The Council unanimously recommended to the President that it be used as a basis for further detailed national policy and military planning studies. The NSC executive director proposed that the JCS be directed to make an immediate detailed study of the armed services force structure. I opposed this proposal on the grounds that the JCS study should follow a careful study of the chiefs' New Look paper by the State Department and the Policy Planning Board. I pointed out that the conclusions reached by the JCS New Look were predicated upon changes in overseas deployments, acceptance by our allies of the policy of atomic deterrence, and acceptance by Congress and the American people of rather drastic changes in national security policy and the structure of the armed forces. As a result of this meeting, the President directed that national policy be reviewed as a matter of priority so that the JCS would have a basis for their review.

In October I received a memorandum from Secretary Wilson in which he said, among other things:

> It is of urgent importance that we determine now the broad outline for the size and composition of our armed forces for some years ahead in the light of foreseeable developments in order to establish a sound basis for planning best to meet the security requirements of the United States for the long pull ahead.
>
> U.S. national policy, strategy and the considerations which lead to their adoption are set forth in NSC 162 and related documents.

On 9 December the JCS agreed to send to the Secretary of Defense the following reply:

> 1) ... The Joint Chiefs of Staff have considered in broad outline and agreed upon a military strategy designed to implement national policies ... They believe that, in the circumstances and under the conditions stated in this paper and enclosures, this strategy and these policies will adequately provide for the security of the United States in 1957 and thereafter as far as the situation can be predicted at this time ... The strategy and other estimates in these papers *reflect our agreed recommendations* under the assumption that present international tensions and threats remain approximately the same (italics herein are mine). Any material increase in danger or reduction in threat would require complete new studies and estimates.
>
> 2) We have also studied and *come to full agreement* upon a general order of magnitude and composition of the total military establishment ... We believe that the recommended establishment, once stabilized, can be maintained thereafter in a qualitatively improved state of readiness over an indefinite period of time. In our opinion, this establishment will also:
>
> a) Furnish an improved mobilization base for a general emergency.
> b) Maintain fully ready forces to counter peripheral aggressions short of general war.
> c) Enable the United States promptly to furnish an atomic contribution to supplement the indigenous forces of our allies.

3) The Joint Chiefs of Staff agree that the total strength of the armed forces should be reduced to about 2,815,000 men, of which the allocation to the services should be in a general order as follows:

Army	1,000,000	Air Force	975,000
Navy	650,000	Marine Corps	190,000

4) Service programs will be based on the following major units:

Army	14 divisions	Marine Corps	3 divisions, 3 air wings
Navy	1,000 active ships	Air Force	137 wings

However, the Joint Chiefs of Staff believe that there should be incentive to achieve maximum combat strength within available resources, and they would not rigidly limit the services to these figures if they can do better. Changes which any service desires to make must be within its approved personnel and budgetary ceilings, and must have prior Joint Chiefs of Staff approval.

Enclosure A to the above gives the "Broad Outline Strategy" in summary, which requires:

a) Changes in the present United States deployments in some forward areas.
b) Emphasis upon the capability of inflicting massive damage upon the USSR by our retaliatory striking power.
c) An adequate continental defense system.
d) Provision of atomic support for the United States forces.
e) Constitution of a strategic reserve with a high degree of combat readiness.
f) Maintenance of control over sea and air lines of communications.
g) Maintenance of mobilization base adequate to meet the requirements of general war, and
h) Maintenance of the qualitative superiority of our armed forces.

Enclosure B is a "Projection of the Federal Budget Receipt and Expenditures" . . .

On 16 December the NSC met to consider the budget for fiscal 1955. I presented the recommendations in the above report. The service secretaries also made statements, the Secretary of the Army protesting the projected cut in army strength because Army missions remained unchanged while a cut of about 20 percent in personnel was planned.

The NSC adopted the projected military program in general for the three-year objectives, and specifically for fiscal 1955, as consistent with national policies. The President "generally approved this decision," with the understanding that the program would be kept under continuous scrutiny in relation to world developments and that any service might request review of its program if developments indicated the necessity thereof.

General Ridgway, Army Chief of Staff, was present but made no statement. Development of the military force structure recommended by the new JCS was gradual. Moving from some 3,500,000 men in the services when the Korean armistice was signed on 27 July 1953 to the approximate total recommended by the Joint Staff study (preliminary to the JCS memorandum above), reached in summer 1956, took about the two years that we expected it to take.

As part of the public information program to introduce and explain our new national military policies, I spoke before the National Press Club in Washington on 14 December 1953. I said, among other things, that I was there to

> summarize frankly for you, and through you for the American people, what the Joint Chiefs of Staff are doing in the way of military planning for the future . . .
>
> . . . The Joint Chiefs of Staff are opposed to radical changes in a hurry because they are militarily undesirable; and from the standpoint of the security of this nation, they are not practicable. By "radical," I mean the dictionary definition— "fundamental."
>
> . . . The Joint Chiefs of Staff do not believe that any fundamental change could develop so fast that one service should be cut in half, and another tripled, all in one brief period. Changes in tactics and strategy do not come that fast . . .
>
> That brings us to what you have called the "New Look." First, let me give you my description. A New Look is a reassessment of our strategic and logistic capabilities in the light of foreseeable developments, certain technological advances, the world situation today, (and with) considerable estimating of future trends and developments. It is a searching review of this nation's military requirements for security.
>
> The motif and the tempo for the New Look stemmed from the directive contained in the President's speech last April when he said that, henceforth, military planning would proceed on the basis of preparations for the long-term pull. Here is the real key to our new planning. With the President's policy as a starting point, economically sound military and mobilization plans, for this nation and for our allies, should result.
>
> The New Look really is not the first such review of military requirements. The JCS since their inception have continuously reviewed security problems and requirements.

In *Mandate for Change*, President Eisenhower says (p. 451):

> Protests against the planned changes came from many quarters . . . When some claimed I was planning to "wreck" the Army and Navy, I decided that anyone familiar with my background and sentiments would know that these charges did not deserve the dignity of a refutation.
>
> Resistance, however, continued in varying degrees throughout 1954, even though I was proposing a defense establishment in which *all three of the services were to remain far larger, stronger and more effective than ever previously* in peacetime . . . My proposed defense budget was three times that of 1950 (my italics here and below).

In January 1954, the President in his State of the Union Message said: "The defense program recommended in the 1955 budget is based on a new military program *unanimously recommended by the Joint Chiefs of Staff* and approved by me following consideration by the National Security Council."

Thus the New Look became the military program for the Eisenhower administration and, as a matter of fact, for the years since that time up to and including 1972—although in the years since August 1964, when the Vietnam War started, all pretense of fiscal responsibility has been disregarded.

Much of my first six months as Chairman of the JCS was taken up with problems of the New Look. In my many contacts with the President I came to respect and admire him more and more. He was the first President who had the courage to insist upon a defense program that was more than half of total national budget expenditures, and this after a costly three years of war.[2] In spite of criticism, he stuck to his guns. His status as an Army general officer made it difficult for General Ridgway to differ with him, and Ridgway often confounded his Army supporters by his support of important JCS proposals. Like President Eisenhower, I understood Ridgway's problems. Although I did not agree with him on many of them I did sympathize with him. What puzzled me was how Ridgway could justify his support of important JCS decisions and then, shortly afterward, make public remarks that in effect indicated his disagreement with these decisions.

☆ ☆ ☆ ☆

Since General Ridgway's agreements and disagreements with certain JCS recommendations received so much prominence in the press, and caused so much difficulty for me personally, I feel that this is the proper place to address them in some detail.

As mentioned earlier, when the new chiefs reported for duty in July 1953, President Eisenhower told each one individually of his ideas about military planning, emphasizing that in his opinion this planning should be long-term. He emphasized also his belief that the country's economic strength was a most important part of its total strength and was thus significant in planning for our national security. I agreed with the latter, although I well knew that in military circles this was not generally accepted. Many senior officers liked to say that the military had to tell the civilians what forces were required, leaving to the latter the problem of finding the money to pay for them.

When the new chiefs met on *Sequoia* we came back with a unanimous paper—an agreement that surprised me, especially General Ridgway's agreement.

During some of the autumn NSC sessions, when the New Look was being discussed, there were times when I felt that both Admiral Carney and General Ridgway were about to kick over the traces; but they did not.

About 1 December, Lt. Gen. Frank Everest, Director of the Joint Staff, submitted his committee's report on the new military force structure, the force structure outlined by the New Look, and its costs. (This was the preliminary report to the JCS memorandum.) Everest had himself put together a force structure with costs that was a compromise between the extreme positions of his committee members. I felt that his recommendations were the best, and in presenting his committee's report to the JCS I suggested that we make them the basis for our recommendations to the Secretary of Defense.

The JCS wrestled with the New Look Force Structure from the first of December, meeting once a day and sometimes twice. On 9 December we reached unanimous agreement and gave Secretary Wilson the paper he had requested.

The Secretary of the Army, in his protest during the December NSC meeting of the 20-percent cut, maintained that the Army's mission had not been reduced; but he obviously did not understand the new force structure. The principal Army forces were to be in the strategic reserve located in the United States, not abroad. At this meeting General Ridgway, who had approved the paper, said nothing.

Some indication of the line General Ridgway would take regarding the New Look decisions had appeared in an address on 24 October at Lafayette College, Pennsylvania. He is reported to have stated that the nation could not gamble with its safety by rushing a substitution of "new and untried weapons for its foot soldiers." He went on to say that military commanders would "loyally" accept whatever security measures were decided upon by the Secretary of Defense and other civilian authorities, but that they would point out the consequences of "any failure to provide the requirements they consider essential."

On 11 November the *New York Times* quoted General Ridgway as having said at Cleveland the day before that the foot soldier is still the dominant factor in war, and that any weakening of United States ground forces now could be a "grievous blow to freedom." He continued to say that some people were espousing "new and untested devices, machines and weapons, in the hope that these can substitute for men." Such hopes were, in his opinion, premature at best; and the presence of American troops abroad was one of the greatest deterrents to war.

On 8 February 1954, Secretary of the Army Robert Stevens and General Ridgway testified before the Subcommittee on Armed Services of the House Committee on Appropriations. In reading his prepared statement General Ridgway said, "The Army has been guided in the preparation of this budget by basic economic and strategic decisions which have been made at a higher level." He also said:

> These [the Army's missions and commitments] are of particular concern, since we are steadily reducing Army forces—a reduction through which our capabilities will be lessened while our responsibilities for meeting the continuing enemy threat remain unchanged. In the long range view, it is contemplated that the execution of these missions may be modified by complementary means being developed within the military establishment. In the development of these new means we must not lose sight of the Army's missions and commitments of today

which must properly be met if our military posture is to be maintained . . .

The imposition of expenditure ceilings for fiscal year 1954 and fiscal year 1955 has required a reappraisal of our material readiness objectives.

Congressman Richard B. Wigglesworth posed this question: "I understand, General, from the testimony of Secretary Wilson and Admiral Radford, that this overall military program, of which the Army program now before us is a part, is a result of the New Look and has the unanimous endorsement of the President, the National Security Council, and the Joint Chiefs of Staff. That is correct, is it not?"

General Ridgway replied, "Yes, sir. So far as the Joint Chiefs of Staff are concerned it was on stated assumption and limitations."

On 15 March, General Ridgway testified before the subcommittee of the Senate Committee on Appropriations. Following are excerpts from his testimony.

> SENATOR MAYBANK: . . . I saw some articles in the paper that the Army was concerned that they had been cut too much. Are you perfectly satisfied that the Army has sufficient funds?
>
> GENERAL RIDGWAY: That would be a pretty broad statement.
>
> SENATOR MAYBANK: Maybe it is too tough a question.
>
> GENERAL RIDGWAY: I accepted it.
>
> SENATOR MAYBANK: You were consulted?
>
> GENERAL RIDGWAY: Yes, sir.
>
> SENATOR MAYBANK: And you agreed to these funds insofar as the Army was concerned?
>
> GENERAL RIDGWAY: It was not a question of agreeing to funds. It was a question of force levels, and then the costs followed.
>
> SENATOR MAYBANK: Were you satisfied with the force levels?
>
> GENERAL RIDGWAY: I accept this program as a sound one.
>
> SENATOR MAYBANK: You accept it, but are you satisfied?
>
> GENERAL RIDGWAY: I am satisfied now, sir.
>
> SENATOR MAYBANK: I just wanted to get the record perfectly clear . . .

General Ridgway continued to indicate at times that he was not completely satisfied with appropriations and manpower allocated to the Army, but he did not disavow his agreement with important documents on which these appropriations and figures were based. Had his position been that of an isolated individual it would not have mattered, but he was the Army Chief of Staff. He disturbed the President and the Secretary of Defense. He certainly disturbed me. He convinced me that I had made a mistake in originally trying to achieve agreement on controversial matters brought before the JCS. As a result, I changed my tactics and tried to develop real differences when I thought they existed.

Undoubtedly, the Army as a whole followed General Ridgway's lead during these months of controversy, and as a result the President did not reappoint him when his first two-year term expired. I was not happy about this, but I considered that there was no other choice. I also concluded that General Ridgway himself preferred to retire.

☆ ☆ ☆ ☆

In fall and winter 1953 I made two trips abroad. The first, to Europe, was essential because I had been there only once since World War II. My responsibilities as Chairman of the JCS required a familiarity with European and NATO problems that I did not have and that I felt I could acquire only by meeting the people who were running things. The President and Secretary Wilson agreed.

The second and shorter trip was a surprise: a visit to the Far East over Christmas to attend the inauguration on 30 December of my friend Ramon Magsaysay as President of the Philippines.

The German portion of my European tour was a very busy six days. I had briefings by all major commands and an opportunity to inspect all major units of the Army and Air Force. One of my principal objectives was to find out if possible what could be done to expedite the formation of German army and air force units that were to be assigned to EDC if and when that organization was approved by the French Chamber of Deputies. I found EDC in a complete "snafu" [situation normal, all fouled up]. It was blocked at almost every turn by regulations, directives, and customs, each of which seemed susceptible of correction but was so linked with the others that nothing seemed possible. Behind all these complications was the French-dominated EDC Interim Committee. The U.S. Command Headquarters told me that they had "not been fully informed on the plans that the French EDC-IC have developed. Thus inaction by EDC-IC serves as a block to further progress in other fields." The French wanted no action until they had made up their minds in regard to EDC, and they were able to successfully block advance arrangements that would have expedited it. On the other hand, answers to my questions at various briefings led me to infer that U.S. commanders preferred to let nature take its course than to force the issue. The roadblock had to be broken in Washington if at all.

On this trip we toured Berlin, both east and west zones. I was told that the East Berlin authorities had not been notified in advance of our visit, but an escort was waiting for us at the gate and stayed with us while we were in communist territory.

East Berlin was most depressing. Little rebuilding had taken place, and there was practically nothing in the shops. Few people and little traffic were on the streets. The one showpiece, on Stalin Allee, the principal thoroughfare, was a block or two of high-rise apartments that at first glance seemed quite impressive but on a closer look were obviously poorly built. A prominent building contractor from the United States whom I met at a reception later that day informed me that the apartments would not last long unless they were practically rebuilt.

One day I drove to Bonn for a call on our High Commissioner to Germany, Dr. James Conant; together we called on Chancellor Konrad Adenauer. This was my first meeting with the Chancellor, and he impressed me very much. Later I got to know him quite well.

Flying to London following a quick trip to Oslo, I was planning my English visit when a sudden sharp explosion brought us all to attention. I saw what looked like a ball of fire roll to the end of the wing on the port side and disappear. The pilot informed me that our plane had been struck by lightning. The only damage was a small hole in the bow where the charge either hit or left the plane. It was the only such experience I have had in many hundreds of hours in the air, and it occurred on a cold day with, so far as we know, no thunderstorms in the vicinity.

I was surprised and pleased to see Ambassador Nelson Aldrich in the group waiting for us at the airport that morning. On the way into London he told me he had just received an invitation for me to call on Prime Minister Churchill at 12:30. Asking if he could accompany me there, he said, "I haven't seen the Prime Minister since last spring, and he has been reportedly quite ill." I told him I was very surprised by the invitation and would be happy to have him accompany me.

Ambassador Aldrich and I were greeted at 10 Downing Street by a secretary who led us into a rather dark hall. We turned, still in the dark, to the entrance of what seemed like a large room on the front of the house—the cabinet room, I learned later. Several small, high windows on one wall provided the only illumination, but I could faintly see three figures sitting on the opposite side of what appeared to be a long table. We were seated on the near side, and as my eyes became accustomed to the light I could make out the Prime Minister as the center figure. I had met him briefly once before, in Washington, soon after the end of World War II. In the dark room I thought I recognized him but his head seemed larger than I remembered.

With few preliminary remarks the Prime Minister began questioning me, mainly about the operations of our carriers in the Pacific against the Japanese. His questions involved rather complicated answers, which I tried hard to simplify. He made things more difficult by sometimes asking an additional question before I had finished my answer to a previous one. We were not there more than half an hour when Mr. Churchill thanked me for my call and indicated that the meeting was over. The Ambassador and I were led out, still in the dark, and made our way back to his office.

I was puzzled and so was Ambassador Aldrich. He, too, had noticed that the Prime Minister's head seemed larger. We concluded that this might have resulted from taking cortisone and agreed reluctantly that Mr. Churchill was nearing the end of his great career. Certainly the interview had made little sense to me, although I had to admit that the Prime Minister seemed to know what he wanted in the way of information.

At that time, the problem of Trieste was on everyone's mind. Italians and Yugoslavs seemed unable to agree on a reasonable settlement. In Washington, our diplomats considered it a tinderbox. I wanted to see for myself and so traveled to Trieste, where I called on a number of civil and military officials, ending with Maj. Gen. B. M. McFadden, Commander U.S. Forces Trieste, who joined me for coffee and cakes at Miramar Castle. General McFadden surprised and pleased me with his optimistic views about the local situation, which he felt could be settled. I carried his suggestions to Washington, and they helped in establishing the basis for arrangements that finally settled the problem in October 1954.

In Rome my official schedule commenced with a cake-cutting ceremony celebrating the U.S. Marine Corps' 178th birthday.

Ambassador Clare Boothe Luce briefed me on the general situation in Italy, including for good measure her observations on the political situation in Europe as a whole. I do not remember having received a more comprehensive, intelligent and interesting survey.

In the next three hours I paid official calls on Prime Minister Giuseppe Pella, Minister of Defense Paolo Taviani, and Chief of the Defense Staff Gen. Efissio Marras. That evening Mrs. Radford and I were the guests of honor at a lovely dinner given by the Minister of Defense.

One morning my party was received by Pope Pius XII at his summer residence. The Pope chatted with each member of the party and gave me an interesting outline of his feelings on important world political and military problems. Pius XII was evidently well-informed on every aspect of world affairs. He was a most intelligent man whom I felt could not have been better fitted for his position.

Our visit to Madrid had seemed quite difficult to arrange at one stage. For reasons that were never clear to me, I was told that my party would have to wear civilian clothes on arrival and while in Spain. The answer was easy: I would not stop there under those conditions. Probably as a result of this statement they were removed. Our brief stop turned out to be enjoyable and, more important, helpful in finalizing our new base agreements.

It was the Chief of the Joint U.S. Military Group in Spain, Maj. Gen. August Kissner, who took us in tow when we arrived in Madrid and made our stay so pleasant. I give him full credit for establishing the excellent relations with Spanish government and military officials that had followed a rather long and difficult period.

On a visit to Generalissimo Francisco Franco, I found him cordial, interested, and talkative. He appeared to be in excellent physical condition and mentally alert. He spoke in Spanish and we used interpreters.

General Franco spoke at considerable length on what he had done for the Spanish armed forces since the civil war, emphasizing his plan for expanding the educational background of the regular and reserve officers; he felt that his officer corps had reached a high state of efficiency. The General dwelt at length on the materiel problems of the armed forces. By stimulating production of material goods, it had been possible to take care of many basic requirements of the Spanish army and navy, he said, but there had been great difficulty in coping with the production of modern equipment, particularly electronic, and aircraft. He knew the Spanish forces had marked materiel deficiencies and hoped that as a result of relations established between the United States and Spain it might be possible to alleviate some of them.

The second point made by General Franco was about utilization of the excess productivity of the West. He felt that, since many Western industrial nations had serious problems finding adequate markets for their commercial products, these nations might consider "supporting" for a temporary period less fortunate nations. This would in time serve to build up the strength of the latter and thereby create real and enduring markets. He seemed, I thought, to be thinking primarily of Spain, which badly needed industrial expansion.

Franco then moved to the question of trading with the communist bloc. He was emphatic on the necessity for a tight economic blockade against the Soviet Union and its satellites. He said that if such a blockade were truly enforced it would create divisive forces within the Soviet bloc—that the Soviet Union would be forced either to satisfy the demands of its satellites for consumer goods or to face the possibility of their breaking away from Soviet control.

I thanked General Franco for the cooperation shown by Spain in concluding the recent bases agreements with the United States, and expressed the hope that this success would be the first of several areas of agreement. I concurred in principle with his point regarding the importance of economic blockade but stressed the obvious difficulties Western nations face in implementing such a program. I said that the blockade was under active and continuous study and much progress had been made, but it was clear that it was not anywhere near 100 percent effective.

My principal comments on the European situation after this trip covered the following:

> The German contribution to NATO: clearly, the defense of not only central but also northern Europe was dependent on an adequate German contribution. I felt that the planned contribution was only half as large as it should be, but I realized that such an increase could not be proposed then.
>
> The lack of real effort in Europe toward getting EDC going, and toward planning

in detail for the utilization of German forces, appalled me. I fully appreciated that the French government was primarily responsible for the delay, but I felt that U.S. efforts left much to be desired and that the British were willing to let our people set the pace.

Withdrawal of some U.S. ground forces from NATO, a specific requirement of the New Look and a necessary step in provision of a strategic reserve in the United States, could not take place until German forces were available. At the rate we were moving, withdrawal of our ground forces was three or more years away, certainly not a pleasing prospect for President Eisenhower. I felt strongly that his plan to consistently and aggressively pursue a course leading to the provision by European members of NATO of most ground forces for the defense of Europe must be carried out at the earliest practicable date. Only then could we have in the United States the ground reserve so important to quickly counter Russian aggressions elsewhere. Furthermore, the existence of such a mobile strategic reserve would pose a threat for Soviet planners greater than that of existing U.S. ground forces in Western Europe, inasmuch as the Russians would not know into which area the reserve might be projected.

I concluded also that we must resist pressure from our allies to augment their air forces beyond presently agreed goals. Certainly, the bulk of air power would have to be provided by the United States, Britain, and Germany. To attempt to fill established air requirements of NATO with contributions from all other countries would require duplication of training facilities for both pilots and maintenance personnel, as well as a large increase in U.S. aid.

I felt that our new relations with Spain were a distinct asset. The spirit and cooperation evidenced by the Spaniards were hearty in comparison with that in certain other countries. While the Spanish army lacked types and quantities of equipment necessary to make it a first-class fighting force, the potential was there, and we should be alert that this reserve of trained manpower existed and could be valuable in the future.

I returned to Washington aware of the tremendous problems involved in maintaining NATO as a viable concern.

☆ ☆ ☆ ☆

On the day before Christmas 1953, Assistant Secretary of State Walter Robertson and I were in Korea, visiting President and Mrs. Rhee at their bungalow on a hill overlooking the sea near Pusan. They stayed there whenever they could get away from Seoul and this year were spending the Christmas holidays there.

I shall never forget that meeting with the President of Korea, in his bedroom, apparently the best place for complete privacy. There were only two small chairs in the room, so I sat on the edge of the bed for our talk, which lasted over an hour. I'm certain that President Rhee expected bad news from us, so in a sense he was prepared.

We told the President that President Eisenhower had decided to reduce our Army forces in Korea, by two divisions in the immediate future and progressively thereafter as circumstances warranted. While we were acting in good faith to preserve the armistice, we would remain alert to all possibilities. President Eisenhower also wanted to emphasize that the withdrawals would not impair our readiness to deter future aggression and, if aggression did occur, to oppose it with even greater effect than heretofore. We went on to explain in detail why our President felt he had to take this action and why he hoped our Korean allies would understand.

President Rhee at first seemed stunned; he then reacted strongly and emotionally, to the effect that the United States was letting him down, that we simply did not understand the situation facing him as the President of Korea.

Both Walter Robertson and I were great admirers of President Rhee, and we talked long and earnestly to convince him that, as the leader of the free world, President Eisenhower had to look at the world picture in his efforts to contain the communist threat. Only after thorough studies had the JCS recommended to our President that we begin to reduce our strength in Korea, pointing out at the same time that the South Korean army was now a powerful force, the *third largest* army in the free world.

Finally, with all three of us nearly exhausted, President Rhee agreed to the reductions and said he trusted us on further moves. We left that little house on the hill with still greater admiration for a courageous little man who had been a wonderful leader of his country in peace and in war. We were glad we had come to tell him in advance of our moves. I am certain there would have been a blowup had the announcement been made in Washington without that preliminary.

My plan for Christmas Day was to join Gen. Maxwell Taylor (Commander Eighth Army) in visiting all major Army units still on the Korean front. We would fly to the eastern end of the line in the morning and work our way back to Seoul in the afternoon.

It was gray, overcast, and cold that morning as we were off shortly after daylight. Traveling by helicopter, we started our visit at units of the First ROK Field Army. Continuing across Korea, we visited several divisions, then had Christmas dinner with the Thirty-Fifth Infantry—turkey and all the trimmings. I don't recall ever having had a better one, for by that time I had worked up a tremendous appetite.

I had had some misgivings about how our visits would be taken by the troops, who were being kept on in Korea months after the fighting had stopped and were suffering through another miserable winter. I was pleasantly surprised. All the troops seemed in excellent spirits and health. Good food, plenty of exercise, and a program of rebuilding Korean schools and other public works projects kept morale high. I had plenty of opportunity to talk to young men whom I picked out myself, at random, and I felt they represented a good sample. It was obvious that a visitor from Washington, especially the top military man, was appreciated and indicated to the troops that they were not forgotten.

After dinner we continued by helicopter, but it started to snow hard and we gave up flying for jeeps. I believe we had to curtail a few visits and eliminate some, but we did the best we could.

In Taiwan the next day, a comprehensive briefing was the first order of business at our Embassy. The Embassy staff was followed by representatives of MAAG, CIA, and the U.S. Information Agency. It was about the most complete and well-organized affair I had ever attended. Walter Robertson felt the same way, and we both expressed special appreciation to Ambassador Karl Rankin. Too often, our diplomatic missions abroad prefer the question-and-answer approach to providing information for visitors, a sure way to leave a lot of loose ends.

On this visit, we enjoyed two informal dinners with President and Madame Chiang. At one of them Walter Robertson surprised all of us by putting on quite a sleight-of-hand show after dinner. None of us had had any idea of his talents.

Secretary Robertson and I were able to meet in Manila with our Ambassador to Vietnam, Donald Heath, and with Brig. Gen. Thomas Trapnell, USA, Chief of our MAAG in Vietnam, who came from Saigon at our request. Their reports, which took up one afternoon, were depressing. The French, under their new Commander-in-Chief, General Navarre, were doing no better than before. The "Navarre plan" for aggressive action was proving to be a repeat of General Salan's defensive tactics, but General Navarre was more difficult to deal with. General Trapnell felt increasingly concerned about the French position at Dien Bien Phu, doubting that they would be able to hold it. Both men said that French requests for additional material support were becoming much larger, in many cases with little or no justification.

Robertson and I could find few if any bright spots in the report from Indochina. Our efforts in material support, and they were *tremendous*, seemed to have had little or no effect. When we tried to augment these efforts with trained advisers in order to insure proper use of our equipment, we were rebuffed more often than not.

On Wednesday 30 December, Ramon Magsaysay was inaugurated as President of the Republic of the Philippines. The ceremonies were impressive. It was obvious from the emotional outbursts of the thousands of Filipinos present that Magsaysay was their one and only hope.

We departed Manila that night for Honolulu, where we met with Adm. Felix Stump, who had relieved me as CINCPAC, to exchange information and discuss the reports we had received from Ambassador Heath and General Trapnell. Much of their adverse news was confirmed by Admiral Stump and his staff.

A long New Year's weekend at the beach on the north coast of Oahu gave us all the rest we badly needed before plunging again into the Washington whirl.

☆ ☆ ☆ ☆

Before my Far Eastern trip I had discussed with Secretary Dulles a talk he was preparing that would give Americans and the rest of the world an outline of President Eisenhower's foreign policy and national security plans as they had developed in the first year of his presidency. The Secretary spoke before the Foreign Policy Association in New York on 12 January 1954. I thought then, and I still think, that this was one of the clearest expositions of the subject ever put forth. I thought it would make a great impression on the American public, as well as on our friends and enemies around the world. It did, but not exactly as I thought and hoped.[3]

Thoughtful citizens who read the speech carefully will appreciate what a powerful statement it was, how clearly it outlined the Eisenhower military policies, and how the new foreign policy objectives fitted into them. The closing paragraphs are particularly impressive more than 19 years after they were spoken: In Russia,

> there are signs that the rulers are bending to some of the human desires of their people. There are promises of more food, more household goods, more economic freedom.
>
> That does not prove that the Soviet rulers have themselves been converted. It is rather that they may be dimly perceiving a basic fact, that is that there are limits to the power of any rulers indefinitely to suppress the human spirit.
>
> In that God-given fact lies our greatest hope. It is a hope that can sustain us. For even if the path ahead be long and hard, it need not be a warlike path; and we can know that at the end may be found the blessedness of peace.

I am confident that readers today will be as impressed by Mr. Dulles' speech as were his listeners in January 1954, but what happened later? I saw the completed draft of the speech once, a day or so before it was given, and asked the Secretary to take out the word "massive" in one spot regarding retaliation, but he evidently did not agree. Our press, and to some extent the world press, chose to accent the statements in the speech about "massive retaliatory power" and "by means and places of our choosing" to the point where the speech became known as "Mr. Dulles' statement on massive retaliation." It was unfortunate. As a result, President Eisenhower's military policy is usually labeled "the policy of massive retaliation," with the further implication that it did not contain strong conventional forces. Kennedy's policies were later described as designed for "gradual response" and as containing "balanced" forces.

President Eisenhower's military policies, with minor modifications, have in fact been the basis for our military structure since 1953; but the phrase "massive retaliation" is still applied critically to the Eisenhower era. The implication sought by critics of that era seems to be of a bloody massacre of innocent people. They wholly ignore the President's stipulation that his orders to retaliate with atomic weapons would only follow confirmed reports of communist attacks on free world forces. During President Eisenhower's eight years in the White House his firm and well-publicized military policies prevented not only World War III, but also the outbreak of further serious lesser but sustained conflicts like the Korean War. On the other hand, history indicates that it did not take the Russian leaders long to assess the fact that President Kennedy was much less sure of himself on the international military and political fields.

24

Indochina Heats Up

B y the end of December 1950, the change wrought by General de Lattre in Indochina, discussed earlier, had already become noticeable.[1] The MAAG reported that "relations between the MAAG and the French Command are unquestionably better than at any previous point in the Indochina program."

In 1950 [Admiral Radford was still CINCPAC], there was general agreement among U.S. government agencies that the peninsula, especially Tonkin, was the keystone of the Southeast Asian arch, without which the free nations in that area would crumble. It was also agreed that all possible must be done to maintain Indochina, although, with its forces tied down in Korea, the United States would have to confine itself to military aid in the form of munitions and equipment. But in Washington it was the Defense Department that was the most anxious about the dangers in Southeast Asia, and this anxiety was stimulated by constant roweling on the part of the JCS. The chiefs seemed to see more clearly than the State Department the threat to the U.S. strategic position in the Far East inherent in a communist Vietnam, and they were more eager to act with the resources at hand to salvage it for the free world.

This advanced position of the JCS became clear when the chiefs were required to comment on an NSC paper entitled "The Position and Actions of the United States with Respect to Possible Further Soviet Moves in the Light of the Korean Situation." How to defeat an offensive by the Vietminh was not the question. Rather, it was what to do should the Chinese provide overt military assistance to Ho Chi Minh, an action that seemed not improbable in view of the Korean example.[2] If, said the JCS, such assistance is given to Vietminh forces, "the United States should increase its MDAP [Mutual Defense Assistance Program] assistance to the French and urge the French to continue an active defense, with the United States giving consideration to the provision of air and naval assistance." Also, the United States should ask the United Nations to call upon its members to make forces available to resist the Chinese aggression.

In August 1950, commenting on a revision of the same NSC paper, the JCS recommended that in the event of overt attack by organized Chinese forces against Indochina the United States should support France and the Associated States, in concert with Britain, accelerate and expand the present military assistance program, and mobilize to the extent necessary to meet the situation. But other government agencies in the NSC drew back from such a strong position. The NSC decision was to accept the recommendation of the JCS on supporting French and Indochinese forces and stepping up MDAP assistance.[3] Mobilization was not accepted and was replaced with a stipulation that if the Chinese attacked in Indochina, the United States should not permit itself to become engaged in a general war with Peking.

A similar difference in attitude appeared during preparations for talks between the foreign ministers of France and Great Britain and the Secretary of State in September 1950. A State Department position paper on Indochina was submitted to the JCS for comment. It recommended that Secretary of State Acheson emphasize to the French the importance of liberal implementation of the Elysée Accords; also that, despite the urgency of the military situation, the political program must not be delayed. The French should be urged to speed the formation of new national armies and to intensify their information activities in Asia. The Secretary was also to recommend military staff talks between the United States, the United Kingdom, and France regarding "pooling and coordination of resources in Southeast Asia in the event of invasion."

The JCS noted that the recommendations

> do not reflect the urgency which, from the military point of view, should be attached to planning, preparing for, and providing adequate means to insure the security of Indochina . . . Intelligence reports indicate that the Vietminh military preparations may be sufficiently complete in the very near future to launch a large scale effort to seize control of all of Indochina. Prior to 1 January 1951, the currently planned level of U.S. military aid to the French and native allied forces of Indochina should increase their capabilities but not to the extent of countering Vietminh capabilities. In view of these considerations, the JCS suggest . . . that the situation in Indochina is to be viewed with alarm and that urgent and drastic action is required by the French if they are to avoid military defeat.[4]

In regard to the proposed staff talks, the JCS asked that the phrase "coordination of resources" be changed to "coordination of operations." They also wished Secretary Acheson to indicate to the French that increases in military aid would be provided in accordance with operational plans acceptable to the United States and compatible with U.S. capabilities. Because of the fluid situation in Korea, the United States would not commit any of its armed forces under present circumstances.

The records of the September tripartite foreign ministers' meetings do not indicate that Secretary Acheson exerted much pressure on the French, as desired by the JCS. He seems instead to have wished to let the JCS work out their problems in the proposed military staff talks. In accordance with NSC policy and the JCS recommendation, the Secretary refused a French request for U.S. tactical air support.

In October 1950, JCS concern for the security of Southeast Asia against communism prompted them to press for a stronger and more precise American policy. They were particularly conscious of the fact that there was no clear statement regarding the contingency of an attack on Indochina by Vietminh forces aided by Communist China. The deteriorating situation in Indochina after the Cao Bang debacle demanded a revision of American policy. And the apparent collapse of communist resistance in North Korea seemed to offer the opportunity. If the Korean conflict could be quickly ended, the U.S. global strategic position would be strengthened and some American armed forces would be freed for employment in other areas.

Also in October, Gen. J. Lawton Collins, Army Chief of Staff, laid before his colleagues in the JCS a written proposal for reappraising the government's stand on Indochina. Stressing the critical importance of Indochina to the United States in the cold war—in contrast to its secondary value in a global war— General Collins advised increasing pressure on the French to take the military and political measures long advocated in Washington. But, should it become clear that those measures were failing, as a last resort the United States should be prepared to commit its own armed forces, subject of course to certain limitations. The commitment must not endanger the U.S. strategic position in the event of a third world war; it must offer a reasonable chance of success; and it should be done in concert with other U.N. members. Plans should be made immediately, General Collins said, to meet this possibility.

The JCS considered General Collins' views in preparing their comments on a proposal by the Southeast Asia Aid Policy Committee for a new NSC decision on U.S. Indochina policy. This proposal roughly conformed to the ideas of the JCS, although it did not provide for the use of American armed forces and, in the JCS view, it did not reflect the urgency of the situation in Indochina. But the chiefs delayed their comments while awaiting a report from General Brink, MAAG Commander in Saigon. They had instructed General Brink to confer with Gen. Alphonse Juin during a visit the latter was about to make to Indochina to estimate the chances of French success against the Vietminh. The chiefs wanted Juin's estimate of the situation.

By the time the JCS were ready to present their recommendations, the Chinese had struck in North Korea, and a longer war, tying down U.S. forces for some time to come, was in prospect. The chiefs therefore could not advise using American combat forces in Indochina in the foreseeable future.

The JCS sent their recommendations to the Secretary of Defense in November. Instead of merely commenting on the Aid Policy Committee's paper, they proposed their own broad policy, which was presented the following month to the NSC for consideration.[5]

An "Analysis," written by the Joint Strategic Survey Committee (JSSC), accompanied the JCS draft policy and explained the strategic concept that kept them from recommending armed intervention: involvement of U.S. forces against Vietminh forces would likely lead to a war with China, which would probably be a prelude to global war. The chief enemy in a global war would likely be the USSR, and the principal theater would be Western Europe. The strength of the Western powers was insufficient to fight a war on the Asian mainland and at the same time accomplish the predetermined Allied objectives in Europe.

Despite the sense of urgency communicated by the strong words of the JCS, the proposal was not adopted by the NSC. Although the chiefs complained intermittently about the lack of a more definite statement of policy, NSC 64 remained the basic American position on Indochina for months. Nevertheless, the JCS strove to realize the objectives that they advocated, and other government agencies gradually moved toward their point of view. The policy enunciated in NSC 64, therefore, although not superseded, was at least modified by prevailing opinion in Washington; this progress toward a stronger stand on Indochina was apparent at the end of 1950.

We were moving into a position in Indochina in which our responsibilities tended to supplant rather than complement those of the French. We could become a scapegoat for the French and be seduced into direct intervention.

Secretary Acheson's record of dealing with the French government in 1950 shows the sincere effort of the United States to support the French in their Indochina operations through this crucial period. The State and Defense Departments did everything they could to help our allies while remaining within the bounds of policies laid down by President Truman and Congress. Our administration based its actions on what they sensed were limitations imposed by the people of the United States. I think it fair to say that the French government tried honestly to stay within the same bounds. Unfortunately, there was a gulf between each government and its people that continued to grow; it is this divergence that is important in the narrative of our involvement in Vietnam.

☆ ☆ ☆ ☆

During 1951, the French military position in Indochina showed a definite but inconstant improvement. Early that year General de Lattre repulsed a series of attacks, inflicting heavy losses on the Vietminh while keeping his own relatively low. In November he undertook a limited, though not well considered, offensive in the Hoa Binh area southwest of Hanoi.

The successes achieved under de Lattre were made possible by American military assistance. The effect of U.S. support in the civil war became apparent in mid-January 1951, when French Union forces defeated the largest offensive yet mounted by the Vietminh. Ambassador Heath reported from Saigon that the French victory could in large part be attributed to the action of French air, artillery (especially 105-millimeter howitzers), and napalm, all of which were provided ... under MAP.

The decisive equipment used to repulse this Vietminh offensive reached Hanoi only in the nick of time and as a result of personal intervention by General Brink, who asked General MacArthur's headquarters to ship material from their stocks, outside the established military aid channels. The value of this assistance was acknowledged by General de Lattre to the American Minister, to the Chief of MAAG, and to the press. His public expressions of gratitude went far toward promoting better relations between the French and Americans in Indochina. The attitude of the French toward MAAG changed from one of suspicion and annoyance to one of qualified approval, easing the future work of that agency.

But too little was happening in Vietnam in developing military power, government responsibility, and popular support. In 1951, though the Vietnamese forces rose to four divisions, they had only 700 Vietnamese officers out of 2,000 required, and the military academy at Dalat was graduating only 200 a year. An American offer of instructors from our military mission in Korea, which was mass-educating officers for twelve Korean divisions, was refused.

Although in 1951 the French perceived an important change in the U.S. government attitude toward the Indochina war, there was little modification of their basic policies. Whatever policy evolution took place resulted from American participation in military and diplomatic conferences and from the setting up of machinery for liaison and consultation between the French, British, and American commands in the Far East. But none of these actions represented or occasioned any considerable alteration in American aims during the year.

The first important international military conference about Indochina was held in Singapore. With JCS concurrence, Secretary Acheson, during the tripartite foreign ministers' meetings in September 1950, had agreed with the British and French that military commanders of the three nations in the Far East should meet to discuss the defense of Southeast Asia. The meeting took place in May 1951, but by this time JCS objections had to be overridden. When the chiefs had originally agreed to participate in the discussions, the Korean conflict had been going well for U.N. forces. But Chinese intervention had placed such heavy demands on American fighting strength that the JCS could visualize no practical means of assisting Indochina other than increasing the flow of supplies in the event of emergency. They felt, therefore, that little could be accomplished by a conference. Considering existing limitations on American action, any matters that might require consultation with the French in Indochina could be handled through General Brink, who had already conferred with Generals Juin and

Marcel Carpentier. Furthermore, the JCS regarded the Chinese intervention as having so changed the general strategic situation in the Far East that new basic decisions on the political level were required.

In February 1951 Secretary Marshall directed the JCS to proceed with arrangements for the meeting. But the chiefs were resolved to limit the scope of the discussions and not permit them to deal with "matters of strategy affecting U.S. global policies and plans." Instead of sending CINCFE, who was preoccupied with Korean operations, the JCS directed CINCPAC to designate an officer from his command to take part in the conference. This officer was to be assisted by General Brink.

As CINCPAC this was my first direct contact with the problems of Indochina—the first of a long series, I might add. I believed it would be best if I attended this conference and tried through Admiral Sherman to get the JCS to change their minds, without success. I cannot say that their refusal to permit me to represent the United States made any great difference, but it may have. Both the British and the French had reason to think that we were trying to avoid really serious discussions, which was true.

General de Lattre, Gen. John Harding, Commander British Forces in the Far East, and Admiral Struble, Commander U.S. Seventh Fleet, were the delegates.

The conference considered the possibility of a Chinese communist invasion of Indochina, including in their report a French estimate of the reinforcements that would be required to defend Tonkin. They made recommendations on certain logistical questions in Indochina; on control of contraband; and on control of shipping in the event the communists were to begin operations by sea.

The important recommendations of the Singapore conference were not immediately effected; instead, they provided subjects for military and political negotiations between the three governments for the rest of the year. For the most part the British and French were anxious to have the recommendations of the report carried out. The JCS, however, were averse to American participation in further military conversations on the defense of Indochina, including periodic conferences on intelligence and logistics problems recommended in the report. They feared that the British and French might try to erect out of such collaborative sessions a new combined chiefs of staff, or an overall three-power command for Southeast Asia. They wished to keep their hands free so that a new global war might not find them encumbered by preestablished combined commands (other than NATO, in which the contribution expected of the European allies justified its establishment). But Allied disagreements over the recommendations of the Singapore report, as well as changing circumstances, obliged the JCS to participate in a new three-power military conference in January 1952.

Even before the Singapore conference had met, and while the JCS were arguing against it, two meetings were held in Washington between American and French officials. The first and more important one took place in January 1951, when Prime Minister René Pleven visited the United States for talks with President Truman. They agreed that, although it was necessary to resist aggression in the Far East, nevertheless the United States and France should not overcommit themselves militarily there, thus endangering the situation in Europe. They also agreed that "interested nations" should maintain continuous contact on the problems of the area, but President Truman declined to establish a British-French-U.S. body to coordinate Far Eastern policies, expressing the U.S. preference for existing mechanisms.

The Prime Minister assured President Truman that France would continue to resist communist aggression in Indochina. Mr. Truman thereupon promised to expedite deliveries of increased quantities of materiel under the aid program. But the French wanted more than this. For the National Armies [of Cambodia, Laos, Tonkin, Cochin China, Annam—the Associated States], they said, 58 billion francs (approximately $166 million) would be required [for development, training, and maintenance], of which the combined budgets of France and Vietnam could supply only 33 billion (approximately $97 million). They therefore made a formal request for the United States to furnish additional aid of $70 million to make up the deficit. President Truman "held out no hope" for the provision of such assistance. As Secretary Acheson informed the NSC later, it is not possible for the United States to become directly involved in local budgetary deficits of other countries. But the Secretary initiated detailed studies concerning this matter, in the hope of devising another method to assure the necessary funds for development of the National Armies. After all, the United States was insisting that these armies be developed as rapidly as possible, and we were already furnishing France with Marshall Plan aid.

The threat of a Chinese invasion of Tonkin, which colored every assessment of the Indochina situation, was also discussed by the President and the Prime Minister. In accordance with JCS advice, the French were informed that in the event an invasion forced the French to retire from Tonkin, the United States would not commit ground troops but would assist in the evacuation of French forces if possible. The JCS had been working on this problem for weeks. On 26 December 1950, General Juin had written to Secretary Marshall saying that if the Chinese came in the French would have to pull out of Indochina. A national intelligence estimate issued a few days later opined that even a relatively small force of Chinese, combined with the Vietminh, could drive the French from the delta in a short time. The JCS therefore, in mid-January 1951, directed me as CINCPAC to plan for U.S. naval and air assistance in case the French requested aid in evacuating their forces from Tonkin under communist pressure. These preparations were not to be disclosed to the French; but, after the Truman-Pleven discussions, and after I had protested the inadvisability of planning without consulting the French, General Bradley recommended to Secretary Marshall that I coordinate my plan with General de Lattre. On 28 March 1951 the JCS authorized me to consult with the French commander.

The most important result of the conversations between the President and the

Prime Minister was a better understanding by each of the other's attitude toward Indochina. President Truman hewed to the line of established American policy. Monsieur Pleven succeeded in planting one new seed in the minds of American officials: France would require direct budgetary support to carry out plans for the National Armies of Vietnam.

Of significance for the development of American policy toward Indochina was the visit of General de Lattre to Washington in September 1951. It was in the preparations made by the JCS for his visit, rather than in the conversations themselves, that its greatest importance lay.

In considering the stance they would take in discussions with the French commander, the chiefs concluded that current U.S. policy had been outmoded by events. They recommended to the Secretary of Defense that a policy revision be made by the NSC.

The considerations that prompted this recommendation were not explicitly stated by the JCS, but in an advance paper adopted for the coming talks one item read: "It would be in the U.S. security interests to take military action short of the actual employment of ground forces in Indochina to prevent the fall of that country to communism." This was a modification of the established policy that no U.S. armed forces would be committed in Indochina other than air and naval forces required to aid in evacuation of Tonkin by the French. It was followed by another important point: "If the Chinese Communist Government intervened in Indochina overtly, appropriate action by U.S./U.N. Forces might include the following: (1) A blockade of the China coast by air and naval forces with concurrent military action against selected targets held by Communist China, all without commitment of U.S. ground forces in China or Indochina, and (2) Eventually, the possible participation of Chinese Nationalist forces in the action."

These ideas were not new. For months the JCS had been considering them in connection with the Chinese intervention in Korea. Since July, however, the armistice negotiations had given them increasing importance, for the conclusion of an armistice would release large communist forces that might be directed against Indochina.

The conversations between General de Lattre and Defense Department officials were largely in connection with the aid program for Indochina. A great deal of time was spent explaining to the General and his aides the limitations imposed by congressional appropriations, under which MDAP operated. Various procedures for administering the program were also agreed upon.

General de Lattre held that the conflicts in Korea and Indochina were actually one war and should be fought as such. The implications of his theory were that there should be a single command for both and a single logistical organization under which requirements of the Indochina war would have equal priority with those of the JCS [for Korea]. The JCS told the Secretary of Defense (now

Robert A. Lovett, since 17 September) that while they recognized the two wars as "but two manifestations of the same ideological conflict between the USSR and the Western world . . . it would be wholly unacceptable . . . to attempt, under existing circumstances, to integrate the forces of the Western World engaged in the two wars."

General de Lattre, in a number of public statements given wide coverage in the press, succeeded in dramatizing for the American people the issues of the Indochina war. He painted a somewhat rosy picture, however, proclaiming that the Associated States were independent, that France had abandoned all rights and privileges but retained the risks and burdens of the war, that the governments of the Associated States were gaining popular support, and that popular elections would be held as soon as the military situation permitted. Nevertheless, his statements were not unwelcome to the U.S. government, since they helped to justify, in the public mind, the material sacrifices the government was making in support of the French and Indochinese.

General de Lattre departed from Washington in an atmosphere of mutual respect and understanding. There were feelings of great loss at the news of his death in January 1952.

In late autumn 1951, it was becoming obvious that the British and French governments were not wholly satisfied with U.S. interpretations of results of the Singapore conference. The British and French said they wanted an overall strategy for the defense of Southeast Asia closely coordinated between the three powers by some sort of tripartite organization. They also wanted the United States to be more deeply committed to defense of the area than our policies would allow. The United States held that cooperation should be achieved generally through existing mechanisms and strove to avoid any definite commitment in Southeast Asia that might limit its military flexibility in the event of a global war.

Early in November the British government brought this issue to the surface in an *aide-mémoire* addressed specifically to the problem of the Chinese threat in Southeast Asia. The British sense was that in the event of a Chinese invasion of Southeast Asia substantial reinforcements would be needed for adequate resistance, and these could only come from outside the area. Such reinforcements involve priorities that could only be settled by agreed tripartite policy for the defense of Southeast Asia and the relation of that defense to the global strategic calculus. Britain believed that a meeting of the United Kingdom, United States and French chiefs of staff should be held to formulate such guidance and to recommend courses of action. They considered that the forthcoming meeting of the NATO Military Committee in Rome would afford a convenient opportunity for such a meeting.

The JCS wanted no part of the suggested meeting. "In effect," they wrote the Secretary of Defense, "this proposal . . . re-opens the entire question of . . . a single military organization for the strategic direction of the armed forces of the Western World in a global war." They would not agree to the formation of such an authority "even by implication at this time." They added that the alignment of the Western nations and their contributions in a future conflict were not rigidly fixed and could not be forecast with sufficient accuracy to justify an immediate decision on a future command organization. They therefore declined the invitation but added that they would not object to discussions on economic and political matters affecting Southeast Asia.

In November, when General Bradley attended the NATO meeting in Rome, the British and French strongly urged him to agree to tripartite discussions on the Singapore report. They proposed to hold a conference in Washington early in January. Despite his protest that the JCS thought such a meeting unnecessary, they prevailed upon him to have the matter reconsidered. On 28 December the JCS, having changed their minds, assented to a conference but with the provision that the discussions involve no commitment on their part.

By the end of 1951 other agencies of the U.S. government had joined the JCS in calling for a review of policy toward Indochina. But almost half a year passed before a new statement of policy was formally approved by the President and the NSC. The ideas that prompted the JCS to urge a revision as far back as September appeared in their actions and planning even before the new NSC decision was made and colored their conversations at the Washington conference in January. Although official policy had not changed perceptibly during 1951, a stronger attitude toward the Indochina problem was in the Washington air.

In May 1951 the French and Vietnamese had expressed considerable anxiety over the delay of expected MDAP shipments for the National Armies. The Vietnamese government offered this as the cause of a seven-month delay in its activation schedule. From Saigon the U.S. legation reported that this was indeed a serious situation, since ultimately the solution of the entire Indochinese problem was dependent on accelerating the development of an adequate Vietnamese national army. Expressions of French concern about the slow arrival of MDAP equipment culminated in General de Lattre's complaints during his visit in September.

This dissatisfaction was not without reason. MDAP shipments had been lagging generally behind schedule, and not only those slated for Indochina, but those programmed for other nations as well. In October, Secretary Lovett listed for President Truman the reasons why deliveries had been sluggish during the preceding eight months. All these shortages occurred, it should be noted, almost a year and a half after the Korean War started and nearly a year after a national emergency had been declared.

Efforts were made to correct this situation, and the results were much better in 1952. The French admitted that the supply situation became virtually sound and the services could function normally. But they never wholly stopped complaining about deficiencies in the aid program.

A summary of the Military Aid Program (MAP) for Indochina at the end of 1951 showed that since the beginning of the program 260,045 measurement tons of supplies valued at $163,600,000 had been shipped. A total of $320,100,000 had been programmed, and this figure rose in January 1952 to $460,000,000.

By mid-1951 the economic aid program administered by the United States in Saigon was making itself felt in support of the military effort. Through it, funds were provided for road construction and improvement, medical supplies, and many other items of aid to the armed services. It was also meeting such civilian needs as housing and medical facilities—important to civilian and therefore army morale. In fighting disease and social unrest, the Economic Cooperation Administration program was contributing much to the battle against communism in the Associated States.

While earlier French complaints about MDAP deliveries had some justification, there was little for those described in legation reports at the end of the year. Such actions might well have given American authorities cause to fear that the French would blame a general defeat in Indochina on an alleged failure of U.S. military aid.

Nevertheless, despite the vastly increased rate of MDAP deliveries in the last two months of 1951, the aid program for the year was not entirely successful. Most material was behind schedule. Although the subsequent history of the Indochina war indicates that the resultant delay in activation of some National Army battalions probably did not affect the final outcome, it does leave room for speculation about what greater contribution those battalions might have made in 1952 and 1953 had they received the benefit of the lost months of training. On the whole, however, the United States did fairly well under the circumstances; and in 1951 the men fighting in Korea had first call on American equipment.

☆ ☆ ☆ ☆

The year 1952 saw little progress in the struggle in Indochina. Neither on the political nor on the military front did the French and Vietnamese achieve an important victory. On neither did they suffer an important defeat. At year-end the situation in Vietnam was about what it had been at the time of General de Lattre's death, a little better in some respects, a little worse in others. Although anticommunist forces had been able to hold their own, the free world's prospects of victory in the area were such that, if they did not go forward, they had to slide back.

The death of General de Lattre deprived the French in Indochina of a commander who had great prestige, energy, and experience, combined with the will to fight. His successor, Gen. Raoul Salan, could not fill his shoes. Conservative, overcautious, and defensive-minded, Salan conducted the war with a "barbedwire strategy" reminiscent of World War I. His concept of operations was to

fortify strong points and wait for the enemy to attack them in the hope of inflicting many more casualties on the attackers than his own forces suffered. He had
only enough success during 1952 to keep his strategy from being discredited.
The Vietminh usually held the initiative.

The extent to which political considerations affected the conduct of operations in Indochina at this time could not be determined, but General Salan did
not have a free hand.

Unfortunately, the new French commander had to contend with a general
letdown in morale following General de Lattre's death, for many in Indochina
had regarded de Lattre as the one man who could end the war. General Salan
had to give up Hoa Binh, thereby acknowledging failure of the one strategic
offensive operation undertaken by the French since autumn 1950.[6] He had to
fight in the shadow of what the French were convinced was a growing threat of
Chinese communist intervention. According to a U.S. intelligence estimate, "the
French [were] apprehensive that substantial French victories would bring about
such intervention, with which the French, because of their limited capabilities,
would be unable to cope."

When dry weather appeared at the end of September 1952, General Salan
was in a position to attack and probably defeat the Vietminh regular forces. He
had a substantial numerical superiority (about 26,000) of troops, he had superior equipment, and he knew the strength and disposition of his enemy. He could
have seized the initiative, but he did not. By default, he permitted the Vietminh
to take the offensive. I came to the conclusion that nothing had really gone
wrong, but that either he had lost his nerve and ordered the force to withdraw or
he had been directed to do so. An operation that started out successfully became
a serious defeat for no good military reasons.

General Salan's only success in fall 1952 was to defend the strongly fortified
position of Na San in western Tonkin. Here the Vietminh began a nine-day
attack in November; they then withdrew, having suffered severe casualties.
From the French view this was a successful battle, and I was convinced that the
lesson they learned there led them to try the same idea again at Dien Bien Phu a
year later. The Vietminh, on the other hand, learned a different lesson: not to
attack a fortified position of this kind unless they could interdict with artillery
fire the airfield, through which all supplies and reinforcements had to come. At
Dien Bien Phu they had the artillery they needed, and topographically Dien
Bien Phu was not as good as Na San. The Vietminh could and did occupy high
ground overlooking the whole French fortress, and they successfully and quickly
interdicted the airfield.

The autumn campaign convinced me and many other American officials
that, unless some drastic change was made in the French conduct of the war,
there would be a prolonged stalemate in Indochina during which the French-
Vietnamese situation might well deteriorate seriously. Two solutions were ad-

vanced. The first was to persuade the French to carry out an aggressive campaign aimed at a decisive defeat of Vietminh forces. The second was to persuade them to give their commanders sufficient forces, preferably by raising the number of Vietnamese regular units, so that even a Salan might be enticed from behind his barbed wire to strike a massive blow at the enemy. During 1953 both solutions were tried.

Granting that, by the end of 1952, the military outlook in Indochina was not good, nothing on the political scene was brighter. The government of Bao Dai had no more popular support in December than it had enjoyed in January and seemed to have few prospects for gaining support. Its appeal to the Vietnamese was not strengthened by the appointment in April 1952 of Jean Letourneau as Minister Resident. Letourneau was known to regard the independence of Vietnam as having already been completed and to oppose any major revision of the Elysée Accords. The French seemed determined to cling to their position in Indochina like a drowning man refusing to let go a sack of gold.

In spite of a history of failures the situation in Indochina did not seem hopeless to the U.S. government, although as 1953 approached the word "stalemate" appeared in many reports from Saigon. But in modern war, unlike chess, stalemate is not the end of the game. American planners in 1952 sought to prevent the introduction of a new red queen, Communist China, and concurrently to strengthen friendly forces so that the stalemate could be broken.

In 1952 four important trends developed in U.S. policy. First, Washington was taking its place with Paris and Saigon as a center of political and military strategic planning for the war. Not only was the vital military aid program determined there; it was also the scene of increasingly numerous tripartite and bilateral conferences between American, British, and French officials concerning Southeast Asia. Second, the U.S. was being drawn into closer cooperation on a high military level with the British and French on the problems of the area. The JCS, fearing that this tendency might lead to a combined command or to increased American responsibility in the Indochina conflict, sometimes protested it. Third, the threat of Chinese intervention was beginning to dwarf other factors in the Southeast Asia scene, especially for the French, who were obsessed with this danger. Finally, France itself was beginning to crack under the triple burden of the Indochina war, European rearmament, and the chronic instability of its own government. Although this tendency was by no means ignored in U.S. planning, the rapid destabilization that led to the Geneva settlement was not generally foreseen at this time.

All of these trends were operating, directly or indirectly, on U.S. policy at the time of the tripartite conference in Washington in January 1952. The problem that received the most attention during the discussions was how to deter Chinese aggression in the area, particularly in Indochina.

But the tripartite chiefs of staff could not reach agreement on the form of retaliation against Chinese aggression. It was obvious that their basic differences would have to be resolved before any contemplated warning to China could be issued. The U.S. JCS knew that before any further negotiations could be carried on, the U.S. government required a new, firm policy toward Southeast Asia. Such a policy had been under study by the NSC since late 1951. It was about to surface, so the chiefs had to wait before undertaking further military talks with the British and French.

The initial draft of the new policy toward Southeast Asia was submitted by the NSC in February 1952. Applied to Indochina, it was directed more toward countering a possible invasion by the Chinese than helping the French and Vietnamese to win their struggle in Tonkin. Further, the measures recommended in the event of overt communist aggression were tied either to the framework of the U.N. or to joint action with the British and French.

In their official comments on the draft, the JCS pointed out that in recent conferences the British and French were opposed to even the concept of military action against China other than in an area of aggression. But without military measures directed against China the local defense of Indochina would have, in the chiefs' opinion, no reasonable chance of success. Therefore, unless the NSC could give assurance that at least the British and French would agree to such measures, the new policy should provide for *unilateral action by the United States* to save Southeast Asia. Only on this basis could the JCS make reasonable plans and determine their costs and requirements.

What the chiefs wanted was a political decision by the NSC on whether the United States, to save Southeast Asia from communism, was willing to take military actions that would in effect constitute war against China. If the answer was affirmative, the chiefs could estimate the costs of specific courses and the NSC could make further decisions concerning them. The JCS alerted the NSC that preparations for the contemplated measures in Southeast Asia could be made only at the expense of other programs, such as that for NATO, unless U.S. military production was stepped up and "forces in being" were increased.

Months of discussions and negotiations ensued between the Departments of State and Defense and the NSC. The NSC decided to give more consideration, in the new statement of policy, to what the United States should do for Indochina in the absence of overt Chinese aggression. Finally, in June 1952, President Truman approved a revision of NSC 124 which, as NSC 124/2, included the first comprehensive U.S. policy toward Indochina.

Our government recognized that the primary threat to Southeast Asia was deterioration of the situation in Indochina as a result of weakening on the part of the French and Associated States in their resolve to continue (or as a result of their becoming unable to continue) opposing the Vietminh rebellion. It also recognized that the successful defense of Tonkin was critical to the retention in noncommunist hands of mainland Southeast Asia.

The JCS now had a firm policy on which to base their planning. In August they directed me as CINCPAC to make plans which, in addition to preparing for unilateral action, would develop a U.S. position should an agreement for Allied combined planning be reached. I had already prepared plans for a naval blockade of Communist China, for supporting participation of Chinese Nationalist forces in hostilities, for assisting in evacuation of the Tonkin Delta, and for military action against selected targets held by Communist China. I was now to develop plans under three different assumptions: first, that the Korean conflict was continuing and no Far East Command (FECOM) naval forces would be available to me; second, that conditions in Korea would permit me to have limited naval forces from FECOM; third, that there was an armistice in Korea and FECOM naval forces above minimum requirements could be used. These plans were to be implemented only upon authorization by the JCS.

The original JCS instructions called for "capabilities" plans, based on the forces available in the Pacific and Far Eastern areas, and as such I considered them of limited usefulness. Upon receiving these orders from the JCS and making some preliminary studies, I flew to Washington in September for consultation. I wanted authority to make "requirement" plans, based on what was required for the tasks to be accomplished. The chiefs took the matter under consideration. I submitted more detailed supporting reasons, and finally, in December, I was instructed to make both capabilities and requirements plans.

Policy NSC 124/2 was a great step forward in national planning, and the JCS were almost entirely responsible for its adoption. For almost the first time, military plans could be made covering specific situations, and they were made. As the operating commander responsible for making them and for carrying them out if directed by higher authority, I was, of course, very familiar with them. They were all completed by spring 1953, before I left for Washington to become Chairman of the JCS. As a result of this background of planning, I was better acquainted with the situation in that part of the world than were the other new members of the JCS when I joined them in August 1953.

A few days after promulgation of the new policy, U.S. representatives at a tripartite foreign ministers' conference in London tentatively assented to holding another five-power military meeting on the problem of Chinese aggression in Southeast Asia. Mindful that an earlier committee had failed owing to lack of agreed political assumptions, the working committee of the conference drew up a set of provisional conclusions which, if approved by the governments concerned, would permit the military representatives to produce a useful report. But the JCS found that these "provisional conclusions" expressed chiefly the usual British and French opposition to action against China outside the area of aggression and their desire for a combined command organization. Further, the conclusions did not fit the provisions of NSC 124/2. The chiefs refused to approve such a meeting, recommending instead a tripartite conference of heads of state, or their representatives and chiefs of staff, that could settle political and military disagreements at the same time.

Once again JCS objections to a military meeting without agreed political guidance were overcome. At a Defense-State conference on 16 July, State representatives had argued that a five-power military representatives' conference would serve as a "step toward bringing the other powers to an acceptance of the U.S. concept of the solution to the problems incident to Southeast Asia," and that the terms of reference proposed by the JCS could not be made acceptable to the other four powers. The JCS consented to soften their position and agreed to more general terms of reference. The conferees were to assume that the five powers had jointly decided to take action against China in the event of its further aggression and that a joint warning had been issued to Peking. From a military point of view they were to determine the available collective military capabilities and recommend military courses of action to make the Chinese cease their aggression.

On 6 October 1952, their governments having agreed to the terms of reference, the military representatives of the U.K., France, Australia, and New Zealand met with the U.S. delegation in Washington. Their report contained overall conclusions that conformed generally with JCS positions of long standing. The representatives agreed that:

> Air, ground and naval action limited only to the areas of aggression and contiguous areas of China offers little prospect of causing Communist China to cease its aggression.
>
> The imposition of a total sea blockade, in conjunction with . . . [such action] . . . might have a significant cumulative effect. This course of action offers little assurance of forcing the Chinese Communists to cease aggression.
>
> A combination of all coercive measures including the defense of the areas of aggression, interdiction of the lines of communication, a full sea blockade and air attacks on all suitable targets of military significance in China, insofar as they are within the allied capabilities, plus such reinforcements in time and scale as may be practicable in the immediate area, offers the best prospect of causing Communist China to cease aggression.

General Bradley opined in a separate report to the JCS that the conclusions represented a step forward from positions established in the earlier meetings; but it was apparent from the discussions, he noted, that the agreement was forced by the terms of reference. When the representatives attempted to settle on a strategy against China that could be undertaken with forces available, the British and French displayed the same interests, attitudes, and fears as in February. Without agreements reached at a high political level, or unless there was a decided change in U.S. policy, further five-power military talks on Southeast Asia would serve no useful purpose.

The JCS concurred on the latter point. But they were encouraged by the conference report. They recommended to the Secretary of Defense that NSC 124/2 be amended to provide for securing assent "under the auspices of the U.N. or in conjunction with France and the U.K. and any other friendly governments" to undertake the "combination of all coercive action" set forth in the report as offering the best prospect of stopping Chinese aggression. They also recommended that the report be used as a basis for securing international agreement on those actions.

The conference report expressed the long-standing desire of the British and French for some sort of staff agency to coordinate the planning of the five powers in Southeast Asia. Insofar as U.S. participation was concerned, CINCPAC could fulfill the U.S. obligation to cooperate in the area. Since this was the position of the JCS, they let the issue rest until French and State Department pressure revived it.

Early in December 1952 the French government, through diplomatic channels, urged the United States to participate in a liaison group drawn from the staffs of the British, French, and U.S. commanders in Southeast Asia. The French had adopted JCS views so far as to project purely liaison, rather than planning or operating, functions for the group. In passing on the French proposal to the JCS, State expressed the view that "it would be advantageous to increase the effectiveness of military liaison arrangements among the countries which have military interests or commitments in Southeast Asia."

The JCS agreed to a liaison in Southeast Asia subject to three conditions. First, it should permit participation "on an on-call and need-to-know basis," not only by each of the five powers but by Southeast Asian countries if this later appeared desirable. Second, it should allow representatives of any participating nation to communicate with representatives of one or more other nations in person or through liaison officers. Finally, it should not result in the establishment of any formal body or committee; therefore, there would be no need for regular meetings or for a permanent chair.

In February 1953 the JCS instructed that CINCPAC invite the principal local military commanders of the other four powers to send representatives to a discussion meeting of liaison arrangements, including machinery for coordinating national plans. This directive led to a five-power military representatives' conference at Pearl Harbor in April.

In pursuing the objectives of NSC 124/2 our government by the end of 1952 was becoming more and more involved in the Southeast Asian struggle against communism. It contrived to keep responsibility for the war in the hands of the French, it refused to be drawn into a combined military command in Southeast Asia, and, while it sidestepped any commitment to participate in a defense of Indochina, it directed that CINCPAC prepare plans for U.S. military action in support of the French.[7] American representatives backed the French position on

Indochina in the U.N. and in international conferences. They assured the French of continued American support of and appreciation for France's efforts in the war. The Truman administration was expanding the military aid program for Indochina and publicizing its contribution to the war. Therefore, when President Eisenhower entered the White House, a considerable part of American prestige rested upon French success in Indochina.

At least one provision of NSC 124/2 was slighted during 1952. That was the obligation to educate the American people concerning the importance of Southeast Asia to U.S. security, in order to prepare them for the courses of action contemplated by this new national policy directive. Government officials seized upon various occasions, such as international conferences, to make statements on the subject but these were few in number. From a recent analysis by the *New York Times* and other news media, it is apparent that no concerted effort was made to arouse public opinion. In an election year, with the unpopular Korean War much at issue, the administration may have feared to present to the public the prospect of another armed action. Nevertheless, this failure was important for the future. In August 1953 [when Admiral Radford became chairman of the JCS], officials of State and Defense estimated that there was no indication that public opinion would support a contribution to the Indochina war other than the current aid program. American military participation, they said, would not be acceptable to the public.

Throughout 1952 France's allies, including the United States, were disturbed by symptoms of weakening in her determination to carry on the war. These symptoms appeared not only in expressions of public opinion but in parliamentary debates and even in statements by government officials. Secretary Acheson's account (in his book, pp. 676–677) of his final tripartite foreign ministers' meeting in Paris, just before the end of the Truman administration, observes:

> In mid-December (1952) [we] noted the rising uneasiness in France about Indochina and a large gap in our government's information about the situation there and about French military plans and . . . recognized as no longer valid an earlier French intention to so weaken the enemy before reducing French forces in Indochina that indigenous forces could handle the situation. It seemed clear to our observers that Vietnamese forces alone could not even maintain the existing stalemate. At the council (meeting) [Foreign Minister Robert Schuman] pleaded for relief from France's "solitude" in Indochina and for "volunteers" to share the burden. He did not ask for "troops" but for financial help (we were already carrying forty percent of it) and for recognition of the equal importance of the struggles in Indochina and Korea . . .
>
> After the council had adjourned . . . Schuman asked Eden and me to come to the Quai d'Orsay . . . three hours before my scheduled departure for Washington. Letourneau spoke for an hour of imminent enemy offensives in Laos and Vietnam and of the need to raise more troops, and for aid; he began to outline plans

... Tired, hungry, and exasperated, I ran out of patience. I asked Schuman for permission to make a brief statement and leave for my plane. We (I said) would be glad to send a working party to Paris after Christmas to get from the French full and detailed information about all aspects of the situation in Indochina. We ·were thoroughly dissatisfied with the information we had been given. This had to be remedied. We must know exactly what the situation was and what we were doing if, as, and when we were to take any further step.

Letourneau and Schuman agreed and suggested that the group go to Saigon where the information was. I said it would go where Letourneau was; if he wanted to work with it in Saigon, that was satisfactory, but we would not struggle any longer to extract information from inferior officials who never seemed to have the authority to give it. He wanted aid; we wanted information. The next move was up to him.

Although the U.S. MAP for Indochina in 1952 left something to be desired, by the end of that year we had given the French equipment for ground, naval, and air forces far superior to that in the hands of the Vietminh. Despite shortages of planes and spare parts, which hampered air operations, it would be difficult to support a contention that French forces would have done much better had those shortages not existed. Wedded to his barbed-wire entanglements, General Salan used his air force too often defensively. More French aircraft would have meant more Vietminh casualties at Na San and the Black River, but it is doubtful that the French could have broken the communist forces in a defensive operation. What seemed most needed in Indochina, and what the United States could not offer under our MDAP, was guts. This is not to say that the French were cowards on the battlefield. On the contrary, their officers and men conducted themselves bravely in action. They were not so brave at the planning board—partly, perhaps, because they felt they were not being supported at home.

Throughout 1952, U.S. equipment supplied under MDAP passed in a steady stream over the docks of Saigon and Haiphong. These deliveries brought the total of end items shipped to Indochina between June 1950 and 31 December 1952 to 539,847 measurement tons with a value of $334,700,000. By the end of 1952, the total value of MDAP materiel programmed under the budgets for fiscal years 1950–1953 had risen to $775,700,000. Obviously, the U.S. contribution to the Indochina struggle was not a small one.

In addition to MDAP, a program for direct support of the French military budget was undertaken by the United States early in 1952. In autumn 1951 the French had announced that their financial difficulties would entail a cut in dollar imports, with resultant injury to their defense program and heavy industry. The United States decided to support the French budget to the extent of $200 million by letting contracts in France, chiefly for end items to be used in Indochina. By 31 December 1952, $127,100,000 worth of this aid had been programmed and $47,100,000 delivered. In July 1952 the United States agreed to support the French budget for fiscal 1953 to the extent of $525,000,000, over half of which was to come from MAP funds.

American participation in training the National Armies was not much discussed in 1952, but for the first time it was considered seriously. In April the service secretaries recommended to Secretary Lovett a program "whereby an expanded MAAG would undertake the training and equipping of a national army capable at least of preserving internal security." Not long thereafter an offer of assistance in training was made, but the French, always skittish over what they might regard as undue American interference, did not take up this offer.

Early in 1952, the British had begun to regard the French internal situation as serious in its possible effects on Southeast Asia. In March the British Embassy in Washington sent an unofficial *aide-mémoire* to the State Department calling attention to recent statements of M. Letourneau, who had said, in reply to a question whether the French were prepared to enter into discussions with the Vietminh, that France could not on principle reject any opportunity to end hostilities. He also indicated that France would not reinforce her troops in Indochina. This followed a statement by Foreign Minister Schuman that France "would not refuse an accord which would put an end to the conflict under conditions which would be honorable for France." The British also felt that French representatives had been in contact with the Vietminh and indeed might be seeking Russian mediation. The JCS were advised by their intelligence committee that, while there was a possibility of an eventual French withdrawal, the British estimate that it might be imminent was exaggerated.

The British predictions were not borne out, but it is difficult to escape the conclusion that the U.S. government in late 1952 and 1953 overestimated the strength of French determination. American officials, while not ignoring the warning signals, seem to have comforted themselves with France's repeated assurances that she would not give up the struggle. They realized, of course, that if the situation in Indochina failed to improve, the French will and ability to resist the Vietminh would eventually weaken. They knew there was a limit to the time the French government would have to win the war before being faced with a collapse on the home front. But as late as June 1953 the belief was expressed that the French would maintain their current troop strength (and by implication their position) in Indochina through mid–1954. And too seldom, during 1952, did U.S. officials, in planning for and supporting the Indochina war, display the sense of urgency that would have been called for had the debacle of early 1954 been foreseen.

25

Stepped-Up Aid to French Indochina

During 1953 the United States took on a large new commitment for financial aid to the French cause. It did so to encourage a program of French military operations that seemed to offer real hope of bringing the Indochina affair to a decisive conclusion. American officials were aware that the present opportunity was probably their last to sustain a positive French effort. The resolute support given by the incumbent French government to its new commander in the field contrasted disturbingly with the steadily declining willingness of the French public to make further sacrifices, and the talk of negotiated settlement that even government leaders had taken up.

At the turn of the year, policy development was virtually suspended. France was without a government, until René Mayer won the endorsement of the National Assembly on 7 January. The United States awaited the inauguration of President Eisenhower and his new administration later in the month.

Dedicated to making a fresh and comprehensive approach to America's problems abroad, the Eisenhower administration nevertheless realized that U.S. aims in Southeast Asia were hardly susceptible of fundamental revision. Reassessment would only highlight anew the national interests and purposes already set forth in the dossier of NSC papers that awaited the incoming officials. Indochina must be defended against Vietminh domination. Unless the United States wished to assume the whole task, its leaders must continue to work with and through the French.

Premier Mayer came to office pledged to lessen the burdens of France in Indochina by seeking greater help from the NATO allies. French spokesmen were intent on wringing every possible advantage from the resolution recently adopted by the NATO Council formally recognizing that French resistance to aggression in Indochina made an essential contribution to the security of the free world and hence deserved "continuing support from the NATO governments." When Secretary of State Dulles arrived in Paris early in February he encountered a request for greater assistance "in order that France may carry out the mission devolving upon her in the common interests of the free world."

For meeting French importunities, the Secretary of State had at hand one telling and legitimate argument. The American people had just installed an administration pledged to government economy; that administration in turn had to deal with a Congress that was even more disposed to reduce expenditures abroad and jettison unproductive programs. Thus, to win authorization for additional U.S. aid, the French requests must in every case be backed by cogent justification and convincing performance in the field.

While the French made much of the heavy losses their entrenched defenders had inflicted on the enemy, April 1953 brought dramatic evidence that the Vietminh still held the initiative. In an entirely new aggression the international repercussions of which nearly carried it to the United Nations, enemy forces invaded Laos. Overrunning the two northeast provinces and surging to within ten miles of the capital, they also posed a threat to Thailand's border. By a major exertion the French command established strong points at the Plaine des Jarres and elsewhere in the path of the invaders. Logistical difficulties and the approach of the rainy season induced the Vietminh to withdraw during May.[1]

Thus the military situation during the first part of 1953 underscored the need for new measures and further effort. As the year began, officials in both Washington and Saigon were considering means of enlarging the forces in Indochina. Since the political conditions that denied any increase in the French manpower contribution seemed unalterable, the troops would have to be Vietnamese. A project for placing 40,000 additional Indochinese under arms received approval from the Franco-Vietnamese Military High Command in February. After training and organization into light battalions, the new forces would free veteran French and Vietnamese army units for an offensive role by replacing them in static defense posts. Americans saw the further advantage that every increase in Vietnamese forces deepened the identification of the native population with resistance to the Vietminh and hastened the time when the National Armies might take over the exclusive defense of their country. Surveys conducted in Washington and by MAAG in Saigon indicated that the United States could readily find MDAP resources to provide arms, ammunition, and other equipment for the additional battalions.

The JCS endorsed this augmentation of the Vietnamese army as an indispensable first step meriting American support, but they listed other necessary measures as well. Defense officials generally were on guard against any French disposition to view the marshaling of more forces as the sole requirement to end the war. They emphasized that plans for the aggressive use of the new battalions must form part of an integrated program encompassing all military, political, economic, and psychological warfare means. From Saigon, General Trapnell warned that the augmentation would be of little worth unless coupled with re-vitalization of the French training system and a genuine shift from defensive to aggressive attitudes among French military planners and commanders.

Material support by the United States for the augmentation project began during March 1953. If the French took the further steps that appeared neces-sary in American eyes, requests for additional aid could be anticipated. Ameri-can leaders were prepared to consider such requests sympathetically, but they insisted that the French must present a comprehensive plan for terminating the Indochinese hostilities within an acceptable period.

French spokesmen had their opportunity in March, when Premier Mayer and his colleagues arrived at President Eisenhower's invitation to hold consultations in Washington. In preparation for the visit Secretary Dulles had pointedly in-formed French officials of the American attitude. He termed unacceptable a continued stalemate in Indochina. The situation required increased effort under a plan envisioning defeat of enemy forces within something like 24 months. Stressing legislative limitations on U.S. executive action, the Secretary declared that administration spokesmen could forcefully present the need for appropria-tions to Congress only if they were convinced that a sound strategic plan for Indochina existed and would be energetically carried out.

President Eisenhower was no less explicit during his first interview with Pre-mier Mayer. He paid tribute to the valiant French defenders and reiterated American recognition that Indochina was of prime significance in the free world's resistance to aggressive communism, but he demanded a plan. In the following sessions Letourneau undertook to sketch at least the military portion of the French program. A rough cost estimate was submitted in writing, but the Minister offered only an oral presentation of the strategic outline.

The Letourneau Plan relied primarily on an expansion of the Vietnamese National Armies during 1954 and 1955 that would add some 80,000 troops to the 40,000 already scheduled for 1953. The program would raise the Viet-namese ground forces to at least 250,000 in 1955, exclusive of local reserve forces. Concurrently, operations would unfold in successive steps. While the re-cruits were being trained, regular French Union forces would pacify the regions outside the Tonkin Delta, working generally from south to north. Later, the newly formed light battalions would occupy the cleared areas, releasing regular units for a striking force in the delta. The last stage of the plan would see a powerful French Union Army engaging and destroying the Vietminh battle corps, compressed by the previous operations into northern Tonkin. This final drive might take place in spring 1955.

The accompanying cost data displayed important gaps, but M. Letourneau's figures indicated that American aid was expected to provide equipment for the expanding Vietnamese armies. In addition, for 1954 and 1955 the fiscal account contained expenditures totaling more than $500 million not covered by the French or Associated States budgets. The French voiced no formal request that the United States assume these deficits, but their intention was clear.

At his final session with Premier Mayer on 28 March the President did not make clear the disappointment with which American authorities viewed the Letourneau Plan, owing particularly to the slowness of its timetable. But he emphasized that the United States remained eager to help; its officials would give the plan thorough study. Premier Mayer suggested that consultations between military technicians would be helpful in establishing more precisely the material requirements, and he invited the dispatch of a U.S. military mission to Saigon for this purpose.

In their appraisal for Secretary Wilson, the JCS displayed marked reluctance to accept the Letourneau Plan as the best that could be hoped for. While they termed it "workable," they considered it wholly lacking in aggressive spirit. Clearing rear areas before concentrating for decisive blows against the main Vietminh forces and supply lines in the north seemed rather like trying to mop up water without turning off the faucet. Pressures against enemy communications with China would be more useful than chasing guerrillas into the hills in central Annam. Further, the extensive French reliance on operations by units of battalion size precluded the type of coordination and concentration of power that American military authorities wished to see.[2] Finally, the Letourneau Plan did not appear to match the expansion of the Vietnamese army with equal emphasis on the training of native military leaders and the prompt transfer of responsibility to their hands.

The JCS concluded that the enlistment of larger Vietnamese forces was vital to this or any other plan to terminate Indochinese hostilities, and they certified the troop augmentation phase of the program as deserving of U.S. material support. But they did not relax their demand for substantial improvement in the French strategic plan. They recommended that political pressure be placed on the French to obtain clear-cut commitments to modernize training methods, expedite the transfer of responsibility to qualified native military leaders, and seize the initiative and act out the plan with determined vigor.

Negotiations with the French by Secretary Dulles and other authorities followed the spirit of the JCS recommendations. Mr. Dulles reemphasized the difficulties faced by administration leaders and clearly implied that they despaired of making an effective appeal to Congress on the basis of the Letourneau Plan. A French overall plan that the JCS could endorse would brighten the prospect of gaining a sizeable appropriation. It was up to the French. "You help us to help you" was the Secretary's charge.

Soon thereafter came the appointment of a new Commander-in-Chief for Indochina, Lt. Gen. Henri Navarre. Although the French pictured General Salan's relief as a routine reassignment, it had decidedly favorable import for the U.S. desire to see the Letourneau Plan recast as a more aggressive concept. General Navarre arrived in Saigon in May exuding a spirit of vigor and determination reminiscent of Marshall de Lattre.

Encouraged, Defense officials readied the U.S. military mission to Indochina suggested by Premier Mayer. Head of the mission was Lt. Gen. John "Iron Mike" O'Daniel, Commander-in-Chief, U.S. Army Pacific, named by the JCS on my recommendation. General O'Daniel was a subordinate in the Pacific command in whom I had great confidence.

The terms of reference given General O'Daniel set the task of his small joint group at considerably more than the mere gathering of information. They were expected to influence General Navarre and his staff to revise the Letourneau Plan along more aggressive lines and with accompanying measures that would silence JCS criticism. Its own efforts would largely control the mission's final estimate of French plans for winning the war and the justification for further American aid.

The O'Daniel mission gave every appearance of success. Following intensive inspections, surveys, and discussions in Indochina from 20 June through 10 July, the group repaired to Hawaii to write its report. Already transmitted to Washington was the prime result of the visit, the Navarre Plan, almost a conscious point-by-point disposal of the previous objections of U.S. military authorities that called for an immediate shift to the offensive. It listed a series of local operations and increasing guerrilla warfare for the remainder of the rainy season. Then General Navarre schemed to anticipate and disrupt the Vietminh autumn campaign by loosing an offensive of his own in Tonkin as early as 15 September. During the remainder of the fighting season [before the monsoon] he intended to operate aggressively, attacking the flanks and rear of the enemy and drawing support from units in areas not directly involved in battle. The high command would also progressively incorporate battalions into regiments and regiments into divisions, creating new supporting units as needed. General Navarre pledged to continue the development of native armies and the transfer to their leaders of responsibility for the conduct of operations.

General O'Daniel hailed the new plan as a design that would accomplish the decisive defeat of the Vietminh by 1955. A still more favorable outlook would result if General Navarre succeeded in his July quest for additional French forces.

General Navarre's personal qualities and the air of confidence and energy that appeared to surround the new high command impressed General O'Daniel. Subsidiary agreements providing for additional U.S. intelligence activity in Indochina, timely sharing of French operational plans with MAAG, and modest American participation in improvement of the French training system only deepened the impression of willing cooperation and receptiveness to advice. As evidence of French sincerity, O'Daniel noted that Navarre and other high officers had invited him to return in a few months "to witness the progress we will have made"; O'Daniel recommended that a follow-up mission under his leadership be scheduled.

General Navarre's plan inspired confidence and conviction in Paris as well, inducing the home authorities to adopt it as official policy. The recently invested government of Premier Joseph Laniel committed itself to enlarged effort and active pursuit of victory in Indochina. Even more extraordinary, it backed this commitment with indications of willingness to send nine infantry battalions plus certain supporting units from metropolitan France.

But all depended on increased assistance from the United States. Commanding no more secure base in the National Assembly than its numerous predecessors, the Laniel government could not face the political hazards of such a course without American support of the French budget far exceeding the current arrangements. When Premier Laniel first broached the matter to Washington in July he mentioned a figure in the neighborhood of $400 million. This sum reflected both the heightened cost of the war owing to activation of the Navarre Plan and the fact that the French military budget of political necessity must be reduced. France would commit more men but less money. Before objections could be voiced the Premier sketched the unpalatable alternative: unless the additional funds were forthcoming, the only prospect was for eventual French withdrawal from Indochina, the only unsettled questions being the method and date.

The U.S. government faced a crucial decision. Yet the very statement of the problem dictated the answer. American officials recognized the Laniel government as the first in seven years that seemed prepared to make the exertion necessary to bring victory in Indochina. If that could be achieved, a favorable train of consequences would ensue. Leaving Southeast Asia secure against any but a major communist aggression, the French could turn their full attention to European and domestic problems. Relief from the drain of the Indochina war should restore French financial stability, end the protracted vacillation over joining EDC, and allow France to assume a confident and active role in the councils of the free world coalition.

Against this bright picture American officials placed the somber conclusion that the Laniel regime was almost certainly the last French government from which a positive approach to the Indochinese conflict could be expected. If Premier Laniel's effort failed, the mounting sentiment in France favoring a negotiated peace would surely find expression in the policy of the next cabinet. Any settlement negotiated under such conditions could hardly fail to spell the eventual loss of all Indochina to communism and confront U.S. policymakers with the momentous decision of whether to intervene with force in Southeast Asia.

Costly though it would be, and undeniably entailing risk, full support of the Laniel-Navarre program seemed the only course compatible with U.S. interests.

The NSC on 6 August agreed to recommend such a policy, providing the Department of State, the Foreign Operations Administration, and the JCS would affirm that the French program held promise of success and could be implemented effectively.

Five days later the JCS advised the Secretary of Defense that "if vigorously pursued militarily in Indochina and supported politically in France," the Navarre Plan offered sufficient promise of success to warrant American aid. But the record of French performance suggested caution in accepting declarations of intention at full value. The chiefs urged that American material and financial support be conditioned on demonstrated French adherence to the plan and continued willingness to receive and act upon U.S. military advice.

Following submission of the 11 August recommendations every member of the JCS was relieved except Gen. Nathan Twining (USAF). I assumed duties as Chairman, Gen. Matthew Ridgway became Chief of Staff, USA, and Adm. Robert Carney became CNO.

Before month's end the new JCS acted to head off Secretary Wilson's transmittal to the State Department of the views of their predecessors. It was not merely that they wished to add an observation on the vital need for creating a political situation in Indochina that would provide the natives with incentive to give wholehearted support to the French. Reports from General Trapnell and the service attachés in Saigon regarding the languid pace of implementation of the Navarre Plan had convinced the new military leaders that even the qualified endorsement of the previous JCS group had been too favorable.

Among other things, General Trapnell had reported profound doubt that the French had either the will or the capability to mount the major offensive listed for 15 September. All three attachés concurred that the French appeared to have no plans for a general autumn offensive. These views were confirmed on 1 September, when General Navarre submitted a new timetable that hardly bore out his previous vows to seize the initiative and operate aggressively.

In various U.S. government consultations during the first days of September the JCS voiced their concern over the modest progress and obviously waning enthusiasm of the French command. But the Laniel-Navarre program offered a chance—and a last chance at that—of putting the Indochina war on the right track. It was hoped that the assurance of wholehearted American support would banish General Navarre's hesitation in carrying forward his plan.

On 1 September the French government submitted its formal statement of the Indochina program and the request for U.S. assistance on which it depended. The total figure now stood at $385 million. Reconsidering the matter, the NSC recommended to the President that the United States give additional assistance to France in an amount not exceeding $385 million, on certain conditions. The French government must give assurance of its determination to put the Navarre Plan promptly into effect and pursue it vigorously, without at the same time retreating substantially from its NATO commitments. The French must also agree to provide a full record of aid expenditures and take into account the comments and advice of U.S. military authorities on campaign plans in Indochina. Assurance was demanded that the French would press forward with their political action program for granting independence to the Associated States. The French must regard the $385 million as the final dollar contribution during 1954 and must recognize the right of the United States to terminate its aid upon invalidation of any of the above understandings. Presidential approval followed, and by 29 September a formal agreement incorporating the above points had been worked out between French officials and our Ambassador in Paris.

Even before the Paris agreement, Washington officials had plunged into the exacting series of resurveys, adjustments, and negotiations necessary to produce the pledged assistance. Congress had already adjourned; besides, seeking a supplemental aid program would have introduced worrisome uncertainties and delays. The task was done by executive decision and the reassignment of funds already in hand.

The President's acceptance of the NSC recommendation involved an important change in the orientation of the foreign assistance program from what had been explained and defended before legislative committees during the recent session, and the program would undoubtedly generate further large requests for appropriations. Consultation now might assure future support, and careful explanation might lessen discontent over the apparent discrepancies between congressional intent and the actual purposes to which some of the funds were now assigned. Whereas a large portion of the present grant was earmarked for the payment and rationing of Vietnamese troops, legislative leaders had hitherto insisted that U.S. aid dollars be expended primarily for "shot and shell." Administration spokesmen had also to explain that concern for proper accounting of the funds had led them to channel the additional assistance through the French. Congressional opinion in the past had strongly favored bypassing Paris to award more aid directly to the Associated States.

While these readjustments continued in Washington the October reports of U.S. military observers in Indochina took on a more encouraging tone. True, there were setbacks such as a severe defeat for some of the new native light battalions in the Tonkin delta area; and it was disturbing too to find General Navarre disclaiming any agreement with General O'Daniel to welcome a small U.S. intelligence team in Hanoi.

But in most respects observers reported modest progress. The activation of Vietnamese units was ahead of schedule and elements of the promised French reinforcements had begun to arrive, including one battalion transferred with American assent from Korea. Unhampered by any extensive enemy activity at the opening of the fighting season, General Navarre had launched an excursion in force southward from the delta. While General Trapnell discounted the French claim that they had inflicted serious losses and disrupted enemy plans, he saw signs that an offensive attitude was creeping into the French command.

The JCS had been closely involved in the months-long American endeavor to commit the French to a plan holding reasonable promise of success. But the comments and evaluations they had supplied for this purpose represented only part of their attention to the Indochina problem. Besides making numerous detailed decisions regarding aid programs, their responsibility included planning for contingencies other than the successful conclusion of the war toward which the main American effort was directed.

The five-power conference in Pearl Harbor in April 1953 had recommended a formal and continuous relationship among designated military representatives of the five nations who would coordinate plans for the defense of Southeast Asia. With the approval of the Secretaries of State and Defense, the JCS late in May had authorized American participation and had designated me the American military representative.

At that time I was completing the series of operations plans called for by the JCS directive of December 1952 and was giving close attention to developments in Indochina. The JCS completed their action on the five-power conference report as a result of my urging that the critical situation in Laos following the Vietminh invasion made it imperative to start coordinated Southeast Asia planning. These same grim estimates undoubtedly influenced Admiral Fechteler to express his concern on 5 May regarding the security of all Southeast Asia in the Laotian crisis. He asked for a study of U.S. options to prevent the spread of communist control.

The resulting paper ranged freely over all the possibilities, including U.S. armed intervention. It omitted previous qualifications about using "as much pressure as is feasible" and listed bluntly all the measures the United States might demand of the French to improve their capabilities in Indochina. These included transferring at least two French divisions to the area, expediting the revision and aggressive implementation of present campaign plans, following American suggestions for expanding and modernizing training, and improving the low rate of aircraft utilization by assigning more French air force personnel and hiring civilian flight and maintenance crews. Short of intervention, the United States might also insist on direct participation in both training and operational planning. Anticipating by more than four months the actual developments of that autumn, the JCS paper suggested speeding and increasing the American aid program and issuing a monitory political announcement stressing American interest in Southeast Asia and indicating concern over continued communist moves there.

Complementary to these brusque considerations were plans, taken up by the JCS a few weeks later, for U.S. military action should the French withdraw.

Estimating that the Vietminh alone did not have the military capability of driving the French out, the chiefs recognized two conditions under which withdrawal might take place: intervention by the Chinese might force an evacuation, or political deterioration in France could bring a government decision to abandon the struggle. There were variations in the two situations depending on the timing. The JCS hoped that French withdrawal would not occur until the expansion of native forces had reached an advanced stage, but they could not count on it.

The gravest possibility, intervention in force by China, led to broader considerations. Military opinion generally agreed that even the extension of full U.S. and Allied counteraction to the portion of China contiguous to the Tonkin border would not suffice to halt the aggression. To succeed, the United States must contemplate applying all available coercive measures against the Chinese mainland, including naval blockade and air attacks on targets of military significance.

Preventing the Far Eastern situation from reaching the flash point was a prime objective of American policy. Our government had met continued French and British reluctance to subscribe to a joint declaration advising China that any further acts of aggression would evoke retaliation that might not observe geographic limitations such as those imposed on the Korean action. Both the Franco-American communiqué at the close of Premier Mayer's visit in March and the public declaration of the July conference of British, French, and American foreign ministers had cautioned the Chinese not to use a Korean armistice as an opportunity to regroup forces for some new adventure in Asia. But on 2 September the American Legion convention in St. Louis heard Secretary Dulles deliver a more pointed admonition. After repeating President Eisenhower's statement that "any Armistice in Korea that merely released aggressive armies to attack elsewhere would be a fraud," the Secretary turned to the risk that "as in Korea, Red China might send its own Army into Indochina" and said: "The Chinese Communist regime should realize that such a second aggression could not occur without grave consequences which might not be confined to Indochina. I say this soberly in the interest of peace and in the hope of preventing another aggressor miscalculation."

In issuing this unilateral warning, Mr. Dulles discreetly gave the Chinese only an oblique view of U.S. strategy. Whereas the Secretary suggested that retaliatory action *might* not be limited to Indochina, the JCS had concluded that such action *could* not be so confined.

☆ ☆ ☆ ☆

A turbulent year in the politics of both France and the Associated States opened in January 1953. The election of village councils in the pacified areas of Vietnam marked a first step toward the establishment of democratic institutions.

Participation by 80 percent of the eligible voters indicated a high level of political interest and a clear rejection of the communist call for an election boycott but showed no striking gain in popular support for the Vietnamese government sponsored by the French.

In Cambodia, King Sihanouk dissolved the National Assembly, arrested "obstructionist" delegates, and assumed personal direction of the government. The King then plunged into a year-long course of unpredictable behavior including the filing of numerous demands and protests in Paris, all designed to win Cambodia independence within the French Union equal to that of India in the British Commonwealth.

The French made halting progress toward satisfaction of native demands for freedom and sovereignty. In February the French command and Minister Letourneau entered into agreements with Bao Dai that provided for freer development of the Vietnamese National Armies. In May, the Mayer government gave pledges to the Cambodians regarding transfer of control over the native army, relaxation of economic restrictions, and acknowledgement of the judicial integrity of the local courts.

Any favor these various moves may have gained was sacrificed when the French devalued Indochinese currency on 10 May. To end government scandals and the financial drain resulting from extensive traffic in piastres, devaluation was long overdue; but when officials set the new rate of exchange with only a few hours' notice to the local governments, they disregarded the pledges of prior consultation given in 1949. The event demonstrated how little true sovereignty the French had accorded the Associated States. Native protests were still resounding when the Mayer government fell on 21 May and France entered a protracted cabinet crisis.

Emerging under the leadership of Joseph Laniel, the French government late in June turned a new face toward Indochina. Laniel declared that it was essential to end the present bad relations between France and the Associated States in a spirit of accommodation and understanding. He began a wholesale replacement of the colonial administrators whose long tenure in Indochina had made them symbols of French arrogance and repression. His ouster of M. Letourneau also ended the curious arrangement whereby the French Commissioner General in Saigon also held membership in the Paris Cabinet as minister for relations with the Associated States.

On 3 July the Laniel government invited the three Indochinese states to enter new consultations during which France intended to "perfect" their independence and complete their sovereignty. Since these proposals differed little from numerous others announced by French officials over the years, native leaders approached them skeptically. But Foreign Minister Georges Bidault informed Secretary Dulles that the statements had been made in earnest. France was prepared to accept virtually any terms that native states demanded so long as

Laos, Cambodia, and Vietnam agreed to continued membership in the French Union.

Secretary Dulles frequently referred to the 3 July declaration as having removed all basis for criticism of French policy. He told the U.N. that, since then, "the communist-dominated armies in Indochina have no shadow of a claim to be regarded as champions of an independence movement." This turn in French policy resulted in successful negotiations with the Cambodians concerning the transfer of control over fiscal matters and the police, army, and judiciary. Negotiations with Laos culminated in October in a treaty of friendship and association that recognized Laos as a "fully independent and sovereign state" while reaffirming its membership in the French Union.

In the state of Vietnam, however, political disorders set aside any immediate hope of orderly progress.

Bao Dai summoned a national congress to define and endorse moderate terms for Vietnamese negotiators in Paris. But when it met on 12 October, the congress displayed its uncompromising character. Its members demanded that France annul the 1949 agreements and grant complete independence forthwith; then negotiations could begin toward a treaty of alliance between equals. Swept on by their nationalistic ardor, the delegates passed a declaration that Vietnam would not participate in the French Union.

The Vietnamese resolutions aroused outrage in Paris. Even spokesmen of the political factions that most actively supported the war now demanded to know what France was fighting for if not the preservation, in some form, of her empire overseas. When seeking larger contributions from Britain and America the government might find it useful to dwell on the role of France in the defense of Southeast Asia against communist domination, but for home consumption this honor was not enough. If France was to be repaid by the very people she sought to defend, her sacrifices in Indochina must end.

No disavowal issued by Chief of State Bao Dai or Premier Nguyen Van Tam could entirely stitch up the damage that had been done to the fabric of French popular and parliamentary support for the war. Large areas of that support had already frayed and given way under the seven-year accumulation of weariness with the apparently endless struggle. While no other party in the (French) National Assembly wished to be identified with the French withdrawal demands chanted by the communist deputies, sentiment for a negotiated settlement in Indochina had grown. An influential portion of the Radical Socialist party had reached the view that a military solution was impossible without an unthinkably large commitment of francs and Frenchmen. Hence political negotiations, during which the bills for past mistakes would have to be paid, seemed the only way out.

To most Frenchmen the case for settlement by negotiation seemed greatly strengthened when on 27 July the U.N. command completed the armistice agreement in Korea. With pardonable exaggeration *Time* reported that a great cry swelled across France: "Finish *la sale guerre* by negotiation ... like the clever Americans in Korea." What was not clear to the French was that the United States had seen to it that the U.N. command was not negotiating from weakness in Korea and that this is exactly what we were trying to persuade them to do in Indochina.

At the end of a debate in which repeated calls for peace by negotiation had aroused few replies favoring continuation of the war, Premier Laniel emphasized that there was no basis for pessimism over the military prospect in Indochina and hence no reason to seek peace merely out of despair. Yet, he said, the government stood constantly ready to undertake negotiations, whether with the Soviet Union, with China, or locally with the Vietminh, on any basis that did not involve abandonment of Vietnam's freedom. "It is true that the war in Indo-China is unpopular," he said. "There is, however, something which is still more unpopular in France ... namely to betray one's friends and to fail in one's duty."

In October the National Assembly endorsed resolutions instructing the government to continue seeking every opportunity for negotiation. The government was also directed to encourage the Associated States to assume a progressively greater share of the military responsibility while completing their independence within the framework of the French Union. Finally, the resolutions called for a more equitable division of the burdens of the Indochina war among the free nations. This may have been included more out of habit than conviction. A new attitude toward foreign assistance was apparent. Whereas in the past American contributions had been welcomed as lifting some of the burdens of French taxpayers, now there were expressions of fear that the acceptance of more aid only committed France to continuing the war indefinitely. When the $385-million grant was announced late in September, *Le Monde* reviewed the prospect in an article entitled "Should We Take the Money?"

The French continued their flat rejection of any recourse to the U.N. Secretary Dulles had urged France to bring the Laotian invasion before the Security Council, thus giving the Indochinese conflict an international standing that would make it more readily subject to negotiation and settlement between the Western powers and the Soviet Union. Refusing to take the action themselves, French authorities were emphatic almost to the point of hysteria in opposing a similar move by Thailand. They appeared to fear that U.N. debate could not be confined to Indochina and might quickly extend to other areas of French colonial administration, particularly in North Africa. Pride in the French military tradition made equally abhorrent any internationalization of the war on the Korean pattern that would transfer control to a U.N. command.

But in another respect the French government saw an intimate connection between the Indochina war and the U.N. action in Korea. As agreement on a Korean armistice drew near, American authorities heard increasing insistence from Foreign Minister Bidault that the political conference scheduled to follow the truce must extend its attention to Indochina. The French people, said Bidault, would be profoundly disturbed by any suggestion that their Western allies regarded a diplomatic solution as proper for Korea but inadmissible for Indochina. The Korean conference must be seized as an opportunity for broader discussions aimed at achieving a general Far Eastern settlement. If [for procedural reasons] this conference under U.N. auspices could not properly add to its agenda a matter that France had always refused to submit to the U.N., then the French would still demand that settlement of the Indochina war be discussed with the Chinese representatives outside the formal sessions.

Adhering at first to a strict interpretation of the purpose of the Korean conference, Secretary Dulles relented in response to the ceaseless agitation of the French. If the negotiations over Korea developed a favorable atmosphere, the conference, with a somewhat different slate of participants, might move on to consideration of Indochina. The Secretary declared in his September American Legion address that the United States wanted peace in Indochina as well as in Korea.

Returning to the question of negotiations, in late October Premier Laniel announced that the French government did not consider that the Indochinese problem necessarily required a military solution. "No more than the United States does France make war for the sake of war," he said. "Like the United States in Korea, [France] would be happy to welcome a diplomatic solution of the conflict."

American authorities could only hope that their constant emphasis on the perils of negotiating from weakness was registering on French minds. If so, the United States might still hope to see a vigorous implementation of the Navarre Plan that would strengthen the French bargaining position.

In January 1953 the French stated that no ground unit had failed to meet its activation date for lack of MDAP equipment. During 1953 the United States enlarged its deliveries of arms, ammunition, and equipment to the French and native forces in Indochina, on a first-priority basis. American aid worked a transformation of the French air force in Indochina from a conglomerate assortment of German, French, and American aircraft into a reasonably standardized organization with modern propeller-driven types.

The general schedule of MDAP equipment deliveries moved forward with relative tranquillity. It was the special requests and accelerated procurements generated by the vicissitudes of war and the recurring inspirations of French military planners in Indochina that demanded unusual exertion and adjustment by American officials.

The Laos emergency provided exasperating evidence of the inability of French air force leaders to assess realistically their capabilities. When French sources released publicity to the effect that all would turn out all right if only the United States would deliver an armada of transport planes to the eagerly waiting French pilots in Indochina, General Trapnell's indignation exploded in a long dispatch to his Washington superiors. Time and again the MAAG Chief had counseled French authorities that the supply and maintenance facilities on which their operations depended were inadequate to support even the aircraft already on hand.

The French Air Ministry had set a limit of 10,000 on personnel assigned to Indochina, including 2,500 guards as well as ordinary laborers. The technicians had been able to maintain the existing planes at an average monthly utilization rate of approximately 40 hours, less than half of U.S. Air Force standards. A desperation effort during the Laos emergency had yielded a higher figure, but only at the cost of virtual abandonment of maintenance and overhaul at echelons above the tactical level. To talk of accommodating more aircraft with these same personnel and facilities was pure fantasy. Yet General Trapnell seemed unable to shake the stolidity of French officials. In the same interview they would acknowledge the critical shortage of skilled mechanics and deplore the arbitrary ceiling imposed by the home authorities but enter an urgent request for more aircraft.

Behind the flight lines there were other French air force deficiencies that even a major increase in personnel would not cure. The French supply system suffered from faulty organization, poor location of facilities, lack of periodic inspections, and absence of modern stock control records and procedures for effective planning. The small Air Force section of the MAAG in Saigon had done what it could to remedy these shortcomings and instill an aggressive attitude toward the correction of malpractices. In July 1953 the effort was reinforced by the arrival on six months' temporary duty of 55 USAF specialists in supply, maintenance, armament, and other logistic functions. Assigned to French units down to the squadron level, they provided instructions in current American procedures on matters ranging from corrosion control to depot organization.

By August 1953 General Trapnell reported that French air force officials presumed they could make virtually unlimited calls on the bounty of the U.S. now that the Korean armistice had removed their only high-priority competitor. They saw a ready solution to French logistic support and maintenance difficulties, proposing that the United States ship spare parts and other materials in such massive quantities that maldistribution in Indochina would pass unnoticed. Further, perhaps used equipment could simply be returned in exchange for new models. The MAAG chief rejected these proposals as too costly and because they contravened a basic purpose of U.S. aid, to assist recipient countries in learning to sustain their own military establishment.

General Trapnell next reported a French request that 25 C47 aircraft and auxiliary equipment be provided within the next 30 days to permit the activation of a fourth transport squadron. For logistic support, 1,000 unskilled native troops and 650 technicians from France were to be used.

The MAAG chief did not concur in this request, feeling strongly that no new air unit should be activated until qualified personnel were actually assembled to utilize and maintain the planes. But he also recognized that the French desire to have sufficient aircraft to mount operations involving a simultaneous drop of three paratroop battalions was justified; any offensive potential must be encouraged and exploited. He offered three alternative plans, and the one accepted by Washington involved an expansion of the C119 arrangement that the O'Daniel mission had worked out in July.

By October detailed arrangements for applying the scheme had been accepted by French authorities. But before October had passed MAAG was receiving new pleas for aircraft. General Trapnell wearily reissued his previous nonconcurrence, noting the reasons for it.

While dealing with French requests for aircraft seemed an endless labor, American officials found time for other aid considerations. Improvement and acceleration of the training given by the French to Vietnamese forces was an objective constantly held in mind by U.S. authorities. Experience qualified the Americans to give advice in this field, but no real opportunity to influence the French training system presented itself.

Earlier in the year the Defense Department had recommended against direct U.S. participation in the Vietnamese training program in the foreseeable future. Repeating General Trapnell's prediction that the French would vehemently oppose any such suggestion, the committee also stressed the language problem that American instructors would encounter. The JCS concurred in March, noting that an exchange of missions between Indochina and Korea was scheduled that should make French officers familiar with the methods used by the United States in training ROK forces.

The results of this exchange were disappointing. French observers returned from Korea with little but a list of reasons why U.S. training procedures could *not* be effectively applied in Indochina. General Trapnell labeled these findings "completely fallacious" and asserted that French authorities had simply fabricated an argument "to justify resistance to any change or modernization of traditional French methods."

The unfavorable report from Indochina led Secretaries Dulles and Wilson to reopen the subject during their visit to Paris in April. Getting the French to observe and adopt the instructional methods so successfully applied in Korea had been one of Mr. Dulles' leading objectives from the moment he assumed office. Maintaining a friendly tone, he said it did not come as a surprise that the initial French reaction had been negative, for the Americans themselves had been slow to realize the capabilities of the South Koreans. Secretary Wilson supported his colleague by pointing to the new faith, confidence, and unity that had flowered in the ROK army when natives were given training and responsibility.

The French response was not encouraging. M. Letourneau spoke of the Korean visits as "very useful," but he dwelt on the standing French assertion that Indochina and Korea presented different problems and conditions.

Committed to supporting the Navarre Plan, American officials and agencies faced a period of exacting decision and increased activity as the fall campaign opened in 1953. There were still occasional failures, such as the deficiencies in Air Force procurement that elicited protest from General Trapnell as late as October, but in many lines the French were receiving not only more material than they could effectively use but more than they could properly store as well. In September the foremost French request was not for more direct material aid but for $385 million in cash.

American officials anticipated that General Navarre's operations would generate further urgent demands for costly equipment. But they did not foresee the Dien Bien Phu emergency, which drove American agencies to extreme exertion and almost doubled the cost of American support of the French.

26

Problems with the French High Command

With the opening of the 1953–1954 fighting season, French Union Forces in Indochina under the command of General Navarre tried to seize the initiative from the Vietminh. Concurrently, the French were employing all available military and diplomatic channels to seek increased American material support. Washington, aware that time was running out, was occupied with satisfying French needs, but also devoted attention to the problem of redrafting American policy toward Southeast Asia.

The provision of material aid for 1953–1954 had been conditioned by the Eisenhower administration on three requirements placed on the French: perfection of the political and economic independence of the Associated States; adoption of a plan for dynamic military action; and expansion and training of indigenous armies.

To determine how well the French were living up to the military conditions, the JCS had directed General O'Daniel and a small joint mission to return to Indochina and check on the findings and recommendations made in his report the past July.

Basically optimistic in tone, General O'Daniel's November 1953 report announced "clear indications of real military progress by French Union Forces since our previous visit to Indochina." If General Navarre had not completely succeeded in wresting the initiative from the Vietminh, he had at least kept the enemy off balance and had established a far better military situation than had existed in 1952–1953. But there were some dark spots. The French continued to be overcautious in the conduct of the war and less than effective in using available means. Progress in training native units remained unsatisfactory. Insufficient naval materiel and inadequate maintenance and logistic support for air units in Indochina were other noted deficiencies.

General O'Daniel concluded that the United States should support General Navarre, yet his recommendations for American action to remedy deficiencies were limited to measures that the French would be willing to accept. They fell short of introducing large-scale American influence in planning operations and the training of Vietnamese forces.

Not all views of the Indochina situation were as sanguine as General O'Daniel's. Commenting on the report, Admiral Stump (CINCPAC) concurred that considerable military progress had been made, but he pointed out additional flaws. Political and psychological factors remained intertwined with purely military aspects of the problem. Little had been done to turn these vital factors to the advantage of the West; therefore it was important that the highest levels of the French and U.S. governments reaffirm their intention of prosecuting the war to a satisfactory conclusion. Admiral Stump also stated that victory was unlikely until there were sufficient native troops to garrison captured areas and until the Indochinese had been won over by French concessions and anticommunist psychological warfare.

Following General O'Daniel's visit the French command took action underscoring Admiral Stump's more reserved optimism. In a move reminiscent of the defensive concepts of previous years, that had not even been mentioned to General O'Daniel during his visit, French Union Forces on 20 November launched operation Castor to seize the Dien Bien Phu basin in mountainous western Tonkin, near the Laotian border.[1] The objective was to consolidate a strong position from which to interdict Vietminh supply routes into Laos, and selection of the site was dictated by the need for an airstrip. Happily, the Japanese had established a pierced-steel planked runway at Dien Bien Phu during World War II. Since the requirements for air support received first consideration, the needs of other arms for good defensive positions were secondary.

Dropping by parachute, the first waves of French troops easily overcame the surprised Vietminh garrison. But repair of the runway was delayed when a heavy bulldozer broke from its parachute and crashed. Succeeding waves of troops had to drop rather than land. A substitute bulldozer was located, and the French began the work of organizing a strong defensive fortress to be manned by 12 battalions.

Pointing to the more active operations, the French high command increased its pressure for American material support. High on General Navarre's list were the oft-sought 25 additional C47s. The request had been turned down in Washington in October, but the November visits of General O'Daniel and Vice President Richard Nixon provided General Navarre with a chance to renew his request.

Vice President Nixon apparently saw the question as largely a political matter and carried it to the President, who decided that political advantages outweighed military objections. Secretary Dulles informed Paris of the decision to provide the C47s and I passed the word to Lt. Gen. Jean Valluy, French representative on the NATO Standing Group in Washington.

President Eisenhower and Secretary Dulles soon had an opportunity to discuss Indochina face-to-face with Premier Laniel and Foreign Minister Bidault when the tripartite French, British, American conference convened in Bermuda on 4–8 December. Although the principal topics were European security and the Soviet proposal for a four-power conference in Berlin, the Big Three found time for one session on the Far East.

In preparation for the conference, the JCS directed the Joint Intelligence Committee to evaluate repetitive French reports that the Chinese might support the Vietminh with jet aircraft. The committee found no justification for these French concerns. It reported that U.S. intelligence did not indicate either an increase in Chinese capability or an intent by them to intervene with jets in Indochina. The JCS agreed and so informed the Secretary of Defense. They took no other part in the Indochina phase of the Bermuda discussions.

By the time the conference turned to Far Eastern matters Premier Laniel was indisposed, so the French position was sketched by the Foreign Minister. He briefed President Eisenhower and Prime Minister Churchill on the military situation, acknowledging American aid and emphasizing French Union sacrifices. The French, he said, were making every effort to establish the Associated States as truly independent nations, but were handicapped by the lack of native leaders capable of participating in government.

The most significant of M. Bidault's remarks dealt with the prospects for negotiations. France, he asserted, would make peace only under conditions that would respect the individual liberty of the Indochinese people. But, he thought that a five-power conference, including China, France, Britain, the United States, and the USSR, called in a specific framework for a discussion of Southeast Asia problems, might be acceptable to France, provided the Associated States could be present. Mr. Churchill praised the French efforts. President Eisenhower seconded the Prime Minister's warm praise, but added that the United States viewed a five-power conference "with a jaundiced eye."

The Bermuda conversations did not resolve questions about the provision of additional American aid to Indochina. General Navarre was in a difficult position: he had to produce military success quickly, and he saw that success threatened by material shortages. Instead of sitting down with General Trapnell for a frank discussion, in mid-December General Navarre dispatched a strong letter to MAAG contrasting promise and performance. He stated that the discrepancy between means in personnel and material threatened to necessitate a complete reexamination of his 1954 operational plan. He wanted Washington to speed deliveries of material programmed in earlier years and to inform him when he could expect 1954 items. In addition, he asked for reconsideration of the reductions applied to the 1954 program.

Since the Office of Military Assistance suspected that this complaint was an attempt to establish an alibi in advance for failure to achieve military success, it so informed General Trapnell, who used the information to register a polite but firm protest against delaying operations. End items programmed in earlier years were on the way and, within budgetary limitations, the 1954 program was being met.

General Trapnell's courteous answer to General Navarre opened the door for American consideration of French battle needs on an ad hoc emergency basis. He assured me during our Christmas week conference in Manila that no deficiencies in the U.S. aid program or deliveries would cause any embarrassment or change in French operational plans in the immediate future.

Perhaps one of the concerns contributing to General Navarre's petulance had been a new political crisis in Vietnam. The world learned on 27 November that Ho Chi Minh had informed the Stockholm newspaper *Expressen* of Vietminh willingness to negotiate with France for an armistice. His terms were cessation of hostilities and real respect for the independence of Vietnam. Coincidentally, President Vincent Auriol of France announced on that day a liberal formula by which the Associated States could be independent yet remain members of the French Union. France would move to carry out the 3 July 1953 declaration and to satisfy American pressure for granting Indochina its independence. The Ho interview and Auriol's statement stirred up anew nationalistic feelings in Vietnam. In early December Premier Tam tried to capitalize on nationalistic sentiment by demanding that Bao Dai establish an anticommunist coalition government to negotiate with the Vietminh and work out terms of association with France. Having failed to win popular support, on 17 December Tam handed his government's resignation to the chief of state. While the resignation may have been little more than the normal Indochinese political ritual, it did nothing to improve the situation.

Against this background of slightly more vigorous French military and political action and a Vietnamese domestic crisis, the JCS gave considerable attention to Indochinese affairs in late December 1953 and early January 1954. We had to decide what action to take on General O'Daniel's recommendations. In addition, the NSC Planning Board was rewriting the statement of U.S. policy by the Eisenhower administration, which until then had been guided by NSC 124/2, the last such paper prepared by the Truman administration in 1952.

First on the agenda was a report on General O'Daniel's mission by the Joint Strategic and Logistic Plans Committee, recommending that the report be accepted as the basis for further planning and seconding the General's principal suggestions. The JCS amended the committee's conclusions and recommendations to reflect comments by Admiral Stump. As amended, the report indicated that the French had made limited progress in carrying out the Navarre Plan but that the military situation had not altered significantly in their favor. The chiefs added that a plausible offer from the Vietminh might lead to a parley, especially in the absence of any real French Union military progress. They also inserted a new conclusion: "Primary military requirements for a French Union victory in

Indochina include the development of large and effective indigenous forces and the effective utilization of psychological warfare among the natives."

Meanwhile, the NSC Planning Board was redrafting the 18-month-old statement of U.S. objectives and options in Southeast Asia because in the interim the French situation in Indochina had deteriorated. A major problem was assessing the probable consequences of a French defeat. In June 1952 the NSC had agreed that the loss of Indochina to communism would have critical consequences for the United States and would probably lead to relatively swift communist domination of the whole area. But in November 1953 the intelligence community would go no farther than to say: "A Vietminh victory in Indochina would remove a significant military barrier to a communist sweep throughout Southeast Asia, expose the remainder of that region to greatly increased external communist pressures, and probably increase the capabilities of local communists." The JCS registered a dissenting view: "The establishment of communist control over Indochina by military or other means would almost certainly result in the communization of all of Southeast Asia."

When the NSC Planning Board submitted its redraft in December, the principal change was increased emphasis on dangers present in the Indochinese situation. It pointed out that the loss of Indochina would have the most serious repercussions on U.S. and free world interests in Europe and elsewhere. The loss might lead to loss of the entire area, with grave economic consequences: it might seriously jeopardize U.S. security interests in the Far East, and subject Japan to severe economic and political pressures leading to her eventual accommodation to communism.

Two agents could transform these threats into reality. First was the new, stronger, hostile and aggressive China. The second was France. A successor government might well accept an improvement in the military situation short of Vietminh defeat as the basis for serious negotiation. If the Laniel-Navarre Plan should fail, or appear doomed to failure, the French might seek to negotiate for the best possible terms whether or not these offered any assurance of preserving Indochina for the free world.

The general U.S. objective, according to the NSC redraft, was "to prevent the countries of Southeast Asia from passing into the communist orbit; to persuade them that their best interests lie in greater cooperation and stronger affiliations with the rest of the free world; and to assist them to the will and ability to resist communism from within and without and to contribute to the strengthening of the free world."

Generalized courses of action were added. Technical assistance, economic aid, and the encouragement of economic cooperation were to be employed to persuade indigenous governments that their best interests lay in cooperation with the free world. It was also essential that the United States encourage and support the spirit of resistance to Chinese communist aggression in all its forms. But this was only one side of the street. The United States had to make China aware of the grave consequences of aggression. Words were not enough; it was necessary to promote the coordinated defense of Southeast Asia, recognizing that the initiative in regional defense measures must come from the governments of the area. Finally, the American people should be made aware of the importance of the region so that they would support the proposed courses of action.

Options toward the nations of Southeast Asia were grouped under two assumptions—one, that Communist China would not overtly intervene in the war; the other, that she would. Should China remain a silent partner of the Vietminh, the main focus for American action would continue to be the French and the Indochinese. In dealing with them the United States was forced to carry water on both shoulders: building up the independence of Indochina, which could only occur at the short-range expense of France, while inducing the French to fight vigorously for the longer-range interests of the free world.

A series of proposals dealt with the possibility that France might sue for peace. France should be allowed no illusions about obtaining acceptable terms short of achieving a marked improvement in the military situation. It would be equally illusory to consider establishing a coalition Vietnamese government with Ho Chi Minh. Drawing upon our Korean experience, it was recommended that the United States flatly oppose any cease-fire prior to opening negotiations because of the probable result: irretrievable deterioration of the French Union military position.

☆ ☆ ☆ ☆

Meanwhile, the military situation in Indochina had not been improving. On Christmas Day 1953 the Vietminh launched its annual invasion of Laos, compelling the French to divert troops for its defense. In early January General Trapnell gloomily reported that the situation bore a striking similarity to last year's campaign, in which sizeable French Union forces were widely dispersed and in defensive attitudes. The French were surprised, moreover, to find that the Vietminh units surrounding Dien Bien Phu were supplied, for the first time, with antiaircraft artillery that could successfully knock down fighter bombers. Only light bombers (B26s) could now be used, and Trapnell warned Washington to expect requests for additional aircraft of this type and for U.S. personnel, both to maintain the C47s, B26s and C119s and to fly C119s on missions to noncombat areas.

Although Admiral Stump had thought General O'Daniel too optimistic, now in January he believed General Trapnell was unduly pessimistic. He recommended to Washington that all possible assistance be given General Navarre. It was his belief that "timely assistance by the United States in this critical period through which General Navarre and the French Union forces are now passing will be instrumental in bringing about ultimate victory."

These two reports from the field arrived in Washington at about the same time the JCS were asked to review the two Planning Board studies, NSC 177 and its special annex. The comments by CINCPAC pointed up the need for early action along lines outlined in NSC 177, which assumed the French would fight on if the United States continued its aid programs. Accordingly, on 6 January the JCS informed the Secretary of Defense that they were in general agreement with the Planning Board draft.

General Trapnell's message emphasized the importance of having plans ready for the possibility of French failure and withdrawal. Such plans, in the annex to NSC 177, came before the JCS for approval also on 6 January. But the JSSC reported that this particular Planning Board study was not explicit. Admittedly, the United States would suffer critical consequences if Indochina fell; therefore, reasoned the JSSC, we should not accept the alternative of writing off the area if the French propose to quit in the absence of American military participation. Instead, the committee recommended that the JCS press for a decision on whether the United States should intervene, if necessary, to preserve Indochina. Such a decision would provide definitive policy for the development of further national diplomatic and military plans. The JSSC recommended that the special annex be revised to reflect the following views:

> Should the French make an arbitrary decision to withdraw from the conflict despite all offers of U.S. assistance, the United States, in any event and as a minimum, should urge the French to phase their withdrawal over a protracted period and to take all practicable measures to prepare the indigenous forces better to assume the responsibilities of their own defense. Additionally, the United States, preferably in connection with its allies, should provide such military assistance to the indigenous forces of Indochina as is . . . feasible in the light of conditions then prevailing, and as is consistent with U.S. objectives both with respect to Southeast Asia and world-wide. The level of military assistance cannot be predetermined, but might encompass anything from a continuation of material aid as a minimum to alternative "A" [vigorous intervention] as a maximum.

The JCS considered the JSSC recommendation on 6 January without reaching a decision. The next day I indicated to Secretary of Defense Wilson that the JCS had hastily prepared some comments on the special annex to NSC 177 but needed more time for proper study. Deputy Secretary Roger Kyes then attacked the accuracy of the logistical requirements set forth under the alternative option of U.S. intervention. He did not address himself to the principal problem at hand, that of being prepared for a French request for U.S. intervention—the problem that the JCS believed should receive timely examination. Nevertheless, Secretary Wilson supported Mr. Kyes and requested that the special annex be withdrawn from further consideration. In addition, *the Defense Department suggested to the NSC that future requests for military advice, such as that contained in the special annex, should be addressed to the Secretary of Defense, not to the JCS* [editor's italics].

When the NSC met on 8 January President Eisenhower sustained the objections of Secretary Wilson and ordered the withdrawal and destruction of the special annex to NSC 177. The Council did, however, touch upon the question of how far the United States would go to stave off French defeat at Dien Bien Phu. I pointed out that the United States had a large share at stake and suggested that American pilots, trained to suppress antiaircraft weapons, could do much even in one afternoon's operations to save the situation there. Although President Eisenhower did not rule out U.S. air and naval intervention at this meeting, he did oppose committing U.S. ground troops. He favored maximum aid short of intervention, including even volunteer air operations like those the Flying Tigers had provided in China prior to World War II.

At my suggestion the Council decided that General O'Daniel should be stationed continuously in Indochina under appropriate liaison arrangements and with sufficient authority "to expedite the flexible provision of U.S. assistance to the French Union Forces." It was intended that he provide the means through which the United States could influence military strategy and the training of native troops.

Six days later the NSC adopted the new Planning Board study of policy toward Southeast Asia, which became NSC 5405 for coordinated implementation: the charter for U.S. action in the months to come, assuming the French fought on. *But the Council had sidestepped the question, raised by the JCS, of what the United States would do if France gave up the struggle* [editor's italics].

The Berlin Conference at the end of January 1954 presented the United States with an abrasive and dual-edged problem: how to parry the expected Soviet demand for a five-power conference including Communist China "to consider measures for the relaxation of international tension" and at the same time persuade France that it should attain a position of strength before negotiating a settlement of the Indochina war.

The stated purpose of the Berlin conference was to settle the German and Austrian questions, and there was no real reason why the Far East should be included. Korea and Indochina were the major sources of tension in Asia, and China had so far shown no disposition to accept a settlement in either country that would preserve the interests of the free world.

The United States had to persuade France that it would be disastrous to open negotiations with the communists before improving its military position in Indochina. The new policy, NSC 5405, reaffirmed that the United States would furnish the French all aid short of actual military participation and would even consider direct military support if the Chinese intervened. On that basis the American task was to strengthen France to the point where it would hold out for a settlement that also protected U.S. security interests in the Far East.

Although the JCS did not participate extensively in preparations for the Berlin Conference, they had been asked by the NSC what the United States should do to improve the French position in Indochina. Replying through the

Secretary of Defense on 15 January the chiefs repeated many of the suggestions received recently from General O'Daniel and Admiral Stump.

Several of their recommendations reaffirmed courses of action to which the United States was already committed. Specifically, the chiefs suggested that the three services expedite undelivered items programmed for the 1950–1954 period and revise programs as necessary in accordance with combat needs. Such revision, they pointed out, might call for additional funds for the 1954 program.

The chiefs also recommended that we reexamine our national strategy toward Indochina, with a view toward developing a unified effort in Southeast Asia to counter communism on a regional basis—the basis on which the communists fought. Further, and this was very important, the United States might consider recommendations to scale down French commitments to NATO to permit deployment of additional forces to Indochina. The chiefs suggested that both France and the United States increase their political warfare activities.

The JCS responded to the recent French requests for additional air power by proposing that the United States provide material and financial support while France augmented her air force in Indochina with maintenance and air crew personnel from France. They now suggested that although the United States should restrict its contribution of manpower to certain specialists, it should also examine the idea of establishing unofficial volunteer air units composed of American personnel.

Before the Secretary of Defense took any action on the JCS recommendations, the question of assisting France again moved up to the highest government levels. Recognizing that a major problem arose from French reluctance to accept American assistance in training native soldiers and improving the conduct of operations, and searching for a way to overcome this reluctance, the President appointed a committee to develop a program for military and political victory without overt American participation in the war. Thenceforth known as the Special Committee on Indochina, it was composed of Allen Dulles, Director of the CIA; Gen. Bedell Smith, Under Secretary of State; Roger Kyes, Deputy Secretary of Defense; C. D. Jackson, White House adviser on cold war strategy; and myself.

While the Special Committee undertook its study events did not stand still. In mid-January Premier Laniel formally requested additional material aid and American maintenance personnel for the French air force in Indochina. He emphasized the temporary nature of this assignment and promised to replace Americans with Frenchmen as soon as possible.

The French request emphasized the need for further and continuous information in Washington. Accordingly, I urged CINCPAC to speed General O'Daniel on a trip he was already planning to Indochina, first to try to win consent from the French high command that he remain in Saigon indefinitely and second to evaluate the adequacy of the American assistance program and list additional requirements.

When the NSC met on 21 January, it considered the latest French request for aid and the JCS recommendations for improving the French position. In presenting these lists and suggestions, I said that some needed further study and others should be approved immediately. We were trying to render maximum material support and to train French Union forces to use our equipment. I pointed out also that additional funds would have to be found to permit adjustment of the current MAAG programs.

On the subject of maintenance personnel, I felt that the French could find the necessary flight and maintenance crews. If necessary, USAF personnel in NATO units could be utilized temporarily to replace and release French air force personnel for service in the Far East. We could also train these French personnel in Europe. I said that I intended to explore this personnel problem in detail with Lt. Gen. Valluy, of the NATO Standing Group.

After discussing the matter with USAF and Defense officials, I informed General Valluy that ten B26s would soon be on their way to Indochina and that we would be willing to supply the 25 aircraft for the third B26 squadron when the French could furnish flight and maintenance personnel. It did not seem feasible for us to furnish maintenance crews: problems of language and accommodations, unfamiliarity with French methods, and the time factor militated against this.

Even while these matters were under discussion, the French command in Saigon was pleading for immediate help. Vietminh forces surrounding Dien Bien Phu were expected to attack soon or to move against Luang Prabang in Laos. To counter either course, the high command needed aircraft and personnel. General Valluy was again instructed to seek our help on an urgent basis.

The General thanked me for the ten additional B26s but announced that France had been able to locate only 90 maintenance specialists. Drawing French personnel from NATO wings would not solve the immediate problem, for these technicians would still need training on American aircraft. He renewed his request for 400 ground crewmen but said that flight crews did not present as great a problem. The French had been able to work out an arrangement with General Gruenther, the NATO Commander, for USAF units to train French pilots in B26s.

When I asked General Valluy to give assurances that Americans, if sent to Indochina, would not be exposed to capture, the General gave me a categorical statement to this effect. He further assured me that these maintenance personnel could be brought home at the end of the fighting season, about 15 June.

With those assurances, I took up the matter of the maintenance personnel with the Special Committee. Since France had no more trained mechanics for the Far East, General Smith favored sending 200 USAF crewmen to Indochina. Roger Kyes objected that this action would commit the United States to such an extent that it would have to prepare for complete intervention. In reply, General Smith distinguished between mechanics and combat troops; he did not think the

United States was taking on any commitment to provide the latter. But he added that Indochina was so important to the United States that we should intervene with naval and air forces, if worse came to worst. I agreed.

The Special Committee agreed that the final decision should be left to the President and recommended that the United States provide a total of 22 B26s (in accordance with the latest French request) and send 200 USAF maintenance personnel to Indochina. They felt we should defer a decision on the third light bomber squadron and on the second contingent of 200 ground crewmen pending General O'Daniel's talks with General Navarre and the outcome of further French efforts to provide the additional mechanics. President Eisenhower accepted all three recommendations. Accordingly, General Twining ordered the Far Eastern Air Force to carry out the President's decisions. I might note that the contribution of these planes and trained men made a distinct and serious reduction in the combat effectiveness of the Far Eastern Air Force. They were *not* surplus planes or *additional* mechanics.

On 27 January, while the Berlin Conference was in session, the fact that the United States had agreed to send maintenance personnel to Indochina was divulged by Joseph and Stewart Alsop. The leak occasioned considerable furor in France and the United States. President Eisenhower found it necessary to intervene personally to calm the uproar. At a press conference in early February he acknowledged that USAF technicians were on their way to Indochina but implied that they would be part of the MAAG group training the French in the use of American equipment. This was technically true, but the furor continued. A week later, permitting direct quotation, he informed newsmen that "no one could be more bitterly opposed to ever getting the United States involved in a hot war in that region than I am. Consequently, every move that I authorize is calculated, so far as humans can do it, to make certain that does not happen." Nor could he conceive of a greater tragedy for America than to become heavily involved in an all-out war in any of these regions, particularly with large units. He told of the French guarantees that Americans would not be exposed to capture, and the French government publicly repeated these guarantees for the benefit of American audiences. When both Republican and Democratic Senators endorsed the President's remarks, the hubbub calmed.

In Indochina, meanwhile, General Vo Nguyen Giap withdrew some of his forces from Dien Bien Phu and moved again in the direction of Luang Prabang. Further depleting their combat reserves in the Tonkin Delta, the French moved to counter this Vietminh thrust. But they bemoaned their lack of troops and aircraft that could have decisively defeated this Vietminh invasion!

This clear indication that the initiative lay with the Vietminh and not with the French brought another somber report from Saigon. Severely indicting General Navarre's defensive concepts, the U.S. Military Attaché likened Dien Bien Phu to another Na San. He reported that the Vietminh command had concentrated its battle corps in western Tonkin, but that the French, with their forces dispersed throughout Indochina, were not in a position to take advantage of the opportunity for offensive operations to destroy the enemy. Although the French Union forces outnumbered the Vietminh two to one and had overwhelming fire power and air transport capability, their tactics remained defensive.[2] Patrolling was the exception, not the rule, for French units. Likewise, French Union forces were not maintaining contact with the Vietminh army, but were waiting to be attacked.

In Laos, too, the French failed to demonstrate tactical initiative. Instead, they were content to let 6 Vietminh battalions tie down 20 French Union battalions rather than capitalize on the chance to defeat the Vietminh forces decisively. The Attaché gave as his opinion that General Navarre had been directed by his government to conduct a minimum-casualty holding operation, improving his position where feasible, with a view to eventual negotiations. The Vietminh seemed to be fighting a clever war of attrition, with time running in its favor. In conclusion, the Attaché reported that "informed U.S. military opinion here" considered the greatest deterrents to successful French action to be lack of energetic support from Paris, inadequate training of combat units and staffs, and a defensive philosophy. These defects could not be remedied by the unlimited provision of modern American military equipment.

Secretary Dulles and Frank Nash of the Defense Department, in Berlin, were so concerned about this report that they asked General Trapnell for his comments. The MAAG chief replied that General Navarre was revealing an increasing tendency to seek "miracle" solutions instead of forthright and energetic action according to "universally accepted principles of war." General Trapnell considered that the French had adequate supplies and equipment for large-scale sustained operations; but, in the absence of any genuine offensive plan, it appeared that they had little intention of moving decisively to defeat the Vietminh.

General Trapnell's comments contrasted strikingly with those of General O'Daniel, who had returned to Washington following his visit to Indochina. O'Daniel pointed out that since the French were bound by treaty to protect Laos, they had no choice but to counter the Vietminh invasion by committing their reserves. But he was still confident that General Navarre would carry out his planned offensive and achieve military success during the 1954–1955 season. Agreeing that more than American supplies were needed, General O'Daniel had arranged for the assignment of five U.S. liaison officers to General Navarre's headquarters, where they could help correct French weaknesses.

These comments reflected O'Daniel's satisfaction with the results of his third visit to Indochina. Although Navarre had not agreed that it would be desirable for the American General to remain at his elbow, he had consented to short visits every four to six weeks. And the agreement to receive five U.S. liaison officers was an encouraging step.

O'Daniel's inspection of Dien Bien Phu and the Tonkin Delta caused him to be optimistic about the immediate military situation.[3] Although he recognized that the Vietminh forces could make Dien Bien Phu untenable if they had medium artillery, and he said that he would have insisted on including the high ground inside the French defense perimeter, he estimated that French Union forces could withstand any attack the Vietminh were capable of launching there.

The French were receiving reinforcements from France, and native troops were being raised and trained. O'Daniel felt that these additional units, supplied with American equipment, would permit the French Union to dominate all areas and bring the Vietminh army to battle by fall 1954. On the whole, in his estimation, the future looked bright.

But Admiral Stump again interjected a note of caution. He did not believe the five liaison officers and occasional short visits by General O'Daniel were an adequate substitute for the continuous assignment of a high-ranking American to Indochina. While he agreed with O'Daniel that there was no immediate danger of the French Union suffering a major military reverse, he viewed with grave concern the French failure to launch an offensive.

I shared CINCPAC's concern and was anxious to have General O'Daniel permanently assigned to Indochina. The French agreed to accept him as General Trapnell's relief (Trapnell was due to leave) as head of MAAG, provided he would surrender one star so that he would not be senior to General Navarre and provided he would have no greater authority than General Trapnell had had.

These terms, dictated by General Navarre, literally meant that O'Daniel would still be unable to exercise any substantial influence on French strategy and training. General Ridgway protested that a distinguished senior officer was being demoted and that the United States was losing prestige in the Far East without gaining compensatory advantages. At JCS instigation, France was again asked to consider increasing the scope of MAAG authority. France again refused. President Eisenhower, after consulting with General O'Daniel—who said he felt the plan worth trying and was willing to accept the temporary demotion—directed O'Daniel's assignment and change of rank. The Defense Department announced the change on 12 March and let it be known that there had been no change in the terms of reference for MAAG Indochina.

While Washington was struggling with General O'Daniel's assignment, the Berlin Conference resumed consideration of the Soviet proposal for a five-power meeting. The United States recognized the very real pressures on the French government and had to give at least the appearance of willingness to negotiate for peace in Indochina. The French felt they had an unassailable argument: the United States had agreed to an armistice in Korea and had consented to meet with the Chinese to negotiate a political settlement. Moreover, Mr. Dulles had publicly stated that if the political talks went well and "the Chinese Communists show a disposition to settle in a reasonable way such a question as Indochina, we would not just on technical grounds say no, we won't talk about that."

The question facing the United States in Berlin, therefore, was whether to let the French go their own way and thereby destroy Western unity, or to attend the conference and seek to influence the terms of the settlement. The latter seemed preferable. The final communiqué regarding the conference announced that the five powers and other countries that had participated in Korean hostilities would meet in Geneva to reach a peaceful settlement of the Korean question. The four foreign ministers further agreed "that the problem of restoring peace in Indochina will also be discussed at the conference, to which representatives of the United States, France, the United Kingdom, the USSR, and the Chinese People's Republic and other interested states will be invited."

In public, U.S. officials expressed satisfaction with the results of the Berlin Conference. Within the privacy of the NSC, however, Secretary Dulles admitted that the United States had little to gain at Geneva, although we would probably lose nothing. He felt it unlikely that the conference would reach an agreement for a free and united Korea. Further, there was some danger that the French might accept a settlement in Indochina contrary to U.S. interests. Yet French domestic political difficulties were so great that the United States had been unable to dissuade the Laniel government from agreeing to the Geneva meeting.

On 2 March 1954 the Special Committee on Indochina submitted its recommendations for further U.S. action to preserve Indochina. The committee had originally only considered steps short of military intervention. Now they recognized that the United States might wish to consider direct military action if the situation drastically deteriorated or if the French rejected a broad program of American advice and aid. But military action had to be considered in its full context, that is, in relation to our Southeast Asian policy as a whole.

The Special Committee reiterated the conclusions of NSC 5405 that Indochina was the keystone of the Southeast Asian arch and that consequently it must not be allowed to fall under communist domination. To prevent such a debacle, the French had to defeat communist military and quasimilitary forces and develop native resistance to communism. The United States should help the French, but help had to be consistent with our own and Allied programs for the Far East. The Committee felt that the United States had already taken all feasible action to furnish assistance that would aid the French to win the coming battle at Dien Bien Phu. By March the Defense Department had expended $123,600,000 beyond the funds allocated in appropriations for aid to Indochina for 1950–1954, to the detriment of programs for other areas. In addition, it appeared that at least another $100 million would be needed to meet French Union requirements.

The Special Committee concluded that delivered and programmed American aid to Indochina, and the potential manpower of the French Union, was sufficient to defeat the communists eventually. It agreed that if political and military reforms that had been suggested were carried out with full French support at an early date, the unfavorable situation in Indochina would be reversed. But significantly and finally, the committee added the suggestion that the Department of Defense be asked to develop a "concept of operations and considerations involved in the use of U.S. Armed Forces in Indochina should such involvement be determined upon."

The Special Committee thereafter turned its attention to studying military intervention and examining the position the United States should take at the forthcoming Geneva Conference, only seven weeks away. Much had to be accomplished in little time if Indochina were to be saved.

☆ ☆ ☆ ☆

Against its best interests, the United States had acceded at Berlin to French demands that the Geneva Conference discuss the Indochina question.[4] The problem then became one of preparing France for the diplomatic struggle awaiting her. The only method likely to bolster the French at the bargaining table was to concentrate on actions to strengthen its military position in Indochina.

American estimates of the military situation were optimistic in their long-range forecasts. There was no theoretical reason why the French should not be able to crush the Vietminh, provided they had the will and the material assistance to do so. Provision of material aid was a relatively simple matter for the United States. Equipment was available, and the pipelines were already established and functioning.

It was in the more nebulous sphere of psychology that the United States encountered real difficulties. Because we wished to stop short of actual intervention with our own armed forces, the fighting and the winning had to be done by the French. The JCS were convinced that, with an aggressive plan for a military offensive, good staff planning, and well-trained native troops, the French would have the situation in hand within a year or two. But French leadership had shown slight inclination and little ability to tackle its basic military problems with energy and foresight. And the French high command, jealous of its traditions and prerogatives, displayed scant desire to accept American assistance in other than a material way.

Well knowing the thankless task they were undertaking, the United States made a concerted effort after Berlin to convince the French that the high road to victory would open before them if they would only allow the United States to increase its aid in training, planning, and unconventional warfare. But even while we were attempting to persuade the French to accept such help, the political climate in France and the military situation in Indochina were crumbling. The will to fight is a thing of the heart, and the French had no heart for the fight. The United States therefore had to decide whether it should commit its own military forces and under what conditions intervention should take place.

The Berlin agreement to discuss peace for Indochina was a signal to the Vietminh to improve their military position. General Giap directed his forces to take the offensive wherever possible, including the beginning of the assault at Dien Bien Phu that commenced on the night of 13 March. Concentrating on one sector at a time, Giap sent two regiments against the northern and north-eastern French positions, each held by one French Union battalion. Employing horde tactics, the Vietminh overran the first French battalion outpost shortly after midnight. Two days later they captured the second. With the capture of these positions, Vietminh forces directly threatened the airfield upon which the isolated fortress depended.

The Vietminh had not been able to capitalize on their new position when Gen. Paul Ely, Chairman of the French Chiefs of Staff, arrived in Washington on 20 March following a visit to Indochina as part of a major survey of the situation by the French government. General Ely came at my invitation to summarize for U.S. officials his impressions drawn from this inspection tour and to hear our suggestions for increasing and improving the scope of our assistance.

During all our meetings I attempted to convince General Ely of the vital importance of winning in Indochina, pointing out that France's position as a world power depended upon what she did in the Far East. I presented arguments for increasing our help along the lines proposed recently by the JCS and the President's Special Committee.

Foremost, I urged acceptance of our proposals to assist in training the Vietnamese army units that were so badly needed. I offered to send well-qualified American officers for that purpose, as well as others to participate in unconventional warfare activities. In regard to improving the French air force, I suggested the formation of an international volunteer air group and offered what we thought were practical ways of improving French aircraft maintenance practices. Despite my best efforts General Ely, after admitting the need for improvements, agreed only to consider and investigate our offers. He did state frankly, however, that increasing the numbers of U.S. personnel in Indochina would jeopardize French prestige there in Indochinese eyes.

General Ely showed no such reluctance about accepting American material aid. In fact, he had come to Washington with a large list of additional emergency requests for airplanes, naval craft, guns, small arms, ammunition, and other supplies.

While we in Washington felt that the real problem was not lack of aircraft but French failure to make efficient use of what they had, President Eisenhower did not want the United States to be in the position of denying any aid critically needed in Indochina. Immediate approval was therefore given to a loan of planes for a third light bomber squadron and to direct gifts of all the other aircraft

General Ely had requested (except C47s and helicopters, which were simply not available).

As a quid pro quo I obtained Ely's consent for the USAF to send a team to Indochina to investigate the low French aircraft utilization rates. The Defense Department also approved Ely's other requests for miscellaneous equipment. While Dien Bien Phu was foremost in General Ely's thoughts, and he frankly gave the French Union only a fifty-fifty chance of staving off defeat there, he shrugged off American suggestions that a relief column be sent overland to the besieged fortress. If the French lost Dien Bien Phu, he said, only 5 percent of their troops in Indochina would be captured, whereas the Vietminh would suffer far heavier casualties. Nevertheless, he admitted that a military defeat at Dien Bien Phu would be a serious blow to morale both in Indochina and at home. He felt that if that strong point fell, Foreign Minister Bidault might not be able to hold out at Geneva for terms acceptable to the United States.

Ely's presentation of his case for practically unlimited assistance from the United States, with few if any concessions in regard to matters that the JCS considered essential to improve the military situation there, was baffling to me. He constantly fell back on the statement that to permit us to do this or that would undermine French prestige with the Indochinese, as if that were sufficient reason to lose the war when he knew full well that if it were lost French prestige would plummet all over the world, not just in Indochina. General Ely was a well-educated, very competent military man. I sensed during our conversations that he really did not, in his heart, support all the French positions that had been given him to present.

General Ely came to Washington with clear instructions, which he outlined at our first meeting. The French government wanted him to impress upon the U.S. government that the United States should not approach the Geneva Conference with the opinion that a military solution to the conflict in Indochina was possible *within a reasonable time*. Ely was to show us that the need for basing any political solution on a favorable military situation required the accelerated development of the Vietnamese army. Finally, they wanted *iron-clad assurances* against the risks they felt they were running of direct Chinese intervention, particularly an aerial intervention. Ely realized that this mission followed the general tenor of the conversations that had been taking place for several years between our two governments with a view to arriving at a common policy and a coordination of our efforts in Southeast Asia. The French hoped that, in anticipation of Geneva, he could expedite congruency of the two positions. He was expected to do this with very little "give" on the French side, and it was a large order. I decided that I wanted him to meet both the President and the Secretary of State because one of the first things he did was to give me a memorandum outlining the French request for assurances of our direct assistance in case of Chinese aerial intervention.

In 1964, General Ely published his reminiscences on Indochina, entitled *Mémoires* (vol. I: *L'Indochine dans la tourmente*), and sent me a copy. The book is a valuable addition to the written history of that period; since I find it generally a very frank and factual account, particularly in connection with our important conferences in March and April 1954, I shall quote from it here.

On 23 March I accompanied General Ely to call on Secretary of State Dulles. The General asked Mr. Dulles frankly if the United States would intervene with air power if the Chinese intervened directly with planes in Indochina. Mr. Dulles replied that a request for such intervention would be received and studied in light of the situation at the time, but added that the General should realize that if in accordance with its constitutional processes the United States did make a decision to intervene, our prestige would be involved to the point where we would want success. He added that if the French wanted American participation they must realize that it would require much greater partnership than had existed up to date. He mentioned agreement to the independence of the Associated States and to U.S. assistance in training the Vietnamese army.

In discussing the memorandum he had given me on arrival, General Ely asked not only whether American aircraft would intervene to counter Chinese planes but also how such intervention would occur. He suggested that precise staff agreements be concluded between CINCPAC and the French command in Indochina "with a view to limiting the air risk which characterizes the present situation." I assured Ely that considerable advance planning for such limited U.S. participation had already been completed and that CINCPAC, in cooperation with the French CINC, had worked out procedures for employing carrier aircraft in Indochina. Any delay in activating such American assistance would occur for other reasons. I pointed out that before the United States would commit these forces it must have firm agreements with the French on such questions as command and organizational arrangements, the duration of support, and basing facilities in Indochina. I asked if the French government was prepared, under these circumstances, to request American air support if the communists intervened and pointed out that if General Ely considered such a request likely, then "prudence dictated that the matter should be explored now on a higher level than ours, in order to be ready for such an emergency."

Ely replied that since he had been instructed by the French Minister of Defense to raise the question of American intervention, it was obvious that France contemplated making such a request if necessary to prevent defeat. He then asked about American constitutional processes governing the commitment of aircraft and informed me that the French Parliament would have to consent to such a request for help. I told Ely that our President had also committed himself to take up such a request with Congress, but that it would take time to arrange for American military intervention for other than military reasons and that it would have to be done at the highest governmental level.

Next General Ely asked what America would do if the French needed help to avert a disaster at Dien Bien Phu. I said the same order of procedure would apply. But if the French government requested such aid and our government granted it, as many as 350 aircraft, operating from carriers, could be brought into action within two days. It would be more difficult and would probably take longer to bring medium bombers into the fight.

The General concluded the discussion by saying that he was certain his government would ask for American air support if the Chinese intervened. But he added that Paris was so fearful of provoking the Chinese that he would not hazard a guess as to whether his government would ask for our help to save Dien Bien Phu.

Before he left Washington, General Ely and I signed the following minute as a record of our conversations in regard to U.S. assistance in the event of Chinese intervention with air power in Indochina.

In respect to General Ely's memorandum of 23 March 1954 it was decided that it was advisable that military authorities push their planning work as far as possible so that there would be no time wasted when and if our governments decided to oppose enemy air intervention over Indochina if it took place; and to check all planning arrangements already made under previous agreements between CINCPAC and the CINC Indochina and send instructions to these authorities to this effect.

The bare bones of this minute were apparently less than General Ely had hoped for, because his original memorandum presented to me that day had included this paragraph: "There was *complete agreement* (italics mine) on the terms of General Ely's memorandum, dated 23 March, dealing with intervention by U.S. aircraft in Indochina in case of emergency, it being understood that this intervention could be either by Naval or Air Force units as the need arises, depending on the development of the situation." In spite of the fact that I had refused to include this statement, General Ely apparently left Washington feeling that a request from the French for American intervention would receive a prompt and affirmative reply.

In preparing for General Ely's visit, and as a result of earlier experiences in negotiating with our allies, particularly the French, I had made elaborate arrangements to keep accurate records of conversations in various meetings. These records for the most part are available to me now, and they confirm the fact that I was very careful to explain to Ely that, regardless of previous joint military planning between our armed forces and the French armed forces in Indochina (started in late 1952), action on such plans by U.S. forces could be instituted only on orders from the President, generally following consultation with Congress. I emphasized the time lag that such consultations might require, to impress upon Ely that the French should not and could not expect quick action on emergency requests.

There are paragraphs in General Ely's *Mémoires* which show that, in spite of my precautions and efforts to be explicitly frank, he left with serious misunderstandings. For instance, in discussing the problem of American aerial intervention in Indochina following a surprise appearance of Chinese MIGs, he wrote (pp. 69–70):

> Defense in Indochina . . . rested on our air superiority . . . A small inter-allied working unit organized in 1952 following an exchange of views with Washington on Southeast Asia and charged with studying various hypotheses on allied intervention in this area, had considered in particular the case of Chinese aerial intervention requiring an immediate response by our allies. Since there was no airstrip usable by MIGs or any similar planes in the areas controlled by the Viet Minh, the appearance of any unidentified aircraft in the sky over Indochina *should have automatically* triggered the American response (my italics throughout). The safety of our Expeditionary Corps depended on this. Maintenance of an anti-communist barrier, whether in Tonkin or farther south on the Indochinese peninsula, also depended on it. The work done by this inter-allied working unit was only a preliminary study carried out at a relatively low level. It was essential that it be confirmed at the *governmental* level and pursued further. *This is what my government wanted me to achieve in Washington.*

> The official report which the Admiral and I signed the final day *showed our agreement on this point. No doubt could exist thereafter of the intent of the United States to carry out the measures provided for if and when the time came.*

> [The translator of passages quoted from Ely's book is unknown.]

The conclusion in General Ely's last paragraph simply is not in consonance with what he was told in Washington. In Mr. Dulles' official biography, the meeting between him and General Ely is reported thus (Gerson, *John Foster Dulles,* vol. XVII: *American Secretaries of State and Their Diplomacy,* p. 157):

> [Ely] asked whether the United States would intervene with air power if Communist China's Air Force attacked French planes bringing supplies to Dien Bien Phu. Dulles replied that "if the United States sent its flag and its own military establishment, land-sea or air, into the Indochina war then the prestige of the United States would be engaged to a point where we would want to have a success." The United States could not "suffer a defeat which would have worldwide repercussions." He went on to say that such a request would be considered in the light of circumstances existing at the time it was received but that if the French wanted American participation they must realize it would require greater partnership than hitherto, notably in relation to independence for the Associated States and for training indigenous groups.

Before this meeting I had warned Secretary Dulles about the request Ely would probably make, so he had time to organize his thoughts. Thinking back on the meetings and conversations that Ely attended and heard, I have concluded that he remembered only the favorable (to him) things. He discounted what he heard Mr. Dulles say that particular day.

Nevertheless, this meeting had important results. With encouragement from the President, Mr. Dulles reviewed with congressional leaders the situation in Indochina and possible American actions. He told them the administration was considering a public call for united (free world) action and would appreciate their endorsement.

Secretary Dulles recognized that a serious situation was developing. Not only was the French military situation in Indochina precarious and potentially dangerous, but the political climate within France boded ill for preserving Indochina at Geneva. On 9 March, before the first serious action at Dien Bien Phu, Radical-Socialist Deputy Pierre Mendès-France called upon the French government to stop the Indochina war immediately by negotiating directly with the Vietminh. He held that it should not wait for an international conference that would prolong for some months "the massacre and anguish of the entire nation." Although this statement captured the views of the noncommunist leftist opposition, Mr. Dulles had reason to be concerned about the attitude of the French government. French hopes were growing that the United States would recognize China or at least loosen the trade embargo as a quid pro quo for a satisfactory settlement of the Korean and Indochinese wars. Premier Laniel expected his government to fall if it returned empty-handed from Geneva. A successor regime would be likely to sell out not only Indochina but also EDC. The question facing the United States was: How far were we prepared to go to prevent further communist expansion in Southeast Asia, either by fighting or by making the concessions sought by China?

Mr. Dulles told the NSC at a meeting on 25 March that before the Geneva Conference opened the United States must have answers to some fundamental questions: what would we do if the French appeared tempted to sacrifice the position of the free world in Indochina by accepting terms unacceptable to us, and what would we do if the French decided to get out of Indochina? Mr. Dulles said he felt the United States had to be prepared either to write off Indochina or to assume responsibility there if the French relinquished their hold.

President Eisenhower listed four conditions to be met before U.S. military intervention might take place: the Associated States would have to request assistance; the U.N. should sanction the response; other nations would have to join the United States in answering; and congressional assent must be given. Mr. Dulles hoped the U.N. would sanction the call for assistance but felt that much more work would have to be done before he presented the case for intervention to Congress.

After discussing the possibility of using the ANZUS pact as an instrument for united action, the NSC directed its Planning Board to recommend the extent to which, and the circumstances and conditions under which, we would be willing to commit resources in support of the Associated States, with the French or with others or unilaterally, to prevent the loss of Indochina.

My talks with General Ely had confirmed my opinion that the United States faced a critical situation. In a memorandum to President Eisenhower outlining my discussions with Ely, I closed by telling him that in my opinion "the measures taken by the French (to improve their military situation) will prove to be inadequate and initiated too late to prevent a progressive deterioration of the situation. The consequences can well lead to the loss of all Southeast Asia . . . I consider that the United States must be prepared to act promptly and in force, possibly to a frantic and related request by the French for U.S. intervention."

27

Negotiations on Indochina

Almost immediately after the National Security Council meeting of 25 March 1954, Secretary Dulles began to prepare the American people and world opinion for possible U.S. intervention in Indochina. In an address entitled "The Threat of Red Asia" to the Overseas Press Club in New York on 29 March, he enumerated ways short of open aggression by which the Chinese were aiding the Vietminh, then clarified the U.S. position as follows:

> Under conditions of today, the impositions on Southeast Asia of the political system of Communist Russia and its Chinese Communist ally, by whatever means, would be a grave threat to the whole free community. The United States feels that that possibility should not be passively accepted but should be met by united action. This might involve serious risks. But these risks are far less than those that will face us a few years from now if we dare not be resolute today.

On 3 April I joined Secretary Dulles and Roger Kyes in a meeting with congressional leaders in the State Department, where I presented a detailed briefing on the military situation in Indochina. Mr. Dulles outlined the French political situation as he saw it and the possibilities of a sudden request from the French government for our military intervention. He then sounded out congressional leaders on the conditions to be met before Congress would sanction American participation in the war.

Above all, the congressional leaders stipulated that the United States *should not intervene unilaterally, but only as a member of an international coalition.* Congress would want assurance that France was granting full independence to the Associated States, that it had developed an effective training program for native troops, and that it would not withdraw its own forces but would prosecute an aggressive plan for military action. It was obvious from this meeting that the government had not yet undertaken a task set forth in 1952 and reaffirmed in 1954: making clear to the American people the importance of Southeast Asia to the security of the United States.

As a result of the meeting, President Eisenhower wrote to Winston Churchill requesting the British to join in organizing a regional grouping of the United States, France, and the Southeast Asian nations. In *Mandate for Change* (p. 347) he quotes from that letter, ending with:

> The important thing is that the coalition must be strong and it must be willing to join the fight if necessary. I do not envisage the need of any appreciable ground forces on your or our part . . .
>
> If I may refer again to history: we failed to halt Hirohito, Mussolini and Hitler by not acting in unity and in time. That marked the beginning of many years of stark tragedy and desperate peril. May it not be that our nations have learned something from that lesson? . . .

Although Prime Minister Churchill's reply showed that the British had little enthusiasm for joining us, President Eisenhower decided as a next step to attempt the organization of a regional grouping before the opening of the Geneva Conference. He arranged for Secretary Dulles to go to Paris and London for that purpose.

Secretary Dulles' resolute call for united action did not deter the Vietminh from pressing their advantage at Dien Bien Phu. At the end of March, General Giap's troops assaulted the main bastions of the fortress. They reduced the French stronghold to a triangle with sides of about 2,500 yards and captured the northern side of the airfield, making it very difficult for the French to reinforce the position even by parachute.

This critical situation brought a new spate of emergency requests for our help. Could the United States airlift two battalions of paratroopers from North Africa to Indochina? Would the United States provide some carrier planes to be flown by French naval aviators? Could the United States furnish 18 C47s to transport a reserve paratroop battalion from Hanoi to Dien Bien Phu? And could six more C119s be loaned to the French air force?

The Department of Defense found ways to meet these new French requests after President Eisenhower reiterated that he wanted to give them all possible assistance, short of outright intervention, that would truly improve the situation. We certainly did our best to cope with this new emergency, but the French government suddenly decided that material aid would not be enough and put forward the "frantic and belated" request for American intervention that I had advised President Eisenhower to anticipate.

On 4 April 1954 Premier Laniel and Foreign Minister Bidault told Ambassador Dillon that "immediate armed intervention of U.S. carrier aircraft at Dien Bien Phu is now necessary to save the situation." Two considerations had moved the French to make this request. First, the Vietminh were throwing fresh troops into the battle at a faster rate than the French could reinforce the garrison with paratroops. Second, General Ely had told his government that I had promised to do my best to obtain help if the situation at Dien Bien Phu required it.

The French leaders further justified their request on the grounds that, in all but name, the Chinese had already intervened in the battle. Premier Laniel admitted that our naval support might bring on Chinese air attacks against the Tonkin Delta but said his government was ready to accept this risk. Foreign Minister Bidault emphasized that speedy American intervention was essential, since the Vietminh were expected to renew their attack within a week. He felt the Geneva Conference would be won or lost at Dien Bien Phu.

After conferring with President Eisenhower early the next morning, Secretary Dulles sent the following message to Ambassador Dillon:

> As I personally explained to Ely in presence of Radford, it is not possible for U.S. to commit belligerent acts in Indochina without full political understanding with France and other countries. In addition, Congressional action would be required. After conference at highest level, I must confirm this position. U.S. is doing everything possible . . . to prepare public, Congressional and Constitutional basis for united action in Indochina. However, such action is impossible except on a coalition basis with active British Commonwealth participation. Meanwhile U.S. (is) prepared, as has been demonstrated, to do everything short of belligerency . . .

Ambassador Dillon's reply was prompt.

> I delivered message to Bidault Monday evening. He asked me to tell Secretary that he personally could well understand position of U.S. Government and would pass on your answer to Laniel.
>
> He asked me to say once more that unfortunately the time for formulating evaluations has passed as the fate of Indochina will be decided in the next ten days at Dien Bien Phu. As I left he said that even though French must fight alone they would continue fighting and he prayed God they would be successful.

In his book (pp. 83–84) General Ely explains in some detail his part in originating this French request. It is a good example of how misunderstandings can take place. He writes that, at the time of his departure from Washington,

> obviously no decision had been made. *Admiral Radford and I had neither the power nor the authority necessary for that.* It had been understood between us that if the French Government officially requested American intervention, Admiral Radford in his official capacity would recommend it very strongly to his government. He thought, quite obviously, that he would have the support of President Eisenhower and, *he assured me that our request would be quickly examined and acted upon by the American authorities* (my italics here and in quotation below).

Apparently General Ely promptly forgot his conversation with Secretary Dulles. I feel certain that his pleasant visit with President Eisenhower gave him the wrong impression. In that visit nothing serious was discussed. The President was interested in hearing from Ely how things were going militarily, and he did tell me to try to give the French everything they asked for. Ely apparently left Washington feeling that President Eisenhower was disposed to do more than Secretary Dulles, not appreciating the fact that the President was *not* meeting Ely with a view to discussing serious matters—that this was more in the nature of a social call.

Ely continues in *Mémoires* that, as he took leave of me, he felt it would be harder for him to get from his own government the request for American support than it would be for me to get an affirmative decision from my government. Nevertheless, he adds:

> I was convinced that the French Government would not hesitate at such a decision, for it was resolved, I knew, to do anything to save Dien Bien Phu ... But I also thought Admiral Radford would finally get the approval of the American Government. *I remembered very well the speed and firmness with which President Truman had decided to intervene in Korea* ... Of course the problem was not the same, since there was no United States commitment directly involved in Indo-China as there had been in Korea. But the fact remained that this decision was just as far reaching as the other *with infinitely smaller risks.*

I wonder how Ely felt it possible to make such a judgment!

On the same day Ambassador Dillon delivered Secretary Dulles' message declining to intervene, the NSC met to consider its Planning Board report on what to do in regard to Indochina. Decision was postponed on the recommendation that the United States should determine now whether to intervene. This action reflected the view of President Eisenhower, who reiterated his opposition to unilateral American intervention. Secretary Dulles reported on his conversations with congressional leaders and also indicated that his discussions with ambassadors of major U.S. allies had not been encouraging. The NSC discussion largely focused on the tangential issue of a Southeast Asia coalition. There was apparently some feeling, shared by the President, that bringing the coalition into existence would so strengthen the bargaining position of the West at Geneva that intervention would become unnecessary.

The NSC also agreed that the United States should attempt to win British support for American objectives in the Far East and should press the French to accelerate their program for granting independence to the Associated States. At the same time, President Eisenhower directed the Defense Department to obtain congressional approval for increasing the number of American maintenance technicians in Indochina and for extending the tour of duty of personnel already there. He felt that if Congress approved these steps the United States could send the French additional aircraft.

The NSC action allowed Defense to intensify its efforts in assisting the French to save Dien Bien Phu, but only by providing material aid. Yet there was very little more material aid that would help. The Air Force Inspection Team and General Trapnell both reported that the factors limiting French utilization of American aircraft were the lack of flight crews and inadequate base facilities, not shortage of aircraft or maintenance deficiencies. General Trapnell informed Washington that the B26 situation was the most critical. The French had only 34 flight crews to fly 43 operational aircraft. But they did have flight crews for the 25 naval Corsairs the United States had agreed to provide, and they could use American maintenance personnel to keep them flying. The U.S. Navy obliged by ordering a few of its ratings to service these planes.

The critical situation had at last produced a change of heart in General Navarre. He finally agreed to use more fully the American officers on his staff and to accept 25–50 Americans to help train native forces. But on the whole, French military authorities in Indochina were doing little to improve Franco-American relations. After receipt of the urgent French request to airlift their paratroops from North Africa to Indochina, I stayed up the better part of a night to make the necessary arrangements, only to be told the next day that the troops would not be ready to leave for two weeks. In addition, the French sent the carrier *Belleau Wood*, loaned by the United States after an urgent request the previous September, to the Far East with a cargo of planes for sale to the Indian government. The carrier would therefore arrive in Indochinese waters at a crucial time without aircraft. Finally, General Ely persisted in his misinterpretation of his March conversations with me. On 7 April he complained to me in this vein:

> The diplomatic exchanges of views stemming from the conditional answer made by the U.S. Government to our request for emergency intervention of the U.S. Air Forces in support of our forces at Dien Bien Phu cause me to fear that this intervention would be subject to time lag which would be too long.
>
> ... [I] wish that requested emergency intervention should not remain subordinated to political exchanges of views which will not fail to take a lot of time, in view of the fact that they must be conducted with several other governments.

I replied by reminding Ely that both the Secretary of State and I had

> made it absolutely clear that the decision to employ U.S. Forces in combat was one that could only be made at the highest government level and in the light of constitutional processes involving Congressional action. I did state that no such participation by U.S. Forces was possible without a formal request by the French Government, and that I was certain that such a request, if made, would receive prompt and thorough consideration by the United States Government.
>
> Events connected with the request have proved my prediction to be true. The Secretary of State is moving with great urgency to cope with the situation. It is receiving continuing attention at the highest levels. Meanwhile, every possible effort is being made to take all action, short of actual intervention by U.S. Armed

Forces, to assist in the defense of Dien Bien Phu until international arrangements involving the nations who are so directly affected, can be completed.

Meanwhile Mr. Dulles was also trying to cope with the situation by attempting to bolster sagging French morale. He pointed out to Foreign Minister Bidault that even if the battle of Dien Bien Phu were lost France would not have lost the war, and he explained again that the United States could not become a belligerent until the American people had been prepared for such a step. His efforts were only partially successful. The French government could recognize the realities of American politics, but it could not overlook French political considerations. Bidault replied that if Dien Bien Phu fell, it would be most unlikely that either the Associated States or France would be willing to continue the war, even with full American military support.

To speed the organization of a Southeast Asia regional defense organization, Secretary Dulles flew to Europe on 10 April. His purpose, he told the American people, was not to extend the fighting, but to end it. He did not intend to prevent the Geneva Conference from arriving at a peaceful settlement; instead, he wanted to create the unity of free wills that was needed to *assure* a peaceful settlement.

Two days earlier, Under Secretary of State Walter Bedell Smith had requested me to acquaint Sir John Whitely, Chief of the British Armed Services Mission in Washington, with the JCS present assessment of the situation in Indochina, so that when Mr. Dulles arrived in London the British government could not say they would have to consult with their military. The memorandum I made of our conversation is of interest.

> ... I outlined the present military situation in Indochina as the U.S. JCS saw it, i.e., at the moment it was very serious ... The JCS feel that while there is no reason from a purely military standpoint to assume that the loss of Dien Bien Phu should prejudice the whole French military position in Indochina, that on the other hand the psychological aspects of a defeat of this magnitude at this time, might cause reactions in Indochina and in France which could lead to a collapse of the whole French effort.

> The U.S. chiefs believe ... that Indochina must be held by the free world ... that its loss would almost certainly result in the ultimate loss of all of Southeast Asia. I reminded General Whitely that beginning with the conference in Singapore in 1951, attended by Marshall de Lattre and General Sir John Harding, and continuing on to the five-power military planners conference in Honolulu last year, there had been no disagreement among these military men as to the importance of Indochina.

> I said that the JCS felt that it was important to hold Dien Bien Phu and as a result ... the United States was providing much additional assistance to the French, particularly in the form of additional aircraft. We hoped that this addi-

tional assistance would be sufficient to enable the French to hold, but we were not sure of it. I said he probably knew we were furnishing more than material assistance, we also had technicians there . . .

General Whitely then asked me if the U.S. chiefs felt that the loss of Dien Bien Phu would result in the loss of Indochina. I said I could not say that the JCS were unanimous in this respect. My own feelings on this matter were probably stronger than some of the others due to my close association with the problems in Indochina during the last three years. In other words, I thought the consequences of a French defeat at Dien Bien Phu . . . would probably involve a collapse of the French military effort in Indochina and ultimately a French compromise at Geneva that would have a great effect on the position of France as a great power and consequently on our NATO arrangements.

General Whitely then asked me just what did I think Mr. Dulles had in mind. I said that I thought Mr. Dulles would represent the feelings of our Congress, and consequently the American public, that Indochina was of great importance to the free world and that the time had come to consider intervention with the French to save the situation, but only in concert with our allies, the principal one of which was Great Britain . . . we realized . . . that [Britain's] military effort in this case would have to be only a token effort as they were already engaged in Malaya, Hong Kong, and Korea, but I thought that in this instance their moral support was more important and a token contribution would suffice if we could also count on contributions from other nations such as Australia, New Zealand, and Thailand.

General Whitely asked if it was intended to issue an ultimatum to China to cease aiding the communists as a part of this collective effort. I said I did not know, but personally thought that would be a mistake . . . because a) even an immediate cessation of aid on the part of the Chinese would have no effect on the outcome at Dien Bien Phu and b) we had no sure way of checking on the Chinese to make sure that they lived up to such an agreement, if they were willing to accept it. I also thought that such an ultimatum might possibly cause the Chinese to intervene overtly, whereas I felt that without such an ultimatum there was little chance that they would intervene. I added, however, that the question of Chinese intervention in case of a united effort to assist the French was a possibility that had to be considered and that among our own military men there were varying opinions as to the seriousness of this particular eventuality. General Whitely expressed the opinion that the issuance of such an ultimatum would have quite an influence on the British position, which I could understand.

General Whitely . . . asked finally if I would consider that in connection with a possible contribution of British Forces they might withdraw some ships from Korea. I told him I thought that would be satisfactory, since if we made a contribution it would have to come from forces we had in the western Pacific.

General Whitely said he would immediately get off a dispatch to the British chiefs . . . He agreed that time was an essential element in the matter since the situation after the fall of Dien Bien Phu might be more complicated from a military point of view. He also agreed that such a situation would have serious ultimate consequences for the British situation in Malaya.

From London Mr. Dulles and Foreign Minister Eden announced that "we are ready to take part with the other countries principally concerned, in an examination of the possibility of establishing a collective defense . . . to assure the peace, security, and freedom of Southeast Asia and the Western Pacific" (see Hoopes, p. 215). A day later the Secretary and Foreign Minister Bidault issued a similar joint declaration. In addition, during early April the Department of State obtained Thai and Philippine acceptance, at least in principle, for the idea of a regional defense organization.

But Mr. Dulles had no more than returned to Washington when the British reneged. Mr. Eden later explained that Commonwealth politics had dictated the change in policy. The Colombo Powers, including India, Pakistan, and Ceylon, were to convene on 26 April, and Mr. Eden felt that it would be "most undesirable" for Britain to give any public indication of membership in a program for united action until that conference had ended. Furthermore, the establishment of the working group of ten nations, which did not include the three Asian Commonwealth members, would produce criticism that Mr. Eden felt would be "most unhelpful" at Geneva. Secretary Dulles privately attributed the reversal to British fear that intervention would bring on overt Chinese participation in Indochina and lead to World War III.[1]

☆ ☆ ☆ ☆

Although the State Department had been unsuccessful in arranging for united action, the first prerequisite for American intervention, Defense pushed ahead with military planning and preparations. The representatives of CINCPAC arrived in Saigon to confer with General Navarre on plans for American air support, should it be authorized. A few days later, Defense publicized the movement of a carrier task force into the South China Sea between Indochina and the Philippines. In Washington, JCS planning machinery was thrown into high gear to recommend policies for the guidance of CINCPAC, CINCFE, and Commander, Strategic Air Command in preparing operational plans to meet possible Chinese aggression in Indochina or Korea. An outline plan was accepted that was based on the assumption that the French Union would continue to supply ground troops while the United States furnished air and naval support.

Although the JCS in 1953 and 1954 had repeatedly approved the concept of limited American intervention in Indochina if circumstances required, in early April 1954 General Ridgway suggested they consider a broader course of action. Returning to a position the chiefs had held in 1952, he recommended that the United States concentrate its strength against Communist China, the true source of Vietminh military power. If the United States was determined to use armed force to hold Indochina and Southeast Asia, it should line up Allied support and warn the communists that military action would be taken to neutralize the sources of Vietminh strength. It should also initiate mobilization and other supporting measures after enlisting the fullest possible military support.

The other chiefs did not immediately accept General Ridgway's analysis. Without approving or disapproving the substance, they noted the views and forwarded them to the Secretary of Defense. Later, after the fall of Dien Bien Phu and the deterioration of the French position at Geneva, they came back to General Ridgway's proposal.

With the Army Chief of Staff calling for action against China, and with the Southeast Asia Coalition foundering on British shoals, the American Vice President took action of his own to test public opinion. Asked a hypothetical question during an off-the-record appearance before the American Society of Editors and Publishers—"What should the country do if the French withdraw from Indochina?"—Mr. Nixon replied that there was no reason why the French could not stay on and win, but, on the assumption that they did withdraw, an assumption he did not accept, Indochina would become communist in a month. The United States, as leader of the free world, could not afford further retreat in Asia. It was hoped that the United States would not have to send troops there, but if we could not avoid it, the administration must face up to the situation and dispatch forces.

Public reaction was so unfavorable that the State Department took pains to point out that the Vice President had been addressing himself to a hypothetical question in an off-the-record talk. The public was reminded that the speech enunciated no new U.S. policy on Indochina and that it expressed full agreement with and support for the policy previously enunciated by the President and the Secretary of State.

I write this 18 years later, with the history of the intervening years laid out before me. The policy of our leaders in 1954 was absolutely sound. If their courageous efforts had been successful we might have avoided altogether the terrible war in Indochina.

With public opinion and the Congress obviously unprepared for unilateral American action, and the British unwilling to internationalize the war, the only course open to the administration was the use of moral suasion to keep the French from selling out at Geneva. There was still hope that the situation could be saved, since the Vietminh had adopted "nibbling" tactics at Dien Bien Phu, reducing the perimeter progressively but not overwhelming the defenders.

Still hoping that he could salvage the Southeast Asia coalition and thereby establish a French bargaining position, Secretary Dulles left for Geneva and Paris on 20 April. I joined him in Europe, and my activities and duties there can best be described by quoting a memorandum prepared on my return entitled "Resume of Conversations with French and British Representatives . . . in Paris and London, 24–26 April 1954, on the subject of Indochina."

[Secretary Dulles] asked me to accompany him to a meeting with Mr. Anthony Eden, British Foreign Secretary. I informed Mr. Eden of the views of the U.S. Chiefs of Staff relative to the deteriorating situation in Indochina and the very serious results [they] . . . believed would ensue. I told Mr. Eden that while the British Chiefs of Staff had been generally informed of the estimates of the U.S. JCS, we had not in turn received their views and I offered to meet with the British chiefs at an early date [Admiral Radford had been requested to do so by the President].

In particular, I pointed out that in the opinion of the United States, Southeast Asia was not militarily defensible after the loss of Indochina. Mr. Eden said that the presentation by Secretary Dulles painted a much worse picture than had been given to the British by the French. Therefore, he . . . would return to London that night in order to talk the matter over with the Prime Minister and the British cabinet before proceeding on to Geneva.

I saw the Secretary of State again following his conversation with Premier Laniel, who again brought forth to the Secretary the seriousness of the French situation in Indochina and the urgency of U.S. intervention to forestall a catastrophe.

. . . In response to an urgent request by General Ely, Chairman of the French Chiefs of Staff, I met with him . . . Apparently he had been sent to talk to me at the direction of M. Bidault and M. Pleven, as one military man to another. He stated that he had come to ask for American intervention, well realizing that such intervention could have no direct bearing on the situation at Dien Bien Phu. The point which he wanted to stress was that American aid should be rendered before Dien Bien Phu fell, for the psychological effect both in France and in Indochina, to prevent a further deterioration of the situation . . . He was not very optimistic as to the number of days Dien Bien Phu could hold out, and therefore urged very prompt action on the part of the United States. He inferred that the refusal of the United States to render aid at such a critical time could have very severe implications in regard to future relations between France and the United States.

I reported this conversation to Ambassador Dillon, who passed it on to Secretary Dulles with his interpretation. Ambassador Dillon felt that the leaders of the French government had never informed their full cabinet of the request for U.S. armed intervention, which had been made by a restricted group of stronger individuals, who (were) willing to take the entire responsibility for the request on the basis that everything possible must be done to save or assist the garrison at Dien Bien Phu. He felt that if such aid were given the French forces would continue to fight in Indochina regardless of the outcome at Dien Bien Phu, but that if it were not rendered, the United States refusal would become public knowledge, with a very adverse reaction on the part of French public. This, in his opinion, would be followed by the overthrow of the Laniel government and its replacement by a government pledged to negotiations with the communists and withdrawal of French forces from Indochina.

I discussed this conversation with General Gruenther, who stated that he had never observed the morale in high French government circles to be so low and pessimistic ... He felt that there would certainly be very adverse reactions in France itself to the fall of Dien Bien Phu and the worsening of the situation in Indochina. This would probably have a bad effect on the French attitude toward NATO, but he believed that, barring the advent of a neutralist government in France, the adverse effect could be overcome in a matter of months.

On Monday afternoon I arrived in London to meet with the British chiefs ... On most points their analysis of ... the situation in Indochina was in accord with that of the U.S. JCS, particularly in respect to ... the serious future possibilities resulting from the loss of all or part of Indochina, either through military action or negotiation. They seemed, however, to maximize the risks of expansion of the war by intervention at this time and the requirements for ground forces to be furnished by the Western powers to achieve a victory. They indicated their confidence in being able to hold Malaya either from external aggression or internal subversion. Their approach to the problem seemed, however, to be on a very narrow basis, strictly in terms of local United Kingdom interest, without adequate regard for the future of other areas of the Far East, including Japan.

On Monday evening I dined with the Prime Minister at Chequers ... Sir Winston appeared in excellent health and in a good conversational mood. He talked with great frankness and also listened attentively. The line taken by him was in exact accord with that expressed to me by the British chiefs and with my understanding of the views expressed by Mr. Eden to Secretary Dulles at Geneva. He is apparently aware of the serious implications stemming from the deterioration of the French position in Indochina, involving the possible loss of the Associated States and later all other areas of Southeast Asia. He realizes that this will probably lead to a worsening of the French position in North Africa and have its effects on NATO, particularly in case a more neutralist-minded government comes to power in France.

While he deplored the foregoing possibilities, he was determined to commit forces and to incur risks only to hold Malaya, both militarily and politically. This he felt could be done. He brushed aside the potential threat to Australia in the event that Indonesia falls into the communist camp and the effect of the loss of the rice-producing areas on the Far Eastern situation generally. He did not seem to appreciate the effect of the loss of Southeast Asia on the future of Japan.

In connection with NATO, he stated that we have waited long enough for the French to make EDC a reality. Therefore the United Kingdom and the United States should "get on with the rearming of the Germans themselves," glossing over the question as to how this should be accomplished.

The Prime Minister repeatedly referred to the loss of India to the Empire, making the point that since the British people were willing to let India go, they would certainly not be interested in holding Indochina for France. He discoursed at length on the threat of atomic weapons to the United Kingdom citing this as a factor which required the utmost caution in dealing with the situation in the Far East. He favors a personal and intimate conversation between President Eisenhower, Mr. Malenkov, and himself to settle the big problems as the only real way to resolve the current world situation.

The Prime Minister reiterated a point mentioned to me by the British chiefs that they regretted that the United States had not stood with them two years ago in coping with their problem in Egypt . . .

The Prime Minister deplored his lack of personal knowledge of the Far East . . . I suggested that it might be helpful to him to have a conversation with Mr. Malcolm MacDonald [U.K. HICOM for Southeast Asia], who is thoroughly familiar with Far Eastern matters. He seemed receptive to this suggestion. On the other hand, he did not react to my suggestion of a possible adverse reaction on the part of U.S. public opinion should Great Britain not join with the United States and other nations in a real effort to stop the spread of communism in Asia.

I gathered . . . that the Prime Minister is presently unprepared to participate in collective action on any matter involving commitments of British resources or incurring any risks unless some British territory is under imminent threat. His personal appraisal of action which can be taken to halt the spread of world communism seems now limited to talks, as he says, "at the summit." Whether this stems from a personal conviction, a real fear of atomic attack on Great Britain, or a fear that the British people will not approve a stronger course of action, I do not know.

The evening at Chequers was one of the most interesting of my career. Sir Winston, who had seemed about to pass from the active political scene only a short five months before when I had met with him in London, was now the genial and fascinating host, full of stories and reminiscences that often kept his small audience in gales of laughter.

This was not the last time I saw this great man, truly one of the world's most distinguished statesmen; but it was the last, and the only, time that I had an opportunity to really talk with him.

The day following our conversation, the Prime Minister made the British position very clear in a public announcement to the House of Commons.

Her Majesty's Government are not prepared to give any undertakings about United Kingdom military commitments. My Right Honorable friend [Eden] has, of course, made it clear to his colleagues at Geneva that if settlements are reached at Geneva, Her Majesty's Government will be ready to play their full part in supporting them in order to promote a stable peace in the Far East.

Confronted with a British statement that gave no hope of strengthening the French bargaining position, Mr. Dulles and the NSC turned their thoughts toward establishing a regional coalition without Britain.

The Secretary of State conferred in Geneva with the foreign ministers of Australia and New Zealand under the terms of the ANZUS pact. He stressed the necessity for a common stand by all countries with interests in Southeast Asia. The Australians indicated willingness to hold military talks immediately, without making any commitments, but they preferred that the discussions be within the framework of the Five-Power Staff Agency, of which Britain was a member. New Zealand was also willing to begin the talks without awaiting the end of the Geneva Conference. Neither country objected to including Thailand.

When the United States began preparing for talks with the Commonwealth, Foreign Minister Eden reversed his field, telling Mr. Dulles that he was ready to recommend that Britain take part in an examination by the Five-Power Staff Agency of the Southeast Asia situation, then and also subsequent to the Geneva Conference. The British, however, would remain opposed to intervention. Mr. Dulles was inclined to feel that such staff talks opened an avenue of hope and that they would have a positive influence at the conference and on public opinion.

Any good effect the announcement of such talks might have had was completely eclipsed two days later when the French Union defenders of Dien Bien Phu capitulated. The surrender came the day before the Indochinese phase of the Geneva Conference began. The French had been saying for weeks that they could not avoid negotiating peace if they lost Dien Bien Phu. The British, also, were prepared to accept a cease-fire. The United States, unwilling to intervene unilaterally, stood alone.

☆ ☆ ☆ ☆

I had no direct and personal connections with the negotiations at Geneva during the time that conference was in session, 26 April–21 July 1954, but as Chairman of the JCS I did. The JCS were almost continuously involved in commenting on or preparing advice to our representatives in Geneva and in studying the long-range implications of possible final actions that might be taken there. I believe that, as a body, the JCS devoted more than half their time during the Geneva sessions to consideration of the problems that developed there.

As Anthony Eden remarked in a statement to the House of Commons on the day following the close of the Geneva Conference, all would probably agree that the proceedings of the conference were of unparalleled complexity.[2] Certainly no one in Washington who had had anything to do with Geneva disagreed with this statement. From the point of view of the JCS and other senior American military men the results at Geneva caused great concern for the future, as they should have.

When the Indochinese phase of the conference opened on 8 May, the main outlines of the U.S. task during the critical days to come were reasonably clear. The French had to be supported, as much as they and harsh reality would permit. There were three areas in which U.S. support could be effective: at the conference table, in Indochina, and on the international scene. The nature of the problems bound to arise, and the nature of the ally, were such that support could not be unqualified. What was, in spite of its gravity, largely a matter of internal affairs to France, was to the United States a major move in its global strategy. There was the risk that, in holding France's chin above the quicksand, America might become inextricably mired in a series of commitments inimical to our own interests. The U.S. position at Geneva was, from the start, difficult and delicate.

The difficulty sprang from the magnitude of the material, psychological, and moral changes the United States wished France and the Associated States to accomplish in order to meet its minimum conditions for really effective support and participation; the delicacy lay in convincing them without alienating them. On the eve of the conference, Ambassador Dillon cabled from Paris that, since the United States had been unable to respond to French requests for military assistance to save Dien Bien Phu, the only available course now was to support fully negotiation of the best possible settlement at Geneva. The Ambassador claimed that it would appear utterly illogical to all Frenchmen were the United States to refuse to associate itself unreservedly with the settlement, and that a refusal would seriously affect our already damaged prestige and have adverse repercussions on NATO and EDC. But the NSC had already established a number of conditions under which the United States would not associate itself with an agreement.

The NSC had decided that the United States ought not to associate itself with any proposal, from any source, directed toward a cease-fire in advance of an acceptable armistice agreement under international controls. The United States could concur in the initiation of negotiations for such an armistice. The NSC urged that France and the Associated States should continue to oppose the Vietminh with all resources at their disposal. In the meantime, to strengthen the position of France and the Associated States during the negotiations, the United States should continue its program of aid and its efforts to organize a Southeast Asian regional grouping to prevent further communist expansion.

The NSC was informed that the Secretary of State intended to indicate to the French government the willingness of the United States to discuss at any time the conditions under which the Indochina conflict might be internationalized. In explaining the administration's position [to the French], Mr. Dulles stated that prerequisites had not been fulfilled and that, therefore, conditions did not exist for a successful conclusion of the war. Under the circumstances, the Secretary said, intervention was not advisable, and in any event the United States would not intervene unless other interested nations joined in.

American intervention was the only ace that France and the United States held between them. The nature of the original French armistice proposals was conditioned by uncertainty about American intentions, while U.S. support depended upon the nature of the proposals. Four days before the conference, a high official of the French Ministry of Foreign Affairs admitted to Under Secretary of State Smith that the French had not advised the United States of their ideas about possible armistice proposals because they had been unable to agree among themselves. He said that the near impossibility of preventing the communists from profiting by a cease-fire or armistice arrangement was fully realized, but that it was necessary to seek the course with the least evil consequences. To an expression of hope that the French proposals would receive American support, Secretary Smith replied that U.S. policy remained that anything short of prosecution of the Navarre Plan to victory was not good enough. The French official observed that that was a "large order," but he believed the United States would not be "too unhappy" over the French proposals when they emerged. He added that if the United States did not like them it would not be in a position to object, unless prepared to intervene militarily.

When finally communicated, the tentative French proposals (not yet authorized by the cabinet) were better than expected. They assumed that the problem of Vietnam was purely Vietnamese, with no question of partition, and that it was only a military struggle for control of the government. Laos and Cambodia were in a totally different category, as victims of external aggression. According to the Berlin Agreement, the purpose of the Geneva Conference was to establish peace in all three countries. To this end, there should be a cease-fire guaranteed by adequate military and administrative controls under supervision. Cease-fire would take effect only when such guarantees had been embodied in armistice conventions, which might be different for all three states, and when control machinery had been established and was in place. Controls would be based upon Premier Laniel's 5 March conditions. When cease-fire occurred, regular troops would be regrouped into delimited areas and all other forces disarmed. The control machinery would be international and would require a considerable body of personnel. After peace had been reestablished by the cease-fire, political and economic problems could be examined.

The French assumed that the USSR would propose an immediate cease-fire, to be followed by a political settlement based on coalition and immediate elections. Such a maneuver would force the West into the position of opposing a cease-fire. In spite of the strong emotional desire of the French public for a cease-fire, the government could defend its proposal on the ground that the conditions demanded were essential for the safety of the troops. Compliance with those conditions would, in effect, delay any cease-fire for a long time, if not indefinitely.

In response to the inquiry whether by "international" the French meant U.N. supervision, it was stated that there was no firm position on the question. But subsequent discussion indicated that the French continued to oppose the use of U.N. machinery for fear it would establish a precedent that could be used against them in North Africa and elsewhere. It was also perceived that the British shared this view.

Although the tentative French terms were not an outright request for a cease-fire, the American delegate [Under Secretary Smith] sensed that unless or until there was firm support in the United States for some other solution, we would not be in a position in Geneva to prevent the French from making such a proposal—far below a successful prosecution of the Navarre Plan. There was doubt whether the French would, in fact, remain firm in negotiations for satisfactory controls. They might slide rapidly toward the almost inevitable communist counterproposal of immediate cease-fire without controls. An important element in blocking French capitulation, as the French themselves observed, would be the degree to which the United States could strengthen the French hand by increasing communist uncertainty of the possibility of American intervention. In the opinion of the American delegate, organizing some form of Southeast Asian coalition would bolster the French.

The comments of the JCS were even more somber. They thought the French proposal would be regarded by Asians as a communist victory, particularly in the light of the current military situation. In their opinion, an armistice under the proposed conditions would lead to a political stalemate attended by progressive deterioration of the French-Vietnamese military position, ultimately resulting in the loss of Indochina.

Judging from past performance, the JCS were skeptical that the communists would enter into a preliminary agreement to refrain from new military operations during the course of negotiations. It was much more likely that they would intensify their operations to improve their bargaining position, whereas the French would be under a strong compulsion to avoid casualties.

The JCS warned that if the United States associated itself with the initial French terms, it would in all likelihood be confronted subsequently with the painful alternatives of continuing to support the French in successively weakened positions, or of extricating itself at some point along the way. The chiefs agreed that it was no longer realistic to insist that the French continue aggressively to prosecute the Navarre Plan. At the same time, they adhered to the view that no satisfactory settlement was possible without a substantial improvement in the military situation of the French Union. In the absence of a settlement that would reasonably assure the political and territorial integrity of the Associated States, any armistice would inevitably lead to eventual loss of the area to the communists.

The JCS considered that the United States should adopt the following as its minimum position:

> . . . The United States will not associate itself with any French proposal directed toward cease-fire in advance of a satisfactory political settlement. The United

States urges the French government to propose that negotiations for a political settlement be initiated at once. During the course of such negotiations, French Union forces should continue to oppose the forces of the Vietminh with all means at their disposal in order to reinforce the French negotiating position. In the meantime, as a means of strengthening the French hand, the United States will intensify its efforts to organize and promptly activate a Southeast Asian coalition for the purpose of preventing further expansion of communist power in Southeast Asia. If the French government persists in its intention of entering armistice negotiations or accedes to immediate cease-fire negotiations, the United States will disassociate itself from such negotiations in order to maintain maximum freedom of action in . . . opposing extension of communist control into Southeast Asia.

To make clear the reason for U.S. refusal to associate itself with a cease-fire in advance of a political settlement, President Eisenhower inserted the phrase "because of the proof given in Korea that the communists will not be bound militarily by the terms of an armistice." He also added a clause to the effect that the United States would continue its aid program to strengthen the French.

The American attitude was hardly helpful to the French government, fighting desperately for the right to negotiate at Geneva at all instead of trying to reach an agreement with the Vietminh immediately. Wits in Paris had prognosticated that the French Assembly would allow the government "to keep its head above water but not show its neck." In the words of the American Embassy, "its neck emerged" when it won a vote of confidence by a better margin than expected. But the government's victory was clearly subject to an implicit caveat: should it fail to find a solution at Geneva along Laniel's lines, it would be faced with almost insurmountable pressure to reach an immediate settlement with the Vietminh on the best terms obtainable.

The French tabled their proposal, now couched in looser terms, on the opening day of the Indochina conference.[3] The JSSC of the Joint Chiefs of Staff displayed little enthusiasm, observing that there were no provisions or safeguards to remove or reduce hazards to U.S. security interests involved in the acceptance of any armistice with the communists that was not preceded by a satisfactory political settlement. If there was good faith on both sides the French terms, subject to the addition of certain safeguards, appeared to constitute a satisfactory basis for negotiation. But there was every reason to expect the characteristic bad faith of the communists. Hence, in the absence of subsequent strong and positive action by the Western powers, an armistice would almost certainly lead to the subjugation of Indochina and eventually the loss of all Southeast Asia. However, in view of the decision of the U.S. government to concur in initiating negotiations, the committee interposed no further objections—providing the French incorporated provisions for international control machinery to be established, in place, and ready to function prior to actual cease-fire, and providing that representatives of the international control commission be guaranteed unrestricted movements in, and free access to, all Indochina.

The recommendations of the JSSC headed the list of principles given the American delegate to guide him in evaluating proposals offered to the conference. The following were considered basic to any acceptable settlement of the Indochina question:

1) Establishment of international control machinery, in place and ready to function, prior to an actual cease-fire.

2) Unrestricted movement in and free access to all of Indochina by representatives of the international control commission.

3) Sufficient military personnel and logistic support by such a commission to discharge its responsibilities in connection with the armistice terms.

4) Provision for U.N. (or some other form of effective international control) responsibility for supervision of the international control commission.

5) Provision for the security of troops and populations, and guarantees against abuses of the cease-fire by either party.

6) Provisions for the humane and orderly liberation of POWs and internees.

7) Evacuation of Vietminh forces from Laos and Cambodia.

8) Provision for the examination of political and economic problems following an armistice agreement.

9) No provisions in the armistice of a political nature, such as for early elections, or for troop withdrawals that would clearly lead to a communist takeover.[4]

American acquiescence in armistice negotiations represented abandonment of the demand for a political settlement first. It was a self-inflicted defeat. The United States had taken too extreme a stand in the beginning by insisting that the French hold out for a political settlement before considering an armistice. The French people were in no temper to throw themselves into an all-out effort to win the war if conference negotiations failed. And, in essence, the American position had been a deliberate invitation to such a failure, in order to give free scope for vigorous prosecution of the war. This approach was based on our strength and confidence and goodwill; it was incomprehensible to the American government that the French should display such a lack of all three of these qualities.

In addition to the specific principles governing armistice negotiations, Secretary Smith was provided with a set of basic instructions approved by the President. He was not to deal with delegates of the Communist Chinese regime or any other regime not then recognized diplomatically by the United States, on any terms implying political recognition or conceding to that regime any status other than that of a regime with which it was necessary to deal on a de facto basis in order to end aggression and obtain peace. The position of the United

States in the Indochinese phase of the conference was defined as that of an interested nation but one that was neither a belligerent nor a principal in the negotiations. The United States was participating to assist in arriving at decisions that would help the nations of that area peacefully to enjoy territorial integrity and political independence under stable and free governments, to expand their economies, to realize their legitimate national aspirations, and to develop security through individual and collective defense against aggression from within and without. This was meant to imply that these people should not be amalgamated into the communist bloc of imperialistic dictatorships.

Secretary Smith was informed that the United States was not prepared to give its express or implied approval to any cease-fire, armistice, or other settlement that would have the effect of subverting the existing lawful governments of the Associated States, or of permanently impairing their territorial integrity or jeopardizing the forces of the French Union in Indochina, or that would otherwise contravene the principles under which the United States was participating. If in his judgment continued participation in the conference appeared likely to involve the United States in a result inconsistent with the above-stated policy, he was instructed to recommend withdrawal or limitation of the American role to that of observer. These instructions had been cleared with the Senate Foreign Relations Committee and the House Foreign Affairs Committee.

Secretary Smith was also to remind the French of the NSC policy concerning the objective of assuring independence and freedom to the Associated States. As far as guarantees were concerned, he was to make it clear that the United States would reserve its position until more was known about the nature of the settlement and the obligations of the guarantors.

28

Time Runs Out for the French

There were few illusions in Washington about the nature of any agreement that would come out of Geneva. The United States was just marking time until France realized that she was facing virtual surrender.

The obvious answer to the problems of France and the Associated States at the Geneva Conference was U.S. military intervention, but the French seemed to dread the cure fully as much, if not more, than the complaint. Twice during April France had sought American intervention to save Dien Bien Phu and twice had been unwilling to pay the going price—independence for the Associated States, and Allied rather than U.S. unilateral participation in the war. British unwillingness to take united action had also blocked Allied participation.

In early May 1954 Secretary Dulles persuaded the NSC and the President that the United States should concentrate on winning consent by Australia and New Zealand for united action, gambling on later British participation. In spite of the need for prompt decisions on internationalizing the war, Secretary Dulles was cautious about imparting to the French the full set of conditions under which the United States would be willing to intervene. He feared that a proposal to internationalize the war would be rejected if the issue were raised before the French were thoroughly convinced that their only choice was between intervention and surrender. Moreover, the British would be more likely to support, or at least acquiesce in, intervention once Geneva had been shown to offer no prospect of a solution. The Australian government would almost certainly not take a position until after elections at the end of May. Nevertheless it appeared desirable for Premier Laniel to know, in general terms, the American conditions because of their influence on current French military decisions in Indochina and political decisions in Geneva. Accordingly, Mr. Dulles informed Ambassador Douglas Dillon that the President would ask Congress for authority to use our armed forces in Indochina to support friendly and recognized governments against aggression or armed subversion fomented from without, providing he could then state that the following conditions had been or would be met:

1) that U.S. military participation had been formally requested by France *and* the Associated States;

2) that Thailand, Philippines, Australia, New Zealand, and Britain had received similar invitations and that we were satisfied that the first two would accept at once; that the next two would probably accept following Australian elections, if the United States invoked the ANZUS treaty; and that the United Kingdom would either participate or be acquiescent;

3) that some aspect of the matter would be presented to the U.N. promptly, such as a request from Laos, Cambodia, or Thailand for a peace observation commission;

4) that the French guarantee complete independence to the Associated States, including an unqualified option to withdraw from the French Union at any time;

5) that France would not withdraw forces from Indochina during the period of united action, so that forces from the United States, principally air and sea, and others would be supplementary and not in substitution;

6) that agreement be reached on training of native troops and on a command structure for united action.

The United States would expect all these conditions to be accepted by the French cabinet and authorized or endorsed by the French National Assembly, because of the uncertain tenure of any French government. Once it agreed to intervene the United States would be fully committed, and would have to be able to rely upon any successor French government to adhere to the conditions. Mr. Dulles characterized the conditions as indispensable as a basis for U.S. action. President Eisenhower approved the message to Ambassador Dillon, and Mr. Dulles authorized communication of these views orally to Premier Laniel *unless,* in the opinion of the Ambassador, it would result in the immediate resignation of the French government or hasten its capitulation at Geneva.

On the whole, according to Ambassador Dillon, Premier Laniel and Foreign Minister Maurice Schumann appeared well pleased by this clarification of the American position. They were particularly impressed by the indication that participation by the United Kingdom was no longer a prerequisite to action by the United States. They pointed out that France had no control over compliance by Thailand and the others and asked to be kept informed of U.S. progress along those lines.

As expected, the one serious objection was to the condition that France publicly accord to the Associated States the right to withdraw from the French Union. To most Frenchmen it was unthinkable that their former colonies would *ever* consider severing their ties with France. At least they said so, not realizing that taking this position was to the rest of the world an indication that France was really unwilling to grant complete independence. Laniel and Schumann buttressed their argument by stressing that even the Vietminh looked toward the possibility of joining the French Union. When Ambassador Dillon reported that American insistence on this point might discourage even the strongest supporters of continued French action, Mr. Dulles noted that it was essential to remove any taint of colonialism in order to attract vital Asian support and forestall opposition by other Asian and Middle Eastern countries. Premier Laniel and his Foreign Minister observed that French public opinion would never understand why it was necessary to make such a statement when it had never been requested by any of the Associated States. In their opinion it also threw into question the whole concept of the French Union as an association of free and independent peoples and cast doubt upon the honor and veracity of France, which had recently stated that Vietnam had been granted independence and had chosen to remain in the Union.

Ambassador Dillon, trying to be helpful, suggested to Mr. Dulles that the matter of independence had been taken care of satisfactorily by the pending treaties between France and Vietnam but that the situation was obscured and complicated by the existence of a state of war. Much of the difficulty was caused by the presence of a large French Expeditionary Corps on Vietnamese soil, by the necessity for a French supreme military commander, and by the absence of a truly powerful Vietnamese national army. The Ambassador recalled that Korea, once regarded as an American puppet, became a demonstrably free and independent nation as soon as its own army was built up. Therefore, suggested the Ambassador, we should press for a publicized agreement with France giving the United States prime responsibility for training and equipping the Vietnamese army. He pointed out that there were manifold advantages: Vietnamese independence could no longer be questionable; doubts about the ability and good faith of the French military command to accomplish the task would be circumvented; and the French would be able to withdraw the Expeditionary Corps after cessation of hostilities. Withdrawal of non-Asian troops, he felt, would also probably have a salutary effect upon the Chinese.

While recognizing virtues in the suggestions, Mr. Dulles responded that we would not be able to wait for the abolition of all deep-rooted abuses and extraterritorial privileges in such times. He continued to explore means of obtaining a public, and preferably international, declaration on the subject of Vietnamese independence, and to press for prompt signature of the draft treaties between France and Vietnam.

Both Ambassador Dillon and Under Secretary Smith were as anxious as Mr. Dulles to see the basic treaties signed. Until that event took place they were forced to occupy an uncomfortably false position at Geneva. Moreover, it was probable that, following signature, Bao Dai would return promptly to Vietnam and, to the extent his energy and ability permitted, attempt to assume national leadership.

Premier Laniel and Vietnamese Prime Minister Prince Buu Loc initialed the

Franco-Vietnamese Treaties of Independence and Association on 4 June 1954. Mr. Dulles cabled Ambassador Dillon to inform the French that initialing the treaties would not conform to the American position concerning independence. M. Schumann explained that this initialing was far more important than the usual initialing of a treaty, since the act permitted Buu Loc to return to Vietnam without the appearance of being empty-handed. Schumann nevertheless gave assurances that the French were ready to sign, but from the Vietnamese chargé it was learned that the conclusion and signature of the related convention, to which the treaty signature was subordinated, had bogged down. The treaties had not been signed by the end of the Geneva Conference, and Bao Dai remained in France.

If the French wanted to use the possibility of American intervention primarily as a card to play at Geneva, it was to their advantage not to come to a firm decision until the conference had run its course. Secretary Dulles tried to impress upon them that, from the point of view of the United States, the practicability of intervention was constantly subject to "consideration in the light of day-to-day developments." Though we were anxious to bolster the French position, the impression was growing that Laniel might be using the U.S. conditions to create an alibi for himself or his successor: capitulation could be blamed on the United States for having presented terms so rigorous as to be unacceptable. This suspicion was shared by American representatives at the conference; but, there was good reason to believe, the French were as confused about the real intentions of the United States as we were about those of France!

Confusion there certainly was. France was loathe to carry out, in any circumstances, the sweeping political changes in Indochina demanded by the United States. France was angling for an American commitment to intervene, without having to reverse overnight a century of ingrained colonial practices. But confusion also arose from other directions. "We make strong statements, then qualify them," said Secretary Smith. Qualification is always necessary where there is not identity of purpose and intent. And the national interests of the United States and France at Geneva were not the same. The French wanted an end to the war, whereas U.S. security interests were best served by its continuation on our terms. Therefore, the attitude of the United States at Geneva was basically negative. We knew precisely what we did *not* want France to do at the conference, because a settlement of any kind represented at least a partial defeat for us. The Geneva Conference was an impediment to the positive contributions the United States had to offer. To the French, American support was of a type that would have been a boon to a fighter in the first few rounds. But France was in the tenth.

Another likely source of misunderstanding was French unfamiliarity with American constitutional processes. There is a certain amount of evidence that high French officials were not familiar with the relationships between our President and Congress. Moreover, at least partly through their misconceptions about the machinery of American government, the French had a tendency to pay too much attention to the pronouncement of individual Americans while disregarding the official statements of the government, and they placed great store on information from other sources that seemed favorable to their point of view.

Much confusion stemmed from the fact that the French would turn immediately to a detailed consideration of exactly what military support they would receive as a result of intervention, instead of first complying with the political prerequisites upon which intervention depended. They thus created the definite impression that they were attempting to "piecemeal us to death" and maneuver the United States into a position where it could be accused of having haggled over minutiae instead of coming to their aid. Once in that position, the United States would have had to enter the war under conditions more suitable to the French, or bear the blame for capitulation.

As a prominent member of Defense observed, it was evident that the French military thought there had already been an agreement to U.S. conditions on the government level. Hence, they could not understand why the United States did not proceed with its commitments. For instance, based on the statement of the United States that *if it intervened* it would commit principally air and sea forces, the French asked for 20,000 Marines, then raised the request to six Marine divisions. When the French Ambassador in Washington reported that there were not six Marine divisions in existence, Paris replied that there had to be some kind of contribution. Minister Schumann was reportedly "excited and dismayed" when informed that I had said there was no intention of using Marines in Indochina. According to Ambassador Henri Bonnet, this answer conflicted with what the French government had hitherto understood to be the intention of the United States in this respect.

This imbroglio, coinciding with several other instances of serious misunderstanding, made evident how correct Secretary Smith had been when he cabled from Geneva that "the U.S. position is not understood here." Secretary Dulles attempted to bring this undesirable state of affairs to an abrupt halt. He told Ambassador Bonnet that the U.S. position had been clear from the start and that we were not willing to make, in advance, a commitment the French could use for internal political maneuvering or for negotiating at Geneva. Such a commitment would, he said, represent a kind of permanent option on U.S. intervention, to be used as best suited French purposes. The U.S. stand was "all or nothing." Ambassador Bonnet expressed surprise that the United States thought the French government had not made up its mind to internationalize the war. He considered the request had already been made! At the same time Under Secretary Smith, in Europe, was still patiently explaining to Messieurs Bidault and Jean Chauvel that the President could not ask Congress to sanction intervention until the basic conditions had been fulfilled by France.

A month earlier, when apprising Premier Laniel of the American conditions,

Ambassador Dillon had been at pains to make clear that they represented high-level thinking in Washington and did not constitute, at that time, any commitment on the part of the whole government. This did not deter M. Laniel from requesting definite assurance, preferably in writing, that American aviation would immediately come to the aid of French forces in the Red Delta if they were attacked by Chinese MIGs.

In March General Ely and I had made arrangements for the preparation of plans to cover the eventuality of Chinese air attack, so that there would be no time wasted if an attack came and the United States decided to intervene. Presumably informed of these arrangements, it was not long before Premier Laniel, Foreign Minister Schumann, and other high French officials were talking as though I had made a commitment of immediate U.S. retaliation in the event of overt Chinese aggression. The French leaders still did not seem to realize that any action would require political approval. On 1 June their inquiries were brought to the attention of President Eisenhower, who expressed himself strongly on the subject: the United States would not intervene in China on any basis except united action. He would not be responsible for going into China alone unless a joint congressional resolution ordered him to do so. He made it very plain that united action was a condition related not merely to regional grouping for the defense of Southeast Asia, but also to U.S. intervention in response to overt Chinese aggression.

☆ ☆ ☆ ☆

On the day after the President had stated his position, and observed it did not differ from that of Mr. Dulles, General Valluy, the senior French officer in Washington, called on me to ask whether it would be possible for the President to obtain some sort of "blank check" from Congress against such a contingency, so that American aid could be provided in a minimum of time. He also wanted to know whether the French could count on our assistance, which might involve the landing of Marines, in case they were forced to evacuate Hanoi and withdraw into the Haiphong redoubt. I gave no direct answer to either question. I first stated that U.S. intelligence did not indicate that the Chinese were preparing for air intervention. I then carefully reiterated the U.S. policy of united action. General Valluy was not satisfied. He likened the French situation to that of a man on a sinking ship. Seven or eight destroyers at a distance were of little help; what he needed was an airplane to come and pick him up.

I tried again to explain that the whole matter was obviously beyond my control since it involved a political decision of grave importance at the highest levels in our government. Concerning the Marines, I reminded General Valluy that any landing could only be pursuant to a political decision to intervene which, in turn, depended upon fulfillment of the conditions already transmitted to the French government. In the event of intervention, the U.S. force contribution would consist principally of "sea and air forces." I admitted that under these circumstances the possible use of Marines would not necessarily be ruled out.

The discussions between General Valluy and myself were in the nature of preliminary conversations in anticipation of bilateral staff talks under cover of the five-power military conference then in session in Washington. General Valluy availed himself of this opportunity to brief me on the military situation in Indochina following the fall of Dien Bien Phu. It was a gloomy report, based on the observations of Generals Ely and Salan after their visit to the theater of operations in May.

Dien Bien Phu, said General Valluy, had left its mark on both civilians and military, particularly in the Tonkin Delta. The troops were tired and their morale visibly low. Effectiveness of the military commanders had markedly decreased; there was controversy between General Navarre and General Cogny (in command in Hanoi) and their respective staffs. There was no close agreement between higher headquarters and commanders of the mobile groups; there was conflict between General Navarre and the French air force; there were differences among the air force commanders and among their staffs. French and Vietnamese troops had lost confidence in one another. Mobilization measures instituted by Bao Dai were a failure. The Vietnamese government was discredited. The situation in Cochin China was not good; there was conflict between the Vietnamese troops and the population of the area.

General Valluy admitted that Vietminh losses at Dien Bien Phu had been considerably less than the French had expected. The Vietminh Battle Corps was still effective, and within ten days their battle-hardened divisions would reach jump-off positions around the perimeter of the Tonkin Delta. There were prospects of a hard battle for Hanoi toward the end of June.

Extraordinary measures were required to make the best of the situation. General Valluy explained that the French were regrouping their forces in order to place the Vietnamese in the static defense of the perimeter, while using French troops as mobile groups. The Vietminh were capitalizing on the delicacy of the regrouping operation to deal hard blows at some of the Vietnamese units.

Although it was the object of the French to hold the Tonkin redoubt at all costs, they were not assured of success. General Valluy claimed the enemy was building up to a strength of 100 battalions, with high morale, exulting in victory, and with the civilian population leaning more and more in their favor. The French were apprehensive about possible intervention by the Communist Chinese air force.[1]

In the meantime, the French military did not hide their desire for American participation, which was the real thrust behind General Valluy's talks with me. On 4 June, three days before his last talk with me, the General made a presentation of the situation in Indochina before the five-power conference.

The General stated that it was not his intention to dramatize, but "only to be realistic among soldiers." If the Tonkin Delta were lost, the military line would not be reestablished anywhere. The Laos bottleneck or the eighteenth parallel had the physiography that should permit reestablishment of a line, but the General affirmed that there would be no forces to man that line. He was not speaking of French forces; he meant to indicate that there were no South Vietnamese who could oppose North Vietnamese.

Ho Chi Minh's objective was Tonkin, General Valluy stated, to be attained either by negotiation at Geneva or by assault on Hanoi. He wished to entangle the French in negotiations by admitting now, for the first time, that there was a communist northern state and a noncommunist southern state, and by saying that both might be incorporated into the French Union. Although, admitted the General, "among military men" Ho was finding receptive French ears across the negotiating table, he was also preparing for military action if it were called for, and his chances for success were good.

"It has been said at this conference," recalled General Valluy, "that if Tonkin is lost, we will fight in the south. However, the French will not fight nor will Vietnam." The General maintained that the conferees would have to provide their own men for the line in the south. Moreover, it would be an artificial line, toward whose defense Laos, Cambodia, and Thailand could contribute nothing. The decisive point was this: if the other conferees did not underwrite the battle for Tonkin, they would fight tomorrow without the French in Saigon. If the Tonkin Delta were lost, no Vietnamese would fight against another Vietnamese and—sooner or later, probably sooner—the whole of Vietnam would become communist.

From Secretary Smith in Geneva to Chargé d'Affaires Robert McClintock in Saigon, there was no American who chose to contest seriously General Valluy's estimate. McClintock cabled that General Valluy's appreciation of the situation was exceedingly good, "in fact almost too good." It was McClintock's impression that Valluy had made his statement under instructions, less with military considerations in mind than with a political objective; he was probably looking as much at the French Parliament as at the Tonkin Delta. General Ely, said McClintock, had twice in his presence stated that it was his keenest desire for the United States to enter the war. McClintock believed that the purpose of Valluy's statement was either to bring the United States, and if possible the other powers at the conference, into the conflict or, failing that, to prepare before history an excuse for an armistice the French would then request of the Vietminh.

General Valluy's presentation of the French plight in Indochina was another in the series of incidents around 9 June that led to emphatic restatement of the American basic position. To Valluy our answer was the same: fulfill the preliminary conditions and the United States will intervene. Moreover, we were well prepared militarily for intervention. The JCS had drawn up and were putting the finishing touches on plans to cover every contingency. They had the strategy worked out, the command structure, the force contributions, plans for training native troops. They awaited only the political agreement at the top.

☆ ☆ ☆ ☆

On 20 May, in discussion between the French and State, the United States had specified that, should intervention be undertaken, France would have to agree not to withdraw its forces from Indochina during the period of united action. Agreement must also be reached on the training of native troops and on command structure for united action. In formulating a Defense position on command structure, and on the size and composition of U.S. force contributions, the JCS had been guided by several factors: the limited availability of forces for military action in Indochina; the current numerical advantage of French Union forces over the enemy (approximately 5–3); the undesirability of basing large numbers of American troops in Indochina; the primary need for an expanded and intensified training problem; the difficulty of superimposing our air forces upon existing facilities in Indochina; the implications of a Chinese reaction to U.S. intervention; and, finally, the fact that atomic weapons would be used when it was to our military advantage.

The JCS considered that no command structure was acceptable that did not permit the United States to influence a future strategy in Indochina. To solve the problem of overall strategic guidance, they suggested a military representative committee, with a steering or standing group along the lines of NATO. The group would be patterned after the U.S. Joint Staff and would be composed primarily of American and French officers. The committee would draw its membership from those nations contributing the principal forces of the coalition. Although the JCS felt that the Allied commander-in-chief should be French, there also had to be an American deputy and an air adviser. The deputy would provide liaison with the French and would coordinate U.S. activities with the overall operations. The JCS were well informed as to the complete subordination of the French air force to the army, hence the air adviser to see that U.S. air power was not misused.

American force contributions, as recommended by the JCS, would be limited primarily to a fast carrier task force and supporting elements, and to USAF units operating from existing bases outside Indochina. It was believed that committing larger naval forces, or basing substantial air forces in Indochina, would reduce readiness to meet probable Chinese reaction elsewhere in the Far East. From the American point of view, with reference to the Far East as a whole, Indochina was devoid of decisive military objectives, and the allocation of more than token armed forces to that area would be a serious diversion of limited U.S. capabilities.

This observation coincided with the central philosophy of the JCS that the real solution to Far Eastern difficulties lay in the neutralization of Communist China. They noted that the principal sources of Vietminh support were "outside Indochina," and that the destruction or neutralization of those outside sources would materially reduce French military problems.

It was unlikely that their strategic calculus would find acceptance at the political level unless the Chinese intervened overtly in the Indochina struggle. In that event, the JCS strategic concept and plan of operations called for destroying effective communist forces and their means of support in Indochina, as well as reducing Chinese communist capability for further aggression. This meant offensive air operations against military targets in China proper, Hainan, and other islands being used by the communists in direct support of their operations, or threatening the security of Allied forces. Simultaneously, French Union Forces, augmented by U.S. naval and air units, would exploit whatever success had been achieved as a result of the massive air operations. Should this not suffice to assure victory, the attack against China would have to be stepped up. It might require a highly selective atomic offensive, in addition to attacks with other weapons systems, accompanied by a blockade of the China coast. Consideration was also given to instituting the blockade from the outset, and increasing it steadily as required. Hainan Island would be seized or neutralized, and operations against the Chinese mainland would be undertaken by the Chinese Nationalists.

All American forces engaged in these operations would be under the unified command of CINCPAC. He would insure the coordination of all operations in Southeast Asia and provide for the necessary ground-air coordination between French Union forces and U.S. naval and air forces. He would also select targets and conduct air operations against military targets in Indochina and against those in China that directly supported Chinese aggression. The Commander Strategic Air Command would support CINCPAC and would, in addition, conduct air operations as directed by the JCS to further reduce the Chinese warmaking capability.

The JCS were by no means oblivious to the possible consequences of their strategy. They recommended that it be accompanied by an appropriate degree of mobilization to provide for the greater risk of a general war, so that the United States might be prudently prepared. Immediate action would have to be taken to strengthen American allies. However, due to the overriding mobilization requirement of U.S. forces, such aid would have to be limited to those allies who could directly support the U.S. strategic concept of a general war. This aid would further have to be limited to combat-essential materiel, essential replacements, and spare parts beyond the capabilities of the individual countries.

Initially, there would be no requirement for materiel and equipment above the current military aid program for France and other Allied forces in Indochina. Within approximately six months, MDAP would have to be increased to take care of three new ROK-type native divisions and thereafter would have to be increased as new divisions were developed. But whether or not the United States intervened in Indochina, the JCS considered it vital that the war there be financed by methods separate and distinct from our worldwide MAP.

Preparation and involvement on such a vast scale would not be necessary if the Chinese did not project themselves openly into the war. In that case, the chiefs recommended a more restricted but equally aggressive, hard-hitting plan, which assumed that the USSR would not enter the conflict openly but would defend Soviet-controlled areas and might covertly supply air and naval forces. The plan also assumed that hostilities in Korea would not be resumed; that French Union Forces would continue to resist in Indochina with American assistance; and that atomic weapons might be used by both sides.

Granted these assumptions, the JCS considered that, regardless of the nationality of the forces engaged, the major courses of action would remain relatively unchanged. Enemy supply lines would have to be interdicted, while sufficient friendly forces were regrouped in the north to conduct coordinated offensive operations there. Territory liberated from the enemy would have to be pacified, following which coordinated ground, air, and naval operations would be undertaken in central Vietnam and northern Laos to destroy enemy forces therein. Finally, attention would be turned to South Vietnam and Cambodia to complete the destruction of the enemy. Throughout, psychological and unconventional warfare operations would be carried out. Basic to all these activities was the building up, training, and equipping of regular and guerrilla indigenous forces.

From the military standpoint, the JCS plan was a good and feasible one for the French themselves to follow, granted continued assistance by the United States as in the past. Could they carry it out without active assistance or intervention of American forces?

It was the opinion of the JCS that, in the face of the rapidly crumbling military situation, support by U.S. air and naval forces, as envisaged and limited to action within the boundaries of Indochina, would not insure decisive military results. Benefit to the French would be mainly psychological. But for the United States it would probably mean that involvement, although initially limited, would continue and expand until it would ultimately require additional naval and air forces and extensive ground forces to prevent the loss of Indochina. Eventually, this could lead to full U.S. responsibility for the outcome of the war.

Again the JCS warned that involvement in Indochina, even on a limited scale, increased the risk of a general war. Accordingly, if the United States decided to intervene the armed forces should be placed in a more suitable state of readiness to meet such an eventuality. Decisions would have to be made on mobilization and logistic, fiscal, and other supporting measures. A major increase in the armed forces, beyond that planned for fiscal 1955, would be required, as well as an expanded draft and the recall of some National Guard and reserve units.

☆ ☆ ☆ ☆

General O'Daniel's permanent assignment to Indochina in April 1954 marked the beginning of intensive attempts to sell the French the notion of requesting our assistance. But really effective assistance would amount to nothing less than our assuming full responsibility for all training. Once committed on that scale, we could find ourselves sharing the blame if the war turned out badly. Hence, responsibility for training without some control over combat employment of native troops and, therefore, a voice in strategy and operational planning would be unacceptable. The French had anticipated this eventuality and feared its consequences, which accounted for much of their reluctance to ask for our help. By the time our arguments and the military situation had softened the French to urgently request assistance, the United States was no longer willing to provide it unless the French complied with all the other conditions upon which full intervention was contingent.

General O'Daniel tackled his job with enthusiasm upon arrival for duty in South Vietnam. By mid-May he had won from Generals Ely and Navarre a considerable degree of acquiescence.

O'Daniel thought it might be possible to create nine Vietnamese and three Cambodian divisions by October. Chargé McClintock in Saigon sounded a note of caution:

> I have the greatest admiration for General O'Daniel's faith, tenacity and bulldog courage. I fear, however, he may be over sanguine as to possibilities of making an effective Vietnamese fighting force in six months' time. Irrespective of General O'Daniel's abundant military virtues, there are many obstacles in his path. Not the least of these is complete apathy of Vietnamese populace coupled with increasing tendency of fence-sitters to go over to enemy, absolute breakdown of mobilization plan, internecine rivalries between the few men capable of showing leadership, and lack of leadership from Bao Dai and his Ministers. I do not say the job cannot be done but that we should take a close look at its dimensions before we come in . . .

General Ely had come a long way since March. He now favored forming native troops into divisional units, although he still felt a U.S. division was not the answer. He also agreed that American advisers should be placed at various levels within a division. On the subject of U.S. participation in operational planning, however, he felt there was need for clarification. There could be no discussion of the United States sharing responsibility for planning operations. There could be only one commander, and he must be French. On the other hand, providing agreement were reached on intervention, American officers could be integrated into French planning staffs. Ely was prepared to discuss in Washington the details of such integration. Although now actively favoring U.S. training, his basic position was that training was only one part of an overall plan that would concern itself with fixing the conditions and the nature of U.S. intervention. They would become pertinent only when an agreement to intervene had been reached, and such an agreement would only take place if the Geneva Conference failed.

General Ely's position was, of course, opposite to that of the U.S. government. Nevertheless, acting on his own, he summoned General O'Daniel and, through him, requested the United States to organize and supervise the training of Vietnamese divisions and to do the same for all other Vietnamese training. This request was promptly transmitted to Washington by General O'Daniel on 9 June [Saigon time]. On the same day General Ely cabled General Valluy in Washington:

> I have not yet made a survey of the military situation—especially in Tonkin. However, it seems to me that the decisions I will have to take regarding the operations will rest on the U.S. intentions, in the present situation, as well as those they anticipate in the future.
>
> Therefore, I would very much like to have either in Paris . . . or here in Saigon, as soon as possible, an exchange of views with a qualified representative of Admiral Radford, in order to know what I can expect on the part of the USA.

These two messages, the mixup over the use of Marines, and a number of other incidents indicating that the French were ignoring the manner in which the United States had conditioned its offer of intervention, precipitated the crisis of 9 June. Both the JCS and State felt it was time to call a halt until the French realized that in regard to intervention it was "all or nothing." While Mr. Dulles was laying down the law to Ambassador Bonnet, I informed General Valluy that he was not in a position to respond to General Ely's request for conversations on the subject.[2] The official U.S. position was this:

> Prior to the French decision to request internationalization of the war, we consider it undesirable to start yet another series of conversations which would inevitably provoke, on the French side, all kinds of hopes and interpretations with regard to basic issues regarding U.S. intervention, which would only cause further confusion; we should not be eased into a series of piecemeal commitments resulting from collateral military conversations, in the absence of an understanding with the French Government based on our general proposal.
>
> With regard to U.S. training of Vietnamese troops, we feel that the situation in Vietnam has degenerated to the point where any commitments at this time to send over U.S. instructors in the near future might expose us to a situation in which it would be contrary to our interests to fulfill such a commitment. Our position accordingly is that we do *not* wish to consider a U.S. training mission or program separately from overall operational plans on assumption that conditions are fulfilled for U.S. participation in the Indochina war.

To keep him from trying to push more requests for aid, General O'Daniel was informed that any agreement on training must be made on a government level. But Ely had already promised to give O'Daniel the request in writing. When it arrived, it turned out to be a statement of agreed principles, not a request for aid, and it came by way of Prince Buu Loc. O'Daniel, commenting on this unexpected channel of communication, cabled:

> Ely gave Buu Loc the copy of the letter knowing that I had no authority to act. He either misunderstood what I wanted, which is possible, or he may in disappointment failure obtain training assistance, desire to show Vietnamese he is trying to obtain aid for them and undesiring be placed in asking position himself— had suggested Buu Loc ask for training assistance by United States.

A less charitable explanation is also possible.

The 9 June decision to defer the training program was a drastic one. General O'Daniel protested vigorously. Secretary Smith, viewing the matter in the light of Geneva, advanced cogent reasons for reconsidering the decision. While appreciating the desirability of an agreement on an overall operational plan for intervention, he pointed out that negotiations were reaching a stage where any indication of U.S. support—particularly a decision to train Vietnamese troops— strengthened the French position. Inasmuch as it looked as though a settlement would result in partition, a national army was going to be needed to protect what was left of Vietnam. A training mission would be needed to strengthen the defenders.

The French had always considered training a separate problem. If the United States was no longer interested in helping with the training of the Vietnamese army, except within the framework of united action in Indochina, Ambassador Dillon felt that the French should be so informed, to prevent misunderstanding. Tactfully, he assumed State had considered the fundamental psychological importance of the decision. The French would most probably consider it meant the definite and final writeoff of Indochina by the United States and might therefore use it as an excuse for accepting Vietminh terms. There was also the probability that opponents of the United States in France might later describe the decision as an attempt to influence the French forcefully to request internationalization of the war. Last, there was the question of Vietnamese morale.

Replying to the Ambassador, Mr. Dulles commented on an apparent discrepancy. The Ambassador had, in one cable, reported Ely as stating that U.S. training of native forces was but one part of an overall plan for intervention. But in his cable protesting the dropping of training, the Ambassador asserted the French had always considered training as a problem separate from possible united action. Mr. Dulles then continued:

> Ely's position seems clear that French have opposed giving U.S. responsibility for training unless U.S. agreed to intervention . . . in effort to draw U.S. into conflict

without having U.S. conditions on intervention met, French military may now seek U.S. training in advance of U.S. commitment to intervene with own combat forces ... We are resolved not to get drawn into training program when, due deteriorating conditions and lack of over-all program to reverse situation, training program has virtually no chance of success.

If the French are going to fight, Dulles continued, for more than protection of the Expeditionary Corps, the possibility could exist for the development of a program to reverse present downhill trends; but this seemed to him most unlikely.

Mr. Dulles believed the United States should try to carry the situation along, avoiding either a formal refusal to train the Vietnamese or a massive commitment of some two to three thousand MAAG personnel. Such a commitment could not help carrying strong political overtones and might raise congressional complications. The French "want, and in effect have, an option on our intervention," said Mr. Dulles, "but they do not want to exercise it and the date of expiry of our option is fast running out."

Time was running out in Indochina, too. General O'Daniel entered plea after plea for a reversal of the decision on training. While the Army Chief of Staff, General Ridgway, told O'Daniel it was imperative that he comply strictly with orders not to negotiate a training agreement, Ridgway absolved the armed forces of blame for the delay. In Washington it was apparent that the French military were not completely aware of the situation and were laboring under the misapprehension that government agreements had been reached, hence that the U.S. military were responsible for the delay. Ridgway told O'Daniel to make clear to the French in Indochina that the delays were in no way an indication that the United States was pulling back.

Unsatisfied, General O'Daniel on 26 June appealed directly to the JCS for permission to go ahead with the training of six divisions. He sketched his plan for accomplishing the task and asked that it be passed to "the highest authority." I informed O'Daniel that, regrettably, more positive action was impracticable in view of the obscure situation, but that his message had been passed to "the highest authority" as requested.

29

Conclusions on Strategic Policy
of the United States

Thus, at least temporarily, came to an end the concerted effort of the United States to build up the indigenous forces of the Associated States. Frustration of this attempt imperiled more than the immediate future of the Indochinese peninsula. It was a body blow to one of the salient features of American strategy toward the Far East as a whole.

In the grand strategy of the United States for developing a position of military strength in the Far East, fostering the growth of the military forces of the Associated States and other noncommunist countries in Asia was second in importance only to rebuilding Japan, Korea, and Nationalist China. Indigenous military power was the heart of America's prime objective in the East, to develop the purpose and capability of the noncommunist countries to act collectively and effectively in opposing the threat of communism. Once this objective had been achieved, the United States might then be able to bring about the establishment of a comprehensive regional security arrangement of these countries, with which the United States, Britain, and possibly France would be associated. By the united action of the coalition, the power and influence of the Soviet Union in the Far East could finally be reduced, primarily through the containment and curtailment of Communist China's relative position of power.

This strategy had not existed, as such, in April 1954 when the NSC called upon Defense to determine means for strengthening our military position in the Far East. Highly relevant to an understanding of U.S. history in this period is the opening comment of the JCS in their reply:

> Since the U.S. military objectives and programs with respect to a specific country or region stem from approved U.S. policy as it affects such country, or region, the development of U.S. military objectives toward the Far East should, in the usual course, be within the context of an overall U.S. policy respecting that area. Although the U.S. policy toward Communist China does set forth certain general

objectives to be sought in the Far East vis-à-vis that country, the United States has not formulated a comprehensive policy in which the Far East is viewed as a strategic entity and which would provide definite direction for the development of a position of military strength in the Far East. Rather, our present policy addresses itself to the individual countries within the area or, in the case of Southeast Asia, to a segment of the area ... Taken in the aggregate, expressions of policy (toward individual countries) make it clear that the United States, from the standpoint of its security interests, attaches major importance to the Far East area and would be prepared to react with military force against an armed aggression by the USSR or Communist China in that region.

To furnish a purposeful answer to the problem posed by the NSC, the JCS were themselves constrained to isolate American objectives in the Far East, relate these objectives to a coherent policy, and then provide courses of action for their attainment. The JCS realized that the United States could not play Atlas forever, supporting the entire world. The noncommunist Far East would have to stand on its own feet, with the confidence that comes from solidarity and the strength that comes from self-reliance. It was the task of the United States to develop the will and strength to oppose further communist aggression.

The policy advocated by the JCS was essentially political and psychological. The development of native armies was only a means toward the greater end of joining all noncommunist Asia into a solid bloc, based upon the real economic interdependence of the various states within the area. Recognizing the magnitude of the undertaking, the JCS suggested approaching it by easy stages. The grand coalition should be formed out of units that the United States could knit together by bilateral and multilateral treaties as time went on. America should be the integrator and the guide.

The security treaties with Japan, the Philippines, South Korea, Australia, and New Zealand all fitted into the pattern. But this was only a beginning. The impending crisis in Indochina naturally sharpened the American desire to hasten the process. Furthermore, Secretary Dulles hoped that the mere knowledge that multilateral talks on mutual defense were being pursued might tend to moderate communist demands at Geneva. Stressing the necessity for a common stand by all the countries in the area, he reminded the foreign ministers of Australia and New Zealand that no agreement on a position toward the Indochina phase of the conference existed among the Western powers. It was, therefore, unclear just what the West would not tolerate from the communists.

The United States announced that it would be willing to participate in an examination of the military situation in Southeast Asia, providing the purpose was to explore, through secret channels in Washington, the means by which the United States, Britain, France, New Zealand, and Australia might assist the countries of Southeast Asia to defend themselves. The United States stressed that this examination was supplementary to continued American efforts to organize a regional grouping, and that it was neither a substitute for, nor the nucleus of, such a grouping.

The British accepted the American viewpoint that they should move forward concurrently on parallel lines. They were prepared to start immediately with military staff talks. Although Britain yielded to the United States, Australia, and New Zealand, there were valid reasons for reluctance. Her Majesty's Government were being played upon by Nehru to back his neutralist proposal for what amounted to a sellout to the communists at Geneva; the British public was terrified at the thought of the hydrogen bomb; and there was a widespread feeling in Britain that, somehow or other, the Geneva Conference was going to settle all the problems of Asia. The British proposal for staff examinations by an already constituted agency was a matter of common prudence. If Geneva succeeded, the talks would not be important; but if Geneva failed, there would be inevitable criticism that staff examinations and long-range planning should have been under way long ago. Presumably, because the talks were secret, the public would not know how long they had been going on.

The United States was not without its own dilemmas. On the one hand, there was the desire to establish collective defense for Southeast Asia as quickly as possible. On the other there was the desire, apparently not shared by the United Kingdom, to avoid planning during the Geneva Conference because it would imply that the Associated States had been written off. To counter with the argument that France would speak for the Associated States at Geneva would merely underline the current skepticism in Asia about their true independence. The problem of the United States was to move rapidly toward the creation of a minimum coalition to cover the possible loss of Indochina, while avoiding the impression that the Associated States had already been given up as lost.

Secretary Dulles, therefore, conceived of forming a Southeast Asian community that would probably not include Vietnam but that might, with luck, embrace Laos and Cambodia. Chargé McClintock, in Saigon, respectfully but firmly dissented against this course. "Most regrettably," he wrote, "there are no human resources in Cambodia nor Laos on which to build a bulwark against communist infiltration or aggression. Furthermore, in the case of Cambodia, there is no geographic barrier against such aggression."

Mr. Dulles found himself facing political disadvantages of a different sort in trying to weld Asian and European powers for concerted action. The issue of colonialism and fear of Communist China acted as a deterrent upon most of the Colombo nations. Although Prime Minister Nehru failed to dominate the conference of prime ministers at Colombo in early May 1954, he succeeded in vitiating any strong support of the Western powers at Geneva.

The Colombo Powers, together with the other countries in South and Southeast Asia, displayed a growing apprehension that Western attempts to solve the Indochina problem might lead to World War III. They showed resentment and frustration over the thought that such a development might be thrust upon them without an opportunity to express themselves or take collective action. They therefore indicated some willingness to help in carrying out an agreed settlement. Mr. Dulles was eager to enlist their services. As the nations most immediately threatened, he felt they should have every opportunity to contribute to a settlement. He sensed that their participation would help mitigate their fears, nurture their self-confidence, increase their prestige, help educate them better about communist intentions, and eventually make them more receptive to the idea of cooperation with Western nations. Mr. Dulles discovered that the East moves in its own inscrutable way.[1]

The five-power military conference met 3–11 June 1954. The conferees agreed that the situation in Indochina was critical and that retention of the Tonkin Delta was of greatest importance to the defense of Southeast Asia. They also agreed that stabilizing the situation in the delta would require outside assistance on the order of three divisions and 300 aircraft. The French indicated that the psychological impact of these reinforcements would be enhanced if they were drawn from the West. And all five representatives concluded that the arrival of reinforcements from the free nations, other than France, would be an important factor in the restoration of Vietnamese confidence. It had been understood that the conclusions of the conferees did not in any way imply a commitment of the governments. None of the governments moved to provide the reinforcements that their military representatives had concluded were necessary.

The conference also studied what would occur should the Tonkin Delta be lost. The conferees recognized: (1) the necessity of considering the establishment of a recovery line in the south; (2) the fact that land forces immediately available would not be sufficient to hold a possible Chinese advance and that, therefore, defensive positions in Thailand and Burma should be considered as well as the recovery line in Indochina; and (3) the fact that maintenance of internal security in Southeast Asia depended upon the support of the people therein. The final conclusion related to the possible cease-fire and called for a guarantee by nations other than those directly involved that they would intervene if the agreement were broken. The United States later ignored this conclusion by refusing to do more than "respect" the cease-fire agreement.

United States military thinking was evident in the acceptance by the conferees of the conclusion that over all Allied strategy should be defensive in Southeast Asia in the event of a global war, and that nuclear attacks should be launched against China if war ensued with her. Acceptance of the concept of blockade also revealed American influence.

Consistent with their thinking for a long time, the JCS on 21 May had informed the Secretary of Defense that they considered a static type of defense for Southeast Asia unsound from a military viewpoint. The chiefs declared that there were two basic military concepts for defense of the area: the static or

Korea type, or an offensive against the source of communist military power being applied in Southeast Asia. So long as Burma and Thailand were not under communist control, the geography of the area and the lack of Chinese capability for a major overseas attack rendered Malaya secure from external threat. Should Burma and Thailand be lost prior to an Allied decision to hold a line in Southeast Asia, the defensive position would have to be established in Malaya. A study of the force requirements and logistic implications of this concept revealed extensive and damaging weaknesses. It would take a minimum of twelve months to build up the base complex and facilities required to support the forces that would be involved. Those forces would have to remain over an extended period of time, and the commitment of manpower and materiel to maintain them would be unacceptable. The presence of large numbers of American, Commonwealth, and French troops in the area would provide the communists with excellent material for anti-Western propaganda.[2] Dissipation of Allied strength on such a scale would be a gift to the USSR. Finally, a static defense plan would result in maldeployment and reduced flexibility in employment of U.S. forces. The support of existing war plans logistically would be seriously jeopardized. The United States should, therefore, adopt the concept of offensive action against Communist China, rather than reacting locally at the point of attack.

☆ ☆ ☆ ☆

Neither these plans, nor America's prolonged efforts to organize a regional grouping, nor the implied threat of the five-power staff meeting served to mar the equanimity of Vyacheslav Molotov, the inscrutable but complacent Soviet foreign minister at Geneva.

Molotov could well afford his complacency. An American representative later remarked to an unhappy Vietnamese, "You can expect no more at the conference table than you have won on the field of battle." There was no doubt about who had the victory in the field.

The Vietminh terms were victors' terms, and they were hard. Either openly or by implication they demanded of the French every concession the United States had sworn was unacceptable. The Vietminh presented their proposal for reestablishing peace in Indochina at the second plenary session of the Geneva Conference on 11 May. The rest of the conference consisted of the vain thrashings of the hooked victim as the Vietminh steadily reeled in the line under the skillful coaching of two experts at fishing in troubled waters.[3]

Americans may find it difficult to understand all the details of the terms. Some difficulties are caused by translation, but many are due to the purposely vague and complicated statements. The Communist Vietnamese in particular were adept at preparing confusing texts that could be accepted as meaning one thing but would later be presented as meaning something almost diametrically opposite. Negotiating with communists, as Admiral Turner Joy found in Korea, is an extremely difficult assignment.

When asked by reporters whether the Vietminh armistice proposal was acceptable to the United States, Mr. Dulles replied that it was certainly unacceptable in its totality. It followed, he said, the same pattern applied in the past to Germany, Austria, and Korea: namely to compel withdrawal of the forces that sustain free society and to set up a system under which the communists could grab the whole area.

I write this at the end of October 1972, just after the North Vietnamese have publicized an agreement to end the latest war in Indochina. I find many resemblances in this latest proposal to the Vietminh proposal of May 1954. We will disregard these warnings at our peril in the negotiations to come.

In the Vietminh proposals there was no provision for international control. Elections "without interference" followed the pattern in Korea. The proposals were also cunningly designed to appeal to the French public. The not unfriendly references to the French Union and arrangements for retention of French economic and cultural interests were obviously designed to win French support. There was reason to believe that the communists might seriously envisage a communist state within the French Union. The proposal made it clear that the Democratic Republic of Vietnam would determine the question of association with the French Union. It was also logical and obivous that the Vietminh would organize the elections and win them quickly. In any event, it would gradually convert Vietnam into a communist state.

Knowledge of the serious military situation in the delta was just becoming public about the time the Vietminh offered their proposal. The political situation in France was deteriorating rapidly. There was an increasing desire for peace at any price. Ambassador Dillon felt that pressure to accept the Vietminh terms as a basis for negotiation would be irresistible unless some new element entered the picture. It was at this time that the United States insisted upon the right of the Associated States to withdraw from the French Union. Ambassador Dillon was not sure that public retraction of this condition by the United States would stop the French parliament from forcing French acceptance of the Vietminh terms, but he did think that retraction would greatly help to clarify our position to the French public and, presumably, to the rest of the world.

☆ ☆ ☆ ☆

The Laniel Government fell on 12 June 1954. Ambassador Dillon pointed out that the successor government, no matter what it said, and although Bidault might remain Foreign Minister, would be under implicit instructions to end the war, even at the cost of major concessions. As far as Geneva was concerned, said the Ambassador, the French bargaining position was so weak (and recently had become still weaker as the United States grew more reluctant to intervene in Indochina) that the fall of the government actually would make little difference.

Pierre Mendès-France accepted the premiership under a four-week "contract" to bring about an honorable settlement of the Indochina war. In spite of repeated assertions that he would not in any event accept a peace that was a surrender to the Vietminh, or even accept a disguised capitulation, Mendès-France was, from the start, identified with peace-at-any-price.

It has been observed that there was little any French government could do at Geneva. It quickly became evident that, in working out the details of cease-fire and regroupment of forces, the negotiators were edging closer and closer to an inevitable partitioning of Vietnam. It was also clear that even though the Vietminh relaxed enough to pay lip service to international supervision of the armistice, the French were in no position to secure a set of controls that would guarantee the effectiveness of such supervision.

On 26 June the United States and Britain received an *aide-mémoire* from the French noting that the communists undoubtedly were afraid of the conflict spreading. The French therefore felt it would be useful for the British and American governments, at that time conducting talks in Washington, to issue a final communiqué stating that a serious aggravation of international relations would result if it were not possible to reach a reasonable settlement at Geneva. The French also hoped they could count on the United States to counsel wisdom and self-control to the Vietnamese, to dissuade them from refusing an agreement. Conversely, the United States was asked not to do anything that might even implicitly encourage a Vietnamese outburst.

The British and American governments drafted an answer in the hope of stiffening the French position, replying that they would be willing to *respect* an agreement that:

1) Preserves the integrity and independence of Laos and Cambodia and assures the withdrawal of Vietminh forces therefrom

2) Preserves at least the southern half of Vietnam and if possible an enclave in the delta; in this connection we would be unwilling to see the division drawn further south than a line running generally west from Dong Hoi

3) Does not impose on Laos, Cambodia, or retained Vietnam any restrictions materially impairing their capacity to maintain stable noncommunist regimes, especially restrictions impairing their right to maintain adequate forces for internal security, to import arms, and to employ foreign advisors

4) Does not contain political provisions that would risk loss of the retained area to communist control

5) Does not exclude the possibility of the ultimate unification of Vietnam by peaceful means

6) Provides for the peaceful and humane transfer, under international supervision, of those people desiring to be moved from one zone to another of Vietnam

7) Provides effective machinery for international supervision of the agreement.

Besides pointing out that the fourth and fifth paragraphs of the statement seemed in contradiction, the French inquired about the meaning of "respect," which struck them as a weak and unclear word.

Secretary Dulles explained that the United States realized that even an agreement seeming to meet all seven points could not guarantee that Indochina would not one day pass into communist hands. The apparent contradiction was merely an attempt to get the best conditions under the circumstances. He further explained that "respecting" the agreement meant that the United States would not oppose a settlement that conformed to the seven points. It did not, of course, mean that the settlement would be guaranteed or necessarily supported in public. "Respect" also meant that the United States would not seek directly or indirectly to upset the settlement by force. Mr. Dulles hastened to add that M. Mendès-France should be under no illusion that observance of the seven points would in itself suffice to elicit a public statement by the United States that it would respect the agreement, unless the Associated States had assented to the settlement. In a personal message to the Premier, Secretary Dulles gave an excellent analysis of the American position, and of the Geneva Conference as a whole, up to that time. He feared that the seven points, which constituted a minimum so far as the United States was concerned would constitute merely an optimum solution so far as France and perhaps the United Kingdom were concerned, and that an armistice could be concluded on less favorable terms than those we might respect.

Dulles thought there was already considerable French thinking about departure from the seven points, such as allowing communist forces to remain in Northern Laos; accepting a Vietnam line of demarcation considerably south of Dong Hoi; neutralizing and demilitarizing Laos, Cambodia, and Vietnam so as to impair their capacity to maintain stable, noncommunist regimes; accepting elections so early and ill-supervised as to risk the loss of the entire area to communism; and accepting international supervision by a body that could not be effective because it included a communist state that had veto power. These were but illustrations of a whittling-away process, he remarked, each stroke of which might in itself seem unessential, but that cumulatively could produce a quite different result from that envisaged by the seven points.

The possibility of complete U.S. disassociation from the final stages of the conference so deeply disturbed M. Mendès-France that Secretary Dulles found it expedient to confer with him personally in Paris on 13 July. The most immediate problem for the French Premier was the refusal of the United States to renew its representation at the conference on the ministerial level. The five foreign ministers recessed a week later, leaving the armistice details to the military negotiators. The American delegation, reduced in size and concept, reverted to an advisory or observer role. Its basic instructions were withdrawn and it functioned on an ad hoc basis, in order to be more responsive to "realities as we see them, not only at Geneva but also in the United States and Indochina."

Premier Mendès-France pointed out that this would be the first time since the war that the United States had not been represented at a level equal to that of other powers at an important conference. He felt it would have catastrophic effects in the Far East and in Europe. There would be no one to take a strong personal position with Molotov. The communists would surely increase their pressure to deepen the obvious rift between the Western powers, whereas, with the Secretary present, the United States would in effect have a veto power on the decisions of the conference.

In spite of the Premier's arguments, Mr. Dulles was more impressed by the probable disastrous effect of a sudden and dramatic severance from the conference at the last moment. Nevertheless, after consultation with President Eisenhower, he went to Paris to thrash the matter out with Mendès-France. From their meeting came an agreed Franco-American position on Indochina:

1) France and the Associated States of Vietnam, Laos, and Cambodia are recognized to be those which, on the non-communist side, are primarily interested in the Indochina phase of the Geneva Conference. The United States is interested primarily as a friendly nation which desires to assist, where desired, in arriving at a just settlement, but who will not seek, or be expected, to impose its views in any way upon those primarily interested.

2) The attached seven points [those of the earlier British-American reply to the French] constitute a result which France believes to be obtainable by negotiation at Geneva and which would be acceptable to France and, France believes, to the Associated States. The United States, while recognizing the right of those primarily interested to accept different terms, will itself be prepared to respect terms conforming to the attached. The United States will not be asked or expected by France to respect terms which in its opinion differ materially from the attached and it may publicly disassociate itself from such differing terms.

3) If the settlement is one which the United States is prepared to "respect," its position will be expressed unilaterally or in association only with non-communist states in terms which apply to the situation the principles of nonuse of forces which are embodied in Article 2(4) and (6) of the Charter of the United Nations.

4) The United States is prepared to seek, with other interested nations, a collective defense association designed to preserve, against direct and indirect aggression, the integrity of the non-communist areas of South East Asia following any settlement.

5) If there is no settlement, the United States and French governments will consult together on the measures to be taken. This will not preclude the United States, if it so desires, bringing the matter before the U.N. as involving a threat to peace as dealt with by Chapter VII of the Charter . . .

6) France reaffirms the principle of independence for the Associated States in equal and voluntary association as members of the French Union.

Following the issuance of the position paper, an exchange of letters took place between Mr. Dulles and M. Mendès-France, in the course of which the French Premier refuted the pro-abstention arguments. Whether or not, as he claimed, Mendès-France was responsible for changing Dulles' mind, the decision to resume participation at the ministerial level was taken, following talks with Britain's Anthony Eden and consultation with President Eisenhower. Under Secretary of State Smith left for Geneva on 16 July.

The United States performed another service requested by France in the 26 June *aide-mémoire*. Ambassador Heath, in Saigon, was instructed to inform Premier Ngo Dinh Diem of the probability of a compromise at Geneva that would slice his country in half. It was Ambassador Heath's unhappy task to make Diem see the futility of resisting the settlement. He was to tell the Premier that the United States and Britain had made clear their strong opposition to any settlement that might be made on terms leading to permanent division of his country. The Ambassador was also to advise Diem of the seven-point British-American note to France. Finally, still speaking in Mr. Dulles' name, he was to state that "while we recognize that settlement along these lines imposes hardships on Vietnam, we fear that the deteriorating military situation and separate negotiations in progress with Vietminh and Chinese Communists could lead to something still worse."

The intent of this demarche was not entirely altruistic. It had been established that the French were not keeping the Vietnamese adequately informed. Besides trying to avert a violent reaction by the bitterly disappointed Vietnamese, the United States wished to place its relations with Diem on a more realistic and confidential basis, if it were later to play a more useful role in Vietnam.

The French had also asked that the final communiqué from the British-American conversations in Washington contain a statement to the effect that the issuing governments would take a serious view of unacceptable communist demands at Geneva. President Eisenhower and Sir Winston Churchill, who headed the British delegation, obliged by inserting this statement: "We are both convinced that if at Geneva the French Government is confronted with demands which prevent an acceptable agreement regarding Indochina, the international situation will be seriously aggravated."

The Anglo-American discussions were held in Washington 25–29 June by President Eisenhower, Mr. Dulles, Sir Winston, and Mr. Eden. There was no formal agenda, but among the topics covered was that of Indochina and the Geneva Conference. Sir Winston had indicated previously his preoccupation with the need to establish a firm front in Southeast Asia. He favored a Southeast Asia treaty organization and a Middle East treaty organization to match NATO. The Americans were less convinced, at least for the time being, that the answer was a NATO-type entente.

Diversity of opinion did not stop here. It appears that the main reason for these extraordinarily high-level talks was that divergence between American and British basic policies in a number of spheres was reaching serious proportions. Certainly the concept of regional grouping, and the attitude toward acceptable conditions at Geneva, were two such areas. Moreover, the French were not the only ones to be bewildered by America's schizo-diplomatics. "Sometimes it is awfully difficult," said Clement Attlee, "to understand what the American line is, as between what members of the government say and what Senators say, and sometimes what generals and admirals say." In spite of bland assurances of solidarity and "intimate comradeship," the concluding declaration issued by the White House on 29 June gave no real indication of how much true mutual understanding had been achieved.

To follow up the Eisenhower-Churchill meetings, a U.S.–U.K. study group on Southeast Asia was established. By 16 July, three sessions had been held and some of the main lines of thought were beginning to emerge. The British felt that a collective security arrangement for Southeast Asia should be considered in two contexts: on the basis of a settlement in Indochina and on the basis of no settlement. In the event of a settlement that posed no immediate military problem, the British preferred a generalized arrangement designed to bring in as many states as possible, including the Colombo Powers. If there were no settlement at Geneva, the British agreed to the immediate establishment of an organization to meet the military threat. This organization, presumably, would be limited to the powers making military commitments.

One thing was clear: the British had no intention of pressing forward with any kind of security organization until the Indochina phase of the Geneva Conference had terminated. They considered that the principal problem in dealing with Southeast Asia after an Indochina settlement would be large-scale economic assistance.[4] Although there was no discussion of support for this program, there was little doubt who the chief contributor would be.

On a number of occasions, the British referred to military force to repel overt communist aggression, but their attitude about countering subversion and infiltration remained vague. The Americans pointed out that the principal danger in the future would probably come through infiltration and subversion, and that the security organization should be in a position to deal with that situation effectively. Also, the organization should be established immediately, to deal with the probable adverse military and political repercussions of an unsatisfactory settlement at Geneva. Even if a pact were signed within a month or so, there would be a time lag of 6–12 months for ratification by the various countries. There had, therefore, to be some kind of interim machinery.

The United States felt it was too early to set up a mechanism like NATO, because it was not yet known whether a NATO-type organization was what was wanted. Instead, we were toying with the idea of an interim council. By making the American Ambassador the U.S. representative and supplementing his staff with political and military advisers, day-to-day business could be conducted without large and possibly unnecessary staffs. The biggest problem still remained that of deciding upon the nature of the basic treaty organization.

Under Secretary of State Bedell Smith, echoing the JCS position, argued strongly for viewing the matter in the light of the whole Far East, not just Southeast Asia. Any organization sponsored by the United States should make room for the inclusion of Japan, the Philippines, and other Asian allies. As long as India remained "neutral" and to a large extent unpredictable, U.S. military men were wary of including her. They feared, with reason, that India would wreck more military plans than ever she abetted. Indian obstructionism could be especially effective in the type of organization the British favored, composed of three elements: a council including all participants, an economic and political council with as many members as possible, and a military organization. Luckily, India would unquestionably not wish to participate in the military aspects per se, but would still be able to do much harm in the other councils.

A side issue of note on the military organization was that the British were reported to be thinking of proposing that the entire command structure in the Pacific, including Southeast Asia, be American. But in return they would suggest complete British control in the eastern Atlantic; unqualified assignment of U.S. Fleet strike forces to Commander-in-Chief Eastern Atlantic; the assignment of U.S. Strike Force South to Commander-in-Chief Allied Forces Mediterranean; and probably, in due time, the appointment of a British officer as Supreme Allied Commander Atlantic. From the American point of view there would be serious disadvantages to such an arrangement.

When the Colombo members were sounded out by the British on their attitude toward the proposed organization, Indonesia replied that its position was one of strict neutrality. Burma protested neutrality but let it be known that it was not averse to the idea. Ceylon took a similar stand. The Indian attitude was assumed to be negative, but it was thought that if the others took a reasonable approach, with time India might not care to be left in an isolated position.

Although the JCS had pressed hard for a long time for some type of Southeast Asian security organization that could be tied in with other of our Far Eastern alliances, it was the military who sounded a note of caution just after the signing of the Geneva settlement. The situation had changed radically. In April it had been assumed that the power of Vietnam would be a factor. But as the situation had developed, there was much talk of a military defensive arrangement where there were no substantive military forces. Except for the British police in Malaya, and negligible Thai and Burmese forces, the only military power was in Korea and Formosa. The cost of developing military might in the area would be tremendous.

It was one thing to make promises and quite another to carry them out. Consequently, the armed forces wished to subject the undertaking to close scrutiny to avoid great mistakes. With limited funds for defense and military aid programs, commitment of huge sums of money to Southeast Asia would mean cutting somewhere else, without generating any real strength. Thailand had produced a plan for an 81,000-man force that would cost the United States $400 million. Adequate for internal security, this force would contribute nothing to mutual defense. The Burmese had a similar plan. Led to think in these terms, Asian peoples would only be disappointed and the United States would have enemies instead of friends. Military aggression would not be countered by the United States in Thailand: it would be cut off at the roots, in China to the north. Aid and materiel poured into Thailand would only reduce that available from the other places where the United States might actually have to fight.

For this reason, consideration had to be given to the type of defense in which the countries of Southeast Asia might be asked to engage. A NATO-type defense was out of the question; each country could not be guaranteed total protection. Moreover, that would require building up the armed forces of each country in the area, a task of staggering proportion and dubious military value. As it was, military aid programs were bleeding the United States and getting out of hand.

One of the worst features of aiding weak or indefensible nations is the great possibility of ending up aiding the enemy instead.[5] Indochina is an excellent case in point. In April 1954 the JCS, anticipating an unsatisfactory settlement at Geneva, had advised the NSC that shipments of military material should be suspended if fighting halted before a controlled armistice could be put into effect. They also suggested that an attempt should be made to recover or destroy equipment already in Indochina. They followed up this suggestion by pointing out that the United States would be justified, despite the fact that the French legally held title to the equipment, in insisting upon its return if no longer employed in the defense of Indochina. They recommended, however, that in the event of partition, units suited to guerrilla operations should not be disarmed. Plans were to be prepared by CINCPAC for salvaging or destroying American materiel. He, in turn, assigned responsibility for these operations to MAAG.

When the diplomats at Geneva formally agreed on 21 July to partition Vietnam, the Defense Department immediately suspended all shipments of materiel to Indochina and diverted those already en route to Japan and allied countries.

Two days later France gave her assurance that American equipment would be evacuated to South Vietnam, and CINCPAC and MAAG collaborated on measures to safeguard the materiel. But at the instigation of the State Department, MAAG was directed not to press plans for recovery and destruction until France had been given sufficient time to determine a course of action in Indochina. Since the French were already evacuating equipment and personnel from the Hanoi area to South Vietnam, American concern was primarily confined to USAF personnel and to aircraft on loan to the French air force.

The Commander Far East Air Force had been concerned for the safety of his air force mechanics in Indochina. Early in July he stated that French C47 capability was sufficient to meet operational requirements and recommended that the 16 C119s and supporting personnel be withdrawn. General O'Daniel opposed this suggestion, recommending that half the C119s and mechanics be withdrawn then and the remainder later. The JCS supported General O'Daniel, and 8 C119s with maintenance support crews were retained in Indochina.

Subsequent to Geneva, the United States adopted an interim policy on aid to the Associated States and to the French in Indochina. Pending further examination of the problem, only common-use items to directly alleviate suffering, prevent disease, and assist in evacuation of military forces and refugees from North Vietnam were to be programmed for Indochina; each case was to be considered individually.

It was our intention to use as much as possible of the materiel rescued from North Vietnam to help equip the native forces of the Associated States. This was in line with the idea that noncommunist nations in the area would have to build up their own forces for internal security, leaving the main fighting to the United States and its more powerful allies.

Corollary to that idea was, of course, the concept that the significant fighting would take place elsewhere. If at all possible, American strategists wished to avoid becoming involved deeply in the militarily unimportant area of Southeast Asia. Hence they tended to oppose the British, who for economic and political reasons preferred a NATO-type security organization, with its implication of limited-area defense. Viewed realistically, such an organization was greatly to the benefit of the British, provided they could induce the United States to pay for it. By late July they had not succeeded in doing so, either through the Eisenhower-Churchill conversations or the subsequent U.S.–U.K. study group.

Although there was still much to cover in smoothing out the difficulties standing in the way of a security organization, the study group accomplished its second purpose more quickly: it had been charged with preparing recommendations on "the terms on which our two countries might be willing to be associated with an agreement which might be reached in Geneva." Britain's policy was much more flexible than that of the United States in this respect. Although both countries had subscribed to the seven criteria for an acceptable settlement, Britain had all along been willing to associate itself with terms falling considerably short of the American ideal. Moreover, Britain preferred a multilateral declaration including Australia, New Zealand, and if possible India and other interested nations in the area. Nor did Britain exclude the possibility that the declaration bear communist signatures. The United States made it plain that it would not participate in any declaration that included Communist China and that it would not compromise with the seven-point statement.[6]

President Eisenhower accordingly announced publicly on 21 July that the United States had not been a party to and was not bound by the decisions taken by the Geneva Conference; it therefore was not prepared to join in the conference declaration. Instead, the following unilateral declaration was presented by Under Secretary of State Smith to the last plenary session of the conference:

> The Government of the United States being resolved to devote its efforts to the strengthening of peace in accordance with the principles and purposes of the United Nations takes note of the agreements concluded at Geneva on July 20 and 21, 1954 . . . [and] declares with regard to the aforesaid agreements and paragraphs that 1) it will refrain from the threat or the use of force to disturb them, in accordance with article 2(4) of the Charter of the U.N. dealing with the obligation of members to refrain in their international relations from the threat or use of force; and 2) it would view any renewal of the aggression in violation of the aforesaid agreements with grave concern and as seriously threatening international peace and security.
>
> In connection with the statement in the declaration concerning free elections in Vietnam my government wishes to make clear its position, which it has expressed in a declaration made in Washington on June 29, 1954, as follows: "In the case of nations now divided against their will, we shall continue to seek to achieve unity through free elections supervised by the U.N. to insure that they are conducted fairly."
>
> . . . the United States reiterates its traditional position that peoples are entitled to determine their own future and that it will not join in an arrangement which would hinder this . . .

Secretary Dulles, in a statement two days after the conference, did not let the French go unscathed. Without naming names, he maintained that one of the lessons of Geneva was that resistance to communism needs popular support, and that this in turn means that people should feel they are defending their own national institutions. One of the positive aspects of Geneva, claimed Mr. Dulles, was that it advanced the independent status of the Associated States. He had been assured by the President of France that French representatives in Vietnam had been instructed to complete by 30 July precise projects for the transfer of authority that would give reality to the independence France had promised.

Both Mr. Dulles and President Eisenhower admitted that the Geneva settlement contained undesirable features. But the President philosophically observed that a great deal would depend on how they worked out. It was not long before the State Department Planning Board produced an estimate of how they would probably work out and what it all would mean to the United States.

It was pointed out that, regardless of the fate of South Vietnam, Laos, and Cambodia, the communists had secured possession of a salient in Vietnam from which military and nonmilitary pressures could be mounted against adjacent and more remote noncommunist areas. *The loss of prestige in Asia suffered by the United States, as backer of France and the Bao Dai government, would raise further doubts about U.S. leadership and its ability to check future communist expansion in Asia. American prestige would inescapably be associated with subsequent developments in Southeast Asia. The communists had increased their military and political prestige, and with it their capacity for extending communist influence without resorting to armed attack. They were now in an excellent posture to exploit the economic and political instability of the free states of Asia.*

It was brought out that the communists were now in a better position for propaganda attacks on the United States. By adopting an appearance of moderation at Geneva, and by having taken credit for the cessation of hostilities in Indochina, they could exploit their political strategy of imputing to the United States motives of extremism, belligerency, and opposition to coexistence. They thus had a focus for their peace propaganda in Asia to allay fears of communist expansion. They now had an opportunity to alienate the United States from its Asian friends and allies, while at the same time establishing for themselves closer ties with the nations of Asia.

One negative aspect of the loss of Southeast Asia was that it might imperil the retention of Japan as a key element of the offshore island chain [Aleutians, Japan, Taiwan, Philippines]. High Commissioner Maurice Dejean, of Indochina, the former French Ambassador to Tokyo, had predicted in May that a communist victory would so enhance the prestige of Communist China that the whole balance of power in the Pacific would be affected and Japanese policy would tend toward rapprochement with a new and powerful Peking.[7]

The Planning Board estimate of July 1954 was very prophetic, and it explains our later difficulties in Vietnam, beginning in 1961. Our government has been generally unable to impress on the majority of our citizens the importance and seriousness of the problems in Vietnam and their relation to real peace in the world. The United States and France did not impress upon their citizens the lesson of Geneva mentioned by Mr. Dulles—that resistance to communism needs popular support, and that this means that the people of free governments should feel that in resisting communism they are defending their own national institutions.

I have covered the history of U.S. involvement in Indochina from its inception under President Truman's administration until the signing of the agreements at Geneva in July 1954. If it appears that I have gone into too much detail, my excuse is that detail is important to show the American people, and the rest of the free world, how diligently their governments worked to find a peaceful solution to the war that international communism chose to fight in Indochina to take over that former French colony after its Japanese captors were forced to leave in 1945.

In the years since the Geneva accords were signed, I have watched with great interest the developments in Indochina and all Southeast Asia. With time I have modified some of the feelings I had in July 1954. At that time I felt, as did many of my military colleagues and a good many of our diplomats up to and including our splendid Secretary of State, that it was too bad we had not found a way to help our French allies militarily. The decision to do this, of course, was shared by our President and the Congress. When the situation became critical in early April 1954, President Eisenhower directed Secretary Dulles to consult with the leaders of Congress; and on 4 April he wrote a personal letter to Prime Minister Churchill in an effort to have the British join us in organizing a regional grouping of the United States, France, and the Southeast Asian nations to defend Indochina. Much of the letter is given in *Mandate for Change,* which I quote here (pp. 346–347):

> I am sure ... you are following with the deepest interest and anxiety the daily reports of the gallant fight being put up by the French at Dien Bien Phu. Today, the situation there does not seem hopeless.

> But regardless of the outcome of this particular battle, I fear that the French cannot alone see the thing through, this despite the very substantial assistance in money and material that we are giving them. It is no solution simply to urge the French to intensify their efforts. And if they do not see it through and Indochina passes into the hands of the communists the ultimate effect on our and your global and strategic position with the consequent shift in the power ratios throughout Asia and the Pacific could be disastrous, and, I know, unacceptable to you and me ... This has led us to the hard conclusion that the situation in Southeast Asia requires us urgently to take serious and far-reaching decisions.

> Geneva is less than four weeks away. There the possibility of the communists driving a wedge between us will, given the state of mind in France, be infinitely greater than at Berlin ... But our painstaking search for a way out of the impasse has reluctantly forced us to the conclusion that there is no negotiable solution of the Indochina problem which in its essence would not be either a face-saving device to cover a French surrender or a face-saving device to cover a communist retirement. The first alternative is too serious in its broad strategic implications for us and for you to be acceptable ...

> Somehow we must continue to bring about the second alternative ...

> I believe that the best way to ... bring greater moral and material resources to the support of the French effort is through the establishment of a new, ad hoc grouping or coalition composed of nations which have a vital concern in the checking of communist expansion in the area. I have in mind in addition to our two countries, France, the Associated States, Australia, New Zealand, Thailand

and the Philippines. The U.S. government would expect to play its full part in such a coalition . . .

The important thing is that the coalition must be strong and it must be willing to join the fight if necessary. I do not envisage the need of any appreciable ground forces on your or our part . . .

If I may refer again to history, we failed to halt Hirohito, Mussolini, and Hitler by not acting in unity and in time. That marked the beginning of many years of stark tragedy and desperate peril. May it not be that our nations have learned something from that lesson?

> *With warm regard*
> IKE

President Eisenhower, in my opinion, thoroughly agreed with the position taken by congressional leaders at the time they were consulted by Secretary Dulles. In the Defense Department, I feel that a majority of senior officers familiar with the details of the Vietnam problem also agreed that it was preferable to have additional allies if we were to intervene militarily. On the other hand there were some, including myself, who thought *we should intervene by ourselves if we could not get additional help*. It was generally understood that the allies we hoped to get could not contribute much in military strength.

After President Eisenhower's decision in regard to intervention—that we needed additional allies, particularly the British; that France and the Associated States had to request our intervention; that France had to promise full freedom to the Associated States as members of the French Union as well as to allow them to withdraw from the Union if they desired; that the French had to promise to maintain their military forces in Indochina in action along with our forces; and finally that we would require that all these decisions be accepted not only by the French cabinet but also be authorized or endorsed by the French National Assembly—I feel that there was no disagreement in the top echelons of his administration. With the benefit of 18 years of hindsight I feel that the President's position was the correct one. Whether, had our conditions been met and had we intervened, we would have been successful in defeating the communists I am not sure. I feel that we would have continued to encounter great problems in getting along with the French.

I believe that the agreements reached between France and the Vietminh at Geneva were greatly influenced by the American position. The communists, as well as the French, were not exactly sure where we stood until the last few days of the negotiations. As a result, I believe that Ho Chi Minh and the Chinese felt it best to get credit for a settlement that was not too harsh. President Eisenhower's reputation as a military leader, coupled with the efforts of his able and articulate Secretary of State, made the communists decide to wait, probably for a new and entirely different administration in the United States.

Epilogue

I n late 1972 Admiral Radford ended his narrative abruptly. The account stopped with the temporary resolution of the Indochina war at Geneva in spring 1954. He had been writing for three long years, using his own notes, letters, and memoranda, as well as official diaries and documents.

It is evident from his notes that he was preparing to write next of the crises that followed Dien Bien Phu; the papers were arranged chronologically, fitted together like the fragments of a jigsaw puzzle, and they reflected the tensions and critical times, the conferences and negotiations, in which he had played a substantive role.

On the Admiral's desk was a sheaf of despatches dealing with the clashes between the Nationalists and Communists in the Formosa Strait area during 1954–1955, and in his hands was Anthony Eden's book on the Suez crisis of 1956. He remarked to his staff that he felt tired and dispirited and believed that a few weeks' respite from the arduous work might restore his flagging energy. He never wrote another word.

On 15 August 1957 Admiral Radford's distinguished career of service to the nation was climaxed when he received from President Eisenhower a fourth Distinguished Service Medal, stepped down as Chairman of the Joint Chiefs of Staff, and retired from the active list of the Navy after 45 years of service. It was at once a poignant moment, a proud occasion, and the happy beginning of a new personal life with his wife, Mariana, to whom he had often confided, "We make a great team."

Many major corporations offered directorships or chairmanships of the board, and inducements in the form of pay and perquisites for the privilege of using the Admiral's name and fame. He responded slowly and with care to avoid even a hint of conflict of interest, ultimately deciding to become a consultant on the development of foreign and domestic business for the Bankers Trust Com-

pany, a position he held from 1957 until his death. He also accepted several directorships. In all these business associations his integrity, sound judgment, and knowledge of world affairs made his assistance invaluable.

Admiral Radford died at Bethesda Naval Hospital on 17 August 1973 and was buried with full military honors at Arlington National Cemetery.

Notes

CHAPTER 1

1 On 15 November 1945 the congressional investigation into the disaster at Pearl Harbor began and for months "was to hold the headlines with its testimony on military disunity, failures of intelligence and conflicts of policy in 1941," Millis, *Arms,* p. 155. Among the best of the many books on Pearl Harbor is Roberta Wohlstetter's *Pearl Harbor.*

CHAPTER 2

1 Before the mirror landing system, naval aviators chosen for the job and trained with their air groups brought the planes aboard with flags by day and lighted wands by night.
2 An officer in the Combat Information Center or another control center who vectors aircraft to intercept enemy aircraft picked up on radar.
3 For a terse but complete assessment of the Gilbert-Marshall Islands campaign, see U.S. Strategic Bombing Survey (USSBS), chap. 9, pp. 191–195; also Morison, vol. VII, chaps. 7–17.
4 In circular formations on a circle 6,000 yards from the center.
5 The only "spirits" legally available aboard ships were under the control of flight surgeons, who at times felt that some tense pilot just back from a mission might relax better with a shot. The pilot would be given a two-ounce bottle of "black death," a brand unnamed but unforgotten.

CHAPTER 3

1 At this time the Imperial Japanese Navy was not capable of such actions, but Admiral Turner and General "Howlin Mad" Smith never ceased to demand—and get—carrier support far beyond what was reasonable and necessary to support their amphibious landings.
2 The Japanese admitted that about 340 planes were damaged at Truk on 16–17 February. See USSBS, p. 202. For extracts see ibid., pp. 198–203, from the official reports of the Imperial Japanese Government on the Gilbert-Marshalls campaign.
3 Ibid., p. 203: The Japanese reported 21 *Marus* sunk plus five unidentified *Marus*.
4 These tasks had devolved upon many entrenched vested interests, and no one was

willing to give ground. The Radford Board was the first hard-nosed attempt to bring order out of chaos.

5 Without the strong naval aviation reserve forces trained and based at these fields, available at short notice, the Navy could not have manned its Korean War requirements in ships and squadrons.

6 For one thing, the horses sometimes wondered whether the returning drivers, rested from their earlier exertions, really were aware of the nerve-wracking, day-in-day-out months at sea put in by the single crews of the ships.

7 This famous dispatch caused Halsey to take umbrage. The padding was after the text, not before as Halsey's *Admiral Halsey's Story* (p. 220) declares. For the complete story of Halsey's part in this battle, see Morison, VII, 290–312.

8 See Karig, pp. 25–26.

9 Halsey notes, "If we had been under the same command, with a single system of operational control and intelligence, the Battle for Leyte Gulf might have been fought differently to a different result" (p. 210). He then notes that he and his staff agreed that the Japanese carriers would attack from the north and east. Actually, the Japanese navy had prepared this lure to draw our carrier forces away from the Leyte area (USSBS, p. 281). Meanwhile, the forces Halsey had attacked all day returned through San Bernardino Strait, and pounced on the helpless escort carriers (USSBS, pp. 284–286, 303, 312–313).

10 USSBS, p. 285.

11 He was also lucky. The enemy carriers had only 30 aircraft between them, the remainder having been sent to defend the Philippines.

CHAPTER 4

1 This letter is in the archives of the Hoover Institution.

2 Jack patrols were antisnooper fighters at low altitudes and at the cardinal points of the compass to ensure against low-flying bandits. Moosetrap exercises were large-scale operations employing enemy tactics, designed to highlight our deficiencies and spur new ideas for countermeasures.

3 See Morison, XIII, 59–84, for a fuller account of the typhoon.

4 Royal Navy battleship and battle cruiser, respectively, sunk off Malaya by Japanese torpedo planes.

5 Protected anchorage and convoy formation center for the Japanese, 1940–1945.

6 For the story of the unsung heroes of this war—the logistics forces who backed up the fighting men and their ships—see Carter, *Beans, Bullets and Black Oil,* and Eccles, *Operational Naval Logistics.*

7 See Morison, vol. XIV, chap. 10, pp. 156–165.

CHAPTER 5

1 For further information, Morison, XIV, 4; also King, U.S. Navy at War, pp. 103–104.

2 The alarm "General quarters, all hands man your battle stations!" is piped over the ship's intercom system, accompanied by the strident ringing of alarm bells.

3 Books, articles, and movies about the *Franklin* have been produced, and few people who saw—or survived—the ordeal can understand how the ship was saved. I was

navigator of *Franklin* and at the conn while Captain Gehres was overcome by smoke.

4 Operation Ten-Go was the fifth (*go* means five in Japanese) operation of the "ten" plan for the defense of the Ryukyu archipelago.

5 *Kikusui* operations were designed to harass and destroy by kamikazes and *baka* bombs as many American ships as possible before the Japanese exhausted their cupboard of both aircraft and pilots. The Japanese admitted that the sweeps cut heavily into their available operational planes. Morison, XIV, 248; Karig, p. 386.

6 Our submarines had orders to send flash reports of ship sightings. The Japanese intercepted the coded messages. Karig, p. 395.

7 This is incorrect; *Yamato* had fueled to 90 percent of capacity by 6 April, and the ships that did manage to escape the carrier aircraft attacks made it back to Sasebo. Interview with Admiral Mitsumasa Yonai, March 1946. Also Karig, p. 394.

8 The *baka* bombs, manned by suicide pilots, were now being used in great numbers. Their small size and great speed (about 500 knots) made them difficult to track and hit.

9 Star shells, fired from guns, open in the air at set altitudes; a parachute slows the burning flare's descent.

CHAPTER 6

1 Failure to consult or heed experienced task group commanders was a common fault of task force and fleet commanders. Their staffs usually provided the provocation.

2 See Morison, XIV, 298–310. Halsey shrugs off this typhoon with a half-page comment in his book, p. 254.

3 This has been done. Many articles on the Halsey typhoons have appeared in various magazines.

4 She had nothing to do with intelligence activities and had been found innocent.

5 Craig, pp. 215–216: Admiral Matome Ugaki and ten other kamikaze pilots took off from Oita airfield for a final kamikaze attack against U.S. ships off Okinawa hours after the Emperor read his surrender message. The eleven planes did not reach Okinawa, and the USN has no record of any suicide attacks against its ships on that day. See also Karig, p. 459. There were about 5,350 aircraft available for suicide attacks in the Japanese army and navy air forces at the end of the war.

6 The Japanese Navy and Army had been warned against any overt effort to obstruct the Emperor's decision to surrender. But extremists in the armed forces indulged in an orgy of plotting, assassination, and preparation for using kamikazes in a final savage and treacherous attack. See Butow, chap. 10; also Craig, chap. 18.

7 Halsey, p. 275.

8 Some of his audience felt that MacArthur's remarks stressing peace and justice removed some of the sting of defeat. See Craig, pp. 299–305, for a good description of the surrender ceremony.

9 Admiral Radford's stepson was lost at Okinawa.

10 See Forrestal, p. 102. The greatest armed forces ever assembled were, in a matter of weeks, a shambles. The Navy's Magic Carpet—transports made out of carriers to get the boys back home—was symbolic of the mindless, almost criminal haste on the part of President Truman and a supersensitive Congress to demobilize without informing the public of growing Russian intransigence.

CHAPTER 7

1 The text of Basic Post War Plan Number 1 and the letters of Admirals Blandy and Hill are in the Naval Historical Archives, Washington Navy Yard.
2 Forrestal, p. 61: Secretary Forrestal had received a letter from Sen. David Walsh on 15 May suggesting inter alia that mere objection to the unification plan would not serve any useful purpose, and adding that the Navy might make "a thorough study" of the whole field.
3 See Truman, II, 46–51, for his purported stand on unification. See also Forrestal, esp. pp. 59–64, 115, 118–121, 200–206, 237, 246–247, 269–271, 274, 291–295, for an active participant's view. Finally, a voluminous but fascinating report is U.S. Congress, House, Committee on the Armed Services, *Hearing on H.R. 234* and *Unification and Strategy,* 81st Cong., 1st session, 1947.
4 Recommended reading for the seeker after truth concerning the exaggerated World War II air damage claims in Europe and Japan are the many vols. of the United States Strategic Bombing Survey.
5 President Truman's famous temper was short-fused on this issue. See esp. Cochran, pp. 118–123. For details of Truman's recommendation, see his *Memoirs,* II, 46, 49–50.
6 For a description of this luncheon meeting, see Forrestal, p. 118.
7 Ibid., pp. 105–106.

CHAPTER 8

1 Forrestal, pp. 159–160. Millis, *Arms,* pp. 170–174. The President (*Memoirs,* II, 48–49) makes it appear that his position was not too different from the Navy thesis. Writing for history, he makes himself appear most reasonable.
2 Forrestal, pp. 160–162.
3 For details see ibid., pp. 163–167.
4 Millis, ed., *American Military Thought,* pp. 445–449: General H. H. Arnold, in his final report as Commanding General of the Army Air Force (12 November 1945) advocated "ruthless elimination of all arms, branches, services, weapons, equipment or ideas whose retention might be indicated only by tradition, sentiment or sheer inertia." Since only the Army and Navy had any traditions it was obvious who the proposed goats were. The Navy questioned whether all military wisdom resided in the "Army's theorists of independent air power—theorists whom the war experience had not too well sustained" (Millis, *Arms,* p. 154). Finally, see Arnold, *Global Mission.*
5 Forrestal, p. 166.
6 Ibid.
7 Ibid., p. 167.
8 *Memoirs,* II, 50–51.
9 Forrestal, pp. 168–170.
10 Ibid., pp. 173–187.
11 Ibid., pp. 203–206, 222.
12 Ibid., p. 222, including Admiral Sherman's notes of this meeting. For Mr. Forrestal's account of the meetings that followed, see ibid., pp. 221–223.
13 Ibid., pp. 228–229.
14 The Collins Plan was the Army plan early on, when a simple merger scheme drawn

up by Lt. Gen. Lawton Collins, without any consultation with the Navy, had been the basis for a bill.

CHAPTER 9

1 Millis, *Arms,* pp. 200–201: the budget for fiscal 1948 launched the Air Force on its career as the dominant element in our armed forces. Increasingly, "the military policy of the nation was to be framed around the dreadful, and in most situations inapplicable, Air Force concept of 'strategic' bombing with mass-destruction weapons."
2 Admiral Radford had been advised by at least five longtime friends that Secretary Symington had done precisely what Forrestal said.
3 See Millis, *Arms,* pp. 209–219: For details of the infighting over "cutting the pie."
4 See Millis, *Arms,* p. 213: Mr. Forrestal was a lone voice until 17 March, when President Truman for the first time identified the Soviet Union as the "one nation" barring every effort for peace. The *Diaries* are replete with Forrestal's concern over Soviet aggrandizement and aggressiveness. See also Roberta Wohlstetter, "Cuba and Pearl Harbor," in Eugene J. Rosi, ed., *American Defense and Detente* (New York: Dodd, Mead, 1973), pp. 262–265, for a description of the Soviet duplicity long practiced against American presidents.
5 *Diaries,* p. 390.
6 Ibid., pp. 390–397, provides the Secretary's diary entries concerning the conference at Key West and his meeting with the President thereafter. The quotations here are his.

CHAPTER 10

1 *New York Times,* 18 March 1948, p. 4.
2 Forrestal, pp. 400–402.
3 Mr. Truman was a cautious politician, preferring to let others discharge politically uncertain or unpopular tasks. Forrestal's *Diaries,* pp. 412–421, contains a more complete recital of the Secretary's efforts and lack of presidential support.
4 For further information on this unusual procedure, see Millis, *Arms,* pp. 217–219. Typically, Truman gave the same task to Budget and to Congress via Forrestal.
5 Forrestal, pp. 429–433 (including Mr. Forrestal's account and quotations of the meetings of 6, 7, and 13 May, described below).
6 Cochran (pp. 186–187) notes: "Marshall, the Army chief of staff throughout the war, represented for Truman the acme of perfection. He [Truman] not only gave him his full confidence and respect, he was in awe of him. He had called him in the past the 'greatest living American,' and it was an opinion he was never to abandon. The man epitomized for him everything he would have liked to have been: a five-star general, solidity of body, steely, craggy, of impassive appearance, an air of martial authoritativeness, a manner of curt decisiveness, of self-control suggesting enormous reserves of power."
7 See Forrestal, pp. 476–477, for all quotations above.
8 Ibid., pp. 498–499.
9 Acheson, p. 405: "It seemed close to certain that the [North Korean] attack had been mounted, supplied, and instigated by the Soviet Union . . ."

10 LaFeber, p. 95: the Russians had supplied the North Koreans with new tanks in April and May 1950. Both the U.S. and the USSR had military advisers in their respective zones.

11 On defense, over and above budgeted funding and appropriated funds.

12 In 1977, 27 years after the Korean War began, President Jimmy Carter announced a proposed gradual reduction in U.S. forces in Korea. Moves that appear logical to American presidents are sometimes regarded as withdrawals, indicators of reduced staying power, and lack of national interest by not only the communist bloc but also by our friends and by neutrals in the region.

CHAPTER 11

1 But the Royal Navy was innovative, especially regarding carriers, having developed angled decks and mirror landing systems.

2 Forrestal, p. 536: Especially with respect to Berlin, the world situation, and China going "from debacle to disaster." See also de Riencourt, pp. 89–91.

3 See Thomas W. Wolfe, *Soviet Power and Europe 1945–1970* (Baltimore: Johns Hopkins Press, 1970), pp. 12–27.

4 Millis, in Forrestal, p. 552, says: "At least one friend came to understand later that . . . this request had been a 'shattering experience.' " Truman does not even mention Forrestal's dismissal in his *Memoirs*. His cavalier handling of the resignation had more than a little to do with Louis Johnson's poor start as Secretary of Defense.

5 Louis Johnson was already in a position of power in the military establishment, and had been Assistant Secretary of War ten years before. Unlike Forrestal, Johnson was a politician with corrosive ambition, unloved and unlamented by the professional armed forces.

6 See Millis, *Arms*, pp. 238–241, for a concise account of the background and of what followed.

7 Truman, in *Memoirs*, p. 53, never accepts responsibility for cancelling the carrier. He writes: "Secretary Johnson cancelled the construction of the Navy's new supercarrier . . . Secretary John L. Sullivan of the Navy resigned in protest of Johnson's cancellation of the carrier contract." The President's remarks add no luster to his credibility.

CHAPTER 12

1 See McLellan, pp. 20–21: The U.S. of course did suture off relations for 33 years.

2 The unsuccessful Hurley, Wedemeyer, and Marshall missions to China only obscured the fact that China was "not ours to lose." The Chinese civil war could not have been won by Chiang even if the U.S. had poured in material and munitions; see Hammond, *The Cold War Years:* American Foreign Policy since 1945 (New York: Harcourt, Brace and World, 1969), pp. 40–41.

3 *China and U.S. Far East Policy: 1945–1966* (Washington: Congressional Quarterly Service, April 1967), pp. 35–219, provides a chronology of events bearing upon American policies (or the lack thereof) in Asia.

4 See James MacGregor Burns, *Roosevelt: The Soldier of Freedom, 1940–1945* (New York: Harcourt Brace Jovanovich, 1970), pp. 573–576: it is possible that Admiral Radford read this out of context. While the war in the Pacific was under way (be-

fore 15 August 1945) no merchant ships with military cargoes were diverted into the Sea of Japan to Vladivostok. Japanese aircraft, including kamikazes, would have sunk them all. It is more likely that "the latter stages of the war" refers to the Chinese civil war, 1945–1949.

5 American policy toward all of Asia was ambivalent and fluctuating. Primary concern had shifted to Western Europe and an aggressive Soviet Union.

6 Lovell, p. 43: "The failure in planning and the general ambiguity of American policies in East Asia at the end of World War II may be accurately described as having contributed directly to the division of Korea in the first place and as having generated conditions conducive to the North Korean attack in June 1950." See also a defense of the same thesis in Cho's *Korea in World Politics: 1940–1950*.

CHAPTER 13

1 The complete record of these presentations is available in most large libraries: U.S., Congress, House, Committee on the Armed Services, *Hearing on H.R. 234* and *Unification and Strategy*, 81st Congress, 1st session, 1949. All quotations below are from this record.

2 The anonymous letter contained allegations that Secretary of the Air Force Symington would benefit from the purchase of the B36. Mr. Cedric Worth, civilian employee of the Navy Department, provided this letter to Congressman Dcane.

3 Admiral Radford was not present. The proceedings are in the public record of the subcommittee's west coast hearings.

4 On 23 September President Truman announced that an atomic explosion had occurred in the Soviet Union. The Russians already had the bomb.

CHAPTER 14

1 See *Present at the Creation*, pp. 430–431, 434: Louis Johnson was not one of Secretary Acheson's favorite people.

CHAPTER 15

1 Millis notes (*Arms*, p. 249) that: "The Navy had advanced a serious criticism of ruling strategic ideas at a moment when those ideas were in a state of utmost uncertainty and when every high policy agency in Washington was looking frantically for guidance. Bradley ... reduced the Navy's case to a mere 'admiral's revolt'—a rebellion by disgruntled sailors—and so the public was largely to accept it."

2 This is so because the committee's report, though bland and judicious, heaped praise and blame equally among the battle-weary participants, and attracted little public notice. The Navy was still in disfavor, and the strategic calculus it had advanced was still unresolved.

3 See Millis, *Arms*, p. 249: "Vinson had stipulated that no Navy witness was to suffer for his testimony, but after Congress adjourned, the President was to manifest his displeasure by abruptly relieving Denfeld, the Chief of Naval Operations. The Navy was in the doghouse." Compare former President Truman's version of the story in *Memoirs*, p. 53: "The battle took on the aspects of a revolt of the entire Navy.

Secretary John L. Sullivan of the Navy resigned in protest of Johnson's cancellation of the carrier contract, and it finally became necessary for me to replace Admiral Louis E. Denfeld as Chief of Naval Operations *in a move to restore discipline"* (editor's italics).

CHAPTER 16

1 See Millis, *Arms,* p. 147. Marshall was also tired and no longer willing to get caught in congressional crossfire.
2 See Acheson, pp. 303–307. It is not clear who the "advisers" were, but their influence was not great compared to that of the China lobby. See also Cochran, p. 310.
3 This is not the whole picture. Admiral Sherman was an officer of unquestioned integrity who would have become CNO in any event.
4 See King's incisive comment on naval air power in *U.S. Navy at War,* p. 47.
5 At Admiral Radford's request, Lt. Comdr. Dorothy Richards was preparing, at the time of this trip, a valuable report on the history of the Navy's administration of the Trust Territory, now in the Naval Historical Archives at the Washington Navy Yard.
6 The Seabees are members of the Navy's Civil Engineer Corps in construction and engineering battalions. They build and defend airfields, harbor facilities, and the like.

CHAPTER 17

1 Millis, *Arms,* p. 260: John Foster Dulles "had been inspecting the South Korean defenses along the 38th parallel. The situation had seemed uneasy and dangerous ever since the withdrawal of the American occupation forces in the previous year. But the recognized peril had not entered into the substance of American military and diplomatic planning." Secretary Acheson in a well-noted speech before the National Press Club in Washington on 12 January 1950 had excluded South Korea from the U.S. "defense perimeter" in Asia; and no less than General MacArthur had pronounced much the same thought some months earlier. In short, with all eyes on NATO and Western Europe, the Far East came to a boil.
2 But see, for a different view, Ridgway, *Soldier,* pp. 190–192; Acheson, pp. 402–415; and Lovell, pp. 28–30, 36–41. Further, see Ridgway, *The Korean War;* MacArthur, pp. 378–380; also Taylor, pp. 14–17, and LaFeber, pp. 96–97.
3 In fact Secretary Johnson, mentally ill, was asked to resign by President Truman in September. Acheson, pp. 373–374.
4 Based on NSC 68, now declassified, this National Security Council planning document became the basis for U.S. foreign policy; Seyom Brown, *The Faces of Power* (New York: Columbia University Press, 1968), pp. 53–56.
5 For details of the conference see Collins, p. 123.
6 Cochran, p. 319: "The Joint Chiefs' instructions to MacArthur on September 27 were a study in bureaucratic canniness, an effort to push off on him responsibilities for decisions that Washington should have faced."
7 See Acheson, p. 454, and Collins, pp. 148–149.
8 An unregistered copy of the transcript, given to Admiral Radford at Pearl Harbor, is among his papers.
9 Cochran, p. 324: "Truman, Acheson, Marshall, the Joint Chiefs, knew the Chinese had armies massed behind the Yalu. Whether the Chinese would choose to use them

was a political estimation for which they were not dependent on MacArthur ... they had made their decision independently before the Wake conference."

CHAPTER 18

1 McLellan, pp. 28–29: Stalin's death, Soviet development of a strategic alternative, and growing U.S. strength were among the factors conducive to "peace" in Korea.

CHAPTER 19

1 Investigation of the reports led to the conclusion that Quirino and Magsaysay were repeating hearsay; no evidence was found to support their statements.
2 The Maginot Line mentality bore heavily on French military planning. The static defense let guerrillas roam between fortified points, and in the evenings when French troops took refuge in the strong points the Vietminh controlled the territory.
3 The French were always ambivalent concerning Indochina, wanting American and British help but fearing they would be replaced politically and economically. Hammer, pp. 11–26: "Defeated in Europe in 1940, France was defeated in Asia in 1941. One day the Vietnamese would cite their failure as proof that France had forfeited its right to protect Indochina."

CHAPTER 20

1 Acheson, p. 598, describes an "infuriating practice of the Navy": the Radford intelligence on British shipping into Communist areas.
2 The text of this report is in the Naval Historical Archives, Washington Navy Yard.

CHAPTER 21

1 Correct, according to anthropologist Ottley Beyer.
2 This thinking was basically in terms of static, positional, defensive operations—a no-win option.
3 The French said it was a success; the Vietcong said it was their victory; the U.S. knew it was a French disaster.
4 Fall, *The Two Viet-Nams,* pp. 120–122: the French intelligence was faulty.

CHAPTER 22

1 Responding to Admiral Radford's request for details of this famous trip, Admiral Johnston in 1972 wrote a summary of his recollections that is now in the archives of the Hoover Institution, for readers who wish to know more about the trip.

CHAPTER 23

1 The Eisenhower New Look paper is in the archives of the Hoover Institution.
2 An excellent treatment of the topic is Warner R. Schilling, Paul Y. Hammond, and

Glen H. Snyder, *Strategy, Politics and Defense Budgets* (New York: Columbia University Press, 1962).
3 This speech is in the archives of the Hoover Institution.

CHAPTER 24

1 Fall, *The Two Viet-Nams*, p. 115: "What changed with de Lattre's arrival in Indochina was the tone . . . a vital element."
2 Hammer, p. 252. Chinese aid increased when the Chinese feared a possible U.N. attack on China.
3 Jackson, p. 30. The NSC serves only in an advisory capacity to the President who alone makes the decision.
4 All quotations from JCS papers are from those papers that have been declassified and are in the Naval Historical Archives at the Washington Navy Yard.
5 The text of this proposal is in the archives of the Hoover Institution.
6 See Fall, *The Two Viet-Nams*, pp. 118–119, for description of the extent of the catastrophe at Hoa Binh.
7 At this very moment the French Commander-in-Chief, General Navarre, had informed his government that the war could not be won in a military sense.

CHAPTER 25

1 Fall, *The Two Viet-Nams*, pp. 121–122, describes the invasion and its effects on the French.
2 This American insistence on making over the Vietnamese army into an image of the U.S. army was a major factor in the ultimate loss of Vietnam.

CHAPTER 26

1 The story of Dien Bien Phu is nowhere better told than Fall's epic, *Hell in a Very Small Place*.
2 See Bell, p. 14, for the defensive tactics of the French.
3 See Fall, *The Two Viet-Nams*, p. 325, for O'Daniel's overoptimism.
4 For details, see Bell, pp. 22–24.

CHAPTER 27

1 Hoopes, pp. 220–221, clarifies the British action, which was wise, moderate, and a carefully chosen course.
2 Eden's book provides an excellent account of British views from a perspective other than American.
3 For the text of this proposal, see Bell, pp. 45–47.
4 The JSSC views were not far from the French initial proposals of M. Bidault (in Bell, pp. 44–56).

CHAPTER 28

1 This despite their non-interference since 1949 and the obvious gains by their Vietminh allies.
2 The U.S. conditions were unacceptable to the French. But in fact, the U.S. government would have added further conditions had the French, out of necessity, ever accepted the original conditions.

CHAPTER 29

1 See Royal Institute of International Affairs, p. xi. Mr. Dulles never subscribed to Sir John Slessor's statement that "to say that the West could not possibly accept the domination of the area by the Communist Powers is not to say that the allegiance of the area must be given to the West."
2 Ibid., p. xiii: "The removal of the fear of Chinese aggression makes the presence of Western forces and the existence of Western inspired military arrangements even less acceptable to the local peoples, who are anxious, so far as possible, to detach themselves from the cold war conflict."
3 See Bell, pp. 45–46, for the text of the Vietminh terms.
4 Ibid.: "The military arrangements developed under the Manila Treaty should be matched by imaginative economic and political policies."
5 As occurred in Vietnam, on the occasion of American withdrawal, when enormous quantities of supplies were seized by the Vietcong. Before that, U.S. supplies captured by the Chinese and North Koreans were given to the Vietminh.
6 See Hoopes, pp. 206–209: "Senator Knowland and the China Lobby had intimidated the administration, and staunch anti-communist Dulles was totally intransigent toward Red China."
7 The Sino-Japanese treaty establishing normal diplomatic and trade relations was signed in August 1978.

Bibliography

Acheson, Dean. *Present At The Creation*. New York: Norton, 1969.

Ambrose, Stephen E., and Barber, J. A., Jr., eds. *The Military and American Society*. New York: Free Press, 1972.

Arnold, Henry Harley. *Global Mission*. New York: Harper, 1949.

Bell, Coral. *Survey of International Affairs: 1954*. London: Oxford University Press, 1957.

Butow, Robert. *Japan's Decision To Surrender*. Stanford: Stanford University Press, 1954.

Carter, W. R. *Beans, Bullets and Black Oil*. Washington, D.C.: U.S. Government Printing Office, 1953.

Cho, Soon Sung. *Korea in World Politics: 1940–1950*. Berkeley: University of California Press, 1967.

Clark, Mark W. *From The Danube To The Yalu*. New York: Harper, 1954.

Cochran, Bert. *Harry Truman and the Crisis Presidency*. New York: Funk and Wagnalls, 1973.

Collins, Joseph Lawton. *War in Peacetime*. New York: Houghton Mifflin, 1969.

Congressional Quarterly Service. *China and U.S. Far East Policy: 1945–1966*. Washington, D.C., 1967.

Craig, William. *The Fall Of Japan*. New York: Dial, 1967.

Davis, Lynn Etheridge. *The Cold War Begins*. Princeton: Princeton University Press, 1974.

De Riencourt, Amaury. *The American Empire*. New York: Dell, 1968.

Devillers, Philippe, and Lacouture, Jean. *End of a War: Indochina, 1954*. New York: Praeger, 1969.

Eccles, Henry, E. *Logistics in the National Defense*. Harrisburg, Pa.: Stackpole, 1959.

———. *Operational Naval Logistics*. Washington, D.C.: U.S. Government Printing Office, 1950.

Eden, Anthony. *Full Circle*. Boston: Houghton Mifflin, 1960.

Eisenhower, Dwight D. *The White House Years*, vol. I: *Mandate for Change, 1953–1956*. New York: Doubleday, 1963.

Ely, Paul/Henri Ronuald. *Mémoires*, vol. I: *L'Indochine dans la tourmente*. Paris: Plon, 1964.

Fall, Bernard. *Hell In A Very Small Place*. New York: Vintage, 1968.

———. *The Two Viet-Nams*. New York: Praeger, 1967.

Feis, Herbert. *The China Tangle*. Princeton: Princeton University Press, 1953.
————. *Churchill-Roosevelt-Stalin*. Princeton: Princeton University Press, 1967.
————. *Contest Over Japan*. New York: Norton, 1967.
Field, James A., Jr. *History of U.S. Naval Operations: Korea*. Washington, D.C.: U.S. Government Printing Office, 1962.
Forrestal, James. *The Forrestal Diaries,* ed. Walter Millis. New York: Viking, 1951.
Gerson, Louis L. *John Foster Dulles,* vol. XVII: *American Secretaries of State and Their Diplomacy*. New York: Cooper Square, 1967.
Halsey, William F., and Halsey, Bryan, J., III. *Admiral Halsey's Story*. New York: McGraw-Hill, 1947.
Hammer, Ellen J. *The Struggle For Indochina*. Stanford: Stanford University Press, 1954.
Hoopes, Townsend. *The Devil And John Foster Dulles*. Boston: Little, Brown, 1973.
Jackson, Henry M., ed. *The National Security Council*. New York: Praeger, 1965.
Joy, C. Turner. *How Communists Negotiate*. New York: Macmillan, 1953.
Karig, Walter. *Battle Report*. New York: Rinehart, 1949.
King, Ernest J. *U.S. Navy At War: 1941–1945*. Official reports to the Secretary of the Navy, United States Navy Department. Washington, D.C., 1946.
King, E. J., and Whitehall, Walter M. *Fleet Admiral King*. New York: Norton, 1952.
La Feber, Walter. *America, Russia, and the Cold War: 1945–1966*. New York: Wiley, 1967.
Lansdale, E. G. *In The Midst Of Wars*. New York: Harper and Row, 1972.
Lovell, John P. *Foreign Policy in Perspective*. New York: Holt, Rinehart and Winston, 1970.
Lyon, Peter. *Eisenhower: Portrait Of The Hero*. Boston: Little, Brown, 1974.
MacArthur, Douglas. *Reminiscences*. New York: McGraw-Hill, 1964.
McLellan, David. *The Cold War In Transition*. London: Macmillan, 1966.
Millis, Walter, with Harvey C. Mansfield and Harold Stein. *Arms and the State*. New York: Twentieth Century Fund, 1958.
Millis, Walter, ed. *American Military Thought*. New York: Bobbs-Merrill, 1966.
Morison, Samuel Eliot. *History Of United States Naval Operations In World War II*. Fifteen vols. Boston: Little, Brown, 1951–1962.
Murphy, Robert. *Diplomat Among Warriors*. New York: Pyramid, 1965.
Parmet, Herbert. *Eisenhower and the American Crusade*. New York: Macmillan, 1972.
Pentagon Papers. New York: New York Times, Bantam ed., 1971.
Public Papers of the Presidents of the United States: Harry S. Truman, 1945. Washington, D.C.: U.S. Government Printing Office, 1961.
Ridgway, Matthew B. *The Korean War*. Garden City, N.Y.: Doubleday, 1967.
Ridgway, Matthew B., as told to Harold H. Martin. *Soldier: The Memoirs of Matthew B. Ridgway*. New York: Harper, 1956.
Royal Institute of International Affairs. *Collective Defence in Southeast Asia*. London: Oxford University Press, 1956.
Serfaty, Simon. *The Elusive Enemy*. Boston: Little, Brown, 1972.
Spanier, John W. *The Truman-MacArthur Controversy and the Korean War*. New York: Belknap Press, 1959.
Stimson, Henry L., with McGeorge Bundy. *On Active Service in Peace and War*. New York: Harper, 1948.
Taylor, Maxwell. *The Uncertain Trumpet*. New York: Harper, 1959.
Turner, Gordon B., and Challenger, Richard D. *National Security in the Nuclear Age*. New York: Praeger, 1960.

Truman, Harry S. *Memoirs by Harry S. Truman,* vol. I: *Years of Trial and Hope.*
   Garden City: Doubleday, 1956.
U.S., Congress, House, Committee on the Armed Services, *Hearing on H.R. 234* and
   Unification and Strategy, 81st Congress, 1st Session, 1949.
U.S. Strategic Bombing Survey (USSBS). *Japan's Struggle To End The War.* Wash-
   ington, D.C.: U.S. Government Printing Office, 1946.
Wedemeyer, Albert. *Wedemeyer Reports.* New York: Devin-Adair, 1958.
Wohlstetter, Roberta. *Pearl Harbor: Warning and Decision.* Stanford: Stanford Univer-
   sity Press, 1962.
Yarmolinsky, Adam. *The Military Establishment.* New York: Harper and Row, 1971.

Index